跨国公司管理

Transnational Corporation Management

主　　编　张秋秋

副 主 编　王婷婷

参编人员　王　丹　刘　莹

中国财经出版传媒集团

经济科学出版社

Economic Science Press

图书在版编目（CIP）数据

跨国公司管理 = Transnational Corporation Management：
英文/张秋秋主编. —北京：经济科学出版社，2019. 12
ISBN 978 - 7 - 5218 - 1141 - 4

Ⅰ.①跨…　Ⅱ.①张…　Ⅲ.①跨国公司 - 企业管理 -
高等学校 - 教材 - 英文　Ⅳ.①F276.7

中国版本图书馆 CIP 数据核字（2019）第 288147 号

责任编辑：于海汛　李　林
责任校对：杨晓莹
责任印制：李　鹏

跨国公司管理

主　　编　张秋秋
副 主 编　王婷婷
参编人员　王　丹　刘　莹

经济科学出版社出版、发行　新华书店经销
社址：北京市海淀区阜成路甲 28 号　邮编：100142
总编部电话：010 - 88191217　发行部电话：010 - 88191522
网址：www. esp. com. cn
电子邮件：esp@ esp. com. cn
天猫网店：经济科学出版社旗舰店
网址：http：//jjkxcbs. tmall. com
北京密兴印刷有限公司印装
787×1092　16 开　32 印张　650000 字
2019 年 12 月第 1 版　2019 年 12 月第 1 次印刷
ISBN 978 - 7 - 5218 - 1141 - 4　定价：78. 00 元
（图书出现印装问题，本社负责调换。电话：010 - 88191510）
（版权所有　侵权必究　打击盗版　举报热线：010 - 88191661
QQ：2242791300　营销中心电话：010 - 88191537
电子邮箱：dbts@ esp. com. cn）

序　言

　　随着经济全球化的快速发展，参与跨国生产经营活动的大型公司越来越多。与此同时，中国经济转型升级的步伐不断加快，技术创新能力进一步提高，中国特色社会主义已经进入新时代，越来越多的国内企业开始向世界优秀跨国公司的行列迈进。根据中国企业联合会、中国企业家协会发布的《中国100大跨国公司榜单》，2019年入围的跨国公司覆盖16个省、自治区、直辖市，经济发达地区所占比重较高，其中北京占43%，广东占12%，上海占9%，山东占7%，浙江占6%，江苏占4%，河南、云南各占3%，安徽、辽宁、湖南、湖北、甘肃各占2%。河北、福建、新疆各占1%。尽管中国跨国公司的入围门槛和跨国指数均稳步提高，但是在复杂的内外部环境下，对企业进行有效的国际化管理，化解投资与经营风险并做出正确的决策，还需要大量不同层次具有创新精神的高级管理人才。要成为跨国公司一名合格的管理者，除了专业知识和实践能力外，对语言水平的要求同样较高，而英语作为跨国贸易与交流活动的世界通用语言，是所有从业者和学习研究者必须要掌握的技能。

　　按照"教育面向现代化、面向世界、面向未来"的要求，教育部在《关于加强高等学校本科教学工作提高教学质量的若干意见》中，提出对发展迅速和应用性强的课程，要不断更新教材内容，积极开发新教材，并积极推进双语教学，满足高等教育与国际接轨的发展要求，培养既精通英语，又有丰富专业知识的高素质"复合型"人才。

　　《跨国公司管理》正是基于上述背景进行编写的，它是工商管理类国际商务方向的一门核心课程。全书共分为十章，主要内容是：跨国公司概述，跨国公司进行生产经营活动的主要理论，基于PEST模型的跨国公司环境分析，跨国公司管理的主要活动，跨国公司的未来发展趋势。尽管已经有很多专家编写了关于跨国公司管理的相关书籍，但是这本教材仍有一些突出特点，主要体现在以下二方面：

　　◎难易适中，教学体系清晰。教材在编写中，除了专业词汇外，避免采用生涩的语言表达方式，语境适合中国学生的理解能力，使学习内容更容易被掌握和吸收。教学体系的构建采用循序渐进的方式，使学生从了解跨国公司的发展历史和相关理论开始，进而掌握跨国经营管理的主体活动，最后介绍未来发展趋势。每章结构分为六个部分，分别是：学习目标、开篇导读、正文、案例分析、扩展阅读和习题，可以有效地巩固教学内容及重要知识点。

◎适用范围较广。随着中国经济全面步入高质量发展的新常态时期，国家和地方经济急需具有创新精神和实践能力的复合型高素质人才。服务于地方区域经济的教育供给侧改革，对高校教学改革中的教材编写提出了更新的要求。这本教材的内容不但适合应用型高校工商管理类本科及以上学生，而且可用于 MBA 教学中的案例分析，并作为跨国企业管理者的参考用书。

◎实用性强，力求培养学习者分析与解决问题的能力。教材在介绍专业理论知识的基础上，通过穿插大量案例的方式，力图还原跨国管理活动的情境。通过这种情境学习方法，把知识和技能置于应用情景中进行传递，使学习者清楚地了解所学的知识将用于哪类具体的实际活动，实现"知行合一，学以致用"教学目标。

这本教材前五章由张秋秋老师编写，后五章由王婷婷老师编写，前期资料收集工作由王丹老师负责，后期出版联系工作由刘莹老师负责。教材在编写过程，广泛吸收了学者们提出的不同观点，为保障案例的准确性主要参阅《中国日报》（China Daily）、《环球时报》（Global Times）等中国权威英文媒体，力求将经典的学习内容呈现给读者。本书在编写中，还有很多不足之处，希望得到读者们的指正，我们将会继续努力。

张秋秋

沈阳大学　商学院

Contents

Chapter 1　Globalization and Transnational Corporation

Learning Objectives

1. Understand the background of globalization
2. Master the definition of transnational corporation
3. Understand the development of WTO, IMF, the World Bank Group
4. Master the differences between MNC and TNC
5. Understand the latest characteristics of transnational corporations development
6. Recognize the operating mode of transnational corporations
7. Master types of Dunning's Transnational Investment and the Influencing Factors

Opening case

IKEA to up China investment, presence to tap home furnishing potential

In 1920s, the founder of IKEA, Ingvar Kamprad, was born. In 1940s, IKEA was founded by Ingvar Kamprad aged 17 in a small farming village in Sweden. The name IKEA was formed from the founder's initials (I. K.) plus the first letters of Elmtaryd and Agunnaryd, the farm and village where he grew up. Originally IKEA sold everything from pens and wallets to picture frames, watches and even ladies stockings! In 1951, the first IKEA catalogue was published and the first IKEA advertisements appeared in local newspapers. Ingvar distributed his products via the country milk van, which delivered them to the nearby train station. IKEA offered flat packaging products. In the late 1950s Ingvar decided to stop selling everything except furniture items—IKEA as we know it today was born! The first IKEA store opened in Almhult, Sweden. In 1960s, first IKEA stores outside Sweden opened in Norway and Denmark. IKEA had a rapid expansion in the 1970s. First store outside Scandinavia opened in Switzerland. More followed in subsequent years in Germany, Australia, Canada, Austria and the Netherlands.

In 1980s, USA and UK opened IKEA first stores. In 1987, IKEA won the Excellent Swedish Design prize. In 1990s, stores opened in Hungary, Poland, Czech Republic, United Arab Emirates, Spain and China. IKEA introduced its range for children. In 2000s, stores opened in Russia and Japan. By reducing use of other transport methods such as large trucks, IKEA has lowered its carbon dioxide emissions. IKEA's vision is 'To create a better everyday life for the many people. '

Global home furnishing giant IKEA plans to increase its investment and presence in China as part of the company's localization strategy to expand its business and cater to the shifting local consumer demands. The Sweden-based company will make its biggest investment in China in fiscal year 2020 and more investment in the following two years as home furnishing is expected to boom in China, IKEA China announced Thursday. The investment plan is part of IKEA China's "Future + " strategy for the local market in the next three years featuring enhanced accessibility, digitalization and home expertise services. "The home furnishings market in China is now in a phase of stable growth. In addition, urbanization, digitalization and people's increasing disposable income are changing the way how people live and consume," said Anna Pawlak-Kuliga, CEO and president of IKEA China. As part of the plan, IKEA will upgrade its existing stores, and will accelerate its expansion in China by opening four new stores in the next four months. Meanwhile, e-commerce coverage will be expanded, while small stores will be opened to create more meeting places close to consumers. To catch up with China's advanced digital adoption, the company will provide digital tools offline to simplify the shopping process, creating an inspiring and convenient shopping experience online. A digital hub was established last month as a brand-new business unit to enable the company's digital capabilities. More diverse business models will be explored to reinforce the company's role as a home furnishing consultant, with key initiatives including launching full-house design services starting from bedrooms and kitchens and upgrading its B2B service to work with commercial real estate companies on furnished apartments, long-term rental apartments and offices. The company opened its first China store in Shanghai in 1998, and now operates 27 stores, two experience centers, four distribution centers and seven parcel delivery centers on the Chinese mainland. It launched e-commerce services in October 2018 covering 227 cities and areas. China is the only market other than Sweden that has a comprehensive IKEA value chain. IKEA has full confidence in the market and a strong belief that the new strategy will help the company to create a better everyday life for even more Chinese people, Pawlak-

Kuliga said, adding, "We are here for the long term. "

(Sources: IKEA official website; IKEA to up China investment, presence to tap home furnishing potential, Xinhua Finance Agency, August 23, 2019.)

1. 1   Overview of Transnational Corporations

1. 1. 1   Definition

Globalization refers to the shift toward a more integrated and interdependent world economy. Globalization has two main features, including the globalization of markets and the globalization of production. The globalization of markets refers to the emerging of historically distinct and separate national markets into one huge global marketplace. Falling barriers to cross-border trade have made it easier to sell internationally. It has been argued for some time that the tastes and preferences of consumers in different nations are beginning to converge on some global norm, thereby helping to create a global market. Consumer products such as Coca-cola's soft drinks, McDonald's hamburgers, Starbucks coffee, IKEA's furniture, and Apple's iPhones are frequently held up as prototypical examples of this trend. The firms that produce these products are more than just benefactors of this trend; they are also facilitators of it. By offering the same basic product worldwide, they help create a global market. A transnational corporation (TNC) is an international corporation or enterprise that sets up branches or subsidiaries in many countries through foreign direct investment (FDI) and engages in economic activities such as manufacturing, sales and service with the purpose of gaining high profits. In many global markets, the same firms frequently confront each other as competitors in nation after nation. Coca-cola's rivalry with PepsiCo is a global one, as are the rivalries between Ford and Toyota, Boeing and Airbus. If a corporate moves into a nation not currently served by its rivals, many of those rivals are sure to follow to prevent their competitor from gaining an advantage. As corporations follow each other around the world, they bring with them many of the assets that served them well in other national markets—their products, operating strategies, marketing strategies, and brand names—creating some homogeneity across markets. The globalization of production refers to the sourcing of goods and services from locations around the globe to take advantage of national differences in the cost and quality of factors of production (such as labor, energy, land, and capital). By doing this, companies hope to lower their overall cost structure or improve the quality or functionality of their product offering, thereby allowing them to compete more effectively. As markets globalize and an increasing proportion of business activity transcends national borders, institutions are needed to help manage, regulate, and police the global marketplace and to promote the establishment of multinational treaties to govern the global business system.

Over the past half century, a number of important global institutions have been created to help perform these functions, including the General Agreement on Tariffs and Trade (GATT) and its successor, the World Trade Organization (WTO), is the only global international organization dealing with the rules of trade between nations. At its heart are the WTO agreements, negotiated and signed by the bulk of the world's trading nations and ratified in their parliaments. The goal is to ensure that trade flows as smoothly, predictably and freely as possible. The International Monetary Fund (IMF) was created in 1945, and is an organization of 189 countries and regions, working on fostering global monetary cooperation, securing financial stability, facilitating international trade, promoting high employment and sustainable economic growth, and reduce poverty around the world. The IMF's primary purpose is to ensure the stability of the international monetary system—the system of exchange rates and international payments that enables countries and regions (and their citizens) to transact with each other. The Fund's mandate was updated in 2012 to include all macroeconomic and financial sector issues that bear on global stability.

The past 70 years have seen major changes in the world economy. Over that time, the World Bank Group—the world's largest development institution—has worked to help more than 100 developing countries and countries in transition adjust to these changes by offering loans and tailored knowledge and advice. The Bank Group works with country governments, the private sector, civil society organizations, regional development banks, think tanks, and other international institutions on issues ranging from climate change, conflict, and food security to education, agriculture, finance, and trade. All of these efforts support the Bank Group's twin goals of ending extreme poverty by 2030 and boosting shared prosperity of the poorest 40 percent of the population in all countries. Founded in 1944, the International Bank for Reconstruction and Development—soon called the World Bank—has expanded to a closely associated group of five development institutions. Originally, its loans helped rebuild countries devastated by World War II. In time, the focus shifted from reconstruction to development, with a heavy emphasis on infrastructure such as dams, electrical grids, irrigation systems, and roads. With the founding of the International Finance Corporation in 1956, the institution became able to lend to private companies and financial institutions in developing countries. And the founding of the International Development Association in 1960 put greater emphasis on the poorest countries, part of a steady shift toward the eradication of poverty becoming the Bank Group's primary goal. The subsequent launch of the International Centre for Settlement of Investment Disputes and the Multilateral Investment Guarantee Agency further rounded out the Bank Group's ability to connect global financial resources to the needs of developing countries. The World Bank Group is one of the world's largest sources of funding and knowledge for developing countries. Its five institutions share a commitment to reducing poverty, increasing shared prosperity, and promoting sustainable development. Today the Bank Group's work touches nearly every sector that is important to fighting against poverty, supporting economic growth, and ensuring sustainable gains in the quality of people's lives in developing countries.

The United Nations is an international organization founded in 1945. It is currently made up of 193 Member States. The mission and work of the United Nations are guided by the purposes and principles contained in its founding Charter. Due to the powers vested in its Charter and its unique international character, the United Nations can take action on the issues confronting humanity in the 21st century, such as peace and security, climate change, sustainable development, human rights, disarmament, terrorism, humanitarian and health emergencies, gender equality, governance, food production, and more. The UN also provides a forum for its members to express their views in the General Assembly, the Security Council, the Economic and Social Council, and other bodies and committees. By enabling dialogue between its members, and by hosting negotiations, the Organization has become a mechanism for governments to find areas of agreement and solve problems together.

All these institutions were created by voluntary agreement between individual members, and their functions are enshrined in international treaties.

1. 1. 2   History of transnational corporations

1. From the origin to the Second World War

The earliest historical origins of transnational corporation can be traced to the major colonising and imperialist ventures from Western Europe, notably England and Holland, which began in the 16th century and proceeded for the next several hundred years. In the late 16th century, for the first time, the corporate form was used in risky "for profit" ventures. It is on these "for profit" forms of corporations that we shall focus. The vast majority of these were incorporated for overseas trade. They were our first "transnational corporations" if you will. During this period, firms such as the British East India Trading Company were formed to promote the trading activities or territorial acquisitions of their home countries in the Far East, Africa, and the Americas.

In the first two decades of the 17th century, some forty companies were granted trading monopolies by their respective governments over much of the known world. A main characteristic of these corporations was that they were granted monopoly powers by their respective governments. The English corporations were typically granted a monopoly over English trade that encompassed specified territory abroad. Additionally, the corporations received power to protect their monopoly and rights over English subjects within the territory. The grant of monopoly status encouraged investors to engage in often highly risky ventures. For the first time, money could be transferred among members and outsiders. Profit was the dominant motive of most of these companies and the commercial risk was high. By the 19th century the public/private distinction was reified. During the wave of colonization by trading company, in the 19th century, public imperium and private dominium had established themselves as seperate categories in international law. As a consequence, the use of the corporate form affected how property was conceived within the colonial encounter. The transnational corporation as it is known today, however, did not really appear until the 19th century, with the advent of industrial capitalism and its consequences: the development of the factory system; larger, more capital intensive manufacturing processes; better storage techniques; and faster means of transportation. During the 19th and early 20th centuries, the search for resources including minerals, petroleum, and foodstuffs as well as pressure to protect or increase markets drove transnational expansion by companies almost exclusively from the United States and a handful of Western European nations. 60% of these corporations' investments went to Latin America, Asia, Africa, and the Middle East. Fuelled by numerous mergers and acquisitions, monopolistic and oligopolistic concentration of large transnationals in major sectors such as petrochemicals and food also had its roots in these years. We can look at the following example: the US agribusiness giant United Fruit Company, controlled 90% of US banana imports by 1899, while at the start of the First World War, Royal Dutch/Shell accounted for 20 percent of Russia's total oil production. Demand for natural resources continued to provide an impetus for European and US corporate ventures between the First and Second World Wars. Although corporate investments from Europe declined somewhat, the activities of US TNCs expanded vigorously. In Japan, this period witnessed the growth of the zaibatsu (or "financial clique") including Mitsui and Mitsubishi. These giant corporations, which worked in alliance with the Japanese state, had oligopolistic control of the country's industrial, financial, and trade sectors.

2. From 1945 to the present

The United States is a represantational country in this period. The US transnational corporations heavily dominated foreign investment activity in the two decades after the Second World War, when European and Japanese corporations began to play ever greater roles. In the 1950s, banks in the US, Europe, and Japan started to invest vast sums of money in industrial stocks, encouraging corporate mergers and furthering capital concentration. Major technological advances in shipping, transport (especially by air), computerisation, and communications accelerated transnational corporations increasing internationalisation of investment and trade, while new advertising capabilities helped transnationals expand market shares. All these trends meant that by the 1970s oligopolistic consolidation and transnationals' role in global commerce was of a far different scale than earlier in the century. Whereas in 1906 there were two or three leading firms with assets of US$500 million, in 1971 there were 333 such corporations, one-third of which had assets of US $1 billion or more. Additionally, transnationals had come to control 70%~80% of world trade outside the centrally planned economies. ①

Over the past 25 years, there has been a virtual increase of transnationals. In 1970, there were some 7,000 parent TNCs, while today that number has jumped to 38,000. And 90 percent of them are based in the industrialised world, which control over 207,000 foreign subsidiaries. Since the early 1990s, these subsidiaries' global sales have surpassed worldwide trade exports as the principal vehicle to deliver goods and services to foreign markets. ②

The large number of TNCs can be somewhat misleading, however, because the wealth of transnationals is concentrated among the top 100 firms which in 1992 had US$3. 4 trillion in global assets, of which approximately US$1. 3 trillion was held outside their home countries. The top 100 TNCs also account for about one-third of the combined outward foreign direct investment (FDI) of their countries

---

①② Greer Jed. Kavaljit Singh (2000) . A Brief History of Transnational Corporations. http: // globalpoling. igc. org.

of origin. Since the mid-1980s, a large rise of TNC-led foreign direct investment has occurred. Between 1988 and 1993, worldwide FDI stock—a measure of the productive capacity of TNCs outside their home countries—grew from US $1. 1 trillion to US $2. 1 trillion in estimated book value. There has also been a great increase in TNC investment in the less-industrialized world since the mid-1980s; such investment, along with private bank loans, has grown far more dramatically than national development aid or multilateral bank lending. In 1992 foreign investment into less-industrialised nations was over US$50 billion; the figure had jumped to US$71 billion in 1993 and US$80 billion in 1994. In 1992-1993, less-industrialised countries accounted for between one-third and two-fifths of global FDI inflows—more than at any time since 1970. These flows have not been evenly distributed, however, with just ten host recipients the majority in Asia accounting for up to 80% of all FDI to the less-industrialised world. On the one hand, economic globalization continues to press forward, bringing up new features; on the other hand, the gradual emergence of many developing countries has made them an important force for world economic development. [1]

In 21st century, great changes have taken place in the forms of international division of labor and capital, China rises to world's largest goods trade country in 70 years. According to the National Bureau of Statistics, goods trade volume stood at only $1. 13 billion in 1950, while the number surged to $4. 6 trillion in 2018. Average annual trade growth remained less than 10 percent from 1950 to 1977 under the planned economy, but quickened to about 14. 5 percent after China started the reform and opening-up drive in 1978. The country's goods trade only accounted for 0. 8% of the global total in 1978, while the number soared to 11. 8% in 2018. China overtook the United States to become the world's largest goods trade country in 2013 for the first time. The Chinese government has taken many positive measures to attract foreign investment and transnational companies. [2]

Haikou introduces preferential policies to boost headquarters economy

Haikou, capital city of China's southernmost Hainan province, has introduced a set of preferential policies to attract global conglomerates and boost the development of its headquarters economy, it was announced at a news conference on Wednesday. The move, targeting Fortune Global 500 companies, leading industrial conglomerates

---

[1] Greer Jed. Kavaljit Singh (2000) . A Brief History of Transnational Corporations. http: // globalpoling. igc. org.

[2] National Bureau of Statistics.

and internationally well-known enterprises and organizations, is an initial step to encourage growth of a headquarters economy in Haikou. Under the preferential policies, a transnational corporation will get 3 million yuan ($470,000) as a reward for establishing its headquarters or regional headquarters in Haikou, and for an international organization, the reward is 2 million yuan. Regional headquarters engaged in tourism and modern service industries will each receive a bonus of 5 million yuan if their first year operations make a contribution of 30 million yuan to local revenue, and headquarters of companies from new and high-tech industries will receive a bonus of as much as 10 million yuan if they contribute 30 million yuan annually to local revenue after registration, according to the incentive measures released at the news conference. Haikou will offer a maximum of 3 million yuan to a new company setting up its headquarters in the city as an office rent allowance within the first five years, and a maximum subsidy of 10 million yuan if it purchases an office in the city. The city is home to a total of 4,384 companies with individual registration capital of 50 million yuan to 1 billion yuan. The provincial capital has also rolled out incentive policies to attract and retain talented individuals. Senior executives whose annual salary exceeds 500,000 yuan, for instance, can get an individual income tax rebate of 50% in the first three years. They will also enjoy special policies related to medical and social security services and education for their children, according to Sun Shiwen, vice-mayor of Haikou. He said the city government would also provide rewards for companies establishing headquarters that would play a key role in helping boost certain local economic sectors, such as tourism, new and high-tech and tropical agriculture. "Haikou will invite well-known professional service firms involved in accounting, law, management consulting and training to serve the development of its local headquarters economy," said the vice-mayor at the news conference. He disclosed that talks are under way with the world's biggest four accounting firms-PricewaterhouseCoopers, Deloitte Touche Tohmatsu, KPMG and Ernst & Young-about opening regional headquarters in Haikou. Alibaba Group Holding Ltd, COFCO Group Ltd, China National Travel Service Group Corp and Suning Corp are also on the list. According to Haikou's plan, the foundation of the city's headquarters economy will be formed by 2020. Haikou will optimize government services to create a better environment for business people and enterprise innovation to support its headquarters economy, the vice-mayor said. In April, China announced a decision to support Hainan in developing the whole island into a pilot free trade zone, and gradually exploring and steadily promoting the establishment of a free trade port with Chinese characteristics. On Sunday, Hainan government announced the establishment of Haikou Jiangdong New District of China

（Hainan）Pilot Free Trade Zone, to promote the development of a free trade zone across Hainan island. Fu Xuanchao, a member of the new district planning and leadership group and director of the Hainan Provincial Development and Reform Commission said, the new district, on the east coast of Haikou, will host the regional headquarters, and will also be built into an international financial trade center and international education base. "The new district will be an international trading venue for energy, shipping, bulk commodities, property rights, stocks and carbon credits," Fu said.

（Source：Ma Zhiping and Liu Xiaoli in Haikou, Haikou introduces preferential policies to boost headquarters economy, China Daily, June 8, 2018.）

In 2018, China, the largest developing economy in foreign direct investment （FDI）recipient, attracted \$139 billion, ranking second worldwide, according to a UN report on June 12, 2019, the United Nations Conference on Trade and Development （UNCTAD）World Investment Report 2019, said FDI to East Asia rose by 4% to \$280 billion in 2018, with inflows to China increasing by 4% to an all-time high. FDI flows to developing economies remained stable in 2018, rising by 2% to \$706 billion, despite the global FDI flows sliding by 13% compared with 2017 to \$1.3 trillion. FDI flows to developed economies reached their lowest point since 2004, declining by 27% to \$557 billion. Table 1-1 shows the top 10 economies for FDI inflows in 2018.

Table 1-1　　　　**Top 10 economies for FDI inflows in 2018**

Ranking	Country/Region	FDI Inflow Amount （USD, Billion）
1	United States	252
2	China	139
3	Hong Kong, China	116
4	Singapore	78
5	Netherlands	70
6	United Kingdom	64
7	Brazil	61
8	Australia	60
9	Spain	44
10	India	42

Source：chinadaily. com. cn, July 8, 2019.

The convenience for the cross-border flows of essential production factors has given more prominence to the effects of comparative advantages and the economies of scale of the transnational production and marketing. The international division of labor has expanded from inter-industrial division of labor to intra-industrial division of labor, while intra-industrial or intra-company division of labor is increasingly broken down and streamlined. Such changes in division of labor are dominated by transnational corporations. Through transnational industrial transfer, transnational corporations have gradually established global or regional production chains and supply chains. Trade volume conducted by transnational corporations has accounted for one-third of the world total. Due to the above-mentioned changes, the relationship of interests among various countries and among different circles of interests within each country is becoming more and more intricate.

1. 1. 3   The distinction of synonyms

1. Multinational corporations

This is a corporation that has assets and facilities in one or more countries, other than the home country, and has a centralized office where global management is coordinated. Decision making hence affects all the subsidiaries globally. A multinational corporation (MNC) is usually a large corporation incorporated in one country which produces or sells goods or services in various countries. The two main characteristics of MNCs are their large size and the fact that their worldwide activities are centrally controlled by the parent companies. Major activities include:
- Importing and exporting goods and services
- Making significant investments in a foreign country
- Buying and selling licenses in foreign markets
- Engaging in contract manufacturing—permitting a local manufacturer in a foreign country to produce their products
- Opening manufacturing facilities or assembly operations in foreign countries

MNCs may gain from their global presence in a variety of ways. First of all, MNCs can benefit from the economy of scale by spreading R&D expenditures and advertising costs over their global sales, pooling global purchasing power over suppliers, and utilizing their technological and managerial know-how globally with minimal additional costs. Furthermore, MNCs can use their global presence to take advantage of underpriced labor services available in certain developing countries, and gain access to special R&D capabilities residing in advanced foreign countries.

One of the first multinational business organizations, the East India Company, was established in 1600. After the East India Company, came the Dutch East India Company, founded March 20, 1602, which would become the largest company in the world for nearly 200 years. The main characteristics of multinational companies are:

● In general, there is a national strength of large companies as the main body, in the way of foreign direct investment or acquire local enterprises, established subsidiaries or branches in many countries;

● It usually has a complete decision-making system and the highest decision-making center, each subsidiary or branch has its own decision-making body, according to their different features and operations to make decisions, but its decision must be subordinated to the highest decision-making center;

● MNCs seek markets in worldwide and rational production layout, professional fixed-point production, fixed-point sales products, in order to achieve maximum profit;

● Due to strong economic and technical strength, with fast information transmission, as well as funding for rapid cross-border transfers, the multinational has stronger competitiveness in the world;

● Many large multinational companies have varying degrees of monopoly in some area, due to economic and technical strength or production advantages.

2. Transnational corporations

These are corporations which operate in other countries, other than the home country, and do not have a centralized management system. Decisions are hence made to suit the operating zone. Similar firms operating in other countries cannot be referred to as subsidiaries, since the management system is not centralized. Transnational companies are also not loyal to the operating country's value system, but are focused on business expansion.

3. Similarities between MNCs and TNCs

(1) Both have foreign affiliates and operate globally.

(2) Both have local services as well as production hence affect employment, standards of living and household incomes.

4. Differences between MNCs and TNCs

(1) Definition. Multinational refers to a corporation that has assets and

facilities in one or more countries, other than the home country, and has a centralized office where global management is coordinated. On the other hand, transnational refers to a corporation which operates in other countries, other than the home country, and do not have a centralized management system.

(2) Operations. While multinationals have subsidiaries in other countries, a transnational does not have subsidiaries in other countries.

(3) Decision making. Decision making in a multinational is made in the mother country and should be effected in all the subsidiaries globally. On the other hand, decision making in a transnational is made by individual transnational corporations.

(4) Local markets. Multinationals face restrictions when it comes to local markets since they have centralized management systems. On the other hand, transnational companies are free to make decisions independently based on local markets.

5. Summary of MNCs VS. TNCs

While both multinational and transnational corporations operate globally, multinational corporations have a centralized global management system while transnational corporations do not have a centralized management system. For this reason, business decisions occur at different levels. This limits decisions that can be made by individual multinational corporations. Both, however, are major contributors to economic development through the provision of goods and services as well as employment creation.

1.2　Characteristics of Transnational Corporations

1.2.1　Characteristics of transnational corporations themselves

(1) Generally, there is a large company with strong national strength as the main body, which sets up subsidiaries or branches in many countries through foreign direct investment or acquisition of local enterprises. According to the report of China Daily, the Goldman Sachs Group Inc is seeking regulatory approval to own a majority stake in its securities joint venture in China, a step that will make it the latest foreign investment bank to take advantage of the further opening of the financial sector by the country. The US bank's plan to boost its stake in Goldman

Sachs Gao Hua Securities Co. to 51% from 33%. Beijing Gao Hua Securities Co. currently owns 67% of the joint venture company. The resilience of the domestic economy, opportunities in the burgeoning capital markets and recent opening-up policies have made the Chinese market a new major arena for global financial institutions. The New York-based financial group will become the latest foreign bank to gain control of its investment banking business in China as the country steps up financial liberalization to give foreign companies greater access to the Chinese market. Swiss bank UBS Group increased its share holding in its China securities joint venture to 51% in 2018. In March, US bank JP Morgan and Japanese financial group Nomura also gained regulatory approval to own a majority stake in their securities venture in China. Morgan Stanley is also seeking regulatory approval to own a majority stake in its China securities JV, information published on the CSRC website showed. Analysts said the move by Goldman Sachs showed that foreign banks remain bullish about the prospects of their business in China as further financial liberalization is expected to bring more business opportunities. Once they get majority ownership in joint ventures, foreign financial institutions will have more say in their management and decision-making, leveraging the advantages associated with a high level of internationalization.

(2) There is a complete decision-making system and the highest decision-making center. Although each subsidiary or branch has its own decision-making organization, it can conduct decision-making activities according to its own business field and different characteristics, but its decision-making must be subordinate to the highest decision-making center.

(3) Transnational corporations arrange their business activities according to the global strategy, seek for the market and reasonable production layout in the world, specialize in production and sell products in designated places, so as to maximize profits.

Bell to focus on technology as demand for helicopters soars

A burgeoning market in China is helping to drive a transformation in US helicopter manufacturer Bell, according to a senior company executive. "Bell is moving beyond being a helicopter manufacturer to becoming a tech company, and the Chinese market is of great significance to our transformation and global presence," said Patrick Moulay, senior vice-president of Bell. "China is the world's most promising market, unique and dynamic. And we are committed to supporting its growth," Moulay said in an interview with Xinhua News Agency. In a complicated global economic environment, China's aviation market keeps growing.

"No other country shows such a trend. Its needs in helicopters and heli-services keep surging," Moulay said. Bell is a global leader in vertical-lift aircraft, including tilt rotors and helicopters. In more than eight decades, it has sold about 35,000 aircraft worldwide.

China is Bell's second-largest market in the Asia-Pacific region after Australia. As of May 2019, more than 160 Bell helicopters were flying in China, taking up about 30% of the general aviation market. China's helicopter market has seen continuous double-digit growth in the past few years with an increase of around 14% year-on-year in 2018. This is amid turbulence in the global market, especially in the offshore oil and gas industry. "The Chinese market is stable. The need is here, and we see incredible growth here," Moulay said. Compared with the market volume of 10,000 turboshaft-engine helicopters in the United States, the existing fleet of under 700 in China "is far away from its needs". He expects China's commercial helicopter market to double in five years with major growth from emergency medical services, law enforcement, utility, tourism and corporate segments. Thanks to their agility, helicopters are the main emergency medical service aircraft and are also favored in other fields that are crucial to public services and commercial operations. Medical rescue is a key focus for China's authorities. The government's decision to boost the general aviation industry is also injecting vitality into the market. "All of these are positive for the heli-market and players worldwide. And we are endeavoring to support its growth," Moulay said. In August 2018, Bell and its Chinese partners jointly launched the Bell 407 reassembly facility in Xi'an, in Northwest China's Shanxi Province. The project followed a purchase agreement for 100 Bell 407 series helicopters from a Chinese customer in 2017. In June, Bell put into operation the Bell China Supply Center. With a bonded warehouse in Shanghai Pudong International Airport, the center is a major move to enhance its customer services capabilities in China. "Our vision for Bell in China is as a local player with local capability," said Moulay. "We support our local partners and are transforming our capability here to grow together with the Chinese market," he added.

Bell Helicopter rebranded to Bell in 2018. "We wanted to move beyond being a manufacturer to becoming a tech company and flight solution provider," said Moulay. With legacy of unique technologies such as the tilt rotor, Bell is gearing up to expand from helicopter manufacturing to providing innovative vertical takeoff and landing vehicles, tilt rotor solutions, and aviation services. The company is developing the Nexus, a new energy-powered aircraft for on-demand aerial transport as a future air taxi. "Being unique and agile, Bell is undergoing a transformation. That is how Bell brings additional value to the market and industry now and in the future," said Moulay. "Bell takes a long-term view of the Chinese market," he added.

(Source: Hu Tao, Bell to focus on technology as demand for helicopters soars, China Daily Global, August 21, 2019.)

(4) Transnational corporations have strong competitiveness in the international market due to their strong economic and technological strength, fast information transmission and fast cross-border transfer of funds. Here is a win-win case. According to Xinhua report: Tencent Music Entertainment Group, one of China's largest media companies, is mulling a purchase of 10% of music monolith Universal Music Group, UMG's parent company Vivendi reported. UMG, with global revenue in excess of $7 billion, is considered one of the "Big Three" music companies in the world, along with Warner Music Group and Sony Music. It was named by Fast Company, a leading business magazine in the United States, as one of the top 50 most innovative companies in the world "redefining what a modern label should look like". "It's a smart business move on Tencent's part," said Eddie Cane, former UMG label representative. "They may dominate the market in China, but UMG dominates the global music market. It's simple math: the more songs you have to license and the bigger the artists, the more money you make." UMG owns global hitmakers such as Lady Gaga, Taylor Swift, Drake, Ariana Grande, Billie Eilish and Kendrick Lamar, but they also has iconic bands like The Beatles, U2, Abba and Queen in its stable. Tencent, owner of the popular and ubiquitous social media WeChat super-app, has bought shares in the past in leading Western companies like Spotify, Tesla and Epic Games. It is a powerful music industry leader in China and owns QQ Music, a leading China-based music site that went public late in one of the largest US offerings, plus a popular online Karaoke platform. Tencent has managed to cash in on Chinese music-lovers' adoption of mobile technology and their willingness to buy music through streaming platforms. Vivendi, a Paris-based media conglomerate controlled by French billionaire Vincent Bollore, announced that negotiations with Tencent were based on a corporate valuation of UMG of $33.6 billion. The Chinese digital giant's potential 10 percent stake would be worth $3.36 billion. Tencent did its homework first, entering into a licensing deal for UMG's content in 2017 to see how well it played in China. Vivendi is eager to explore enhanced cooperation that could help UMG capture growth opportunities offered by the digitization and the opening of new markets, adding the company hoped the Vivendi-Tencent relationship would help promote its artists in China. This deal enables Tencent to make money not just

on the Western artists that they license on their platform in China, but on artists that are selling anywhere in the world. It's a smart kind of double-dipping. If all goes well, the deal also gives Tencent an option to buy an additional 10% of UMG within the next 12 months under the same terms, a move that could pay off for both parties.

(5) Many transnational corporations have varying degrees of monopoly on certain products because of their economic, technological strength or advantages in the production of certain products or in certain regions. For example, XGIMI, China's largest intelligent projector manufacturer in terms of shipments in 2018, is looking to gain a lead in the European market by unveiling a new product toward the end of this year. XGIMI, was founded in 2013. Back to 2014, when XGIMI launched its first generation smart projector, it caused a stir in the projector industry due to its innovative product concept and outstanding user experience. It has sold its products in more than 127 markets including the United States, Singapore and India. XGIMI designs and manufactures high-performance multi-functional smart projectors and laser TV and is determined to improve viewers' audio-visual experience. XGIMI has created a series of giant screen projection products with critical partners like Harman/Kardon, Texas Instrument, Baidu and Google. The fresh product will be in partnership with tech giant Google Inc and will be embedded with brand new functionalities that are designed specifically for European users, said Zhong Bo, CEO of XGIMI. Through beefing up global efforts, the company aim to become the largest intelligent projector firm in the world over two to three years. In Japan, one of its major products, PopIn Aladdin, has already gained great popularity. The product topped other domestic projectors in Japan with a market share of 25%. PopIn Aladdin is a dome light with a built-in projector that the company specifically designed for the Japanese market, where many apartments have limited living space. Such as in Japan, the company tailor their products according to different characteristics in different countries to make them really localized. Recent years have witnessed increasing number of people jumping onto the bandwagon of screenless televisions in the form of high-end projectors that are capable of providing very high-resolution pictures. In China, more than 2.6 million intelligent projectors were sold last year, up 102% year-on-year, according to smart home data provider All View Cloud. The figure is expected to reach 4.2 million this year. The rising demand also led to a fierce competition in the home market where around 30 projector manufacturers are trying to grab a slice of the cake. Facing fierce competition, the firm has made major efforts in research and development of core technologies. XGIMI hopes to gain more users through offering

a high-end tech experience instead of simply lowering prices to attract more customers.

1.2.2 Latest characteristics of transnational corporations development

1. Focus on localization strategy

The localization strategy of multinational companies in the early stage was mainly the localization of raw materials and production. In recent years, localization strategy pays more attention to in-depth research and development and the development of human resource localization. In order to better serve overseas markets, transnational corporations have changed the practice of arranging research and development activities in their home countries and gradually set up R&D centers in host countries with important market positions and certain conditions. China has surpassed the US and India in 2007 as the most attractive destination in the world for research and development (R&D) investment, according to the United Nations report. There are now approximately 1000 R&D centers in China with most of them in the technology sector. The number of centers in the country continues to rise thanks to the ongoing investment by transnational corporations, the increasing need to be closer to local customers and low labor costs. Conscious and clear positioning, competency-based hiring, leadership induction and integration are some of the major factors that transnational corporations look for when expanding or setting up new facilities in China.

Apple plans $160 million on 2nd China data center

Apple Inc will invest at least 1 billion yuan ($160 million) as part of its plan to build a second data center in China, as the United States tech giant accelerates steps to localize its iCloud services in the world's largest smartphone arena, according to a source familiar with the matter. The data center, located in North China's Inner Mongolia autonomous region, will be put into operation in 2020 and Apple's investment into fixed assets related to the project, including buildings and other basic infrastructure, will total around 1 billion yuan, the source said. The figure does not include costs relating to servers, which will account for most of Apple's investment in Inner Mongolia, added the source, who declined to be named as he is not authorized to speak publicly about the matter. The move follows Apple's announcement in July 2017 that it will build its first China data center in Guizhou province, in the southwest of the country. The project will also receive $1 billion in investment and be put into operation in 2020. The two centers will be operated by Guizhou-Cloud Big Data Industry Co Ltd, an enterprise owned by the Guizhou provincial government, the source added. They are designed to comply with China's new cybersecurity laws and to meet local consumers' growing appetite for better cloud services. The Inner Mongolia project, located in Ulanqaab city, will use 100 percent renewable energy sources. The region was listed as one of the country's big data development zones in 2016. Ulanqaab is now home to an ongoing big data center project of Chinese technology giant Huawei Technologies Co Ltd, a big smartphone rival of Apple. The Huawei project is expected to cost 1.5 billion yuan when finished. James Yan, research director with Counterpoint Technology Market Research, a global research firm, said, "Establishing local data centers would further strengthen Apple's ties with the Chinese government, and help reduce the company's operating and maintenance costs of cloud services. " As for data security, he said the Chinese operator GCBD, with disaster recovery capabilities, already has data privacy and security protection in place. GCBD's shareholders include Inspur Group Co Ltd, China's largest server-maker. Apple is ratcheting up investment in China. Last March, the California-based company announced plans to build two research and development centers in Shanghai and Suzhou, Jiangsu province, as part of its broad efforts to tap into the country's manufacturing, design and app development talent pools.

(Source: Zhang Jianfeng, Apple plans $160 million on 2nd China data center, China Daily, February 8, 2018.)

2. Accelerate the global strategy

Transnational corporations pay more attention to enhance strategic coordination and accelerate the allocation of global resources by promoting global strategies, so as to realize the transformation from transnational corporations to global corporations. Accelerate the efficiency of global resource allocation through relocation, mergers and acquisitions. Strengthen overseas branches and improve resource sharing.

Transnational corporations attach importance to increase investment in overseas branches, actively expand local and global research and development, change the mode of single output of knowledge from home country, and promote the efficient flow and sharing of knowledge, information and resources within enterprises. Accelerate the reserve of international talents. Transnational corporations attract talents with their attractive cultural atmosphere, governance mode, favorable treatment and development space, and fully reserve international human resources.

3. Attach great importance to fulfill corporate social responsibility

Corporate social responsibility (CSR) is how companies manage their business processes to produce an overall positive impact on society. One definition of corporate social responsibility is that set of actions which the organisation is not obliged to take, taken for the well-being of stakeholders and the public. With the emergence of global issues such as climate warming, environmental pollution and food safety, transnational corporations, as "corporate citizens" with global industrial chain layout and important role in the world economy and society, have further improved their requirements to fulfill their social responsibilities. In recent years, transnational corporations have made great progress in solving local employment problems, protecting the environment and improving product standards in their supply chains. By raising social responsibility performance standards, transnational corporations directly raise requirements on suppliers and play an important role in promoting global industrial enterprises to fulfill social responsibility.

Huawei donates 98,000 USD ICT equipment to Zimbabwe's leading university

Huawei on Friday donated telecommunications equipment worth 98,000 US dollars to the University of Zimbabwe (UZ) to enable the institution to offer the latest training in information and communication technology. The equipment was handed over to the university by Huawei Zimbabwe (Pvt) Limited managing director Hao Wen to UZ acting vice chancellor Paul Mapfumo. Hao said his company had become a leading ICT player in Zimbabwe since entering the local market in 1998 and was committed to enhancing technical skills training to students. "As a result of this commitment, we will, today, hand over the ICT equipment to the University of Zimbabwe. This laboratory equipment will enable the University of Zimbabwe to offer the latest technical training to students and professionals in the industry. We hope they could help develop local ICT talent and boost ICT industry development of Zimbabwe," he said. He added that the company was committed to building a better connected Zimbabwe, to bridge the digital divide by increasing network coverage and had so far built more than 2,500 km optical cable and serving over 4 million people. "As part of our ongoing investment, Huawei has created over 20,000 jobs directly and indirectly. We would also like to continue to cooperate with Zimbabwean schools, universities and colleges to build capacity and enhance technical skills transfer to students," he said. Hao said the company intended to continue creating continuous innovation and cooperation in the ICT industry through its Seeds for the Future corporate social responsibility program. "We leverage our world-leading ICT technologies in the program to cultivate ICT professionals in the countries where it operates and thus drive the local ICT industry forward. " Hao said. The Seeds for the Future program was launched in Zimbabwe in 2016 and so far more than 40 outstanding students have travelled to China for training. ICT minister Kazembe said the handover of the ICT equipment would enable Zimbabwean universities to produce world class graduates and professionals as it made learning and teaching skills more effective. "This will enhance professional skills and competency in ICT among ICT practitioners and science and technology and engineering students and graduates for the benefit of the country as we move towards an upper middle income economy by 2030," he said. Acting vice chancellor Mapfumo said UZ was looking forward to becoming a center of excellence following the donation of the equipment. He added that given the increasing importance of ICTs, Zimbabwe needed to strengthen its technological base in order to meet the demands of the 21st Century.

(Source: Xinhua, Huawei donates 98,000 USD ICT equipment to Zimbabwe's leading university, May 18, 2019.)

4. Focus on business model innovation

Business model innovation is an activity that changes the basic logic of enterprise value creation to enhance customer value and enterprise competitiveness. For example, the emergence of the Internet has changed the basic business competition environment and economic rules, marking the advent of the era of "digital economy". The Internet has made a lot of new business practices possible, and a number of new businesses have emerged based on it. In general, there are three ways of transnational corporations business model innovation:

(1) Start by changing the way meet customer needs. Nowadays in the megatrend of innovation, the industrial value chain becomes more and more sophisticated and the traditional single-organization innovation mode faces huge challenges. Take Nippon Paint for example, it is the world's leading paint brand. Since its inception in 1881, after hundreds of years of unceasing innovation, has now developed into a major global suppliers of automotive paint and one of the largest suppliers of decorative paints. From October 18 to October 19, Nippon Paint China (Nippon Paint) took part in the 40th anniversary of the establishment of Shandong Wiskind Ltd (Wiskind) and the Future Building Development Forum in Qingdao, during which Wiskind held a signing and launching ceremony,

announcing the establishment of Nippon Paint-Wiskind joint innovation center, in the coil coatings industry. In the new joint innovation center, Nippon Paint and Wiskind, a domestic construction market leader in manufacturing and pre-coated metal (PCM) trading and PCM application products, will cooperate closely along a full innovation process. Both companies collaborate on identifying business opportunities, developing advanced technologies, market promotion with intentions of commercial success. The center will be a platform for integrating value chain players, and actively participate in the innovation eco-system involving coating manufacturers, coil producers, distributors, design institutes, project owners and contractors. The center will provide high value-added solutions for customers in the construction industry. Additionally, this cooperation between Nippon paint and Wiskind will integrate the resources, experience and expertise from both sides in the construction PCM industry to carry out a joint innovation project, developing tailored products to best address the customer needs in the targeted market segments thus creating high value solutions for customers. After many years of market development in China, customer needs in the PCM industry have changed, requiring suppliers to provide more comprehensive, better targeted and higher technology solutions. Nippon Paint China recognized that "We must take the approach of customer-centric open innovation and achieve multiple victories by collaborating with partners along with the entire value chain, even cross-industry or cross-discipline innovation". The cooperation between Wiskind and Nippon Paint will open up a new chapter in the PCM industry. The establishment of the joint innovation center is not only the integration of resources of both sides, but also the starting point of a win-win cooperation. In the future, the company will continue to innovate, make full use of the resource platform, create better products and provide more considerate services to create an integrated, efficient and oriented enterprise, so to play its dual role and contribute to more customers and partners.

(2) Break industry boundaries and redefine customers. Do you know which industry Suning, Gome and JingDong belong to? Innovations in business models tend to break industry boundaries or play with the rules of another industry. Suning and Gome belong to the household appliance trade circulation industry and have achieved great success through the business model of chain stores. However, JingDong, a rising star, did not have a single store. Relying on the virtual Internet, JingDong came into the world and directly attacked the customers with online shopping preferences. With the operation rules of the internet industry, JingDong directly forced the two power giants to jump far away from the traditional storefront model and achieved great success. Breaking the boundaries of the industry

is also a major path for business model innovation under the new economic forces.

Museums join online marketplace

When the British Museum opened its online store on Alibaba's marketplace Tmall on July 1, more than 50 types of products based on the institution's iconic collection sold out within days. Revenue amounted to more than 1 million yuan ($146,000) and the store attracted about 160,000 fans in just one month. Sales were beyond the expectations of both the museum and its Chinese licensee partner, Alfilo Brands Co. "We'd anticipated the museum's online store being a success but never thought it would be so big," said He Yizan, the CEO of Alfilo, which operates the online shop. The bulk of the products that sold out, such as teacups, bags and fans, were tailored solely for the Chinese market. They were inspired mainly by the museum's Egyptian collections and the Rosetta Stone, a slab found in 1799 inscribed with three versions of a decree issued in Memphis, Egypt, in 196 BC during the Ptolemaic dynasty (305-30 BC). The best-selling item was a set of black decorative tape inscribed with words from the Rosetta Stone, the British Museum's signature work, priced at 19 yuan. Consumers posted photos showing creative displays with lipstick, notebooks, perfume bottles and phone covers decorated with the tape to show how much they love it. The majority of these product users were born in the 1990s and 2000s, a generation known for affinity for interesting and "cute" designs. The annual revenue of the museum's Tmall store is expected to be 20 million to 30 million yuan, He said. Later this year, a pop-up store will open under the name of the British Museum, and will run for four months in Shanghai, where art lovers will be able to experience replicas and products in the museum's worldwide collection via high-technology. "When people's income reaches a certain level, the art and culture industry will witness a boom," He said, adding that this point has already been reached in China. Consumers' desire for the British Museum's products is just the tip of the iceberg for China's prosperous museum-related creative and cultural industry.

The past two years have seen the rising popularity of designer products based on cultural references as well as an increasing number of cultural institutions entering this market in China. In 2016, four ministries, including the then Ministry of Culture and the Ministry of Finance, issued a regulation to support museums in developing their collections to sell gifts and souvenirs. According to the Ministry of Culture, as of last year about 2,500 museums and cultural institutions had begun to design and produce merchandise. When Qiu Tong introduced her team's designs based on the Summer Palace-the imperial garden in Beijing listed as a UNESCO world heritage site in 1998-to many brands and e-commerce platforms last year, her targeted consumers were surprised. This was because they still had the impression that the Summer Palace only had an on-site store offering low-priced and poor-quality souvenirs. Qiu set up China Cultural Tourism and Creativity, a company in Beijing, last year to help museums and cultural institutions design and promote brands and products. Her team of about 50 is dedicated to cooperating with the Summer Palace, a must-see destination for travelers to Beijing. The palace, overlooked by mountains and boasting lakes and traditional architecture, is regarded as a masterpiece of Chinese garden design. It was built by the Qianlong Emperor during the Qing Dynasty (1644 ~ 1911) to celebrate the 60th birthday of his mother. "It's common to associate the Summer Palace with the Forbidden City, since both are related to royal families. However, if you look into its history, the Summer Palace is more about females. That's the basis on which we design its products, which are more oriented toward women," Qiu said. Buyers of Summer Palace items are mainly women, ranging in age from 18 to 28, who want beautiful items, Qiu added. While the Forbidden City was China's seat of power and home to emperors, the Summer Palace acted as a resort where emperors and their family members spent their vacations. The former, also called the Palace Museum, now leads the way for China's creative and cultural industry, with millions of fans following its online stores on various e-commerce platforms. The Summer Palace just started its online merchandising business last year. Qiu and her team spent almost a year getting ideas on how to design products for the public. The first items were based on animals, plants and buildings, and included paper tapes, teacups, bookmarks, jewelry and accessories. An online store opened under the name of the Summer Palace on e-commerce giant Alibaba's Tmall in June. Chinese festivals are used to promote its products in cooperation with JD or 360buy, another Chinese e-commerce player. In January, the store sold tens of thousands of red envelops on 360buy before Spring Festival with patterns inspired by buildings at the Summer Palace. During the Dragon Boat Festival in June, the palace launched special boxes for 360buy. Thousands of boxes of zongzi, a Chinese rice dish, sold out within a week, each priced at 188 yuan, doubled the average price. The dish is prepared for the Dragon Boat Festival. Qiu said that working with e-commerce platforms was a quick and effective way to reach more consumers and make them aware that the Summer Palace has its own products. "I think the rise of the Chinese creative and cultural industry can be partly attributed to the boom in China's social media and new media," Qiu said, referring to the rapid spread of information on social media such as instant message app WeChat, microblogs and short-video apps such as Douyin. The Palace Museum's online store opened in 2008 and quickly caught the public eye with a series of interesting promotions on social media. In 2016, a short animation on emperors and their concubines in the Forbidden City went viral on WeChat, quickly attracting numerous fans to the Palace Museum. This also happened when seven museums, including the National Museum of China, the Shanxi History Museum and the Hunan Museum, made a short video depicting iconic antique statues and sculptures performing a pop dance on Douyin in May. The video, which lasted less than two minutes, was watched millions of times, resulting in numerous searches in online stores. Qiu said the Summer Palace is also planning to make short videos on apps such as Douyin to promote its products, while in December the British Museum turned to streamlining platforms in China to promote its products to buyers. Despite these various promotion channels, according to industry insiders the key to the popularity of museum-related products lies in the design and the cultural history behind them. Wang Feiyue, the design manager on Qiu's team, said that although many museums have turned to designing products, the items are similar. All the museum stores have notebooks, fans, key rings, bookmarks and fridge magnets. Making their products different from others requires designers to take time to carry out research and related work.

Most museums do not have in-house studios to design products. They only have one or two workers in charge of the products and brand department. Some have not yet even set up such a department. Wang, who has worked in the industry for 10 years, used to design for other cultural institutions, including the Palace Museum. "A good design does not mean simply printing a pattern from a painting onto a product. Many museums do it in this way, though," Wang, 31, said. "We should combine modern design and traditional patterns. " For instance, Wang and her colleagues made more than 4,000 pictures inspired by buildings, animals and plants at the Summer Palace after visiting it hundreds of times, and finally chose to draw illustrations based on these. Wang referred to the Empress Dowager Cixi, a significant presence for decades in the 19th and early 20th centuries who spent lots of time living at the Summer Palace. As a result, the garden has been used to promote items associated with her lifestyle in certain areas, such as fashion, cosmetics and pets. "Cixi was a dog lover...she had lots of dogs in the garden and she gave each of them a salary," Wang said. Cixi's favorite colors were pink and blue. Most of the porcelain vases in the garden featured a combination of the two colors, which Wang said were "a strange mix of colors for people in her era". But she said that through modern design full use of both colors can be made to make signature products for the Summer Palace-for instance, a vase-shaped pink-and-blue cushion. Wang describes herself as a passionate lover of traditional Chinese culture. She thinks museum items should also be used to spread culture and make young people see that "traditional culture can be cool and chic". That is also the approach taken by designer Xu Chenkang when working with his client, the National Museum of China. Xu, deputy general manager of the culture and creative products trading department with the Shanghai Free Trade Zone, decorated Kentucky Fried Chicken outlets in eight Chinese cities in February with designs from a scroll painting. This depicted people in the Ming Dynasty（1368～1644）taking part in different activities to celebrate the Lantern Festival on the streets. The painting is in a collection at the National Museum of China. In 2016, the museum cooperated with the Shanghai Free Trade Zone to develop cultural and creative products. Xu invited designers from China and abroad to work on the museum's collection, which covers 5,000 years of China's history, ranging from jade and porcelain to bronze and paintings. "It's a vast collection. Antiques from a single dynasty are enough for designers to get inspiration," Xu said. Through these efforts, sales at the museum's online shop on Tmall doubled last year. Thousands of night lamps from the museum's porcelain collection shaped like antique vases were sold. Although Xu's team has come up with some popular designs, he still feels that interpreting collections for modern designs is difficult. The cooperation between the National Library of China and Shanghai Free Trade Zone in June increases the difficulty because turning books into products is harder than turning artworks into them. "It's the first time we have designed products for libraries. To turn books and Chinese characters into creative products is a big challenge and time-consuming," Xu said. The National Library of China has more than 37 million books, many of them are rare and thousands of years old. Xu also uses the free trade zone to help sell museum products overseas. Some items, such as postcards, feature in online stores for foreign buyers, but such sales are still in their infancy, Xu added. For He Yizan, whose company, Alfilo, signed the license contract with the British Museum and the Palace Museum, Chinese museums' business overseas is set to take off. "Museums are major inspirations for designers in the West. I believe there must be passion for the Palace Museum outside China," He said. His team is developing product ideas with the theme "when East meets West", for example, enamel vases and bottles introduced into China's royal families in the 17th century. The technique for creating them was learned by Chinese craftsmen. The Palace Museum has a large collection of such enamelwork, which He considers to be a good inspiration for products tailored for Western consumers. His company has teams in Shanghai and Los Angeles, and he plans to work with retailers and brands in the West to expand the market for museum products from the East. He said Western museums have only relatively recently entered the commercial arena, and although they are leading the way, their Chinese counterparts are catching up. As a museum lover, Feng Wei from Beijing likes to buy museum products. She has bought a yellow duck from the British Museum, a necklace from the Louvre in Paris and bookends from the Museum of Modern Art in New York. Now, she has turned to products from Chinese museums, which she says are considerably more attractive than when they were designed five years ago, when most museums only had an on-site store selling low-quality souvenirs. "All my female friends buy museum products on Tmall. They are very beautiful and practical," she added. She buys teacups, bags, bookmarks, paper tapes, notebooks and even aprons. When she visits her foreign friends, she hands them over as gifts. "They love it and I feel proud to share a taste of my culture," Feng said. The mother of a 3-year-old boy, Feng added that her only regret is that there are not enough museum products for children in China and they are not well-designed or are "too childish".

(Source: Deng Zhangyu, Museums join online marketplace, China Daily, August 9, 2018.)

1. 2. 3　Operation characteristics of transnational corporations

(1) The strategic goal of transnational corporations is to realize the maximization of global profits by taking the international market as the orientation, while domestic enterprises take the domestic market as the orientation.

(2) Transnational corporations control foreign enterprises by holding shares, while domestic enterprises control their foreign economic activities by contract.

(3) The foreign-related activities of domestic enterprises do not involve the establishment of economic entities in foreign countries. The relationship between domestic and foreign economic activities is loose and has great contingency. Their foreign-related economic activities are often terminated immediately after the completion of the transaction and no longer participate in the subsequent reproduction process. And transnational corporations in all areas within the scope of world, full of capital, goods, talent, technology, management and information, such as trading activity, and the "package" activities shall conform to the company overall strategic goals and under control, the parent company, its subsidiary or branch, as well as foreign enterprises to participate in the local reproduction process. Therefore, transnational corporations must implement highly centralized and unified management of their branches.

1.2.4 Operation mode

(1) Horizontal diversification. Such companies are mainly engaged in the production and operation of a single product. There is little specialized division of labor between the parent company and its subsidiaries, but the amount of intangible assets such as production technology, sales skills, trademark and patent transferred by the company is relatively large.

(2) Vertical diversification. Such companies can be divided into two categories according to their business content. One is that the parent company and subsidiaries produce and operate products in different industries but related to each other. They are cross-industry companies, mainly involved in the production and processing industries of raw materials and primary products, such as mining and planting, refining, processing and manufacturing, sales and other industries. For example, Exxon Mobil, one of the world's largest publicly traded energy providers and chemical manufacturers, develops and applies next-generation technologies to help safely and responsibly meet the world's growing needs for energy and high-quality chemical products. It is engaged in the exploration and exploitation of oil and gas worldwide, transporting oil and gas by pipelines, oil tanks and vehicles and ships, operating large refineries, refining the final products from crude oil, wholesale and retail hundreds of oil derivatives.

The other is that the parent company and subsidiaries produce and operate products with different processing degrees or process stages in the same industry, mainly involving automobile, electronics and other industries with a high level of specialized division of labor. For example, PSA (Peugeot Société Anonyme) is founded in 1966. Ten years later, the merger of Citroën S. A. and Peugeot S. A. gives rise to the PSA Peugeot Citroën group. The Group harnesses its solid results to buy out Chrysler Europe in 1978, making it Europe's number-one group and world number-four. Creation of the PSA Peugeot Citroën group through the merger of Citroën S. A. and Peugeot S. A. The PSA Peugeot Citroën holding company owns 100% of the two companies Automobiles Peugeot and Automobiles Citroën. Present in 107 countries or regions, the Group is a leader in its sector. Six strategic regions are key to Groupe PSA's industrial and commercial ambitions today: China, the Group's No. 1 market; Europe, central to its growth momentum; the Middle East and Africa, the third mainstay of the PSA Group's global activities, particularly with its return to Iran; India-Pacific, one of the most dynamic growth markets looking ahead to 2021; Eurasia, where Groupe PSA is seeking greater local integration of its production, notably in Russia; and Latin America, where the Group is focusing on Brazil and Argentina. The company carries out the specialized division of labor internally, its 84 subsidiaries and sales organizations abroad are engaged in the business of various processes such as casting, casting, engine, gear, reducer, machining, assembly and sales, realizing the integration of vertical production and operation.

(3) Mixed diversification. Such companies handle a variety of products. The parent company and subsidiaries produce different products and conduct different businesses, and they are not connected with each other. Such is the case with Japan's Mitsubishi heavy industries. The companies of the Mitsubishi zaibatsu that formed the Mitsubishi keiretsu were predominantly heavy industrial companies. This gave the Mitsubishi keiretsu a product base that was weighted toward the slow-growing or declining industries. These were also the industries which were energy-intensive. This was a liability when the price of energy increased substantially in the 1970s. The Mitsubishi group is close-knit. Of the 29 firms belonging to Mitsubishi's presidents' council, 23 are named Mitsubishi. The Mitsubishi group firms are managed relatively conservatively. The main bank for the group, Mitsubishi Bank, merged with the Bank of Tokyo, a quasi-governmental bank that was set up in the Meiji Period to handle foreign exchange transactions. The general trading company for the group is Mitsubishi Shoji, which is important enough to be part of the core of the group. The other member of the core of Mitsubishi is Mitsubishi Motors.

1.3   Development Trend of Transnational Corporation

1.3.1   Strategic technology alliance of transnational corporation rising continuously

Today, the market's demand for technology has become the core of major transnational corporations to fight for and consolidate market competitiveness. Due to the invisibility of technology itself, high investment, high risk of technology research and development, through division of labor, joint competition, choosing combination, adopting the ways of technological alliance and cooperation among enterprises to reduce the operating cost and make up for their own strategic gap. This trend has become the best choice for transnational corporations. In 2015, the Bluetooth Special Interest Group, which oversees the development of the wireless communication standard, announced that Apple has become a "promoter member" of the group, giving the company new power to guide Bluetooth's development. Promoter members are given a continual seat on the group's board of directors, and are also the only membership class that can vote on its corporate matters. Apple has been an associate board member of the group since 2011, and the company's senior wireless architect, Joakim Linde. currently serves as the board's secretary. In the past, Apple's board membership was term limited. The current promoter members—Ericsson, Intel, Lenovo, Microsoft, Nokia, and Toshiba—voted unanimously to have Apple join their ranks. The company's upgraded membership makes sense given how important Bluetooth is to so many of its products. The Apple Watch relies on Bluetooth to exchange information with the iPhone it's paired to, and many of the continuity features introduced to iOS and OS X last year use Bluetooth to exchange information between Apple devices so users can transfer their work back and forth. Apple first introduced Bluetooth support in Mac OS X at the 2002 Macworld Expo in Tokyo, along with a $49 Bluetooth adapter that allowed users to begin testing the wireless communication technology. Starting in 2003, users were able to purchase new Macs with Bluetooth built in. Since then, Bluetooth use has exploded, fueled by the popularity of mobile devices and wearable tech. Those markets represent one of the tech industry's new frontiers going forward, and today's decision means that Apple will have a front seat to help guide the Bluetooth standard going forward. Interestingly, Google isn't currently one of the interest group's board members, even though it's building technology like Android Wear that also relies on Bluetooth.

In addition, through extensive strategic technology alliances with upstream and downstream companies, transnational corporations have achieved both technological innovation and reduced R&D costs. Massive export-oriented assembly activities have formed a great demand for the upstream industries. Over the past two decades, foreign investors have massively transferred their export-oriented labor-intensive activities to China. As a result, a huge assembly capacity has been formed, which has in turn produced a huge demand for the upstream spare parts industries. In order to reduce cost and enhance competitiveness, more and more upstream spare parts have been produced in China, leading to the formation of industrial clusters between upstream and downstream industries. This trend will become an important direction for foreign investors to transfer their industries to China. In fact, this "import substitute" is completed under the conditions of opening to the outside world, which will result in a continuous extension of the value chain of the processing trade production in China. Massive export-oriented assembly activities have formed a great demand for the upstream industries. Over the past two decades, foreign investors have massively transferred their export-oriented labor-intensive activities to China. As a result, a huge assembly capacity has been formed, which has in turn produced a huge demand for the upstream spare parts industries. In order to reduce cost and enhance competitiveness, more and more upstream spare parts have been produced in China, leading to the formation of industrial clusters between upstream and downstream industries. This trend will become an important direction for foreign investors to transfer their industries to China. In fact, this "import substitute" is completed under the conditions of opening to the outside world, which will result in a continuous extension of the value chain of the processing trade production in China.

1.3.2   Industry scope of cross-border mergers and acquisitions become extensive and monopolistic

Established business models across traditional industries are changing at a breakneck pace due to technological advancements, changing consumer preferences and cross sector convergence. At the current speed of change, many businesses may be unable to keep up due to lack of internal capability to generate innovation. Increasingly, market leading companies are turning to Disruptive M&A in responding to disruption and growth challenges. According to the Hurun China Cross-border M&A Report, a total of 323 overseas cases of mergers and acquisitions were registered in 2018, with a value reaching 738 billion yuan, a decrease of 23% from a year earlier. Energy and mining were the focus areas of Chinese companies' overseas investment last year. Seven of the top 50 M&A cases targeted overseas energy companies, while another six eyed mining. High-tech industries, Internet and E-commerce, computer science, radio and biological science were also of great interest to Chinese companies.

Why do transnationals choose overseas merges and acquisitions? What is the mechanism for Chinese enterprises increase their overseas investment rapidly while their technologies and business capacity are relatively poor? According to Dunningh's OLI theory, three primary factors are affecting or deciding on transnational investment by enterprises: Ownership of resource skills (O, business resource advantages such as technology and the basis for overseas investment owned by multinational enterprises), Location (L, which can bypass the trade barriers and is accessible to market and to interests of low-cost bases), and Internalized advantages (I, costs saved by turning transnational trade into intra-company transactions through transnational investment). This theoretical framework can be used to analyze the factors affecting transnational investment and can also be used to analyze the factors affecting transnational merger and acquisition. It's the only principle whether the cost of merger and acquisition can be $1 + 1 > 2$ after the merger and acquisition. If the M&A profit and welfare is bigger than M&A cost, then the merger and acquisition is make sense.

People used to think that enterprises conduct transnational investment only with the business resources and technological advantages. Dunning pointed out that enterprises can also form their advantages by combining different objectives and factors, at the same time the transnational investment strategies and models adopted by transnational corporations can differ. By giving examples, Dunning pointed out that there can be different models. We can see the following types of dunning's transnational investment and the influencing factors written by Asakawa Kazuhiro (2003):

① Gaining of natural resources. To use self-owned funds, technologies, marketing management and relevant supplementary resources as the basis (O) instead of market transactions to gain access to resources with lower cost (I) in countries rich in natural resources and relevant facilities (L).

② Gaining of market. To use self-owned funds, technologies, business organizations, economies of scale and brand formation as the basis (O) to reduce transaction costsby directly producing and supplying on the market of the country (I) where trade barriers exist and policies encouraging investment are carried out (L).

③ Pursuit of efficiency. To use self-owned funds, technologies, business organizations and marketing management and the gained resource capabilities characterized by economies of scope and geographical advantages as the basis (O) to gain access through internalization to economies of scale and governance co-efficiency (I) in countries where products are specialized and economically low wages are distributed (L).

④Gaining of strategic resources. To reduce risks and raise efficiency (I) through internalized efficiency based on the above-mentioned capabilities (O) and in countries where needed technologies, markets and other assets are available (L).

⑤Commercial intercourse. To use self-owned superior products and marketing management ability as the basis (O) to stabilize through internalization the production of superior products and reduce contradictions between the agents on the markets that are attractive and have potential customers (L).

⑥Service Support. To use rich customer service experiences accumulated in the native country as the basis (O) to provide customers on valuable customer markets (L) through internalization with services (I) in a more stable and effective way.

We can see from the above: Models ② and ⑥ are virtually used to make overseas investment by making use of the comparative advantages (O) of enterprises in terms of technology and service; Model ③ is similar to the aforesaid two models, that is, investors must have comparative advantages (O), but should also pay close attention to applying economies of scale brought about by investment, merger and acquisition to increase such comparative advantages (O); Model ④ is actually used by enterprises to acquire such strategic resources as technologies owned by other countries through investment. Merger and acquisition (L) and to gain efficiency and development through internal integration; Model ① is virtually used to gain direct access through investment, merger and acquisition to the needed natural resources (L) exclusively possessed by other countries so as to step up those advantages (O).

According to the theory of value chain and competitive advantage put forward by Porter, the competitive advantages are related to various links of the value chain, including R&D, designing, procurement, manufacturing, marketing and service, and to the whole of the chain (including coordination and financial resources), and the competitive advantages of different enterprises probably come from different links and their combinations. It suggests that enterprises may increase the advantages of some links in advance through strenuous efforts or merger and acquisition, then form the overall advantages and capitalize on the overall advantages to improve the weak links and further develop the overall abilities. For example, Zhejiang Geely Holding Group acquired a 9.69% stake in Daimler AG, for 600 billion yuan in 2018, becoming the largest shareholder of Mercedes-Benz's parent company. The Chinese carmaker acquired the stake valued at around $9 billion through an investment fund, according to a regulatory filing. Geely, one of the most successful carmakers in China, has been on a shopping spree. In December 2017, it became the biggest shareholder in Sweden's Volvo AB. In the same year, it acquired a 49.9% stake in Malaysian automaker Proton and bought flying car company Terrafugia Inc. Geely also owns Volvo Cars, which it purchased from Ford in 2010. Take the global strategies of Geely and Great Wall vehicle makers for example:

China's carmakers are speeding up their expansion into overseas markets, especially in the Belt and Road economies, which is expected to boost their sales and more importantly help improve the local automotive industry. Zhejiang Geely Holding Group, owner of Volvo Cars, purchased a 49. 9% stake in Malaysian carmaker Proton in June 2017. Within two years, the brand has shown encouraging signs of fast recovery. In May, Proton sold 10, 711 vehicles, a 46-month high. From January to May, its sales totaled 36, 157 units, up 70% year-on-year. By the end of April, it had become the second best-selling brand in Malaysia. Daniel Donghui Li, chief financial officer of Geely, said one reason why Proton singled out Geely from others was that the Chinese carmaker had a unique vision for Proton's future development. "We set a goal to help it to become the No. 1 brand in Malaysia and a top three brand in the ASEAN region. The results so far are showing that we are on the right path," said Li, who is also a Proton board member, in late April.

Proton's burnished performance was mainly thanks to its model X70 launched in December. Made at one of Geely's plants in Zhejiang Province, the model was built based on its popular Boyue sport utility vehicle but tweaked to meet Malaysian customer demands. Geely said the model is just part of the story. In fact, it has introduced for Proton a comprehensive strategy covering aspects from personnel, product quality and cost control to research and development and plant renovation. Proton engineers are also joining Geely's research teams in Ningbo, Zhejiang province, and the two sides are working to find solutions that will enable Proton to benefit most from Geely's proven system. Ahmad MuzaimiZainol, a Proton project manager, said after two years of cooperation, they have seen encouraging progress. Geely is helping Proton to revamp its plants as well. The facility in TanjungMalim is now ready to produce the X70 SUV later this year, as local assembly trials had started on June 12. Proton Chairman Syed Faisal Albar said that the two companies' partnership has proved to be a shining example of cooperation between both countries. He also suggested that Chinese companies use Malaysia as a gateway to the ASEAN market, which has a population of 650 million. China's Industry and Information Technology Minister Miao Wei said during the plant's opening ceremony that Geely and Proton should seize the opportunities provided by the Belt and Road Initiative, and urged them to deepen cooperation to offer globally competitive products. Besides Malaysia, Geely has built plants in countries like Belarus, the UK and Sweden and is selling its models in more than 20 countries and regions.

Another leading Chinese carmaker, Great Wall Motors, is reaping fruits of its going-global efforts in Russia. On June 5, a Haval F7 SUV rolled off its plant in Tula, a city 193 kilometers south of Moscow. Haval is one of Great Wall Motors' three automotive brands. The $500 million plant is the company's largest ever investment overseas. It is also the first overseas wholly-owned full-process manufacturing plant by any Chinese carmaker. The plant has a designed annual capacity of 150,000 vehicles, and in accordance with the carmaker's vision, around 65 percent of components will be purchased locally in Russia. The carmaker hopes the plant will better serve local demands but also work as a base for its foray into eastern European markets, including the adjacent countries of Belarus, Ukraine and Moldova. Great Wall Motors said it would like to make the most of the plant by producing models of other Chinese brands aiming to expand their footprint overseas. "Going global is an inevitable trend for Chinese brands," said Wei Jianjun, founder and chairman of the company. "The Haval plant in Russia is one of the most important parts of Great Wall Motors' overseas strategy, and it starts a new era for Chinese carmakers to sell their technology and standards to foreign markets," he said. Great Wall Motors President Wang Fengying said the global market will become the main battlefield for the company. "Thus, we have made a global development strategy, sped up planning internationally and expanded investment in the overseas markets," she said. Great Wall Motors is currently selling its SUVs and pickup trucks to more than 50 countries and regions, said Wang.

(Source: Li Fusheng, Chinese vehicle makers to tap potential in global markets, China Daily, June 25, 2019.)

1.3.3   The participation of transnational corporations promotes the aggregation effect of industry and knowledge

There are three types of transnational corporation participation, namely, manufacturing knowledge clusters, tech-based knowledge clusters and market-oriented knowledge clusters.

1. Manufacturing knowledge clusters

Manufacturing knowledge clusters are mainly concentrated in manufacturing industries represented by tabulating areas in Switzerland, Toyota city in Japan, and semiconductor hardware in Taiwan Hsinchu of China, etc. They are mainly in regions with lower factor costs, and more emphasis is put on the smooth division of labor and cooperation network among regional enterprises. The way of transnational corporations to participate in the main points is two kinds. One kind is through the outsourcing of productive value chain, although the transnational corporations not directly enter because the market is mainly composed of local small business network, transnational corporations can use the outside information which passed to the production system in the region form the cluster in the global market network and provide most of the industry's customer service. The other kind is the cost or efficiency advantage obtained by transnational corporations as participants. For example, Toyota city in Japan and the just-in-time system jointly developed by Toyota and supplier clusters.

2. Tech-based knowledge clusters

Tech-based knowledge clusters are concentrated in areas such as silicon valley in the United States, triangle science park in north Carolina, and Bangalore in India. Here gathered mainly for high-tech companies, highlighting the dissemination of tacit knowledge, diffusion, innovation and high-tech talents. In order to acquire local tacit knowledge and global or regional talents, it is necessary to establish a direct participant network. Silicon valley in the United States, many international business companies like Microsoft and other international well-known transnational corporations give the financial and material resources, human capital investment to the area, or to support the supplier's activities in this region, or the company headquarters in this place, or will be moved into the region's global research and development center, only because participating in the regional innovation network can get together the set of competitive advantage. Talent is an important factor of tech-based knowledge clusters, especially for the fast developing China.

In recent years, Lanzhou, the capital of Gansu Province, has fully utilized its unique resources, developed new talent recruitment models and broadened the channels for attracting talent, which not only stems the outflow of talent but also promotes the construction of its talent pool. Several measures have been taken to attract and sustain talent, according to the Lanzhou Talent Office. Flexible measures have been carried out to attract high-end talent. In the past four years, Lanzhou has introduced 375 well-known domestic experts and academic leaders, including 29 academicians and 30 experts from the "Thousand Talents Program". Projects are also effective to pool innovative talent. Lanzhou has organized the talent support program on innovation and entrepreneurship since 2014. Up to now, it has invested a total of 190 million yuan to gather innovative teams to advance the development of key areas and emerging industries. Lanzhou has explored new mechanisms for institutional cooperation. Several plans have taken effect to boost cooperation with different areas and research institutes. Technology transfer centers have been established with Shanghai Zhangjiang, the National Center for Technology Transfer, Peking University, the University of Science and Technology of China, University of Lausanne of Switzerland and Nanyang Technological University in Singapore. It has also established cooperative ties with more than 40 universities. To the end of 2018, the city had 405,900 in its talent pool, accounting for 10.95% of the total population—2.57% points higher than the provincial level, according to statistics from the municipal departments. The number increased 39.49% compared with the same period three years ago, and 45.38% compared with the end of 2012. Those with bachelor's degrees or above account for nearly half the total, and those under the age of 45 make 64.41%. On July 5, the Lanzhou City Talent Office held the awarding ceremony for overseas talent stations, also the Matchmaking Meeting of the Gansu Chamber of Commerce to attract investment and invite talent. National Guidance on Promoting the New Pattern of Western Development in the New Era has approved a series of policies, such as the development plans of urban agglomeration in West Lanzhou and the Lanbai National Independent Innovation Demonstration Zone, said Municipal Talent Work Group chairman Wang Xu said during the meeting of the Lanzhou Municipal Committee. Restrictions on urban residency have been lifted in cities whose population is less than 5 million, providing more opportunities for talent to start their own businesses in Lanzhou. Preferential policies such as research funding, platform operating subsidies, living subsidies and relevant services are also available.

(Source: MaJingna, Lanzhou continues building talent pool, ChinaDaily. August 19, 2019.)

3. Market-oriented knowledge clusters

Market-oriented knowledge clusters is generally concentrated in world-class cities, and the leading industries are mainly financial service industries such as banking and securities, like London financial hub in Britain, Frankfurt financial hub in Germany and Hong Kong financial hub in China. Transnational corporations enter these regions not only to obtain important information from the whole world and meet the needs of the regional market, but also to provide comprehensive information services to subsidiaries and their corresponding branches in the surrounding areas. Hong Kong has been ranked among the top 3 global financial hubs, following New York and London according to the 25th edition of the Global Financial Centers Index report launched in Dubai. China's financial center Shanghai grabbed fifth position on the list ahead of Tokyo, Toronto and Zurich, according to the report jointly released by the city of London's think tank Z/Yen Group and Shenzhen's China Development Institute. Beijing ranked ninth ahead of Frankfurt, putting three Chinese cities in the top 10 world hubs. The index tracked 112 financial centers globally, with 102 centers in the main index and 10 in the associate list, according to their business environment, human capital, infrastructure, financial sector development and reputation. Top 10 global financial hubs include: New York, London, Hong Kong, Singapore, Shanghai, Tokyo, Toronto, Zurich, Beijing, Frankfurt.

1.3.4 Brand marketing has become the focus of transnational marketing

The integration of global markets has led to a convergence of consumer preferences, encouraging organizations to search for more competitive global corporate locations. The global efforts of transnational corporations lead to the development and promotion of global brands. Therefore, with the increasing globalization of competition, the success of transnational corporations depends on the positioning of their capabilities and the management of their brands in many countries. Brand value, not to be mistaken with brand equity, is a phrase used in the marketing industry to describe the value of brands based on the implication that the owner of a well-known brand name can generate more money than from products with a less well known name, brand valuation is the estimation of a brand's total value. ISO (International Organization for Standardization) 10668 maps out the appropriate process of valuing brands by adhering to six key requirements: transparency, validity, reliability, sufficiency, objectivity and financial, behavioral and legal parameters. A brand is an intangible asset (name, term, design, symbol or any other feature) which identifies one seller's product from another. Usually, a brand is the corporation's most valued asset. Strong brands enhance business performance primarily through their influence on three key stakeholder groups: (current and prospective) customers, employees and investors. They influence customer's choice and create loyalty; attract, retain, and motivate talents; and lower the cost of financing. For example, Google is one of the most recognized brands in the world. Use the data of Statista, in North America alone, the brand's value amounted to approximately 302 billion U. S. dollars in 2018. Ultimately, brands help shaping perceptions and purchasing behavior, making products and service less substitutable. Therefore, brands create economic value by generating higher returns and growth and mitigating risk.

The United States was the world's most valuable nation brand by a distance in 2018, with a value of 25.9 trillion U. S. dollars. To give this figure some context, China was second in the ranking valued at 12.8 trillion U. S. dollars, less than half the nation brand value of the United States (see Figure 1-1). From the perspective of objective facts, many of the world's most valuable brands come from the United States. The impact of a country's national image on a country's economy and the brands based in the country cannot be understated. A good national image can bring many positives such as encouraging investment from outside of the country, adding value to a country's exports, as well as attracting tourists and skilled migrants to the country. On the other hand, a country may incur significant economic damage from poor nation brand management or global events. The evidence of the impact of a nation's brand value can be seen in the retail industry. As a result of globalization and various trade agreements between markets and countries, many retailers are capable of doing business on a global scale. As such, the national image associated with the brand's home market is important. Many of the world's leading retailers are companies based in the United States, the world's most valuable nation brand. Walmart and Amazon are examples of American retailers doing business around the world. The success of U. S. retailers can also be seen through their performance in online retail. Amazon is a prime example of this, with the company's sales revenue flourishing over the previous years.

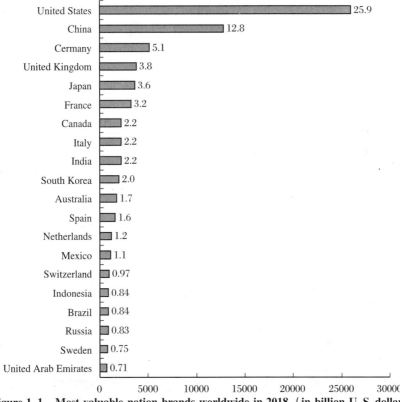

Figure 1-1   Most valuable nation brands worldwide in 2018 (in billion U. S. dollars)

Source: Statista, 2019.

This statistic presents the brand value of the 25 most valuable brands worldwide as of 2019. As of 2019, Amazon was the most valuable brand in the world with an estimated brand value of about 187. 905 billion U. S. dollars. Apple, which was the second leading brand in the world, had a brand value of about 153. 634 billion U. S. dollars. See Figure 1-2 below for details:

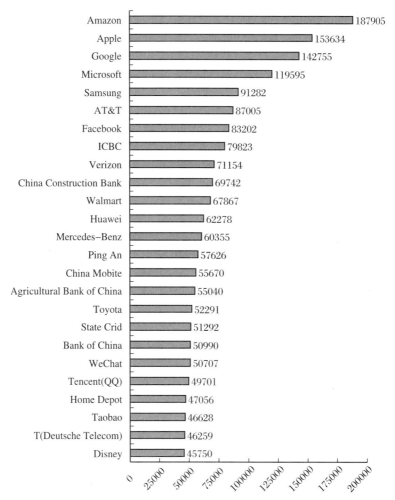

Figure 1-2 Brand value of the 25 most valuable brands in 2019 (in million U. S. dollars)
Source: Statista, 2019.

The statistic shows the the largest brand value change of the biggest brands in the world in 2019 compared to 2018 (see Figure 1-3). The brand value of Instagram increased 95% in 2019 compared to 2018, which was the highest increase of the year.

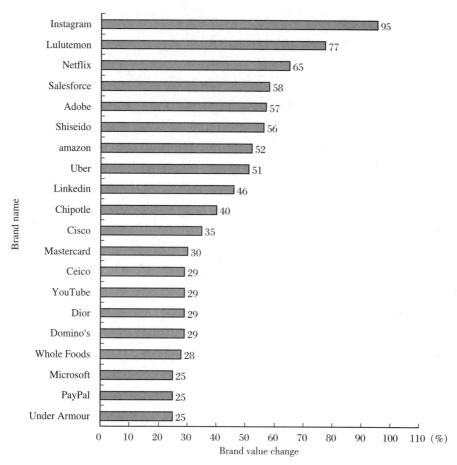

Figure 1-3   Largest brand value change of the largest brands in the world 2019 value compared with 2018 value-(in percent)

Source: Statista, 2019.

More Chinese companies have been striving to build stronger brands in a global arena. Their brand value rises rapidly, primarily propelled by technology-driven innovation and overseas consumers' acknowledgement, some researchers and reports showed. Many Chinese brands overall have experienced a massive growth. According to the Xinhua's report, Chinese brands have the characteristics below:

1. Surge in brand value

A total of 15 Chinese brands gained their footholds in the 2019 BrandZ Top 100 Most Valuable Global Brands ranking this year, according to an annual report released on Tuesday by global communication services provider WPP and Kantar. Among them, e-commerce heavyweight Alibaba and internet giant Tencent entered the global top 10, ranking No. 7 and No. 8 respectively. 9 brands made their debut in the highly competitive list. BrandZ is what it describes as the world's largest database for brand equity, which refers to a brand's value based on consumer perception of and experiences with the brand. Besides, the total value of the top 100 most valuable Chinese brands leaped a record 30% to 889. 7 billion US dollars, making the largest annual rise since the ranking for Chinese brands was launched in 2011, according to another report titled 2019 BrandZ Top 100 Most Valuable Chinese Brands released in May. In particular, Chinese technology brands dominate the top 10 in terms of overseas presence. Six brands, including Huawei, smartphone maker Xiaomi, drone maker DJI, AI and humanoid robotic company UBTECH Robotics, double their figures of last year.

2. Stronger brand power overseas

A separate study also showed that the brand power—a BrandZ measure of brand equity—of Chinese brands in the global market, expanded by 15% year on year, compared with the 5% growth last year. The strongest growth of brand power appeared in mobile gaming, E-commerce and smartphone. Huawei, Lenovo, and Alibaba are the top three in the 2019 Top 50 BrandZ Chinese Global Brand Builders ranking released in April. The study also found that brand power has been rising fastest in Japan, France and Spain. Other countries with massive future import potential for Chinese brands involve the United States, Britain, Germany and Australia. These products and platforms are Chinese owned, designed, or originate from China. They adhere to global standards.

3. Better perception, tech-driven innovation

The remarkable growth in total brand value of Chinese firms was propelled by various brands' speedy expansion into China's lower-tier cities. Rising purchase power among consumers and more positive comments from overseas consumers towards Chinese consumers are some other factors behind, according to the ranking report in May. Many people have to recognize that the perception of (overseas) consumers toward Chinese brands has changed significantly, those brands were not just getting into local markets, but also setting up a cool image of being leading innovators. Particularly, innovators in E-commerce, video streaming and social media fields have performed quite well, which made western companies like YouTube and Facebook "start to look at the east" to learn how to twine social network with commercial patterns. Chinese video streamers iQiyi and Youku achieved some of the fastest growth in brand value last year, rising 158% to 5.6

billion dollars and 136% to 5 billion dollars respectively, according to the May report. YouTube is studying (from) iQiyi and TikTok. Facebook is also studying (from) Wechat and how it connects social network with commerce. Nowadays when we ask overseas consumers, they think Chinese brands are innovative and creative, especially young consumers in Spain, the UK and the United States. China's Belt and Road Initiative has given Chinese brands some "real guidance and a lot of support," so that they can "get their products there and promote their presence to local consumers. People are seeing lots of Chinese brands start to increase cultural and social influence in overseas markets, especially countries alongside the Belt and Road.

4. Localization is necessary

Some experts also pointed out what challenges Chinese companies are facing in the global brand landscape, as the overall recognition of Chinese brands abroad is still relatively low. For example:

"Having your products there in the market does not mean that you have a brand. Brand building is not happening overnight. So that's why (when) we're seeing Chinese brands, like Alibaba, Tencent, Meituan and Didi, they are all working very hard to build their equity day in and day out. There is a long way to go." To strengthen brand building in international markets, experts suggested that Chinese companies should improve their ability in story-telling about their products and how the products would make a difference to the lives of their consumers, so as to promote their brands' reputations. "We highly recommend the Chinese brands to really explore local lifestyles, local insights, and local media habits. How to deliver great customer experience and how to generate more bonding with consumers are key." Experts said and further noted that they found Chinese brands with greater popularity overseas have used "mainstream media to interact with their target consumers. Consumers are willing to pay more for a unique and differentiated product and service that they could not find elsewhere. In this regard, a possible way for consumers to pay more for a brand is through not only a differentiated product, but the employment of communication channel, delivery, packaging, etc. to create this point of difference. Going forward, Chinese brands must be clearer about what makes them different and build up brand recognition, if they are to compete successfully against strong global brands." experts stressed.

(Source: Chinese companies try to build stronger brands with more value overseas. Xinhua, June 14, 2019.)

1. 4   Case

Case-1

Apple，Goldman Sachs start issuing Apple Cards to consumers

Apple Inc. and Goldman Sachs Group Inc. rolled out a virtual credit card on Tuesday, which would help the iPhone maker diversify from device sales and also built out the Wall Street bank's new consumer business. With the card, Apple aims to draw in iPhone owners with 2% cash back on purchases with the Apple Pay service, no fees and an app to manage related finances. For Goldman, the card will enhance the bank's focus on its Marcus consumer banking brand, which it started in 2015 to even out volatile results from businesses such as trading and investment banking. Apple shares were up about 1 percent at $195. 30 in trading before the bell. The company said a limited number of the people who had expressed interest in Apple Card would start receiving sign-up invitations on Tuesday. "The Apple Card doesn't play in the same league as premium rewards credit cards like the Chase Sapphire Reserve or AmEx Platinum," said Sara Rathner, an expert on credit cards at NerdWallet. "Those cards charge ultra-high fees, but in return, you get some pretty sweet perks: massive sign-up bonuses, annual statement credits, free Global Entry, and a higher point-earning rate for travel expenses. " Apple will offer an option for a physical card made of titanium, but with no visible number. Instead, the card's number is stored on a secure chip inside the iPhone, which will generate virtual numbers for online or over-the-phone purchases that require a number. Apple said purchase information would be stored on the user's iPhone and that it cannot see the data. Goldman will not be allowed to use data for marketing purposes, even for selling its other products. Gene Munster, managing partner with Loup Ventures and a longtime Apple watcher, said the card's adoption is likely to be low in the first year, but it could generate about $1. 4 billion of high-margin revenue by 2023. That would add about 1. 8% to Apple's overall earnings and complement the much larger Apple Pay business for total payments revenue of $5. 38 billion by 2023. Apple has roughly 50 million US Apple Pay users now. But at Apple's size— $265. 6 billion in sales for fiscal 2018— the revenue matters less than the effect on keeping Apple customers tied to its brand, said Ben Bajarin, an analyst at Creative Strategies. "If it works, it's one more thing that causes you to stay deeply loyal and entrenched in the Apple ecosystem, even if something better comes along," he said.

(Source: China Daily, August 7, 2019.)

Questions:

1. Why did Apple Inc. and Goldman Sachs Group Inc. roll out a virtual credit card?

2. Through this collaboration, what did Apple Inc. gain from a strategic perspective?

Case-2

Nestle and Starbucks launch new coffee products in nation

Nestle has teamed up with coffee giant Starbucks to launch a new series of coffee products on Thursday for the Chinese mainland market, which are also the alliance's first products in the market since it was established in August last year. The new products feature capsule coffee and allow consumers to make coffee at home or in the office by themselves, which is part of the alliance's efforts to tap such groups amid fierce competition in the coffee delivery sector. All of the new products will be available on e-commerce platforms and gradually be promoted in grocery stores, including stores on Tmall, JD and Suning. com. Belinda Wong, chairman and CEO of Starbucks China, said the alliance with Nestle will better suit the daily lives of consumers outside of its retail stores. "This is just the beginning," said Wong. "The coffee market in China is large and still growing, and coffee consumption here is still at an early stage." It also marks the first move by Starbucks to promote its coffee retail products in the at-home and foods service segments in China. Nestle is seeking to accelerate the innovation and development of China's coffee categories with the launch of the new products and attract more consumers with customized designs. Rashid Aleem Qureshi, chairman and CEO of Nestle in China, said the partnership with Starbucks would integrate benefits of three top coffee brands in Nescafe, Nespresso and Starbucks to develop business opportunities in China, the second largest market for the alliance. "Overall, the coffee category is exciting in China," said Qureshi. "We saw momentum in different coffee product categories. The cooperation with Starbucks will help transform and upgrade the Chinese coffee industry." Jason Yu, general manager of the Kantar Worldpanel China, said the country's coffee market has massive potential, especially in instant coffee, capsule coffee and coffee stores. "The competition among these coffee makers will further upgrade the Chinese coffee market and will offer consumers more options in coffee consumption," Yu said.

(Source: Wang Zhuoqiong, Nestle and Starbucks launch new coffee products in nation. China Daily, August 9, 2019.)

Questions:

1. What are the characteristics of transnational corporation development through activities of Nestle and Starbucks?

2. For the transnational marketing, what is the significance for corporation to build brand value?

1.5 Expanding Reading

Reading-1

Amazon to shift focus of its business in China

US-based tech giant Amazon. com Inc plans to shut down its third-party seller services on its Chinese online marketplace in July as it shifts its focus to the more lucrative businesses of cross-border e-commerce, cloud services and e-reader devices in the country. Starting from July 18, customers logging in to Amazon's Chinese web portal will only see a selection of overseas goods from its global store, rather than products from local third-party sellers. "We are working closely with our sellers to ensure a smooth transition and will continue to deliver the best customer experience possible. Sellers interested in continuing to sell on Amazon outside of China are able to do so through Amazon Global Selling," Amazon said in a statement. Amazon emphasized it won't exit the Chinese market and will continue to invest and grow in China across its cross-border shopping business Amazon Global Store, Global Selling, which helps Chinese merchants sell products abroad, cloud service platform Amazon Web Services, Kindle devices and content. "Over the past few years, we have been evolving our China online retail business to increasingly emphasize cross-border sales," Amazon said, adding that it continues to make operational adjustments to focus its efforts on cross-border sales in China and to keep improving the experience for both Chinese customers and global selling partners. The US tech heavyweight is facing increasingly fierce competition from homegrown e-commerce rivals such as Alibaba Group Holding Ltd and JD, as well as group buying app Pinduoduo Inc, which went public in New York last year. Statistics from market consultancy iResearch showed Alibaba's

Tmall marketplace and JD controlled 81.9% of the Chinese market last year. Amazon entered China in 2004, when it bought a local online shopping website Joyo. com for $75 million. Since then, it has invested in warehouses, data centers, and programs to teach Chinese sellers how to get their goods to Amazon customers. Amazon launched Amazon Prime in China, the first unlimited free cross-border shipping membership program globally in October 2016, in an attempt to lure the rising number of quality-conscious Chinese buyers to buy foreign products. A Chinese third-party seller who sells books via Amazon China's online marketplace said he hasn't got the notice on closure of the third-party seller service yet, and his sales revenue at Amazon is lower than that from Tmall and JD. "Amazon did not gain an upper hand in China. The Chinese e-commerce business is a small part in the company's global layout and its competitive edge in China mainly lies in its abundant overseas products from its global e-store," said Yu Jian, general manager of shopper behavior specialist from Kantar Worldpanel China. Amazon is struggling to contend with local leaders including Alibaba, JD and NetEase Kaola, which have ramped up their efforts in cross-border shopping, Yu added. Chen Tao, an analyst at the Beijing-based consultancy Analysys, said Amazon has strong competitiveness and a good reputation in its global logistics, warehouses and supply chain, but it faces some challenges in its localization efforts in China. "Amazon lags behind its rivals in marketing promotion and business operations in China. If its Seattle headquarters gives more operating and decision-making power to the China unit, the situation might be much better," Chen added. Chen also said compared with Amazon, domestic online retailers have a better understanding of local consumers' needs and how to operate in accordance with local market conditions.

(Source: China Daily, April 19, 2019.)

Reading-2

Foreign marketing, analytics companies are looking to meet strong data tracking demand as Chinese firms expand overseas. China is gearing up to be one of the few truly mobile-first economies in the world, which is spurring foreign mobile marketing and analytics companies like AppsFlyer to target opportunities in the country.

Oren Kaniel, CEO and co-founder of AppsFlyer, said that in China, the firm's development is "much faster than they can grow the team. Chinese companies think bigger. One notable thing is that when doing business in China, we get direct feedback from companies and leverage those suggestions to improve our businesses worldwide," Kaniel said. With 15 offices and more than 4,000 partners around the world, the Israeli company is rated by multiple market agencies as the top player in terms of market share in market attribution, an important niche of mobile marketing. At this year's Mobile Attribution and Marketing Analytics, or MAMA, a leading mobile marketing conference, at the end of June, China Daily spoke to Kaniel in an exclusive interview about his insights into the Chinese mobile marketing market, the firm's growth strategy and its future investment plans in the country.

How do you see the role of the Chinese market in your global business strategy and layout?

The Chinese market is important to us—it has become one of AppsFlyer's most successful regional markets. In recent years, increasing numbers of Chinese companies are thriving globally and we are happy to see Chinese customers who use our products succeed on a global level. This is consistent with our mission: to help our customers gain global success through our technology, support, service and premium experience. On one hand, with these successful global companies, the growing demand in the Chinese market has driven the development of AppsFlyer's business in China and we have now gained the trust of many mobile companies. On the other hand, we also benefit from cooperating with such great companies. Their high standards and expectations strongly motivate and inspire us to keep improving our product, customer experience and data accuracy. It helps us better serve our clients worldwide. In Israeli culture, people are straightforward. This is a shared value that we appreciate in our daily work with Chinese companies. When I ask for product feedback, they tell us what they like and what they'd like us to improve, what challenges they are facing and how we can help them. Based on this feedback, we can develop and improve our products to better meet the market and evolving market dynamics. This is one great example of the culture fit between Israel and China.

What are your views of the Chinese mobile market? What are some of the latest changes? What opportunity does it bring to your company?

The China market is truly mobile-first-and it is thriving. According to a CNNIC (China Internet Network Information Center) report, there are 829 million netizens in China, 98.6% of whom access the internet using mobile devices. The support of emerging infrastructure-for example, the fast development of 4G and 5G in China, plus cheaper data packages and the greater accessibility of smartphones and apps for developing populations-has meant an influx of heavy downloads and app activity that is predicted to continue. In addition, China is also a dominant leader in terms of both app downloads and in-app consumer spending. With its strong international presence, China's potential as an app market has jumped exponentially in the past year or two and is expected to hit 120 billion downloads and $62.4 billion in consumer spending by 2022. Under the trend of more refined advertising, AppsFlyer can help advertisers determine which campaigns are successful, where and when-serving as a go-to resource for deciding how to select efficient distribution platforms for advertisers. We see a huge opportunity in the China market, reflected in the strong demand for data tracking and marketing attribution, and the strong willingness of Chinese companies to enter the global market. With the common goal of making Chinese companies successful, this will be a win-win cooperation for us and our Chinese customers.

Since more and more firms are targeting overseas markets, what major challenges do you think they are facing?

It depends on the regions they are targeting and the media partners they are cooperating with. Different markets bring different opportunities and challenges. Through our partnerships with 5,000 media sources and technology integrations, we can help marketers and advertisers achieve their goals in practically every corner of the globe. In short, this is a platform that allows any company to go global. We also encourage companies to experiment and test their products, to measure almost every aspect of their marketing activities so they can see what's working, what isn't, and how everything works together. This is the essence of attribution, and it's essential in enabling brands and businesses to make the best data driven decisions possible. With our measurement and attribution, we can tell them whether the decisions they've made are good or not. In this way, they can always learn and grow. So, one of our main pieces of advice for companies is to experiment, find the mistakes they've made, and improve to be more competitive in the global market. At the same time, retention continues to be a major challenge for Chinese advertisers with only 4% ~ 5% of their acquired users sticking around after 30 days. As such, a focus on post-install metrics, not on installs, is the key to success. Ad fraud remains one of the biggest challenges for mobile marketers in China. These are the problems we can help Chinese customers solve.

What's your near-term plan in China? Do you plan to increase investment or expand your presence in the Chinese market this year?

First, since we're seeing increasing demand, we definitely plan to continue to invest and expand our team in China, as the business is growing faster than we can grow our team. We also plan to continue to develop a robust platform for domestic

Chinese advertisers. We've set up an AppsFlyer Academy project, which will entail one month of training for new employees in a local learning center. Afterward, these employees will join our training center in Tel Aviv for a further three months of training. This ensures that we have professional, high-quality employees. In terms of business development, our plan is simple: we will continue doing what we are doing now. Our core business is clear: we will maintain our unbiased market positioning. Remaining independent is critical for us, as we have no economic relationships with media services. We only represent our clients' interests-the marketers, advertisers and developers. Because we stick to our principles, we have earned a lot of trust, especially from major companies like Alibaba, Tencent, Bytedance Pinterest, Baidu, and more. Also, we will continue to invest in our technology and product development to help our customers achieve success.

What are the differences between the Chinese market and those in other Asian countries and the West in the mobile marketing sector?

I would say the major difference is that the Chinese market has much more potential to grow. The advanced mobile infrastructure, mature measurement technology, and robust mobile payment culture, all put China at the forefront of growth potential for app developers and marketers worldwide. Another important factor I'd like to mention here is our cultural fit. I think Chinese culture and Israeli culture are a good fit because we share many common values. We have the courage, creativity, and strong enterprising spirit to create something new. At the same time, feedback is also crucial for us. Our Chinese customers are usually straightforward about their needs, which makes communication with customers easier and clearer. They tell us what challenges they are facing and what they want from us.

How was AppsFlyer's performance in China during the past year?

Since we entered the Chinese mainland market in 2013, we have grown alongside this fast-growing market, and we now have more than 60% market share in China. Over the past few years, we have served thousands of customers in China, and have docked almost all the mainstream advertising platforms like Tencent, Bytedance, UC, Baidu, Weibo, iQIYI, Kuaishou, and Xiaomi. Many major companies and smaller companies in China use our technology and product. Our team in China has also grown from five to more than 50. We take our responsibilities seriously. And in the meantime, we're excited about industry growth.

How is AppsFlyer special from other similar companies? What's your unique selling point?

There are four points that make us different: data accuracy, privacy security, the richness of our platform and the fact that we are customer-focused.

(Source: Cheng Yu, Mobile-first efforts creating opportunities, China Daily, August 23, 2019.)

Quick Quiz

1. A transnational corporation is an international corporation or enterprise that sets up branches or subsidiaries in many countries through _____ and engages in economic activities such as manufacturing, sales and service with the purpose of gaining high profits.

2. What's the latest characteristics of transnational corporations development? (   )

A. Focus on localization

B. Accelerate the global strategy

C. Centralized management system

D. Encourage business model innovation

3. The two main characteristics of MNCs are (   ).

A. Large size   B. The world wide activities

C. Selling licenses   D. Significant investment

4. Which one is not the operation characteristics of transnational operations? (   )

A. Maximization of global profits by taking the international market as the orientation

B. Control foreign economic enterprises by holding shares

C. Control foreign economic enterprises by contract

D. The relationship between domestic and foreign economic activities is loose and has great contingency

5. There are three types of transnational corporation participation, namely (   ).

A. Manufacturing knowledge clusters

B. Tech-based knowledge clusters

C. Market-oriented knowledge clusters

D. Investment-oriented knowledge clusters

Answers:

1. foreign direct investment （FDI）

2. ABD

3. AB

4. C

5. ABC

Endnotes

[1] Doob, Christopher M.. Social Inequality and Social Stratification in US Society, Pearson Education Inc., 2013.

[2] "Role of Multinational Corporations". T. Romana College. Archived from the original on 27 November 2016. Retrieved 3 January 2018.

[3] Eun, Cheol S., Resnick, Bruce G.. International Financial Management, 6th Edition, 2013.

[4] Medard Gabel, Henry Bruner. An Atlas of The Multinational Corporation, GlobalInc., New York: The New Press, 2003.

[5] John Dunning. Multinational Enterprises and the Global Economy, Addison-Wesley Publishing Company, Reading, Massachusetts, 1993.

[6] FrederickClairmonte, John Cavanagh. The World in Their Web The Dynamics of Textile Multinationals, Zed Press, London, 1981.

[7] For the facts and figures on TNCs and FDI in this section, see: "Trends on Foreign Direct Investment—Report by the UNCED secretariat," Commission on Transnational Corporations, 20th session, March 1994; World Investment Report 1994—Transnational Corporations, Employment and the Workplace, UNCTAD Division on Transnational Corporations and Investment, Geneva, 1994, chapter 1; "Ongoing and Future Research: Transnational Corporations and Issues Relating to the Environment," United Nations Centre on Transnational Corporations, April 1989; and "Activities of the Transnational Corporations and Management Division and Its Joint Units," Commission on Transnational Corporations, 19th session, April 1993.

[8] Mark Lehrer, Kazuhiro Asakawa. Managing Intersecting R&D Social Communities: A Comparative Study of European 'Knowledge Incubators' in Japanese and American Firms, Organization Studies, 2003, 24 (5): 771-792.

[9] Fan Zengqiang. The new trend and characteristics of the development of multinational corporations, China's circulation economy, 2013 (9): 70-76.

[10] Long Guoqiang. New Opportunities for China's Industrial Upgrading and Recommended Strategies and Policies, Development research center of the state council of the people's republic of China, December 17, 2015.

[11] Dunning, J. H.. Multinational Enterprises and the Global Economy, Addison-Wesley, Boston, 1993.

[12] Porter (1985) has divided the value chain into 5 main links, 3

subsidiary links and 1 infrastructure (finance, plan and quality, etc.). This paper has not adopted Porter's categorization and only tells about the importance of the links. See Chapter 2 of Competitive Advantage (1988 Chinese version) by Porter (1985), China Financial & economic Publishing House.

[13] Chen Xiaohong, Wang Jicheng. Business Model for Chinese Enterprises to Make Overseas Investment, Merger & Acquisition: Types and Conclusions, Research Team on "Study on Approaches to and Policies for Promoting Corporate Mergers and Acquisitions in Economic Adjustment Period", the DRC, 2010.

Chapter 2　Transnational Corporate Management Theory

Learning Objectives

1. Master the definition of international trade.
2. Understand Leontief Parodox.
3. Recognize the meaning of absolute advantage.
4. Master the opportunity cost.
5. Master the definition of comparative advantage.
6. Understand and apply the competitive advantage.

Opening case

Mengniu in $1 billion Bellamy bid

Chinese dairy giant aims to gain further access to lucrative overseas markets. China's dairy giant Mengniu announced on Monday it had made an acquisition offer to Australian infant formula producer Bellamy in a deal valued at $1 billion, to further penetrate the infant formula and food market while expanding its reach overseas. Hong Kong-listed Mengniu said it proposed to acquire 100 percent of the issued share capital of Bellamy Australia Limited. Under the proposed deal, Mengniu would pay A $12. 65 ($8. 69) per share plus a shareholder dividend, marking a 59% premium on Bellamy's closing price. Bellamy's share price soared by 54. 9% on Monday to a peak of A $12. 98. The CEO of Bellamy, Andrew Cohen, said: "Mengniu is a preeminent dairy company in China and an ideal partner for our business. It offers a strong platform for distribution and success in China, and a foundation for growth in the organic dairy and food industry in Australia. " Lu Minfang, the CEO of mengniu said: "Bellamy's leading organic brand position and Bellamy's local operation and supply-chain are critical to Mengniu. " According to Euromonitor International, China's milk formula market is growing steadily and fast from $23. 9 billion in 2018 to a forecast of $32 billion in 2024. Nestle, Feihe International Inc and Danone are top three in the sector in

2019, while Mengniu and Bellamy ranked 12th and 24th respectively. Song Liang, an independent dairy analyst, said the move shows Mengniu's strong ambition to penetrate into the organic dairy market, which is booming in China and it is also a chance to build an infant and baby nutrition and food system. The possible takeover of Bellamy is also an entry ticket for Mengniu to expand its supply chain and capital operations in Australia. In July, Mengniu agreed to sell all of its 51% holding in baby formula and yogurt maker Shijiazhuang Junlebao Dairy Co Ltd as it seeks to concentrate on its core business. In 2018, Junlebao contributed 13.6% of Mengniu's revenue and 9.58% of its profits. For Bellamy, the deal is vital for entry into China's formula market, as the Australian brand has not been eligible for infant and baby formula registration in China. It means it cannot manufacture or sell such formula in China. Its 2019 fiscal report shows that Bellamy's revenue was A $266 million, down 19%. Bellamy is likely to benefit from the acquisition of dairy manufacturer Burra Foods in 2016 by Mengniu. Bellamy and Burra are both Australian companies and the latter can provide OEM service to the former, said Miranda Zhou, an analyst at Euromonitor International. China's dairy industry has been expanding its reach to global markets in recent years. Inner Mongolia Yili Industrial Group-the largest dairy producer in China and Asia-has prioritized global dairy resource security capacity and a management team with global vision, covering areas including raw materials, global cooperation and overseas dairy source development, as well as an international management team. In August, Yili acquired New Zealand's second-largest dairy cooperative Westland Co-operative Dairy Co Ltd after finally clearing all the regulatory hurdles. Yili products are sold under more than 1,000 brands and Yili owns more than 130 branches or subsidiaries. Yili acquired Oceania Dairy Group of New Zealand in 2013. It has since invested approximately $660 million in establishing milk powder, infant formula and UHT production lines for Oceania.

(Source: Wang Zhuoqiong, Mengniu in $1 billion Bellamy bid, China Daily, September 17, 2019.)

In this section, you'll learn about the different trade theories that have evolved over the past century and which are most relevant today. Additionally, you'll explore the factors that impact international trade and how businesses and governments use these factors to their respective benefits to promote their interests.

2. 1 International Trade Theory

What Is International Trade?

International trade theory is a sub-field of economics which analyzes the patterns of international trade, its origins, and its welfare implications. Trade is the concept of exchanging goods and services between two people or entities. International trade is then the concept of this exchange between people or entities in two different countries. International trade theory and economics itself have developed as means to evaluate the effects of trade policies.

2. 1. 1 Classical or Country-Based Trade Theories

1. Mercantilism

Mercantilism, emerged in England in the mid-sixteenth century. The principle assertion of mercantilism was that gold and silver were the mainstays of national wealth and essential to vigorous commerce. Mercantilism was one of the earliest efforts to develop an economic theory. It advocated economic development by the enrichment of the country by means of foreign trade. This theory stated that a country's wealth was determined by the amount of its gold and silver holdings. In its simplest sense, mercantilists believed that a country should increase its holdings of gold and silver by promoting exports and discouraging imports. In other words, if people in other countries buy more from you (exports) than they sell to you (imports), then they have to pay you the difference in gold and silver. The objective of each country was to have a trade surplus, or a situation where the value of exports are greater than the value of imports, and to avoid a trade deficit, or a situation where the value of imports is greater than the value of exports.

A closer look at world history from the 1500s to the late 1800s helps explain why mercantilism flourished. The 1500s marked the rise of new nation-states, whose rulers wanted to strengthen their nations by building larger armies and national institutions. The bulk of what is commonly known as "mercantilist literature" appeared in Britain from the 1620s up until the middle of the eighteenth century. The concept of "mercantilism" first appeared in print in Marquis de Mirabeau's Philosophie Rurale in 1763 as system mercantile, although it was used by other physiocrats during the same period as well. In a mercantilist system, the

State plays a major role through the implementation of protectionist policies building barriers and tariffs and encouraging exports. By increasing exports and trade, these rulers were able to amass more gold and wealth for their countries. One way that many of these new nations promoted exports was to impose restrictions on imports. During the 19th century, the policies of "protection for young industries" that depart from the perspective proposed by Adam Smith that were focused on trade and the allocation of resources are inspired by conceptions based on the economic and political power of States in international trade relations. This strategy is called protectionism and is still used today.

People or entities do busness because they believe that they will be benefit from the exchange. They may need or want the goods or services. While at the surface, this may sound very simple, there is a great deal of theory, policy, and business strategy that constitutes international trade. Nations expanded their wealth by using their colonies around the world in an effort to control more trade and amass more riches. The British colonial empire was one of the more successful examples; it sought to increase its wealth by using raw materials from places ranging from what are now the Americas and India. France, the Netherlands, Portugal, and Spain were also successful in building large colonial empires that generated extensive wealth for their governing nations.

Although mercantilism is one of the oldest trade theories, it remains part of modern thinking. Countries such as Japan, China, Singapore, and even Germany still favor exports and discourage imports through a form of neo-mercantilism in which the countries promote a combination of protectionist policies and restrictions and domestic-industry subsidies. Nearly every country, at one point or another, has implemented some form of protectionist policy to guard key industries in its economy. While export-oriented companies usually support protectionist policies that favor their industries or firms, other companies and consumers are hurt by protectionism. Taxpayers pay for government subsidies of select exports in the form of higher taxes. Import restrictions lead to higher prices for consumers, who pay more for foreign-made goods or services. Free-trade advocates highlight how free trade benefits all members of the global community, while mercantilism's protectionist policies only benefit select industries, at the expense of both consumers and other companies, within and outside of the industry.

New mercantilism, just like the old one, is a system which impoverishes debtors. At all times, the most powerful economies (the ones with foreign accounts showing a surplus and/or with a common currency used as legal tender for international transactions) pour their surpluses (goods and capital) into other countries while carefully selecting their purchases from those countries. Thus, they further their own national economies and levels of employment. Nowadays, we can explain the new phase of mercantilism, by analysing the behaviour of big firms—inescapable agents in the definition of protectionist policies. Transnational corporations notonly redefine and reorganize international exchanges by the way of their networks and strategies, but they also introduce new models of governance, as well as new rules and principles in the places where they act (within and outside the markets). Competition thus becomes global and systemic, and the relations between firms and States are part of this new mercantilism, governed by a global framework of accumulation benefiting to the most powerful economic centres of interest, being private or public.

Multilateralism faces the wrecking ball

US pressure on WTO to rid some members of developing-country status is its latest attack on multilateral institutions that support fairness and inclusiveness.

The United States continues to attack China and the World Trade Organization. A memorandum from the US president to the US trade representative, dated July 26, calls on the latter to use every available means to reform the developing country status in the World Trade Organization, to prevent self-declared developing countries, such as China, Turkey, Mexico, the United Arab Emirates and Qatar, from availing themselves of special treatment and taking on weaker commitments. The memo threatens the US will unilaterally revoke the special and preferential trade treatments granted to these countries unless substantial progress is made in reforming the WTO developing country status within 90 days. The move once again tries to replace global rules with US law. It has cast a dark shadow over multilateralism, but is destined to hit a wall of opposition and end in failure.

Special and differentiated treatment is the basic and legitimate right endowed to WTO members with developing-country status. The benefits include longer time frames to implement commitments, greater flexibility in adopting measures such as export subsidies to adapt to global markets and procedural advantages for WTO disputes. Given the gaps between developing and developed countries, developing country status is a basic principle and pillar of the WTO, embodying the inclusiveness of the multilateral trading system. Many developed countries of today benefitted from long periods of special and differentiated treatment from GATT rules before. It goes without saying that the US is attempting to deprive some developing countries such as China of the legitimate rights and interests they are entitled to by overstressing selective indicators, for example the size of their economies. It is undeniable that, after being admitted to the WTO in 2001, China is much richer as a whole than it used to be and much closer to developed countries than before, and that China has become the world's second-largest economy. However, the gap between China and developed countries is too yawning to miss in terms of economic and social development. In fact, the development level of a country cannot be assessed by total GDP alone. Broad-based indicators, including per capita income, technological strength, economic structure and quality of development, to name a few, also need to be considered.

Multilateralism must address the needs of those who have been left behind. According to the World Bank World Development Indicators database, China's GDP per capita in purchasing power parity (constant 2011 international dollar) was $16, 186.79, only 29% that of the US in 2018. It has prominent imbalanced development and income inequality across regions, with 40.85% of the total population living in rural areas and over 10 million people still living in extreme poverty. China ranked 25th out of 119 countries in the 2018 Global Hunger Index, and 24th out of 101 countries in the 2018 Multidimensional Poverty Index. In contrast, countries such as Singapore and South Korea did not feature on either list.

The US' demand to change the status quo of multilateral institutions has some merit. Over decades, the WTO has helped many countries around the world lift millions of people out of poverty, raise living standards and achieve unprecedented levels of economic growth, especially for the richest developing economies and regions such as Singapore, South Korea, Saudi Arabia, Brunei and Qatar. But the global rules indeed appear increasingly outdated; accordingly, there is a need to fuse those aspects of the existing multilateralism that remain useful into new arrangements that are better aligned with today's world. However, the underlying WTO rules and principles of multilateral institutions-that issues be addressed multilaterally rather than bilaterally-should be respected and not be trampled on. By changing the WTO rules for its own benefit, the US would make multilateralism a relic from a distant past. Since taking office, the US leader has rolled out his "America first" agenda, which is against the underlying values and principles of multilateralism. His administration has embraced inward-looking nationalism, its trade agenda being driven by a narrow mercantilism that privileges the interests of US corporations above those of all others. With rising populism and protectionism, tariffs are being unilaterally imposed on adversaries and many longtime allies alike, based on the grounds of national security. Multilateralism is in retreat, which is due, more than anything else, to the changed attitude of the US. The US leader is apparently cynical toward the international order and has vowed to destroy such multilateral institutions as the WTO. The US withdrawals from one international agreement after another have astounded and embittered its allies, causing the trans-Atlantic alliance to visibly and rapidly weaken. As regards the WTO, the US was its principal architect, and it has been the WTO's principal backer and principal beneficiary. But the US leader has at times complained that it treats the US unfairly and has threatened to pull out of the international trade body. The US administration has blocked the appointment of judges to the WTO's trade court in protest against its rulings, which it regards as having favored China over the US. The multilateral institutions that support core values such as fairness, inclusiveness, and sustainability are currently under increasing threat and being called into question, posing a serious risk to future prosperity. Facing today's complex global challenges, we will all lose in a divided world. We need multilateral settings more than ever to provide us with platforms to communicate ideas, resolve differences, reach consensus in terms of common rules of the game and to draw up the action plans of joint forces. Only when we work together and recommit to the core values and principles of key multilateral organizations, principally the WTO and the United Nations, can we shape a brighter, more prosperous and sustainable future for everyone.

（Source：Huang Yongfu, Multilateralism faces the wrecking ball, China Daily Global, August 8, 2019. ）

2. Absolute advantage

In 1776, Adam Smith questioned the leading mercantile theory of the time in The Wealth of Nations. Smith offered a new trade theory called absolute advantage, which focused on the ability of a country to produce a good more efficiently than another nation. Adam Smith describes trade taking place as a result of countries having absolute advantage in production of particular goods, relative to each other.

3. Comparative advantage

The challenge to the absolute advantage theory was that some countries may be better at producing both goods and, therefore, have an advantage in many areas. In contrast, another country may not have any useful absolute advantages. To answer this challenge, David Ricardo, an English economist, introduced the theory of comparative advantage in 1817. Ricardo reasoned that even if Country A had the absolute advantage in the production of both products, specialization and trade could still occur between two countries. We will discuss this part in more detail in section 2. 2.

4. Heckscher-Ohlin Theory（Factor Proportions Theory）

The theories of Smith and Ricardo didn't help countries determine which products would give a country an advantage. Both theories assumed that free and open markets would lead countries and producers to determine which goods they could produce more efficiently. In the early 1900s, two Swedish economists, Eli Heckscher and Bertil Ohlin, focused their attention on how a country could gain comparative advantage by producing products that utilized factors that were in abundance in the country. Their theory is based on a country's production factors— land, labor, and capital, which provide the funds for investment in plants and equipment. They determined that the cost of any factor or resource was a function of supply and demand. Factors that were in great supply relative to demand would be cheaper; factors in great demand relative to supply would be more expensive. Their theory, also called the factor proportions theory, stated that countries would produce and export goods that required resources or factors that were in great supply and, therefore, cheaper production factors. In contrast, countries would import goods that required resources that were in short supply, but higher demand.

Leontief Paradox

Wassily W. Leontief was an American economist known for his research on input-output analysis and how changes in one economic sector may affect other sectors. Leontief is credited with developing early contributions to input-output analysis and earned the Nobel Prize in Economics (1973) for his development of its associated theory. He has also made contributions in other areas of economics, such as international trade where he documented the Leontief paradox. He was also one of the first to establish the composite commodity theorem. And four of his doctoral students have also been awarded the prize (Paul Samuelson 1970, Robert Solow 1987, Vernon L. Smith 2002, Thomas Schelling 2005).

Leontief's paradox in economics is that a country with a higher capital-per worker has a lower capital/labor ratio in exports than in imports. This econometric find was the result of Wassily W. Leontief's attempt to test the Heckscher-Ohlin theory empirically. In 1953, Leontief found that the United States—the most capital-abundant country in the world—exported commodities that were more labor-intensive than capital-intensive, in contradiction with Heckscher-Ohlin theory ("H-O theory"). His analysis became known as the Leontief Paradox. Leontief used this result to infer that the U. S. should adapt its competitive policy to match its economic realities. In subsequent years, economists have noted historically at that point in time, labor in the United States was both available in steady supply and more productive than in many other countries; hence it made sense to export labor-intensive goods. Over the decades, many economists have used theories and data to explain and minimize the impact of the paradox. However, what remains clear is that international trade is complex and is impacted by numerous and often-changing factors. Trade cannot be explained neatly by one single theory, and more importantly, our understanding of international trade theories continues to evolve.

2.1.2 Modern or Firm-based trade theories

Failure of Leontief and other researchers to empirically validate Heckscher-Ohlin theory. In contrast to classical, country-based trade theories, the category of modern, firm-based theories emerged after World War II and was developed in large part by business school professors, not economists. Firm-based theories have developed for several reasons: (1) the growing importance of TNCs in the postwar international economy; (2) the inability of the country-based theories to explain and predict the existence and growth of intra-industry trade; and (3) the failure of Leontief and other researchers to empirically validate the country-based Heckscher-Ohlin theory. Intra-industry trade means a country exports and imports in the same industry, in contrast to inter-industry trade.

Unlike country-based theories, firm-based theories incorporate factors such as quality, technology, brand names, and customer loyalty into explanations of trade flows. Because firms, not countries, are the agents for international trade, the newer theories explore the firm's role in promoting exports and imports. The country-based theories couldn't adequately address the expansion of either TNCs or intra industry trade, which refers to trade between two countries of goods produced in the same industry. For example, Japan exports Toyota vehicles to Germany and imports Mercedes-Benz automobiles from Germany.

1. Country similarity theory

Inter-industry trade is the exchange of goods produced by one industry in country A for goods produced by a different industry in country B, such as the exchange of French wines for Japanese clock radios. Yet much international trade consists of intra-industry trade—trade between two countries of goods produced by the same industry.

In 1961, Swedish economist Steffan Linder sought to explain the phenomenon of intra-industry trade, as he tried to explain the concept of intra-industry trade. He hypothesized that international trade in manufactured goods results from similarities of preferences among consumers in countries that are at the same stage of economic development. Linder's theory proposed that consumers in countries that are in the same or similar stage of development would have similar preferences. In this firm-based theory, Linder suggested that companies first produce for domestic consumption. When they explore exporting, the companies often find that markets that look similar to their domestic one, in terms of customer preferences, offer the most potential for success. Linder's country similarity theory then states that most trade in manufactured goods will be between countries with similar per capita incomes, and intra-industry trade will be common. This theory is often most useful in understanding trade in goods where brand names and product reputations are important factors in the buyers' decision-making and purchasing processes. Linder's theory is particularly useful in explaining trade in differentiated goods such as automobiles, expensive electronics equipment, and personal care products, for which brand names and product reputations play an important role in consumer decision making. ①

2. Product life cycle theory

Raymond Vernon, a Harvard Business School professor, developed the product life cycle theory in the 1960s. According to Vernon's theory, the international product life cycle consists of three distinct stages: new product, maturing product, and standardized product.

In Stage 1, the new product stage, a firm develops and introduces an innovative product in response to a perceived need in the domestic market. The existence of a profitable market for the product is uncertain, so marketing executives must monitor customer reactions closely. Furthermore, the firm often minimizes its investment in manufacturing capacity for the product, and sells mostly to the domestic market.

In Stage 2, the maturing product stage, demand for the product expands dramatically as consumers recognize its value. The innovating firm builds new factories to expand its capacity and satisfy domestic and foreign demand for the product. Domestic and foreign competitors begin to emerge, lured by the prospect of lucrative earnings.

In Stage 3, the standardized product stage, the market for the product

---

① Undifferentiated goods, such as coal, petroleum products, and sugar, are those for which brand names and product reputations play a minor role at best in consumer purchase decisions.

stabilizes. The product becomes more of a commodity, and firms are pressured to lower their manufacturing costs as much as possible by shifting production to facilities in countries with low labor costs. As a result, the product begins to be imported into the innovating firm's home market (by either the firm or its competitors). In some cases, imports may result in the complete elimination of domestic production.

The theory assumed that production of the new product will occur completely in the home country of its innovation. In the 1960s this was a useful theory to explain the manufacturing success of the United States. US manufacturing was the globally dominant producer in many industries after World War II.

It has also been used to describe how the personal computer (PC) went through its product cycle. The PC was a new product in the 1970s and developed into a mature product during the 1980s and 1990s. Today, the PC is in the standardized product stage, and the majority of manufacturing and production process is done in low-cost countries in Asia and Mexico.

The product life cycle theory has been less able to explain current trade patterns where innovation and manufacturing occur around the world. For example, global companies even conduct research and development in developing markets where highly skilled labor and facilities are usually cheaper. Even though research and development is typically associated with the first or new product stage and therefore completed in the home country, these developing or emerging-market countries, such as India and China, offer both highly skilled labor and new research facilities at a substantial cost advantage for global firms.

3. New Trade Theory

New trade theory (NTT) is a collection of economic models in international trade which focuses on the role of increasing returns to scale and network effects, which were developed in the late 1970s and early 1980s by Helpman, Krugman, and Lancaster. According to this theory, economies of scale occur if a firm's average costs of producing a good decrease as output of that good increases. Like Linder's approach, the new trade theory predicts that intra-industry trade will be commonplace. It also suggests TNCs within the same industry, such as Caterpillar and Komatsu, Unilever and Procter & Gamble, and Airbus and Boeing, will continually play cat-and-mouse games with one another on a global basis as they attempt to expand their sales to capture scale economies. Often they seek to harness some sustainable competitive advantage they enjoy as a means of leveraging their own strengths and neutralizing those of their rivals.

Firms competing in the global marketplace have numerous ways of obtaining a sustainable competitive advantage. The more popular ones are owning intellectual property rights, investing in research and development (R&D), achieving economies of scope, and exploiting the experience curve.

Owning intellectual property rights. A firm that owns an intellectual property right—a trademark, brand name, patent, or copyright—often gains advantages over its competitors. R&D is a major component of the total cost of high-technology products. Because of such large "entry" costs, other firms often hesitate to compete against established firms. According to the global strategic rivalry theory, trade flows may be determined by which firms make the necessary R&D expenditures. Thus the firm that acts first often gains a first-mover advantage.

Achieving economies of scope. Economies of scope occur when a firm's average costs decrease as the number of different products it sells increases. These lower costs give the firm a competitive advantage over global rivals. Exploiting the experience curve. For certain types of products, production costs decline as the firm gains more experience in manufacturing the product. Experience curves may be so significant that they govern global competition within an industry.

4. Global strategic rivalry theory

Global strategic rivalry theory emerged in the 1980s and was based on the work of economists Paul Krugman and Kelvin Lancaster. Their theory focused on MNCs and their efforts to gain a competitive advantage against other global firms in their industry. Firms will encounter global competition in their industries and in order to prosper, they must develop competitive advantages. The critical ways that firms can obtain a sustainable competitive advantage are called the barriers to entry for that industry. The barriers to entry refer to the obstacles a new firm may face when trying to enter into an industry or new market. The barriers to entry that corporations may seek to optimize include:

- research and development
- the ownership of intellectual property rights
- economies of scale
- unique business processes or methods as well as extensive experience in the industry
- the control of resources or favorable access to raw materials

5. Porter's national competitive advantage theory

In the continuing evolution of international trade theories, Michael Porter of

Harvard Business School developed a new model to explain national competitive advantage in 1990. Porter's theory stated that a nation's competitiveness in an industry depends on the capacity of the industry to innovate and upgrade. His theory focused on explaining why some nations are more competitive in certain industries. To explain his theory, Porter identified four determinants that he linked together. We will learn it in later section.

2.2　Absolute, Comparative Advantage and Protectionist

Early 19th century, with the development of textile technology and a growing population, the United States was a highly effective producer of cotton shirts. For more than a century it was the world's biggest clothing manufacturer. Since then, the U. S. population has grown larger, and manufacturing technology has improved even more. So, why do many American clothing brands outsource their manufacturing to other countries? More and more clothes are labelled as made in Vietnam or China today.

Let's imagine this scenario, if there is no trade between countries, then the United States can consume only those goods that it produces on its own. In the real world, however, goods are made all over the world. If Americans want to buy more shirts than the United States produces, they can get them from somewhere else. Under these conditions, how can we predict which countries will produce which goods?

Understanding how resources are allocated among multiple producers is a step toward understanding why big firms work with specialized suppliers, or why a wealthy, productive country like the United States trades with much poorer, less-productive countries. To see why, let's turn to the question of why many T-shirts sold in the United States today are made in Vietnam.

2.2.1　Case of absolute advantage

Suppose that taking into account all the improvements in shirt-making and soybean-planting technology over the last two centuries, an American worker can now make 100 shirts or grow 400 kilograms of soybean per day. A Vietnam worker, on the other hand, can produce only 50 shirts (perhaps because U. S. workers use more advanced sewing tools) or 100 kilograms of soybean (maybe because U. S. farmers have agricultural mechanization and use fertilizers and pesticides that farmers in Vietnam don't). In other words, given the same number of workers the United States can produce twice as many shirts or four times as much soybean as Vietnam.

If a producer can generate more output than others with a given amount of resources, that producer has an absolute advantage. In our example in this section, the United States has an absolute advantage over Vietnam at producing both shirts and soybean, because it can make more of both products than Vietnam can per worker.

So, we can give the definition of absolute advantage: the comparison among producers of a good according to their productivity.

2. 2. 2　Comparative advantage and opportunity cost

It is only common sense that countries will produce and export goods for which they are uniquely qualified. But there is a deeper principle underlying all trade—in a family, within a nation, and among nations—that goes beyond common sense. The principle of comparative advantage holds that a country can benefit from trade even if it is absolutely more efficient (or absolutely less efficient) than other countries in the production of every good.

Let's go back to the example we had in the last part, the example of United States and Vietnam. We need to think about the opportunity cost. In a word, opportunity cost means a benefit, profit, or value of something that must be given up to obtainor to achieve some item. Since every resource (land, money, time, etc.) can be put to alternative uses, every action, choice, or decision has an associated opportunity cost. Opportunity cost is the value of the next best use for an economic good, or the value of the sacrificed alternative. Opportunity costs are fundamental costs in economics, and are used in computing cost benefit analysis of a project. Such costs, however, are not recorded in the account books but are recognized in decision making by computing the cash outlays and their resulting profit or loss.

In our simplified model, the opportunity cost of making one shirt in the U. S. is 4 kilograms of soybean (400 kilograms ÷ 100 shirts = 1 kilograms per shirt), the opportunity cost of making one shirt in Vietnam is only two kilograms of soybean (100 kilograms ÷ 50 shirts = 2 kilograms per shirt). So, for the United States, the best option is to outsource the production of shirts, because it has to give up more to make a shirt than Vietnam does.

So, we can give the definition of comparative advantage: the comparison among producers of a good according to their opportunity cost. This means that when a producer can make a good at a lower opportunity cost than other producers, it has a comparative advantage at producing that good.

The United States, on the other hand, has a comparative advantage over Vietnam at growing soybean. Each time the U. S. produces a kilogram of soybean, it gives up the opportunity to produce one-quarter of a shirt $\left(100 \text{ shirts} \div 400 \right.$ kilograms $= \dfrac{1}{4}$ shirt per kilogram $\left. \right)$. For Vietnam, however the opportunity cost of growing a kilogram of soybean is larger: it's one-half of a shirt $\left(50 \text{ shirts} \div 100 \right.$ kilograms $= \dfrac{1}{2}$ shirt per kilogram $\left. \right)$. The United States has a lower opportunity cost for producing soybean than Vietnam, and therefore we say it has a comparative advantage at soybean production. In real life, a country can have a comparative advantage without having an absolute advantage.

If we assume that the United States has higher output per worker (or per unit of input) than the rest of the world in making both software and grain. But suppose the United States is relatively more efficient in software than it is in grain. For example, it might be 60% more productive in software and 10% more productive in grain. In this case, it would benefit the United States to export that good in which it is relatively more efficient (like software) and import that good in which it is relatively less efficient (like grain). Or consider a poor country like Ethiopia. Ethiopia, country on the Horn of Africa. The country lies completely within the tropical latitudes and is relatively compact, with similar north-south and east-west dimensions. Ethiopia is underdeveloped in scientific research and development, agricultural production tools are not advanced and productivity is only a fraction of that of industrialized countries, hope to export any of its soybean? Surprisingly, according to the principle of comparative advantage, Ethiopia can benefit by exporting the goods in which it is relatively more efficient (like soybean) and importing those goods which it produces relatively less efficiently (like computers and smart phones).

Botswana looks to investment from China to develop economy

Botswana is a landlocked country located in the southern African continent. In recent years, the country has been looking to China's investment to boost its social and economic development. Global Times reporter Xing Xiaojing (GT) talked to Reginald Selelo (Selelo), chief operating officer of the Botswana Investment and

Trade Center (BITC), to discuss the potential of Chinese investment in Botswana.

In 2017, bilateral trade reached $267 million. At the end of 2017, Chinese companies had signed $10.16 billion worth of contracts in Botswana.

GT: Total Chinese investment in Africa has topped $6 billion. What would be Botswana's comparative advantage?

Selelo: Botswana imposes no controls over the flow of foreign exchange and the country's central bank since last year has cut the basic lending rate to a historic low of 5%. Companies in manufacturing industries are entitled to a 15% income tax rate, in contrast to a global average of 23.6% and an African average of 27.46%. The country's safe society is another positive factor for foreign investors.

Also, English is widely spoken, meaning there are lower language barriers for Chinese investors. The flow of people is also smooth as Botswana has implemented a visa-on-arrival policy to global tourists. On the downside, there are no direct flights between China and Botswana, but we hope a Chinese carrier could fill the gap as we do not have the ability to open up long-haul flight route. BITC will also open an office in Shanghai soon to promote business opportunities in Botswana to Chinese investors.

GT: Which sector does the Botswana government want to develop with investments from Chinese companies?

Selelo: Chinese companies have already undertaken many infrastructure projects in Botswana such as building roads, hospitals, and schools. They are also investing in manufacturing and energy. We are interested in developing the high-tech sector and we have been in contact with Alibaba Group. We hope to develop digital infrastructure facilities such as mobile payments and e-commerce and with these tools create a better future for small and medium-sized companies.

We think it would be great if Alibaba chose to build a data center in Botswana. This would not only bring advanced ideas to our country but also allow more Chinese companies to become aware of Botswana, which is currently little-known among Chinese businesses.

Tourism and the diamond industry are also the "treasures" of Botswana and unfortunately most Chinese have never heard about it. Agriculture, textiles and mining are other sectors that present good opportunities for Chinese investors.

(Source: Global Times, December 11, 2018.)

2.2.3 Applications of comparative advantage

The principle of comparative advantage explains interdependence and the gains from trade. Because interdependence is so prevalent in the modern world, the principle of comparative advantage has many applications. We can illustrate it by interesting examples.

Robyn Rihanna Fenty is a very famous pop music female singer. Born in Barbados, she grew up listening to reggae music and began singing when she was quite young. A very successful artist was still in the prime of her youth, she has already sold over 41 million albums and 150 million songs worldwide, becoming one of the best-selling artists of all time. She is the recipient of eight Grammy Awards from 24 nominations. Pretty, young and highly talented, today she is regarded as a teen idol and a fashion icon. Rihanna also puts her fame to good use and is actively involved with several charitable causes. With the exception of music, Rihanna is so successful with beauty and fashion that she can do anything. So what about Rihanna weeding her lawn?

To answer this question, we can use the concepts of opportunity cost and comparative advantage. Let's say that Rihanna can weed her lawn in 2 hours. In that same 2 hours, she could film a television commercial for lip balm and earn $50,000. By contrast, Emily, the girl next door, can weed Rihanna's lawn in 4 hours. In that same 4 hours, she could work at KFC and earn $40.

In this example, Rihanna's opportunity cost of weeding the lawn is $50,000, and Emily's opportunity cost is $40. Rihanna has an absolute advantage in weeding lawns because she can do the work in less time. Yet Emily has a comparative advantage in weeding lawns because she has the lower opportunity cost.

The gains from trade in this example are tremendous. Rather than weeding her own lawn, Rihanna should make the commercial and hire Emily to weed the lawn. As long as she pays her more than $40 and less than $50,000, both of them are better off.

2.2.4 Protectionist

From the definition of "Encyclopedia Britannica", "Protectionism" is the policy of protecting domestic industries against foreign competition by means of tariffs, subsidies, import quotas, or other restrictions or handicaps placed on the imports of foreign competitors. Protectionist policies have been implemented by many countries despite the fact that virtually all mainstream economists agree that the world economy generally benefits from free trade. Government-levied tariffs are the chief protectionist measures. They raise the price of imported articles, making them more expensive (and therefore less attractive) than domestic products.

Throughout history wars and economic depressions (or recessions) have led to increases in protectionism, while peace and prosperity have tended to encourage free trade.

The theory of comparative advantage shows how countries can benefit from specialization and international division of labor. Notwithstanding this established economic finding, legislatures are continuously besieged by groups lobbying for protective measures in the form of tariffs or import quotas. For example, in the United States, Congress and the President struggle every year over whether to enact measures to protect domestic industries from inexpensive imports. Is protectionism sound economic policy? Economists generally agree that it is not. They believe that free trade promotes a mutually beneficial division of labor among nations and that free and open trade allows each nation to expand its production and consumption possibilities, raising the world's living standard.

1. Trade barriers

For centuries, governments have used tariffs and quotas to raise revenues and influence the development of individual industries. Tariff, also called customs duty, tax levied upon goods as they cross national boundaries, usually by the government of the importing country. The words tariff, duty, and customs can be used interchangeably. The objectives of tariffs may be levied either to raise revenue or to protect domestic industries, but a tariff designed primarily to raise revenue also may exercise a strong protective influence, while a tariff levied primarily for protection may yield revenue. Gottfried von Haberler in The Theory of International Trade (1937) suggested that the best way to distinguish between revenue duties and protective duties (disregarding the motives of the legislators) is to compare their effects on domestic versus foreign producers. If domestically produced goods bear the same taxation as similar imported goods, or if the foreign goods subject to duty are not produced domestically, and if there are no domestically produced substitutes toward which demand is diverted because of the tariff, then the duty is not protective. A purely protective duty tends to shift production away from the export industries and into the protected domestic industries or other industries producing substitutes for which demand is increased. On the other hand, a purely revenue duty will not cause resources to be invested in industries producing the taxed goods or close substitutes for such goods, but it will divert resources toward the production of those goods and services upon which the additional government receipts are spent.

From the standpoint of revenue alone, a country can levy an equivalent tax on domestic production (to avoid protecting it) or select a relatively small number of imported articles of general consumption and subject them to low duties so that there will be no tendency to shift resources into industries producing such taxed goods (or substitutes for them). If, on the other hand, a country wishes to protect its home industries, its list of protected commodities will be long and the tariff rates high. Political goals often motivate the imposition or removal of tariffs. Tariffs may be further classified into three groups—transit duties, export duties, and import duties. Tariff, also called customs duty, tax levied upon goods as they cross national boundaries, usually by the government of the importing country. The words tariff, duty, and customs can be used interchangeably. Transit duties is levied on commodities that originate in one country, cross another, and are consigned to a third. As the name implies, transit duties are levied by the country through which the goods pass. The most direct and immediate effect of transit duties is a reduction in the amount of commodities traded internationally and an increase in the cost of those products to the importing country. Export duties are duties levied by the customs of the exporting country on exporters or individuals leaving the country when their goods and articles are exported abroad. Export duties are no longer used to a great extent, except to tax certain mineral, petroleum, and agricultural products. Import dutiesare the duties imposed by the customs of the importing country on the import of foreign goods.

Huawei to continue challenging constitutionality of US ban

China's tech giant Huawei said on Thursday, it would continue to challenge the constitutionality of the latest US ban on agencies from purchasing the company's telecom gears. The US government on Wednesday issued an interim regulation, prohibiting its federal agencies from purchasing telecommunications equipment and services from five Chinese companies, including Huawei, according to an official website run by General Services Administration, the US government agency was responsible for contracting. In a media statement, the Shenzhen-based company called the action "not unexpected" as it was the continued promulgation of the rules laid out by the National Defense Administration Act (NDAA) of 2019. The NDAA, signed by President Donald Trump last year, included a ban on US government agencies and those receiving federal grants and loans from doing business with Huawei and companies substantially using Huawei products. "The NDAA law and its implementing provisions will do nothing to ensure the protection of US telecom networks and systems and rather is a trade barrier based on country-of-origin," the company said. Huawei said it would continue to challenge the constitutionality of the ban in the US federal court. "Ultimately, it will be rural citizens across the US that will be most negatively impacted as the networks they use for digital connectivity rely on Huawei," the company said. On May 27, Song Liuping, Huawei's chief legal officer, wrote in an opinion article in the Wall Street Journal that Huawei had sued and would file a motion for summary judgment asking a US court to declare the NDAA law unconstitutional.

(Source: Huawei to continue challenging constitutionality of US ban, China Daily, August 8, 2019.)

2. The economic costs of tariffs

In general, there are three effects of economic costs of tariffs: (1) The domestic producers, operating under a price umbrella provided by the tariff, can expand production; (2) Consumers are faced with higher prices and therefore reduce their consumption; (3) Government gains tariff revenue. Tariff create economic inefficiency. When tariffs are imposed, the economic loss to consumers exceeds the revenue gained by the government plus the extra profits earned by producers. We can use the following example to understand. According to the China Daily's recent report, the United States and China have benefited greatly from cooperation in science, technology and innovation, a senior Chinese science strategist said, lamenting the recent protectionist turn in the US. An objective appreciation of such accomplishments would help ease recent technology and trade frictions and reveal new grounds for win-win cooperation between the countries. China and the US had been close partners in integrated research and development for most of the past four decade. From 2012 to 2015, the number of collaborative research projects involving Chinese and US institutions increased by more than 80%, according to a blue paper on China's contribution to STI and global governance published by the academy last year. Chinese and US scientists had co-authored more than 55,000 papers by 2014. Moreover, scientists from both countries had cooperated on climate change, clean energy, environmental protection, health, agriculture and other fields related to sustainable development and people's livelihoods, the blue paper said. It added that Chinese enterprises had set up research and development facilities in the US, while US companies had established more than 800 R&D centers in China covering industries including electronics, information technology, software, food manufacturing, cosmetics, home furnishing and finance. These interactions have created a flow of talent and know-how to provide better products and services for the people of both countries and the world. Over time, China and US had developed different but crucial positions in the global industrial system and value chain. The US was at the top, given its leading position in STI and emerging industries, while China was at the middle and lower end of the industrial and value chain, but striving to climb up. Like Japan, Singapore, South Korea and other countries before it, China was improving its people's living standards through education, trade, infrastructure investment and technologies. These feats mean China will inevitably close its gap with developed countries. But it does not mean China wants to or is capable of challenging the US's global dominance. Historically, China's technological rise was not an issue that troubled the US, because the US maintained its lead role by attracting the best talent from around the world to fuel its STI efforts-pushing new frontiers, making new products and climbing up the industrial value chain. However, STI development is an arduous process, and the US has grown increasingly anxious that its lead is being eroded. So instead of staying ahead via continued innovation, it has turned protectionist toward China and other developing countries and used unconventional means, from tariffs to travel restrictions, in the hope of keeping them behind. At the same time, the US was plagued by many domestic issues, ranging from growing social inequality to rising corporate influence, and ordinary US people, notably those from Midwestern states, felt disenfranchised by globalization and technological progress because "the fruits of these trends have been mostly reaped by the elites from coastal states". When internal issues become too difficult to handle, politicians often rely on scapegoating to divert public frustration and attract support, especially during election years. But the US public must realize that blaming China and other countries for its economic, social and existential woes will not solve its issues, it will only exacerbate them to disastrous levels for all. Despite the US's effort to disconnect with China, full detachment was unlikely in the long run because it would not be in the interests of either country. China's market and its pivotal role in the global industrial chain are too important for US companies to give up. In addition, science requires the exchange of ideas and collaboration to progress. When faced with common challenges, from climate change to changing ethical landscapes in artificial intelligence and biosciences, it will require a global joint effort to find the best solution to tackle these emerging issues. Dividing the scientific community and the world, as some politicians are implying, is dangerous and counterintuitive to maximizing the potential of science and its benefit for the people. Given the unpredictability of the current US administration, China needs to "keep a rational, objective outlook and focus on improving its own capability at its own pace". We must have the confidence and patience to get through turbulent times.

　　The Trump administration raised the stakes in a trade dispute with China by proposing 10% tariffs on $200 billion of Chinese goods on July 10, 2018, on top of $50 billion of tariffs that were officially imposed on China. The Ministry of Commerce of China immediately responded by warning of similar retaliation. In the latest World Economic Outlook (IMF, 2018a) and G-20 Surveillance Note (IMF, 2018b), the IMF estimates that the global economy will be 0.5% (or roughly US$430 billion) smaller by 2020 if the various tariffs threatened by the US, China, Europe, Mexico, Japan, and Canada were to be implemented.

　　In the world of global value chains, firms are intertwined in input-output relationships. While tariffs can reduce competition from foreign firms at home, they will also raise the costs of imported inputs for domestic firms, and hence backfire. Domestic consumers and firms that depend heavily on goods produced in a foreign country suffer the most. Moreover, the costs of import tariffs on production can get amplified as tariff-induced increases in input costs are compounded down the supply chains until the final stage when goods are sold to consumers. Thus, the overall economic effect of tariff protection in the world of global value chains is hard to predict.

　　So what are the costs of the trade war? Most of the recent discussions mainly focus on the trade flows and trade policy (Crowley et al., 2017; Bown, 2017, 2018; Frankel, 2018). In a recent paper (Huang et al., 2018), we study instead firms' financial market responses to the various announcements in 2018 by both the US and Chinese governments of their intentions to raise tariffs over a comprehensive lists of goods imported from each other.

　　As Figure 2-1 illustrates, the sharp fall in the stock market index on March 22 2018 suggests that the presidential memorandum based on Section 301 of the Investigation of China's Laws, Policies, Practices, or Actions was a largely unanticipated event. The Dow Jones index dropped by 4.7%, while the S&P 500 index dropped by 4.5% between March 21 and 23. Public interest in the trade war also peaked on March 22. Similar declines in the S&P 500 index and corresponding spikes in public interests are also observed for the other two announcement dates (April 3 and 4).

　　(1) Evidence from the financial markets. We exploit this unexpected and abrupt policy announcement by the US government on March 22, 2018, applying an event-study approach to examine publicly listed firms' market responses to the announcement in both nations. Several new datasets are built to assess a US (Chinese) firm's direct exposure to imports from and exports to China (US). We also gauge a US firm's indirect exposure to trade with China through its engagement

in global value chains, using US input-output tables and trade data.

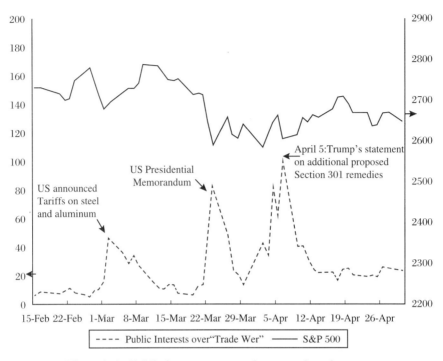

Figure 2-1 Public interests over trade war and stock returns

Notes: The solid curve indicates the S&P 500 index (right scale). The dashed curve shows the public interest over trade war as measured by Google Trends (left scale). The information on Google Trends was accessed on July 11, 2018.

We find significant heterogeneous responses to the announcement of tariff hikes across listed firms in both countries. Around March 22, 2018, the date when the Trump administration made the first announcement which triggered a sequence of trade-war type events between the two nations, US firms having imports from or exports to China experienced relatively lower stock returns, weaker bond performance, and higher default risks. Specifically, in a three-day window around March 22, we find that after controlling for standard firm-level characteristics, a 10 percentage-point increase in a firm's share of sales to China is associated with 0.8% lower average cumulative returns, while firms that directly offshore inputs from China have a 0.8% lower average cumulative return than those that do not. In addition, firms that are more exposed to the trade experienced higher default risks gauged by the growth rate in the implied CDS spread over the same three-day period.

We also find that a firm's indirect exposure through global value chains matters. In particular, an industry that has a 10% higher average share of imports across its upstream industries is associated with a 1.2% lower average cumulative raw return, suggesting significant indirect effects of (perceived) tariff-induced increases in input costs.

The effects are equally significant on the Chinese financial market. Chinese listed firms that are more dependent on sales in the US tend to have lower cumulative returns around March 22. Specifically, after controlling for the standard firm characteristics, a 10% increase in the share of exports to the US in total sales (in 2013) is associated with a 0.4% larger drop in the firm's cumulative return in the three-day event window. However, Chinese firms that import inputs from the US do not experience lower stock returns. We find in both countries' stock markets the same patterns of heterogeneous firms' market responses to the June 18 announcement by the US government about additional tariff hikes against Chinese products.

(2) Winners and losers from globalisation 2.0. The findings show that whether a firm will win or lose during the US-China trade war depends on the extent of its participation in the global value chains shared by the two countries. While raising the prices of imported goods can transfer profits from foreign to domestic businesses, our study shows that this benefit is far outweighed by the (perceived) increases in input costs. Given the complex structure of US-China trade, most firms in both countries would not be isolated from such negative cost shocks.

2.3   Competitive Advantage

First we need to understand the concept of competitive advantage. Every business, large or small, needs a competitive advantage to distinguish itself from the competition. In the aggressive business world, especially in global economy. Without a competitive advantage, your business has no unique method of drawing in customers. A competitive advantage is simply a factor that distinguishes your business from others and makes customers more likely to choose your product over the competition.

2.3.1   Porter's diamond system

Michael Porter, the famous Harvard strategy professor, with his team looked at 100 industries in 10 nations. For Porter, the essential task was to explain why a nation achieves international success in a particular industry. Why does Japando so well in the automobile industry? Why does Switzerland excel in the production and export of precision instruments and pharmaceuticals? Why do Germany and the United States do so well in the chemical industry? These questions cannot be answered easily by the Heckscher-Ohlin theory, and the theory of comparative advantage offers only a partial explanation. The theory of comparative advantage would say that Switzerland excels in the production and export of precision instruments because it uses its resources very productivelyin these industries. Although this may be correct, this does not explain why Switzerland is more productive in this industry than Great Britain, Germany, or Spain. Porter tries to solve this puzzle.

They found that four broad attributes of a nation shape the environment in which local firms compete, and these attributes promote or impede the creation of competitive advantage. See the Figure 2-2:

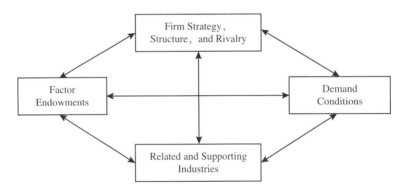

Figure 2-2　Determinants of National Competitive Advantage: Porter's Diamond

● Factor endowments—a nation's position in factors of production, such as skilled labor or the infrastructure necessary to compete in a given industry.

● Demand conditions—the nature of home demand for the industry s product or service.

● Related and supporting industries—the presence or absence of supplier industries and related industries that are internationally competitive.

● Firm strategy, structure, and rivalry—the conditions governing how companies are created, organized, and managed and the nature of domestic rivalry.

Porter speaks of these four attributes as constituting the diamond. He argues that firms are most likely to succeed in industries or industry segments where the diamond is most favorable. He also argues that the diamond is a mutually reinforcing system. According to Porter's theory, the favorable demand conditions will not result in competitive advantage unless the state of rivalry is sufficient to cause firms to respond to them. Companies gain advantage against the world's best competitors because of pressure and challenge. They benefit from having strong domestic rivals, aggressive homebased suppliers, and demanding local customers. Porter maintains that two additional variables can influence the national diamond in important ways: chance and government. Chance events, such as major innovations, can reshape industry structure and provide the opportunity for one nation's firms to supplant another's. Companies achieve competitive advantage through acts of innovation. They approach innovation in its broadest sense, including both technologies and new ways of doing things. They perceive a new basis for competing or find better means for competing in old ways. Innovation can be manifested in a new product design, a new production process, a new marketing approach, or a new way of conducting training. Much innovation is mundane and incremental, depending more on a cumulation of small insights and advances than on a single, major technological breakthrough. Chance or innovation of ten involves investments in skill and knowledge, as well as in physical assets and brand reputations. Some innovations create competitive advantage by perceiving an entirely new market opportunity or by serving a market segment that others have ignored. When competitors are slow to respond, such innovation yields competitive advantage. Government, by its choice of policies, can detract from or improve national advantage. For example, regulation can alter home demand conditions, antitrust policies can influence the intensity of rivalry within an industry, and government investments in education can change factor endowments. In a world of increasingly global competition, nations have become more, not less, important. As the basis of competition has shifted more and more to the creation and assimilation of knowledge, the role of the nation has grown. Competitive advantage is created and sustained through a highly localized process. Differences in national values, culture, nomic structures, institutions, ancontribute to competitive success. There are striking differences in the patterns of competitiveness in every country; no nation can or will be competitive in every or even most industries. Ultimately, nations succeed in particular industries because their home environment is the most forward-looking, dynamicand challenging.

1. Factor Endowments

Factor endowments lie at the center of the Heckscher-Ohlin theory. This theory means if two countries produce two goods and use two factors of production (say, labour and capital) to produce these goods, each will export the good that makes the most use of the factor that is most abundant. Simply put, countries with plentiful natural resources will generally have a comparative advantage in products using those resources.

While Porter does not propose anything radically new, he does analyze the characteristics of factors of production. He recognizes hierarchies among factors, distinguishing between basic factors (e. g, natural resources, climate, location, and demographics) and advanced factors (e. g, communication infrastructure, sophisticated and skilled labor, research facilities, and technological know-how). Heargues that advanced factors are the most significant for competitive advantage. Unlike the naturally endowed basic factors, advanced factors are a product of investment by individuals, companies, and governments. Thus, government investments in basic and higher education, by improving the general skill and knowledge level of the population and by stimulating advanced research at higher education institutions, can upgrade a nation's advanced factors but the relationship between advanced and basic factors is complex. Basic factors can provide an initial advantage that is subsequently reinforced and extended by investment in advanced factors. Conversely, disadvantages in basic factors can create pressures to invest in advanced factors. An obvious example of this phenomenon is Japan, a country that lacks arable land and mineral deposits and yet through investment has built a substantial endowment of advanced factors. Porter notes that Japans large pool of engineers (reflecting a much higher number of engineering graduates per capita than almost any other nation) has been vital to Japan's success in many manufacturing industries

2. Demand Conditions

Porter emphasizes the role home demand plays in upgrading competitive advantage. Firms are typically most sensitive to the needs of their closest customers. Thus, the characteristics of home demand are particularly important in shaping the attributes of domestically made products and in creating pressures for innovation and quality. Porter argues that a nation's firms gain competitive advantage if their domestic consumers are sophisticated and demanding. Such consumers pressure local firms to meet high standards of product quality and to produce innovative products. Take 5G as example, it is defined as the 5th generation of mobile phone and data communication standards. 5G is a real opportunity to share and for dialogue and make the Internet of everything is possible. The huge economic value, wide impact and importance to national security of 5G have led some major countries to speed up 5G layout. In 2019, nearly 20,000 5G base stations have been built in China by the end of June, with 90 percent of these base stations in Beijing, Shanghai, Guangzhou and Shenzhen, business news portal 21jingji reported on Friday. Beijing has constructed 7,863 5G base stations by the end of July, Shanghai, Guangzhou, and Shenzhen have set up 3,000, 5,000 and 3,777 5G stations by the end of June, respectively, said the news portal, citing public data. 5G not only can download a 10G video in 9 seconds, but also can deeply integrate with industry, transportation and medical care to form the strategic emerging industries such as industrial internet, automatic driving, and telemedicine. The well-developed regions have pressing needs to industry transformation and upgrading. Guangdong, one of China economic powerhouses, enhanced its annual target to build 5G base stations to 32,000 from 20,000 after the country granted 5G licenses for commercial use in June. China will build 150,000 5G base stations this year, 50 percent higher than expected at the beginning of the year, citing the CCID Consulting. The cities, including Beijing, Shanghai, Chengdu, Shenzhen, Wuhan and Hangzhou, plan to build more than 10,000 5G base stations by the end of this year, according to the CCID Consulting. The commercial use of 5G is expected to directly bring 10.6 trillion yuan in economic output between 2020 to 2025, and will create 2.9 trillion yuan in value-added economy, 8 million jobs and contribute 6% of GDP by 2030, said the China Academy of Information and Communications Technology. The revenue from network equipment and terminal equipment will reach 450 billion yuan at the 5G commercial use initial stage, the revenue from the terminal equipment will be 140 million yuan at the medium term, and the revenue from service provided by 5G internet companies will hit 2.6 trillion yuan at the middle and later periods. However, the cost to build the 5G base station is also high, said 21jingji. com. As the coverage radius of the 5G base station is about 100 ~ 300 meters, that is less than the 4G base station's coverage radius, the 5G base station will be more intensive, citing an industry expert. China had 3.72 million 4G base stations in 2018, according to the Ministry of Industry and Information Technology. Calculating based on two time of the 4G base station's number, the country will build at least seven million 5G base stations in the future, said the 21jingji. com. Moreover, the investment of a 5G base station is about 1.5 to 3 times of a 4G base station. China Mobile plans to invest 17.2 billion yuan to operate 30,000 to 50,000 5G base stations to realize 5G commercial use in over 50 Chinese cities by the end of 2019. In addition, China Unicom will invest 6 billion yuan to 8 billion yuan to build 20,000 5G base stations to cover 33 Chinese cities, and China Telecom's investment will be 9 billion yuan to build 20,000 5G base stations in more than 40 Chinese cities in 2019. To achieve the same coverage as the 4G network, the investment to build 5G networks will hit 4 trillion yuan, and the electricity consumption will account for more than 40 percent of 5G network operating costs. The 5G base stations sharing should be increased to avoid repeated construction on 5G base stations to reduce financial waste. [1]

3. Related and Supporting Industries

The third broad attribute of national advantage in an industry is the presence of suppliers or related industries that are internationally competitive. The benefits of investments in advanced factors of production by related and supporting industries can spill over into an industry, thereby helping it achieve a strong competitive position internationally.

For many firms, the presence of related and supporting industries is of critical importance to the growth of that particular industry. A critical concept here is that national competitive strengths tend to be associated with "clusters" of industries. For example, Silicon Valley in the USA and Silicon Glen in the UK are techno clusters of high-technology industries which includes individual computer software and semi-conductor firms. Swedish strength in fabricated steelproducts has drawn on strengths in Sweden's specialty steel industry. In Germany, a similar cluster exists around chemicals, synthetic dyes, textiles and textile machinery. Technological leadership in the U. S. semiconductor industry provided the basis for U. S. success in personal computers and several other technically advanced electronic products. Similarly, Switzerland's success in pharmaceuticals is closely related to its previous international success in the technologically related dye industry. Knowledge flows occur when employees move between firms within a region and when national industry associations bring employees from different companies together for regular conferences or workshops. With industrial transformation and upgrading, technology cluster brings huge benefits for many countries.

China moves up in global innovation ranking

China is ranked 14th among more than 100 economies worldwide in a benchmark innovation ranking in 2019, moving up three spots from last year and

---

[1] Zhang Jie. Around 20,000 5G base stations constructed across the country. China daily and 21 jingji. com, 2019-08-09.

strengthening its position as a leading innovative nation. The 2019 edition of the Global Innovation Index (GII) report, jointly released by the World Intellectual Property Organization, Cornell University and several other organizations on Wednesday, gave China an overall score of 54.82 out of 100 with top ranks in patents by origin, industrial designs and trademarks by origin, as well as high-tech and creative goods exports. It noted China has remained the only middle-income economy in the top 30 and continues to be top-ranked in quality of innovation among middle-income economies for the seventh consecutive year. Of the top 100 science and technology clusters, China has racked up 18, second only to the United States. The highest overall ranking this year goes to Switzerland with a score of 67.24, the ninth straight time the European country has topped the GII. Sweden, the United States, the Netherlands and Britain followed Switzerland in the ranking accordingly. The GII 2019 gauges levels of innovation in 129 economies based on 80 indicators, from traditional measurements like research and development investments and international patent and trademark applications to newer indicators including mobile-phone app creation and high-tech exports. Themed "Creating Healthy Lives-The Future of Medical Innovation," the 2019 ranking aims to explore the role of medical innovation as it shapes the future of healthcare. Despite signs of slowing economic growth and shadows from protectionism, innovation continues to blossom, particularly in Asia, the report has noted.

(Source: China moves up in global innovation ranking, Xinhua net, July 26, 2019.)

4. Firm strategy, structure, and rivalry

The fourth broad attribute of national competitive advantage in Porters model is the strategy, structure, and rivalry of firms within a nation. Porter makes two important points here. First, different nations are characterized by different management ideologies, which either help them or donot help them build national competitive advantage. For example, German companies tend to be hierarchical. Italian companies tend to be smaller and are run more like extended families. Such strategy and structure helps to determine in which types of industries a nation's firms will excel. He linked this to U. S. firms' lack of attention to improving manufacturing processes and product design. He argued that the dominance of finance led to an over-emphasis on maximizing short-term financial returns. According to Porter, one consequence of these different management ideologies was a relative loss of U. S. competitiveness in those engineering-based industries where manufacturing processes and product design issues are all-important (e. g, the automobile industry). Porter's second point is that there is a strong association between vigorous domestic rivalry and the creation and persistence of competitive advantage in an industry. Vigorous domestic rivalry induces firms to look for ways to improve efficiency, which makes them better international competitors. Domestic rivalry creates pressures to innovate, to improve quality, to reduce costs, and to investing upgrading advanced factors. All this helps create world class competitors.

China's SOEs, private companies race to produce more satellites

China's state-owned enterprises (SOEs) and private companies are racing to build up their capacity to produce more commercial satellites for their own ambitious networks, as the country's policy support for the industry attracts more capital. Ground was broken on April 24 for a satellite industry park, where annual production is expected to exceed 100 satellites, in Wuhan, Central China's Hubei Province. That park plans to build the first intelligent production line in China by 2020, according to a press release China Aerospace Science and Industry Corp Space Engineering Development Co sent to the Global Times. The facility will produce satellites for the company's Hongyun project, which aims to construct a vast space-based communications network capable of covering the globe with broadband internet service. Under the project, the company launched its first satellite in December 2018. Another production line operated by a satellite start-up, Spacety, based in Changsha, Central China's Hunan Province, began construction in January. It aims to reach annual production capacity of more than 100 satellites starting next year, according to local media reports. SOEs and the private sector have accelerated efforts to expand capacity since the country gave policy support to the commercial satellite sector in 2015, according to analysts. The National Development and Reform Commission and other departments jointly issued a support policy for civil space infrastructure development in October 2015, and the first batch of commercial space companies were established in the same year. According to a report by the Xinhua News Agency in December 2018, in the first 10 months of the year, private companies launched five space missions. An increasing number of enterprises have moved into areas including rockets, satellites, telemetry and control. Although the domestic market's value is estimated to reach 800 billion yuan by 2020, the profit model of the business is still not clear, Xinhua has reported. According to a report published by Futureaerospace, an industry think tank, the number of private space companies in China reached 141 by the end of 2018. The policy support will drive more capital into the commercial space sector, and a favorable business environment is taking shape, Huang Zhicheng, an expert in space technology, told the Global Times. As more private capital is encouraged to join the market, fierce domestic competition will definitely drive technology upgrading and development in the space sector, said Huang. "However, total demand is limited, and only the fastest movers will survive. "

(Source: Wang Yi, China's SOEs, private companies race to produce more satellites, Global Times, May 8, 2019.)

2.3.2　Generic competitive strategies

Michael Porter wrote a book in 1985 which identified three strategies that businesses can use to tackle competition. This book was named the ninth most influential management book of the 20th century. These approaches can be applied to all businesses whether they are product-based or service-based. He called these approaches generic strategies. They include cost leadership, differentiation, and focus. These strategies have been created to improve and gain a competitive advantage over competitors. These strategies can also be recognized as the comparative advantage and the differential advantage.

1. Overall cost leadership strategy

Cost leadership is a business' ability to produce a product or service that will be at a lower cost than other competitors and (or) distributor in the industry. If the business is able to produce the same quality product but sell it for less, this gives them a competitive advantage over other businesses. Company strategies aimed at controlling costs include construction of efficient-scale facilities, tight control of costs and overhead, avoidance of marginal customer accounts, minimization of operating expenses, reduction of input costs, tight control of labor costs, and lower distribution costs. Therefore, this provides a price value to the customers. Lower costs will result in higher profits as businesses are still making a reasonable profit on each good or service sold. The low-cost leader gains competitive advantage by getting its costs of production or distribution lower than those of the other firms in its market. The strategy is especially important for firms selling unbranded commodities such as beef or steel.

2. Differentiation strategy

The second generic strategy, differentiating the product or service, requires a firm to create something about its product or service that is perceived as unique throughout the industry. Michael Porter recommended making those goods or services attractive to stand out from their competitors. The business will need strong research, development and design thinking to create innovative ideas. If customers see a product or service as being different from other products, consumers are willing to pay more to receive these benefits. Whether the features are real or just in the mind of the customer, customers must perceive the product as having desirable features not commonly found in competing products. The customers also must be relatively price-insensitive. Adding product features means that the production or distribution costs of a differentiated product may be somewhat higher than the price of a generic, non-differentiated product. Customers must be willing to pay more than the marginal cost of adding the differentiating feature if a differentiation strategy is to succeed.

Differentiation may be attained through many features that make the product or service appear unique. Possible strategies for achieving differentiation may include:

- warranties (e. g., Sears tools)
- brand image (e. g., Coach handbags, Tommy Hilfiger sportswear)
- technology (e. g., Hewlett-Packard laser printers)
- features (e. g., Jenn-Air ranges, Whirlpool appliances)
- service (e. g., Makita hand tools)
- quality/value (e. g., Walt Disney Company)
- dealer network (e. g., Caterpillar construction equipment)

Differentiation does not allow a firm to ignore costs; it makes a firm's products less susceptible to cost pressures from competitors because customers see the product as unique and are willing to pay extra to have the product with the desirable features. Differentiation can be achieved through real product features or through advertising that causes the customer to perceive that the product is unique. For example, Ralph Lauren, founder and CEO, has been the guiding light behind his company's success. Part of the firm's success has been the public's association of Lauren with the brand. Ralph Lauren leads a high-profile lifestyle of preppy elegance. His appearance in his own commercials, his Manhattan duplex, his Colorado ranch, his vintage car collection, and private jet have all contributed to the public's fascination with the man and his brand name. This image has allowed the firm to market everything from suits and ties to golf balls. Through licensing of the name, the Lauren name also appears on sofas, soccer balls, towels, tableware, and much more.

3. Focus on a particular market niche

The generic strategies of cost leadership and differentiation are oriented toward industry-wide recognition. The final generic strategy, focusing (also called niche or segmentation strategy), involves concentrating on a particular customer, product line, geographical area, channel of distribution, stage in the production process, or market niche. The underlying premise of the focus strategy is that a firm is better able to serve a limited segment more efficiently than competitors can serve a broader range of customers. Focus strategy ideally tries to get businesses to aim at a few target markets rather than trying to target everyone. This strategy is often used for smaller businesses since they may not have the appropriate resources or ability to target everyone. Businesses that use this method usually focus on the needs of the customer and how their products or services could improve their daily lives. In this method, a firm concentrates on meeting the specialized needs of its customers. Products and services can be designed to meet the needs of buyers.

This strategy can also be called the segmentation strategy, which includes geographic, demographic, behavioral and physical segmentation. By narrowing the market down to smaller segments, businesses are able to meet the needs of the consumer. Many automobile dealers advertise that they are the largest volume dealer for a specific geographic area. Other car dealers advertise that they have the highest customer satisfaction scores within their defined market or the most awards for their service department. Similarly, customers are allowed to design their own automobiles within the constraints of predetermined colors, engine sizes, interior options, and so forth. Burger King advertises that its burgers are made "your way," meaning that the customer gets to select from the predetermined options of pickles, lettuce, and so on.

2.4　Case

Case-1

Diverse trade helps China weather trade war

According to the General Administration of Customs of China on Thursday, China's US dollar-denominated exports in July rose 3.3% year-on-year, beating expectations. Imports fell by 5.6%; the fall is also lower than expected. China's overall trade surplus in July was $45.06 billion, expanding by 63.9% from a year ago. These numbers are widely believed to show that although the trade war is having a negative effect on China's foreign trade, the resilience of China's trade is far beyond people's expectations. Chinese export enterprises are making swift adjustment, and have made progress in minimizing the effects of US tariffs. In the first seven months of 2019, China's trade in major markets, including the EU, ASEAN and Japan, has increased. China's trade growth rate in countries along the Belt and Road Initiative is higher than the overall level. The trade of private enterprises has grown rapidly, with electromechanical and labor-intensive products all maintaining growth. The Chinese economy is now more capable of shunning the impact of a US-launched trade war. China does not want a long-term trade war. But if this is unavoidable, the Chinese economy can open a new path and explore room for maneuvering.

China's foreign trade will remain difficult in the second half of 2019 amid the potentially worsening China-US trade war and the global economic downturn. But previous experiences have shown that the Chinese economy is among those with the strongest resilience. Some in the US have been eager to knock China down. They will be increasingly disappointed in the global economic context. China has learned new capabilities in every field where the US strong-armed it. China has not experienced economic shocks which the US had anticipated. This is the great society's unique natural endowment. China has mastered complete industrial capabilities and opened up numerous channels to connect to the outside world.

There is an obvious distinction between China and the US: China, practical and realistic, has prepared for the worst; but the US has kept making unrealistic promises and lying to the public. The US is taking a wrong path and placing itself in a dilemma. Many of the US lies are intended to bolster US stock markets. The exuberance of the US economy is partly supported by bubbles, hot money and financial leverage. US investors will pay the price sooner or later. The China-US trade war will be a protracted one and Chinese society is firm about it. The US trade war won't weaken China, but will promote China's all-round rejuvenation. Economic data may be mixed, but China is getting stronger, a trend which the world clearly perceives. The Chinese economy's resilience comes from the country's huge potential and strong ability to tap this potential. There is no outside force that can disrupt the process as long as China doesn't stop by itself. Some people in Washington refuse to accept this trend, but time will teach them.

(Source: Global Times, August 8, 2019.)

Questions:

1. What's trade war? What impact will the trade war have on our economy and daily life?

2. Tell the history of protectionist, and what are the implications of protectionism?

Case-2

Why West has begun to learn from China?

"Seek knowledge even if you have to go as far as China" is a popular adage in the Muslim world. It has its origin in the hadith-traditions related to Prophet Muhammad, the founder of Islam. Now the West has begun to take the same road.

Why should the West seek knowledge from China? The answer lies in the clear comparison between the two: The West is in relative decline compared to its previous glory, while China enjoys stability and development. With comprehensive reforms, China has been the pillar of world economic growth after the 2008 global financial crisis. Besides, China has proposed the Belt and Road Initiative (BRI) and the concept of community of shared future for mankind. The West's demand for better understanding China's intention has pushed Western countries to learn from the East Asian nation, a way to get the key to China's success so that they can use it to contain China's rise.

What the West can learn from China includes governance and innovation. China's experience in poverty alleviation, unemployment, wealth gap, and fighting against corruption can set an example for the West, which is confronted with all such problems.

Reform is no longer aimed at catching up with the world. It is now an important move to improve China's competitiveness. China is the second-largest spender on research and development after the US. German Chancellor Angela Merkel visited Wuhan, a hub for innovation in Central China's Hubei Province, during her China trip in early September, to seek knowledge from the country's digital revolution. On the one hand, Western countries want to learn from China; but on the other, they often point an accusing finger at China. What they criticize is precisely China's competitiveness and the things they want to learn. Western countries want China to change so that it can become less competitive. For example, the EU said China is "a systemic rival" and proposed a strategy on connecting Europe and Asia, trying to compete with the China-proposed BRI. The US and Australia have helped develop infrastructure in the Indo-Pacific region with an attempt to counter BRI's influence. By learning from China, the West is actually learning things that it gave birth to. China has learned industrial policies and subsidies from the West. Christian culture, market economy and Western model of governance are becoming less relevant, and are even reaching the end of the rope. Thus, Western countries have to learn from China to reform, whether they want to or not. Learning is innovation, not imitation. Learning is not only a virtue, but also a source of competitiveness. When Western countries learn from us, China is still learning from the world, drawing lessons from all the outstanding achievements of human civilization, reforming our system and implementing modern governance practices. Reform has become China's best choice to integrate with the international community, seize the opportunity of globalization and unleash systematic vitality and creativity. The competitiveness of China's system comes from reform. As President Xi Jinping once said, "The reform and opening-up is a game-changing move not only in making China what it is today, but also for the Chinese people to achieve the country's two centenary goals and its great national rejuvenation. " In the context of profound changes unseen in a century, development models and international rules are changing. No country can boast that its model is absolutely right. Globalization has its uncertainties. Reform not only reshapes, but also has become, China's international comparative advantage. The mission of comprehensively deepening reform is to resolve China's current challenges, reshape international comparative advantages and lay the foundation for it to become a world leader. The reason why Western countries learn from China's reform is that they face internal problems and are afraid of being surpassed by China. We sincerely hope all countries can learn from each other's civilization, overcome ideological differences, and work together to build a community with a shared future for mankind.

(Source: Wang Yiwei, Why West has begun to learn from China, Global Times, September 24, 2019.)

Questions:

1. According to the case, what are the new changes in the reformation of China?

2. Try to use Porter's Diamond theory analysis the national competitive advantage in China.

2.5　Expanding Reading

New economy companies offer key to growth

Editor's Note: China's economy has maintained stable growth, increasing 6.3% year-on-year in the first half of 2019. China Daily invited senior executives of multinational companies to share their views on the nation's economic development and outlook.

China is investing more in cutting-edge technologies and innovation, as well as expanding in emerging industries.

Q1: Overall Chinese economic growth has slowed in recent years, but the top-line numbers remain relatively robust. This means some sectors are growing well to compensate for any hard-hit sectors. In what areas of the Chinese economy do you plan to increase investment or employment?

Q2: Retail sales and consumption have been a bright spot of the Chinese economy. What business opportunities do you see as China continues to pursue higher-quality growth, which is increasingly driven by services and consumption?

Q3: What do you see as the most resilient part of the Chinese economy and how do you plan to align your business with it?

Q4: Uncertainty about trade with the United States has created risks in the Chinese and global economies. How has your company adjusted to these uncertainties? Which sectors of the economy are the most promising and which are most affected by trade conflicts?

Q5: The government has announced a series of policies to further open the economy to foreign investment, to transform finance, and to promote private enterprises. How are you planning to take advantage of these policy changes?

Q6: Many observers believe China is on the brink of a significant technological transformation. How does your company plan to take advantage of tech opportunities in China over the next decade?

Zhu Wei, senior managing director and chairman of Accenture China.

A1: Clearly consumption plays a big role in spurring the Chinese economy and enterprises' growth. Meanwhile, strategic emerging industries like high-end equipment manufacturing, new information technologies, new energy and high-tech industries have been expanding faster in the first half of this year.

We believe that government bodies, businesses and others will increase investments in such areas, speed up the pace of transformation and drive innovation further in more sectors. And we also believe that during the process more value can be released from the value chain from R&D to delivery, from prototype to application, from best case sharing to open innovation.

In such a context, Accenture works with Chinese companies to practice what we call wise pivot-to transform their core business and scale the new business activities. We have opened an innovation hub in Shenzhen and a digital hub in Shanghai this year. Together with some investments and acquisitions in the fields of artificial intelligence, digital marketing and industry design in recent years, they are our latest efforts to build innovation abilities in China and take root in the local ecosystem partnering with clients, startups, institutes and other players.

A2: China's economy is shifting from being investment to consumption driven. In the future the pace in consumer markets will be faster and the competition more intense. New trends led by digital and intelligent technologies, and consumer behaviors are reshaping services.

Both international and Chinese companies are investing to improve their insights and capabilities to take advantage and stay relevant to Chinese consumers. Accenture helps clients to become "living businesses" -stay relevant and generate new revenue streams by becoming more human-centric, delivering individualized relationships, pursuing new customer experiences and protecting customer data-and more importantly, building digital trust without creating new bias by technology.

A3: China is demonstrating its great resilience, switching gear from its old growth model to high-quality growth. It's not only about removal of overbuilt capacities, it also focuses on investing in advanced technologies and innovation, as well as expanding in emerging industries.

The courage to take reforms and the continued pursuit of the new driving forces are the backbone of such resilience in the Chinese economy, whether it is to facilitate enterprise transformation, upgrade industries, unleash consumption potential or restructure development models.

So for consultancies like us, we are determined to explore uncharted waters together with our clients in China. We are investing heavily to build or acquire new capabilities to help Chinese enterprises apply innovation to unlock the value trapped in limited use of digital technologies, in underused assets, and in failure to engage in profitable partnerships in ecosystem.

We are also making changes to become more resilient ourselves, especially how we operate and how we deliver our services. We are becoming leaner in structure and nimbler in the digitally contested consulting and IT services market.

We can move toward deeper engagement to co-create and share tangible outcomes with our clients.

A4: Forty years into its reform and opening-up, China is deepening the market-oriented reform, encouraging innovation, supporting the private sector and attracting foreign investment with all these policies.

Accenture has witnessed many such initiatives and has benefited from them, growing into a team of some 15,000 people in China today. We have witnessed the State-owned enterprise reforms, the rise of privately owned companies, the globalization of Chinese companies, industrial upgrading, and today's digital transformation.

We feel confident that past experience can prepare us to cater to economic uplift and serve Chinese clients both locally and globally. We are fostering innovation within the local ecosystem, exploring next-generation disruptive technologies, going deeper in industrial applications, building up inclusivity, helping the workforce adapt to the new digital environment and ensuring the fair use of data and personal information.

A5: Technological revamp led by digital technologies is indeed bringing disruptions to various industries and constantly changing the competition landscape- and the winner won't necessarily take all. As Chinese companies embrace the digital transformation that is proliferating in more fields, many imperatives still need to be addressed properly and in a timely manner for them to take full advantage of the dynamics of the Chinese economy.

Companies will harness digital technologies to enhance operational efficiency and innovate at scale, support a new way of working, and maintain perpetual relevance through constant intelligent engagement. Only companies able to transform from traditional growth to new growth will become market champions.

A6: At Accenture, we are looking deeper into such opportunities and seeing rising demands from Chinese companies to apply new technology combinations at scale and at speed to increase agility and efficiency. Moreover, we are always practicing at the intersection of business and technology to bring the latest management concepts to life, apply new technologies such as applied intelligence, analytics and robotics, tailor innovative new products and services, and streamline organizational changes in every aspect of the transformation journey with holistic and comprehensive approaches.

Guo Ruyi, managing partner, China TH Capital.

A1: Over the past decade, we have seen the consumer sector give a big boost to the Chinese economy, but as the benefits of population growth and mobile internet penetration fade, we are seeking new opportunities in three areas.

Better lives-education and healthcare will be our focus for the next 3 to 5 years, as these two sectors are important aspects of people's lives, and we need both technological breakthroughs and more capital to develop the foundations of our society. We have already witnessed increasing numbers of venture capital and private equity firms looking into investment opportunities in these two areas, and new unicorns are emerging.

Better work-efficiency should be the key word for the next 5 to 10 years for the Chinese economy. To enhance efficiency in all industries, we need improvement in reorganizing supplies and promoting tech-driven businesses. New technologies, such as artificial intelligence, big data, cloud computing, 5G and automation, and supply-side reform, should always be our focus and we need more talents to understand the technology and help entrepreneurs translate their business to the capital market.

Globalization-we still believe that the trend of globalization is unstoppable. We now have the most Fortune 500 companies in the world, more and more Chinese products and business models are recognized all over the world. As the Chinese government promotes the Belt and Road Initiative and our products and services become more competitive, we believe that a lot of entrepreneurs will seek opportunities to expand their business to other regions of Asia, and eventually build up global businesses. We need international talents to help understand the local market, and to help our clients reach out, or help business leaders from other regions learn from their China counterparts.

A2: China's consumption is entering the next stage of competition with three key concepts.

Consumption stratification-different people in different situations have different demands. More specifically, those who live in the suburbs purchase cheaper products via Pinduoduo, while those who live in first-tier cities prefer to pursue more sophisticated lifestyles. There is no "winner takes all" scenario in the consumer industry, but diversity and uniqueness will be key.

The rise of brands-brands boom if a country's per capita GDP exceeds $8,000. China's new brands in the next few years will enter a blowout type of explosive growth stage, as GDP per capita in China achieves the right level.

Spiritual needs-since the post-90s and post-00s generations are more willing to build self-identity through consumption, consumption that expresses individuality and personality is becoming more important. We believe that trendy products and ACGN (animation, comic, game and novel) culture will present exciting opportunities for new growth.

Based on these areas, massive opportunities in China's consumer sector are expected to release more industry dividends. In addition, service consumption such as travel and education will develop.

A3: We have gone through several economic cycles in the past seven years, yet one trend remains stable-technology is gaining importance in business.

On the supply side, R&D expenditure in relation to GDP has grown at a compound annual growth rate of 6% in recent years, the highest among developed countries globally, especially considering the speed at which China's GDP itself is growing.

More than 75% of R&D personnel and funds are distributed to business enterprises, also the highest among major global economies, in line with our observation of talents flowing from academia to industry.

On the demand side, on a macro level, IT and artificial intelligence comprised almost a quarter of the private equity and venture capital investments in the first quarter this year, highest among all sectors. On a micro level, we see all kinds of capital coming into the sector. Most of our private equity and venture capital partners have set up tech teams, and about 50% of tech deals we closed in the past year involved corporate venture capital, and some sovereign-backed funds invested solely in the tech sector in 2018.

To capture this long-lasting opportunity, we have been investing heavily in tech startups since 2016, which now comprise of about 30% of our customer base. We expect the number to rise further.

A4: There are some uncertainties about trade, but for our clients, most "new economy" companies are less affected. We have observed different responses throughout the sectors we cover. For healthcare and education, there is strong demand in the domestic market, so service providers are less affected. For transportation and logistics, there is a strong requirement for infrastructure upgrading and intelligent transportation.

Logistics in China will see strong growth, and investors are starting to show interest in this sector. For tech innovation, we believe that China now has an abundance of talents, and a willingness to support proprietary innovation, so even if some companies in this sector are under pressure from Sino-US trade friction, it is essential to have as many Fortune 500 tech companies of our own in the long run as possible.

For the consumer sector, the situation is different for companies with global businesses. Consumer brands that have large US market needs face the greatest uncertainty and investors are more cautious about investing in these companies. However, companies that are content driven or offering products and services to other overseas markets than the US are still drawing more attention from investors.

Institutional investors are constantly shifting their interests among different sectors, so it is not unusual that we make some adjustments in our approach to help our clients. First, we focus on talking to new investors. Second, we reach out to some of our clients' global partners to seek investments from them, which can hedge some of the risks caused by trade uncertainty. Last, we do more market research and try to advise our clients on their strategic plans, especially the steps they should take to expand businesses outside of China.

We believe certain trends will never change-globalization and technology evolution, so we will continue to serve new economy companies and invest heavily in these two trends.

A5: We have observed that these policy changes have already come into play in some sectors, such as cloud computing, healthcare, enterprise services, AI, automated driving and the internet of things. We are glad that our investor pool has grown, as the government guide fund, sovereign funds, pension funds and direct investment funds from banks and insurance companies are joining the group.

As a financial adviser, it is always our duty to help clients find the right investors. Now that there is new capital emerging in the market, we should keep a close relationship with them, to better understand the investment criteria and decision-making process of the funds, and to help our clients get financing from the capital market.

A6: Since the reform and opening-up, the Chinese economy has been benefiting from technological advancement, but what has changed is where it comes from. In the past 40 years, most came from imports, from following mature technology bought or exchanged via international trade. Looking ahead, technology will come from proprietary innovation. In this sense, we believe the statement is true.

We believe that China's huge population base contributes to a large data set, a large talent pool, and large user density-all of which are key prerequisites for tech investment success. We plan to focus on sectors already benefiting from these factors as well as policy guidance-AI to start with, 5G and semiconductors to follow.

(Source: New economy companies offer key to growth, China Daily, August 8, 2019.)

Quick Quiz

1. New trade theory (NTT) is a collection of economic models in international trade which focuses on the role of increasing returns to _____ and _____, which were developed in the late 1970s and early 1980s by Helpman, Krugman, and Lancaster.

2. If a producer can generate more output than others with a given amount of resources, that producer has an (   ).

    A. absolute advantage   B. comparative advantage

    C. opportunity cost   D. protect cost

3. What are the three economic costs of tariffs? (   )

    A. Public gains tariff revenue

    B. The domestic producers, operating under a price umbrella provided by the tariff, can expand production

    C. Consumers are faced with higher prices and therefore reduce their consumption

    D. Government gains tariff revenue

4. According to Porter's Diamond theory, determinants of National Competitive Advantage are (   ).

    A. Factor endowments

    B. Demand conditions

    C. Related and supporting industries

    D. Firm strategy, structure, and rivalry

5. Michael Porter wrote a book in 1985 which identified three strategies that businesses can use to tackle competition. In this book, he wrote the approaches that can be applied to all businesses whether they are product-based or service-based. He called these approaches generic strategies. They include (   ).

    A. Overall cost leadership strategy

    B. Differentiation strategy

    C. Focus on a particular market niche

    D. Market leading strategy

Answers:

    1. scale, network effects

    2. A

    3. BCD

    4. ABCD

    5. ABC

Endnotes

［1］ Zhang Zhihao, Science expert laments US protectionist trends, China Daily, August 6, 2019.

［2］ Chad P. Bown, Will the Proposed US Border Tax Provoke WTO Retaliation from Trading Partners?, Policy Briefs PB17-11, Peterson Institute for International Economics, 2017.

［3］ Chad P. Bown, Trump has announced massive aluminum and steel tariffs, Washington Post, 2018.

［4］ M. Crowley, H. Song and N. Meng, Protectionist threats jeopardise international trade: Chinese evidence for Trump's policies, VoxEU. org, 10 February, 2017.

［5］ Da, Z., Engelberg, J. and Gao, P. J., In search of attention, Journal of Finance, 2011: 66 (5), 1461-1499.

［6］ Frankel, J., Trump's on-again, off-again trade war with China, Jeffrey Frankel's Blog, 31 May, 2018.

［7］ Y. Huang, C. Chen, S. Liu and H. Tang, Trade Linkages and Firm Value: Evidence from the 2018 US-China 'Trade War', SSRN e-Library, 26 August, 2018.

［8］ IMF, Less Even Expansion, Rising Trade Tensions", World Economic Outlook Update, 2018.

［9］ IMF, G-20 Surveillance Note, Group of Twenty IMF Note, Finance Ministers and Central Bank Governors' Meetings, 2018.

［10］ Zhang Jie, Around 20,000 5G base stations constructed across the country, chinadaily. com. cn, 9 August, 2019.

［11］ "Porter's Generic Strategies: Choosing Your Route to Success". www. mindtools. com. Retrieved April 1, 2016.

［12］ "Generic Competitive Strategies—strategy, levels, system, advantages, school, company, business, system". www. referenceforbusiness. com. Retrieved April 1, 2016.

［13］ "Oxford Learning Lab—Watch it. Learn it. Badge it". www. oxlearn. com. Retrieved April 1, 2016.

［14］ "Business Strategies for a Competitive Advantage". smallbusiness. chron. com. Retrieved April 1, 2016.

Chapter 3   Political-legal Environment

Learning Objectives

1. Understand the fiscal policy.
2. Master the types of monetary policy.
3. Recognize the instruments of trade policy.
4. Understand the essential-industry arguments.
5. Understand the infant industry argument.
6. Master the four initiatives of comparative advantage.

Opening case

Russia, Belarus may partially merge economies from 2021: report

MOSCOW-Russia and Belarus may partially merge their economies starting from January 2021, Russia's Kommersant business daily reported Monday. "This degree of integration is higher than in the European Union. Basically the talk is about the creation of a confederate state at the level of economies in 2022," Kommersant said, quoting a draft economic integration program, initialed by the parties in early September, but not made public. The merger will involve the introduction of unified Tax and Civil Codes, foreign trade regime, accounting of property and similar socialguarantees, joint banking supervision but with two central banks, a single regulator of oil, gas and electricity markets and harmonized state regulation of industries, the report said. The merger is unlikely to be on equal grounds with the Russian economy 29 times larger than that of Belarus, according to the newspaper. The Treaty on the Creation of a Union State of Russia and Belarus was signed on Dec 8, 1999. After being ratified by the Russian State Duma and the National Assembly of Belarus, the Treaty and the Union came into effect in January 2000. Kommersant said that practical negotiations at the presidential and government levels have been ongoing since spring 2019. On Sept 3, the Belarusian government submitted the draft action program for the integration of Belarus and

Russia to the Belarusian president for approval. The document does not contain specific agreements on a "single" budget of the Union State, and it is too early to assess whether there would be tax risks for Russia, Kommersant said. The draft does not affect such areas as defense, state security, courts, law enforcement, the internal structure of the executive branch in Russia and Belarus, as well as the executive power of the Union State, it said. The parties agreed that "other provisions of the treaty" on the Union State may also be discussed, the newspaper said. There is no reason to talk about the actual unification of the two countries at least until 2022, as the document deals only with economic integration, Kommersant said.

(Source: Russia, Belarus may partially merge economies from 2021: report, Xinhua net, September 16, 2019.)

3.1 The Policy Instrument

Government policy influences the economic environment, the framework of laws, industry structure and certain operational issues. Political instability is a cause of risk. Different approaches to the political environment apply in different countries. International trade is subject to a further layer of international law and regulation. The political environment affects the firm in a number of ways:

(1) A basic legal framework generally exists.

(2) The Government can take a particular stance on an issue of direct relevance to a business or industry.

(3) The Government's overall conduct of its economic policy is relevant to business.

A country or government's policies will have a greater impact on the economy. From the perspective of economic research, the government uses economic, legal and necessary administrative means to change the current economic structure so as to rationalize and perfect it and further adapt it to the process of the development of productive forces. All modern governments are expected to manage their national economies to some extent. In general, there are four main objectives of macroeconomic policy:

(1) To achieve economic growth, and growth in national income per head of the population. Growth implies an increase in national income in real terms. Increases caused by price inflation are not real increases at all.

(2) To control price inflation. This has become a central objective of many

countries' economic policy.

　(3) To achieve full employment. Full employment does not mean that everyone who wants a job has one all the time, but it does mean that unemployment levels are low, and involuntary unemployment is short term.

　(4) To achieve a balance between exports and imports over a period of years.

3.1.1　Fiscal policy

　Fiscal policy provides a method of managing aggregate demand in the economy, mainly include taxation, public borrowing and public spending. Fiscal policy is often used to stabilize the economy over the course of the business cycle, specifically by using of government revenue collection (mainly taxes) and expenditure (spending) to influence the economy. It needs to make a plan in order to establish how much taxation there should be, what form the taxes should take and so which sectors of the economy (firms or households, high income earners or low income earners) the money should come from. This formal planning of fiscal policy is usually done once a year and is set out in the Budget. There are three possible scenarios of fiscal policy:

　(1) Neutral fiscal policy is usually undertaken when an economy is in neither a recession nor a boom. This occurs when there is a large tax revenue and a balanced economy. Government spending is not financed by issuance of debt, and the fiscal policy has a neutral effect on the level of economic activity. The government is essentially choosing not to use the income earned from taxation to directly influence the economy.

　(2) Expansionary fiscal policy involves government spending exceeding tax revenue by more than it has tended to, and is usually undertaken during recessions. It is a form of fiscal policy that involves decreasing taxes, increasing government expenditures or both, in order to fight recessionary pressures. This is a situation where government spending is larger than tax revenue, thus the government needs to borrow money. This policy involves government attempts to increase aggregate demand (total demand for final goods and services in the economy.) The policy involves lowering taxes and (or) higher government spending.

　A decrease in taxes means that households have more disposal income to spend. Higher disposal income increases consumption which increases the gross domestic product (GDP). Further, a decrease in taxes communicates to the businesses that the government is interested in reviving the economy. It increases their confidence which in turn increases the private investment component of GDP. Since government expenditures form a component of GDP, an increase in government expenditures increases GDP directly. Further, such an increase also results in indirect increase in consumption and other components of GDP. The bottom line is that increase in GDP resulting from a decrease in taxes and increase in government expenditures is much more than the initial decrease in taxes or increase in government expenditures due to the multiplier effect. The multiplier effect is a phenomenon used to describe an expansion in the money supply within a specific nation. With this effect, the ability of banking institutions to make loans to individuals and businesses increases.

We can learn the following example:

Abigail Noble is an economist assisting the IMF in developing policy recommendations for different economies. Currently she is meeting with finance ministers of newly formed states of Sacramento and Salamia. Sacramento has inflation rate of 7% as compared to historical average of 3%, unemployment rate of 2% as compared with natural unemployment rate of 4%, budget deficit of 5% and a GDP growth rate of 6% as compared with average growth rate of 3%. Salamia on the other hand has 1% inflation, 8% unemployment as compared to historical average of 4%, budget surplus of 4% and GDP growth rate of 1.5%. For which country Abigail would most likely recommend expansionary fiscal policy?

Low inflation, high unemployment, a budget surplus and low GDP growth rate indicates that Salamia is facing recessionary pressures which makes it an ideal candidate for expansionary fiscal policy. Salamia can achieve this by either decreasing taxes, increasing its government expenditures or both. This will eliminate the budget surplus, increase growth rate, increase inflation and decrease unemployment rate. Sacramento on the other hand, is facing inflationary pressures and expansionary fiscal policy will only worsen her problems.

(Source: Obaidullah Jan, Expansionary Fiscal Policy, XPLAND, 2019)

(3) Contractionary fiscal policy occurs when government deficit spending less than the total tax revenue it receives. The policy is a result of raising taxes and (or) reducing spending. It gets its name from the way it contracts the economy. It reduces the amount of money available for businesses and consumers to spend. The purpose of contractionary fiscal policy is to slow growth to a healthy economic level. When governments cut spending or increase taxes, it takes money out of consumers' hands. That also happens when the government cuts subsidies, transfer payments

including welfare programs, contracts for public works, or the number of government employees. Shrinking the money supply decreases demand. It gives consumers less purchasing power. That reduces business profit, forcing companies to cut employment and cut down their investment expenditures. Consumption and private investment are part of the Gross Domestic Product (GDP), which falls as a result. However, this fall is magnified by the multiplier effect. A decrease in government expenditures decreases GDP directly because government expenditures is a part of GDP (i. e. GDP = consumption + private investment + government expenditures + net exports). But, such a decrease is worsened as a result of indirect decrease in consumption and other components of GDP. Let us reuse the example from the article on expansionary fiscal policy.

Abigail Noble is an economist assisting the IMF in developing policy recommendations for different economies. Currently she is meeting with finance ministers of newly formed states of Sacramento and Salamia. Sacramento has current inflation rate of 7% as compared to historical average of 3% , unemployment rate of 2% as compared with natural unemployment rate of 4% , budget deficit of 5% and a GDP growth rate of 6% as compared with average growth rate of 3% . Salamia on the other hand has 1% inflation, 8% unemployment as compared to historical average of 4% , budget surplus of 4% and GDP growth rate of 1. 5% . For which country Abigail would most likely recommend contractionary fiscal policy?

High inflation, low unemployment rate (relative to natural rate of unemployment), a budget deficit and high GDP growth rate indicates that Sacramento is facing inflationary pressures which makes contractionary fiscal policy appropriate. Sacramento can achieve this by either increasing taxes, decreasing its government expenditures or both. This will reduce the budget deficit, decrease growth rate, decrease inflation and increase unemployment rate. Salamia on the other hand, is facing recessionary pressures and contractionary fiscal policy will only worsen her problems.

(Source: Obaidullah Jan, Expansionary Fiscal Policy, XPLAND, 2019)

Fiscal policy is connected to the government's budget. The budget is simply the government's financial "roadmap" for the upcoming year, and is similar to an individual or corporate budget in the sense that it determines projected income and spending. The three components of the budget which the Government determines and through which it exercises its fiscal policy are:

(1) Expenditure. The expenditure aspect, outlining how much money the

government expects to spend during the fiscal year. The Government, at a national and local level, spends money to provide goods and services, such as a health service, public education, a police force, defence, roads and public buildings, and to pay its administrative workforce.

(2) Revenue. The revenue aspect, which is an estimate of the total amount of money it expects to collect. Expenditure must be financed, and the government must have income. Most government income comes from taxation, although some income is obtained from direct charges to users of government services, such as National Health Service charges.

Weakening German economy needs a dose of tax cuts

A weakening economy has rekindled an old debate: Does Germany need tangible tax relief for its workforce and enterprises in order to remain internationally competitive? Or should taxes go up to provide more funds for social programs and public investment? Higher taxes create more room for government expenditure, while lower taxes limit the state's spending capacity. The choice between these options is a political matter. But one general approach that might garner cross-party support in Germany would be to ensure that the share of economic output claimed by the public sector neither increases nor decreases over the medium term. In fact, the ratio of taxes and social security contributions to GDP in Germany has been increasing for years. A reference point for deciding the overall tax burden could be the year 2014, in which net new debt for the federal budget fell to zero. At that time, tax revenue (including contributions) amounted to 38.6% of GDP. By 2018, the ratio had risen to 39.8%. Similarly, the tax-to-GDP ratio, excluding social contributions, has also increased significantly, from 22.1% in 2014 to 22.8% last year. By 2020, it will exceed 23 percent. The main reason for this is that inflation and earnings growth are pushing increasing numbers of income-tax payers into higher rate brackets. Bringing the tax-to-GDP ratio back to its 2014 level would require tax relief in 2020 to the tune of 34 billion euros ($ 38 billion) . Even to reach the 2017 level, the government would have to lower the tax burden by 22 billion euros. But which particular taxes should be cut? Canceling the solidarity tax, a surcharge on income tax, would be a good place to start. This tax was introduced on the understanding that it would be levied only temporarily to finance the reconstruction of the former East Germany following reunification. Thirty years on, it's time to make good on this promise. The argument that the end of the solidarity tax would be an unwelcome "gift to the rich" skews the facts. The truth is that its introduction was a special measure that predominantly hit the "rich" . Any German political party eager to tax higher-wage earners more heavily should be campaigning to reform income tax rates, not block the overdue retirement of the solidarity tax. The view that it would make more sense to direct the money raised from the solidarity tax toward public investment is also unconvincing, because there is no shortage of funds available for investment. At the same time, government final-consumption expenditure is increasing massively, and redistribution programs often fail to target the poor. The failure of infrastructure projects in Germany owes more to protracted planning processes and resistance from local communities than to a lack of funds. Urgent action is also required on corporate tax. In Germany, the standard tax rate for companies' retained earnings is around 30%, which is significantly higher than in similar countries. Among the G7, only France's 33% rate is higher, and this will drop to 28% in the coming years, with further reductions to 25% already agreed. To prevent a reduction in tax revenue through companies shifting profits abroad, and to keep investment and jobs in Germany, the federal government should follow France's lead and also gradually reduce the corporate-tax burden toward 25%. Opponents of corporate-tax reform assert that Germany's high export surplus shows there is no need to make its economy even more competitive. But this is simply wrong. Anyone making that argument is confusing companies' export potential with Germany's attractiveness as a location for investment and jobs. Germany's export surplus is accompanied by net capital exports, because more investments are being made abroad than at home. Lowering corporate taxes would change that. According to current estimates, if the tax rate were to drop from 30% to 25%, companies in Germany could increase investment by up to 14%. What's more, owing to reduced tax avoidance, profits recorded in Germany would rise by some 4%. All in all, this means corporate-tax reforms could be roughly revenue-neutral. And there is a final compelling argument for tax relief. It would force German politicians to reexamine existing government expenditure and priorities, instead of always readily serving up new spending programs simply because abundant funds seem to be available.

(Source: ClemensFuest, Weakening German economy needs a dose of tax cuts, Global Times, March 24, 2019.)

(3) Borrowing. It's the third element of the fiscal policy. To the extent that a government's expenditure exceeds its income it must borrow to make up the difference, this is a budget deficit. Money borrowed by the government through issuance of securities, bonds and bills. The government borrows money to make up the difference between revenues and expenditures. The money comes from lenders within the country and from foreign lenders. According to China Daily's news, the

White House and congressional Democrats have reportedly moved close to a budget deal that would prevent the US federal government from breaching its debt ceiling, as the Congress' August recess draws near. The deal, which would raise the US debt ceiling for two years, is "near final". White House officials and congressional leaders have been engaged in heightened negotiations for a debt ceiling increase as well as setting overall spending levels after the current budget deal expires on Oct. 1, the start of the next fiscal year. The budget agreement is expected to include parity between increases in defense spending, demanded by the Republicans, and domestic outlays including on veterans' health care, sought by the Democrats. House Democrats want to package the debt ceiling with a budget bill, believing that will give them more leverage in spending negotiations. House Speaker Nancy Pelosi, who set Friday as the deadline for an agreement, rejected the Trump administration's latest two-year budget proposal requesting that Democrats select $150 billion in spending cuts from a list of $574 billion of saving opportunities, according to earlier report from the Bloomberg. The White House has revised the fiscal year 2019 budget deficit to a projected $1 trillion, the highest since 2012, Office of Management and Budget (OMB) said in its recently released Mid-Session Review. Without reform, trillion-dollar deficits will continue throughout the budget window, and will drive debt to more than $33 trillion by 2029, the OMB report said. "The trend of growing deficits can be reversed only through concerted efforts of spending restraint and restoring government to the proper size," it said.

3.1.2　Monetary policy

Monetary policy is associated with interest rates and availability of credit. Instruments of monetary policy have included short-term interest rates and bank reserves through the monetary base. Monetary policy is the macroeconomic policy laid down by the central bank. It involves management of money supply and interest rate and is the demand side economic policy used by the government of a country to achieve macroeconomic objectives like inflation, consumption, growth and liquidity. Together with fiscal policy, monetary policy is used to save the economy from severe ups and downs. It is relatively more responsive than the fiscal policy because central banks can react to economic changes more quickly than the government and the legislature.

1. Three objectives of monetary policy

Central banks have three monetary policy objectives. The most import is to manage inflation. The secondary objective is to reduce unemployment, but only after controlling inflation. The third objective is to promote moderate long-term interest rates.

When the economy is under recessionary pressures, the central bank increases the money supply which in turn decreases the cost of borrowing. Low cost of borrowing stimulates consumption and investment which increases GDP. Higher investment by businesses reduces unemployment rate and all this helps the economy move out of recession. On the other hand, when the economy is under inflationary pressures, the central bank decreases money supply which increases cost of borrowing. Higher cost of borrowing dampens consumption and investment which reduces inflation.

2. Types of monetary policy

（1）Contractionary monetary policy. Central banks use contractionary monetary policy to reduce inflation. They reduce the money supply by restricting the amount of money banks can lend. The banks charge a higher interest rate, making loans more expensive. Fewer businesses and individuals borrow, slowing growth.

Contractionary monetary policy is when a central bank uses its monetary policy tools to fight inflation. It's how the bank slows economic growth. Inflation is a sign of an overheated economy. It's also called restrictive monetary policy because it restricts liquidity. The bank will raise interest rates to make lending more expensive. That reduces the amount of money and credit that banks can lend. It lowers the money supply by making loans, credit cards, and mortgages more expensive.

The purpose of restrictive monetary policy is to ward off inflation. A little inflation is healthy. A 2% annual price increase is actually good for the economy because it stimulates demand. People expect prices to be higher later, so they buy more now. That's why many central banks have an inflation target of around 2%.

If inflation gets much higher, it's damaging. People buy too much now to avoid paying higher prices later. This causes businesses to produce more to take advantage of higher demand. If they can't produce more, they'll raise prices further. They take on more workers. Now people have higher incomes, so they spend more. It becomes a vicious cycle if it goes too far. It creates galloping inflation where inflation is in the double-digits. Even worse, it can result in hyperinflation, where prices rise 50% a month. To avoid this, central banks slow demand by making purchases more expensive. They raise bank lending rates. That makes loans and home mortgages more expensive. It cools inflation and returns the economy to a healthy growth rate of between 2% and 3%. Let's continue with the example above.

James Traina works as Assistant Economist at World Bank. He is developing policy recommendations for Estovakia and Estrovia. Estovakia has unemployment rate of 7% as compared to natural unemployment rate of 3%, inflation rate of-1% and a growth rate of 0.5% as compared to average of 4%. Estrovia has unemployment rate of 1% as compared to natural unemployment rate of 3%, inflation rate of 9% as compared to average of 4% and a growth rate of 7% as compared to average of 3.5%. For which country James would most likely recommend a contractionary monetary policy?

Contractionary monetary policy is used to reduce inflation. Since Estrovia has inflation rate of 9% as compared with average of 4%, her central bank should implement a contractionary monetary policy to lower the inflation rate, otherwise the economy will heat up and hit a severe recession. However, such a change will increase the unemployment rate and reduce the growth rate. But, such a sacrifice is inevitable for sustainable growth.

(Source: Obaidullah Jan, Contractionary Monetary Policy, XPLAND, 2018)

These are the three main tools that are used by Central Bank to implement the contractionary monetary policy:

①Open market operations: Buying and selling of government securities by the central bank are referred to as open market operations. This changes the reserve amount the banks have on hand. A higher reserve means banks can lend less. Under this, central bank influences interest rates by selling government debt in the market which results in reduced cash in investor account, excess reserves with banks, fewer funds available for lending and reduced money supply thereby sucking liquidity from the system and led to tightening of the amount of money in circulation. However, it is pertinent to note that in the absence of a liquid market in government debt securities it is difficult to implement open market operations.

② Reserve requirements: Minimum amount of cash or cash-equivalents (computed as a percentage of deposits) that banks and other depository institutions (credit unions, insurance companies) are required by law to keep on hand, and which may not be used for lending or investing. Reserve requirements serve as (a) a safeguard against a sudden and inordinate demand for withdrawals (as in a run on a bank), and (b) as a control mechanism for injecting cash (liquidity) into, or withdrawing it from, an economy.

③Policy rate: Policy rate is basically the monetary tool used by the Central bank to control the money supply in the country. Prominent Policy rates are Repo Rate and Reverse Repo Rate. Repo Rate is the rate at which central bank lends money to Banks and Reverse Repo rate is the rate at which central bank borrows funds from the banks. By increasing the repo rate as part of contractionary monetary policy implement exercise, central bank makes the cost of borrowing high for banks which in turn compel banks to increase their lending rates resulting in the reduced supply of money. The discount rate at which a central bank repurchases government securities from the commercial banks, depending on the level of money supply it decides to maintain in the country's monetary system. To temporarily expand the money supply, the central bank decreases repo rates (so that banks can swap their holdings of government securities for cash). To contract the money supply it increases the repo rates. Alternatively, the central bank decides on a desired level of money supply and lets the market determine the appropriate repo rate. Repo is short for repossession. Reverse repo rate refers to the borrowing rate for a short term period. Reverse repo rate is a kind of monetary instrument. It plays a vital role while framing the existing monetary policy of the country. Its main purpose is to monitor the money supply in a particular country.

(2) Expansionary monetary policy. Expansionary monetary policy is when a central bank uses its tools to stimulate the economy, lower unemployment and avoid recession. That increases the money supply, lowers interest rates, and increases aggregate demand. It boosts growth as measured by gross domestic product. Businesses borrow more to buy equipment, hire employees, and expand their operations. Individuals borrow more to buy more homes, cars, and appliances. That increases demand and spurs economic growth. It lowers the value of the currency, thereby decreasing the exchange rate. It is the opposite of contractionary monetary policy. Expansionary monetary policy deters the contractionary phase of the business cycle. But it is difficult for policymakers to catch this in time. As a result, you typically see expansionary policy used after a recession has started.

The U. S. central bank, the Federal Reserve, is a good example of how expansionary monetary policy works. The Fed's most commonly used tool is open market operations. That's when it buys Treasury notes from its member banks. Where does it get the funds to do so? The Fed. simply creates the credit out of thin air. That's what people mean when they say the Fed is printing money. By replacing the banks' Treasury notes with credit, the Fed gives them more money to lend. To lend out the excess cash, banks reduce lending rates. That makes loans for autos, school, and homes less expensive. They also reduce credit card interest rates. All of this extra credit boosts consumer spending. When business loans are more affordable, companies can expand to keep up with consumer demand. They hire more workers, whose incomes rise, allowing them to shop even more. That's usually enough to stimulate demand and drive economic growth to a healthy 2%~ 3% rate. The Federal Open Market Committee may also lower the Fed. funds rate. It's the rate banks charge each other for overnight deposits. The Fed. requires banks to keep a certain amount of their deposits in reserve at their local Federal Reserve branch office every night. Those banks that have more than they need will lend the excess to banks who don't have enough, charging the Fed. funds rate. When the Fed. drops the target rate, it becomes cheaper for banks to maintain their reserves, giving them more money to lend. As a result, banks can lower the interest rates they charge their customers. The federal's third tool is the discount rate. It's the interest rate the Fed. charges banks that borrow from its discount window. But banks rarely use the discount window because there is a stigma attached. The Fed. is considered to be a lender of last resort. Banks only use the discount window when they can't get loans from any other banks. Banks hold this viewpoint, even though the discount rate is lower than the Fed. funds rate. The Fed. lowers the discount rate when it decreases the Fed. funds rate. The Fed. hardly ever uses its fourth tool, lowering the reserve requirement. Even though this immediately increases liquidity, it also requires a lot of new policies and procedures for member banks. It's much easier to lower the Fed. funds rate, and it's just as effective. During the financial crisis, the Fed. created many more monetary-policy tools.

Benefits of globalization must be better shared

If trade tensions continue and escalate, China and the US will suffer the largest hurt, but other economies will also feel pain. The trade frictions instigated against China by the United States administration will profoundly reshape the global economy. The raising of tariffs on US imports of Chinese goods followed by China's retaliatory measures is having negative impacts on output, investment, employment, productivity not only in both economies, but also in bystanders up and down global value chains. In the short term, the direct economic losses are not negligible for both sides. Since the trade sector and manufacturing sector account for a bigger share in China's GDP, the estimated loss on the Chinese side in the short term is larger, ranging from 0.5% to 1.5% of GDP, and 0.3% to 0.6% of GDP on the US side, according to the latest World Economic Outlook of the International Monetary Fund. However, in the long term, the negative effects will become larger for the United States, as higher tariffs, often followed by real exchange rate appreciation, will lower the returns on capital. Among all the economic factors, China-US bilateral investment has been affected most and may suffer more in the future. Chinese foreign direct investment in the United States dropped 84% in 2018 compared to 2017, from $29.4 billion to $4.8 billion, according to a report by Rhodium Group. And US FDI in China stagnated at $26.9 billion, with the annual growth rate dropping from 11% to 1.5% in 2018. Several factors have played a role here, largely on the US side. First, the uncertainty of economic prospects and investment policies brought about by trade tensions has made some investors shy away. Second, the US administration has imposed new restrictions on Chinese FDI into the United States. Regulators such as the Committee on Foreign Investment in the United States and the Federal Communications Commission have blocked or reversed several investment deals in the name of national security. Third, the Chinese government has also imposed some restrictions on capital outflows, although not specifically targeted at the US. If trade tensions continue and escalate, China and the US will suffer the largest losses from tariff increases. And the impact on trade will be materialized in the years to come. In the worst case scenario, in which the US imposes 25% tariffs on all imports from China and China retaliates, an IMF simulation suggests that the trade volume between China and the US may slump by around 70%. One explanation of this result is the trade pattern. Processing trade accounts for roughly one-third of China's exports to the US, while general trade related with importing core intermediates from the US accounts for another significant share. Therefore, China's exports to the US and imports from the US are closely linked. So, when higher tariffs raise costs, some of this trade will be replaced by domestic supply or get diverted to a third country. Thus, other countries not directly involved in disputes will also be affected due to the disruption of global production chains. Studies suggest that the global manufacturing sector will experience a significant contraction. Economies with both relatively big and fragmented manufacturing sectors, such as Germany and Japan, will also suffer heavy losses if this course is taken. Although some economies will benefit from the trade disruption, such as Canada and Mexico given their geographical and economic proximity to the US, simulation results show that the overall effects are small but negative in every region in the long run. The spillover effects also include sectoral reallocation across countries and repositioning of global value chains. The US agricultural sector will experience a considerable contraction. And the electronics and other manufacturing capacity in China will partly relocate to Mexico and other Asian countries such as Vietnam and Indonesia, while the service sector will substantially expand in China and contract in other countries. This will imply job losses in specific sectors in China, which will tend to be bearable with the right policy reactions, since the losses can be accommodated with structural change to the economy. Two main policy implications emerge here. First, it is important for China's central bank, the People's Bank of China, to maintain a moderate expansionary monetary policy to act as a buffer against the negative effects of the slowdown in the growth of exports, investment and consumption, and take measures to stabilize expectations of the exchange rate. To achieve this, it is essential to balance cross-border capital flows. This means further tightening capital controls if necessary and opening up the domestic financial market to encourage more portfolio investment inflows when direct investment staggers. Meanwhile, the central bank will need to closely monitor and strengthen regulations on short-term capital flows to avoid financial risks. Second, China should keep seeking close trade relations with other valuable trading partners, for instance with European countries and the members of the Association of Southeast Asian Nations, and explore the trade potential with the Belt and Road economies. Since a driving force behind the recent anti-globalism is unevenly shared benefits from trade and the burden of structural adjustment across countries and sectors, it is important to have coordination mechanisms and policies in place to make sure economic costs do not fall on just a few.

(Source: Zhang Ying, Benefits of globalization must be better shared, China Daily Global, June 20, 2019.)

3.2　Instruments of trade policy

Trade policy means laws related to the exchange of goods or services involved in international trade including tariffs, subsidies, import quotas, local content requirements, voluntary export restraints, antidumping duties, and import or export regulations.

3.2.1　Tariffs

Tariff, also called customs duty, tax levied upon goods as they cross national boundaries, usually by the government of the importing country. In a word, a tariff is a tax levied on imports (or exports). It is a policy that taxes foreign products to encourage or protect domestic industry. The tariff is historically used to protect infant industries and to allow import substitution industrialization.

Tariffs fall into two categories. Specific tariffs are levied as a fixed charge for each unit of a good imported. Import tax expressed in an amount of money per unit imported. Specific tariffs are trade barriers designed to reduce imports into countries. Ad valorem tariffs are levied on an item on the basis of its value of the imported good and not on the basis of its quantity, size, weight, or other factor. In most cases, tariffs are generally introduced as a means of restricting trade from particular countries or reducing the importation of specific types of goods and services.

US toy prices may rise due to additional tariff

For the US toy industry, President Donald Trump's threatened 10% tariff on an additional $300 billion worth of Chinese goods starting from Sept 1 would come during the peak holiday shipping month, when many Chinese toy manufacturers send their products to the United States.

Though some US toy companies have come up with contingency plans, like lowering their reliance on manufacturing in China, many will still make the US consumer pay more if the tariffs hit. "Hasbro will have no choice but to pass along the increased costs to our US customers," said Brian Goldner, CEO of toy company Hasbro. He said the Pawtucket, Rhode Islandbased company, the maker of popular products such as Monopoly and GI Joe, was working to reduce its reliance on manufacturers in China, but he also said it has built up extra inventory, incurring additional storage costs, as it braces for tariffs. It's hard to tell whether companies will alleviate the impact of a new tariff before the holiday season arrives, Linda Bolton Weiser, a senior research analyst at financial services firm D. A. Davidson Companies, told China Daily. But she said that they will try to find alternative suppliers, and work with their procurement teams to optimize product mix and sourcing options. Many also will continue to move manufacturing from China to countries like Vietnam. "They will do as much as they can to mitigate or offset the impact of the tariffs through all the different measures, but it's uncertain now to what extent they will be able to either partially or fully offset the impact," Weiser said. "The good news is that the tariff is only 10% , so a product-price increase of 5% is needed to keep gross profit dollars unchanged. However, the gross margin would decline," she said.

Around 85% of the toys sold in the US are manufactured in China. Major players, such as Hasbro and El Segundo, California-based Mattel, will bear less of a tariff burden then the rest of the industry because only two-thirds of their products are manufactured in China. For many smaller companies, however, almost all of their products are made in China, Weiser said. The US toy industry is still reeling from last year's liquidation of the major retailer chain Toys R Us. After four straight years of growth, toy sales in the US in 2018 fell 2% to $21.6 billion, from $22 billion in 2017, according to market researcher NPD Group. "This is supposed to be the year of recovery. To continue to play this guessing game of whether there's going to be a cost increase, how much that cost increase is going to be, when is it going to go into effect, has been a really troubling environment for companies to try to make business decisions that are long term," said Rebecca Mond, vice-president of federal government affairs at the New York-based Toy Association. The US toy industry supports more than 680,000 US workers, and it accounts for $110 billion in economic value, according to data from the association. Overall, tariffs on the toy industry would reduce its economic impact on the US economy by approximately 10%, or $10.8 billion. The new tariff would be in addition to the 25% tariff that Trump levied on a separate $250 billion worth of Chinese imports over the past year. While the previous tariffs affect inputs, components and raw materials for domestic toy production, the latest tariff will likely hit finished toys and other toy-related items not yet subject to tariffs. With the tariffs implemented, the retailers would want to avoid paying the tariffs themselves, which would in turn force toymakers like Hasbro or Mattel to bring in more imports, Weiser said. "It changes the nature of the business, and it changes the makeup of the revenue, so it's going to put more burden for more shipping capacity onto the toymaker," she said.

(Source: LIU YINMENG, China Daily, August 10, 2019.)

3.2.2　Subsidies

A subsidy is a government payment to a domestic producer. Subsidiestake many forms, including cash grants, low-interest loans, tax breaks, and government equity participation in domestic firms. By lowering production costs, subsidies help domestic producers in two ways: (1) competing against foreign imports and (2) gaining export markets. Agriculture tends to be one of the largest beneficiaries of subsidies in most countries.

3.2.3　Import quotas and voluntary export restraints

An import quota is a different restriction on the quantity of some good that may be imported into a country. A tariff quota permits the import of a certain quantity of a commodity duty-free or at a lower duty rate, while quantities exceeding the quota are subject to a higher duty rate. An import quota, on the other hand, restricts imports absolutely. A quota of this type is designed to help to maintain an equitable balance in the marketplace, allowing domestic producers to compete with producers who manufacture the goods outside the country.

Proponents of the import quota feel this approach is necessary in order to protect the economy of the nation receiving the goods. Placing limits makes it possible for part of the demand for those goods to be met by products produced within the country, a move that helps to ensure jobs are provided for citizens who are engaged in the production of those goods. At the same time, the measure helps to prevent domestic or imported goods from overpowering the consumer market, and ensures that consumers have several options on which products to purchase.

Critics feel that the need for an import quota to protect the interests of consumers is unnecessary. Limiting the quantity of goods imported has the potential to limit consumer options, rather than expand them. In addition, the limits may actually have a negative impact on the economy, since consumers may pay a higher price for the readily available domestic products and thus be unable to afford other types of products that they would otherwise buy.

While there is disagreement on the effectiveness of the import quota, there is often agreement on how the quota compares to the application of tariff rate surcharges on imports. Typically, the tariff is seen as a more efficient way to place limits on the inflow of international goods without placing undue hardship on producers who import goods. For many, tariffs represent the best solution when it comes to maintaining a healthy economy, providing consumers with a variety of purchase options, and in promoting healthy competition among suppliers.

A variant on the import quota is the voluntary export restraint. A voluntary export restraint (VER) is a quota on trade imposed by the exporting country, typically at the request of the importing country's government. One of the most famous historical examples is the limitation on auto exports to the United States enforced by Japanese automobile producers in 1981. A response to direct pressure from the U. S. government, this VER limited Japanese imports to no more than 1. 68 million vehicles per year. The agreement was revised in 1984 to allow 1. 85 million Japanese vehicles per year. The agreement was allowed to lapse in 1985, but the Japanese government indicated its intentions at that time to continue to restrict exports to the United States to 1. 85 million vehicles per year. After entering the 21st century, trade conflicts between countries occur from time to time. Chinese Ambassador to the World Trade Organization (WTO) in May 2018 said, the lately imposed tariffs by the United States on steel and aluminum do not aim at protecting the so-called "national security", but serve to protect commercial interests of US domestic industries. Despite worldwide objection, the US administration decided in March to impose a 25% tariff on steel imports and a 10% tariff on aluminum imports. The U. S. then provided temporary exemptions for EU member states as well as Argentina, Australia, Brazil, Canada, Mexico and South Korea. It is reported that the United States sought quotas or voluntary export restraints during its negotiations with economies requesting permanent exemption from US steel tariffs.

3. 2. 4 Local content requirements

The term "localisation barriers to trade" applies to a range of measures that favour domestic industry at the expense of foreign competitors. While many localisation barriers have been around for a number of years, they are being applied with increasing frequency. The fastest growing of these measures are local content requirements (LCRs), which are policies imposed by governments that require firms to use domestically-manufactured goods or domestically-supplied services in order to operate in an economy. Local content requirement is a requirement that some specific fraction of a good be produced domestically. There has been a substantial increase in the use of these measures in recent years, as governments try to achieve a variety of policy objectives that target employment, industrial, and technological development goals.

Local content regulations have been widely used from the simple assembly of products whose parts are manufactured elsewhere into the local manufacture of component parts. They have also been used in developed countries to try to protect local jobs and industry form foreign competition.

US, India to go back to WTO in solar power dispute: source

India has failed to comply with a World Trade Organization ruling on solar power, the US will tell the WTO's dispute settlement body (DSB) next month, triggering a fresh round of litigation, according to an agenda issued on Wednesday. Renewable energy has become a hot area of trade friction as major economies compete to dominate a sector that is expected to thrive as reliance on coal and oil dwindles. India unveiled its national solar program in 2011, seeking to ease chronic energy shortages in Asia's third-largest economy without creating pollution. But the US complained to the WTO in 2013, saying the program was discriminatory and US solar exports to India had fallen by 90 percent from 2011. The US won the case last year, when WTO appeals judges ruled India had broken the trade rules by requiring solar power developers use Indian-made cells and modules. Such "local content" requirements are banned as they discriminate in favor of domestic firms and against foreign rivals. Under an agreement with the US, India had until December 14 to comply with the ruling and it told the DSB last week that it had done so. If India is found not to have complied, Washington could ask the WTO for permission to impose trade sanctions on India. But the WTO dispute system is struggling to process a large number of complex disputes. The process is likely to continue for a year or more.

(Source: Global Times, December 20, 2017.)

3. 2. 5   Antidumping policies

Dumping is variously defined as selling goods in a foreign market at below their costs of production or as selling goods in a foreign market at below their "fair" market value. For example: In November 2017, the Trump administration imposed an 18% tariff on Canada's $5. 9 billion of softwood lumber exports. It said some provinces allowed loggers to cut down trees on government-owned land at reduced rates. The U. S. Commerce Department said the dumping injured the American lumber industry. The action sent lumber prices to a 23-year high. Trump first announced the tariff in April 2017. The threat was enough to reduce imports of Canadian softwood lumber. The tariff was retroactive for 90 days. Many companies hesitated to purchase lumber that could face a 20% surcharge. Canadian loggers say there is no unfair subsidy. They pay the government for the logs and plant trees to replace the ones taken. In April 2019, the World Trade Organization ruled that the United States violated international trade rules in the way it calculated the tariff. Frankly speaking, dumping is when a country's businesses lower the sales price of their exports to gain unfair market share. They drop the product's price below what it would sell for at home. They may even push the price below the actual cost to produce. They raise the price once they've destroyed the other nation's competition.

Antidumping policies are designed to punish foreign firms that engage in dumping. The ultimate objective is to protect domestic producers from unfair foreign competition. Many governments take action against dumping in order to defend their domestic industries. The WTO agreement does not pass judgement. Its focus is on how governments can or cannot react to dumping—it disciplines anti-dumping actions, and it is often called the "Anti-Dumping Agreement". [1]The legal definitions are more precise, but broadly speaking the WTO agreement allows governments to act against dumping where there is genuine ("material") injury to the competing domestic industry. In order to do that the government has to be able to show that dumping is taking place, calculate the extent of dumping (how much lower the export price is compared to the exporter's home market price), and show that the dumping is causing injury or threatening to do so.

Agreement on Implementation of Article VI of GATT allows countries to take action against dumping. The Anti-Dumping Agreement clarifies and expands Article VI. They allow countries to act in a way that would normally break the GATT principles of binding a tariff and not discriminating between trading partners— typically anti-dumping action means charging extra import duty on the particular product from the particular exporting country in order to bring its price closer to the "normal value" or to remove the injury to domestic industry in the importing country.

Calculating the extent of dumping on a product is not enough. Anti-dumping measures can only be applied if the dumping is hurting the industry in the importing country. Therefore, a detailed investigation has to be conducted according to specified rules first. The investigation must evaluate all relevant economic factors that have a bearing on the state of the industry in question. If the investigation shows dumping is taking place and domestic industry is being hurt, the exporting company can undertake to raise its price to an agreed level in order to avoid anti-dumping import duty.

Detailed procedures are set out on how anti-dumping cases are to be initiated, how the investigations are to be conducted, and the conditions for ensuring that all interested parties are given an opportunity to present evidence. Anti-dumping measures must expire five years after the date of imposition, unless an investigation shows that ending the measure would lead to injury.

Recently, China raises anti-dumping duties on alloy-steel pipes from US, EU. China's Ministry of Commerce (MOC) announced will raise anti-dumping duties on imports of alloy-steel seamless pipes from the United States and the European Union. US producers of the tubes and pipes for high temperature and pressure service are subject to anti-dumping duties of between 101% and 147.8%, while rates for EU companies range between 57.9% and 60.8%. The adjusted rates took effect on 14 June. China started to impose anti-dumping duties ranged between

---

① This focus only on the reaction to dumping contrasts with the approach of the Subsidies and Countervailing Measures Agreement.

13% and 14. 1% on imported alloy-steel seamless pipes from those regions in 2014 on the grounds that the products were being dumped on the Chinese market at below market prices. The latest decision follows a review last year that found such dumping still existed. High temperature and high pressure alloy steel and seamless steel tubes are mainly used in supercritical and ultra-supercritical boilers and steaming-water pipes in power stations.

3. 2. 6   Administrative barriers

There are several different variants of the division or classification of non-tariff barriers. In general, there are three main categories. The first category includes methods to directly import restrictions for protection of certain sectors of national industries: licensing and allocation of import quotas, antidumping and countervailing duties, import deposits, so-called voluntary export restraints, countervailing duties, the system of minimum import prices, etc. Under second category follow methods that are not directly aimed at restricting foreign trade and more related to the administrative bureaucracy, whose actions, however, restrict trade, governments sometimes use informal or administrative policies to restrict imports and boost exports, for example: customs procedures, technical standards and norms, sanitary and veterinary standards, requirements for labeling and packaging, bottling, etc. The third category consists of methods that are not directly aimed at restricting the import or promoting the export, but the effects of which often lead to this result.

1. Embargo

An embargo is when a government refuses to trade with a country or a certain part of a country. This is usually because of a political problem inside the country. It differs from a blockade in not requiring a state of war or obliging other countries to stop trading. Embargoes may be put in place for any number of reasons. For instance, a government may place a trade embargo against another country to express its disapproval with that country's policies. Embargoes are outright prohibition of trade in certain commodities. As well as quotas, embargoes may be imposed on imports or exports of particular goods in respect of certain goods supplied to or from specific countries, or in respect of all goods shipped to certain countries. Although an embargo may be imposed for phytosanitary reasons, more often the reasons are political (see economic sanctions and international sanctions). Embargoes are generally considered legal barriers to trade.

Seoul rejects Tokyo's remarks on sanctions

SEOUL-Moon Jae-in, president of the Republic of Korea, on Wednesday criticized comments by Japanese officials who questioned the credibility of Seoul's sanctions against the Democratic People's Republic of Korea when they justified Tokyo's stricter controls on high-tech exports to the ROK. The issue has become a full-blown diplomatic dispute between the neighboring US allies in Asia. In a meeting with ROK business leaders at Seoul's presidential palace, Moon said his government was committed to resolving the matter diplomatically and urged Japan to refrain from pushing the situation to a "dead-end street". Tokyo last week tightened the approval process for Japanese shipments of photoresists and other sensitive materials to ROK companies, which need the chemicals to produce semiconductors and display screens used in TVs and smartphones. Japanese officials say such materials can be exported only to trustworthy trading partners, hinting at security risks without citing specific cases. Tokyo hasn't elaborated, but Japanese Prime Minister Shinzo Abe and his conservative aides have hinted there may have been illegal transfers of sensitive materials from the ROK to the DPRK. Moon spoke hours after ROK officials told a WTO meeting in Geneva that the Japanese measures would have repercussions for electronics products worldwide and called for their withdrawal. Japanese officials countered that the measures didn't amount to a trade embargo, but rather a review of export controls based on security concerns. The ROK, which has an export-reliant economy, sees the Japanese trade curbs as retaliation for ROK court rulings that ordered Japanese firms to compensate aging ROK plaintiffs for forced labor during World War II and plans to file a complaint with the WTO. Japanese officials have rejected any link to historical disputes. "(Our) government is doing its best to resolve the issue diplomatically…(I call for) the Japanese government to respond. It should no longer walk straight toward a dead-end street," Moon said in a meeting with senior executives from 30 of the country's biggest companies, including Samsung, Hyundai and SK. "The Japanese government's move to inflict damage on our economy to serve political purposes and link (the issue) with sanctions against North South Korea (DPRK) without any evidence is surely not ideal for the friendship and security cooperation between the two countries," Moon said. He called for the ROK government and private companies to form an "emergency response system" to deal with the impact of the Japanese trade curbs. Analysts said the Japanese measure won't have a meaningful impact immediately on ROK chipmakers Samsung Electronics and SK Hynix, which both have sufficient supplies of the materials for now, given the slowdown in demand for semiconductors. But there's concern that Japan might expand the restrictions to include other sectors. Shin Hakcheol, the CEO of LG Chem, said on Tuesday the company was planning for possible restrictions on battery materials.

(Source: Seoul rejects Tokyo's remarks on sanctions, China Daily, July 11, 2019.)

2. Import deposits

Another example of foreign trade regulations is import deposits. Import deposits is a form of deposit, which the importer must pay the bank for a definite period of time (non-interest bearing deposit) in an amount equal to all or part of the cost of imported goods. At the national level, administrative regulation of capital movements is carried out mainly within a framework of bilateral agreements, which include a clear definition of the legal regime, the procedure for the admission of investments and investors. It is determined by mode (fair and equitable, national, most-favored-nation), order of nationalization and compensation, transfer profits and capital repatriation and dispute resolution.

3. License

The most common instruments of direct regulation of imports (and sometimes export) are licenses and quotas. Almost all industrialized countries apply these non-tariff methods. The license system requires that a state (through specially authorized office) issues permits for foreign trade transactions of import and export commodities included in the lists of licensed merchandises. Product licensing can take many forms and procedures. The main types of licenses are general license that permits unrestricted importation or exportation of goods included in the lists for a certain period of time; and one-time license for a certain product importer (exporter) to import (or export). One-time license indicates a quantity of goods, its cost, its country of origin (or destination), and in some cases also customs point through which import (or export) of goods should be carried out. The use of licensing systems as an instrument for foreign trade regulation is based on a number of international level standards agreements.

4. Standards

Standards take a special place among non-tariff barriers. Countries usually impose standards on classification, labelling and testing of products to ensure that domestic products meet domestic standards, but also to restrict sales of products of foreign manufacture unless they meet or exceed these same standards. These standards are sometimes entered to protect the safety and health of local populations and the natural environment. Take China's fruit imports as example. Thanks to the fast-growing demand in China for quality fruits, Egypt has witnessed a rapid increase in its citrus exports to China in the past years, which has led many Egyptian citrus farms to prosper. Now Egypt, famous for producing sweet juicy oranges, has become the third largest exporter of citrus to China after South Africa and the United States. Use the data of Horticultural Export Improvement Association (HEIA), Egypt began citrus export to China with over 23,000 tons in the first year in 2015, which then increased to more than 36,000 tons in 2016 and finally jumped to exceed 101,000 tons in 2017, which is more than three times increase since it started Egypt's. HEIA, founded in 1996, is in charge of selecting certified farms and arranging citrus exports to several parts of the world including European and Asian states in coordination with concerned agricultural authorities home and abroad. Egypt inspect the farms and choose the best of them to export to China, in cooperation with officials from the Chinese Ministry of Agriculture. HEIA also holds training programs for Egyptian citrus farmers to raise the quality of their fruits to be exported to China. Han Bing, economic and commercial counselor at China's Embassy in Cairo, noted that Egypt's orange exports to China hit 20 million U. S. dollars in 2015 and sharply increased to 80 million dollars in 2016. He said he expected to see further increase in the exports of Egyptian agricultural products to China in the future. According to the interview of Xinhua and Han, "Chinese market is a big, open and highly-competitive. Our imports from all over the world will reach 10 trillion dollars in the next five years. We help Egyptians improve the quality of products to reach our import standards and we expect to see more Egyptian agricultural products in the Chinese market. " Maghrabi Agriculture (MAFA), one of Egyptian citrus farms approved for exports to China, exported 2,500 tons of oranges to the world's most populous country in 2017. Stretched on a vast reclaimed desert area in the Beheira province to the north of Cairo, MAFA looked like a piece of art with its rows and rows of aligned citrus trees bearing shinning round-shaped golden fruits waiting to be harvested and sent to the packing facility before exporting. China rises as a very important market with very good potentials for Egyptian citrus exports. Egypt's orange exports to China to gradually increase to higher levels in the near future. Based on the success of citrus exports to China, Egyptian exporters are now working to increase exports of grapes and dates, another two local quality fruits, to China to meet the fast-growing demand there.

3.3   Political Arguments for Government Intervention

3.3.1   Essential-industry argument

Commonly, the government used trade restrictions to protect its national economy and livelihood industries. This is the so-called protection of the national economy and the livelihood of the industrial perspective. Since the costs of protecting inefficient industries or high-cost domestic alternatives are extremely high, a country must carefully assess the costs, real needs, and alternatives before considering whether to protect. Once one industry is protected by the government, it is often difficult to stop because the protected companies and their employees support politicians who continue to subsidy it, even when the original justification for the subsidy is no longer valid. For example, Lebanon's Health Minister Jamil Jabak vowed in 2019 to support the manufacturing of local pharmaceutical drugs to offer them to citizens at affordable costs. The boost in local production of pharmaceutical drugs will reduce their prices to become more affordable for citizens. Jabak added that he will make sure to offer high quality of locally manufactured pharmaceutical drugs to guarantee their effectiveness. His remarks, came during his meeting with Industry Minister Wael AbouFaour to discuss the importance of supporting local industries to minimize the import of foreign products. Lebanon-based pharmaceutical production is weak due to high local production costs. As a result, imports constitute over 95% of the total available pharmaceutical products in the market which are even more expensive than locally produced drugs. The Lebanese have in the past few years resorted to buying their medical needs from nearby countries such as Turkey and Egypt which have strong pharmaceutical markets and low cost of production. It is important for Lebanon to protect and support the development of its pharmaceutical industry.

New China-Japan cooperation models build tech strength

The escalating trade row between Japan and South Korea seems unlikely to be resolved in the short term. Although China is not involved in their dispute, there is still something worthy of attention as regards aspects like semiconductor material development and high-tech industrial competition. Since the 1990s, the South Korean semiconductor industry has built a significant market in the global semiconductor industry. In particular in 2017 Samsung overtook Intel to become the world's largest semiconductor company and the latter had previously ranked first for 25 consecutive years. South Korea's DRAM memory accounted for about 70% of the global market, with its NAND flash memory accounting for about 50%. The rapid development of South Korean semiconductor companies inevitably pointed to a rapid increase in demand for components and raw materials for the semiconductor production. South Korea's component and raw material sectors are far from meeting the development need of the domestic semiconductor industry in terms of type, quality and technical level. Thus South Korea has long relied on imports of Japanese components, raw materials and technology, and this reliance is difficult to abandon in the short term. For example, South Korea buys 91.9% of its photoresists and 93.7% of its polyamides from Japan. Japan was a leading producer of consumer electronics such as computers and video recorders for a long time. The often-overlooked fact is that Japan was also the biggest supplier of intermediate products including many key components and raw materials. Among Japan's exports of industrial products, the proportion of durable consumer goods is less than 20%, while that of production materials is as high as 80%. In June, a Japanese media report found that of 1,631 parts in the Huawei P30 Pro smartphone, 859 were from Japan, or 53%. Japan's strength in component technology lies in companies committed to developing and manufacturing products that other countries cannot produce. Smaller companies specialize in a certain technology for decades or even generations. Statistics show that as of 2015, there were 21,666 companies that had been operating in Japan for more than 150 years. By comparison, China had less than 100. As South Korean companies have been cut off from supplies of Japanese semiconductor materials, many Chinese people are concerned about whether China might one day face a similar situation. In my opinion, in the era of globalization, while we Chinese are trying to improve our own technology, we should not shun cooperation. Two new models for Sino-Japanese technological cooperation have emerged: Japan's new technology plus China's new market and China's capital plus Japan's smaller companies. For the first model Japan's hydrogen energy vehicles and chip technology could combine with China's fast growing new-energy car market. For instance, the Mirai hydrogen fuel cell vehicle manufactured by Toyota can travel 500 kilometers on a tank of hydrogen, with the fuelling process taking three minutes. Due to the high costs of research and development in its early stage, the car is priced relatively high, at about 460,000 yuan ($66,880). If China and Japan can cooperate to promote the practical development of hydrogen fuel cell vehicles, the rapid expansion of China's new-energy car market would probably drive down the price of hydrogen fuel cell cars, making it a new type of transport for the public by 2025. Most of the electric cars in China are using lead-acid batteries, creating worries as waste batteries lead to serious environmental pollution, violating the original intention of green vehicles. In this sense, it is necessary to accelerate the development of hydrogen fuel cell vehicles for the protection of the environment. The second model is a new approach to scientific and technological cooperation between China and Japan. Japan has experienced small manufacturers with long-term, specific skills and technologies. With an aging population, such companies face the future with the worry of a lack of successors or sluggish sales. Chinese capital has recently started to flow into some Japanese companies with operating difficulties or even facing bankruptcy, helping them establish sales channels in Asia and thus regaining vitality. China and Japan have cooperated for decades in science and technology. We should make good use of this experience, learn lessons and build on networks to further that cooperation.

(Source: Feng Zhaokui, New China-Japan cooperation models build tech strength, Global Times, July 28, 2019.)

3. 3. 2   Encourage foreign acceptance of certain practices

Countries sometimes argue that it is necessary to protect certain industries because they are important for national security. Defense-related industries often get this kind of attention (e. g, aerospace, advanced electronics, and semiconductors). Although not as common as it used to be, this argument is still made.

Governments may also try to force changes in the policies or capabilities of foreign governments by restricting trade. And the basis for that is reduce the benefits of foreign sales or limit the availability of needed products, thereby weakening the economy of the country. For example, U. S. Secretary of State Hillary Clinton on Wednesday reiterated American calls for Iran to give up its nuclear ambition for the sake of its own security in 2009. Addressing a Senate subcommittee overseeing State Department funding, Clinton said that "our goal is to persuade the Iranian regime that they will actually be less secure if they proceed with their nuclear-weapons program. A nuclear-armed Iran with a deliverable weapons system is going to spark an arms race in the Middle East and the greater region. That is not going to be in the interests of Iranian security," she noted. Iran resumed its uranium enrichment in early 2006, and has since refused to suspend the nuclear activity despite three sanctions resolutions adopted by the United Nations Security Council resolutions.

Restrictions are effective only if the exporting country believes that they will not invite retaliation from other countries, or that they will harm their trading partners more than themselves. Even so, it is possible for trading partners to find alternative markets and sources of supply, or to produce their own products.

The aim of trade regulation is to force foreign governments to change their positions on everything from human rights to environmental protection to the production of products that importing countries consider dangerous or immoral. Of course, import restrictions on unacceptable products are obvious, but they are often combined with other economic restrictions, such as restricting trade in other products, restricting the use of bank accounts, cutting off foreign aid or granting consent as incentives. Indeed, efforts to limit harmful products, such as drugs, often aim to reduce supply rather than demand. For example, the Japanese cabinet approved a partial amendment to the Export Trade Control Order on Friday, removing South Korea from a "white list" of trade partners with preferential treatment. According to the Global Times' report, the order will be implemented on August 28, 2019. Countries on the "white list" are identified by Japan as its trusted partners in view of national security. They enjoy preferential treatment with simplified procedures when importing strategic technologies and materials from Japan. South Korea was listed in 2004 as the only Asian country, but it is now the first country to be taken off the list. South Korean importers from Japan will face cumbersome inspections, leading to lower efficiency and higher operating costs. Two rounds of trade sanctions that Tokyo had launched against Seoul have seemingly hit the South Korean economy, but the impact on Japan has also begun to unfold. Since early July, South Korean customers' boycott of Japanese goods has caused a decline in sales of beer, clothing and cosmetics produced in Japan. A survey by pollster Gallup South Korea published on July 26 revealed that 80% of respondents were reluctant to purchase goods from Japan. South Koreans' boycott is likely to last for a long time, probably giving rise to a rapid decline in Japanese products' market shares in South Korea and negatively affect Japan's exports to its peninsular neighbor. The decrease in the number of South Korean tourists will also have an effect on the Japanese economy. South Korea is the second-largest source of tourists to Japan, following China, contributing greatly to the Japanese economy. But amid soured relations, fewer South Korean tourists are traveling to Japan. Japan's Sankei Shimbun reported that an airport in Tottori prefecture, a county famous for the museum of Detective Conan, which called Gosho Aoyama Manga Factory (Gosho Aoyama is the author of Detective Conan), received 424 South Korean tourists in June but only 211 in July. It is estimated that the number of South Korean tourists will keep dropping, harming tourism in Japan. Since Japan restricted the export of three semiconductor materials to South Korea on July 4,

Seoul has made several attempts to avoid being excluded from the "while list," including sending high-ranking officials and members of parliament to mediate and requesting the US to intervene. But South Korea's restrained response failed to change Japan's mind. Tokyo's tough attitude against Seoul might be a bid to ensure the ruling party's election victory in July, but its current decision to remove Seoul from the list shows the Japanese Prime Minister Shinzo Abe administration's resolve to hammer bilateral ties. And there is no sign of improvement in ties. With the rise of nationalist sentiment in both countries, the trade dispute will inevitably spread to military and other domains. The stability of the US-Japan-South Korea alliance may be impacted. The US has played a special role in Japan-South Korea ties since World War II. It was US mediation in 1965 that facilitated the normalization of diplomatic relations between Japan and South Korea. But as Washington's allies, Tokyo and Seoul failed to forge an alliance due to historical and territorial reasons. In 2016, due to the Korean Peninsula nuclear crisis and US mediation, Japan and South Korea signed the General Security of Military Information Agreement (GSOMIA), marking that the bilateral relationship has turned into a quasi-alliance. In late August, Japan and South Korea need to decide whether to renew the GSOMIA in accordance with relevant regulations. Although the Abe administration has repeatedly asked Seoul to renew the agreement in spite of trade disputes, some in South Korean political circles have called for termination of the deal. South Korean people's dissatisfaction over Japan is also growing. Given the semblance of stability on the Korean Peninsula and the abated Korean Peninsula nuclear crisis, it is less likely for the two countries to renew GSOMIA. If the agreement, to which the Abe administration attaches great importance, fails to be renewed, Japan will highly likely adopt new tough measures against South Korea. If this is the case, not only the Japan-South Korea quasi-alliance will come to an end, diplomatic relations between the two might even be severed. It is worth noting that several senior US officials have recently proactively mediated Japan-South Korea disputes, though US President Donald Trump showed little interest. US National Security Advisor John Bolton, US Secretary of State Mike Pompeo, and US Secretary of Defense Mark Esper, who will visit the two countries in early August, have all tried to improve Tokyo-Seoul ties. But judging from Tokyo's decision to jettison Seoul from its trusted trade partners, the Abe administration did not care about Washington's feelings this time. This is a sign that US influence over its allies as well as US prestige are declining. Whether it is an accidental event or a long-term trend might be gauged form future Japan-South Korea relations.

3. 3. 3　Maintain or expand the scope of influence

Typically, governments use trade to cement their global influence, by providing aid or loans to countries that join political coalitions or vote yes in international institutions, and by encouraging imports from those countries. For example, the Cotonou Agreement is a treaty between the European Union and the African, Caribbean and Pacific Group of States ("ACP countries"). It was signed in June 2000 in Cotonou, Benin's largest city, by 78 ACP countries (Cuba did not sign) and the then fifteen Member States of the European Union. The Cotonou Agreement is aimed at the reduction and eventual eradication of poverty while contributing to sustainable development and to the gradual integration of ACP countries into the world economy. The Cotonou Agreement wishes to give a stronger political foundation to ACP-EU development cooperation. Therefore, political dialogue is one of the key aspects of the arrangements and addresses new issues which have previously been outside the scope of development cooperation, such as peace and security, arms trade and migration. Furthermore, the element of "good governance" has been included as an "essential element" of the Cotonou Agreement, the violation of which may lead to the partial or complete suspension of development cooperation between the EU and the country in violation. It was furthermore agreed that serious cases of corruption, including acts of bribery, could trigger a consultation process and possibly lead to a suspension of aid. robably the most radical change introduced by the Cotonou Agreement concerns trade cooperation. Since the First Lomé Convention in 1975, the EU has granted non-reciprocal trade preferences to ACP countries. Under the Cotonou Agreement, however, this system was replaced by the Economic Partnership Agreements (EPAs), a new scheme that took effect in 2008. These new arrangement provide for reciprocal trade agreements, meaning that not only the EU provides duty-free access to its markets for ACP exports, but ACP countries also provide duty-free access to their own markets for EU exports. True to the Cotonou principle of differentiation, however, not all ACP countries have to open their markets to EU products after 2008. The group of least developed countries is able to either continue cooperation under the arrangements "Everything But Arms" regulation. Non-LDCs, on the other hand, who decide they are not in a position to enter into EPAs can for example be transferred into the EU's Generalized System of Preferences (GSP), or the Special Incentive Arrangement for Sustainable Development and Good Governance.

FOCAC to enhance voice of emerging nations

The Beijing Summit of the Forum on China-Africa Cooperation (FOCAC) comes at a critical juncture for global trade marked by disruptions caused by the US'protectionist measures and the increased investment flow created by the implementation of the Belt and Road initiative. These shifting global dynamics create opportunities for an enhanced South-South cooperation, as demonstrated by the growing China-Africa relationship. Today, China is investing more in Africa than any other country, and its trade volume is four to five times that between Africa and the US. China's Ministry of Commerce has also committed to opening its market even more to African products. Already, 97% of imports from 33 African countries enjoy duty-free access to China's market. In addition, although China and the African continent are not exclusive partners, many aspects of their relationship are unique in the world.

The FOCAC is an ever-evolving entity. Since its first edition in October 2000, when 44 African countries had sent their foreign ministers and those responsible for economic affairs to Beijing, it has grown into a large official summit between the Chinese president and African heads of state that would shape China's relations with the African continent in the near future. The ongoing FOCAC sees more than 50 heads of state and government from Africa gather.

In parallel, its scope has been continuously expanding. FOCAC tackled several areas of cooperation such as industrialization, agricultural modernization, poverty reduction, public health, education and scientific and academic cooperation. In 2015, peacekeeping was added to the table when China announced it would provide a total of $100 million of free military assistance to the African Union in the next five years. Since the 2015 FOCAC, China also played a critical role in the battle against Ebola, conducted its first overseas deployment of peacekeepers to South Sudan and signed a lease for its first overseas military installation in Djibouti. Besides, the reduction in foreign aid currently affecting developing countries has increased their awareness of the need for reducing dependence on developed countries. The concept of South-South cooperation exists since the 1950s, but has returned to the forefront since China has emerged to play a bigger role in international affairs thanks to its considerable economic clout and strategy of forging partnerships in new markets, particularly in Africa and Asia. In a departure from classic donor-to-recipient relations, China openly recognizes looking for new suppliers and new markets for its goods, especially now that the country is in the middle of a trade war with the US. Research shows that Chinese investors benefit from investments and trade in Africa. Ten of

China's 15 fastest-growing export markets since 2009 are in Africa: Djibouti, Kenya, Ethiopia and Tanzania, Senegal, Ivory Coast, Guinea, Ghana, Cameroon and Mozambique. Africa is also the only big regional grouping that recently recommitted to free trade with the signing of the African Continental Free Trade Area in March. Many African countries like Rwanda and Ethiopia are lobbying for China to continue to play an active role in their industrialization. Total Chinese FDI stock is continually growing in Africa, from $491 million in 2003 to $40 billion in 2016. South-South trade has more than tripled between 2005 and 2015 and is a vital force in world economic development today. By 2010, developing countries accounted for around 42% of global merchandise trade, with South-South flows making up about half of that total. And 52.6% of the African continent's exports were to Europe in 1995, yet this share had declined to 37.3% by 2015.

In contrast, the percentage of Africa's trade with developing economies almost doubled in the same period-from 25.6% in 1995 to 49.8 percent by 2015. The increase was driven by the growing share of exports to China (from 1.2% to 10.6%), but also intra-Africa exports (from 12.4% to 17.7%). In the future, this growing economic power could translate into political influence and change the balance of power as well. As developing countries become less dependent upon traditional donors and Western partners for their economic wellbeing, they could emerge with a stronger voice on the global stage. In this emerging global landscape, African countries would gain much from looking for common ground between their own goals expressed in the Agenda 2063 and China's foreign policy strategies like the Belt and Road initiative-especially as the US is reducing its economic and military engagement on the continent and the EU is reviewing the Cotonou Partnership Agreement, its overarching framework for relations with African, Caribbean and Pacific countries. With its considerable scope and tangible impact, the FOCAC could just be the right place to do so.

(Source: Laetitia Tran Ngoc, FOCAC to enhance voice of emerging nations, Global Times, September 3, 2018.)

3.3.4 Protecting national culture and consumers

Part of the cohesion of a country comes from the identity of its citizens, and that is what distinguishes its inhabitants from those of other countries. To maintain this collective identity, a country bans the export of art and historical objects that are considered part of its national heritage. At the same time, a country will restrict the import of products and services that conflict with the mainstream national values (such as moral codes), and restrict the import of products and services that substitute for the production that is the cornerstone of the country's traditional values. China has become a more and more mature market for global luxury brands. In 2019 French fashion house Christian Dior announced to launch its e-commerce website in China. According to a report released in January by Bain & Company, a US-based management consulting firm, Chinese accounted for 33% of the global personal luxury goods market in 2018, and the proportion is expected to be 46% in 2025. To cater to a more mature Chinese market, foreign luxury brands started to roll out corresponding promotion strategies. Setting up online stores has been one of the steps, given that Chinese customers' online shopping for luxury goods has shown a rising trend. Many renowned luxury brands have already established online stores in China, including Gucci, Prada and Louis Vuitton. Hermès only has two e-commerce websites in Asia, one in China and one in Japan. Moreover, foreign luxury brands' experience of losing the Chinese market has been a lesson. Italian brand D&G is still suffering from a racist video that insulted China, as Chinese people didn't accept its insincere apology, Bloomberg reported. The brand was removed from online retailers in China such as Alibaba's Tmall and JD. com after the event. Data from D&G's February show in Milan, Italy demonstrated a decrease of $8 million worth of exposure on social media and press on a yearly basis. Apparently, public censure cannot awaken the foreign companies to realize the seriousness of their "mistake", which is actually suspected of violating China's foreign investment laws. To ensure a smooth operation in overseas markets, luxury brands need to respect local culture and abide by local laws and regulations. All foreign businesses that operate in China are obliged to follow all the relevant laws of the country, which is an important guarantee for the country to maintain the order of its business environment, and protect the rights and interests of consumers and law-abiding companies.

Government has responsibility use regulations to protect consumers from unsafe products. The indirect effect of such regulations often is to limit or ban the importation of such products. In 2013, Center for Food Safety of Hong Kong announced that the importation of poultry and poultry products, including eggs, from Catalonia, Spain have been banned with immediate effect. The move has been made to protect both public and animal health in view of a notification from the World Organization for Animal Health[1]about an outbreak of low pathogenic H7N1 avian influenza on a poultry farm in Catalonia. In the same year, China's drug

_____

① Formerly the Office International des Epizooties (OIE).

watchdog has banned imports of a set of antibiotic injection products manufactured by a Republic of South Korea (ROK) pharmaceutical company due to its refusal to accept spot checks. According to a statement issued by the China Food and Drug Administration (CFDA), the body has ordered all ports to stop importing cefmetazole produced by the ROK's Daewoong Pharmaceutical Co., Ltd. The statement quoted an unnamed CFDA official as saying that the administration plans to inspect the production facilities of some imported goods, including Daewoong Pharmaceutical's cefmetazole, in order to strengthen management of such products, a policy which is in line with the CFDA's annual arrangements. However, Daewoong Pharmaceutical did not accept checks according to a prearranged schedule. The CFDA therefore decided to ban its cefmetazole until it can make sure the product meets Good Manufacturing Practice (GMP) standards after conducting spot checks. Implementing GMP standards is a credible measure to ensure the quality, safety and efficiency of drugs. Drugs sold in China must meet the standards of the country's drug manufacturing quality norms and be subject to the supervision of China's drug regulator. Drug manufacturers that refuse or fail the examination will be severely dealt with according to the law.

3.4　Economic Arguments for Government Intervention

3.4.1　Protecting jobs and industries

Perhaps the most common political argument for government intervention is that it is necessary for protecting jobs and industries from unfair foreign competition. In March 2018, Europeans, IMF tell Trump to back off unilateral tariffs. Trump plans to impose a duty of 25% on steel and 10% on aluminium to counter cheap imports, especially from China, that the policy undermine US industry and jobs. But the move risks retaliatory measures against US exports and further complicates efforts to save the North American Free Trade Area (NAFTA). IMF chief Christine Lagarde said: "In a so-called trade war…nobody wins, one generally finds losers on both sides." The International Monetary Fund head said Canada—the largest supplier of steel and aluminium to the US—and Europe—whose car exports Trump has threatened to target—are both likely to impose retaliatory tariffs on US goods. If world trade were jeopardized by such measures, they would become a vector for lower growth and a slowdown of commerce. The impact on growth would be a formidable. The European Union has drawn up a list of US products—from bourbon to Harley Davidson motorbikes—on which to apply tariffs if Trump goes ahead. A trade war has no winners and if it does not happen, for the better, then we can work with our American friends and other allies on the core issue of this problem, overcapacity, but if it does happen we will have to take measures to protect European jobs, European Commissioner for Trade Cecilia Malmstrom said.

3. 4. 2　The infant industry argument

The infant-industry theory is the supposition that emerging domestic industries need protection against international competition until they become mature and stable. In economics, an infant industry is new and in its early stages of development, and not yet capable of competing against established industry competitors.

The infant industry argument is by far the oldest economic argument for government intervention. It is said to be an economic argument that favors a protectionist approach to trade. The infant-industry theory, first developed in the early 19th century, by Alexander Hamilton and Friedrich List, is often a justification for protectionist trade policy. The basic idea is that young, emerging industries need protection from more established, substantial industries elsewhere.

According to a paper in the Journal of International Economics, titled "When and how should infant industries be protected?" the theory was later improved on by the economist and philosopher John Stuart Mill, who said that infant industries should only be protected if they can mature and then become viable without protection. Charles Francis Bastable, added a simple condition, that the cumulative net benefits provided by the protected industry must exceed the cumulative costs of protecting the industry.

Infant-industry theorists argue that industries in developing sectors of the economy need to be protected to keep international competitors from damaging or destroying the domestic infant industry. Infant industries, they argue, don't have the economies of scale that older competitors in other countries may have, and should be protected, just until they have built an economy of similar scale. In response to these arguments, governments may enact import duties, tariffs, quotas, and exchange rate controls to prevent international competitors from matching or beating the prices of an infant industry, thereby giving the infant industry time to develop and stabilize. The infant-industry theory holds that once the emerging industry is stable enough to compete internationally, any protective measures introduced, such as tariffs, are intended to be removed. In practice, this is not always the case because the various protections that were imposed may be difficult to remove.

The basic argument is that when an industry develops, particularly in non-industrialized areas, it has specific disadvantages. It lacks what are called economies of scale, which are financial advantages accruing when an industry is big that help to lower costs. These advantages could include being able to purchase in bulk, get better loan rates, and allocate personnel resources more efficiently. Given this disadvantage, it's thought by some economists that the best way to tackle the matter is by limiting importation of similar goods into the country, and this is usually addressed via a government that imposes tariffs (importation taxes) or limits, that make imported goods less attractive or available to consumers in the less industrialized country.

Protectionist reasoning that industrial startups need safeguards against established foreign manufacturers and cutthroat competitors, especially in developing economies. This protection is commonly sought by enacting high import duties and/or import quotas. Although frowned upon by the World Trade Organization in this era of globalization, virtually every country, at one time or another and in one form or other, has instituted such measures to protect its threatened enterprises.

VR industry ready to take off as government gets behind sector

The woman screamed and was too afraid to take one step further. In her field of view, she was standing on the top of the Empire State Building in New York. But in reality, she was standing on a plank placed on the floor in a room in a Beijing suburb, with VR goggles on. In China, there were more than 3,000 such VR arcades in 2016. The source that provided the figure, iResearch Consulting Group, has not given the Global Times the updated statistics. According to a report by Shenzhen-based research firm Askci Corp, the market size of VR in China is expected to reach 30.09 billion yuan ($4.36 billion) next year.

With policy support from the government, China is showing that it intends to lead the VR industry by 2025, according to a document on how to accelerate the development of the industry released by the Ministry of Industry and Information Technology (MIIT) at the end of last year. The guidance pointed out that VR technology and products should be applied in manufacturing, education, culture, healthcare, commerce and trade. In addition to strengthened policy support, MIIT called for VR talent training, international exchanges and cooperation as the country strives to lead a technological revolution in terms of artificial intelligence and intelligent manufacturing.

Desire to lead

The world's largest VR theme park opened to the public in the city of Nanchang, capital of East China's Jiangxi Province last December. Covering 13,000 square meters, the park can accommodate 120 pieces of advanced recreational VR equipment, the Xinhua News Agency reported in December 2018. The report noted that in a bid to embrace the emerging industry, Jiangxi launched China's first industrial VR base in 2016, and more than 200 VR-related firms have since settled in the province. Microsoft also located its first VR/MR (mixed reality) incubator in the province last year, Xinhua said in October 2018. "China's role [in VR development] has been on the rise-95% of the world's VR equipment is produced in China," Alvin Graylin, president of HTC China, told Xinhua at the 2018 World Conference on the VR industry held in Nanchang in October 2018. "China has a huge market, and the Chinese people are passionate about new technologies," he told Xinhua, "China has the largest number of viewers of Ready Player One [a film set in a future VR game] in the world. " Even though America delivered more AR (augmented reality) /VR revenue than China in 2017, Chinese growth in the next five years could see it dominate AR/VR in the long-term-and not by a small margin, according to a report by Silicon Valley consultancy Digi-capital in May 2018. "China has the potential to take more than $1 of every $5 spent on AR/VR globally by 2022," said the company. In another report by Canalys released in June 2018, the VR headset market grew by 200% in China in the first quarter of 2018. "Thanks to active participation from local vendors, China now dominates the standalone VR headset market, accounting for 82% of global shipments," said Canalys.

Early stages

Wang Xin, in his 20s, is one of the owners of the VR arcade "Triple Reefs," located in Shunyi district in northeastern Beijing. He started the arcade due to his love of VR. "VR is an emerging thing with huge potential to grow. I believe the VR market will remain for some time in China," Wang told the Global Times. After opening last year, he said the peak business time was the Spring Festival period, when his arcade was visited more than 100 times in one month. Charging 128 yuan per hour, "Triple Reefs" provides four sets of VR headsets and equipment. Unlike China's gaming sector, which felt the pinch as regulations tightened last year, VR is benefiting from preferential policies and even understanding from Chinese parents.

"Most of our customers are elementary school children who come with their parents. People in their 20s are also frequent customers," Wang said. Some Chinese parents are going against the traditional mindset which frowns on their children taking up recreational activity and puts more emphasis on studying hard. Now, some Chinese parents are more willing to let their children experience cutting-edge technology as part of their development. Lai Zhen, a VR analyst at iResearch Consulting Group, told the Global Times that VR applications in the educational sector are in their early stages in China, since the industry is waiting for the government's instructions on how to develop it in preschool education and improve children's all-round development. Some experimental exploration has been carried out in Chinese schools. Recently, VR goggles were used in the classroom at the Second High School Attached to Beijing Normal University. Students used them to dive into the sea, hurtle through outer space and witness a smoke-filled battlefield. Scenes normally only described in words in text books were brought to life in front of the students' eyes. Lai said that in the subjects of natural science and arts, VR could be an invaluable tool to assist teaching. "3D creation brings richer cognition in teaching practice compared with 2D. Children will be more interested to explore and will have a greater enjoyment learning through the use of VR in the classroom," Lai said. As an example, she cited a chemistry experiment that was too dangerous to be conducted by young children. A teacher could demonstrate the experiment in front of the classroom, but the students sitting in the back row would not be able to see it clearly. Even though most classrooms in China use projectors to show teacher's instruction is doing, such methods may not gain the students' full attention. "However, if every student puts VR goggles on, they can all have an immersive and interactive experience," Lai noted, saying VR has the power to create more interest and broaden students' horizons. In China, VR applications are used in a wide variety of fields, from adjuvant therapy to training pilots. Other uses in healthcare, precision and advanced industries, filming and television have all been explored on a trial basis.

Challenges ahead

One major factor that will influence the development of China's VR will be content. In Chinese app stores, a search for "VR" will mostly yield results related to VR content platforms supported by big video companies, such as iQiyi and Youku (Chinese YouTube). With a set of VR goggles and a screen, a girl at college can enjoy the effect of watching an IMAX movie in her dormitory. But in Google Play Store, there are a large number of VR games, which means developers are dedicated to creating content. VR content creation is extremely difficult due to its three-dimensional features, Lai told the Global Times. She acknowledged content development in China's VR industry is lagging behind that of other countries. Wang also pointed out that VR is not as popular in China as it is abroad. "Foreign VR players already have the equipment and headset in their homes. It will be hard for Chinese people to dedicate a particular room in their home to enjoy VR," Wang said. However, revolutionary changes brought by a combination of cloud and 5G connectivity may bring opportunities to the industry, according to industry analysts. 5G can offer the extremely low latency needed to deliver high-bandwidth services and removing limits on where devices are situated, according to Huawei iLab. Paul Brown, the general manager for Europe for VR pioneer HTC Vive, said that he believes 5G could bring mobile VR into line with experiences enjoyed by consumers using high-end home PCs, and his company has already begun testing VR through 5G with very encouraging initial results, according to Huawei iLab. Lai also noted that the introduction of 5G in VR could help solve the problem of feeling like you are spinning when wearing VR goggles. "Compared with VR arcades in Japan and the US, the profitability of Chinese VR arcades is improving. More than 5,800 companies have registered VR related businesses in China as of May," Lai said this year, adding that China's VR industry is waiting for a surge on the customer side.

（Source：Zhang Dan, VR industry ready to take off as government gets behind sector, Global Times, May 28, 2019. ）

3. 4. 3　Promote industrialization level

A country with a strong manufacturing base tend to have higher per capita GDP. The United States and Japan, for example, have built strong industrial bases and imposed massive restrictions on imports. Many countries have also adopted this strategy, using trade protection to promote their own industrialization. Specifically, they all follow the following assumptions：

（1）Surplus Labour is more productive in industry than in agriculture.

（2）The inflow of foreign capital into the industrial sector can promote the sustainable growth of the industrial sector.

（3）Prices and sales of agricultural products and raw materials fluctuate widely, and they are bad for economic structures that rely too much on one or a few commodities.

（4）The growth rate of industrial product market is faster than that of commodity market.

（5）Industrial growth has led to lower imports and/or higher exports.

（6）Industrial activities contribute to nation-building.

3.4.4 Enhance comparative advantage

Every country monitors its economic interests, compares itself with others and, of course, takes steps to improve its relative position. Four of these initiatives are particularly important:

1. Maintain the balance of international payments

For countries with small foreign exchange reserves, trade deficits cause problems. A trade deficit is an amount by which the cost of a country's imports exceeds the cost of its exports. It's one way of measuring international trade, and it's also called a negative balance of trade. A trade deficit occurs when a country does not produce everything it needs and borrows from foreign states to pay for the imports. That's called the current account deficit. A trade deficit also occurs when companies manufacture in other countries. Raw materials for manufacturing that are shipped overseas to factories count as exports. The finished manufactured goods are counted as imports when they're shipped back to the country. The imports are subtracted from the country's gross domestic product even though the earnings may benefit the company's stock price, and the taxes may increase the country's revenue stream.

If a country's balance of payments is in trouble and continues to remain unresolved, the government will take measures to balance the budget by reducing imports or encouraging exports. There are two main options:

(1) Currency devaluation. A currency devaluation occurs when a country allows the value of its currency to drop in relation to other currencies. It would help to reduce a country's trade deficit. If a currency's value drops, then exports will become less expensive and imports will become more expensive to people living in the country. A country can also choose to allow their currency to strengthen, which would make their exports more expensive and their imports less expensive.

(2) Through the regulation of fiscal policy and monetary policy, the price of domestic products grows slower than that of other countries.

2. Comparable access argument

According to the view of comparable access argument, enterprises and industries enjoy the same rights as foreign enterprises and industries to access foreign markets. If enterprises cannot enter competitors' market equally, it is difficult to gain cost competitive advantage by expanding sales.

3. Use restrictions as bargaining chips

The threat or actual imposition of import restrictions can be retaliatory measures to persuade other countries to reduce trade barriers. The risk is that if countries scramble to increase restrictions, there will be a trade war, with negative consequences for all economies. If restrictions are to be used successfully as a bargaining chip, it is necessary to choose carefully the target products that threaten other countries with restrictions.

4. Price controls

Price controls are governmental restrictions on the prices that can be charged for goods and services in a market. The intent behind implementing such controls can stem from the desire to maintain affordability of goods, to prevent during shortages, and to slow inflation, or, alternatively, to ensure a minimum income for providers of certain goods or a minimum wage. There are two primary forms of price control, a price ceiling, the maximum price that can be charged, and a price floor, the minimum price that can be charged. For some products that are in short supply worldwide, one country restricts exports to meet the needs of its own consumers. Usually, an increase in domestic supply will cause the domestic price to be lower than the international market price. Of course, a country also fears that foreign producers keep prices artificially low, forcing importing producers out of the market.

3.5   Case

New list system provides legal protection to tech security amid trade war

China has been mulling over list systems to provide the legal basis to protect its national technology security and safeguard the legitimate interests of Chinese firms amid an escalating trade war with the US. The move shows Chinese authorities are preparing for another round of countermeasures against the brutal US crackdown on Chinese tech firms to inflict serious harm on American firms, industry observers said. They predicted that technologies in rare earths, 5G, nuclear, drones and the aerospace industry could be included in the export control list.

The National Development and Reform Commission, China's economic planner, announced late Saturday that it has been tasked with organizing a study to establish a national technological security management list system to "more effectively forestall and defuse national security risks," the Xinhua News Agency reported. The move is based on China's National Security Law and other related laws and regulations. Detailed measures will be unveiled in the near future, the Xinhua report said. "Certain countries have taken extreme measures to hinder global technological cooperation, and the establishment of the list will help ... prevent certain countries from using China's technologies to suppress its development," Xinhua said in an editorial. While the US has frequently targeted Chinese tech firms, citing "national security", and has an Entity List to control exports during the yearlong trade war, the soon-to-be released list is widely considered a move to leverage China's legal means to provide the legislation framework for protecting domestic tech companies and hitting back at US suppression, industry observers said. The timing of the list, which also comes ahead of the reported meeting between Chinese and US leaders at the G20 later this month, also mirrors Chinese officials' urgency to "up the ante" and devise new measures as the trade war intensifies.

Getting prepared legally

On May 15, the US Commerce Department placed Huawei and its 70 affiliates on an "Entity List" on grounds of national security, which will ban the Chinese telecom giant from accessing US-made components and parts. "Without the list system, China was defending passively to US tech offensives. But with such a list, China will become more legally prepared so that it can hit back swiftly and intelligently against the US," Huo Jianguo, vice chairman of the China Society for World Trade Organization Studies, told the Global Times on Sunday. Huo predicted that the list system will be a dynamic one with a small scope of strategically important "technologies that are at the heart of US firms, such as rare earths, nuclear technology, 5G technology, drones and the aerospace industry, that are subject to export control. As the "international situation and China-US relations change," the list could include more or exempt others. The management list is in line with international norms and rules to protect a nation's security, which technology security is an indispensable part of, analysts said. Major Western economies came up with a similar approach years ago. "Economic globalization is irresistible as every country has integrated deeply into the global industrial chain. No country has neglected their economic safety, and China is no exception," a People's Daily editorial said Sunday.

China's National Security Law also states that China should strengthen the capacity to protect technology confidentiality and guarantee the safety of major technologies and projects. "As a technological powerhouse, China has been drafting the list for a very long time. Changes in the international situation just provided the right timing," said Mei Xinyu, an analyst close to the Ministry of Commerce (MOFCOM).

Collateral damage

The new management list also comes days after MOFCOM announced on May 31 that it will soon release a list of unreliable foreign entities that undermined Chinese firms' interests. Xiang Ligang, director-general of the Beijing-based Information Consumption Alliance, said that the two schemes could work together to "generate collateral damage" on foreign firms that have cut off supplies to Chinese tech companies. "From a tech security perspective, foreign companies from certain countries have pocketed profits from Chinese markets by dumping products, such as auto parts, auto motors and computer central processing units, which led to a delayed growth in homegrown industries. The Chinese government could prioritize national security and impose quotas to restrict such imports," Xiang noted. That way, foreign suppliers that distance themselves from Chinese firms could face restricted market access and see their revenues slump, Xiang said. Following the US government ban in May, some US tech firms have yielded to the pressure and halted cooperation with Huawei. For example, semiconductor-maker ARM Holdings announced that it was cutting ties with Huawei. US tech giant Google also restricted Huawei's Android license. Last week, the Chinese government met with representatives of major tech companies from the US, UK and South Korea, urging them to honor their partnerships with Chinese firms, the New York Times reported. Microsoft, Dell, Samsung and ARM were reportedly among the foreign companies summoned. Representatives of those firms have not responded to interview requests from the Global Times as of press time. "This is a warning to foreign companies. But China's door is always open to foreign firms and China's will never abuse its legitimate rights by targeting foreign firms who respect their cooperation with their Chinese peers," Huo said.

(Source: Li Xuanmin, New list system provides legal protection to tech security amid trade war, Global Times, June 9, 2019.)

Questions:

1. What's the trade policy? In this case, which trade policy does the US adopt?

2. Can you write the main categories of administrative barriers? Try to give some examples.

3.6　Expanding Reading

Reading-1

US must respect China's digital sovereignty: analyst

Foreign technology companies' moves to store data locally in China are in compliance with the nation's Cybersecurity Law, which aims to protect the country's network safety, and the US must respect China's cyberspace sovereignty and users' demand for information security, experts said on Monday. The US has demanded that China stop discriminating against foreign cloud computing providers, curb requirements for companies to store data locally and ease limitations on the transfer of data overseas, the Financial Times reported on Sunday. The report, citing three people briefed on the talks, said that China had yet to offer "meaningful concessions" on these requests. Experts said that the US'attempt to gain access to more Chinese data is "unfair" and creates "unilateral benefits" and the US must respect China's internet sovereignty. China's Cybersecurity Law, which came into effect on June 1, 2017, requires critical information infrastructure operators to store personal information and important data collected and generated in China within the country. If it is necessary to provide this information abroad to meet the needs of businesses, a company must conduct a safety assessment in line with the methods formulated by relevant departments of the State Council, China's cabinet. The cloud computing services of US companies including Apple Inc, Microsoft Corp and Amazon were localized in the Chinese market through setting up data centers and seeking cooperation with local companies. Apple announced in July 2017 that it would set up its first local data center in Southwest China's Guizhou Province, which the local government said was a cooperative effort with a global technology giant based on China's Cybersecurity Law. Starting on February 28, 2018, the operations of Apple's iCloud services in China were transferred to Guizhou-Cloud Big Data Industry Co, a Chinese internet services company. The new data center will help resolve many problems that Chinese iPhone users have faced, including data synchronization failures and internet connection errors, Lisa Jackson, an Apple senior executive, said in a report published in January 2018. The US companies' operations in China, conducted while storing data locally, guarantee that they can maintain a core technological advantage and better help them localize their business in the Chinese market, said Zhang Shuang, a Beijing-based independent industry analyst. The Cybersecurity Law is China's coping strategy against global network competition and a necessary method of protecting the network information security of the country and its people, Zhang told the Global Times on Monday.

Safeguard sovereignty

Digital trade is among the issues expected to be on the table when US Trade Representative Robert Lighthizer and Treasury Secretary Steven Mnuchin arrive in Beijing on Thursday to resume bilateral trade talks after a nearly month-long pause, according to the Financial Times. China made an initial offer on digital trade that the US judged as insufficient, the report said. China has paid more attention to digital trade regulations and played a vital role in this activity, but its digital applications now mainly focus on the services industry and the trade itself is still at the starting phase, Zhang said, noting that more efforts are needed in intellectual property rights protection and cybersecurity. "What matters is that China's basic position in digital trade is to protect network security, maintain cyberspace sovereignty and promote the sound growth of economic and social information," said Zhang. "China's internet sovereignty is a basis to secure the sound development of its internet industry and companies. Foreign firms must respect it and Chinese users' demand for internet data and information security," Zhang noted.

Unilateral interests

As China increasingly participates in global digital services, some countries are keeping a wary eye on data services from China. China will surpass the US to be the largest datasphere by 2025, driven by faster growth of data from the Internet of Things and productivity in the country, read a report from International Data Corp and data storage firm Seagate, which was released in January. The US can have more contact with Chinese data as China uses lots of US software and databases. Meanwhile, the US-citing data security concerns-does not want Chinese companies to access its data sources, which can be seen in the Huawei case, said Han Xiaoping, a chief analyst from energy industry website china5e.com. "Such an imbalance would create unilateral benefits for the US and would also be unfair to Chinese firms," Han told the Global Times. The Chinese data industry has great growth potential thanks to the nation's large internet user base and the huge amount of time these people spend online. The sector is expected to further open up in the future, according to Han. The US is trying to impose pressure on China before the trade talks, he said. The Ministry of Industry and Information Technology and

Amazon did not reply to the Global Times request as of press time.

(Source: Huang Ge, US must respect China's digital sovereignty: analyst, Global Times, March 25, 2019.)

Reading-2

How the Trump administration launched a multi-front trade war

Since U. S. President Donald Trump came to office, the U. S. has engaged in a trade fight with almost all major economies, ranging from allies like the EU and Japan, to its major trading partner China. Though Trump trumpets that trade wars are "easy to win", American consumers and industries have felt the pinch from the tariff hike, with jobs losses and price spikes. As the U. S. and China engage in a trade dispute, we take a look at how small-scale trade friction between U. S. and a few selective countries has blown into a multi-front trade war under the Trump administration.

Tariffs on solar panels and washing machines

The first shot was fired when Trump ordered an investigation into the imports of solar panels and washing machines in late 2017, claiming the imports hurt domestic manufacturers. A statement published by the Office of the U. S. Trade Representative said that surging global production and falling prices led to substantial injuries to U. S. companies. It accused South Korean, Mexican and Chinese corporations of pursuing an aggressive downward pricing strategy. Following the investigation, in February 2018, the Trump administration approved a tariff of 20% on the first 1.2 million washing machines and 50% on all subsequent imported machines in the following two years. A 30% tariff on solar panels, with the rate declining over four years was also approved. Trump's move immediately raised alarm of rising trade protectionism. In an op-ed for the Washington Post, Chad P. Bown, senior fellow at the Peterson Institute for International Economics, pointed out that before Trump's tariffs on all imports of solar panels and washing machine, the U. S. had already imposed similar special import tariffs on all those products, but only on selected foreign sources. "His decision could trigger a tsunami of new requests for trade barriers," Bown wrote, raising the fear that this could lead to further tit-for-tat actions from countries subject to the tariff hike.

Tariffs on steel and aluminum

As trade tensions escalate, the Trump government's appetite for tariffs has only increased. In March 2018, Trump announced a 25% tariff on steel and 10%

on aluminum would be imposed based on national security grounds. Trump granted Mexico and Canada temporary exemption from the steel and aluminum tariffs, hoping to gain a bargaining chip as the U. S. continued its negotiations with the two countries over the North American Free Trade Agreement (NAFTA). He later added the EU and a few other countries in the exemption with the expectation that a separate bilateral deal may be reached. But Trump's move drew ire from countries all over the world, with U. S. allies at the forefront. Canadian Prime Minister Justin Trudeau said it was inconceivable that Canada could be considered a national security threat, while Jean-Claude Juncker, the president of the European Commission, criticized the move as pure and simple protectionism. In this case, retaliations from countries subject to Trump's tariff hike were immediate. Canada, the largest exporter of steel and aluminum to the U. S., announced a counter-tariff of 25% on American steel exports, and a 10% tariff on other goods. Mexico responded with a retaliation against American goods worth around three billion U. S. dollars, and the EU announced tariffs against a long list of signature goods that are produced in parts of the U. S. that are supportive of Trump. Tariffs were also used by Trump to further his political goals. In August 2018, Trump decided to double the steel and aluminum tariff on Turkey to 50% and 20% respectively, amid a diplomatic dispute between the two over the detention of an American pastor.

The auto war

The car industry is a main point of contention between the U. S. and its key allies. On Friday, the White House issued a proclamation regarding a Section 232 report submitted by the Department of Commerce in February. It concluded that imports of automobiles and automobile parts, mainly from Japan and the EU, "threaten to impair the national security of the United States." The investigation was the third under Trump into autos and parts, following the steel and aluminum cases. The tariffs would affect 208 billion U. S. dollars worth of imports, nearly all from U. S. allies. Companies including Toyota, BMW, Volvo, Honda and Hyundai, which have built large assembly plants in the U. S., would be hardest hit. Japan's Minister of Economic Revitalization Toshimitsu Motegi said Japan opposes any measure that distorts free and fair trade. Toyota said in a statement that Friday's proclamation sends a message that "our investments are not welcomed, and the contributions from each of our employees across America are not valued." As for the EU, Trump renewed his complaints saying the bloc treats his country "worse than China, they are just smaller." EU Trade Commissioner Cecilia Malmstrom rejected the notion that EU car exports are a national security threat in a tweet on Friday. EU officials have also prepared to target U. S. exports worth of 23 billion U. S. dollars with retaliatory tariffs if Trump follows through on his threat. Trump had his way with auto trade before, when replacing NAFTA with the new U. S. -Mexico-Canada Agreement (USMCA). Canada and Mexico reportedly agreed to a cap on their own auto exports to the U. S. to prevent threatened auto tariffs. Another deal was renegotiated last year with South Korea, which agreed to double the number of U. S. car imports without restrictions from local safety standards.

The U. S. against the world

One of the few things both Democrats and Republicans in the U. S. government overwhelmingly agree on is being tough with China. When it comes to economic relations, the U. S. political establishment and Trump's inner circle want to see China singled out, not the U. S. being pitted against the rest of the world. But, the Trump administration has waged a trade war against all major U. S. trading partners. Central to those trade fights is a misguided view about how trade and tariffs work and a handful of people in Trump's inner circles share this view, including Commerce Secretary Wilbur Ross and U. S. Trade Representative Robert Lighthizer. Peter Navarro, director of the White House's Office of Trade and Manufacturing Policy, the man widely believed to be the central architect of Trump's trade policy, articulated this most clearly when he wrote in a paper that laid out Trump's economic plan during the 2016 campaign that "when a country runs a trade deficit by importing more than it exports, this subtracts from growth." Yet the view that trade deficits drag down growth has been debunked repeatedly by economists. Neither is the view that tariffs inflicts more pain on foreign exporters than on domestic consumers and producers proven true by reality. A recent report by the National Bureau of Economic Research finds that the tariffs reduced real incomes in the U. S. by about 1. 4 billion U. S. dollars per month in 2018, with domestic consumers and producers who buy imported goods bearing the brunt of the burden. Driven by the displaced belief that trade deficits are proof of unfair practices by other countries, Trump has been using the trade war to force through so-called economic reform in other countries, that he thinks would "allow the international trade system to become fairer to the U. S. ". But acting without Congressional restraint and bypassing the multilateral framework of the WTO, Trump has inflicted heavy blows to the global economic framework that countries have spent decades building.

(Source: How the Trump administration launched a multi-front trade war, ECNS, May 21, 2019.)

Quick Quiz

1. The political environment affects the firm in a number of ways, includes (   ).

A. A basic legal framework generally exists

B. The Government can take a particular stance on an issue of direct relevance to a business or industry

C. It does not rely on market governments to make all its policies

D. The Government's overall conduct of its economic policy is relevant to business

2. Fiscal policy is connected to the government's _____ .

3. The two components of the budget which the Government determines and through which it exercises its fiscal policy are (   ).

A. Expenditure   B. Revenue

C. Export   D. Import

4. Tariffs fall into two categories (   ).

A. voluntary export restraints   B. Specific tariffs

C. antidumping duties   D. Ad valorem tariffs

5. (   ) is when a government refuses to trade with a country or a certain part of a country.

A. Embargo   B. Standards

C. License   D. Import deposits

Answers:

1. ABD

2. budget

3. AB

4. BD

5. A

Endnotes

[1] Liu Yinment. US toy prices may rise due to additional tariff, China Daily, 2019-8-10.

[2] Marc J. Melitz. When and how should infant industries be protected? Journal of International Economics, 66 (2005) 177-196.

[3] Evans G., Newnham J. Dictionary of International Relations, Penguin Books, 1998.

[4] Filanlyason J., Zakher M. The GATT and the regulation of Trade

Barriers: Regime Dynamic and Functions; International Organization, 1981: 35 (4).

[5] Frieden J., Lake D. International political economy: perspectives on global power and wealth, London: Routledge, 1995.

[6] Mansfield E., Busch M. The political economy of Non-tariff barriers: a cross national analysis; International Organization, 1995: 49 (4).

[7] Oatley T. International political economy: interests and institutions in the global economy; Harlow: Longman, 2007.

[8] Roorbach G. Tariffs and Trade Barriers in Relation to International Trade; Proceedings of the Academy of Political Science, 1993: 15 (2).

[9] Yu Zhihao. A model of Substitution of Non-Tariff Barriers for Tariffs, The Canadian Journal of Economics, 2000: 33 (4).

[10] World Trade Organization Website, Understanding the WTO: The Agreements, 2019.

[11] Xinhua. Citrus farms prosper in Egypt as country becomes 3rd largest orange exporter to China, February 1, 2018.

[12] Chen Yang. Chips are down for South Korea-Japan ties, Global Times, August 5, 2019.

Chapter 4　Economic Environment

Learning Objectives

1. Understand the definition of economic growth
2. Master the main factors affecting economic growth
3. Recognize the phase of economic growth
4. Master GDP, GNP, global competitiveness index
5. Understand inflation, deflation and stagflation

Opening case

CPI: No sign on continued inflation rise

China's consumer inflation picked up more than expected in August, mainly driven by food price increases because of seasonal factors. Amid worries about inflation pressure caused by African swine fever and tariff tensions with the United States, there are no major concerns for significant inflation pressure in the coming months, pointing to mild inflation toward the end of this year, according to analysts and officials. The consumer price index, a main gauge of inflation, rose 2.3% year-on-year in August, up from 2.1% in the previous month, the largest increase since February, according to the National Bureau of Statistics on Monday. China is aiming to keep annual CPI growth at around 3% this year. NBS statistician Sheng Guoqing attributed the higher than expected CPI growth to higher food prices in August that have been pushed up by adverse weather and the relatively limited supply of pork. Food prices went up by 2.4% year-on-year in August, according to Sheng. Those prices jumped in August as hot, wet weather and an outbreak of swine fever in some regions decreased supplies in vegetables and pork, while seasonal factors also led to some price increases, Haitong Securities analysts Jiang Chao and Li Jinliu wrote in a note. "We expect CPI in September to increase slightly to 2.5% year-on-year, led by a continued rise in pork prices and moderate growth of prices of vegetables and fruits," they said. The producer price index grew by 4.1% year-on-year in August, which is 0.5 percentage points slower than in the previous month, according to the National Bureau of Statistics. The latest data come as worries of possible stagflation have emerged amid rising expectations for continued inflation and downward economic pressure. Stagflation is characterized by slower economic growth and increased inflation. Nevertheless, no signs have appeared to indicate a continued rise of inflation pressure, nor is the economy facing a hard landing later this year, according to a the National Development and Reform Commission official who declined to be identified. Despite some downward pressure ahead, the government is not likely to proceed with a major policy easing to fend off financial risks, which means the monetary environment does not point to a sharp increase in inflation, according to the official. As for additional tariff threats by the United States, the overall pressure remains by far under control, reflected by a monthly decline in edible oil prices in August despite a drop in soybean imports, according to Wang Qing, chief economist with Golden Credit Rating. The two countries have already slapped tit-for-tat tariffs on $50 billion worth of goods, and the US is eying additional tariffs on $200 billion in Chinese imports.

（Source：Wang Yanfei, CPI：No sign on continued inflation rise. Chinadaily, September 10, 2018）

4.1　Economic Growth, Measurements and Phases

4.1.1　Economic growth

Economic growth is an increase in the production of goods and services over a specific period, and it represents the expansion of a country's potential GDP or national output. Economic growth creates more profit for businesses. As a result, that gives companies capital to invest and hire more employees. Investment is one of the most important way to improve economy growth, it heavily influence the economy development of the country, the region, and the company. With economic development, people's living standards rise accordingly, households have more money to buy additional products and services and generate more borrowing and aggregate demand, which leads to the growth of demand for consuming, then drive higher economic growth. For this reason, all countries' priority are to promote economic development and growth. According to the China Daily and the report of "China's economy：Taking stock of 2018", China's economy ended 2018 on firm footing amid a complex external environment, with better quality and improved structure (See Figure 4 – 1 to Figure 4 – 15)① . Gross domestic product totaled 90. 03 trillion yuan ($13. 28 trillion) in 2018, more than half of which was from the service sector. Consumption remained the major economic growth driver, contributing 76. 2% to GDP growth last year. Retail sales, a main gauge of consumption, rose 9% from a year earlier. China's economy performed within a reasonable range in 2018, with economic growth being generally stable and improvement achieved in performance, based on the data of National Bureau of Statistics (NBS). Contributing to nearly 30% of the world's economic growth, the country's economy remained the largest contributor to global economic growth.

1. GDP expands 6. 6%

China's economy advanced 6. 6% year-on-year in 2018 (see Figure 4-1), in line with the official target of about 6. 5 percent, data from the NBS showed. The reading was lower than the 6. 8-percent growth registered in 2017. Growth in the fourth quarter came in at 6. 4%, down from 6. 5% seen in the third quarter, according to the NBS.

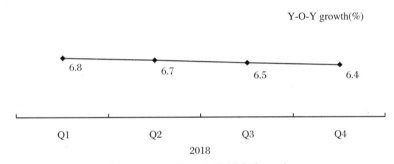

Figure 4-1   Trend of GDP Growth

Source: National Bureau of Statistics of China.

2. CPI up 2. 1%

China's consumer price index, a main gauge of inflation, rose 2. 1% year-on-year in 2018 (see Figure 4-2), staying within the range of mild growth, said the NBS in its report. The reading was lower than the yearly control target of 3%. In December, the figure stood at 1. 9% year-on-year, remaining flat the previous month, according to the bureau.

---

① China's economy: Taking stock of 2018. Chinadaily. www. chinadaily. com. cn/business/2018 novcnecodata/index. html.

Y-O-Y growth(%)

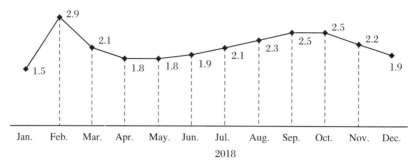

Figure 4-2 Trend of Consumer Price Index

Source：National Bureau of Statistics of China.

3. PPI grows 3.5%

For all of 2018, producer price index, which measures costs for goods at the factory gate, climbed 3.5% from one year earlier. In December alone, producer price inflation rose 0.9% year-on-year, retreating from November's 2.7% (see Figure 4-3), the NBS data showed; on a monthly basis, the figure dropped 1%.

Y-O-Y growth(%)

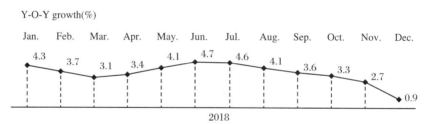

Figure 4-3 Trend of Producer Price Index

Source：National Bureau of Statistics of China.

4. PMI at 50.9%

The purchasing managers' index, an indicator of manufacturing sector health, stood at 50.9% on average for 2018, compared with 51.6% the previous year. And the figure in December came in at 49.4% (see Figure 4-4), decelerating 0.6 percentage points in November and falling below the boom-bust line of 50%, according to the NBS. A reading above 50% indicates expansion, while a reading below reflects contraction.

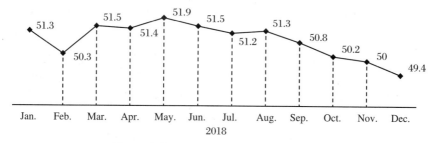

Figure 4-4   PMI of Manufacturing Sector

Source: National Bureau of Statistics of China.

5. Fiscal revenue rises 6. 2%

China's fiscal revenue rose 6. 2% year-on-year to 18. 34 trillion yuan in 2018, according to the Ministry of Finance. The central government collected more than 8. 54 trillion yuan in fiscal revenue, up 5. 3% year-on-year, while local governments saw fiscal revenue expand 7% to top 9. 79 trillion yuan.

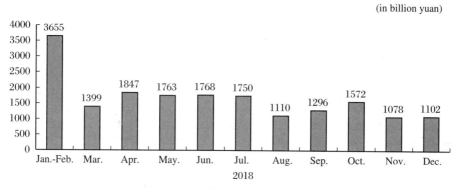

Figure 4-5   China's Fiscal Revenue

Source: Ministry of Finance.

6. Industrial output develops steadily

China's industrial output gained 6. 2% last year, with slow yet stable growth, official data showed. The figure for December was 5. 7% (see Figure 4- 6), accelerating 0. 3 percentage points from the number recorded in November. Industrial output, officially called industrial value added, is used to measure the activity of designated large enterprises with annual turnover of at least 20 million yuan.

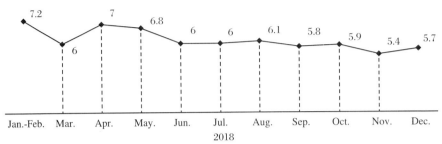

Figure 4-6   Trend of Value-added Industrial Output

Source：National Bureau of Statistics of China.

7. FAI increases 5.9%

Fixed-asset investment grew 5.9% over the course of 2018, remaining flat with that of the first 11 months and down from a rise of 7.2% in 2017. Month-on-month, December saw a 0.42% increase in FAI (see Figure 4-7), while private investment expanded 8.7% compared with previous year.

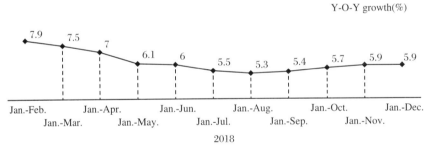

Figure 4-7   Trend of Urban Fixed-asset Investments

Source：National Bureau of Statistics of China.

8. Retail sales up 9%

China's retail sales of consumer goods rose 9% to more than 38 trillion yuan in 2018, with the number in December increasing 8.2% year-on-year to 3.59 trillion yuan (see Figure 4-8), according to the NBS. Notably, online retail sales in 2018 reached over 9 trillion yuan, an increase of 23.9% compared with that of last year.

Y-O-Y growth(%)

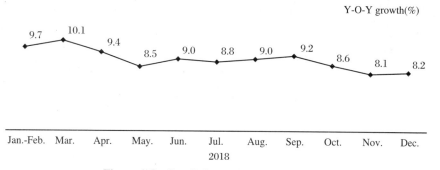

Figure 4-8   **Retail Sales of Consumer Goods**

Source: National Bureau of Statistics of China.

9. Imports and exports set a new record

China's foreign trade volume rose 9. 7% year-on-year to surpass 30 trillion yuan, a record high, said the NBS. Among the figures, exports climbed by 7. 1% to total 16. 42 trillion yuan, while imports surged 12. 9% to 14. 09 trillion yuan. Thus, the trade surplus was 2. 33 trillion yuan, shrinking 18. 3% from the previous year. Total imports and exports achieved the set goal of stable and positive development with increased volume and optimized structure (see Figure 4-9).

Figure 4-9   **Total of Import and Export Volume**

Source: General Administration of Customs.

10. FDI and ODI rise

Foreign direct investment rose 0. 9% in 2018 to reach 885. 61 billion yuan in 2018, the Ministry of Commerce said. According to the MOC, 60, 533 foreign-funded companies were set up in China during the whole year, up 69. 8% from a year before. The statistics from MOC and State Administration of Foreign Exchange showed outbound direct investment across industries reached $129. 83 billion, an increase of 4.2% on a yearly basis. Breaking it down, financial outbound direct investment lifted 105.1% year-on-year to $9.33 billion, while non-financial ODI rose by 0.3%, with amount of $120.5 billion.

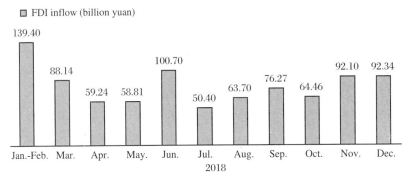

Figure 4-10   Trend of FDI Inflow

Source: The Ministry of Commerce.

11. New yuan loans improve

In 2018, new yuan-denominated lending totaled 16.17 trillion yuan, 2.64 trillion yuan more than the previous year, according to the People's Bank of China. The M2, a broad measure of money supply that covers cash in circulation and all deposits, reached 182.67 trillion yuan at the end of December, up 8.1% from a year earlier, the central bank said, adding the growth rate was the same as

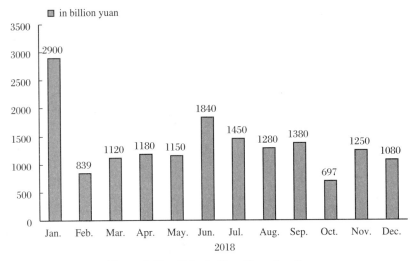

Figure 4-11   China's New Yuan Lending

Source: People's Bank of China.

the same period last year. The narrower measure of money supply, or M1, which covers cash in circulation plus demand deposits, rose 1.5% year-on-year to 55.17 trillion yuan at the end of December. M0, the amount of cash in circulation, was up 3.6% year-on-year to 7.32 trillion yuan.

12. Property investment climbs 9.5%

China's real estate investment went up 9.5% year-on-year to exceed 12 trillion yuan, said NBS. Its newly released data showed that growth figure was lower by 0.2 percentage point from that in the first 11 months, while lifting 2.5 percentage points from a year earlier (see Figure 4-12).

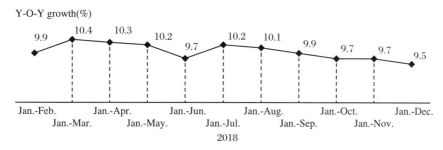

Figure 4-12   Trend of Real Estate Investment

Source: National Bureau of Statistics of China.

13. Growth of disposable income keeps pace with GDP

China's per capita disposable income stood at 28,228 yuan in 2018, up 6.5% year-on-year in real terms, NBS figures showed, compared with the GDP growth of 6.6% in the year. Separately, urban and rural per capita disposable income reached 39,251 yuan and 14,617 yuan, respectively, in 2018, up 5.6% and 6.6% in real terms after deducting price factors.

14. Jobs market remains stable

A total of 434.19 million people worked in urban areas at the end of 2018, the number was 9.57 million more than that of 2017. From January to December, China's surveyed unemployment rate in urban areas stayed in the range between 4.8% to 5.1%, with most of the 12 months having lower rate than in the same period previous year. In December, the surveyed unemployment rate in urban areas stood at 4.9%, slightly up by 0.1 percentage point from November and maintaining below 5% in the straight fourth month.

(%)

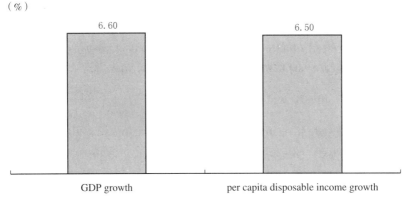

GDP growth   per capita disposable income growth

Figure 4-13   Growth of per capita Disposable Income VS GDP in 2018

Source: National Bureau of Statistics of China.

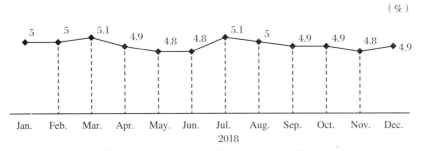

Figure 4-14   Trend of Unemployment Rate

Source: National Bureau of Statistics of China.

15. Power consumption hits peak high

China's power consumption saw a faster growth in 2018, according to the National Energy Administration. Electricity use increased 8.5% year-on-year to 6.84 trillion kilowatt hours over the year, 1.9 percentage points higher than a year before and reaching peak consumption since 2012.

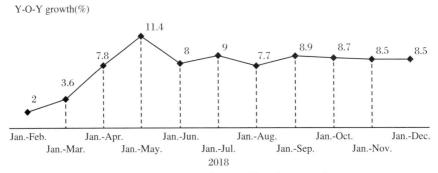

Figure 4-15   Trend of Electricity Consumption

Source: National Energy Administration.

4. 1. 2   Main factors affecting economic growth

In the 1800s, Britain became the pioneer of the Industrial Revolution, became the economic leader and got the great success. The same fundamental process of economic growth and development that helped shape Britain and Japan is at work today in developing countries like China and India. Studied these success, economists have found four basic elements stimulate economic development. These factors of growth are:

- Labor (labor supply, education, discipline, motivation).
- Natural resources (land, minerals, fuels, environmental quality).
- Capital (machines, factories, roads).
- Technology and innovation (science, engineering, entrepreneurship).

On the basis of "Economics" (Samuelson, Nordhaus, 2002), economics write the relationship in terms of an aggregate production function (or APF), which relates total national output to the inputs and technology. The APF is

$$Q = AF(K, L, R)$$

Q = output, K = productive services of capital, L = labor inputs, R = natural-resource inputs, A represents the level of technology in the economy, and F is the production function.

1. Labor

Labor inputs refers the quantity and quality of the workforce. For the company means finding, screening, recruiting, training job applicants, administering employee-benefit programs and dealing with labor relationships. As companies reorganize to gain a competitive edge, HR plays a key role in helping companies deal with a fast-changing environment and the greater demand for quality employees. With the improvement of medical treatment and living level, the aging of population has become a dilemma faced by many countries.

From "World Population Day 2019" data, demographic discrepanciesmay threaten the regions' economic gains, especially in Asia, have to tackle a demographic paradox. East Asia, Europe and elsewhere are confronted with rapid aging that can pressure their resources and public services. The pace of aging in Asia is faster and happening at a much earlier stage of development compared with the more industrialized economies. It took France 115 years and the United States 69 years to move from an aging to an aged society, but Japan took only 24 years to become an aged society. China is expected to make the transition in 25 years and

Singapore in 22 years. the pace of aging in Asia is faster and happening at a much earlier stage of development compared with the more industrialized economies. At the same time, East Asians face a different problem: falling birth rates and a growing number of elderly people. This trend will greatly affect the future labor force and economic growth.

2. Natural Resources

Land, oil and gas, forests, water, mineral and other resources called important resources. If a country has enough natural resources, like large output in agriculture, fisheries and forestry, they will have the advantage of economic development. But the possession of natural resources is not necessary for economic success in the modern world. As Singapore is a city-state with not much land area, it is not particularly rich in natural resources. For example, water itself being a scarce resource, Singapore has come up with an efficient water management policy, to ensure sustainability of water resources over a period of time. The Government in Singapore has taken initiatives by investing in infrastructure, thrived by concentrating on sectors that depend more on labor and capital than on indigenous resources, upgrading technology, devising water management strategies to manage precious natural resources.

3. Capital

From macroeconomics' view, it refers to a measure of the net additions to the (physical) capital stock of a country (or an economic sector) in an accounting interval, or, a measure of the amount by which the total physical capital stock increased during an accounting period. In accounting, capital goods are treated as fixed assets. They're man-made objects like machinery, equipment and chemicals that are used in production, also known as "plant, property and equipment." Capital differentiates from consumer goods. Financial capital is the money, credit, and other forms of funding that build wealth. Individuals use financial capital to invest, by making a down payment on a home or creating a portfolio for retirement.

In the business world, there are three types of financial capital. The first is debt. Take the United States as example, companies receive capital now that they pay back with interest. At first, many entrepreneurs borrow from family members or their credit cards. As these businesses continue to grow, they become large enough to issue individual bonds to investors. The advantage of debt is that owners don't have to share the profits. The disadvantage is that they must repay the loan even if the business fails. The second type of capital is equity. The business receives cash now from investors for a share of the profits later. Most entrepreneurs use their own cash to get started. They put their own equity into the business in hopes of receiving 100 percent of the return later. If the company is profitable, they forgo spending some of the cash flow now and instead invest it in the business. A larger firm gets equity from partners, venture capitalists, or angel investors. It must give up some control and ownership of the business in exchange for the cash. A larger firm gets equity from partners, venture capitalists, or angel investors. It must give up some control and ownership of the business in exchange for the cash. Angel investors typically investing involves a high degree of risk, so angel investors have the expectation of doing more than just getting their money back when they invest in an enterprise. They are looking for a higher return on their investment than they can get on the stock market. The third type of capital is specialty capital. It's extra cash flow that comes from managing the company's operations better.

To connect new firms with cash-flush investors, ToJoy enlarges its footprint

ToJoy, a startup accelerator, expects to set up offices across Europe and Asia to help more new Chinese enterprises to go global by connecting them with a vast network of investors. Founded in 1991, ToJoy is an online-to-offline platform matching startups with investors. It has about 700,000 registered entrepreneurs and investors.

Typically, investors registered on ToJoy seek to plough their surplus capital into potentially profitable ventures or already proven ones like unicorns (startups valued at $1 billion each). They target startups with potential to grow into unicorns or local unicorns that can grow into global enterprises.

ToJoy opened a new office in Paris earlier this month to target West European markets. It had set up similar branches in New York and Vienna last year. Company executives said ToJoy plans to complete its global expansion by the end of this year. By then, it would likely cover East Europe and much of Asia, including Japan, South Korea, Indonesia and India. "Though many Chinese companies grow rapidly, few of them succeed in entering global markets," said Ge Jun, global CEO of ToJoy. "We select projects with innovative ideas, technologies or business models that have already proved successful but lack market penetration and funds. We will connect such startups with suitable investors so they could expand locally, nationally and internationally."

But ToJoy will steer clear of early stage startup financing that is usually done by angel investors, series A investors or private equity firms. Instead, it will focus on proven local success stories to help replicate their success on a larger canvas or mass scale. Over the last three years, ToJoy has helped more than 40 unicorns or potential unicorns to grow. Among its beneficiaries are Sousoushenbian, an app that can provide community delivery service within eight minutes; Hanbond, a provider of customized men's garments; and the industrial water treatment branch of OriginWater.

Investors registered on ToJoy have assets surpassing 10 million yuan ($1.44 million) each. They buy rights shares, intellectual property of target startups; or help in marketing or supply-chain services; conduct chain-store operations in cooperation with other companies, Ge said.

Wang Haifeng, founder and CEO of Hanbond, said its offline stores have increased from 4 to 122 across the country within 20 months, after joining ToJoy in 2017. The average revenue of each store is 150,000 yuan to 200,000 yuan per month. Wang's dream is to "create a Chinese men's clothing brand with taste" and the target customers are male professionals in the 26-40 age-group who can afford suits priced 1,000 yuan to 8,000 yuan each. "Compared with traditional retail business, tailored production will have no pressure of overstocked products. Besides, the demand is continuous," he said. When it first expanded operations, the company incurred losses for eight months due to high costs like store decorations and wages. But those expenses were necessary, he said. "Though there are more than 20,000 customized men's clothing brands in China, few of them get high recognition. We want to be a brand with scale and market influence," Wang said.

Investors listed on ToJoy picked up a 45% stake in Hanbond for about 30 million yuan, and helped promote its sales, leveraging their connections. Hanbond recruits local employees to run new stores that are set up as part of its expansion. Its shareholders reap rich dividends, he said. "Hanbond's expansion (on the back of ToJoy-registered investors' support) has been 10 times quicker than I could have imagined. Had we explored those cities by ourselves, it would have taken much longer," Wang said. He also said Hanbond plans to open 10 stores in 10 cities in Europe. It is eyeing France, Spain and Austria to sell affordable customized clothing with Chinese styles to Europeans. "The go-global strategy is a necessity for Chinese brands," he said, adding investors will pay franchisee fee to operate Hanbond-branded chain of stores locally.

According to Ge, the number of Sousoushenbian stores surged from about 1,000 to 350,000 over an eight-month period (August 2018 ~ April 2019). Similarly, estimated valuation of a coffee brand grew five times to reach 1 billion yuan after coming onboard ToJoy. "Rapid expansion is good for startups that wish to get listed and raise further capital," Ge said. ToJoy itself has benefited from its business of matching startups and investors. It charges a service fee after a startup and an investor sign a contract. It also picks up equity up to 25% in the startups that register on the platform, and when they expand the number of their stores, it stands to benefit.

The central government's projects such as the Belt and Road Initiative also encourage companies to go global, which makes ToJoy more promising, he said. ToJoy is also working on helping foreign companies, mainly in entertainment, lifestyle, catering and high technology, to enter China. About 150 overseas-originating projects are on the anvil, he said. Annette Nijs, economist, China watcher and the founder of The China Agenda, a provider of information on China, said ToJoy is a unique and innovative business model for scaling up entrepreneurial businesses.

Over 2,000 potential unicorns are eagerly waiting in line to have their growth accelerated on ToJoy. By the end of 2025, ToJoy aims to strengthen 3,000 unicorns in total, making it potentially the largest unicorn business accelerator in the world, Nijs said. Felix Ma, principal at consultancy firm Roland Berger, said incubators and accelerators in China have many revenue streams. They rent out office space, receive government subsidies, invest in startups, or provide entrepreneur-enabling services. The last two streams will likely be the mainstays in the future. "To do that, they have to spot in advance promising startups and evaluate their potential returns and risks," he said. Ma also said many startups are still exploring the domestic market, and sense some risks in entering overseas markets prematurely as the business environment there could be very different from China's, and pose stiff challenges. "They have to be successful in terms of market share and profitability in the Chinese market first, so that it is safe for them to offer their products and services, as well as deploy their capital, human resources and business models, in other countries. "

(Source: Chen Meiling, "Accelerating local startups' expansion across the world", China Daily, June 24, 2019.)

4. Technology and innovation

Nowadays, technology and innovation become one of the most determinant for economic growth. They can provide goods and services in more efficiency and effective ways. We take the agriculture as an example, hundreds years ago, most people worked on farms, because farm technology required a high input of labor in order to feed the entire population. But now, thanks to the development of agricultural technology, a small fraction of the population can use agricultural machinery produce enough food to feed the entire country.

Entrepreneurship is the drive to develop an idea into a business. China government is beefing up efforts to provide favorable policies and support for promote entrepreneurial innovation, especially for youth.

Huawei to hold biggest-ever developer conference

Chinese tech giant Huawei recently announced that it will hold its annual developer conference from Aug 9 to 11 in Dongguan city, Guangdong province in South China. Approximately 1,500 partners and 5,000 developers from around the world will participate in the event, which is expected to be Huawei's largest-ever developer conference since the company was founded in 1987.

Huawei is now working to troubleshoot its self-developed operating system, Hongmeng, according to the Chinese news portal, The Paper. It is still unknown if Huawei's new operating system will be ready in time for launch at the conference. Hongmeng is an operating system designed for the internet of things. It can even be applied to autonomous transport and industrial automation, as it can control processing delays below five milliseconds. The Hongmeng system is not a substitute for the Google-developed Android operating system used in smartphones and tablets, Huawei founder and CEO Ren Zhengfei said in June. He made the remarks after Google announced it would partially cut off Huawei devices from its Android operating system to comply with US restrictions on Huawei. Washington accused Huawei of posing risks to US national security, and banned it from accessing any American technologies without special approval. Huawei has repeatedly denied the accusation, saying the charge was not supported by any factual evidence.

Huawei is one of the world's largest investors in innovation. Its expenditure on R&D exceeded $15 billion in 2018, and is expected to reach $100 billion in the next five years.

(Source: "Huawei to hold biggest-ever developer conference", Chinadaily. July 9, 2019.)

4.1.3 Measure economic growth

1. GDP

Gross domestic product (GDP) is the best way to measure economic growth. GDP is the market value of all final goods and services produced within a country in a given period of time. GDP takes into account the country's entire economic output, measures final production. It includes all goods and services that businesses in the country produce for sale. As a broad measure of overall domestic production, it includes exports because they are produced in the country. It can be adjusted for inflation and population to provide deeper insights. Imports are subtracted from economic growth. Most economists agree that GDP (which we denote as y) is divided into four components: consumption (C), investment (I), government purchases (G), and net exports (NX).

$$Y = C + I + G + NX$$

There are several types of GDP measurements:

• Nominal GDP uses current prices to place a value on the economy's production of goods and services, so it is the measurement of the raw data.

• Real GDP uses constant base-year prices to place a value on the economy's production of goods and services, takes into account the impact of inflation and allows comparisons of economic output from one year to the next and other comparisons over periods of time. Real GDP is not affected by changes in prices, changes in real GDP reflect only changes in the amounts being produced. Thus, real GDP is a measure of the economy's production of goods and services. The most accurate measurement of growth is real GDP. It removes the effects of inflation.

• GDP growth rate is the increase in GDP from quarter to quarter.

2. GNP

The World Bank uses gross national income instead of GDP to measure growth. Gross national product (GNP) is an estimate of total value of all the final products and services turned out in a given period by the means of production owned by a country's residents. Any output produced by foreign residents within the country's borders must be excluded in calculations of GNP, while any output produced by the country's residents outside of its borders must be counted. GNP is commonly calculated by taking the sum of personal consumption expenditures, private domestic investment, government expenditure, net exports and any income earned by residents from overseas investments, minus income earned within the domestic economy by foreign residents. GNP does not include intermediary goods and services to avoid double-counting since they are already incorporated in the value of final goods and services.

GNP and GDP can have different values, and a large difference between a country's GNP and GDP can suggest a great deal of integration into the global economy. GNP is the total output produced with labor or capital owned by one country residents, while GDP is the output produced with labor and capital located inside the country. GDP doesn't include unpaid services. It leaves out child care, unpaid volunteer work, or illegal black-market activities. It doesn't count the environmental costs. For example, the price of plastic is cheap because it doesn't include the cost of disposal. As a result, GDP doesn't measure how these costs impact the well-being of society. A country will improve its standard of living when it factors in environmental costs. A society only measures what it values.

3. Global Competitiveness Index

The World Economic Forum, the international organization for public-private collaboration, invite policymakers, business leaders, young entrepreneurs, and the public at large to consult the performance of their countries in the Global Competitiveness Index and seeks to provide guidance, inform future-oriented solutions. It remains critically important to monitor closely the factors that determine economic growth, which enables countries to offer more equal opportunities and higher living standards.

There is wide spread agreement that economic growth is important for human development and well-being. Growth creates the resources needed for better education, health, and security, and for higher incomes. economic growth should not be an end in itself. It should contribute to human welfare, be rooted in political legitimacy, and be defined and measured based on a multidimensional notion of economic progress that includes values such as:
- a broad-based distribution of economic gains,
- environmental sustainability,
- intergenerational equity for young people and futuregenerations.

We define competitiveness as the set of institutions, policies, and factors that determine the level of productivity of an economy. Global Competitiveness Index (GCI) are grouped into 12 pillars: institutions, infrastructure, macroeconomic environment, health and primary education, higher education and training, goods market efficiency, labor market efficiency, financial market development, technological readiness, market size, business sophistication, and innovation. These pillars are in turn organized into three subindexes: basic requirements, efficiency enhancers, and innovation and sophistication factors. The three subindexes are given different weights in the calculation of the overall Index, depending on each economy's stage of development, as proxied by its GDP per capita and the share of exports represented by raw materials.

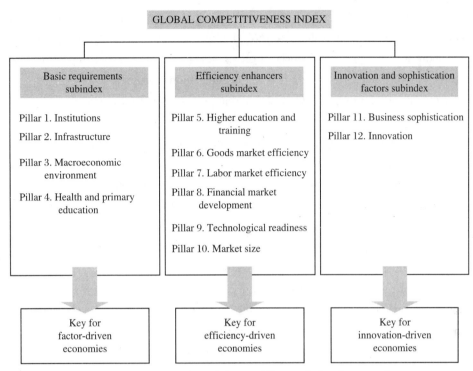

Figure 4-16   The Global Competitiveness Index framework

The Global Future Council on Economic Progress

The evolution of the global economy has been largely motivated and justified by its enormous contribution to economic growth over the past few decades. To the extent that broad-based social inclusion was given any consideration in that process, it was primarily limited to an ex-post re-distribution of any economic gains. With the evolving global political context and the advent of the Fourth Industrial Revolution, that approach will need to change-not only to make globalization work for more people than it has benefited to date, but also to ensure that globalization has a large enough constituency going forward to allow it to continue driving economic growth in the first place. We must shift the economic policy debate and interventions to unlock productivity and deliver broad-based prosperity by simultaneously solving for economic growth and social inclusion before the fact, not after it. This must be the case even if it results in a substantially modified form of globalization with potentially dampened growth but more buy-in and inclusion. In order to succeed, we must also establish modern venues and means for deliberating about the impacts of future policy efforts that include a fuller set of stakeholders than currently play a role in driving change. To that end, the World Economic Forum's Global Future Council on Economic Progress has identified and is exploring four interrelated themes:

● Making globalization more inclusive, which includes proposals to improve skilling, re-skilling, and dealing with job displacements; taxation, social protection, and addressing inequality; financial markets that work for all; competition and avoiding capture; and fostering a new era of international cooperation.

● Unleashing productivity and economic potential in the context of the Fourth Industrial Revolution, which is fundamentally changing the constructs and limits of productivity growth, and raising questions about the future potential for improved well-being and how to best capture and share the rewards of new efficiencies, especially in light of the evolving nature of employment and jobs.

● Promoting and achieving multidimensional inclusion, notably by developing a multidimensional tool that is informed by tested aggregate-level indices of inclusive growth and well-being and that can be used to evaluate the degree to which countries and communities are inclusive at the household level.

● Evolving communications, connectivity, and organizations to incorporate new developments in social media, counteracting self-reinforcing echo chambers and the increasing polarization of ideas, thus expanding the set of channels and messages that resonate with people whose lives are affected in order to improve broad-based engagement and ensure buy-in for sound policy choices.

(Source: Diana Farrell, The Global Future Council on Economic Progress, The Global Competitiveness Report 2017-2018.)

4.1.4 Phase of economic growth four phases in the business cycle

Economic growth has the stage of the business cycle. Business cycles or trade cycles are the continual sequence of rapid growth in national income, followed by a slowdown in growth and then a fall in national income (recession). After this recession comes growth again, and when this has reached a peak, the cycle turns into recession once more. Four main phases of the business cycle can be distinguished:

(a) Recession.

(b) Depression.

(c) Recovery.

(d) Boom.

We can see the figure 4-17, and give the diagrammatic explanation. Recession is a period of falling economic activity spread across the economy, lasting more than a few months, may be a long time. At point "a" in the diagram below, the economy is entering a recession. In the recession phase, consumer demand falls and many investment projects already undertaken begin to look unprofitable. Orders will be cut, inventory levels will be reduced and business failures will occur as firms find themselves unable to sell their goods. Production and employment will fall. The general price level will begin to fall. Business and consumer confidence are diminished and investment remains low, while the economic outlook appears to be poor. Eventually, in the absence of any stimulus to aggregate demand, a period of full depression sets in and the economy will reach point "b".

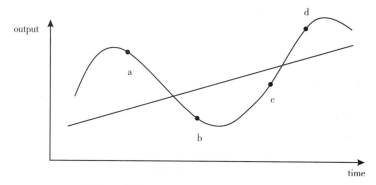

Figure 4-17   Phase of Economic Growth

Point "b" is a severe and prolonged downturn in economic activity that lasts two or more years. A depression is characterized by economic factors such as substantial increases in unemployment, a drop in available credit, diminishing output, bankruptcies and sovereign debt defaults, reduced trade and commerce, and sustained volatility in currency values. At last, depression causes the economy to shut down.

At point "c" the economy has reached the recovery phase of the cycle. Once begun, the phase of recovery is likely to quicken as confidence returns. Output, employment and income will all begin to rise. Rising production, sales and profit levels will lead to optimistic business expectations, and new investment will be more readily undertaken. The rising level of demand can be met through increased production by bringing existing capacity into use and by hiring unemployed labor. The average price level will remain constant or begin to rise slowly. In the recovery phase, decisions to purchase new materials and machinery may lead to benefits inefficiency from new technology. This can enhance the relative rate of economic growth in the recovery phase once it is underway.

As recovery proceeds, the output level climbs above its trend path, reaching point "d" , in the boom phase of the cycle. During the boom, capacity and labor will become fully utilised. This may cause bottlenecks in some industries which are unable to meet increases in demand, for example, because they have no spare capacity or they lack certain categories of skilled labor, or they face shortage key material inputs. Further rises in demand will, therefore, tend to be met by increases in prices rather than by increases in production. In general, business will be profitable, with few firms facing losses. Expectations of the future may be very optimistic and the level of investment expenditure high.

It can be argued that wide fluctuations in levels of economic activity are damaging to the overall economic well-being of society. The inflation and speculation which accompanies boom periods may be inequitable in their impact on different sections of the population, while the bottom of the trade cycle may bring high unemployment. Governments generally seek to stabilise the economic system, trying to avoid the distortions of a widely fluctuating trade cycle.

4.2　Economic Systems

4.2.1　Market economy

A market economy is a system where the laws of supply and demand direct the production of goods and services. Supply includes natural resources, capital, and labor. Demand includes purchases by consumers, businesses, and the government. In the archetypal pure market economy, all productive activities are privately owned, as opposed to being owned by the state. The goods and services that a country produces are not planned by anyone. Everyone is free to live, work, produce, buy and sell whatever they choose (as long as it's legal). Production is determined by the interaction of supply and demand and signaled to producers through the price system. If demand for a product exceeds supply, prices will rise, signaling producers to produce more. If supply exceeds demand, prices will fall, signaling producers to produce less. Businesses sell their wares at the highest price consumers will pay. Self-interest drives the buying and selling of goods and services, including employment. At the same time, employers look for the lowest prices for the goods and services they want. Employees bid their services at the highest possible wages that their skills allow. Employers seek to get the best employees at the lowest possible price. In a word, sellers want the highest price and buyers want the best value for their money. The primary role of government is to make sure that everyone has free access to a free market. The government makes the laws about market economy operation. The law protects competition, that means the law protects ownership of private property.

We can take the United States as an example to understand market economy. The market economy has six defining characteristics:

• Private Property. Most goods and services are privately-owned. The owners can make legally-binding contracts to buy, sell, or lease their property. In other words, their assets give them the right to profit from ownership. But U. S. law excludes some assets. Since 1865, you cannot legally buy and sell human beings. That includes you, your body, and your body parts.

• Freedom of Choice. Owners are free to produce, sell and purchase goods and services in a competitive market. They only have two constraints. First is the price at which they are willing to buy or sell. Second is the amount of capital they have.

• Motive of Self-Interest. Everyone sells their wares to the highest bidder while negotiating the lowest price for their purchases. Although the reason is selfish, it benefits the economy over the long run. This auction system sets prices for goods and services that reflect their market value. It gives an accurate picture of supply and demand at any given moment.

• Competition. The force of competitive pressure keeps prices low. It also ensures that society provides goods and services most efficiently. As soon as demand increases for a particular item, prices rise thanks to the law of demand. Competitors see they can enhance their profit by producing it, adding to supply. That lowers prices to a level where only the best competitors remain. This competitive pressure also applies to workers and consumers. Employees vie with each other for the highest-paying jobs. Buyers compete for the best product at the lowest price. There are three strategies that work to maintain a competitive advantage.

• System of Markets and Prices. A market economy relies on an efficient market in which to sell goods and services. That's where all buyers and sellers have equal access to the same information. Price changes are pure reflections of the laws of supply and demand.

• Limited Government. The role of government is to ensure that the markets are open and working. For example, it is in charge of national defense to protect the markets. It also makes sure that everyone has equal access to the markets. The government penalizes monopolies that restrict competition. It makes sure no one is manipulating the markets and that everyone has equal access to information. But, the contents and forms of market economy are different strikingly in different economic backgrounds, and they vary greatly from country to country and from area to area. You can see the article below:

China's Market Is Fundamentally Different

China's evolving approach to marketing is different from that of developed economies because its market is different, in four key respects:

Channel-straddling media giants. The first and most important difference is the presence of channel-straddling media powerhouses. These include, most notably, Baidu, Alibaba, and Tencent, which together are known by the acronym BAT. To put this in a Western context, imagine if Amazon, Bank of America, Google, Facebook, Activision Blizzard, CNN, and ESPN were all owned by one company. That's essentially how the big conglomerates work in China, with the BAT companies controlling most of the digita lcontent across industries. For example, Tencent owns the world's largest gaming platform, a wide array of news agencies, the dominant social media platforms in China (Weixin and WeChat), financial services platforms (WeChat Pay and QQ Red Envelope Mobile Pay), retail investments (Tencent is the second-biggest shareholder in JD. com, one of China's largest online retailers), Tencent Video (the largest streaming service in China, with over 43 million subscribers), and Tencent Sports (China's number one online sports-media platform). Almost all media activity in China is consolidated on mobile devices, with consumers spending, on average, seven hours a day looking at their phones—approximately twice as much time as Americans spend. Remarkably, 55% of all online time spent by Chinese consumers is within the Tencent ecosystem of companies, according to data from Kleiner Perkins. The regulatory environment in the West prohibits such concentration, and as a result, Western marketers have been trained to use highly fragmented, channel-centric strategies to reach consumers. Marketing theories developed in this kind of media landscape don't easily translate to China—and perhaps more important, they may blind Western companies to the opportunities that exist when data is aggregated within a single, channel-straddling company.

A world of closed-loop data. In the West, marketers typically analyze data from, for instance, Facebook, CNN, People, and the Wall Street Journal separately, because information isn't easily connected across different channels at the consumer level. However, as much as privacy advocates dislike the linking, selling, and integrating of information, companies need access to closed-loop data at the individual level across every aspect of a person's life in order to develop deep consumer understanding and improve marketing relevancy. This is precisely the kind of integrated data that the BATs have. Marketers can see how a particular customer approaches banking, entertainment, gaming, social media, and news, and then create more-relevant and engaging experiences for them.

A mobile-first market development. In the West, media developed sequentially over the past century, with radio giving way to TV, followed by the personal computer and then mobile. In China, the evolution happened much more rapidly, essentially leapfrogging the PC to move straight to mobile. Thus, the marketing theory, principles, and methods developed in China were built on the assumption that mobile devices are the primary way to reach consumers. Tsuyoshi Suganami, president of Amplifi China (Dentsu AegisNetwork), pointed out that on China's biggest shopping day, known as Double Eleven or Singles Day, consumers bough tover $25 billion worth of merchandise—more than U. S. customers bought on Black Friday and Cyber Monday combined—with 90% of the purchases made on mobile phones. In contrast, China's mobile-centric platform has enabled marketers to focus on content-based experiences that will connect with consumers and change behavior quickly.

A focus on speed. Marketers in China make decisions more quickly than their Western counterparts do, mainly because firms in that fast-growing economy need to show momentum to keep investors on board. Scott Beaumont, head of Google's China and South Korea sales operations, put it this way: "Companies are in a race to determine which two or three will be left standing, and as soon as it's clear that a company won't be, funding dries up. " Marketers, he noted, recognize that a campaign needn't be perfect as long as it makes clear progress toward driving awareness and traffic. Western marketers do not aim to be slow, of course. But there is a central difference in approach, with large Western firms emphasizing scale and efficiency (a profit mindset) while Chinese marketers focus on speed and growth (a revenue mindset). Among the China-based teams of Western multinational firms I've met, this is a significant tension.

(Source: "China's Market Is Fundamentally Different", Harvard Business Review, May-June 2019.)

1. Market demand

In market economy, prices are allowed to float along with supply and demand. Demand describes how much of something people are willing and able to buy under certain circumstances. The demand for a good or service is defined as: Quantities of a good or service that people are ready to buy at various prices within some given time period, other factors besides price held constant.

- Price of the good or service. There is a relationship between the quantity demanded and the price, we called "law of demand". If the price increases, people buy less. The reverse is also true. If the price drops, people buy more.

- Consumer preferences, tastes and fashion.

Consumer preferences are the personal likes and dislikes that make buyers more or less inclined to purchase a good. We don't need to know why people like what they like or to agree with their preferences.

Luckin eyes tea market, expansion

Luckin Coffee, the Chinese answer to Starbucks, has diversified its beverage offerings by adding tea at its more than 3,000 stores in 40 cities to cash in on the country's latest trend of hand-brewed tea-based beverages. On July 8, the coffee chain announced its new strategy of entering the tea category in Beijing. Guo Jinyi, senior vice president of Luckin, said after fast development in 20 months, Luckin Coffee has improved its customer buy rate and brand awareness.

"Tea beverages and coffee are the top two beverages most popular among young people at work. Getting into tea beverages is a sound strategy for us," Guo said. Luckin Coffee's stores have been stationed at more than 2,000 office buildings and more than 100 universities and colleges. Guo said their new offering is targeted to solve challenges in the hand-brewed tea-drinking market including inconsistent quality and taste resulted from franchised models and insufficient capacity in supply management, as well as hygiene concerns raised by hand-brewing.

(Source: Wang Zhuoqiong, "Luckin eyes tea market, expansion", Chinadaily, June 8, 2019.)

- Price of other related goods. There are two kinds of related goods—substitutes and complements. Substitute goods are goods that are alternatives to each other, so that an increase in the demand for one is likely to cause a decrease in the demand for another, Switching demand from one good to another "rival" good is substitution. Examples of substitute goods and services:

(1) Apple and pear.

(2) Rival brands of the same commodity, like Coca-Cola and Pepsi-Cola.

(3) Tea and coffee.

(4) Some different forms of entertainment.

So the goods are substitutes when they serve similar-enough purposesthata consumer might purchase one in place of the other—for example, apple and pear. If the price of apple doubles while the price of pear stays the same, demand for pear will increase. That's because the opportunity cost of pear has decreased: You can buy less apple for the same amount of money, so you give up less potential apple when you buy pear. If the two goods are quite similar, we call them close substitutes.

Complements are goods that tend to be bought and used together, so that an increase in the demand for one is likely to cause an increase in the demand for the other. Related goods that are consumed together, so that purchasing one will make a consume more likely to purchase the other. Examples of complements:

(1) Cars and gasoline

(2) Cups and saucers

(3) Bread and butter

(4) Motor cars and the components and raw materials that go into their manufacture

• Households' income. Household income is an economic measure that can be applied to one household, or aggregated across a large group such as a county, city, or the whole country. The amount of income people earn affects their demand for goods and services. The household has the more money they can afford to spend more on the things they want. The smaller their paycheck, the more they have to cut back. We use income elasticity of demand measures the responsiveness of demand to changes in household income. The income elasticity of demand for a good indicates the responsiveness of demand to changes in household incomes.

$$\text{Income elasticity of demand} = \frac{\%\text{ change in quantity demanded}}{\%\text{ change in income}}$$

(1) Elastic. Demand for a good is income elastic if income elasticity is greater than 1. If quantity demanded rises by a larger percentage than the rise in income. For example, if the demand for overseas travel will rise by 15% if household income rises by 9%, we would say that the demand for overseas travel is income elastic.

(2) Inelastic. Demand for a good is income inelastic if income elasticity is between 0 and 1, and the quantity demanded rises less than the proportionate increase in income. For example, if the demand for basic food stuffs rises by 5% if household income rises by 9%.

(3) Negative. If income elasticity is negative, the commodity is called an inferior good since demand for it falls as income rises, such as: instant noodles, inter-city bus travel, cheaper cars. Inferiority in this sense is an observable fact about the consumer's demand preferences, rather statement about the quality of the

good itself.

A special type of inferior good may exist known as the Giffen good, which would disobey the "law of demand". Quite simply, when the price of a Giffen good increases, the demand for that good increases. This would have to be a good that is such a large proportion of a person or market's consumption that the income effect of a price increase would produce, effectively, more demand. The observed demand curve would slope upward, indicating positive elasticity. It was noted by Sir Robert Giffen that in Ireland during the 19th century there was a rise in the price of potatoes. The poor people were forced to reduce their consumption of meat and expensive items such as eggs. Potatoes still being the cheapest food, in order to compensate they started consuming more even though its price was rising. This phenomenon is often described as "Giffen's Paradox".

Household wealth to surge in next decade: Report

China's household wealth will rise to $51.8 trillion by 2028, surging 120% from 2018, according to Global Wealth Migration Review 2019, published by the research company New World Wealth. During the past 10 years, China has been the best-performing wealth market, with its private wealth skyrocketing 130% to $23.6 trillion in 2018, taking the second spot in the world's top 10 richest counties. The latest Global Wealth Migration pointed out worldwide private wealth has steadily increased since the 2008 financial crisis. In 2018, total worldwide private wealth reached $204 trillion in 2018, increasing 26% from 2008. The private wealth of the top 10 richest countries-the US, China, Japan, the UK, Germany, India, Australia, Canada, France and Italy-accounted for 74% of global private wealth in 2018. Driven by strong growth in Asia, global private wealth will jump to $291 trillion by 2028, and private wealth in China and India will post triple-digit growth in the next decade.

As developed countries' economies slowdown, the private wealth growth of the UK, Germany, France and Italy will slacken to 10% in the next 10 years, and growth will be a little higher in North America, the report said.

(Source: Zhang Jie, "Household wealth to surge in next decade: Report", Chinadaily. com. cn, June 9, 2019.)

● Expectations of future price changes. Changes in consumers' expectations about the future-especially future prices-can also affect demand. Consumers choose not only which products to buy but also when to buy them. For instance, if enough consumers become convinced that houses will be selling for lower prices in three months, the demand for houses will decrease now, as some consumers postpone their purchases to wait for the expected price decrease, causing current demand to decrease. Conversely, if consumers expect prices to rise in the future, they may wish to purchase a good immediately, to avoid a higher price.

● Number of potential buyers. In general, an increase in the number of potential buyers in a market will increase demand; a decrease in the number of buyers will decrease it.

2. Market supply

The supply of a good or service is defined as: Quantities of a good or service that people are ready to sell at various prices within some given time period, other factors besides price held constant.

● Costs of inputs. These include raw materials costs, which ultimately depend on the prices of factors of production.

● Prices of related goods. The price of related goods determines supply because it affects the opportunity cost of production. When a supplier can switch readily from supplying one good to another, the goods concerned are called substitutes in supply. An increase in the price of one such good would make the supply of another good whose price does not rise less attractive to suppliers. When a production process has two or more distinct and separate outputs, the goods produced are known as goods in joint supply or complements in production. Goods in joint supply, It the price of one rises, the joint part more will be supplied and there will be an accompanying increase in the supply.

● Technology. Technological developments which reduce costs of production, increasing the quantity producers are willing to supply at each price. Improved technology has played a huge role in almost industries.

Smart tech transforming medical sector

Online platforms open new channels for patients to purchase medicines, allowing doctors to focus more on patients. Chinese hospitals, especially those with good reputations in big cities, are always crowded, with patients who have traveled long distances to wait for several hours, or even all night, just for a few minutes' consultation with a doctor. Many patients visit hospitals not because they are in urgent need of medical care, but because they want follow-up treatment for chronic conditions or simply to get medicine. This is because doctors in China are only allowed to prescribe medicines in limited doses: usually in third-tier hospitals only enough to last up to two weeks and in community hospitals prescriptions only last one month maximally, and patients cannot buy prescription drugs without a prescription. Thanks to the internet and smart hospital technologies, a change is under way that is making it easier for patients to get the medicines they need. Bestyoo, an enterprise affiliated to Chinese pharmaceutical company Baheal Pharmaceutical Group, has been cooperating with local governments and hospitals to establish online prescription transferring and sharing systems to solve such problems by diverting patients' drug purchases from hospitals to offline pharmacies. Bestyoo has designed two information system products-one for local governments and the other for hospitals. The system for local governments incorporates real-time prescriptions information from medical institutions, medical insurance billing information, and drug sales information in a region. The prescription information, once verified and approved by a pharmacist, will be transferable between different medical institutions, or from medical institutions to approved pharmacies, drug delivery services, and online sales terminals, if patients authorize the transfer with text message verification codes. The system for hospitals is designed to connect to a hospital's existing information system, or HIS, allowing prescription information to be transferred to approved pharmacies with the permission of patients.

（Source：Liu Zhihua, Smart tech transforming medical sector, China Daily, June 9, 2019.）

• Expectations of price changes. If a supplier expects the price of a good to rise in the future, they are likely to try to reduce supply while the price is lower so that they can supply more of their product or service once the price is higher.

• Number of sellers. The market supply curve represents the quantities of a product that a particular number of producers will supply at a various prices in a given market. For example, Taobao, the Chinese largest e-commerce platform, said its sales generated through live streaming reached 100 billion yuan in 2008, a fourfold increase from 2017. Such sales typically involve a celebrity demonstrating a product and answering real-time questions from a digital audience using smartphones. More and more sellers use both the flashlight and camera lens on their phones show the goods on the e-platform.

• Other factors. These include changes in the weather, natural disasters or industrial disruption, and the quantity supplied will change in response to a change in price. For example：fruit prices recorded the most notable rise mainly in China because bad weather hammered supplies, with the price of fresh fruit up 26.7% year-on-year in May, 2019.

If we want to have the deep understanding of market demand and supply, the

"Determinants" are necessary knowledge points（see table 4-1）.

Table 4-1　　　　　　**Factors determining demand and supply**

Determinants of demand	Determinants of supply
Price of the good or service	Costs of inputs
Consumer preferences	Prices of related goods
Prices of related goods	Technology
Households' income	Expectations
Expectations	Number of sellers
Number of buyer	Other factors

4.2.2　Command economy

A command economy is where a central government makes all economic decisions. It plans the goods and services that a country produces, the quantity in which they are produced and the prices at which they are sold. Either the government or a collective owns the land and the means of production. Consistent with the collectivist ideology, the objective of a command economy is for government to allocate resources for "the good of society. " All businesses are state-owned, the rationale being that the government can then direct them to make investments that are in the best interests of the nation as a whole rather than in the interests of private individuals. It doesn't rely on the laws of supply and demand that operate in a market economy. A command economy also ignores the customs that guide a traditional economy. In the late 1980s, the number of command economies has fallen dramatically. France and India both experimented with extensive government planning and state ownership, although government planning has fallen into disfavor in both countries. While the objective of a command economy is to mobilize economic resources for the public good, the opposite often seems to have occurred. In a command economy, state. owned enterprises have little incentive to control costs and be efficient because they cannot go out of business. Also, the abolition of private ownership means there is no incentive for individuals to look for better ways to serve consumer needs; hence, dynamism and innovation are absent from command economies. It cannot effectively promote economic grow, and the economy tend to stagnate. In recent years, many centrally-planned economies began adding aspects of the market economy. The resultant mixed economy better achieves their goals.

From the definition, we can find some characteristics of command economy (see table 4-2):

● The government creates a central economic plan. Central government sets economic and societal goals for every sector and region of the country for a long term, and shorter-term plans convert the goals into actionable objectives.

● The government allocates all resources according to the central plan. It tries to use the nation's capital, labor, and natural resources in the most efficient way possible. It promises to use each person's skills and abilities to their highest capacity. It seeks to accomplish the ambition of full employment.

● The central plan sets the priorities for the production of all goods and services. That includes quotas and price controls. Its goal is to supply enough food, housing, and other basics to meet the needs of everyone in the country. It also sets national priorities. These include mobilizing for war or generating robust economic growth.

● The government owns monopoly businesses. These are in industries deemed essential to the goals of the economy. That includes finance, utilities, and automotive. There is no domestic competition in these sectors.

● The government creates laws, regulations, and directives to enforce the central plan. Businesses follow the plan's production and hiring targets. They can't respond on their own to free market forces. We can draw the conclusion of advantages and disadvantages from Command economy.

Table 4-2　　Advantages and Disadvantages from Command Economy

	Advantages	Disadvantages
Command Economy	● concentrate resources for large projects ● industrial power is created and massive projects completed while attaining imperative social goals ● transform the society to conform to the government's vision for the country or society ● society as a whole benefit from the success and not just a select few individuals	● lack of Competition Inhibits Innovation ● inefficiency and discourage innovation ● supply will not have enough to support the economic needs

4.2.3　Mixed economy

Between market economies and command economies can be found mixed economies. We can say "a mixed economy" is a system that combines characteristics of market, command and traditional economies, reflecting characteristics of both market economies and planned economies. In a mixed economy, certain sectors of the economy are left to private ownership and free market mechanisms, while other sectors have significant state ownership and government planning. A mixed economy has some characteristics of a command economy in strategic areas. For example, it allows the government to safeguard its people and its market. The government has a large role in the military, international trade and national transportation. The basic plan of the mixed economy is that the means of production are mainly under private ownership; that markets remain the dominant form of economic coordination; and that profit-seeking enterprises and the accumulation of capital would remain the fundamental driving force behind economic activity. However, the government would wield considerable indirect influence over the economy through fiscal and monetary policies designed to counteract economic downturns and promote social welfare. Sometimes mixed economies allow the government to own key industries. These include aerospace, energy production, and even banking. The government may also manage health care, welfare, and retirement programs. In some cases, the government creates a central plan that guides the economy.

A mixed economy has all the advantages of a market economy.

• First, it distributes goods and services to where they are most needed. It promote efficiency in both the private sector and the public sector. it allows prices to measure supply and demand. It rewards the most efficient producers with the highest profit. That means customers get the best value for their money.

• Second, it encourages innovation to meet customer needs more creatively, cheaply or efficiently., it automatically allocates capital to the most innovative and efficient producers. That means efficiency resource allocation and customer demand orientated production would be maintained, in turn, people can invest the capital in more businesses like them.

• Third, to some extent, the mixed economy can control the crisis. Because the private ownership is still well protected and private sector is still dominating the economy, therefore the advantages of the market economy such as efficiency resource allocation and customer demand orientated production would be maintained; and on the other hand, when there should be any market irregularities and obvious risks, the government could intervene and keep a good order of market to avoid market failures such as financial crisis in which some large market players were knowingly contributing to the economic bubbles because they were benefiting from creating such bubbles. In this way, both the private sector and public sector are functioning and helping the national economy to develop in an efficient but well managed way which would promote overall efficiency.

Every coin has two sides. A mixed economy can also take on all the disadvantages of the other types of economies. Some disadvantages could happen in a mixed economy if the two different frameworks operate and function at the same time. For example, it would be inefficient if the both forces do act against each other and also it would be difficult to judge which forces should play the major role under certain circumstances. It just depends on which characteristics the mixed economy emphasizes. For example, if the market has too much freedom, it can leave the less competitive members of society without any government support. However, ? central planning of government industries also creates problems. The defense industry could become a government-subsidized monopoly or oligarchy system. That could put the country into debt, slowing down economic growth in the long run. Successful businesses can lobby the government for more subsidies and tax breaks. The government could protect the free market so much that it doesn't regulate enough. For example, businesses that took on too much risk could receive taxpayer-funded bailouts.

4.3　Economy Analysis

4.3.1　Inflation, deflation and stagflation

US Public Debt Reaches Record High of More Than $22 Trillion

WASHINGTON-The US public debt has reached a record high of more than $22 trillion, according to data released by the US Treasury Department. Total outstanding public debt stands at $22.01 trillion as of Feb 11, the Treasury Department's daily statement showed Tuesday. "The national debt has now eclipsed $22 trillion, as we added $1 trillion in debt over just the last 11 months," said Michael A. Peterson, CEO of the Peter G. Peterson Foundation, a non-partisan organization dedicated to addressing America's long-term fiscal challenges. "Reaching this unfortunate milestone so rapidly is the latest sign that our fiscal situation is not only unsustainable, but accelerating," Peterson said in a statement. Analysts said the Trump administration's $1.5-trillion tax cut and increased government spending have fueled the rapid increase in budget deficits and public debt. The Congressional Budget Office (CBO) last month estimated that federal budget deficit is about $900 billion in 2019 and exceeds $1 trillion each year beginning in 2022. Because of persistently large deficits, the public debt is projected to grow steadily, reaching 93% of US gross domestic product (GDP) in 2029 and about 150% of US GDP in 2049, according to the CBO. "As we borrow trillion after trillion, interest costs will weigh on our economy and make it harder to fund important investments for our future," Peterson said. "We already pay an average of $1 billion every day in interest on the debt, and will spend a staggering $7 trillion in interest costs over the next decade," he said, adding "we must put our fiscal house in order and begin to manage our national debt." Former Federal Reserve Chairman Alan Greenspan has warned that the rising public debt in the United States could lead to the next economic recession. During an interview with Bloomberg Television in November 2018, Greenspan said he saw "a lot of talk but no realistic movement" to address the problems of rising deficits and debt, which could drag the US economy into a period of stagflation with rising inflation and high unemployment. Greenspan believed that the next US economic recession is going to come "sometime" and it's going to be driven by "dramatically" rising debt.

(Source: Xinhua, "US public debt reaches record high of more than $22 trillion", Chinadaily, February 14, 2019.)

From the opening vignette, we look several key words about "US Public Debt" which are stagflation, inflation, unemployment. They are important economic indicators, so it is necessary for us to learn first.

1. Inflation

Inflation is the name given to an increase in price levels generally. It is also manifest in the decline in the purchasing power of money. According to economy research, inflation has three categories: low inflation, galloping inflation and high inflation. Low inflation is characterized by prices that rise slowly and predictably. We might define this as single-digit annual inflation rates. When prices are relatively stable, people will have confident to the economic growth. They believe the relative prices of goods they buy and sell will not get too far out of line. Galloping inflation becomes entrenched, serious economic distortions arise. In these conditions, money soon loses its value, so people hold only bare-minimum amount of money needed for daily transactions, and Capital flees abroad. While economies seem to survive under galloping inflation, hyperinflationoccurs. It appears when a country experiences very high and usually accelerating rates of inflation, rapidly eroding the real value of the local currency, and causing the population to minimize their holdings of local money. The population normally switches to holding relatively stable foreign currencies. Under such conditions, the general price level within an economy increases rapidly as the official currency quickly loses real value. Nothing good can be said about a market economy in which prices are rising a million or even. Take Venezuela as example: Given the dearth of official data for inflation, different indicators from official and non-official sources are used as proxies to measure the evolution of price levels in the South American country. Developments throughout 2016 suggest that the inflationary spiral has intensified enormously since the latest official inflation data from December 2015 showed that prices had grown by 180.9% annually. In particular, price pressures seem to have intensified greatly in the second half of 2016. Large increases in the money supply, a sharp weakening of the bolivar in the parallel market, the depletion of international reserves and the dysfunctional price control scheme in the country are among the main reasons behind Venezuela's spiraling inflation. The latest Central Bank data show that the money supply increased by 159.2% in December 2015, up from 144.6% in November 2015 and marking the fifth consecutive triple-digit increase. The money supply is expected to have increased sharply in January thanks to a 50% salary hike, the fifth since the start of 2016, and the introduction of larger denomination bills. According to figures from the Venezuelan Center of Documentation and Analysis for Workers, inflation is seen ending 2017 at 724.5%. So, Venezuela has signs of hyperinflation looming.

High inflation will be a big problem for one's country economy. Some studies have found that the adverse influence of inflation on economic growth and level of investment in short term, and it could affect a country's standard of living fairly significantly over the long term. Such a mindset is mainly reflected in five aspects:

(1) Redistribution of income and wealth. Inflation leads to a redistribution of income and wealth in ways which may be undesirable debts lose 'real' value with inflation. When people owe money, a sharp rise in prices is a wind fall gain for them. Redistribution of wealth might take place from accounts payable to accounts receivable. For example, if you owed $5,000, and prices then doubled. This is because would still owe $5,000, but the real value of your debt would have been halved. In general, in times of inflation those with economic power tend to gain at the expense of the weak, particularly those on fixed incomes. If you are a lender and have assets in fixed-interest-rate mortgages or long-term bonds, the shoe is on the other foot. An unexpected rise in prices will leave you the poorer because the money repaid to you are worth much less than the money you lent.

(2) Balance of payments effects. If a country has a higher rate of inflation than its major trading partners, its exports will become relatively expensive and imports relatively cheap. As a result, the balance of trade will suffer, affecting employment in exporting industries and in industries producing import-substitutes.

Eventually, the exchange rate will be affected.

(3) Uncertainty of the value of money and prices. If the rate of inflation is imperfectly anticipated, no one has certain knowledge of the true rate of inflation. As a result, no one has certain knowledge of the value of money or of the real meaning of prices. If the rate of inflation becomes excessive, and there is hyper inflation, this problem becomes so exaggerated that money becomes worthless, so that people are unwilling to use it and are forced to resort to barter. In less extrem e circumstances, the results are less dramatic, but the same problem exists. As prices convey less information, the process of resource allocation is less efficient and rational decision-making is almost impossible.

(4) Resource costs of changing prices. A fourth reason to aim for stable prices is the resource cost of frequently changing prices in times of high inflation, substantial labor time is spent on planning and implementing price changes. Customers may also have to spend more time making price comparisons if they seek to buy from the lowest cost source.

(5) Economic growth and investment. Some studies have found inflation is harmful to a country's economic growth and level of investment in short term, but it could affect a country's standard of living fairly significantly over the long term.

2. Deflation

Deflation is the general decline in prices for goods and services occurring when the inflation rate falls below 0%. Monetary deflation can only be caused by a decrease in the supply of money or financial instruments redeemable in money. In a situation where there is unemployment of resources there is said to be a deflationary gap. Pricesare fairly constant and real output changes as aggregate demand varies. Deflation is caused by a number of factors but is largely attributed to two: a decline in aggregate demand and increased productivity. A decline in aggregate demand typically results in subsequent lower prices. A deflationary gap can be described as the extent to which the aggregate demand function will have to shift upward to produce the full employment level of national income. Take Switzerland as example, in March 2013, consumer prices rose 0.2% over the previous month, which represents the second consecutive monthly increase after three consecutive drops. The reading fell short of market expectations of a 0.3% increase and mainly reflected higher prices for clothing and footwear as well as for recreation and culture. Despite the monthly increase, however, annual consumer prices fell 0.6% in March, which came in below both the 0.3% fall registered in February as well as market expectations of a 0.5% decline. As a result, the inflation rate sits well below the Swiss National Bank's 2.0% inflation target. Annual average consumer prices fell 0.6% in March. The Swiss National Bank expects consumer prices to drop 0.2% this year. So, from the data Switzerland economy remains mired in deflation.

3. Stagflation

The term "stagflation" was first used during a time of economic stress in the United Kingdom by politician Iain Macleod in the 1960s while he was speaking in the House of Commons. At the time, he was speaking about inflation on one side and stagnation on the other, calling it a "stagnation situation." It was later used again to describe the recessionary period during the 1970s following the oil crisis, when the U. S. underwent a recession that saw five quarters of negative GDP growth. Inflation doubled in 1973 and hit double digits in 1974; unemployment hit 9 percent by May 1975. Stagflation is a condition of slow economic growth and relatively high unemployment, or economic stagnation, accompanied by rising prices, or inflation. It can also be defined as inflation and a decline in gross domestic product (GDP). Stagflation is a combination of unacceptably high unemployment, unacceptably high inflation and low/negative economic growth.

From the definition, what's the difference? Inflation is a term used to define broad increases in prices. Inflation is the rate at which the price of goods and services in an economy increases. Inflation also can be defined as the rate at which purchasing power declines. Stagflation is a term used to define an economy that has inflation, a slow or stagnant economic growth rate, and a relatively high unemployment rate. With stagflation, a country's citizens are affected by high rates of inflation and unemployment. High unemployment rates further contribute to the slowdown of a country's economy, causing the economic growth rate to fluctuate no more than a single percentage point above or below a zero growth rate. From Angela Bouzanis, the lead economist, take the data of Brazil Central Bank's Monetary Policy Committee (COPOM), in September 2014, COPOM decided to leave the benchmark SELIC interest rate unchanged at 11.00%, where it has been since April. The decision was consistent with market expectations. The Bank's statement was almost exactly the same as the one that followed the prior meeting that took place on 16 July and COPOM's choice to keep the SELIC interest rate at 11.00% was voted unanimously by the committee. The decision reflects the Bank's commitment to curb inflation, even amidst contracting economic growth rates. Last week, Brazil released Q2 data that confirmed that the country is now in a technical recession after contracting in both Q1 and Q2 of this year. The combination of negative growth and high inflation has gained presence within the economic debate in the country. Presidential elections are taking place in October, and candidates have been debating the fact that the country might be approaching a "stagflation" scenario, although Central Bank Governor Alexandre Tombini denied this possibility in a speech at the Senate on 5 August. Moreover, Brazil's Central Bank is not independent from the government, and the head of the Bank is likely to change if the government does. Looking forward, the market expects the SELIC interest rate to remain unchanged until after the new government is formed. Latin Focus Consensus Forecast participants see the SELIC rate ending 2014 at an average of 11.11%. Panelists see the SELIC rate ending 2015 at an average of 11.92%.

4. CPI

Inflation refers to an overall increase in the Consumer Price Index (CPI), which is a weighted average of prices for different goods. CPI is a measure of the overall cost of the goods and services bought by a typical consumer. The set of goods that make up the index depends on which are considered representative of a common consumption basket. Therefore, depending on the country and the consumption habits of the majority of the population, the index will comprise different goods. Some goods might record a drop in prices, whereas others may increase, thus the overall value of the CPI will depend on the weight of each of the goods with respect to the whole basket. Annual inflation, refers to the percent change of the CPI compared to the same month of the previous year. So, we can use the steps of Bureau of Labor Statistics (US), understand how the consumer price index calculated.

(1) Fix the basket. The first step in computing the consumer price index is to determine which prices are most important to the typical consumer. If the typical consumer buys more A goods than B goods, then the price of A is more important than the price of B, therefore, should be given greater weight in measuring the cost of living.

(2) Find the prices. The second step in computing the consumer price index is to find the prices of each of the goods and services in the basket for each point in time.

(3) Compute the baskets cost. The third step is to use the data on prices to calculate the cost of the basket of goods and services at different times.

(4) Choose a base year and compute the index. The fourth step is to designate one year as the base year, which is the benchmark against which other years are compared. To calculate the index, the price of the basket of goods and services in each year is divided by the price of the basket in the base year, and this ratio is

then multiplied by 100. The resulting number is the consumer price index.

（5）Compute the inflation rate. The fifth and final step is to use the consumer price index to calculate the inflation rate, which is the percentage change in the price index from the preceding period.

4. 3. 2　Unemployment

Unemployment occurs when a person who are not employed but actively searching for work or waiting to return to work. The rate of unemployment is the number of unemployed at any time measured by government statistics, and it can be calculated in an economy as:

$$\text{Unemployment} = \frac{\text{Number of unemployed}}{\text{Total workforce}} \times 100\%$$

There are two types of people flow into unemployment:

（1）Members of the working labour force becoming unemployed; redundancies, voluntarily quitting a job, lay-offs;

（2）People out of the labour force joining the unemployed: school leavers without a job, Others rejoining the workforce but having no job yet.

There are three types of people flow out of unemployment:

（1）Unemployed people finding jobs.

（2）Laid-off workers being re-employed.

（3）Unemployed people stopping the search for work.

High unemployment is both an economic and a social problem. Unemployment represents waste of a valuable resource. At the same time, it is a major social problem because it causes enormous suffering as unemployed workers struggle with reduced incomes and affect the people's family life.

India's Economy-Time for a Makeover

India's new finance minister, Nirmala Sitharaman, is an unusual figure in the country's politics. She is the first woman to head the finance ministry since Indira Gandhi seized the post（while also serving as prime minister）50 years ago, after nationalising many of India's banks. She is an economist. But unlike most in her Bharatiya Janata Party（bjp）she hails from the country's south, having grown up in Tamil Nadu, one of the few big states to resist the bjp's advances in the recent election. She claims a humbler background than her predecessor, Arun Jaitley. Her father worked for India's railways and she spent a month selling home furnishings at Habitat, a shop in London. Ms Sitharaman thus embodies the bjp's broadening appeal to aspirational Indians outside its traditional heartlands. But will she help it fulfil those aspirations? On the day she was appointed, India's statistical authority reported that growth in the first quarter of the year had slipped to 5.8%, its slowest since Narendra Modi was elected prime minister in 2014. The government also belatedly released a report it had with held showing that unemployment had risen to 6.1% in the year ending June2018. In India, the jobless are often not the poorest, who cannot afford not to work, but the newly educated, qualified for better jobs that have yet to arrive. The prospects for a quick economic recovery depend partly on the banks Ms Gandhi nationalised. They are responsible for most of the bad loans that have long clogged lenders' balance-sheets. Optimists point out that the share of bad loans has begun to fall. And several troubled banks have been permitted to expand credit after a more lenient official was put in charge of their regulator, the Reserve Bank of India (rbi), the country's central bank. The rbi cut interest rates for the third time this year on June 6th. It must also keep a close eye on India's lightly regulated "nonbank" lenders. They have kept credit flowing to households and industry in recent years, financing themselves by selling bonds and commercial paper to yield-hungry mutual funds, until one lender defaulted in September 2018. The prospects for a cyclical recovery seem brighter than the chances of deeper reform. Ms Sitharaman is unlikely to enjoy the same autonomy given to Mr Jaitley, a cabinet heavy weight who helped pave Mr Modi's path into national politics. His departure due to ill health may mean his boss takes a closer interest in economic affairs. That is not necessarily a good thing. As chief minister of Gujarat, Mr Modiexcelled at drumming up investment from big corporations and breathing down civil servants' necks. But that approach has translated less well to the role of prime minister, which requires more indirect methods, such as creating the right incentives and delegating to the right people. Abureaucrat quoted in "The Lost Decade", a new book by Puja Mehra, talks of long, tedious meetings, in which Mr Modi would monitor his policies' implementation and the civil servant would scoff the peanuts and chickpeas. After Mr Modi's first victory in 2014, liberals hoped the pro-business tub-thumper would become a pro-market prime minister, encouraging investment by liberalizing labour and land laws, relying on statecraft, not stagecraft. Instead he became what Indians call "pro-poor", providing a multitude of redistributive welfare schemes, such as cash handouts for small farmers. These schemes seemed inspired by thegovernment's lingering fear of being out-flanked on the left. It largely abandoned its efforts to ease the acquisition of land for industrial purposes after Rahul Gandhi, the leader of the opposition Congressparty, accused it of being a "suit-boot ki sarkar" — a government for suited-and-booted corporations. It was slow to help public-sector banks write off their bad loans, inpart because it did not want to appear soft on crony capitalists. Since this timidity helped win it a second landslide, Mr Modi would seem to have little reason to abandon it. But perhaps his victory has finally killed his fear of the opposition. Ms Sitharaman was described as a "one-person demolition squad" after her impassioned response inparliament to Mr Gandhi's accusations of government cronyism. Having bulldozedt he opposition, perhaps Mr Modi will now feel emboldened not to copy it.

(Source: "India's Economy-Time for a Makeover", The Economist, June 8th, 2019.)

1. Consequences of Unemployment

Unemployment results in the following problems:

(1) Loss of output. If labour is unemployed, the economy is not producing as much output as it could. Thus, total national income is less than it could be.

(2) Loss of human capital. If there is unemployment, the unemployed labour will gradually lose its skills, because skills can only be maintained by working.

(3) Increasing inequalities in the distribution of income. Unemployed people earn less than employed people, and so when unemployment is increasing, the poor get poorer.

(4) Social costs. Unemployment brings social problems of personal suffering and distress, and possibly also increases in crime, such as theft and vandalism.

(5) Increased burden of welfare payments. This can have a major impact on government fiscal policy.

2. Causes of unemployment

(1) Real wage unemployment. This type of unemployment is caused when the supply of labour exceeds the demand, but real wages do not fall for the labour market to clear. This type of unemployment is normally caused by strong trade unions which resist a fall in their wages. Another cause of this type of unemployment is the minimum wage rate, when it is set above the market clearing level.

(2) Frictional unemployment. Frictional unemployment arises when a person is in between jobs. It is inevitable that after a person leaves a company, it naturally takes time to find another job, making this type of unemployment short-lived, some unemployment is caused because of difficulty in matching quickly workers with jobs, caused perhaps by a lack of knowledge about job opportunities. In general, it takes time to match prospective employees with employers, and

individuals will be unemployed during the search period for a new job. Frictional unemployment is a natural result of the fact that market processes take time and information can be costly. Searching for a new job, recruiting new workers, and matching the right workers to the right jobs all take time and effort to do, resulting in frictional unemployment. Frictional unemployment is temporary, lasting for the period of transition from one job to the next, movement of people between regions and jobs or through different stages of the life cycle. Even if an economy were at full employment, there would always be some turnover as students search for jobs when they graduate from school or parents reenter the labor force after having children. Because frictionally unemployed workers are often moving between jobs, or looking for better jobs, it is often thought that they are voluntarily unemployed. It is also the least problematic from an economic standpoint.

(3) Seasonal unemployment. This occurs in certain industries, for example building, tourism and farming, where the demand for labour fluctuates in seasonal patterns throughout the year. According to Economic Forecasts from the World's Leading Economists news, unemployment in Spain rose from an over seven-year low of 18.6% in Q4 to 18.8% in the first quarter of 2017, traditionally a weak period for the country's labor market due to the end of temporary jobs linked to the winter holiday. Compared to the same period of last year, this quarter's reading marked a notable improvement over the 21.0% recorded in Q1 2016. In absolute terms, the number of unemployed totaled 4.26 million people in Q1, an increase

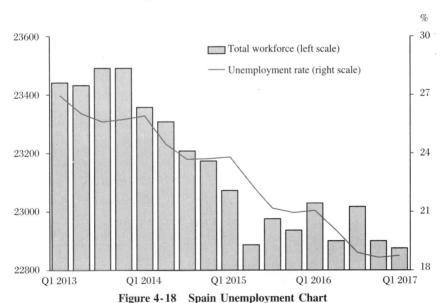

Figure 4-18　Spain Unemployment Chart

Note: Total workforce in thousands and unemployment rate as % of active population.
Source: National Statistical Institute (INE).

from the 4. 24 million recorded in the previous quarter. Although the seasonal components argue against reading too much into this quarter's data, unemployment still remains one of the economy's weakest flanks and stands as the second highest in the Euro zone.

Meanwhile, the country's workforce decreased by 52,600 people in Q1 to 22. 7 million. Although the reading was smaller than Q4's figure, when the workforce shrank by 102,400 people, the Spanish workforce now sits at its lowest level since the financial crisis.

（1）Structural unemployment. Structural unemployment refers to a mismatch between the supply of and the demand for workers. Generally speaking, mismatches can occur because the demand for one kind of labor is rising while the demand for another kind is falling, and supplies do not quickly adjust. Structural unemployment comes about through technological change in the structure of the economy in which labor markets operate.

Technological unemployment is a form of structural unemployment, which occurs when new technologies are introduced, such as old skills are no longer required, or with machines doing the job that people used to do. With robots are widely used in the automobile industry, employment levels in an industry can fall sharply, even when the industry's total output is increasing. Technological development like the research on automatic speech recognition has seen great achievement in the passed twenty years, lead to unemployment among workers displaced from jobs that are no longer needed. Most of these workers belong to the lower-skilled and semi-skilled workforce from lower tiers of the talent market, retraining these workers can be difficult, costly, and time consuming, and displaced workers often end up either unemployed for extended periods or leaving the labor force entirely. This occurs where long-term changes occur in the conditions of an industry. A feature of structural unemployment is high regional unemployment in the location of the affected. The primary cause is a significant reduction in the level of demand.

（2）Cyclical or demand-deficient unemployment. Cyclical unemployment exists when the overall demand for labor is low. As total spending and output fall, unemployment rises virtually everywhere. It has been the experience of the past that domestic and foreign trade go through demand cycles of boom, decline, recession, recovery, then boom again, and so on.

①During recovery and boom years, the demand for output and jobs is high, and unemployment is low.

②During decline and recession years, the demand for output and jobs falls, and unemployment rises to a high level.

Cyclical unemployment can be long term, and a government might try to reduce it by doing what it can to minimise a recess. Cyclical unemployment is the variation in the number of unemployed workers over the course of economic upturns and downturns. Cyclical unemployment occurs during recessions, when employment falls as a result of an imbalance between aggregate supply and demand. The distinction between cyclical, frictional, and structural unemployment helps economists diagnose the general health of the labor market. High levels of frictional or structural unemployment can occur even though the overall labor market is in balance. Unemployment rises during recessionary periods and declines during periods of economic growth. Preventing and alleviating cyclical unemployment during recessions is a major concern behind the study of economics and the purpose of the various policy tools that governments employ on the downside of business cycles to stimulate the economy.

4. 3. 3　Poverty

Poverty is a state or condition in which a person or community lacks the financial resources and essentials for a minimum standard of living. Despite a high and growing global average income, billions of human beings are still condemned to life-long severe poverty, with all its attendan tevils of low life expectancy, social exclusion, ill health, illiteracy, dependency, and effective enslavement. Though constituting 44% of the world's population, the 2, 735 million people the World Bank counts as living below its more generous $2 per day international poverty line consume only 1. 3% of the global product, and would need just 1% more to escape poverty so defined. The poverty gap is the average shortfall of the total population from the poverty line. This measurement is used to reflect the intensity of poverty. The poverty line used to measure this gap is the amount typical to the poorest countries in the world combined with the latest information on the cost of living in developing countries.

A poverty trap is a mechanism that makes it very difficult for people to escape poverty. A poverty trap is created when an economic system requires a significant amount of capital in order to earn enough to escape poverty. When individuals lack this capital, they may also find it difficult to acquire it, creating a self-reinforcing cycle of poverty. Many factors contribute to creating a poverty trap, including: limited access to credit and capital markets, extreme environmental degradation (which depletes agricultural production potential), corrupt governance, capital flight, poor education systems, disease ecology, lack of public health care, war and poor infrastructure.

Demographic Discrepancies Cause Worry

As the international community observes this year's World Population Day on Thursday, policymakers across continents, especially in Asia, have to tackle a demographic paradox. The United Nations estimates the global population may hit 9. 7 billion in 2050 from about 7. 7 billion today. However, a wide discrepancy among subregions is apparent across the world. Southern Asia and Africa are struggling with providing jobs for the growing number of young people as a result of higher fertility rate, but East Asia, Europe and elsewhere are confronted with rapid aging that can pressure their resources and public services. The ramifications of this divergent demographic trend may threaten the regions' economic gains and the UN's 2030 Sustainable Development Goals, analysts noted. The 17 goals include eradication of extreme poverty, halting deforestation and promotion of gender equality. Sivananthi Thanenthiran, executive director of the Kuala Lumpur-based Asian-Pacific Resource and Research Center for Women, said meeting these SDGs is crucial for Asian countries with a huge youth population. Such "sizable youth power" needs quality education, skills and job opportunities. The United Nations Population Fund said the total fertility rate for Asia is close to the replacement level of 2. 1 births per woman. In East Asia, fertility rate is 1. 7 births, while in South Asia, the rate is 2. 5 births. According to the UNFPA, the Asia-Pacific region has nearly 1 billion young people aged 10 to 24 years. More than half of these young Asians live in India, China, Indonesia, Pakistan and Bangladesh. In most "young" countries, youth unemployment is a problem and faster development can ease the pain. In contrast, East Asians face a different problem: falling birth rates and a growing number of elderly people. According to the United Nations Economic and Social Commission for Asia and the Pacific, over 12% of the Asian population is 60 years or older. This is projected to rise to more than 20% by 2050. In East Asia, over 30% of the population is expected to be 60 years or older by 2050. Peter Mcdonald, professor at the School of Population and Global Health, University of Melbourne in Australia, said having fewer children has served East Asian countries well. Parents with one to two children were able to invest in quality education and produce a more skilled workforce. Apart from lower birth rates, UNESCAP said the improved living standards and access to health care and nutrition also boosted the number of the elderly. But the pace of aging in Asia is faster and happening at a much earlier stage of development compared with the more industrialized economies. It took France 115 years and the United States 69 years to move from an aging to an aged society, according to UNESCAP. In contrast, Japan took only 24 years to become an aged society. China is expected to make the transition in 25 years and Singapore in 22 years. East Asian policymakers did not anticipate birthrates would fall at such low rates, Mcdonald said, noting that they enjoyed a "nice big dividend in the short-term (but will have a) big problem in future". Bussarawan Teerawichitchainan, deputy director of the Center for Family and Population Research at the National University of Singapore, said policymakers in the region need to take note of how to ensure the health and financial security of the elderly. "How will people support themselves during old age, especially if they don't work. They also need long-term care because as people live longer, those added years may not be healthy years," she said. Moreover, developing Asia has to tackle another burden of their young women besides joblessness: the lack of family planning policies and cultural bias against women's reproductive health. "Never-married women, including adolescents and young women, have a great disadvantage in obtaining contraceptives largely due to the stigma attached to being sexually active before marriage," Thanenthiran said. She cited this year's World Population Day theme which focuses on the progress made after the 1994 International Conference on Population and Development held in Cairo, Egypt. Participants of the 1994 conference recognized that reproductive health and gender equality are essential for achieving sustainable development. Thanenthiran said most women in South and Southeast Asia still struggle with unwanted pregnancies and forced marriages. She said that 63% of the adolescent pregnancies in Asia are unplanned. "People need to recognize that women have to understand and have control over their reproductive health," said Junice Melgar, executive director of the Manila-based Likhaan Center for Women's Health. Melgar said that sex education and access to contraceptives are important in order to reduce high adolescent fertility rate that usually push women to drop out of school and remain jobless and poor.

(Source: Prime Sarmiento, "Demographic discrepancies cause worry", China Daily Global, June 11, 2019.)

4. 4   Case

Case-1

China Can Withstand Economic Headwinds

Despite downside pressure, the Chinese economy is expected to remain stable in the second half of this year. The year-on-year GDP growth rate for 2019 is expected to be no lower than 6.2%. Several factors will help China withstand headwinds from global slowdown and other external instabilities. First, as the country is a developing economy with lots of weak links, investments in numerous areas still offer prospects of relatively high returns. Second, consumption is expected to continue a steady growth, given the stimulus of recently implemented large-scale tax cuts. Additional policies to boost consumption are probably on the horizon. Also, macro policies still have room for maneuver toward steady growth. Proactive fiscal policy will continue in the second half. Meanwhile, monetary policy could be adjusted to counter downside pressure, as inflationary risks are controllable and as the US Federal Reserve may cut interest rates in the coming months. Against the backdrop of increasing policy support for the real economy, an upside for the A-share market can be expected in the second half of the year, given the relatively cheap valuations of listed firms. Fluctuations in the bond market may offer investment opportunities as the room for further interest rate falls is limited. In the long term, China will rely on new growth points to achieve a healthy development. The shift in driving forces, however, takes time to realize, making it important to foster the new economy and vitalize traditional growth engines for the purpose of stabilizing growth. The launch of the Nasdaq-style tech board STAR Market is conducive to helping new-economy enterprises develop themselves, and provides a new channel for domestic investors to share the benefits of economic upgrading. Infrastructure investment currently grows fairly slowly as financing condition has tightened. Policy support is expected to strengthen, to meet local governments' reasonable financing needs relating to infrastructure investment. In addition, financing difficulty faced by enterprises has been eased to some extent this year with quickened credit expansion. But structural obstructions in financing channels remain, making more policies to facilitate financing of small businesses necessary.

(Source: Xu Gao, China Can Withstand Economic Headwinds, China Daily, July 16, 2019. Xu Gao is chief economist of BOC International (China) Co Ltd. The analysis above is based on his recent interview with China Securities Journal.)

Questions:

1. What helps China withstand headwinds from global slowdown and other external instabilities?

2. What is fiscal policy and monetary policy?

3. In the long run, how can China achieve healthy economic development?

Case-2

GDP Data Seen As "Reasonable" Despite Pressure

Country still has room to render policy support for economic growth, World Bank official says China's GDP growth slowed to 6.2% year-on-year in the second quarter, its slowest pace in the 27 years since quarterly record keeping began. But analysts said the brisk retail sales growth and stable employment, together with possible support measures to be rolled out in the second half, will help bolster full-year growth. Growth in the April-June period was 0.2 percentage point lower than the first quarter. GDP growth came in at 6.3% in the first half, the National Bureau of Statistics said on Monday. Retail sales rose by a higher-than-expected 9.8% year-on-year in June, the fastest since March 2018, and increased by 8.4% year-on-year in the first half, compared with 8.3% in the first quarter. Industrial output rose by 6.3% year-on-year in June, beating general market expectations, compared with 5% in the previous month, the NBS said. But in the first half, industrial output growth dropped to 6%, down from 6.5 percent in the first quarter. Fixed-asset investment growth was 5.8% in the first six months, compared with 6.3% in the first quarter, the NBS said. Mao Shengyong, a spokesman for the NBS, said that "growth remained on track despite increasing external uncertainties and new downward growth pressure". "The 6.3% growth in the first half is in line with our expectations and our full-year forecast of 6.2% growth," said World Bank Country Director for China Martin Raiser. In fact the data suggest "some stabilization of domestic demand, which is welcome", Raiser added. "The growth rate in the first half is within a reasonable range," said Liang Haiming, dean of the Hainan University Belt and Road Research Institute. "It's not a very poor reading. " Yan Se, an economist at Peking University's Guanghua School of Management, warned that downward pressure remains heavy, and he cited uncertainties arising from the Sino-US trade dispute, significant local government debt weighing on investment and a lackluster property sector. "We think that in the third quarter, growth could continue to dip to about 6.1%," he said. Yan added that the central government will likely further resolve local government debt risks, increase infrastructure investment and resort to monetary expansion to stimulate growth. "Those efforts will help the Chinese economy bottom out in the fourth quarter," he said. Liang expected authorities will lower banks' reserve requirement ratio by 100 basis points in the second half as part of growth-stabilizing measures. "If growth further weakens, interest rate cuts would not be ruled out," said Liang, who is also chairman of the China Silk Road iValley Research Institute. Raiser said that China still has some room to render more policy support if the situation continues to deteriorate, although "at this stage, this seems unwarranted". Apart from short-term fiscal and monetary policy reactions, China needs to carry out structural reforms to boost productivity growth by further reducing distortions such as those in the allocation of land and capital. Promoting competition and opening-up to encourage greater diffusion of technologies, and stimulating discovery through investment in R&D, including basic research, is also necessary, he said.

(Source: Xin Zhiming, GDP Data Seen As "Reasonable" Despite Pressure, China Daily, June 16, 2019.)

Questions:

1. What is GDP? What is the difference between real GDP and nominal GDP?

2. What is fixed-asset investment growth and how does it affect economic growth?

3. At present, which factors affect economic growth is the focus of many countries?

Case-3

Digital Economy can Drive up Domestic Demand

Data shows that Chinese imports declined by 2.5% year-on-year in May. Some interpret the decrease as a sign of a lack of domestic demand, as reflected by the sharp decrease in imports. Also, the prospects of global trade improvement are less certain under the "Trump slump. " If China fails to boost domestic demand, will it be able to keep reaching the 5.5 to 7.5% medium-high growth interval? The answer is yes. But, the further question is what kind of policy should be adopted to achieve this? China should determine which institutional factors and policy mechanism are holding back domestic demand. What short and long-term policies can be introduced to address these problems? China's growth is dependent on industrial and policy paths, reflecting some of the institutional reasons holding back domestic demand. This dependence has increased the cost of economic transformation. The US is a benchmark that China is trying to match in terms of economic development after the introduction of reforms and opening-up. But in China, the investment-driven and export-orientated industrial policy has made the investment cycle outrun the inventory cycle, which is the main cause of economic fluctuation. The US'economic fluctuation, by contrast, is mainly due to the business cycle. China's investment cycle rises and falls together with the domestic producer price index (PPI) and the consumer price index (CPI). Meanwhile, the export-oriented policy links the two indexes to the international market. As long as other markets worldwide can consume the exports manufactured by China, the export-oriented growth model can withstand the US'economic stagnation. But China's inflation can hardly break the economic cycle and the capacity build-up within the country. Once there is an economic downturn or certain products have saturated the market, the overcapacity will start to show. Take the steel industry as an example; the demand for steel in China has outweighed the supply since 2003; and since then, every year, the overcapacity has increased by 5% or higher. With the policy dependence formed in several decades, in order to stimulate the domestic demand, the country should search for a new industrial structure that caters to the demands of Chinese consumers. Without radically changing the industrial structure, stimulation will continue to generate overcapacity. The industries that will get the most monetary and fiscal support will be those that take up more weight in the economy. Policies targeted at firing up domestic demand exacerbate overcapacity, keep creating the assets bubble and bring down overall economic growth.

These are the institutional factors and policy mechanisms that inhibit domestic demand, and supply-side reform is a prescription to addressing this problem. Although supply-side reforms undertaken in the past five years have been beneficial, they have, however, paid more attention to eliminating financial risks, rather than effectively solving the structural problems that occurred during the industry transformation and upgrade. In the past few years, measures, like tightening control on money supply to ward off inflation, pushing through deleveraging without being selective about the type of financial institutes and revoking the licenses of non-banking institutions, have squeezed medium, small and micro-sized enterprises on liquidity. The effects have impacted consumers as well. The policy itself has hindered domestic demand, therefore, a more open and reasonable currency liquidity policy in the next three quarters will be imperative. Traditional industries-real estate and automobile-have run out of their ability to stimulate domestic demand. More support should be given to innovation, research and development in strategic products and processes. Since the 18th century, every technological and industrial revolution has brought fundamental changes to the world development pattern. As artificial intelligence develops with the emergence of robots, the super economy that combines human and superhuman will prevail. The total value of the digitized economy has reached 3.13 billion yuan ($452 million), making up 34.8% of China's GDP last year. The digital economy has become the driving force of domestic demand. After many years of implementing economic transformation, the Chinese economy will have unlimited prospects.

(Source: Cao Heping, Digital Economy can Drive up Domestic Demand, Global Times, June 16, 2019.)

Questions:

1. What is producer price index (PPI) and the consumer price index (CPI)?
2. What are the consequences of the inflation?

4.5　Expanding Reading

Reading-1

China's coordinative development economics powers up economy, global governance

Chinese culture is tenacious enough to grow continuously and prosper due to its core value, coordination. With coordinative measures, China has pushed for progress and the evolution of history. Following the coordinative principle, the country has dealt with many historical issues and built up a foundation for modernization. In the 40 years since China's reform and opening-up began, its economic miracle has amazed the world. Many have tried to decipher the code of China's successful economic development. China's reform and opening-up has given coordinative development economics a solid platform. Some may say China's success in reform and opening-up has benefited from a cheap labor force, hard-working Chinese people and wise government policy, but one thing that should not be ignored is that the economics of coordinative development spawned tremendous creativity. Creativity and innovation have filled the Chinese economy with vitality and helped it succeed by overcoming difficulties.

In the 30 years from 1949 to 1979, with coordinative development economics, China implemented joint state-private ownership and promoted its five-year plans. Those efforts restored China's economy, which was on the brink of collapse, and put it on the right track. The coordinative policy saved China's economy. Each of the four decades of China's reform and opening-up has had its own theme. The first 10 years were right after the Cultural Revolution (1966-1976) and great effort was required to change the old rules and regulations. Coordinative policy refurbished the old mechanism and after the change, China was ready to take off. After the old rules and regulations were changed, it was necessary to remove barriers impeding productivity. China entered into a new phase of reform. A new set of problems, such as a balance between industrial and agricultural development, the interconnected foreign exchange and the yuan, as well as the structure of imports and exports, started to emerge. Policies favoring coordinative development once again served as an anchor to solve problems. The second 10 years had great significance to China's reform. China's role became increasingly important on the international stage. As the first two phases were carried out smoothly, China opened its arms wider to the international market. However, with no experience and a weak economic foundation, China, in the first 20 years of reform and opening-up, was not bold or open enough although it had always had an eye on the global market. Especially since China became a WTO member, a new stage of opening-up has been unlocked. What triggered the opening was the coordination method the country had been sticking with. This development concept worked to unravel issues brought by urbanization and industrial transformation. It also reconciled the conflict between development and environment, state-owned enterprises and private firms. Overall, it assisted China to steer away from an economic hard landing so that it could gradually blend into the international market, production chain and supply chain, and build up its own prestige and honor. During the fourth 10 years, the Chinese economy faced many challenges, including how to better foster innovation, eco-friendly development and sustainable development. While continuously opening-up, China had to give the market more freedom. Some industries and sectors had been opened but still faced market access restrictions. This situation has cooled down the enthusiasm for Chinese companies to go abroad. The Chinese government has implemented a large number of policies to free up the market. Foreign Investment Law and a shortened negative list have attracted more foreign investment. Strategies like launching multiple free trade zones have pumped up the Chinese economy to an unprecedented level. China is the second largest economy in the world and keeps moving forward. Despite the US adopting protectionism and blocking the Chinese technology industry, coordinative development economics has become a powerful weapon of the Chinese economy. China's march toward reform and opening-up will not slow down. This development philosophy not only makes tremendous contributions to China's economic development, but has also been learned by other countries. The Belt and Road Initiative has brought the idea to the world. China's economy bears the mark of coordinative development and has provided a model for economies elsewhere. The miracle of Chinese economic development is fundamentally to coordinate every factor and make each factor function well. In this way, the innate impetus will drive up the country's economy.

Coordinative development has become a term that attracts worldwide attention. China's coordination philosophy has become a key concept for global governance. The economics of coordinative development will definitely provide the world with policy solutions and strength.

(Source: Liu Zhiqin, China's coordinative development economics powers up economy, global governance. Global Times, June 11, 2019.)

Reading-2

More leeway needed for creativity to flourish in China

Editor's Note:

China, long known as the world's factory, has increasingly been referred to as an engine powering global technology sphere. As Jean-Pierre Bourguignon (Bourguignon), president of the European Research Council (ERC), put it, China is already a global science and technology powerhouse.

In an exclusive interview with Global Times reporter Li Qiaoyi (GT) on Monday at the World Economic Forum's Summer Davos in Dalian, Northeast China's Liaoning Province, the French mathematician called for more leeway to enable creativity to flourish in China, and advocated an open attitude toward academic exchanges to shake some suspicions surrounding the academic environment. Bourguignon chairs the organization created by the European Commission in 2007 to fund frontier research.

GT: Is China in the driver's seat when it comes to 5G and artificial intelligence (AI)? Is China already a global science and innovation powerhouse?

Bourguignon: I think it is. We know that for AI, there are several components. Part of it is technology and software. The other part is how you implement it in society. At the moment, the way AI is used is not so visible, but people anticipate it will be increasingly visible through transportation systems and other things. A very important element in AI is the new approach reliant on big data, using past data to anticipate what you should be doing. From that point of view, China's huge population and well-organized systems put it in a good position to develop AI applications. At some point, the nation needs some scientists to be involved for the technology to mature further. 5G will change the approach that people are having with networks, as it will probably alter a number of things which for the moment are difficult, for example, controlling traffic and enabling a smart home makeover.

GT: How innovative are Chinese technology companies?

Bourguignon: I think in China and other countries there are very innovative companies and less innovative ones. Only the most innovative ones will survive and probably gain a significant part of the market. One company I've been following for some years is Huawei, because I visited some of its labs in China and I was very impressed by the quality and diversity of people they have in their labs in terms of their training and exposure to different things. I'm sure some of the leading companies will be Chinese. But there will be non-Chinese companies which is healthy for competition. In my own country, France, some companies are doing very well in terms of innovation, some others are much more traditional. The key point for innovation is to take risks. This depends on the environment. In France, people tend to think they are not taking enough risks and therefore they do good things, but not disruptive things. The key point for the future, I think for many companies, will be to invest enough into disruptive innovation. This is not easy, because you have to take risks. For the first new development, the US did fantastically well in Silicon Valley in the 1990s and at the beginning of this century. For the new wave which is coming, 5G and AI, there would be other places where this would happen. I'm sure some of them will be in China. It's almost inevitable.

GT: Both Yale and MIT presidents have recently posted open letters staking support for academic exchanges amid growing unease in the academic community over unfair suspicion. What do you think of the current academic atmosphere?

Bourguignon: For scientists, it's a fundamental truth that there are no borders. With the new relationship between scientific discoveries and economic development, the question of intellectual property becomes very important. Even if you want to raise borders, it's not going to work, because for scientists, fundamentally knowledge is knowledge; it's not Chinese knowledge, American knowledge or French knowledge. It's totally normal if companies invest in developing new products, and they want rewards. It's the same with countries. The countries invest in research as they feel this will bring about some good things for their people. It could create situations of tension, but it's fundamental that we overcome this tension. I think in the end, nobody would be able to develop things for themselves, ignoring the rest. Having an open attitude toward this is fundamental for a successful future.

GT: What are the areas for future cooperation between China and the EU in the science and technology arena?

Bourguignon: I'm in charge of the European Research Council, which basically has no priorities. We just rely on initiatives and researchers. If you broaden this to Europe, the EU has agreed on investment in some joint projects with China. This is regularly rediscussed, and new priorities appear. Some of these relate to climate change. In the same way, food security is of great importance for both. But the areas would be regularly revised. It's not something which is frozen or decided forever. It's just evolving.

GT: What is still missing in China's drive toward innovation?

Bourguignon: What makes a difference is always people. Efforts are required to train the people, both in terms of knowledge and space for development. For instance, if some students have initiatives to develop new activities, they have to be encouraged and supported and have access to resources. This is maybe a slight change from the spontaneous culture shared by Chinese students. They must have space to develop their own ideas. I think some universities are doing that very well. This is slightly different from the tradition in China highlighting extremely respectful attitudes toward teachers.

GT: What do you think of China's stellar performance at the International Mathematical Olympiad competitions?

Bourguignon: I've repeatedly seen some extremely high-level Chinese students in mathematics. Some of them are even my students. There are some other countries that are doing well in this regard. An example is Iran which has been producing a number of very good mathematicians. The only woman who got the Fields Medal, maths' top prize, is from Iran. I know several other Iranian women with very high level in maths. India has a tradition in mathematics. My discipline is not an obvious one to develop businesses. But some did it and they did it very successfully. This shows young people who can do science might do something else across the market. If they have interest and capacity to do it. It should not be compulsory and people should feel comfortable to do that. China's achievements in mathematical competitions can be attributed to a great tradition in the nation for knowledge, in the present generation as well as previous generations. At the same time Chinese students are extremely hard working which will help them become successful, but we should be careful to make sure students have enough room for creativity. Learning is not just about what the teacher knows; your own ideas should be respected and encouraged. The students sometimes expect too much from their teachers. Sometimes they should really take the lead themselves.

(Source: Global Times, June 3, 2019.)

Reading-3

Countries need to engage in the digital economy and cyberspace through trust, cooperation

As our societies have stepped into the era of the information technological revolution, a few nations that were slow to embrace the revolution and the new political environment are now taking the lead in international relations so that they can avoid being sidelined this time. China is a good example of a nation that has not only made major and historic achievements in political reform but also embraced the industrial revolution, succeeding in a matter of 40 years in catching up with the new economic world order. China has now projected itself well into the future of the fifth industrial revolution. And that is making waves in the West. Having lost their lead, some developed nations are trying desperately to regain the advantage in the new era of internet communications and AI. As we entered the 21st century, China was in a position to bring forward a new balance in the international economic and political order, offering a genuine alternative to support developing nations and south-south cooperation to advance their needs in infrastructure and trade opportunities. The success of the Belt and Road Initiative can be seen as a concrete manifestation of the shift that has happened in the global order; a balanced, equitable diversified one. However, for different reasons including the 2008 financial crisis, most Western nations have found themselves preoccupied with weak economic growth, high unemployment rates, and bankrupt governments. During this time, China was ready to take its rightful place in the world, and instead of pushing inward, its policymakers took the decision to support the global economic order by pushing investment and opening new trade routes and financial packages for developing nations, especially those in Africa, the Middle East and North Africa region, South America, and South Asia. Alerted by the new shift, Western policymakers, and especially some hardliners in the US administration, took notice of China's capabilities and spectacular advancement, especially in the field of fifth-generation network technologies. When facing the risk of losing their economic advantage, or the fear of a new world powered by Chinese innovation, they started using outmoded tactics such as protectionism under the label of national security, imposing tariffs, and coercing allies to take sides. This is dangerous, because if we take, as an example, the ban on Huawei entering the US market and the warnings to other nations about the dangers of using Huawei 5G equipment, it could lead to a unipolar technological drive that would not only limit innovation across the world, but would also create a new gap above the financial, ecological and structural ones that already exist-a technological gap. We are at a crucial point in our societal evolution. Are we leaning toward an era of shared technological infrastructure, integrating existing and future technological innovation into one hub, and free access to networks, in which all stakeholders have a say in the way forward and participate actively in shaping the future? Or will we divide humanity and thus our economic order between network access origins? We understand the security and peace issues that the world faces. Nations need to protect their core interests, and of course their cybersovereign rights. But this is the 21st century; we are past ideological confrontations. Our economies are connected whether we appreciate it or not, and economic leadership is no longer about GDP percentages. The future lies in shared innovation and technological know-how. So when we talk about stopping sharing information if US allies choose a Chinese provider for their network upgrade, this is a message from the last century's security order. We have accomplished so much since World War II, thanks to the US, the Europeans and the Chinese. Our societies have thrived and our economies are better off today. With about 800 million people lifted out of poverty in a matter of 50 years, China has helped to achieve the UN goals of social progress. Security threats are not the issue. China and America and the rest of the world do not need an arch enemy or a new bipolar technological divide. Security today means engagement in the digital economy and cyberspace through trust and maybe new understanding and cooperation within the era that we are in. China is right to question the nature of Huawei's ban, and to strike back-but not as a retaliatory action, but rather to defend the future of technology and knowledge-sharing. Developing nations should appreciate Chinese efforts to ensure that technology is not the cause of the next cold war. Innovation should not be limited to two blocs: the US and Europe. The rest of the world should not just be consumers. They should be part of the innovation process, at a minimum offering local solutions for a global purpose. We hope global policymakers take the Huawei case seriously, and try to find an alternative to confrontation, bans, access limits for markets and opportunities, and dividing the world between technological walls. The truth is that the world needs connectivity and we cannot undo the digital economic integration that is shaping the future.

(Source: Toumert AI, Global Times, June 1, 2019.)

Quick Quiz

1. Economic growth is an increase in the production of goods and services over a specific period, and it represents the expansion of a country's (　　) or national output.

A. potential GNP   B. real GNP

C. potential GDP   D. real GDP

2. What are the main factors affecting economic growth? (   ).

A. Labor   B. Natural resources

C. Capital   D. Technology and innovation

3. (   ) is the best way to measure economic growth.

A. Consumer price index（CPI）

B. Gross domestic product（GDP）

C. Gross national product（GNP）

D. Retail price index（RPI）

4. Demand for a good is income elastic if income elasticity is greater than （   ）.

A. 1   B. 100

C. -1   D. 0

5. The term (   ) was first used during a time of economic stress in the United Kingdom by politician Iain Macleod in the 1960s while he was speaking in the House of Commons. It is a condition of slow economic growth and relatively high unemployment, accompanied by rising prices.

A. inflation   B. deflation

C. stagflation   D. hyperflation

Answers:

1. CD

2. ABCD

3. B

4. A

5. C

Endnotes

［1］China's economy: Taking stock of 2018, Chinadaily. com. cn, 2019.

［2］Chen Meiling. Accelerating local startups' expansion across the world, China Daily, June 24, 2019.

［3］Huawei to hold biggest-ever developer conference", Chinadaily. com. cn, June 9, 2019.

［4］Diana Farrell, The Global Future Council on Economic Progress, The Global Competitiveness Report 2017-2018.

［5］China's Market Is Fundamentally Different, Harvard Business Review,

May-June 2019.

［6］ Wang Zhuoqiong. Luckin eyes tea market, expansion, Chinadaily. com. cn, July 8, 2019.

［7］ Zhang Jie. Household wealth to surge in next decade: Report, Chinadaily. com. cn, July 9, 2019.

［8］ Liu Zhihua. Smart tech transforming medical sector, China Daily, July 9, 2019.

［9］ China's economy: Taking stock of 2018, Chinadaily. com. cn, 2019.

［10］ Bon Kristoffer G. Gabnay, Roberto M Remotin, Jr., Edgar Allan M. Uy, editors. Economics: Its Concepts & Principles, Rex Book Store: Manila, 2007.

［11］ William M. Pride, Robert J. Hughes and Jack R. Kapoo. Business (12th Edition), South-Western College Pub, 2010.

［12］ Thomas Pogge. World Poverty and Human Rights, Ethics of International Affairs, 2005: 19 (1).

［13］ Shaohua Chen and Martin Ravallion. How Have the World's PoorestFared since the Early 1980s? World Bank Research Observer, 2004: 19 (2).

Chapter 5　Society Environment

Learning Objectives

1. Understand ten key findings of World Population Prospects.
2. Master the background of the ageing workforce.
3. Master the relationship of culture and business.
4. Master the definition of values.
5. Understand the four major market segments in electronic commerce.
6. Recognize the types of social structures and class.

Opening case

E-commerce giant strikes gold in cultural creative industries

Do you remember the innovative and irresistible starry lollipops, a hit snack that swept China's social media during the past Qixi festival (aka Chinese Valentine's Day)? The credit for this business miracle goes to Tmall. Backed by Chinese ecommerce behemoth Alibaba, Tmall boasts 500 million monthly active users as of Feb 2018, making it the world's second-largest e-commerce website after Taobao, which it spun off from in 2008. Thanks to the facilitation of the Tmall Neo-Culture Creativity Plan 1. 0 launched in January, Crafted, a hand-made sugar brand, has partnered with China's Lunar Exploration Project in a bid to woo more customers. The day the starry lollipop was launched on Tmall, more than 100,000 boxes were sold. Another crossover money spinner generated by this plan is the spring tea branded "The Four Scholars". Inspired by the Ming Dynasty (1368 ~ 1644) household legends of the four scholars headed by Tang Yin, Tmall teamed up with the Suzhou Museum in East China's Jiangsu province and eight tea brands to orchestrate a marketing campaign, "Modern Spring Outing of the Four Scholars". The campaign bore sweet fruit. Statistics show the sales of major spring teas increased by about 60% year-on-year on Tmall, and the eight participating tea brands also saw a nearly 100% rise in the number of their new patrons. "2019 has witnessed the huge momentum of the collaborations between museums and private companies," said Jia Luo, general manager of Tmall's operation center. Recently, the e-commerce giant added more fuel to this momentum by launching the Tmall Neo-Culture Creativity Plan 2.0 on Aug 15. According to the plan, in the coming three years, it will facilitate the world's prestigious museums, such as Russia's Winter Palace, to join hands with nearly 10,000 brands that are currently available. They'll be working together to make crossover products such as clothes, accessories, and kitchenware that feature collection highlights housed in each of the world's museums. The drive behind the e-commerce giant's ambitious move can be largely explained by the boom in China's online museum-related merchandise market, which has been growing at a jaw-dropping rate. So far a total of 24 museums, including the Palace Museum and the British Museum, have opened their flagship stores on Tmall and Taobao. The sales of museum goods nearly tripled in the first half of 2019 from the same period last year, according to a report jointly released by Tmall and the Institute of Cultural Economy of Tsinghua University on Aug 15. The report also revealed that last year, over 1.6 billion people in China patronized museums' Tmall flagship stores, 50% more than those who visited the museums across the country. Plus, among all of museums' online store patrons, 100 million of them were born in the 1990s. Above all, the report found that the younger generation has grown tired of those vanilla products, like notebooks and refrigerator magnets, sold on museums' online flagship stores. Instead, they are always willing to foot the bill for novel and creative crossover products, the sales of which account for as much as 72% of the entire sales of the cultural and creative products in China. Guided by the Tmall Neo-Culture Creativity Plan 2.0, Tmall looks to build a bridge between consumers, museums, and brands, adding fuel to the development of China's cultural and creative industry, as well as instilling life into Chinese traditional culture, Luo added. Neo-Culture Creativity, a concept first put forward by Chinese internet titan Tencent in April 2018, is about mutually promoting the cultural and industrial value of content through a centralized connection of channels to achieve higher efficiency for the creation of digital culture and the development of intellectual property.

(Source: Yang Xiaoyu, E-commerce giant strikes gold in cultural creative industries, chinadaily; September 3, 2019.)

5. 1   Demographic Factor

5. 1. 1   Population Structure

Population structure is a component of the environment for the members of the population and provides information that affects individual physiology and behavior. Whereas population structure can be measured by sampling the population, estimates of natality, mortality, and dispersal require measurement of changes through time in overall rates of birth, death, and movement. For example, latest figures suggest that China's population is set to peak at 1. 442 billion in 2029, beginning a steady decline in the following years. The Green Book of Population and Labor released by the China Academy of Social Sciences on January 3, 2019 estimates that by the middle of the century, the population would drop to 1. 36 billion, which could mean a 200 million decrease in the labor force. If fertility rates remain unchanged, the population could drop to 1. 17 billion by 2065. The stagnating working population as well as the rapidly rising number of elderly people could lead to very unfavorable social and economic outcomes, says the report. Nonetheless, the negative population growth will not necessarily have an adverse impact on the country. The aging of population is an inevitable global trend marking social and economic development. With advances in healthcare, social security and gender equality in China, it is normal to see the population and labor force gradually decline after reaching a peak. A large population has indeed provided abundant human resources. But looking at China's four decades of reform and opening-up, the dramatic change has definitely not been driven solely by the huge population, but has come about more as a result of reforms and improvements in economic and social systems as well as education and technology. Other than fears of domestic consequences, there are concerns about China's competitive power in the world. The World Population Prospects released by the United Nations in 2017 indicates that India will surpass China in 2024 and become the world's most populous country. Some believe that China's advantage of more hands to work may by then disappear. These concerns are as well superfluous. With worldwide educational and technical progress, will a vast labor force poll still be needed in India and the global market? Moreover, China can still hold on to its favorable position backed by the continuous optimization of the quality of workforce, the improvement of policies, and the ramping up of technological advantages. Therefore, the thinking that economic development relies simply on labor growth must be got rid of. Decline in the size of labor requires attention, but is not something one should panic about. To cope with the shrinking labor force and aging population, the country should be prepared. First, changes in China's population structure must be watched to avoid large fluctuations in a short period of time. Second, concrete measures should be taken to fill the human capital gap caused by the dwindling workforce. The country must further develop education to improve the quality of labor, and increase investment in science and technology such as artificial intelligence to replace manpower to an extent. Third, increasing fertility is urgent. With the development of society, there does seem to be an ineluctable tendency to have fewer children or stay childless.

A relaxed family planning policy is one solution, although it can have limited effect. According to data from the National Statistics Bureau, the size of newborn population in the country in 2017 decreased by more than 630,000 compared with the previous year in which the two-child policy was officially implemented, with more than half the total births attributed to the second child. The family planning policy requires coordination with specific and comprehensive social services. For instance, the country needs to narrow the gap in the distribution of educational resources and improve maternal and child health facilities. Only by focusing on these services can people's worries be alleviated and they can help increase fertility rates.

Population affects an organisation's supply of labour and hence its policies towards recruiting and managing human resources. According to the United Nations' data, within little more than a decade there are likely to be around 8.5 billion people on earth, and almost 10 billion by 2050, compared to 7.7 billion in 2019. A small number of countries will account for most of the increase. While some countries continue to grow rapidly, others are seeing their populations decline. At the same time, the world is growing older, as global life expectancy continues to rise and the fertility level continues to fall. Such changes in the size and distribution of the world's population have important consequences for achieving the Sustainable Development Goals and ensuring that no one is left behind. From the UN "World Population Prospects 2019: Highlights", there are ten key findings:

（1）The world's population continues to increase, but growth rates vary greatly across regions. The world's population is projected to grow from 7.7 billion in 2019 to 8.5 billion in 2030 （10% increase）, and further to 9.7 billion in 2050 （26%） and to 10.9 billion in 2100 （42%）. The population of sub-Saharan Africa is projected to double by 2050 （99%）. Other regions will see varying rates of increase between 2019 and 2050: Oceania excluding Australia/New Zealand (56%) , Northern Africa and Western Asia (46%) , Australia/New Zealand (28%) , Central and Southern Asia (25%) , Latin America and the Caribbean (18%) , Eastern and South-Eastern Asia (3%) , and Europe and Northern America (2%) .

(2) Nine countries will make up more than half the projected population growth between now and 2050. The largest increases in population between 2019 and 2050 will take place in: India, Nigeria, Pakistan, the Democratic Republic of the Congo, Ethiopia, the United Republic of Tanzania, Indonesia, Egypt and the United States of America (in descending order of the expected increase) . Around 2027, India is projected to overtake China as the world's most populous country.

(3) Rapid population growth presents challenges for sustainable development. Many of the fastest growing populations are in the poorest countries, where population growth brings additional challenges in the effort to eradicate poverty, achieve greater equality, combat hunger and malnutrition, and strengthen the coverage and quality of health and education systems.

(4) In some countries, growth of the working-age population is creating opportunities for economic growth. In most of sub-Saharan Africa, and in parts of Asia, Latin America and the Caribbean, recent reductions infertility have caused the population at working ages (25 ~ 64 years) to grow faster than at other ages, creating an opportunity for accelerated economic growth. To benefit from this "demographic dividend", governments should invest in education and health, especially for young people, and create conditions conducive to sustained economic growth.

(5) Globally, women are having fewer babies, but fertility rates remain high in some parts of the world. Today, close to half of all people globally live in a country or area where fertility is below 2. 1 births per woman over a lifetime. In 2019, fertility remains above this level, on average, in sub-Saharan Africa (4. 6) , Oceania excluding Australia/New Zealand (3. 4) , Northern Africa and Western Asia (2. 9) , and Central and Southern Asia (2. 4) . The global fertility rate, which fell from 3. 2 births per woman in 1990 to 2. 5 in 2019, is projected to decline further to 2. 2 in 2050.

(6) People are living longer, but those in the poorest countries still live 7 years less than the global average. Life expectancy at birth for the world, which increased from 64. 2 years in 1990 to 72. 6 years in 2019, is expected to increase further to 77. 1 years in 2050. While considerable progress has been made in closing the longevity differential between countries, large gaps remain. In 2019, life expectancy at birth in the least developed countries lags 7. 4 years behind the global average, due largely to persistently high child and maternal mortality, as well as violence, conflict and the continuing impact of the HIV epidemic.

（7）The world's population is growing older, with persons over age 65 being the fastest-growing age group. By 2050, one in six people in the world will be over age 65 （16%）, up from one in 11 in 2019 （9%）. Regions where the share of the population aged 65 years or over is projected to double between 2019 and 2050 include Northern Africa and Western Asia, Central and Southern Asia, Eastern and South-Eastern Asia, and Latin America and the Caribbean. By 2050, one in four persons living in Europe and Northern America could be aged 65 or over. In 2018, for the first time in history, persons aged 65 or above outnumbered children under five years of age. The number of persons aged 80 years or over is projected to triple, from 143 million in 2019 to 426 million in 2050.

（8）Falling proportions of working-age people are putting pressure on social protection systems. The potential support ratio, which compares numbers of working-age people aged $25 \sim 64$ to those over age 65, is falling around the world. In Japan, this ratio is 1. 8, the lowest in the world. An additional 29 countries, mostly in Europe and the Caribbean, already have potential support ratios below three. By 2050, 48 countries, mostly in Europe, Northern America, and Eastern and South-Eastern Asia, are expected to have potential support ratios below two. These low values underscore the potential impact of population ageing on the labour market and economic performance as well as the fiscal pressures that many countries will face in the coming decades as they seek to build and maintain public systems of health care, pensions and social protection for older persons.

（9）A growing number of countries are experiencing a reduction in population size. Since 2010, 27 countries or areas have experienced a reduction in the size of their populations of one percent or more. This is caused by low levels of fertility and, in some places, high rates of emigration. Between 2019 and 2050, populations are projected to decrease by one percent or more in 55 countries or areas, of which 26 may see a reduction of at least ten percent. In China, for example, the population is projected to decrease by 31. 4 million, or 2. 2%, between 2019 and 2050.

（10）Migration has become a major component of population change in some countries. Between 2010 and 2020, Europe and Northern America, Northern Africa and Western Asia, and Australia/New Zealand will be net receivers of international migrants, while other regions will be net senders. Fourteen countries or areas will see a net inflow of more than one million migrants, while ten countries will see a net outflow of more than one million migrants. Some of the largest migratory movements are driven by the demand for migrant workers (Bangladesh, Nepal and the Philippines) or by violence, insecurity and armed conflict (Syria, Venezuela and Myanmar) . Belarus, Estonia, Germany, Hungary, Italy, Japan, the Russian Federation, Serbia and Ukraine will experience a net inflow of migrants over the decade, helping to offset population losses caused by an excess of deaths over births.

5. 1. 2   Population and the labour market

There is a close relationship between population and labor market. In this part, we will talk about the impact of youth, woman, and ageing population on labour market.

1. Youth population and labour market

Increasing birth rates mean more young people, growing populations offer a larger labour market. The number and quality of young people has an important impact on the workforce. Fewer young people might mean that young people become more expensive. According to the United Nations department of economic and social affairs population division's report, we can find some youth population facts.

(1) Social sustainable development needs high-quality youth population.

From the data, there were 1. 2 billion youth aged 15 ~ 24 years globally in 2015, accounting for one out of every six people world wide. By 2030, the target date for the sustainable development goals, the number of youth is projected to have grown by 7%, to nearly 1. 3 billion. Youth can be a positive force for development when provided with the knowledge and opportunities they need to thrive. In particular, young people should acquire the education and skills needed to contribute in a productive economy, and they need access to a job market that can absorb them into its labour force. Among the greatest challenges facing many countries today are inadequate human capital investment and high unemployment rates among youth. Some countries are struggling currently to educate and employ their young people, while also anticipating substantial growth in the number of youth. These countries will be doubly challenged in their efforts to assure universal high-quality education, productive employment and decent work for all. So the challenges of sustainable development for all countries are educating and employing their youth.

（2）In the future, almost all countries face a decline in the number of young people but Africa.

The size of the youth population has peaked in all regions but Africa. In Latin America and the Caribbean, Europe, Northern America and Oceania, youth populations have stabilized in size and are projected to change little over the coming decades. By contrast, Asia and Africa are in the midst of substantial changes in the size of their youth populations. After rapid and sustained growth through the latter half of the twentieth century, the number of young people aged 15 ~ 24 years in Asia is projected to decline from 718 million in 2015 to 711 million in 2030 and 619 million in 2060. Still, Asia will be home to more youth than any other region until around 2080, when it could be surpassed by Africa according to United Nations projections. In Africa, the number of youth is growing rapidly. In 2015, 226 million youth aged 15 ~ 24 years lived in Africa, accounting for 19% of the global youth population. By 2030, it is projected that the number of youth in Africa will have increased by 42%. Africa's youth population is expected to continue to grow throughout the remainder of the twenty-first century, more than doubling from current levels by 2055.

（3）Many countries with rapidly growing youth populations are struggling already to educate their young people.

The education systems of many countries are leaving behind a substantial proportion of the population. According to the most recent data available, in 32 countries, fewer than 80% of 15 ~ 24 year-olds are literate. Of these 32 countries, 18 countries are projected to see amore than 40% increase in the number of youth between 2015 and 2030. In six of these low-literacy countries, all in sub-Saharan Africa, the growth of the youth population in this period is projected to exceed 60%. In Niger, for example, where just 24% of youth were literate in 2014, the youth population is projected to growby 92% within the next 15 years. Angola, Burkina Faso, Chad, Mali, Nigeria, the United Republic of Tanzania and Zambia, among others, are also anticipating rapid growth of the population aged 15 ~ 24 years in a context of low youth literacy rates. Inadequate investment in the health and education of young people limits their ability to reach their full productive potential and to contribute to economic development. Rapid growth in the number of youth further compounds that challenge, requiring countries to improve the quality and reach of their education systems not only to make up for existing deficiencies, but also to serve the rapidly growing number of young people. By contrast, many countries that have experienced fertility reductions in recent decades now have an opportunity to improve the education available to their young people without needing simultaneously to serve a rapidly growing population of youth. In Pakistan, for example, where 71% of the population aged 15 ~ 24 years was literate in 2011, the number of youth is projected grow by only 5% between 2015 and 2030. Similarly, in Haiti, with a youth literacy rate of 72% in 2006, the youth population is projected to increase by 7% over the next 15 years. In some parts of the world, girls and young women do not have the same access to education and training as their male peers, depriving them of their rights and the ability to make decisions about their lives, including the pursuit of higher education and formal employment. Empowering women and girls and ensuring equitable investments in their human capital are essential for sustainable development.

(4) Some countries anticipating rapid growth in numbers of youth are among those with very high youth unemployment rates.

In Jordan, Iraq and Saudi Arabia, for example, youth unemployment rates are very high, above 30%, and the youth populations are expected to grow by more than 20% over the coming 15 years. By contrast, a number of countries, such as South Africa, Spain and Greece, face extremely high youth unemployment, with rates above 50%, but are projected to see a slower growth of the youth population, with increases around 10 percent or less between 2015 and 2030. Even in countries where youth unemployment rates are comparatively low, rapid growth in the number of youth over the coming years could challenge sustainable development, if labour markets are unable to absorb rapidly increasing numbers of young workers. In Mali, for example, a large fraction of the labour force is still engaged in subsistence agriculture. Even though the youth unemployment rate in 2015, at just under 11%, is substantially lower than in many other countries, the number of youth aged 15 ~24 years in 2030 is projected to be 70% larger than in 2015. Thus, Mali's economy will need to grow to accommodate a substantially larger number of youth seeking to enter the labour force. Similarly, Nigeria and Zambia, with youth unemployment rates of 14% and 24% respectively in 2015, are projected to see their youth populations grow by 60% over the next 15 years. If youth are provided with sufficient education, training and jobs, then the growth in their numbers could be highly beneficial for development. If instead they are unemployed or underemployed in subsistence agriculture, the growing number of youth will pose a challenge to the achievement of sustainable development, and could prove socially or politically destabilizing as well. Moreover, current unemployment among youth impedes social and economic development not just for today but also for the future, since youth who experience a delayed start in the labour force tend to continue to lag behind in terms of earnings and income growth once they become employed. Several countries with comparatively low youth unemployment rates are projected to see declines in the number of youth in the coming 15 years. In Thailand, for example, youth unemployment is projected to be just 3% in 2015 and the population aged 15 ~ 24 years is expected to shrink by 22% by 2030. Cuba, Japan and Viet Nam are also projected to see declines in the number of youth in a context of low youth unemployment. These economies must prepare for an ageing labour force in the coming decades.

（5）Youth education and employment are essential to harnessing the opportunities for economic growth associated with the demographic dividend. When a population experiences a sustained decline infertility rates, the share of the population composed of children declines while the share in the working ages grows larger. Demographers and economists have heralded the window of opportunity presented by this "demographic dividend", where in the relative abundance of working-age people can lead to increased savings, higher productivity and more rapid economic growth. However, the ability of countries to harness the demographic dividend depends critically on their investments in human capital, particularly amongst young people poised to enter the labour force, whose productivity, entrepreneurship and innovation will drive future economic growth. If human capital investment falls short or if the labour market is unable to absorb new workers, the opportunity of this demographic dividend may be squandered. The importance of investment in youth for a full realization of the demographic dividend is evident in a comparison of recent trends in population age structure, youth employment and gross domestic product（GDP）per capitain Tunisia and the Republic of South Korea. Both countries are experiencing historic highs in the proportion of the population in the working ages, owing to fertility declines that took place over the latter half of the twentieth century. The share of persons aged 15 ~ 64 years rose from just over 50% the late 1960s to around 70% in 2015 in both countries. The two countries differ markedly, however, with respect to youth employment. In Tunisia, the proportion unemployed amongst persons aged 15 ~ 24 years has hovered around 30% or more since the early 1990s, whereas in the Republic of South Korea only around 10% of youth were unemployed over the same period. Trends in economic growth have likewise differed markedly since the early 1980s: in Tunisia, per capita GDP tripled between 1980 and 2010, whereas for the Republic of South Korea it increased by a factor of 12. Although a host of factors help to determine the pace of economic growth for a given country, the lack of employment opportunities for large fractions of youth in Tunisia and elsewhere has limited the economic potential offered by the favourable population age structure associated with the demographic dividend.

2. Aging population and labour market

Persons aged 65 or over make up the world's fastest-growing age group. Virtually all countries are anticipating an increase in the percentage of older persons in their populations.

（1） Aging changes the socio-economic structure. Population ageing—the increasing share of older persons in the population—is poised to become one of the most significant social transformations of the twenty-first century, with implications for nearly all sectors of society, including labour and financial markets, the demand for goods and services, such as housing, transportation and social protection, as well as family structures and inter-generational ties.

（2） The present situation and future development trend of aging. United Nations Department of Economic and Social Affairs Population Division analyzed the data. In 2018, for the first time in history, persons aged 65 years or over worldwide out numbered children under age five. Between 2019 and 2050, the number of persons aged 65 or over globally is projected to more than double, while the number of children under five is projected to remain relatively unchanged. Consequently, the projections indicate that in 2050 there will be more than twice as many older persons as children under five. Moreover, it is expected that in 2050 the 1. 5 billion people aged 65 years or over worldwide will outnumber adolescents and youth aged 15 to 24 years （1. 3 billion）. Whereas the overall numbers of males and females globally are about equal, women outnumber menat older ages owing to their longer average life expectancy. According to the medium-variant projection virtually all countries and areas are experiencing population ageing. In 2019, women comprise 55 percent of those aged 65 years or over and 61% of those aged 80 years or over globally.

All 201 countries or areas with at least 90, 000inhabitants in 2019 are projected to see an increase in the proportion of persons aged 65 or over between 2019 and 2050. At the global level in 2019, approximately nine per cent of people are aged 65 or over （see table 5-1）. The proportion of older persons in the world is projected to reach nearly 12% in 2030, 16% in 2050 and it could reach nearly 23% by 2100. Europe and Northern America have the most aged population in 2019, with 18% aged 65 or over, followed by Australia／New Zealand （16%）. Both regions are continuing to age further. Projections indicate that by 2050 one in every four persons in Europe and Northern America could be aged 65 years or over. According to the medium-variant projection, the data can be seen in the Table 5-1.

Table 5-1   **Percentage of population aged 65 years or over for the world, SDG regions and selected groups of countries, 2019, 2030, 2050 and 2100**

Region	2019	2030	2050	2100
World	9.1	11.7	15.9	22.6
Sub-Saharan Africa	3.0	3.3	4.8	13.0
Northern Africa and Western Asia	5.7	7.6	12.7	22.4
Central and Southern Asia	6.0	8.0	13.1	25.7
Eastern and South-Eastern Asia	11.2	15.8	23.7	30.4
Latin America and the Caribbean	8.7	12.0	19.0	31.3
Australia/New Zealand	15.9	19.5	22.9	28.6
Oceania*	4.2	5.3	7.7	15.4
Europe and Northern America	18.0	22.1	26.1	29.3
Least developed countries	3.6	4.2	6.4	15.3
Land-locked Developing Countries (LLDC)	3.7	4.5	6.4	16.8
Small Island Developing States (SIDS)	8.7	11.9	16.1	23.7

Source: United Nations, Department of Economic and Social Affairs, Population Division (2019). World Population Prospects 2019.

* excluding Australia and New Zealand.

The designations employed and the presentation of material on this map do not imply the expression of any opinion whatsoever on the part of the Secretariat of the United Nations concerning the legal status of any country, territory, city or area or of its authorities, or concerning the delimitation of its frontiers or boundaries. Dotted line represents approximately the Line of Control in Jammu and Kashmir agreed upon by India and Pakistan. The final status of Jammu and Kashmir has not yet been agreed upon by the parties. Final boundary between the Republic of Sudan the Republic of South Sudan has not yet been determined. A dispute exists between the Governments of Argentina and the United Kingdom of Great Britain and Northern Ireland concerning sovereignty over the Falkland Islands (Malvinas).

Populations in other regions are also projected to age significantly over the next several decades. For Latin America and the Caribbean, the share of the population aged 65 years or over could increase from 9% in 2019 to 19% in 2050. Similarly, the proportion aged 65 or over in Eastern and South-Eastern Asia is expected to increase from 11% in 2019 to 24% in 2050. Sub-Saharan Africa, which has the youngest age distribution of the eight SDG regions, is also projected to experience population ageing over the coming decades, but to a much lesser extent, with the percentage of the population aged 65 or over rising from three percent in 2019 to around five percent in 2050. The number of people above age 80 years is growing even faster than the number above age 65. In 1990 there were just 54 million people aged 80 or over in the world, a number that nearly tripled to 143 million in 2019. Globally, the number of persons aged 80 or over is projected to nearly triple again to 426 million in 2050 and to increase further to 881 million in 2100. In 2019, 38% of all persons aged 80 or over reside in Europe and Northern America, a share that is expected to decline to 26% in 2050 and to 17% in 2100 as the older populations of other regions continue to increase in size. Population ageing will have a profound effect on the potential support ratio, defined here as the number of people of working age (25 to 64 years) per person aged 65 years or over. In 2019, sub-Saharan Africa has 11. 7 persons aged 25 to 64 for each person aged 65 or over. This ratio is 10. 2 for Oceania*, 8. 3 for Northern Africa and Western Asia, 8. 0 for Central and Southern Asia, 5. 8 for Latin America and the Caribbean, 5. 0 for Eastern and South-Eastern Asia, 3. 3 for Australia and New Zealand, and 3. 0 for Europe and Northern America. At 1. 8, Japan in 2019 has the lowest potential support ratio of all countries or areas with at least 90, 000 inhabitants. An additional 29 other countries or areas, mostly in Europe and the Caribbean, have potential support ratios below three. By 2050, 48 countries, mostly in Europe, Northern America, Eastern Asia or South-Eastern Asia, are expected to have potential support ratios below two. These low values under score the potential impact of population ageing on the labour market and economic performance as well as the fiscal pressures that many countries are likely to face in the coming decades in relation to public systems of health care, pensions and social protection schemes for older persons. Trends in population size and age structure are shaped mostly by levels of fertility and mortality, which have declined almost universally around the globe. In some countries, international migration also has become an important determinant of population change. According to the medium-variant projection, the figure 5-1 give the details of persons aged 65 years or over make up the fastest-growing age group.

Globally, the rapid ageing of populations has profound implications for employers, the labour market and society as a whole. Both the Madrid International Plan of Action on Ageing, 2002, and the World Health Organization have endorsed goals for "active ageing", which includes the full participation and better social integration into society of older persons as citizens with full rights, as well as health, security and dignity as people age. The participation and integration of older persons also implies the removal of barriers that exclude or discriminate against them.

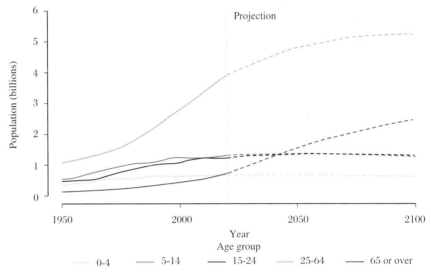

Figure 5-1   Estimated and projected global population by broad age group（1950～2100）

Source：United Nations, Department of Economic and Social Affairs, Population Division（2019）. World Population Prospects 2019.

（3）Intelligent use the aging workforce. Based on the data above, for the most countries, workforce is likely to contain a higher proportion of older workers. In some development countries, the situation is particularly significant, mainly in Europe, North America and Japan. Because of factors such as increased life expectancy, removal of the default retirement age and raising of the State Pension Age, which means that many people will need, and want to continue working. In order to make better use of these "silver" human resources, employers have the same responsibilities for the health and safety of older employees as they have for all their employees. So the Health and Safety Executive of US published some rules for the employers and employees, and enacted laws. These guidance maybe the model for other countries.

①For employers. Older workers bring a broad range of skills and experience to the workplace and often have better judgement and job knowledge, so looking after their health and safety makes good business sense.

Review the risk assessment for old workers if anything significant changes, not just when an employee reaches a certain age. Not assume that certain jobs are physically too demanding for older workers, many jobs are supported by technology, which can absorb the physical strain.

Think about the activities older workers do, as part of your overall risk assessment and consider whether any changes are needed. This might include: allowing older workers more time to absorb health and safety information or training, for example by introducing self-paced training; introducing opportunities for older workers to choose to move to other types of work; designing tasks that contain an element of manual handling in such a way that they eliminate or minimise the risk. Think about how your business operates and how older workers could play a part in helping to improve how you manage health and safety risks. This might include having older workers working alongside colleagues in a structured programme, to capture knowledge and learn from their experience. Avoid assumptions by consulting and involving older workers when considering relevant control measures to put in place. Extra thought may be needed for some hazards. Consultation with your employees helps you to manage health and safety in a practical way.

②For old workers. As an employee, you have a duty to take care of your own health and safety, and that of others who may be affected by your actions. You must cooperate with your employer and other employees to help everyone meet their legal requirements. If you have specific queries or concerns about your health and safety or if you are experiencing difficulty in carrying out your work, you should raise this with your employer.

③The law and regulation of US. Under health and safety law, employers must ensure, so far as is reasonably practicable, the health and safety of all their employees, irrespective of age. Employers must also provide adequate information, instruction, training and supervision to enable their employees to carry out their work safely.

(a) Management of Health and Safety at Work Regulations 1999 (MHSWR). Under the Management of Health and Safety at Work Regulations 1999, employers have a duty to make a suitable and sufficient assessment of the workplace risks to the health and safety of his employees. This includes identifying groups of workers who might be particularly at risk, which could include older workers.

(b) Equality Law. Discrimination in respect of age is different from all other forms of direct discrimination in that it can be justifiable if it is a proportionate means of achieving a legitimate end, such as considering changes to work that may be needed to ensure older workers can remain in the workforce.

3. Female and labour market

With the progress of society and the development of economy, more and more women are participating in social production and business activities. According to the data of Global Times, the female labor participation rate (FLPR) in China has surpassed higher-income countries such as the US, Japan and France. According to statistics on the labor force market by the World Bank in 2017, the FLPR in China has reached 61.5%, higher than 55.74% in the US, 50.5% in Japan and 50.56% in France.

(1) Women are under more pressure in the workplace. Take Chinese female labour as example, World Bank survey shows more than 60% of the respondents from China's urban women in the workplace are "moderately satisfied" and "very satisfied" with their current job. However, 50% of the respondents said they are disturbed by sleeping problems, and the survey shows that sleeping problems has become the top health issue among women in the workplace for all ages ranging from 20 to 60. Compared to men and women in the workplace face more health issue, work stress, excessive sitting, irregular sleeping hours, excessive screen time and life pressure.

(2) Compared to male, female workers face greater inequality. In developing country, especially China, marriage and raising children are the main reasons for the unfair treatment of women in the job market. From China Daily's survey, female employees called for equal opportunities in the job market as surveys by recruitment firms showed bias against married women or those with children has led to stagnation in their pay and chances for promotion. Women have taken on more responsibility, including family and work. A report by Zhaopin, an online recruitment platform based in Beijing, shows the average salary of Chinese women was 23% lower than men's last year, with the income disparity seeing a 1% increase in 2018 compared with 2017. Also, women have fewer opportunities for promotion than men. The report said that among the companies surveyed, women occupied an average of only 18.7 percent of board seats while men occupied 81.3%.

Another report focusing on the situation of Chinese women in the workforce by LinkedIn, an employment-oriented website based in Sunnyvale, California, shows that one-third of the surveyed Chinese women registered with the site changed jobs or chose to freelance after having a baby, and 46% said they either turned down job offers or failed to get a job because of pregnancy.

(3) More and more national laws and regulations published to protect female

workers. Equal participation in economic activities and equitable access to economic resources are the basic conditions for the well-being and development of women. While pressing forward with a strategic adjustment of its economic structure and reform and innovation of its growth model, China fully protects the economic interests of women, promoting women's equal participation in economic development and equal access to the fruits of reform and development. The Ministry of Human Resources and Social Security and the Ministry of Education as well as other departments have recently released a notice prohibiting any discrimination against women in the workplace. Companies are not allowed to require any marriage or pregnancy-related information when interviewing female job-seekers.

5. 2　Culture and Values

5. 2. 1　Culture

1.　What is culture?

The meaning of culture is very broad, and scholars have never been able to agree on a simple definition of culture. We can use the definition from the Merriam-Webster dictionary, Culture means the set of shared attitudes, values, goals, and practices that characterizes an institution or organization, also the characteristic features of everyday existence (such as diversions or a way of life) shared by people in a place or time.

From the perspective of management, Harvard Business Review (January-February, 2018) presents, culture is the tacit social order of an organization. It shapes attitudes and behaviors in wide-ranging and durable ways. Cultural normally define what is encouraged, discouraged, accepted, or rejected within a group. When properly aligned with personal values, drives, and needs, culture can unleash tremendous amounts of energy toward a shared purpose and foster an organization's capacity to thrive. Cultural changes have a significant impact on business management, especially transnational operation. For the successful transnational corporation, strategy is typically determined by the C-suite, culture can fluidly blend the intentions of top leaders with the knowledge and experiences of frontline employees.

At same time, culture can evolve flexibly and autonomously in response to changing opportunities and demands. The academic literature on the subject is vast. Our review of it revealed many formal definitions of organizational culture and avariety of models and methods for assessing it. Agreement on specifics is sparse across these definitions, models, and methods, but through a synthesis of seminal work by Edgar Schein, Shalom Schwartz, Geert Hofstede, and other leading scholars, we have identified four generally accepted attributes:

(1) Shared. Culture is a group phenomenon. It cannot exist solely within a single person, nor is it simply the average of individual characteristics. It resides in shared behaviors, values, and assumptions and is most commonly experienced through the norms and expectations of a group—that is, the unwritten rules.

(2) Pervasive. Culture permeates multiple levels and applies very broadly in an organization; sometimes it is even conflated with the organization itself. It is manifest in collective behaviors, physical environments, group rituals, visible symbols, stories, and legends. Other aspects of culture are unseen, such as mindsets, motivations, unspoken assumptions, and what David Rooke and William Torbert refer to as "action logics" (mental models of how to interpret and respond to the world around you).

(3) Enduring. Culture can direct the thoughts and actions of group members over the long term. It develops through critical events in the collective life and learning of a group. Its endurance is explained in part by the attraction-selection-attrition model first introduced by Benjamin Schneider: People are drawn to organizations with characteristics similar to their own; organizations are more likely to select individuals who seem to "fit in"; and over time those who don't fit in tend to leave. Thus culture becomes a self-reinforcing social pattern that grows increasingly resistant to change and outside influences.

(4) Implicit. An important and often overlooked aspect of culture is that despite its subliminal nature, people are effectively hard wired to recognize and respond to it instinctively. It acts as a kind of silent language. Shalom Schwartz and E. O. Wilson have shown through their research how evolutionary processes shaped human capacity; because the ability to sense and respond to culture is universal, certain themes should be expected to recur across the many models, definitions, and studies in the field. That is exactly what we have discovered in our research over the past few decades. For example: impact of culture on health and diet issues, life style, environmentalism and so on.

2. Culture and Business (Trade)

When companies do cross-border business, they will meet the collision of business and culture.

Chinese story with universal appeal

The trailer for Mulan, a Disney movie based on its previous animation about the ancient Chinese legend, has been released and Chinese viewers have been quick to criticize it. China Daily writer Zhang Zhouxiang comments: There are two main points that Chinese audiences are unhappy with. First, in the trailer there are shots of Fujian, which is about 3,000 kilometers away from historical home of Mulan in history. Second, the heroine Mulan, starring Crystal Liu, wears heavy makeup that is appealing to Westerners' eyes, not Chinese eyes. Perhaps the criticism is unfair as Disney has designed the movie to please Western audiences, who care more about the story than the historical facts. That's why Chinese audiences should not expect the film to have accurate Chinese elements even though the story is Chinese and almost all the leading actors are Chinese or at least ethnic Chinese. It shows Chinese elements through the eyes of Westerners. Yet the differences cannot hide the points where the Chinese and Western elements and values can find common ground. A good example being the part in the trailer where the matchmaker describes the qualities that make for a good wife, namely a woman being "quiet, composed, graceful, disciplined". This is said with Mulan appearing in two images. One has her dressing as a woman, the other with her practicing sword. Obviously Disney described Mulan as a warrior, an independent female who can save herself instead of waiting for someone to save her. That's a good point where Chinese and Western values are similar because gender equality and female independence are now valued in both cultures. It will strike a chord with both Chinese and Western audiences.

But whatever styles her clothes and makeup follow, Mulan is a Chinese legendary heroine and she embodies the virtues of Chinese women. Disney's Mulan should also prompt the Chinese movie industry to make better use of Chinese stories. Chinese script writers and directors can well tell stories about Chinese ancient heroes to the world, instead of waiting for Disney or Hollywood to tell them. Good stories move audiences of the whole world because their hearts are interconnected.

(Source: Zhang Zhouxiang, Chinese story with universal appeal, China Daily Global, June 11, 2019.)

(1) Impact of culture on health and diet issues. There have been significant changes in some countries in attitudes to diet and health. Some people are slowly moving to a healthier diet. In addition, there has been an increase invegetarianism, and "green consumerism". This includes a concern with "organic food" now found

in many supermarkets.

①Growing market. There is a growing market for sports-related goods (even though, as is the case with running shoes, sporting goods might be purchased as fashion accessories).

②Employee health. The health of employees is related to the production efficiency and work quality of enterprises, so the employers are concerned with the effect of ill-health on productivity. The State Council, China's cabinet, has issued a new guideline to implement the country's Healthy China initiative and promote people's health. Employers are concerned with the effect of ill-health on productivity. Some multinationals provide gyms and physical recreation facilities. Others offer counselling program to employees who may be struggling with stress or health problems, that's what we call EAP (Employee Assistance Program). With a focus on disease prevention and health promotion, government encourage many special campaigns to "intervene in health influencing factors, protect full-life-cycle health and prevent and control major diseases".

③New foods. The health food and supplement market has grown significantly over the past decade. Some food and supplements claim health benefits including improved mental focus and concentration.

④Convenience food. There is a market for new sorts of convenience food.

⑤ Organic foods. Organic foods (grown without artificial pesticides, hormones etc.) are more popular. This could lead to a healthier workforce, or on the other hand may increase days lost to issues of food health (e.g. food poisoning).

(2) Lifestyle. From business dictionary, lifestyle is a way of living of individuals, families (households), and societies, which they manifest in coping with their physical, psychological, social, and economic environments on a day-to-day basis. Lifestyle is expressed in both work and leisure behavior patterns and (on an individual basis) in activities, attitudes, interests, opinions, values, and allocation of income. It also reflects people's self image or self concept; the way they see themselves and believe they are seen by the others. Lifestyle is a composite of motivations, needs, and wants and is influenced by factors such as culture, family, reference groups, and social class.

In recent time, Work-life balance is a problem for many companies and employees. Hard work and diligence over the past four decades have played a role in building the economic miracle that China is today. However, along with recent contention over "996" culture-a work schedule that starts at 9 am and finishes at 9 pm, six days a week, has been the topic of heated debate for days after a few IT industry staffers complained about their long working hours earlier this month with the slogan "996 ICU. " More and more employees in China have changed the way of lifestyle, and there has been a demand for leisure travel time indicates higher living standards. Changes in lifestyle have a huge impact on cross-border business.

(3) Environmentalism. With the development of society, people's behavior of environmental grab has gradually become the protection of the environment. Environmental protection has become the focus of social and cultural trend in many countries. Take China as example, Regulations on the Administration of Domestic Waste in Shanghai came into effect on July 1, 2019. This shows that Shanghai is carrying out the most ambitious garbage revolution in history. China has carried out bagged garbage collection since the mid-80s and in 1995 began exploring the classification of garbage. The Ministry of Housing and Construction in 2000 selected eight major cities, including Beijing, Shanghai and Hangzhou, to classify and recycle garbage. After 19 years of this pilot, the expected results have not been achieved. Municipal garbage disposal has become a bottleneck problem restricting China's development. Shanghai is on par with cities like New York, London, Tokyo and Paris when considering its economy and finance, shipping, trade, and science and technology industries. Today incineration accounts for about 36% of Shanghai's domestic waste treatment, landfills about half and recycling less than 10%. The figures for London are 40, 30, and nearly 30%, respectively, with Tokyo registering about 75, 3, and 20%. Compared with these global first-tier cities, the gap in urban waste classification in Shanghai is not only down to infrastructure, but the humanism of its residents.

Waste Disposal Revolution Of Shanghai

After entering a new era, Shanghai encountered unprecedented opportunities in domestic garbage treatment, reflected in three later-developing advantages.

(1) Shanghai has the advantage of "overtaking in bends". Four first-tier cities across the world established modern garbage classification systems about 50 years ago. These systems were first carried out from the perspective of the circular economy. Shanghai, as a catcher, started to classify and recycle municipal garbage through comprehensive integration. Today garbage in Shanghai is classified into four categories: harmful; recyclable; organic; and other. This integrates waste recycling, composting, incineration and landfills, and has the advantage of overtaking in bends. Shanghai for example provides a fixed subsidy for the construction of wet garbage resource facilities.

(2) Shanghai has the advantage of "backward force". Shanghai's waste treatment sets the maximum capacity of landfill and incineration facilities, reverses the

front-end classification collection and resource utilization, and reduces quantity at the source. The city encourages classification by disposing of organic garbage for free and calculating the cost of other garbage disposal. Shanghai also promotes quality control and both rewards and punishes district treatment facilities through its garbage treatment fee system.

(3) Shanghai has the advantage of "governance orientation". Shanghai residents participate in making waste classification a bottom-up action. Enterprises strengthen market-oriented changes and fulfill their corporate social responsibility. The integration of waste-sorting networks and renewable-resource recycling networks meanwhile helps accelerate the realization of the urban circular economy.

The paths towards garbage classification in Shanghai are:

(1) Establishing a garbage classification guarantee system. Shanghai should establish a whole-class classification guarantee system covering the three functions of front, middle and end. The city should exert influence in planning, construction, equipment development, process transformation, preparation, and intelligent sanitation. For the front end Shanghai should anchor more than 4 million green accounts and build recycling service points in each of its districts. The city should integrate resources collected by the front end of recyclable materials. At the middle end Shanghai should rely on Hongkou, Huangpu, Changning, Yangpu, Qingpu, other district-level transfer stations and the two container transport bases in Xupu and Hulin to achieve classification, compression, classified transportation and classified transit of domestic garbage. At the end meanwhile, the city should adhere to the strategic positioning of solid garbage disposal and bottoming protection. It should build the Laogang ecological and environmental protection base and the organic garbage, construction garbage and other disposal facilities in the Songjiang, Qingpu, Jiading, Jinshan, Fengxian and Chongming districts. Shanghai promotes the classification of urban domestic waste, according to the goal of "reduction, resource, and harmlessness". Reduction means supplementing and updating classification facilities in Shanghai. More than 40,000 road waste bins in public areas have been classified and labeled, for example. Using the internet, the integration of waste-sorting networks and renewable-resource recycling networks will be formed, and a "garbage sorting and recycling platform" will be established to form a large-scale map of Shanghai domestic waste with community as a unit. To this end, a garbage classification reward and punishment mechanism will be established to guide and encourage residents to separate their waste. The comprehensive coverage pattern of domestic waste classification has taken shape, and more than 70% of residential areas achieve the set waste-classification standard. Shanghai has simultaneously followed the construction

period of nine domestic garbage treatment projects and accelerated work on three organic garbage projects and four other garbage projects. By the end of 2019, the other garbage incineration capacity will reach 19,300 tons per day and organic garbage capacity will reach 5,500 tons per day.

(2) Adhering to the four categories method and forming the Shanghai model. Shanghai's waste classification standard has changed many times. Today the city's standard is set to the aforementioned four categories of waste. Regulations on this standard clearly categorize the whole process: units and individuals should be classified at source; property companies should be classified and transferred; receiving enterprises should be classified and transported; and the final disposal enterprises should be classified and disposed. Clarifying the purpose of the four categories establishes a social responsibility system so that garbage producers, government departments, managers, collection, transportation and disposal units and social organizations can perform their duties and responsibilities. This is all with the goal of putting in place the Shanghai model of Chinese domestic waste classification.

(3) Forming a system based on the rule of law. Shanghai in 2000 became China's first pilot for municipal solid waste classification. To ensure the pilot's success, the Shanghai Municipal Government in 2014 issued ten policies and documents. Laws and regulations are obviously crucial to any waste management system, and on July 1, 2019, Regulations on the Management of Domestic Waste in Shanghai indicated that Shanghai is now in line with the world's first-tier cities in the classification of domestic waste. Shanghai's per-capita GDP reached $20,000 in 2018, placing the city in the high-income ranks. To catch up with the world's first-tier cities, build an eco-friendly international city and achieve the goal of less than one kilogram of garbage per capita, Shanghai must enforce its regulations and adopt both restraint and incentive measures. After more than 20 years' work, Shanghai can take the lead in incorporating garbage classification into the rule of law. The regulations for example say that people can be fined up to 2,000 yuan for mixed garbage and 50,000 yuan for mixed transportation by units. The regulations also hold that disposable cups and utensils cannot be used in the Shanghai Party internal office and government organs. Hotels will no longer provide disposable household necessities or they'll be fined at least 500 yuan and less than 5,000 yuan. Caterers cannot provide disposable tableware-if they do and fail to make corrections within a time limit, they will be fined the same amount.

(Source: Chen Xinguang, How establishing the Shanghai model of waste disposal can be revolutionary, chinadaily, June 20, 2019.)

5. 2. 2 Values

1. What is values?

Business Dictionary give the meanings of values that important and lasting beliefs or ideals shared by the members of a culture about what is good or bad and desirable or undesirable. Values have major influence on a person's behavior and attitude and serve as broad guidelines in all situations.

Cultural values represent the implicitly or explicitly shared abstract ideas about what is good, right, and desirable in a society (Williams, 1970). These cultural values (e. g. freedom, prosperity, security) are the bases for the specific norms that tell people what is appropriate in various situations. The ways that societal institutions (e. g. the family, education, economic, political, religious systems) function, their goals and their modes of operation, express cultural value priorities. Cultural values have three aspects on work: work centrality, societal norms about work, and work values or goals.

(1) Work centrality. The International Research Team (1987) defined work centrality as the importance and significance of work in a person's total life. Their index of work centrality includes both a general question about the importance of work and a question about the importance of work relative to four other life areas—leisure, community, religion, and family.

(2) Societal norms about working. In some country, societal norms are expected to define work more as an entitlement where Egalitarianism and Intellectual Autonomy values are especially important, like US. Others societal norms are expected to define work more as an obligation where Conservatism and Hierarchy values are especially important, like Japan.

(3) Work values or goals. Work values refer to the goals or rewards people seek through their work. They are expressions of more general human values in the context of the work setting. A review of the literature points to four broad types of work values that are distinguished implicitly by respondents. Listed with their core goals in parentheses, these are: intrinsic (personal growth, autonomy, interest, and creativity), extrinsic (pay and security), social (contact with people and contribution to society), power (prestige, authority, influence).

2. Values and trade

Some successful transnational corporations' business values are fairness, innovation and community involvement. Take Cognizant as example, it is an American multinational corporation that provides digital, technology, consulting, and operations services. It is headquartered in Teaneck, New Jersey, United States. It was the first software services firm listed on the NASDAQ. Cognizant has the special principles between values and business.

(1) Transparency. We succeed through open exchange of information. Cognizant is built on a foundation of open and honest communication. We believe the only way to ensure success for our clients and ourselves is to operate in a fully transparent manner. We encourage associates to listen to ideas and share feedback that can make us a better, stronger, more able company.

(2) Passion. We have a collective can-do attitude, with the enthusiasm and commitment to go the extra mile. Everything we do at Cognizant we do with passion—for our clients, our communities and our organization. Each associate has the drive and commitment to do whatever it takes to help our customers succeed and we apply that passion to help sustain our communities and environment.

(3) Empowerment. Figure out how to get things done and make them happen. We de? ne ourselves by our ability to deliver results. That means taking the initiative to find new ways to get the job done. We encourage end-to-end ownership, responsibility, accountability and recognition. Cognizant is entrepreneurial and fast-growing, offering numerous opportunities to shape our roles and careers.

(4) Collaboration. Work together to achieve a common goal. A corner stone of Cognizant's success is the interconnectivity of our associates and teams across business units. We believe that the better we share knowledge and work together, the more we can achieve for our clients and ourselves.

(5) Customer focus. The customer is our true north. Our customers' delight powers our success, and exceeding customer expectations is our belief. No matter how big or small a project is, it will be delivered with the highest quality. Every associate knows that the customer is why we are here and that we place unwavering focus on customer satisfaction.

(6) Integrity. We act with integrity in every decision we make. We never compromise on integrity, and we take every decision accordingly. Integrity means doing the right things, always. Integrity also means that we treat our colleagues and clients with respect and value their opinions.

Context, Conditions, and Culture

Context matters when assessing a culture's strategic effectiveness. Leaders must simultaneously consider culture styles and key organizational and market condition if they want their culture to help drive performance. Region and industry are among the most germane external factors to keep in mind; critical internal considerations include alignment with strategy, leadership, and organizational design.

● Region. The values of the national and regional cultures in which a company is embedded can influence patterns of behavior with in the organization. (This linkage has been explored in depth by GeertHofstede and the authors of the GLOBE study.) We find, for example, that companies operating in countries characterized by a high degree of institutional collectivism (defined as valuing equity within groups and encouraging the collective distribution of resources), such as France and Brazil, have cultures that emphasize order and safety. Companies operating in countries with low levels of uncertainty avoidance (that is, they are open to ambiguity and future uncertainty), such as the United States and Australia, place a greater emphasis on learning, purpose, and enjoyment. Such external influences are important considerations when working across borders or designing an appropriate organizational culture.

● Industry. Varying cultural attributes may be needed to address industry-specific regulations and customer needs. A comparison of organizations across industries reveals evidence that cultures might adapt to meet the demands of industry environments. Organizational cultures in financial services are more likely to emphasize safety. Given the increasingly complex regulations enacted in response to the financial crisis, careful work and risk management are more critical than ever in this industry. In contrast, nonprofits are far more purpose-driven, which can reinforce their commitment to a mission by aligning employee behavior around a common goal.

● Strategy. For its full benefit to be realized, a culture must support the strategic goals and plans of the business. For example, we find differences between companies that adopt a differentiation strategy and companies that pursue a cost leadership strategy. Although results and caring are key cultural characteristics at both types of companies, enjoyment, learning, and purpose are more suited to differentiation, whereas order and authority are more suited to cost leadership. Flexible cultures— which emphasize enjoyment and learning—can spur product innovation in companies aiming to differentiate themselves, whereas stable and predictable cultures, which emphasize order and authority, can help maintain operational efficiency to keep costs low. Strategic considerations related to a company's life cycle are also linked to organizational culture. Companies with a strategy that seeks to stabilize or maintain their market position prioritize learning, whereas organizations operating with a turn around strategy tend to prioritize order and safety in their efforts to redirect or reorganize unprofitable units.

• Leadership. It is hard to overestimate the importance of aligning culture and leadership. The character and behaviors of a CEO and top executives can have a profound effect on culture. Conversely, culture serves to either constrain or enhance the performance of leaders. Our own data from executive recruiting activities shows that a lack of cultural fit is responsible for up to 68% of new-hire failures at the senior leadership level. For individual leaders, cultural fit is as important as capabilities and experience.

• Organizational design. We see a two-way relationship between a company's culture and its particular structure. In many cases, structure and systems follow culture. For example, companies that prioritize team work and collaboration might design incentive systems that include shared team and company goals along with rewards that recognize collective effort. However, a long-standing organizational design choice can lead to the formation of a culture. Because the latter is far more difficult to alter, we suggest that structural changes should be aligned with the desired culture.

(Source: Context, Conditions, and Culture, Harvard Business Review, January-February, 2018.)

5.3　Social Structures and Class

5.3.1　Definition

1. Social structure

The early study of social structures has informed the study of institutions, culture and agency, social interaction, and history. Alexis de Tocqueville was apparently the first to use the term social structure; later, Karl Marx, Herbert Spencer, Max Weber and other scholars all contributed to structural concepts in sociology. One of the earliest and most comprehensive accounts of social structure was provided by Karl Marx, who related political, cultural, and religious life to the mode of production (an underlying economic structure). Marx argued that the economic base substantially determined the cultural and political superstructure of a society. Subsequent Marxist accounts, such as that by Louis Althusser, proposed a more complex relationship that asserted the relative autonomy of cultural and political institutions, and a general determination by economic factors only "in the last instance". From the dictionary of Merriam-Webster and Social Science, social structures mean the internal institutionalized relationships built up by persons living within a group (such as a family or community) especially with regard to the hierarchical organization of status and to the rules and principles regulating behavior.

Based on the review of definition, social structure has been identified as:

• relationship of definite entities or groups to each other;

• enduring patterns of behaviour by participants in a social system in relation to each other;

• institutionalised norms or cognitive frameworks that structure the actions of actors in the social system.

Based on the point view of sociology, social structure can also be divided into three contents, from the macro view, social structure is the system of socioeconomic stratification (e. g. the class structure), social institutions, or other patterned relations between large social groups. From the medium view, it is the structure of social network ties between individuals or organizations. From the micro view, it can be the way norms shape the behavior of individuals within the social system.

2. Social class

Social class means "The basic idea of class is that a society can be divided into broad strata which comprise individuals, whose members share common features, such as type of occupation, income level, education background and other variables". The common stratum model of social class divides society into a simple hierarchy of working class, middle class and upper class. Within academia, two broad schools of definitions emerge: those aligned with 20th-century sociological stratum models of class society, and those aligned with the 19th-century historical materialist economic models of the Marxists and anarchists.

5. 3. 2　Types of social structures and class

1. Types of social structures

Talcott Parsons has described 4 principal types of social structure. His classifications is based on four social values-universalistic social values, particularistic social values, achieved social values and ascribed social values. Universalistic social values are those which are found almost in every society and are applicable to everybody. Particularistic social values are the features of particular societies and these differ from society to society. When the statuses are achieved on the basis of efforts it means that such societies attach importance to achieved social values. When the statuses are hereditary even the society gives importance to ascribed social statuses.

(1) Universalistic-achievement pattern. This is the combination of the value patterns which sometimes opposed to the values of a social structure built mostly around kinship, community, class and race. Under this type of social structure, the choice of goal by the individual must be in accord with the universalistic values. His pursuits are defined by universalistic moral norms. Such a system is dynamically developing norms. Such a system is dynamically developing system with an encouragement for initiative.

(2) Universalistic-ascription pattern. Under this type of social structure the elements of value-orientation are dominated by the elements of ascription. Therefore in such a social structure strong emphasis is laid on the status of the individual rather than on his specific achievements. The emphasis is on what an individual is rather than on what he has done. Status is ascribed to the group rather than to the individuals. The individual derives his status from his group. In this type of social structure all resources are mobilized in the interest of the collective ideal.

(3) Particularistic-achievement pattern. This type combines achievement values with particularim. The primary criterion of valued achievement is found not in universalistic terms such as conformity to a generalized ideal or efficiency but these are focused on certain points of reference within the relational system itself or are inherent in the situation. The emphasis on achievement leads to the conception of a proper pattern of adaption which is a product of human achievement and which are maintained by continuous efforts.

(4) Particularistic-ascription pattern. In this type also the social structure is organized around the relational reference points notably those of kinship and local community but it differs from the particularistic achievement type in as much as the relational values are taken as given and passively adapted to rather than make for an actively organized system. The structure tends to be traditionalistic and emphasis is laid on its stability.

2. Types of social class

In sociological terms, a class is more than a group of people with various things in common, however. Classes fit into a social structure, in which some classes have advantage over others:

- Access to power;
- Inherited wealth;
- Educational attainment;
- Status or esteem;
- Income.

Generation Z

Following millennials, China's next demographic cohort share interests, struggles, with Americans. Zhang Yunyi, a 19-year-old male student in Beijing, and Conall Curran, a young American man born in 1998, are both trying to save money for their favorite pastimes, but in two totally different ways. Saving part of his pocket money every month, Zhang dreams of buying a new camera lens, which may cost about 20,000 yuan ($2,875). Curran, however, is working extra part-time jobs to cover his car expenses. He finds everything about cars interesting, including road trips. Take a look at any social media platform in the world and you'll find millions of young people like Zhang and Curran complaining about their generation's financial pressures. Despite financial support from parents, many youth today find themselves troubled by steep tuition fees, expensive rent and other high expenses for entertainment and hobbies. Generation Z-a term referring to those born between the mid-1990s and mid-2000s-are on track to becoming not only the largest group of consumers, but also the backbone of our respective economies. Thus, it is important to understand how Generation Z earn and spend money. The Metropolitan recently interviewed some young adults in Beijing and New York City who identify as Generation Z to glean some insight into this subject. Despite financial support from their parents for tuition, rent and other daily expenses, some try to earn money through part-time jobs. Shaped by an internet-driven environment and a more inclusive world, there are also some behavioral patterns of consumption and views shared among the youths of this generation in China and the US. For Generation Z youth born in the US and China after the year 2000, tuition and rent are naturally the biggest chunk of their daily expenses. "I'm very lucky that my parents have the resources and are willing to support me like they do," said 20-year-old Conall Curran, who studies at a private school in Michigan. His total tuition is about $60,000 each year, though an academic scholarship means his parents only have to pay half that amount. "It's extremely expensive as far as Michigan goes, but schools will give students some discounts based on family income and how much you deserve your scholarship," he said.

Supported by parents and government. According to data from US News, the average cost of tuition and fees for the 2018-2019 school year was $35,676 at private colleges, and $9,716 for state residents at public colleges, which have seen a surge in enrollment since the late-1990s. Such is the steep cost of higher education in the US that increasing numbers of youths are choosing to study overseas at less expensive institutions-or simply skip college altogether. In 2018, Americans are burdened by student loan debt more than ever, with 44 million borrowers owing $1.5 trillion in student loans, according to Forbes. Meanwhile, the problem is nonexistent in China. Student loans are not as common in China as in the US. Hu Yuchen, who recently turned 18, is a vocational college student at Beijing International Studies University. Hu spends only 1,800 yuan ($259) per year on her tuition. "A vocational education is supported by the government," Hu explained to Metropolitan. Generally speaking, the tuition for Chinese students at institutions of higher education is about 5,000 yuan ($719) per year on average, according to figures published on sina.com. Many American youth do not have the time or energy to secure a part-time job, despite the financial incentives in doing so. A 22-year-old Generation Z student named Kevin Brew tried to combine studying with part-time work while attending college in New York City. He took his first job as a lifeguard during his senior high school year in his hometown of Rhode Island. Curran noted that while it is possible for Generation Z students to get a part-time job as early as high school, he acknowledged that the pay is hardly enough for them to become independent from their parents. According to Zhang Yunyi, whose tuition is 6,000 yuan ($863) per year, many Chinese students his age prefer to concentrate on their studies instead of work. "I choose not to work because I don't want to," said Hu. "This is the right time for me to absorb as much knowledge as I can during my school years by reading and learning." But Zhang will be seeking an internship next year, though his primary motivation is to gather work experience in his chosen field, rather than simply earning money. "I don't think [working] means that American youth are more independent than Chinese," Zhang told Metropolitan.

Surpassing millennials. According to a 2016 survey release by an entrepreneurship lab at Zhejiang University, out of 10,000 local college students, 21% had part-time jobs while attending school. But with Chinese tuition fees being much lower than those in the US, neither Hu nor Zhang's family bear too much debt for their education. "I want to be a journalist for a car magazine after graduation," said Curran, who spends at least $40 per week on gasoline alone for his road trips. Hu and Zhang likewise said that a majority of their expenses after tuition and food go toward their personal hobbies. It was in his senior year of high school, in 2016, that Zhang purchased his first digital camera lens at a price of 9,000 yuan ($1,294). "It was worth it," he said. With Generation Z increasingly spending more money on their hobbies, the rising number of young adults suggest that this pattern of consumption is likely to continue rising. From a consumer spending point of view, new information from Bloomberg reveals that by 2019, Generation Z will comprise 32% of the global population (7.7 billion), surpassing millennials for the first time. Although rent in Beijing and New York are similarly high, "the biggest difference between the two countries is that the middle class in China is growing, but in the US it is shrinking," according to Curran. In such an era, Generation Z are being shaped more by technology than social class. "To tell the truth, we are the generation who have experienced the internet from very young ages, so we are more sophisticated and inclusive than others," Hu said.

(Source: Li Jieyi and Yin Lu, Generation Z, Global Times, November 15, 2018.)

5.3.3　Social structures and business

While there are some real differences between the groups, "social class" for marketing or planning purposes should be used with caution. Sometimes people's lifestyles are a reflection of their economic condition in society, not the reason for their position. Buying behaviour is an important aspect of marketing. Many factors influence the buying decisions of individuals and households. Demography and the class structure are relevant in that they can be both behavioural determinants and inhibitors.

(1) Behavioural determinants encourage people to buy a product or service. They include the individual's personality, culture, social class, and the importance of the purchase decision (e. g. a necessity such as food or water, or a luxury).

Foreign firms target night market success with niche offerings

It is not a surprise that KFC's latest product innovation is chicken-related. But a bucket full of spicy chicken offal for night snack deliveries has shocked Chinese consumers. The feedback was explosive. Photos of the KFC kebab spicy dipping sauce have gone viral on the internet. On July 15, KFC started to sell late night treats including spicy kebabs and stewed fowl, traditional late night treats in southern China. The kebab bucket has cooked chicken heart, chicken stomach, agaric and bean curd and aorta of livestock. The stewed category has stewed chicken wings, chicken heart, chicken stomach and chicken pieces. The products were available on

KFC's mobile application, priced at 59 yuan ($8.5) for 12 pieces of kebabs and 39 yuan for the stewed fowl. Though KFC and McDonald's have previously experimented with including Chinese food on their menus such as porridge and fried twisted cruller, it is the first time that foreign fast food chains have put offal products on their menus. Consumers in Shanghai, Chengdu, Chongqing, Harbin and Shenyang can buy the products currently. Beijing is not included in the list. "It is an attempt by KFC to localize its offerings especially for late nights in summer," said Jason Yu, general manager of Kantar World panel. "By doing so it can appeal to younger consumers." The two offerings are also considered easier for quality control and taste. According to reports from the Ministry of Commerce, about 60% of dining consumption occurs at night. More than six out of 10 Chinese consumers have gone for food at night at least once, and the night food delivery market's growth has been much higher than others, according to data from the China Dining Association. Foreign companies in China have faced fierce pressure from local players, pushing them to roll out more localized products at a faster speed. For example, Skittles-a brand from US chocolate major Mars-has launched jasmine and rose flavored candies to attract local consumers. Nestle's local research team launched a series of new instant coffee products with three flavors-peach, pineapple and green apple-to attract younger Chinese consumers. According to the latest China Shopper Report from Bain & Company and Kantar World panel in June, Chinese brands grew by 15% since 2016, contributing 76% of market growth in 2018. By comparison, foreign brands grew more slowly-by 9% since 2016-and contributed 24% to last year's market growth. The encouraging news for foreign brands is that despite being outpaced by domestic companies, the 24% growth in market share is actually double the rate in 2017. Foreign brands are learning what it takes to win in China, according to the report. It requires keeping pace with the market's rapid changes, the report said.

(Source: Wang Zhuoqiong, Foreign firms target night market success with niche offerings, China Daily, July 24, 2019.)

(2) Inhibitors are factors that make the person less likely to purchase something (eg low income). Socio-economic status can be related to buying patterns in a number of ways, both in the amount people have to spend and what they spend it on. It affects both the quantity of goods and services supplied and the proportion of their income that households spend on goods and services.

(3) E-commerce. Electronic commerce or e-commerce is a business model that lets firms and individuals conduct business over electronic networks, most notably: the Internet. Electronic commerce operates in all four of the following

major market segments:

- Business to business (B to B).
- Business to consumer (B to C).
- Consumer to consumer (C to C).
- Consumer to business (C to B).

E-commerce has helped businesses establish a wider market presence by providing cheaper and more efficient distribution channels for their products or services. E-commerce in China is developing very fast. Chinese e-commerce giants, technology device producers and financial solution providers are shaping the retail industry in China and the world at large. China's cross-border e-commerce imports rose 24.3% year on year to 45.65 billion yuan ($6.64 billion) in the first half of 2019, according to a bureau for duty collection of the General Administration of Customs (GAC). Imports of cosmetics, milk powder, diapers, food and other daily necessities rank the top among all of 1,321 cross-border e-commerce items, according to the Customs National Supervision Bureau for Duty Collection (Shanghai) of GAC. The soaring imports reveal that more Chinese customers are engaging in cross-border e-commerce, whose lives are more closely connected to cross-border trade. As of 2018, multinational conglomerate Alibaba.com is the most successful e-commerce company in China. Alibaba dominates the B2B market and it's Tmall and Taobao websites also enjoy the biggest market share of the B2C and C2C markets respectively. Fortune Global 500 (2019) shows six of the top 10 companies with the fastest growth are from China, including Alibaba Group Holdings, Tencent Holdings and Suning.com; companies that have benefited from China's rapidly expanding domestic consumption market, especially the rapid development of e-commerce.

E-commerce culture clash tests foreign online retailers

Global internet vendors have found the going rough in China. As Edith Lu reports, foreign enterprises have yet to get used to local consumer habits and preferences, let alone fine-tuning their strategies. Nobody can say no to a $1.50 hot dog with unlimited drinks, a $4.99 roast chicken, or a tire replacement service for only $15-especially Chinese consumers. Their enthusiasm for bargains has put e-commerce platform Pinduoduo on the Nasdaq Stock Exchange, and has also attracted the attention of Costco Wholesale Corp, the second-largest retailer in the world. Famous for selling good-quality products at low prices, Costco announced in May that it is set to open its first brick-and-mortar store on the Chinese mainland at the end of August, marking its first foray into the competitive market. The membership-driven warehouse-club retailer dipped its toe into the Chinese market in 2014 by selling on Tmall Global, a cross-border business-to-consumer (B2C) platform under Alibaba. But Costco no longer has its traditional pricing advantages in China due to the import tariffs. The key to its expansion now is whether it can adapt to the retail realities of China-a goal that has eluded other foreign retailers.

A tough market to crack for foreign companies. For foreign companies, breaking into China's retail market-and the world's largest e-commerce market-has always been a tough nut to crack. Even global e-commerce giant Amazon could not escape the challenges and consequences. Amazon has declared that it plans to shut down part of its Chinese marketplace business in mid-July, which means that Chinese customers will no longer be able to buy domestic merchants' goods on Amazon. Many local merchants on Amazon China, including Momax, are ending their e-commerce business on the platform these days. The Hong Kong-and Shenzhen-based smartphone-accessories maker used to operate its major online business on Amazon, as well as Tmall and JD. com. But withdrawing from Amazon isn't a major setback, company officials said. Momax Sales Director Aden Li Dong said the impact of closing is minimal to the company since Amazon is not Momax's key e-commerce platform. The cost of inventory and manpower is next to nothing, as Momax's warehouse does not serve only Amazon. According to Li, sales from Amazon and other cross-border platforms account for less than 10% of the company's total e-commerce income. The biggest earners are Tmall and JD, occupying 40% and 30% , respectively. He said Momax cooperated with Amazon mainly for its cross-border business, as Momax hoped to leverage the platform to lure more overseas buyers. Amazon described its partial retreat as a focus shift so that it can do a better job offering Chinese consumers overseas products. Meanwhile, it will continue to run businesses such as Kindle e-books, Amazon Web Services, and other cross-border operations in China. The company has been operating in China for almost 15 years. In 2004, Amazon got a toehold in China when it bought local online book seller Joyo. com for $75 million.

Amazon's success in China short-lived. As a leader in the e-commerce sector, Amazon was an up-and-comer at the very start. With the well-known brands and quality products in its self-operated stores, Amazon China saw sales approach nearly $7 billion for its first year. At that time, Alibaba had not launched Tmall, its B2C division, and JD had not yet raised its first round of funds. But Amazon's good times did not last long. The e-commerce industry expanded rapidly. Platforms based on third-party merchants such as Alibaba's Taobao sprang up and priced out the competition, while Amazon did not introduce third-party merchants to its platform until 2012. "The market share of Amazon has dropped from its peak of 15% to, at one time, less than 1% ," said Michael Cheng Woon-yin, PwC consumer markets leader of Asia Pacific, Hong Kong and the Chinese mainland. He questioned Amazon's competitiveness in China, as its promotion events are not attractive enough to woo Chinese customers compared with its local rivals. And most of its business model, including its payment method and membership discount, just copies its US website without localization. When Amazon founder Jeff Bezos visited China in 2007, he was asked why so many global internet companies failed here, including eBay and Yahoo. Bezos said it was terrible to see these multinational firms come just to satisfy their foreigner bosses rather than local customers. However, years later, the company of the world's wealthiest man stumbled in China for the same reason. "Amazon China does not have much power to make decisions," said Jin Tai (not her real name), a former Amazon China account manager who was based in Shanghai. "All the decisions need to be reviewed by the headquarters in the US. " She cited product information displays as an example. When people search a certain item, local online platforms display all merchants that are selling the product. However, Amazon automatically designates one seller as the item's default seller. This means that the other sellers have no chance to be visited unless customers specifically click through to see them. Amazon's reason for doing this was to improve the shopping experience by providing the most cost-effective product. But that method is unfamiliar to Chinese consumers and does not match their shopping habits. "We have reported these kinds of problems to the US, but they just insist websites of different marketplaces should have a consistent style," said Jin, paraphrasing what she was told during her training. Jin left the company after a year because she found she could learn little from the work.

Retailers must adapt to changing market. However, localization by itself is not enough to conquer the Chinese market. Retailers have to adapt to the dynamic changes rapidly and catch targeted consumers' attention, Cheng said. He summarized the preferences of the main forces in e-commerce: The post-'80s shoppers liked cost-effective products; the post-'90s generation valued the brand more; and the post-'00s preferred an integrated platform. These features explain the rise of a group of new e-commerce platforms. On one hand, people go gaga over products at fire-sale prices on Pinduoduo. On the other hand, girls in their 20s are addicted to the small bourgeois world created by Xiaohongshu, an e-commerce platform operating like a mash-up of Instagram and Amazon. It provides a channel for its young consumers to buy luxury items or expensive skin-care products as soon as they check some bloggers' recommendations. "Although sales from these kinds of new e-commerce platforms now account for only 20% of our total e-commerce income, the proportion is going up," Li said, adding that Momax has started to tap deeper into these platforms, as social e-commerce platforms and live promotions are becoming increasingly popular. Even traditional e-commerce giants such as Taobao have included some social media elements. Sellers can update new posts every day to increase exposure and maintain the relationship with regular customers. Live promotion for new-arrived goods is also needed, which could greatly increase the sales of products. Jeffrey Huang, a Zhejiang-based e-commerce retailer, saw the business model of these new e-commerce platforms as a trend. As a retailer, he must go after to "gain more volume and more turnover". The household-slipper retailer, whose business runs across every major e-commerce platform, ventured into Pinduoduo in 2017. But soon his store shifted the emphasis to other platforms, since the rock-bottom prices on Pinduoduo provide too small a profit. Now it mainly focuses on social ones. But Huang is still positive about traditional platforms. "The rise of new platforms doesn't mean there's no market for traditional ones. Though new forms are springing up, many shut down quickly," he said. Thus, the retailer will continue the business on traditional platforms such as Tmall.

Online, offline selling platforms integrate. In addition, many platforms are integrating their online and offline platforms. Alibaba is transferring its business from one that is solely online to an online-to-offline (O2O) platform as well. Its offline supermarket chain, Hema Xiansheng, allows consumers to order groceries online and have them delivered to their doorstep, or they can shop at the physical stores and ask to have the goods delivered to their homes. Once an e-commerce platform focusing mainly on electronic appliances, Suning. com has been gearing up its offline presence in recent years and realized its transformation through its O2O business model. It announced earlier this year that it will acquire all Wanda Department Stores to expand its offline presence. Last month, Suning agreed to buy an 80-percent stake in the Chinese unit of Carrefour for 4. 8 billion yuan ($698 million). The French supermarket chain has been searching for a local partner for a long time, trying to save its struggling operations in China. Before the deal with Suning, Carrefour had been in discussions with Tencent and Yonghui Superstores regarding a potential investment and cooperation to bring together its retail knowledge with Tencent's digital expertise and innovation capabilities. According to the company's annual report, sales of Carrefour China slumped almost 10% to 3. 65 million euros ($4. 11 million) last year. Chinese Commerce Ministry spokesman Gao Feng said the purchase is simply a strategic collaboration as a normal market behavior. He stressed the retail sector in China is a perfectly competitive market. The ministry will take affirmative steps to promote the integration of online and offline, as well as consumption transformation and upgrading, he added. Like Carrefour, a growing number of foreign retailers are tying up with local players in order to survive in China. Walmart, which has a network of around 400 outlets, relies on JD for its delivery service, while Germany's Metro AG is trying to offload a majority stake in its Chinese business. "Different companies just have different global strategies," said Phil Lai, consulting partner of PwC China. "Some retailers are beginning to step back their globalization, focusing more on their home markets. But there are also other companies quite bullish about their march into the Chinese market-for example, Costco. " Lai agrees that collaboration with major local partners is a key to success in China since it will be easier for them to create so-called "customer stickiness" and read the hearts of Chinese consumers. "For all of the multinational brands, they need to find a balance between localization and retaining multinational DNA," Lai said.

（Source：Edith Lu, E-commerce culture clash tests foreign online retailers, ChinaDaily, July 12, 2019. ）

5.4　Case

Alibaba and the Future of Business

Alibaba hit the headlines with the world's biggest IPO in September 2014. Today, the company has a market cap among the global top 10, has surpassed Walmart in global sales, and has expanded into all the major markets in the world. Founder Jack Ma has become a household name.

From its inception, in 1999, Alibaba experienced great growth on its e-commerce platform. However, it still didn't look like a world-beater in 2007 when the management team, which I had joined full-time the year before, met for a strategy off-site at a drab seaside hotel in Ningbo, Zhejiang province. Over the course of the meeting, our disjointed observations and ideas about e-commerce trends began to coalesce into a larger view of the future, and by the end, we had agreed on a vision. We would "foster the development of an open, coordinated, prosperous e-commerce ecosystem. " That's when Alibaba's journey really began. Alibaba's special innovation, we realized, was that we were truly building an ecosystem: a community of organisms (businesses and consumers of many types) interacting with one another and the environment (the online platform and the larger off-line physical elements). Our strategic imperative was to make sure that the platform provided all the resources, or access to the resources, that an online business would need to succeed, and hence supported the evolution of the ecosystem. The ecosystem we built was simple at first: We linked buyers and sellers of goods. As technology advanced, more business functions moved online— including established ones, such as advertising, marketing, logistics, and finance, and emerging ones, such as affiliate marketing, product recommenders, and social media influencers. And as we expanded our ecosystem to accommodate these innovations, we helped create new types of online businesses, completely reinventing China's retail sector along the way. Alibaba today is not just an online commerce company. It is what you get if you take all functions associated with retail and coordinate them online into a sprawling, data-driven network of sellers, marketers, service providers, logistics companies, and manufacturers. In other words, Alibaba does what Amazon, eBay, PayPal, Google, FedEx, wholesalers, and a good portion of manufacturers do in the United States, with a healthy helping of financial services for garnish. Of the world's 10 most highly valued companies today, seven are internet companies with business models similar to ours. Five of them—Amazon, Google, and Facebook in the United States and Alibaba and Tencent in China—have been around barely 20 years. Why has so much value and market power emerged so quickly? Because of new capabilities in network coordination and data intelligence that all these companies put to use. The ecosystems they steward are vastly more economically efficient and customer-centric than traditional industries. These firms follow an approach I call smart business, and I believe it represents the dominant business logic of the future.

What is Smart Business?

Smart business emerges when all players involved in achieving a common business goal—retailing, for example, or ride sharing—are coordinated in an online network and use machine-learning technology to efficiently leverage data in real time. This tech-enabled model, in which most operational decisions are made by machines, allows companies to adapt dynamically and rapidly to changing market conditions and customer preferences, gaining tremendous competitive advantage over traditional businesses. Ample computing power and digital data are the fuel for machine learning, of course. The more data and the more iterations the algorithmic engine goes through, the better its output gets. Data scientists come up with probabilistic prediction models for specific actions, and then the algorithm churns through loads of data to produce better decisions in realtime with every iteration. These prediction models become the basis for most business decisions. Thus machine learning is more than a technological innovation; it will transform the way business is conducted as human decision making is increasingly replaced by algorithmic output. Ant Microloans provides a striking example of what this future will look like. When Alibaba launched Ant, in 2012, the typical loan given by large banks in China was in the millions of dollars. The minimum loan amount—about 6 million RMB or just under $1 million—was well above the amounts needed by most small and medium-size enterprises (SMEs). Banks were reluctant to service companies that lacked any kind of credit history or even adequate documentation of their business activities. As a consequence, tens of millions of businesses in China were having real difficulties securing the money necessary to grow their operations. At Alibaba, we realized we had the ingredient for creating a high functioning, scalable, and profitable SME lending business: the huge amount of transaction data generated by the many small businesses using our platform. So in 2010 we launched a pioneering data-driven micro loan business to offer loans to businesses in amounts no larger than 1 million RMB (about $160,000). In seven years of operation, the business has lent more than 87 billion RMB ($13.4 billion) to nearly three million SMEs. The average loan size is 8,000 RMB, or about $1,200. In 2012, we bundled this lending operation together with Alipay, our very successful payments business, to create Ant Financial Services. We gave the new venture that name to capture the idea that we were empowering all the little but industrious, ant-like companies.

Today, Ant can easily process loans as small as several hundred RMB (around $50) in a few minutes. How is this possible? When faced with potential borrowers, lending institutions need answer only three basic questions: Should we lend to them, how much should we lend, and at what interest rate? Once sellers on our platforms gave us authorization to analyze their data, we were well positioned to answer those questions. Our algorithms can look at transaction data to assess how well a business is doing, how competitive its offerings are in the market, whether its partners have high credit ratings, and so on. Ant uses that data to compare good borrowers (those who repay on time) with bad ones (those who do not) to isolate traits common in both groups. Those traits are then used to calculate credit scores. All lending institutions do this in some fashion, of course, but at Ant the analysis is done automatically on all borrowers and on all their behavioral data in real time. Every transaction, every communication between seller and buyer, every connection with other services available at Alibaba, indeed every action taken on our platform, affects a business's credit score. At the same time, the algorithms that calculate the scores are themselves evolving in real time, improving the quality of decision making with each iteration. Determining how much to lend and how much interest to charge requires analysis of many types of data generated inside the Alibaba network, such as gross profit margins and inventory turnover, along with less mathematically precise information such as product life cycles and the quality of a seller's social and business relationships. The algorithms might, for example, analyze the frequency, length, and type of communications (instant messaging, e-mail, or other methods common in China) to assess relationship quality. Alibaba's data scientists are essential in identifying and testing which data points provide the insights they seek and then engineering algorithms to mine the data. This work requires both a deep understanding of the business and expertise in machine-learning algorithms. Consider again Ant Financial. If a seller deemed to have poor credit pays back its loan on time or a seller with excellent credit catastrophically defaults, the algorithm clearly needs tweaking. Engineers can quickly and easily check their assumptions. Which parameters should be added or removed? Which kinds of user behavior should be given more weight? As the recalibrated algorithms produce increasingly accurate predictions, Ant's risk and costs steadily decrease, and borrowers get the money they need, when they need it, at an interest rate they can afford. The result is a highly successful business: The micro lending operation has a default rate of about 1%, far below the World Bank's 2016 estimate of an average of 4% worldwide. So how do you create that kind of business?

Automate All Operating Decisions

To become a smart business, your firm must enable as many operating decisions as possible to be made by machines fueled by live data rather than by humans supported by their own data analysis. Transforming decision making in this way is a four-step process.

Step 1: "Datafy" every customer exchange.

Ant was fortunate to have access to plenty of data on potential borrowers to answer the questions inherent in its lending business. For many businesses, the data capture process will be more challenging. But live data is essential to creating the feedback loops that are the basis of machine learning. Consider the bike rental business. Start-ups in China have leveraged mobile telephony, the internet of things (in the form of smart bike locks), and existing mobile payment and credits ystems to datafy the entire rental process. Renting a bike traditionally involved going to a rent allocation, leaving a deposit, having someone give you a bike, using the bike, returning it, and then paying for the rental by cash or credit card. Several rival Chinese companies put all of this online by integrating various new technologies with existing ones. A crucial innovation was the combination of QR codes and electronic locks that cleverly automated the checkout process. By opening the bike-sharing app, a rider can see available bicycles and reserve one nearby. Once the rider arrives at the bicycle, he or she uses the app to scan a QR code on the bicycle. Assuming that the person has money in his or her account and meets the rental criteria, the QR code will open the electronic bike lock. The app can even verify the person's credit history through Sesame Credit, Ant Financial's new online product for consumer credit ratings, allowing the rider to skip paying a deposit, further expediting the process. When the bike is returned, closing the lock completes the transaction. The process is simple, intuitive, and usually takes only several seconds. Datafying the rental process greatly improves the consumer experience. On the basis of live data, companies dispatch trucks to move bikes to where users want them. They can also alert regular users to the availability of bikes nearby. Thanks in large part to these innovations, the cost of bike rentals in China has fallen to just a few cents per hour.

Most businesses that seek to be more data-driven typically collect and analyze information in order to create a causal model. The model then isolates the critical data points from the mass of information available. That is not how smart businesses use data. Instead, they capture all information generated during exchanges and communications with customers and other network members as the business operates and then let the algorithms figure out what data is relevant.

Step 2: "Software" every activity. In a smart business, all activities—not just knowledge management and customer relations—are configured using software so that decisions affecting them can be automated. This does not mean that a firm needs to buy or build ERP software or its equivalent to manage its business—quite the opposite. Traditional software makes processes and decision flows more rigid and often becomes a strait jacket. In contrast, the dominant logic for smart business is reactivity in real time. The first step is to build a model of how humans currently make decisions and find ways to replicate the simpler elements of that process using software—which is not always easy, given that many human decisions are built on common sense or even subconscious neurological activity.

The growth of Taobao, the domestic retailing website of Alibaba Group, is driven by continuous softwaring of the retailing process. One of the first major software tools built on Taobao was an instant message tool called Wangwang, through which buyers and sellers can talk to each other easily. Using the tool, the sellers greet buyers, introduce products, negotiate prices, and so on, just as people do in a traditional retail shop. Alibaba also developed a set of software tools that help sellers design and launch a variety of sophisticated online shop fronts. Once online shops are up and running, sellers can access other software products to issue coupons, offer discounts, run loyalty programs, and conduct other customer relationship activities, all of which are coordinated with one another. Because most software today is run online as a service, an important advantage of softwaring a business activity is that live data can be collected naturally as part of the business process, building the foundation for the application of machine-learning technologies.

Step 3: Get data flowing. In ecosystems with many interconnected players, business decisions require complex coordination. Taobao's recommendation engines, for example, need to work with the inventory management systems of sellers and with the consumer-profiling systems of various social media platforms. Its transaction systems need to work with discount offers and loyalty programs, as well as feed into our logistics network. Communication standards, such as TCP/IP, and application programming interfaces (APIs) are critical in getting the data flowing among multiple players while ensuring strict control of who can access and edit data throughout the ecosystem. APIs, a set of tools that allow different software systems to "talk" and coordinate with one another online, have been central to Taobao's development. As the platform grew from a forum where buyers and sellers could meet and sell goods to become China's dominant e-commerce website, merchants on the site needed more and more support from third-party developers. New software had to be broadly interoperable with all other software on the platform to be of any value. So in 2009, Taobao began developing APIs for use by independent software suppliers. Today, merchants on Taobao subscribe to more than 100 software modules, on average, and the live data services they enable drastically decrease the merchants' cost of doing business. Getting the technical infrastructure right is just the beginning. It took tremendous effort for us to build a common standard so that data could be used and interpreted in the same way across all of Alibaba's business units. Additionally, figuring out the right incentive structures to persuade companies to share the data they have is an important and ongoing challenge. Much more work is needed. Of course, the degree to which companies can innovate in this area will depend in part on the rules governing data sharing in the countries they're operating in. But the direction is very clear: The more data flows across the network, the smarter the business becomes, and the more value the ecosystem creates.

Step 4: Apply the algorithms. Once a business has all its operations online, it will experience a deluge of data. To assimilate, interpret, and use the data to its advantage, the firm must create models and algorithms that make explicit the underlying product logic or market dynamics that the business is trying to optimize. This is a huge creative undertaking that requires many new skills, hence the enormous demand for data scientists and economists. Their challenge is to specify what job they want the machine to do, and they have to be very clear about what constitutes a job well done in a particular business setting. From very early on, our goal for Taobao was to tailor it to each individual's needs. This would have been impossible without advances in machine learning. Today, when customers log on, they see a customized webpage with a selection of products curated from the billions offered by our millions of sellers. The selection is generated automatically by Taobao's powerful recommendation engine. Its algorithms, which are designed to optimize the conversion rate of each visit, churn data generated across Taobao's platform, from operations to customer service to security.

A milestone in Taobao's growth, in 2009, was the upgrade from simple browsing, which worked reasonably well when the platform had many fewer visits and products to handle, to a search engine powered by machine-learning algorithms and capable of processing huge volumes of inquiries. Taobao has also been experimenting with optical-recognition search algorithms that can take a photo of a desired item supplied by the customer and match it to available products on the platform. While we are still in the early stages of using this technology to drive sales, the function has proved very popular with customers, boasting 10 million unique visits daily. In 2016, Alibaba introduced an AI-powered chatbot to help field customer queries. It is different from the mechanical service providers familiar to most people that are programmed to match customer queries with answers in their repertoire. Alibaba's chatbots are "trained" by experienced representatives of Taobao merchants. They know all about the products in their categories and are well versed in the mechanics of Alibaba's platforms—return policies, delivery costs, how to make changes to an order—and other common questions customers ask. Using a variety of machine-learning technologies, such as semantic comprehension, context dialogues, knowledge graphs, data mining, and deep learning, the chatbots rapidly improve their ability to diagnose and fix customer issues automatically, rather than simply return static responses that prompt the consumer to take further action. They confirm with the customer that the solution presented is acceptable and then execute it. No human action by Alibaba or the merchant occurs.

Chatbots can also make a significant contribution to a seller's top line. Apparel brand Senma, for example, started using one a year ago and found that the bot's sales were 26 times higher than the merchant's top human sales associate.

There will always be a need for human customer representatives to deal with complicated or personal issues, but the ability to handle routine queries via a chatbot is very useful, especially on days of high volume or special promotions. Previously, most large sellers on our platform would hire tempworkers to handle consumer inquiries during big events. Not anymore. During Alibaba's biggest sales day in 2017, the chat-bot handled more than 95% of customer questions, responding to some 3.5 million consumers. These four steps are the basis for creating a smart business: Engage in creative data fication to enrich the pool of data the business uses to become smarter; software the business to put workflows and essential actors online; institute standards and APIs to enable real-time data flow and coordination; and apply machine-learning algorithms to generate "smart" business decisions. All the activities involved in the four steps are important new competencies that require a new kind of leadership.

The Leader's Role

In my course on smart business at Hupan School of Entrepreneurship, I show a slide of 10 business leaders and ask the students to identify them. They can easily pick out Jack Ma, Elon Musk and Steve Jobs. But virtually no one can identify the CEO of CitiGroup or Toyota or General Electric. There is a reason for this. Unlike GE, Toyota, and CitiGroup, which deliver products or services through optimized supply chains, digital companies must mobilize a network to realizetheir vision. To do that, their leaders have to inspire the employees, partners, and customers who make up that network. They must be visionaries and evangelists, outspoken in a way that the leaders of traditional companies do not have to be. At the highest level, the digital evangelists must understand what the future will look like and how their industries will evolve in response to societal, economic, and technological changes.

They cannot describe concrete steps to realize their companies'goals because the environment is too fluid and the capabilities they will require are unknowable. Instead, they must define what the firm seeks to achieve and create an environment in which workers can quickly string together experimental products and services, test the market, and scale the ideas that elicit a positive response. Digital leaders no longer manage; rather, they enable workers to innovate and facilitate the core feedback loop of user responses to firm decisions and execution. In the smart business model, machine-learning algorithms take on much of the burden of incremental improvement by automatically making adjustments that increase system wide efficiency. Thus, leaders' most important job is to cultivate creativity. Their mandate is to increase the success rate of innovation rather than improve the efficiency of the operation.

Digital-Native Companies such as Alibaba have the advantage of being born online and data-ready, so their transformation to smart business is quite natural. Now that they have proven the model works and are transforming the old industrial economy, it is time for all companies to understand and apply this new business logic. That may look technologically intimidating, but it is becoming more and more feasible. The commercialization of cloud computing and artificial intelligence technologies has made large-scale computational power and analytic capabilities accessible to anyone. Indeed, the cost of storing and computing large quantities of data has dropped dramatically over the past decade. This means that real-time applications of machine learning are now possible and affordable in more and more environments. The rapid development of internet-of-things technology will further digitize our physical surroundings, providing ever more data. As these innovations accumulate in the coming decades, the winners will be companies that get smart faster than the competition.

(Source: Ming Zeng, Alibaba and the Future of Business, Harvard business review, September-October, 2018.)

Questions:

1. Have you ever had shopping experience on Alibaba? Do you think shopping online is a new way of consumption?

2. What is culture? Can lifestyle changes change the structure of consumption? Take Alibaba for example, give your reasons?

3. How does Alibaba adapt to the changing consumer culture? Give your reasons.

5.5   Expanding Reading

A change in people's lifestyle will bring new business. Take garbage sorting in Shanghai, residents in the metropolis have developed a variety of new dining habits. Since Shanghai's domestic waste management regulation implementation began on July 1, new business has emerged.

Reading-1

Waste management becoming big business

Regulations requiring Shanghai households and enterprises to sort their trash will create opportunities in circular economy. Trash sorting was a hot topic in

Shanghai in the weeks before a new municipal regulation on waste management took effect on July 1, requiring everyone, from households to businesses, to sort their trash into recyclable, kitchen, hazardous and residual waste. Though the regulation inconveniences people while they form new habits and those who don't comply face fines, it has boosted existing waste treatment business and will create new opportunities in the circular economy. Dealing with waste is big business as 200 billion yuan ($29 billion) in investment will be needed if the current trash-sorting program in Shanghai is to be implemented across China, according to a recent report by Orient Securities. The report calculated a 7. 56-billion-yuan market for Shanghai in the whole industrial chain-education, monitoring of garbage disposal, transportation, and construction of waste treatment facilities. It then projected the Shanghai model to the national level, and estimated the market size will be around 200 billion yuan. China plans to set up domestic waste classification systems in 46 major cities by next year, and all the cities at prefecture level and above, about 300, should have similar systems to classify and dispose of trash by 2025, according to the Ministry of Housing and Urban-Rural Development. Zhang Lequn, deputy director of the urban development department at the ministry, said in a news conference in June that the government will inject 21. 3 billion yuan into the building of waste treatment facilities. As the trash-sorting program is implemented in Shanghai, more kitchen and food waste, which will demand proper treatment facilities, is being separated from residual waste. According to the Shanghai Municipal Administration of Landscaping and City Appearance, Shanghai now has more than 6,000 metric tons of kitchen waste every day, but the existing kitchen waste treatment facility can only process about 5,000 tons. The administration is responsible for the city's domestic waste management, and it aims to increase the capacity of waste treatment in Shanghai to handle more than 20,000 tons of residual waste through incineration and to utilize 7,000 tons of kitchen waste every day next year. Hua Yinfeng, general manager at Shanghai Liming Resources Reuse Co, told local news portal Shanghai Observer: "All the people sorting trash have given us confidence to expand our plant. " The company operates an organic waste treatment center in Pudong New Area that turns kitchen waste into electricity. Its current capacity is 300 tons of kitchen waste per day, and the plant expansion will allow it to process another 700 tons. The plant uses correctly sorted organic waste to produce biogas, but when it started in 2017, about 30% to 40% of the waste it received contained other waste such as plastic bottles, construction trash and paper, which needed to be removed first to avoid lower efficiency during the anaerobic procedure. The purity of the kitchen waste rose significantly in 2018 when Shanghai announced an action plan for trash sorting, and now after the implementation of the regulation, 99% of the waste it receives meets the minimum quality level, said Hua. The expansion of Liming Resources is just one example of the acceleration of the capacity building taking place in Shanghai. A biological kitchen waste treatment center is due to open by the end of July on Chongming Island, Shanghai, that will use kitchen waste to feed fly maggots, which on maturity can be used as animal feed and their droppings as fertilizer. The center is operated by Shanghai Yuanshi Environment and will work as a biotechnology demonstration area. "If our technology meets market requirements, we hope it can be applied in other districts in Shanghai," said Na Chenning, co-founder of Shanghai Yuanshi Environment, adding that the profit from processing 1 ton of kitchen waste through this technology is about 700 to 800 yuan. Apart from waste treatment, many startups are eyeing opportunities in other parts of the long value chain. Yang Fei, a lecturer of economics at Zhejiang University of Science and Technology, said the compulsory trash sorting will make once valueless trash profitable. According to the National Bureau of Statistics, China produced 215 million tons of domestic waste in 2017, up nearly 60% from 2001. The State Council plans to reach a recycling rate of at least 35% of domestic waste in the 46 major cities by 2020. Heather Kaye, an American fashion designer, has started using recycled materials to make swimwear. She and her friend Indian designer Itee Soni registered a company called Golden Finch in Shanghai in 2010, and they launched a new brand Loop Swim in 2019 to highlight the company's sustainable production. "Ten plastic bottles can make one set of Bikini top and bottom, and 14 plastic bottles can make a sun protective shirt," said Kaye. "We prefer to manufacture locally as much as possible, so all of our Asia, Australia and Middle East production is proudly-and beautifully-made in China. " Kaye said she was excited to see Shanghai's trash-sorting program taking effect, and the incredible level of commitment from the government and the citizens wanting to use resources wisely impressed her. "We know China has studied recycling systems around the world before implementing the current plans, and is looking for ways to make recycling profitable for the private companies who will likely take it over," she said. "When waste has value, people see opportunities. " Gao Cheng, a former veteran private equity investor from Hong Kong, is also digging for gold in the recycling industry. She founded a startup EcoEasy in July, and wants to introduce biodegradable food containers into the fast-growing food delivery market. "The trash-sorting program is good news for us, because it is an important step toward building a circular economy in China," Gao said. Chinese people used an average 60 million take-away containers per day in 2018, and the number is still growing, but most of them have not been recycled because the containers are usually contaminated by food and oil, she said. "Although the existing kitchen waste treatment centers in China might not have the facility and standards to process biodegradable plastics together with food waste, this is what we are working to solve," she said. Song Ya'nan, an environment industry researcher at Guotai Junan Securities, said the trash-sorting program has created a social consensus on supporting businesses related to environmental protection, and that will help the industry grow in the long term. "The upgrade of waste treatment facilities will push the growth, and new technologies in waste processing will receive more investment," Song said.

(Source: Xing Yi, Waste management becoming big business, China Daily, July 25, 2019.)

Reading-2

Museums mint money from merchandise

Assorted modern souvenirs retell past stories to cultural buyers, boost revenue.

Museums in China are increasingly exploiting the power of the intellectual property they own through merchandise. Art, figurines, icons, replicas of jewelry, and various products printed with designs or images of ancient objects are all finding buyers in the souvenir market. Zhao Xinhao, 31, is one such cultural consumer. A government employee, she recently parted with 199 yuan ($29) to buy a pair of earrings in shape of guzheng (Chinese zither) strings. The earrings make her feel more Chinese, Zhao said. Among her other favorites are a notebook with printed quotes of Emperor Yongzheng (1722-35) in Qing Dynasty (1644-1911), Chinese princess dolls, and adhesive tapes painted with images of Beijing's Palace Museum.

To own souvenirs with Chinese cultural elements has become something of a fashion. More and more museums are jumping on the bandwagon, using their collections to create goods that can meet market demand. "Such products convey a sense of delicate design. They are affordable and their quality isn't bad. New products are released every month. I just can't stop buying them," Zhao said. Li Yuanyuan, 31, an entrepreneur in the cultural industry in Beijing, said her personal "collection" now includes the entire range of collectibles related to the Palace Museum. She spends more than 10,000 yuan on average annually on such goods. Her favorites include limited-edition bags and necklaces with intricate patterns, which she wears to events overseas, so that "people can tell where I come from at first sight". Guo Ying, 21, a collegian in Xianyang, Shaanxi province, said although she buys loads of animation products and games-related dolls or pillows, what give her true joy are the adorable little objects she bought at various museums.

The Palace Museum, also known as the Forbidden City, houses 1. 86 million cultural items. China's imperial palace from 1420 to 1911, the museum is popular among tourists, artists, architects, researchers and historians alike. In recent years, the museum began harnessing the potential for revenue from souvenirs. Its limited-edition set of lipstick cases has colorful miniature imagery of butterflies, deer and blossoms. They showcase traditional Chinese royal aesthetics. No sooner had their online sale begun in December than they sold out. Sales of the museum's cultural and creative products grew from 600 million yuan in 2013 to 1 billion yuan in 2016. Merchandise revenue for 2018 is estimated to reach about 1. 5 billion yuan. Liu Dongming, a marketing expert from Tencent's intelligent marketing division, said the museum's fame, coupled with the large number of its visitors, has laid a solid base for the merchandise business to boom. Besides, the newly launched products are very creative and have utility value, he said.

In May 2016, the government released a document to encourage culture and relics-related institutions, such as museums, galleries, libraries, and memorial halls, to develop cultural and creative products, in a bid to integrate traditional culture into modern life and meet demand among consumers for cultural merchandise. By the end of 2017, about 2, 500 museums and other cultural institutions have produced such products, which include earphones in the shape of court beads, scarves decorated with famous paintings, and funny emojis such as a Chinese emperor holding a rose and a thick paper fan emblazoned with the words "I miss you too". "Generally, the idea of a museum conveys a sense of heavy or dull historical objects covered with dust. But using modern design and technology, the power in such objects to stir cultural pride can be harnessed. Merchandise, in turn, gives such objects added significance," said Ji Gang, partner of consultancy firm Roland Berger.

From January to October 2018, the number of netizens who searched for "museum" on Tmall and Taobao, China's major e-commerce platforms, rose 2. 15 times from the same period in 2016. Among them, about 90% were looking for cultural and creative products, data from Tmall showed. About 76% were female consumers and more than 30% were people aged 19 to 25, it said. Ji further said some museums now have teams of designers and salespeople dedicated to their merchandising business. Some institutions cooperate with other firms to develop such products, earning copyright fee in the process. Although nascent in China, cultural products are a popular business in the West. About one-third of revenue of the Museum of Modern Art in New York comes from IP-related products. Similarly, British Museum's revenue from merchandise reached about $ 200 million in 2015. Without entrance fee, a large part of its revenue comes from cultural and creative products. The museum sells about 60 products that are based on the Rosetta Stone alone, Ji said. So, museums must try to make use of their most famous collections with the help of top global experts in the field. They should research consumer demand, and come up with products that can retell past stories to the new generation, Ji said. According to He Yizan, CEO of Alfilo Brands, a Shanghai-based firm dealing in IP-related products, China's per-capita GDP in 2017 exceeded $8,000, which is considered the threshold when citizens start to care more about aesthetics, culture and spiritual life. Clearly, China has entered a boom period for art consumption, he said.

(Source: Chen Meiling, Museums mint money from merchandise, China Daily, January 1, 2019.)

Reading-3

Cultural elements bring vitality to products

Brands exploit tradition-related themes and IP to pack a punch in marketing. In early January, a shopping center in Guangzhou, capital of South China's Guangdong province, hosted a candy and snack fair themed on the Qing Dynasty (1644-1911). What made the fair stand out were its red lanterns and candy made using the "royal kitchen method". Chinese confectionary maker Hsu Fu Chi International Limited, which was acquired by Nestlé Group in 2011, chose this event to kick off its marketing campaign for the Chinese Lunar New Year, which begins on Tuesday. With television serials about the Qing Dynasty period, such as The Story of Yanxi Palace and Ruyi's Royal Love in the Palace proving popular among the younger generation last year, Hsu Fu Chi has developed a series of royalty-and palace-themed entertainment content and gift packs. "The move is to better communicate with younger consumers by emphasizing popular traditional elements, given that the atmosphere of Spring Festival or Nian (year) festivities has grown somewhat weaker each year," said Qiao Ruilin, marketing manager of Hsu Fu Chi. For this year's week-long holiday, has rolled out 43 varieties of candy, cakes and chocolates. In addition to renovating displays at its offline stores, it has introduced its new products on its online stores. "The palace-themed packaging is not just to be in line with a recent trend but, more importantly, an attempt to pass on China's significant cultural heritage to the younger generation during the Spring Festival holiday," said Qiao.

Meanwhile, Beijing-based tea maker Xiao Guan Tea has partnered with the Prince Kung's Palace Museum to introduce Spring Festival gift packs of tea, as part of the company's efforts to attract younger Chinese back to tea consumption. The tea gift packs, themed Good Fortune, are a joint work with one of the most renowned museums, a move showing that Xiao Guan Tea aims to integrate intangible cultural heritage into modern Chinese people's lives, Mei Jiang, general manager of marketing at Xiao Guan Tea, said. The company plans to develop more products for younger consumers this year. On the anvil are convenient tea packs and colorful wrapping, Mei said. The age of consumers buying Xiao Guan Tea online is between 18 and 35, lower than the average age of consumers of the traditional tea products, Mei said. Launched in 2012, Xiao Guan Tea, which sells small-sized and convenient tea packs, has expanded quickly to more than 600 franchised stores and is available at 5,000 other retail stores in the country. Its e-commerce distribution has expanded to Tmall and JD. In 2018, Xiao Guan Tea's retail sales reached 2 billion yuan ($295 million), making it the No 1 tea brand in the country. Zhu Danpeng, an independent fast moving consumer goods analyst, said the challenge of selling history-themed products to younger consumers requires new techniques of marketing. Tradition-related merchandise these days is seen as intellectual property as it can get younger consumers' attention and unlock their purchasing power. The IP rights of the Palace Museum and the Prince Kung's Palace Museum are part of the rare and renowned resources that have an overwhelming fan base nationwide, Zhu said. Therefore, it would benefit the brands to be associated with such popular IP, he said. In addition to working with the Palace Museum on ancient royalty themes, the biggest intellectual property of the year is the adorable pig image, as the 12-month lunar period beginning Feb. 5 is regarded the Year of the Pig. It has become the most-sought-after IP for numerous marketing campaigns of retail brands. For instance, the Disney store launched its Chinese New Year-themed products specially designed for the Chinese market. A large portfolio of products with various characters of pig in Disney's animations was launched by working with licensee partners. The brand crossovers included Lao Feng Xiang's gold accessories and Chow Tai Fook jewelry. Allen Au Yeung, vice-president of creative and product development in the Asia-Pacific region for The Walt Disney Company, said: "Disney's lovable characters such as Piglet, Pumba, Hamm, Ms Piggy and the Three Little Pigs have been part of many childhood memories across generations. " With Chinese New Year upon us, a celebratory occasion that brings families together, we are thrilled to bring fans a fun collection of products adorned with these playful characters to usher in the Year of the Pig. "The US-based food and snack maker Mondelez International has also joined the efforts to attract younger consumers with Spring Festival elements in its product design, packaging and marketing. Holly Yuan, vice-president of marketing, biscuit category, Mondelez China, said various kinds of merchandise for the Year of the Pig have already been launched one after another, in order to let Chinese consumers spend a joyous Spring Festival. Yuan said consumers have expressed great interest in its Spring Festival series of products with sales higher than that of last year. " Mondelez China knows that Spring Festival is an important consumption occasion for Chinese people, "said Yuan. " Therefore, it puts much emphasis on the product development and marketing for the Spring Festival occasions, and launches novel customized products during this period to win consumers' hearts. For example, Lu cookies, Mondelez's French cookies, were introduced two years ago in the Chinese market. Lu has joined hands with China's famous fashion photographer and visual artist Chen Man to produce two gift boxes. The gift boxes reproduced two classic posters of Lu using the modern artistic approach in connection with the elements of traditional Chinese culture. It is the first time for Lu to be wrapped in red and round shaped package to go with the Chinese New Year atmosphere. However, analyst Zhu said despite the frenzy in promoting brands with Chinese traditional elements and other kinds of IP like cultural heritage elements, the challenge for such marketing of brands is to maintain the product's top quality, to meet the expectations raised by the new marketing strategy. "If their product quality is not as exciting and updated as their marketing or packaging, the consumers would not stay with them," Zhu said.

(Source: Wang Zhuoqiong, Cultural elements bring vitality to products, China Daily, February 1, 2019.)

Quick Quiz

1. Cultural values have three aspects on work (   ).

A. work centrality

B. societal norms about work

C. work values or goals

D. person values

2. (   ) is a component of the environment for the members of the population and provides information that affects individual physiology and behavior.

A. Population trend   B. Population development

C. Population gender   D. Population structure

3. Based on the review of definition, social structure has been identified as ( ).

A. relationship of definite entities or groups to each other

B. enduring patterns of behaviour by participants in a social system in relation to each other

C. institutionalised norms or cognitive frameworks that structure the actions of actors in the social system

D. universalistic-achievement pattern

4. The common stratum model of social class divides society into a simple hierarchy of ( ).

A. working class   B. middle class

C. diamond class   D. upper class

5. Electronic commerce operates in all four of the following major market segments ( ).

A. Business to business (B to B)

B. Business to consumer (B to C)

C. Consumer to consumer (C to C)

D. Consumer to business (C to B)

Answers：

1. ABC

2. D

3. ABC

4. ABD

5. ABCD

Endnotes

[1] Du Peng. Why slower population growth should not drive us to press panic button, Global Times, January 14, 2019.

[2] Population data from United Nations World Population Prospects：The 2012 Revision, 2013.

[3] Urdal, H., A Clash of Generations? Youth Bulges and Political Violence, International studies quarterly, 2006：50, 607-629.

[4] Gregg, Tominey. The wage scar from male youth unemployment, Labour Economics, 2005 (12)：4, 487-509.

［5］Andrew Mason. Demographic dividends: the past, the present, and the future, Contributions to economic analysis, 2007 (281): 75-98.

［6］Xinhua. Full Text: Gender Equality and Women's Development in China, September 22, 2015.

［7］Boris Groysberg, Jeremiah Lee, Jesse Price, J. YoJud Cheng. The Leader's Guide to Corporate Culture, Harvard Business Review, January-February, 2018.

［8］Chen Xinguang. How establishing the Shanghai model of waste disposal can be revolutionary, Chinadaily. com. cn, June 20, 2019.

［9］Williams, R. M.. American society: A sociological interpretation (3rd Edition), Knopf, New York, 1970.

［10］Shalom H. Schwartz. A theory of cultural values and some implications for work, Applied psychology: an international review, 1999: 48 (1), 23-47.

［11］MOW International Research Team, The meaning of working, New York: Academic, 1987.

［12］Surkis, S.. Work values: influences of basic individual values and education level on their importance, Unpublished Masters thesis, The Hebrew University, Jerusalem, 1992.

［13］Vincent N. Parrillo. Encyclopedia of social problems, SAGE Publications, 2008.

［14］Gilbert, Dennis. The American class structure, New York: Wadsworth Publishing, 1998.

［15］Williams, Brian, Stacey C. Sawyer, Carl M. Wahlstrom. Marriages, families and intimate relationships, Prentice Hall (2nd Revised edition), 2005.

［16］Edward A. Tiryakian, Talcott Parsons. Politics and social structure, American Sociological Review, 1971: 76 (5).

Chapter 6　Technological Environment

Learning Objectives

　1. Recognize the trends in technology, communication, and innovation

　2. Master the connotation of technology transfer

　3. Master the Forms TNCs choose for technology transfer

　4. Understand policies of technology transfer

　5. Understand the determinants of overseas R&D

　6. Recognizethefeatures of TNCs' technological R&D

　7. Understand forms of TNCs' technological R&D

Opening case

In Search of Balance: Intellectual Property and Technology Transfer

　　This June the EU issued a formal communication following the dispute settlement procedures of the World Trade Organization. The EU is requesting consultations with China relating to Article 64 of the Agreement on Trade-Related Aspects of Intellectual Property Rights. The EU alleges China imposes restrictions on foreign intellectual property rights holders, who, because of restrictions, cannot freely negotiate market-based contractual terms of licensing and other technology-related contracts. The EU claimed that in the context of joint ventures, China imposes mandatory contract terms that are discriminatory to foreign enterprises and restrict the ability of foreign companies to protect intellectual property rights in China.

　　These allegations will be the subject of "consultations" between the EU and China within the framework of the WTO's dispute settlement system. However, consultations are not litigation. Their value is in the opportunity for an exchange of arguments and for an eventual compromise. This situation has to be understood as an opportunity to move the international debate on transfer of technology to a new level.

Historically, every rising nation seized the ideas of those who were at the time technologically more advanced—often at displeasure of the latter. Martin Wolf, a prominent columnist at the Financial Times, recently reiterated this fact. He then emphasized: "The idea intellectual property is sacrosanct is wrong. It is innovation that is sacrosanct. Intellectual property rights both help and hurt the effort. A balance has to be struck between rights that are too tight and too loose. "

Balance in technology transfers is not a new aspiration but it is of particular significance now, at the time of the fourth technological revolution. The US and the EU are insisting on stricter protection of intellectual property rights. China, in its legitimate pursuit of technological advancement, is trying to limit what it perceives as adverse effects of strict intellectual property protection.

The resulting tensions reach beyond relations among states, or, as is the case with the mentioned communication, beyond the relations between the EU and the government of China. European and American companies have an important role as stabilizers of relations with China. Their legitimate interests have to be taken into account and appropriate balance has to be found. This is increasingly understood in China.

So, what is the path toward balance and to the compromise needed in the EU-China dispute? It would be important to start with the understanding China's development is part of the global transformation in knowledge, science and technology. The challenge is to devise a system that will enable all sides to take advantage of future technological development.

The objective should be to build "win-win outcomes". For this to happen, all relevant participants have to take an open-minded approach and work to better understand China's innovation system and development plans. The WTO consultations initiated by the EU should be used as an instrument for this purpose.

Another interesting question is how to take advantage of China's ability to provide knowledge opportunities through mutually beneficial exchange and cooperation in research and education. Let's recall that innovation is more important than protection of intellectual property. And innovation is closely related to education and culture. So, it would be important to include the development of higher education and research cooperation into the equation, while keeping in mind the centrality of the trading system itself and the WTO.

There are good reasons to do whatever it takes to find a genuine compromise to the EU-China dispute on intellectual property.

There are some signs of hope. This June, China and the EU reached an agreement to launch a group that will work to update global trade rules to address technology policy, subsidies and other issues characterizing the current debate on global trade. Subsequently, in the joint statement of this year's EU-China Summit, a joint working group on WTO reform was established. The world is at a threshold of a new era. While the prospect of an old-fashioned trade war remains a real possibility, so does the process of consultations within and outside the WTO leading to better and more balanced global cooperation in the field of innovation.

(Source: Danilo Türk[1], In Search of Balance: Intellectual Property and Technology Transfer. Chinadaily, August 9, 2018.)

6.1　Trends in Technology, Communication, and Innovation

The innovation of the microprocessor could be considered the foundation of much of the technological and computing advancements seen today. The creation of a digital frame work allowed high-power computer performance at low cost. This then gave birth to such breakthroughs as the development of enhanced telecommunication systems, which will be explored in greater depth later in the chapter. Now, computers, telephones, televisions and wireless forms of communication have merged to create multimedia products and allow users anywhere in the world to communicate with one another. The Internet allows one to obtain information from literally billions of sources.

Global connections do not necessarily level the playing field, however. The challenge of integrating telecom standards has become an issue for TNCs in China. Qualcomm Corporation had wanted to sell narrowband CDMA (Code Division Multiple Access) technology; however, Qualcomm was initially unsuccessful in convincing the government that it could build enough products locally. Instead, China's current network the world's largest mobile network, uses primarily GSM technology that is popular in Europe. By 2009, however, CDMA had gained a foothold in China. According to statistics released by market research firm Sino-MR, sales volume of CDMA handsets topped 1.29 million during December 2008, up 33.6% year on year and 183% month on month, marking a five-year high.

Furthermore, concepts like the open-source model allow for free and legal sharing of software and code, which may be utilized by underdeveloped countries

---

[1]　Danilo Türk was President of the Republic of Slovenia from 2007 to 2012. He is currently a non-resident senior fellow at the Chongyang Institute for Financial Studies at Renmin University of China.

in an attempt to gain competitive advantage while minimizing costs. India exemplifies this practice as it continues to increase its adoption of the Linux operating system (OS) in place of the global standard Microsoft Windows. The state of Kerala is shifting the software of its 2,600 high schools to the Linux system, which will enable a user to configure it to his or her needs with the goal of creating a new generation of adept programmers. In 2008, Microsoft unveiled DreamSpark, a software giveaway for an estimated 10 million-plus qualified students in the country. DreamSpark will provide students access to the latest Microsoft developer and designer tools at no charge to unlock their creative potential and set them on the path to academic and career success. The program is aligned to Microsoft Unlimited Potential, the company's global effort to creating sustained social and economic opportunity for everyone. More broadly, a number of for profit and nonprofit firms have been aggressively working to bring low cost computers into the hands of the hundreds of millions of children in the developing world who have not benefited from the information and computing revolution.

One initiative—One Laptop Per Child (OLPC) is a U. S. nonprofit organization set up to oversee the creation of an affordable educational device for use in the developing world. Its mission is "to create educational opportunities for the world's poorest children by providing each child with a rugged, low-cost, low-power, connected laptop with content and software designed for collaborative, joyful, self-empowered learning. " Its current focus is on the development, construction and deployment of the XO-1 laptop and its successors, notably the release of the so-called XO-3, the long-awaited upgrade to the nonprofit's XO, the so-called "hundred-dollar laptop" launched in 2007. The organization is led by chairman Nicholas Negroponte and Charles Kane, President and Chief Operating Officer. OLPC is a nonprofit organization funded by member organizations such as AMD, eBay, Google, News Corporation, Red Hat. and Marvell. As of March 2010, there are 2 million free books available for OLPC computers. Most recently, the One Laptop Per Child foundations aim is to create the world's most innovative tablet computer for the developing world, priced at less than $100. The new device is modeled in part on the education-focused Moby tablet Marvell introduced earlier in 2010, with modifications to keep the price low ($100 or less) and make the device usable in challenging environmental conditions.

There also exists a great potential for disappointment as the world relies more and more on digital communication and imaging. The world is connected by a vast network of cables which we do not see because they are either buried underground or under water. One disruption occurred off the shores of Asia on December 26,

2006, when undersea cables were destroyed by rock slides, cutting phone and Internet connections in South Korea, Japan, and India. The fact that so many were reliant on a mere 4-inch-thick shows the potential risks associated with greater global connectivity. Restoration of same services to most of the affected areas was accomplished within 12 hours of the earthquake by rerouting digital traffic through Europe to the United States with other network cables.

We have reviewed general influences of technology here, but what are some of the specific dimensions of technology and what other ways does technology affect international management? Here, we explore some of the dimensions of the technological environment currently facing international management, with a closer look at biotechnology, e-business, telecommunications, and the connection between technology, outsourcing, and offshoring.

1. Biotechnology

The digital age has given rise to such innovations as computers, cellular phones, and wireless technology. Advancements within this realm allow for more efficient communication and productivity to the point where the digital world has extended its effect from information systems to biology. Biotechnology is the integration of science and technology, but more specifically it is the creation of agricultural or medical products through industrial use and manipulation of living organisms. At first glance, it appears that the fusion of these two disciplines could breed a modern bionic man immune to disease, especially with movements toward technologically advanced prosthetics, cell regeneration through stem cell research, or laboratory-engineered drugs to help prevent or cure diseases such as HIV or cancer.

Pharmaceutical competition is also prevalent on the global scale with China's raw material reserve and the emergence of biotech companies such as Genentech and the newMerck, after its acquisition of Swiss biotech company Serono. India is emerging as a major player, with its largest, mostly generic, pharmaceutical company Ranbaxy's ability to Produce effective and affordable drugs. While pharmaceutical companies mainly manufacture drugs through a process similar to that of organic chemistry, biotech companies attempt to discover genetic abnormalities or medicinal solutions through exploring organisms at the molecular level or by formulating compounds from inorganic materials that mirror organic substances. DNA manipulation in the laboratory extends beyond human research. As mentioned above, another aspect of biotech research is geared toward agriculture. Demand for ethanol in the United States is on the rise due to uncertain future oil supplies, making corn-derived ethanol a viable alternative. Yet, using corn as a fuel alternative will not only increase the cost of fuel but also create an imbalance between consumable corm and stock used for biofuel. For this and many other reasons, global companies like Monsanto are collaborating with others such as BASF AG to work toward creating genetically modified seeds such as drought-tolerant corn and herbicide-tolerant soybeans. Advancements in this industry include nutritionally advanced crops that may help alleviate world hunger.

Aside from crops, the meat industry can also benefit from this process. The outbreak of mad cow disease in Great Britain sparked concern when evidence of the disease spread throughout Western Europe; however, the collaborative work of researchers in the United States and Japan may have engineered a solution to the problem by eliminating the gene which is the predecessor to making the animal susceptible to this ailment. Furthermore, animal cloning, which simply makes a copy of pre-existing DNA, could boost food production by producing more meat or dairy-producing animals. The first evidence of a successful animal clone was Dolly, born in Scotland in 1996. Complications arose, and Dolly aged at an accelerated rate, indicating that while she provided hope, there still existed many flaws in the process. While the United States is the only country that allows cloned animal products to be incorporated in the food supply, other countries actively cloning animals include Australia, Italy, China, South Korea, Japan and New Zealand. The world is certainly changing, and the trend toward technological integration is far from over. Whether one desires laser surgery to correct eyesight, a vaccine for emerging viruses, or more nutritious food, there is a biotechnology firm competing to be the first to achieve these goals. Hunger and poor health care are worldwide issues, and advancement in global biotechnology is working to raise the standards.

2. E-Business

As the Internet becomes increasingly widespread, it is having a dramatic effect on international commerce.

Tens of millions of people around the world have now purchased books from Amazon. com, and the company has now expanded its operations around the world. So have a host of other electronic retailers (e-tailers) which are discovering that their home-grown retailing expertise can be easily transferred and adapted for the international market. Dell Computer has been offering B2C (electronic business-to-consumer) goods and services in Europe for a number of years, and the automakers are now beginning to move in this direction. Most automotive firms sell custom cars online. Other firms are looking to use e-business to improve their current operations. For example, Deutsche Bank has overhauled its entire retail network with the goal of winning affluent customers across the continent. Yet the most popular form of e-business is for business-to-business (B2B) dealings, such as placing orders and interacting with suppliers worldwide. Business-to-consumer (B2C) transactions will not be as large, but this is an area where many MNCs are trying to improve their operations.

The area of e-business that will most affect global customers is e-retailing financial services. For example, customers can now use their keyboard to pay by card, although security remains a problem. However, the day is fast approaching electronic cash (e-cash) will become common. This scenario already occurs in a number of forms. A good example is prepaid smart cards, which are being used mostly for telephone calls and public transportation. An individual can purchase one of these cards and use it in lieu of cash. This idea is blending with the Internet, allowing individuals to buy and sell merchandise and transfer funds electronically. The result will be global digital cash, which will take advantage of existing worldwide markets that allow buying and selling on a 24-hour basis.

Some companies, such as ING DIRECT, the U. S. s largest direct bank, are completely "disintermediating" banking by eliminating the branches and other "bricks" and "mortar" facilities altogether. ING has more than 7. 6 million savings customers and $89. 7 billion in assets. ING DIRECT has developed a comprehensive social media "Savers Community," including Twitter, Facebook, and its "We, the Savers" blog. And so far, not one of the 275-plus bank failures in the U. S., since the financial crisis began in 2008, have been online banks. HSBC and other global banks are learning from ING'S success and growing their Internet banking globally. AirAsia, a growing regional airline in Southeast Asia, has distributed tickets electronically since its inception, demonstrating that even in regions where Internet penetration had not been extensive, electronic distribution is possible and profitable.

3. Telecommunications

One of the most important dimensions of the technological environment facing international management today is telecommunications. To begin with, it no longer is necessary to hardwire a city to provide residents with telephone service. This can be done wirelessly, thus allowing people to use cellular phones, pagers, and other telecommunications services. As a result, a form of technologic leapfrogging is occurring, in which regions of the world are moving from a situation where phones were unavailable to one where cellular is available everywhere, including rural areas, due to the quick and relatively inexpensive installation of cellular infrastructure. In addition, technology is merging the telephone and the computer. As a result, Growing numbers of people in Europe and Asia are now accessing the Web through their cell phones. Over the next decade, the merging of the Internet and wireless technology will radically change the ways people communicate. Wireless technology is also proving to be a boon for less developed countries, such as in South America and Eastern Europe where customers once waited years to get a telephone installed.

One reason for this rapid increase in telecommunications services is many countries believe that without an efficient communications system their economic growth may stall. Additionally, governments are accepting the belief that the only way to attract foreign investment and know-how in telecommunications is to cede control to private industry. As a result, while most telecommunications operations in the Asia-Pacific region were state-run a decade ago, a growing number are now in private hands. Singapore Telecommunications, Pakistan Telecom, Thailand's Telecom Asia, South Korea Telecom. and Globe Telecom in the Philippines all have been privatized, and TNCs have helped in this process by providing investment funds. Today, NYNEX holds a stake in Telecom Asia; Bell Atlantic and Ameritech each own 25 percent of Telecom New Zealand; and Bell South has an ownership position in Australia's Optus. At the same time, Australia's Telestra is moving into Vietnam, Japan's NTT is investing in Thailand, and South Korea Telecom is in the Philippines and Indonesia.

Many governments are reluctant to allow so much private and foreign ownership such a vital industry; however, they also are aware that foreign investors will go elsewhere if the deal is not satisfactory. The Hong Kong office of Salomon Brothers, a U. S. investment bank, estimates that to meet the expanding demand for telecommunication service in Asia, companies will need to considerably increase the investment, most of which will have to come from overseas. TNCs are unwilling to put up this much money unless they are assured of operating control and a sufficiently high return on their investment.

4. Technological Advancements, Outsourcing, and Offshoring

As TNCs use advanced technology to help them communicate, produce, and deliver their goods and services internationally, they face a new challenge: how technology will affect the nature and number of their employees. Some informed observers note that technology already has eliminated much and in the future will eliminate even more of the work being done by middle management and white-collar staff. Mounting cost pressures resulting from increased globalization of competition and profit expectations exerted by investors have placed pressure on TNCs to outsource or offshore production to take advantage of lower labor and other costs. In the past century, machines replaced millions of manual laborers, but those who worked with their minds were able to thrive and survive. During the past three decades in particular, employees in blue-collar, smoke-stack industries such as steel and autos have been down sized by technology, and the result has been a permanent restructuring of the number of employees needed to run factories efficiently. In the 1990s, a similar trend unfolded in the white-collar service industries (insurance, banks, and even government). Most recently, this trend has affected high-tech companies in the late 1990s and early 2000s, when after the dot-com bubble burst, hundreds of thousands of jobs were lost, and again in 2008 ~ 2010, when many jobs were lost in finance and related industries as a result of the financial crisis and global recession. According to the U. S. Bureau of Labor Statistics, on a net basis, more than 400,000 finance jobs were lost in the U. S. from July 2008 to 2009, and nearly1. 5 million jobs were lost in professional and business services.

Some experts predict that in the future technology has the potential to displace employees in all industries, from those doing low-skilled jobs to those holding positions traditionally associated with knowledge work. For example, voice recognition is helping to replace telephone operators; the demand for postal workers has been reduced substantially by address-reading devices; and cash-dispensing machines can do 10 times more transactions in a day than bank tellers, so tellers can be reduced in number or even eliminated entirely in the future. Also, expert systems can eliminate human thinking completely. For example, American Express has an expert system that performs the credit analysis formerly done by college-graduate financial analysts. In the medical field, expert systems can diagnose some illnesses as well as doctors can, and robots capable of performing certain operations are starting to be used.

Emerging information technology also makes work more portable. As a result, TNCs have been able to move certain production activities overseas to capitalize on cheap labor resources. This is especially true for work that can be easily contracted with overseas locations. For example, low-paid workers in India and Asian countries now are being given subcontracted work such as labor-intensive software development and code-writing jobs. A restructuring of the nature of work and of employment is a result of such information technology.

The new technological environment has both positives and negatives for TNCs and societies as a whole. On the positive side, the cost of doing business worldwide should decline thanks to the opportunities that technology offers in substituting lower-cost machines for higher-priced labor. Over time, productivity should go up, and prices should go down. On the negative side, many employees will find either their Jobs eliminated or their wages and salaries reduced because they have been replaced by machines and their skills are no longer in high demand. This job loss from technology can be especially devastating in developing countries. However, it doesn't have to be this way. A case in point is South Africa's showcase for automotive productivity as represented by the Delta Motor Corporation's Opel Corsa plant in Port Elizabeth. To provide as many jobs as possible, this world-class operation automated only 23%, compared to more than 85% auto assembly in Europe and North America. Also, some industries can add jobs. For example, the positive has outweighed the negative in the computer and information technology industry, despite its ups and downs. Specifically, employment in the U. S computer software industry has increased over the last decade. In less developed countries such as India, a high-tech boom in recent years has created jobs and opportunities for a growing number of people. Additionally, even though developed countries such as Japan and the United States are most affected by technological displacement of workers, both nations still lead the world in creating new jobs and shifting their traditional industrial structure toward a high-tech, knowledge-based economy. In addition to the trends discussed above, other specific ways in which technology affect international management in the next decade include:

(1) Rapid advances in biotechnology that are built on the precise manipulation of organisms, which will revolutionize the fields of agriculture, medicine and industry.

(2) The emergence of nanotechnology, in which nanomachines will possess the ability to remake the whole physical universe.

(3) Satellites that will play a role in learning. For example, communication firms will place tiny satellites into low orbit, making it possible for millions of people, even in remote or sparsely populated regions such as Siberia, the Chinese desert, and the African interior, to send and receive voice, data, and digitized images through handheld telephones.

(4) Automatic translation telephones, which will allow people to communicate naturally in their own language with anyone in the world who has access to a telephone.

(5) Artificial intelligence and embedded learning technology, which will allow thinking that formerly was felt to be only the domain of humans to occur in

machines.

(6) Silicon chips containing up to 100 million transistors, allowing computing power that now rests only in the hands of supercomputer users to be avail-able on every desktop.

(7) Supercomputers that are capable of I trillion calculations per second, which will allow advances such as simulations of the human body for testing new drugs and computers that respond easily to spoken commands.

The development and subsequent use of these technologies have greatly benefited the most developed countries in which they were first deployed. However, the most positive effects should be seen in developing countries where inefficiencies in labor and production impede growth. Although all these technological innovations will affect international management, specific technologies will have especially pronounced effects in transforming economies and business practices. The following discussion highlights some specific dimensions of the technological environment currently facing international management.

6. 2　Technology Transfer

6. 2. 1　Connotation of Technology Transfer

Technology transfer is the activity that the technology supplier transfers certain technology and related rights to the recipient by certain means. Technology is a kind of knowledge body that can be transferred by learning process. When technologies are transferred from one country to another, the situation may be complicated, and it may happen even within transnational corporations (TNCs). Technology has become the prime driving force for modern economic growth. In an era of knowledge economy, with new technologies constantly emerging and technological advancement and update speeding up, ownership and application of advanced technology means powerful competitive edge.

International technology transfer is the transfer of three technological factors, namely skill, techniques and knowledge, from one country to another or from one company to another. This transfer can be done through technological assistance, technology trade or interchange of technical personnel and joint R&D, etc.. Technology transfer is technology export from the standpoint of a supplier and technology import from the standpoint of a recipient. Technology transfer can be free or for a fee. Usually, technology transfer for economic benefit is called non-gratuitous transfer. The rapid development of international technological trade has proved that non-gratuitous technological transfer is exerting a growing important effect in the diffusion of world technologies.

There are four reasons for TNCs to undertake technology transfer:

(1) TNCs implement global strategy through international technology transfer. TNCs aim at world market, maximizing global interest through resource allocation worldwide. The tactics of technological innovation, monopoly and competition is the core of TNCs'global strategy. This is for the needs to constantly develop new product and maintain or enlarge their market share, and more importantly to struggle for or maintain their monopoly position in the industry, that is, for survival and development.

(2) TNCs earn huge profit by international technology transfer. Technology transfer not only pays for the work of technological innovation, but also brings in value increase of profit and cost. Because technology is a kind of creative production, which has high added value, and the price is indefinable, TNCs with monopoly position usually transfer technologies at high price, thus earning large profit. This is one of the most important sources of income for TNCs.

(3) TNCs readjust their industrial structure through technology transfer, thus stimulating the development of new technologies. To keep in line with the development of high-tech industries, TNCs are all actively readjusting their industrial structure and transferring traditional industries and technologies to developing countries with a view to achieving the transfer of sunset industries. Meanwhile, it is difficult for TNCs to dominate a certain technological area for along time. Therefore, TNCs maintain their leading position only by concentrating on the development of most promising technologies, which requires them to transfer minor technologies and concentrate resources on new technology.

(4) TNCs seize host countries' markets by technology transfer. The eagerness of developing countries to develop domestic economy by introducing foreign technology and their policy of market-for technology go a long way to help TNCs to enter local market and facilitate technology transfer. TNCs with advanced technologies can rapidly seize large local market shares in certain sectors with the help of technology.

China-Arab States Expo Unlocks Potential for Win-win Cooperation

The rising popularity of a water-saving irrigation system in Oman and Egypt, designed by Northwest China's Ningxia University, serves as a witness to the China-

Arab win-win cooperation in science and technology.

Comprised of underground pipes, wind and solar power equipment and mobile intelligent control devices, the system enables water to spread to targeted spots more accurately compared with many surface drip irrigation systems currently deployed in Arab countries.

"It is more water-efficient and can be controlled remotely with just a smartphone," said Sun Zhaojun, dean of the school of resources and environment at Ningxia University and head of a China-Arab joint laboratory on resources and environmental governance in arid areas. "It is labor-saving, cost-effective and very popular in Arab countries."

The third China-Arab States Expo held in 2017 saw the signing of a technology transfer cooperation agreement between Ningxia University and a university in Oman. So far, more than a dozen sets of such water-saving irrigation equipment have been exported from China to Oman.

It was followed by similar cooperation on water-saving irrigation technology between China and Egypt, with an agreement signed during the fourth China-Arab States Expo that ran from Thursday to Sunday.

Ahmed Galal, dean of Faculty of Agriculture at Ain Shams University in Egypt, said the Chinese water-saving irrigation system is "very impressive, particularly because the system can be used in desert areas" that lack electricity and water.

Welcoming the cooperation, Galal said the Egyptian government is seeking to replace outdated traditional irrigation methods with modern ones to save irrigation water.

This is only a part of broader China-Arab science and technology cooperation for mutual benefit highlighted at the China-Arab States Expo, which, held biennially since 2013, has become an important platform for China and the Arab states to jointly pursue Belt and Road cooperation.

High-tech cooperation

This year's expo featured a number of exhibitions displaying high-tech innovations in the fields of artificial intelligence, aerospace, new energy and Internet Plus healthcare to showcase the latest achievements in China-Arab sci-tech cooperation.

Among the exhibitors at the event was Huawei, which presented a series of equipment with 5G technology, including security robots.

Abdullah Ahmed Al Saleh, undersecretary for Foreign Trade and Industry of the Ministry of Economy of the United Arab Emirates, said during the expo that there is huge potential for China and Arab nations to cooperate in science and technology, with the rapid development of state-of-the-art technologies such as 5G, AI, blockchain and the internet of things.

"This is in line with the interests of both sides," he added. "It helps open up new markets for Chinese commodities and also contributes to the implementation of Arab states' own development plans. "

Notable progress has been observed in the development and application of AI and 5G technology in recent years in China, which boasted a mobile internet population of more than 840 million as of June 2019.

In 2018, China's digital economy totaled 31.3 trillion yuan ($4.4 trillion), accounting for 34.8% of its GDP, according to the latest statistical report on China's internet development.

Khaled Hanafy, secretary-general of the Union of Arab Chambers, expressed the hope that Arab countries would take advantage of the fourth industrial revolution to cooperate with China in more areas than just trade, such as IoT, 3D printing and Internet Plus.

"The close cooperation between China and Arab states in science and technology will contribute to the all-round development of both sides," Hanafy said.

Mutual benefit

China-Arab economic and trade cooperation has gained steam in recent years. Last year, the bilateral trade volume reached $244.3 billion, jumping 28% year-on-year.

The China-Arab States Technology Transfer Center was inaugurated at the 2015 expo to facilitate technology cooperation.

The Ningxia-based organization over the past four years has formed eight sub-centers in Arab countries, including Saudi Arabia, the United Arab Emirates, Jordan and Morocco, according to GuoBingchen, head of the sci-tech department of the Ningxia regional government.

The technology transfer network has played a "pivotal role" in training personnel and matching technology with needs from both sides, Guo said.

A report unveiled by Xinhua Silk Road, a brand of the China Economic Information Service, at the expo identifies the great potential for China-Arab cooperation in areas of infrastructure construction, energy, international shipping, 5G and AI.

"Effective policy communication, sound economic and trade relations and strong economic complementarity are favorable conditions for deepening China-Arab third market cooperation," it says.

Addressing Thursday's opening ceremony of the expo, Cao Jianming, vice-chairman of the Standing Committee of the National People's Congress, called for concerted efforts from both sides to pursue Belt and Road cooperation to benefit more people.

（Source：China-Arab States Expo unlocks potential for win-win cooperation. Xinhua net, September 10, 2019.）

6. 2. 2　Forms TNCs Choose for Technology Transfer

TNCs technology transfer has different modes such as license transaction, technical co-ordination, projects contract of complete plants, cooperative production, equity joint-venture and wholly-owned subsidiaries.

1. License Transaction

Technology supplier (also licenser) sells patent technologies, proprietary technologies, use-right of trademark, and manufacture or sales right to recipient (also licensee or buyer) by signing license contract, permitting licensee the use of the sold object under certain conditions.

The objects of license transaction are patent technology, proprietary technology and product. So, there are three relevant license modes, patent license, proprietary technology license and trademark license.

（1）Patent license. Patent license is the main form of technology transfer, by which the owner of patent confers the use-right of approved patent to the licensee. While signing patent license contract, TNCs must make clear following terms：

①Licenser must specify that this patent has been approved by and registered with the authorities and the licenser is responsible for the reliability of the patent.

②Licenser must list proprietary name, register date and valid period of the patent.

③Licenser must specify that he has vested the licensee the manufacture, use and sales right of the patent.

④Licenser is responsible for protecting the patent from infringement in both export country and the country where the licensee is located.

⑤Licenser should guarantee that the licensee can make full use of the patent right before the expiry date.

⑥Licenser should make clear whether the licensee has the right to use the patent after the expiration of the technology transfer agreement.

⑦Licenser should provide more favorable patent royalties for the licensee than for other rivals.

⑧Licenser should promise conferring use right of modified technology patent without asking for extra royalties.

（2） Proprietary technology license. Holder of a technology, except when applying for a patent to get the exclusive right, pays more attention to guard the secret of core technologies, in order to monopolize this technology. As a result, proprietary technology license is very popular in international technology trade, and even gaining higher importance. In this kind of contract, these terms should be specified:

①Licenser vests licensee only the use right of the proprietary technology, viz. the right to use the technology, not the exclusive right.

②Licensee uses the proprietary technology only in the territory stipulated by the contract.

③Licensee uses the proprietary technology only in the department stipulated by the contract, and should not expand the territory at will.

④Licensee uses the proprietary technology only in the production stipulated by the contract, and should not expand the range of use at will.

⑤Licensee cannot use the proprietary technology to manufacture licensed product beyond the capacity that stipulated in the contract.

⑥Licensee should designate certain person to contact and use proprietary technology, and to make detailed record after each use. Any copy, publication and breach of confidence are prohibited. Licensee should also keep the secret of acquired technological data or return blueprint and data at any time.

⑦Punishment terms should be specified in case that licensee breaches the secrecy.

⑧Technological advancement, acquired by licensee while uses the proprietary technology, should be gratis transferred to licenser.

⑨Licensee shall not be entitled to transfer the proprietary technology to others.

（3） Trademark license. One of the important issues concerning trademark license is to keep the reputation of it, protect it from being blemished. Accordingly, licensers need to constrain the licensee under certain condition in the contract. According to general provision, licenser has the approval or supervision right for the quality of the product manufactured by the licensee under licenser's trademark. Similarly, in the trademark license contract, licensee requires licenser to undertake such obligations:

①To state clearly that he is the owner of the trademark of certain type of products in a certain country's market.

②To allow licensee to use trademark of this type of product in a certain country's market.

③Licenser is responsible to make licensee the trademark's' registered user.

④Licenser is responsible to ensure validity of the trademark and file suit against possible infringement.

⑤Licenser cannot require the licensee to accept any mandatory obligation, such as to purchase raw material and components from licenser, etc.

⑥Licenser cannot constrain licensee's distribution of products not under licenser's trademark.

⑦Licenser should not restrain licensee from using licensee's own trademark on products that ought to have the licenser's trademark.

In license contract, licenser can choose different degrees of license to transfer technology. There are five types of license contracts with different authorization degrees as follows:

(1) Exclusive License: Within certain region and authorized duration, licensee owns exclusive use right to the licensed technology. Within the duration of the contract, licenser should not use that technology in production or distribution activities within that area, and should not transfer the same technology to the third party or even more.

(2) Sole License: Within certain region and contract duration, licensee owns exclusive use right to the licensed technology, and the third party should not use that technology to undertake production or distribution. But licenser keeps the right to produce and sell products of the technology as well as to apply the technology.

(3) Non-exclusive License: Within certain region and contract duration, licensee owns use right to the licensed technology in production and distributionproducts. Meanwhile, licenser reserves the right to use or transfer that technology.

(4) Sub-License: Licensee has the right to transfer the technology use right to third party in certain region.

(5) Cross-License: Under this license both sides vest reciprocal technologies that equal in worth to each other. Rights of both sides can be independent or non-independent.

License transaction has pros and cons for both licenser and licensee.

For licenser, there are such advantages: realize technology capitalization through investment using technology as stocks; transfer the technology for many times, thanks to the reservation of ownership; easily open international market. Its disadvantages are: constrained from other fields of host country and limited only in technology transfer; have no share in licensee's future profits; every time of transfer means cultivating competitors.

For licensee, there are such advantages: gain access to needed technology in short time, saving time and cost; help speed up technology update of the host country; realize the update of industrial structure of the host country. Its disadvantages are: brings in higher risks while new technologies are constantly emerging and lifecycles shortening; possibly cause a loss because sometimes evaluation of technology import is difficult.

2. Technical Co-ordination

Technical co-ordination is a transfer form in line with the complexity of transfer and technological receptivity of licensee. More specifically, it has such types: Personnel Training. Licenser is in charge of training professional technical staff and administrative staff; technological Consultancy Services. Licenser provides technological consultancy service to licensee or licensee entrusts technological consultancy agents with technological service, hereby absorbing foreign advanced technologies and making full use of imported technologies; Marketing Service. Licenser provides services in technology promotion and marketing service, creating better economic benefits to licensee.

The advantage of technical co-ordination is that it can overcome possible barriers to technology application and services and allow the licensee to master the imported technology.

3. Projects Contract of Complete Plants

It's often carried out when TNCs in developed countries transfer large manufacture facility technologies to corporations in developing countries. TNCs provide package transfer of technologies facilities, and workshops, including project design, installation, modification and even marketing service.

Licensers would like to choose project contract, because they can gain much more profits than only selling technology products Besides, they can keep a firm grip of the technology. For licensee, on the one hand, the technology can be put into production in a short time; on the other hand, the cost is enormous. Meanwhile, there are risks in the advancement, adaptability and operation skills, and to some extent, they are under technological control of licensers after import.

4. Joint Production

Technology seller and buyer jointly manufacture certain goods on the basis of joint production agreement. Technology in joint production can be provided by licenser or jointly developed. There are three major forms: Licenser provides technology and production facilities and both sides produce products components separately in line with; Licenser supplies components while assemblage takes place in host country; Cooperation contracting, viz. Licenser takes complete charge of needed technologies an both sides manufacture products separately according to the division of labor.

By this means, licenser can take full advantage of licensee's cheap labor force save transportation fees and import tax and reduce production cost. For licensees, on the one hand, they can safe import fees and reduce equipment import; on the other hand, they can increase comprehensive productivity of their home countries' production facilities.

5. Equity Joint-Venture

Equity joint-venture is mix of direct investment technology transfer. It is a joint-venture funded by TNC and local enterprises (two or more) based on host country's relevant laws. All parties of equity joint-venture can invest by various means, including in cash, in kind or all sorts of property rights.

By this means, TNCs can gain a good knowledge of the host country's politics, economy, technology, market and labor and make preparations for seeking sustainable profit. Meanwhile, TNCs can take full advantage of host country's resources to achieve their global strategic goals.

For the host country, they can invest with existing factories, equipments and land-use right as capital and reduce cost; they are able to learn TNCs' advanced management experience and method with insurance of the advancement and adaptability of imported technology; they can understand and get access to international market, and gradually enlarge and gain international popularity.

TNCS'selection of transfer forms depends not only on TNCs themselves, but also on many factors including the host country. More specifically, the choice depends on:

First, home country's policy. Home country's policy for FDI and license trade affects technology transfer forms Home country often encourages TNCs to transfer technologies in the form of FDI when home country and host country have signed Bilateral Investment Agreement.

Second, nature of the technology. TNCs often choose different transfer forms according to the different natures of hardware technology, software technology, operative technology or leading-edge technology. For example, TNCs often choose joint research or license for computer software development, and projects contract of complete plants for chemical production.

Third, TNCs' own global development strategy.

Fourth, host countries' political, economic and cultural environment, including political stability, Infrastructure, legal system, favorable policy, market openness, limitation on profit remittance, will affect the selection of transfer forms.

Usually TNCs choose license trade and then FDI to transfer technology, in order to gain optimum benefit. Actually, TNCs' selection for transfer forms is flexible and always combine more than one forms.

6. 2. 3   Policies of Technology Transfer

One important characteristic of international technology transfer nowadays is the increasingly stronger national intervention. Every country has formulated a series of policies and taken strict control measures banning the export of leading-edge technologies under the pretext of national economic and military security. However, technology transfer brings about both positive and negative effect Therefore, it should be a serious task to transfer technology under national control along the right track of technology and economic rules. Technology transfer policies in developed countries are different from those of developing countries. The differences are mainly manifested on three kinds of policies: encouragement policies, restriction policies and prohibition policies.

1. Encouragement Policies

（1）Encouragement policies for technology transfer of western developed countries.

① Direct government policies for technology dissemination. Developed countries not only invest huge annual R&D capital（engage in joint development with private enterprise or fund R&D activities of private enterprises）to translate technology achievements into social productivity as soon as possible. In this process, the results can be fully used by enterprises and governments promote globalization of technology development.

②Policies for institution for technology dissemination. Developed countries not only pay attention to technology dissemination, but also strengthen the building of institution for technology dissemination. With advanced communication technology and knowledge consulting industry and well-organized institutes for technology dissemination, the United States has become the world center of technology market. Advanced modern communication technology and instruments accelerate technology dissemination.

③ Policies for Science and Technology Consulting and Technology Education. Developed countries and enterprises establish technology consulting network and strengthen consulting management system through consulting and processing, transmission, management and other related technologies.

（2） Encouragement policies for technology transfer of developing countries.

①Encourage developed countries to invest and build factories in the host countries in order to promote technology in-flow from foreign enterprises, which can be developed in host countries. Meanwhile, foreign enterprises are encouraged to employ local staff by means of granting labor license visa. Government of The Republic of Panama has such rules that foreign enterprises in Panama must employ local staff with a 1 : 8 ratio, that is, a foreign company must have eight local workers against one foreign worker. Foreign technical staff are not included in this rule.

②Favorable policies for foreign scientists and technologists.

③Create good investment environment and provide warrant for the investment and technology of foreign enterprises. Developing countries do not only update infrastructure like transportation, communication, energy, education, etc., but also focus on the construction of material equipment. The infrastructure, material equipments building and technology facilities in developing countries are backward and cannot meet the requirement of modern establishment. Therefore those countries must invest large amount capital in infrastructure development to get ready for technology introduction.

④ Import countries grant tax preferences to badly needed and advanced technology project.

2. Restriction Policies and Measures

There are differences between developed and developing countries regarding restriction polices for technology transfer.

By technological advancement, it means not only that the technology introduced should be more advanced than existing technologies of the host country, but also that the protection period of the patent technology has not expired or it has not been disclosed. Technological applicability is mainly determined by the specific needs and technological development level of the host country and its capability to digest and absorb the new technology.

Economical effectiveness means that the import country should not only consider whether introduction of the technology can bring in economic benefit to its enterprises, but also analyses the impact of the introduced technology on local industries, economy and natural environment. Whether the price of the introduced technology is rational depends on such factors: the effective value of the technology, performance of products, volume of market and to what extend the recipients obtain the technology, etc. .

Legal feasibility means that the content of technology introduction contract must be in conformity with the law of the import country, in particular, be void of restrictive clause. Some developing countries have special stipulation that the introduction contract should be governed only by the law of the import countries, Mexico, India and some other countries even stipulate that, when disputes of technology introduction contract are to be submitted for arbitration, they must be arbitrated by the arbitrators of the import country.

US Politics and Technology Policy Paradigms

The history of US technology policy includes three competing paradigms, the market failure paradigm, the mission paradigm, and the cooperative technology paradigm. Table 6-1 summarizes the three technology policy paradigms.

Table 6-1　　　　　　**Three competing technology policy models**

Market failure	Mission	Cooperative technology
Core assumptions (1) Markets are the most efficient allocator of information and technology.	(1) The government role should be closely tied to authorized programmatic missions of agencies	(1) Markets are not always the most efficient route to innovation and economic growth
(2) Government laboratory role limited to market failures such as extensive externalities high transaction costs: and information distortions Small. Mission domain, chiefly in defense. Universities provided basic research, in line with private sector under-supply due to market failure (inability to appropriate directly the results of basic research).	(2) Government research and development (R&D) is limited to missions of agencies, but not confined to defense University R&D supports traditional roles of land grant universities such agricultural or engineering extension, manufacturing assistance andcontract research for defense or energy research.	(2) Global economy requires more centralized planning and broader support for civiliantechnology development.
(3) Innovation flows from and to private sector, minimal university or government role.	(3) Government should not compete with private sector in innovation and technology. But a government or university r&d role is a	(3) Government laboratories and universities can play a role in developing technology, especially pre-competitive technology, for use in the private sector.

Continued

Market failure	Mission	Cooperative technology
Peak influence Highly influential during all periods	complement 1945-1965; 1992-present	1992-1994
Policy examples De-regulation; contraction of government role; R&D tax credits; capital gains tax roll back. Little or no need for federal laboratories except in defense support.	Creation of energy policy R&D, agricultural labs and other such broad mission frameworks	Expansion of federal laboratory roles and university role in technology transfer and cooperative research and other technology-based economic development programs.
Theoretical roots Neo-classical economics	Traditional liberal governance with broad definition of government role.	Industrial policy theory, regional economic development theory.

1. The market failure technology policy paradigm

The market failure technology paradigm is based on familiar premises: the free market is the most efficient allocator of goods and services, and left to its own devices. an unfettered market will lead to optimal rates of science production technical change and economic growth. The market failure policy paradigm recognizes that there may be a role for government in science and technology policy when there are clear externalities (i. e, that benefits cannot be captured in the market); when transactions costs are extremely high; and when information is unavailable or there are distortion in information so that market signals are not clear.

2. The mission technology paradigm

In the Us, the mission paradigm has for many years influenced the government technology policy role, including early efforts in agriculture research and extension and setting of standards and intellectual property policy (Dupree, 1986), but the mission paradigm has been most influential in the post-World War II period (Reingold, 1994). The mission paradigm assumes that the government should perform R&D in service of well-specified missions in which there is a national interest not easily served by private R&D. In the US, the most important element of the mission technology policy paradigm is defense and national security-related R&D, but such missions as energy production and conservation, medicine and public health, space and agriculture have expanded the role of universities and federal laboratories.

3. The cooperative technology policy paradigm

The cooperative technology policy paradigm features an active role for government actors and universities in technology development and transfer. According to this paradigm, government's role can be as a research performer, including supplying applied research and technology to industry, or as a broker, developing policies affecting industrial technology development and innovation. Thus, the cooperative technology paradigm is an umbrella term for a set of values emphasizing cooperation among sectors (Larsen and Wigand, 1987; Wigand and Frankwick, 1989)-industry, government, and university and cooperation among rival firms in development of pre-competitive technologies and "infratechnologies" (Link and Tassey, 1987).

(Source: Barry Bozeman. Technology transfer and public policy: a review of research and theory [J]. Research Policy, 2000 (29): 630-632.)

6.3   Technology R & D of New Product

To a large extent, overseas R&D by transnational corporations (TNCs) is explained by the need to adapt products and processes to foreign markets. Multinational enterprises still perform the major part of their R&D at home, because of scale economies in R&D, proximity to the company headquarters, and maintaining the secrecy of firms' technologies, to name a few of the main reasons. Yet, a trend of increased internationalization of their R&D activities has been observed over time. Production in foreign affiliates the size of the host country market, and the technological intensity of the TNCs have been shown to be positively related to the internationalization of R&D.

R&D Crucial to Developing New Technology

Chinese tech giant Huawei plans to invest more than $300 million every year for research at universities, which supports those in basic science and technology, as well as innovation. "The amount [of funds] will only increase, not decrease, from now on," Xu Wenwei, director of the company's board, said during an event at the 5th Asia-Pacific Huawei Innovation Day on Tuesday. Amid suppression from the US on the company, all-round cooperation with the world is the company's strategic choice to break through the siege.

Funding universities in research is a wise strategic move of Huawei, which allows the company to be more closely linked to global development. One reason Huawei can become one of the world's leaders in telecommunications is that it attaches great importance to innovation research.

The giant tech company established the Huawei Innovation Research Program (HIRP), formerly known as the Huawei College Fund, in 1999, to improve cooperation with universities and institutions. Benefiting from such cooperation, Huawei got opportunities to share insights into the industry with distinguished research fellows and senior engineers, hold comprehensive and in-depth discussions to help translate technology innovation into tangible results.

Huawei said the HIRP has covered over 300 universities from more than 20 countries and funded more than 1,200 projects. Huawei has learned from others, completed breakthroughs and innovations, and successfully grown to a global communications giant.

Huawei is not the only party which benefits from the program. As cooperation is bidirectional and win-win, every side can get what it wants. Universities and institutions have also gained much from the program.

US President Donald Trump's crackdown on Huawei has forced some universities such as MIT and Oxford University to suspend ties with the Chinese company. This will probably negatively affect these institutions' innovation research in relevant fields in the long term.

The era of globalization determines the trend of inevitable globalization in science and technology as well as the flow of technological concepts and talent from around the world. In almost every advanced institution, there are fellows with different cultural backgrounds.

This trend shows the US is bound to fail if it intends to suppress Huawei by elbowing it out of global research and development. By doing so, the US is actually setting itself against the world's technological advances. The US ban would have an impact on Huawei in the short run, but would ultimately harm US interests.

Huawei's story shows that research and development is crucial to developing new technology. As China takes the fast lane of technological development, we would like to see more Chinese high-tech enterprises follow the footsteps of Huawei to create more technology and tangible results, which will benefit not only China but also the whole world.

(Source: R&D Crucial to Developing New Technology. Global Times, September 5, 2019.)

6.3.1　Determinants of Overseas R&D

Three factors which mainly relate to the adaptation motive of overseas R&D have been examined in the literature:

First, production in affiliates requires overseas R&D to adapt a TNC's products and processes to local conditions. Consequently, overseas R&D to a large extent will be found where overseas production is taking place. Production in foreign affiliates turns out to be the most powerful determinant of overseas R&D. Pearce and Singh (1992), employing a patent based proxy for internationalization of R&D, obtain a positive association between this proxy and the share of production abroad for European-based TNCs as well.

Second, a positive relationship is expected between market size of the host country and overseas R&D. A larger market should provide incentives to perform overseas R&D for the purposes of adapting products and processes to local conditions, which may not be worth while in a small host country. Zejan (1990) finds a positive association between the R&D intensity of Swedish foreign affiliates and the host country GDP. It could be argued that market size is already accounted for in a measure of affiliate production since there should be incentives to locate more production to larger countries. Yet, a large market size, given the location of production, may have a separate positive effect on the location of R&D, e. g. to adapt products in view of an expected higher future potential in a larger market.

Third, firms with more technologically advanced products or processes should have a greater need to undertake overseas R&D for adaptation. Lall (1980) reports a positive and significant influence of R&D intensity on the share of R&D located abroad for US firms. Another study by Zejan (1990) suggests a positive relationship between parent company and affiliate R&D intensity.

6. 3. 2   Features of TNCs' Technological R&D

Nowadays, globalization of TNCs'technology R&D is marked with the following features:

First, in total R&D cost, the proportion of TNCs' overseas R&D investment shows rising tendency. In recent years, increasing overseas R&D investment has played an important role in the global operation strategy of TNCs from developed countries. Since 1970's, American TNCs have steadily increased their investment in overseas technology R&D, with the spending on overseas subsidiaries' R&D increasing all the time. In 1977, the overseas R&D spending of American TNCs was 2. 075 billion dollars, which reached 3. 647 billion dollars in 1982 and 10. 187 billion dollars in 1990. But in 1993, it was only 10. 954 billion. Instead of basing R&D in home countries, TNCs in developed countries have increasingly globalized their general operation flow, R &D included, from long-term strategic perspective in order to keep pace with technological advancement and economic globalization. To a certain extent, this has produced a positive impact on the economic development and technology advancement of countries across the world.

Second, the proportion of R&D staff in TNCs-invested oversea enterprises is rising. TNCs are attaching more and more importance to recruiting local high-quality technical staff, engineers, scientists and experienced administrative staff to work on the development of Hi-Tech industries and make business decision. Therefore, the number of R&D and administrative staff in TNCs' oversea branches is seeing a sharp increase, which has far exceeded the number of employees in traditional industries and sectors. With Technology R&D being more and more important in economic development and international competition, TNCs will adjust industrial structure of FDI and demand structure for local human resources drastically. As a result, competition for human resources between TNCs and local enterprises will be more and more fierce.

Third, the internationalization of TNCs' technological R&D centers in Western developed countries, and they will cross-invest in high-tech sector with investment focused on the sophisticated technology. Western developed countries have solid industrial foundation, superb research equipment and a great storage of technology talents, a strong magnet attracting research resources from abroad. When TNCs choose a host country for research investment, they must consider: ① host country's technological human resources, scientific development level and the ability to engage in high-tech innovation; ②host country's comparative advantages in certain traditional and high-tech areas, particularly the specialty of project research while undertaking research investment. These will make TNCs and the host country achieve mutual complementarity regarding technological advantages, thus optimizing the allocation of technological resources worldwide.

Fourth, TNCs' choice tends to be countries with liberal research policy, complete service facilities, and great market potential for innovative technological products. The massive high-tech research investment can be met with considerable rate of return only in international markets with strong consumer demand and great consuming potential. Meanwhile, host counties' favorable policies for high-tech product can stimulate TNCs to undertake research and development while convenient and efficient service facilities can help TNCs to acquire necessary information, thus increasing their R&D efficiency.

6. 3. 3   Forms of TNCs' Technological R&D

While organizing technological R&D, TNCs usually choose three forms: to set up transnational strategic alliance, to undertake merger and acquisition, to establish oversea research institute.

First, setting up transnational strategic alliance. With the development of technology and intensified competition the cost, difficulty and risk of new product and technology rise accordingly. Meanwhile, with rising degree of product standardization and shortening of product lifecycle, TNCs cannot solely afford the massive cost of technological innovation and accompanied huge risk. To maintain and enlarge the room for survival and development, major TNCs are setting up different forms of international strategic alliance to strengthen communication and cooperation in high-tech research, thereby promoting globalization of TNCs' R&D. Transnational strategic alliance is a kind of cooperative partnership set up by two or more rival companies by signing an agreement based on equality and mutual benefit, with the aim of achieving certain strategic objectives. Through this partnership TNCs can exchange proprietary technologies, fully absorb and make use of the most advanced technologies of the world and increase the scientific and technological content in innovative products, thus increasing the difficulties and cost for their competitors to copy or emulate, extend the lifecycle of innovative product and earn a high return rate of investment. They can also reduce the cost and risk of new product R&D and increase the success rate of technological innovation.

Second, merger and acquisition. TNCs can enter directly into host countries' markets and engage in production and operation through merger and acquisition. With the loosening of government control over merger and acquisition in western countries, merger and acquisition has become one of the most direct and important instrument for TNCs to undertake oversea technological R&D. By merger and acquisition, TNCs keep a firm hand on the R&D institutes, personnel, facilities, distribution channel and other resources of the local enterprises, thus creating favorable conditions for reorganization of technological R&D. Meanwhile, TNCS can acquire key technologies, research achievements of related industries, existing production capability and stable distribution network from host countries, thus improving the technological sophistication and competitiveness of TNCs. Moreover, TNCs can take advantage of local human resource to employ S&T personnel who are familiar with local consuming preference and purchasing power, to engage in new product R&D, which will help TNCs better target for the innovative products and timely develop suitable and marketable products that can meet different requirements of consumers hence boosting the success rate of technological innovation.

Third, establishing overseas research institute. There are two types of oversea R&D institutes established by TNCs. One is research institute attached to TNCs' oversea branches or companies merged by TNCs whose research activities are closely related to production and can meet the requirement of expanding local consuming market and therefore mainly focus on applied research. The other is research institutes separated from productive enterprises, targeting mainly at fundamental research or studies tracking host countries' high-tech development. Locations of these institutes are usually close to renowned universities, especially technological universities, and high-tech research institutes or laboratories of the host countries, or just in high-tech industrial parks of foreign countries. This kind of arrangement not only helps keep track of high-tech development of nowadays and adjust R&D strategies and directions accordingly, but also engages the in various exchanges and cooperation with research personnel from different countries, and the absorption of advanced technologies and research achievements from related companies, thus improving TNCs' capability and level of high-tech research.

6. 4　Case

Case-1

A Chinese Venture

The Darby Company is a medium-size communications technology company headquartered on the west coast of be the United States. Among other things, Darby holds a patent on a mobile telephone that can operate effectively ta within a 5-mile radius. The phone does not contain state-of-the-art technology, but it can be produced extremely cheaply. As a result, the Chinese government has expressed interest in manufacturing and selling this phone throughout its country.

Preliminary discussions with the Chinese government reveal some major terms of the agreement that it would like to include: (1) Darby will enter into joint venture with a local Chinese firm to manufacture the phones to Darby's specifications; (2) these phones will be sold throughout China at a 100 percent markup, and Darby will receive 10% of the profits; (3) Darby will invest $35 million in building the manufacturing facility, and these costs will be recovered over a five-year period; and (4) the government in Beijing will guarantee that at least 100,000 phones are sold every year, or it will purchase the difference.

The Darby management is not sure whether this is a good deal. The company also is concerned that once its technology is understood, the Chinese will walk away from the agreement and start making these phones on their own. Because the technology is not state-of-the-art, the real benefit is in the low production costs, and the technological knowledge is more difficult to protect.

For its part, the Chinese government has promised to sign a written contract with Darby, and it has agreed that any disputes regarding enforcement of this contract can be brought, by either side, to the World Court at the Hague for resolution. Should this course of action be taken, each side would be responsible for its own legal fees, but the Chinese have promised to accept the decision of the court as binding.

Darby has 30 days to decide whether to sign the con-tract with the Chinese. After this time, the Chinese intend to pursue negotiations with large telecommunications firm in Europe and try cutting a deal with it. Darby is more attractive to the Chinese, however, because of the low cost of producing its telephone. In any event, the Chinese are determined to begin mass-producing cellular phones in their country. "Our future is tied to high-tech communication", the Chinese minister of finance recently told Darby's president. That is why we are so anxious to do business with your company; you have quality phones at low cost. Darby management is flattered by these kind words but still unsure if this is the type of business deal in which it wants to get involved.

(Source: Fred Luthans. International Management. China Machine Press, 2018: 51.)

Questions:

1. If a disagreement arises between the two joint-venture partners and the reneges on its promises, how well protected is Darby's position? Explain.

2. Are the economic and technological environments in China favorable for Darby? Why or why not?

Case-2

Africa—A Crucible for Creativity

How many companies in africa earn annual revenues of $1 billion or more? Most global executives we speak with guess there are fewer than a hundred many answer "zero. " The reality? Four hundred such companies exist and they are, on average, both faster growing and more profitable than their global peers.

We have advised many of these companies as they have spread rapidly across africa and beyond, and we've observed an unexpected side effect of this growth burst: Africa has become an important test lab for global innovation. If you can build a product, a service, or a business model that's cost-effective and robust enough to succeed in Africa, chances are it will be competitive in many other regions of the world.

We don't mean to minimize the challenges of doing business in Africa (challenges of which successful entrepreneurs are well aware). In adequate infrastructure may mean that companies need to build their own supply chains, for example, and inadequate public education may mean they need to train workers in basic skills and mindsets. But as we shall see those challenges also provide opportunities for value creation.

To help global executives and entrepreneurs pinpoint the Africa-born innovations they can learn from, partner with, or invest in, we have sketched a taxonomy of six innovation types, which we describe in the following pages. Technology is the golden thread running throughout: More than perhaps any other region, Africa is piloting digitally enabled breakthroughs that can aid companies in surmounting entrenched barriers and unlocking exponential progress.

LOW-and High-Tech Moves Toward Financial Inclusion

In emerging economies, 2 billion individuals and 200 million businesses lack access to savings and credit and many of those with access pay dearly for a modest range of products (see Figure 6 – 1). The problem is by no means limited to the developing world. In the United States, one in 14 households-some 9 million in all-lacks a checking or savings account, often for reasons of affordability another 24 million are underbanked. Although they have accounts, they also resort to costly financial products and services outside the banking system, such as payday loans.

To serve excluded households-and to do so in a profitable, sustainable way-banks and other firms must use technology-based solutions and low-tech work arounds African companies provide compelling examples of both. Consider Equity Bank, born of a small building society in Kenya in 2004. By 2017 it had more than 12 million clients across East Africa, more than \$5 billion in assets, and reported pretax profits of \$270 million. James Mwangi, the founding CEO, told us that the bank's very purpose is "to solve a social problem: lack of access to financial services. " That problem is deeply personal for him. I grew up in aural area, and my mother didn't have a bank account he said. The nearest bank branch was 50 kilometers away, and the minimum opening balance was equivalent to several years of her earnings. Kenyans' response was to keep their money under the mattress.

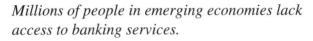

Millions of people in emerging economies lack access to banking services.

Financially excluded, as a share of the adult population and in millions, 2017

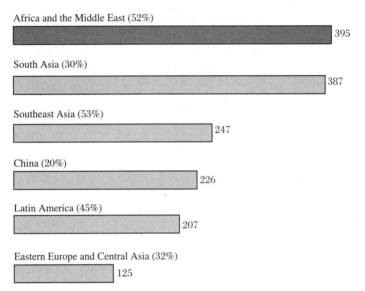

Africa and the Middle East (52%)   395

South Asia (30%)   387

Southeast Asia (53%)   247

China (20%)   226

Latin America (45%)   207

Eastern Europe and Central Asia (32%)   125

Figure 6-1   Countries and Regions of Financially Excluded

Source: The World Band's Global Findex Database, 2017; McKinsey Global Institute analysis.

Fewer than one in 10 Kenyan adults had a bank account at the turn of the 21st century. Today, thanks in large measure to Equity Bank's innovations, two-thirds do. "We knew we had to address the needs of people like my mother," Mwangi said. Well before cell phone-based banking came along, Equity Bank introduced what it called mobile banking: mini bank branches that fit in the back of a land rover and were driven from village to village. The bank's best-known innovation, though, is its agency banking model: It has accredited more than 30,000 small retail outlets across the country as bank agents, able to accept deposits and dispense cash.

Alongside these low-tech innovations, Equity Bank has harnessed the exponential growth in mobile telephony in Africa. In 2000 the entire sub-Saharan region had fewer telephone lines than the island of Manhattan. By 2016 there were more than 700 million mobile phone connections across the continent-roughly one for every adult Cell phones have transformed Africans' lives in important ways, such as by replacing cash transactions with instant and secure mobile payments. There are now 122 million active mobile money accounts in sub-Saharan Africa-more than in any other region of the world (see Figure 6 – 2). That growth enabled Equity Bank to move beyond Land rovers and create true mobile banking via its Equitel cell-phone banking application, launched in 2015.

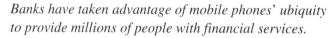

Banks have taken advantage of mobile phones' ubiquity to provide millions of people with financial services.

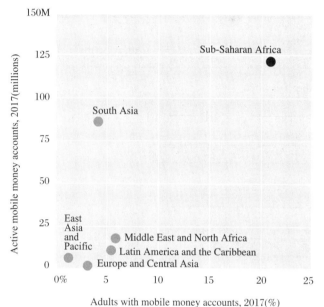

Adults with mobile money accounts, 2017(%)

Figure 6-2   Mobile Money in Africa

Source: GSMA Mobile Money Deployment Tracker; GSMA State of the Industry Report on Mobile Money, 2017; The Wrold Bank's Global Findex Databaes, 2017.

Equitel now handles the vast majority of the bank's cash transactions and loan disbursements, helping to make the bank extremely cost-efficient.

New Partnerships for Infrastructure Development

Both developed and developing countries have glaring gaps in transportation, power, and water infrastructure and in soft infrastructure such as health care facilities. Our McKinsey colleagues estimate that the global gap between current and required infrastructure spending is $350 billion a year; unless it is closed, growth will slow and fast-growing cities will come under enormous strain. Nowhere is the gap bigger than in Africa; for instance, nearly 600 million people there lack access to electricity. The deficit has spurred some bold public-private collaborations that could serve as a model for other regions.

A case in point: the "company to country" agreements between GE and various African governments. These represent a new frontier in the company's approach to public-sector clients. For example, GE's agreement with Nigeria supports the financing, design, and building of vital infrastructure, with projects including the development of 10,000 mega watts of power generation capacity, upgrades to airports the modernization and expansion of the national railway corporation's locomotives, and the construction of public hospitals and diagnostic centers. Jay Ireland, the recently retired president and CEO of GE Africa, describes the approach as "an umbrella agreement matching our capabilities as a company with the issues the country was facing, including putting more power on the grid, strengthening logistics, and improving health care outcomes."

Other African innovators are harnessing mobile money, along with advances in solar power and battery storage, to leapfrog the continent's gaps in electric power generation. One example is Kenya-based M-KOPA, which provides affordable solar-powered electricity generation and storage solutions to households that lack access to the grid-and finances payment over a 12-month period via mobile money accounts. Since its founding, in 2011, M-KOPA has sold more than 600,000 household kits and garnered investments from multinationals including Japan's Mitsui. Another example is Uganda-based Fenix, which has sold 140,000 solar power kits, also enabled by mobile money. In late 2017 Fenix was acquired by Engie, a major global energy company based in France, as part of a drive to use digital technologies to provide 20 million people around the world with decarbonized decentralized energy by 2020.

Smart Approaches to Industrialization

Manufacturing represents another class of african innovations relevant to other regions seeking to build or revitalize their industrial base to meet local demand and create stable jobs. One pioneer is Nigeria's Aliko Dangote, whose Dangote Industries achieved the seemingly impossible task of building large-scale manufacturing businesses when the country was plagued by chronic power outages, exchange rate volatility, and other impediments, including underdeveloped local supply chains and shortages of technical skills. "We knew that everyone who had tried industrialization in Nigeria had gone out of business," Dangote told us. So he built a shock-proof manufacturing model that included vertical integration, on-site power generation, robust engagement with the government, and an internal manufacturing academy. Today his group produces pasta, sugar, salt, flour, plastics, and cement in large volumes, and it will soon add refined petroleum and fertilizers-all commodities that Nigeria has historically imported. The company has created 30, 000 jobs and made Dangote Africa's richest person.

Africa is also home to a growing group of innovative industries, from car making to chemicals, that meld the latest technologies with the continent's labor force advantages to meet both African and global demand. An analysis by the McKinsey global institute suggests enormous potential to increase the production of such "global innovations," which could enable Africa to double its manufacturing output in a decade. In Morocco, for example, the automotive industry has multiplied its export revenue by a factor of 12, taking it from $4 billion in 2004 to $5 billion in 2015, and added 67, 000 jobs during that time. The French automakers Renault and Peugeot have together invested more than $2 billion to create assembly capacity for 650, 000 cars and 200, 000 engines. Morocco has also built industries in aerospace and other advanced sectors. In these high-tech African industries, companies make use of both automation and skilled labor. That makes sense: In Morocco, for example, labor costs are about one-third those in even the lowest-cost European countries. And Africa's labor force is expanding fast; by 2034 it will surpass China's and India's. By 2050 the continent's working-age population will exceed 1. 5 billion (see Figure 6-3).

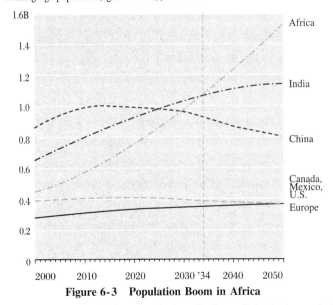

The continent is expected to have a larger working-age population than China's or india's by 2034.

Figure 6-3   Population Boom in Africa

Source: IHS Markit; International Labour Organization; McKinsey Global Institute analysis.

New models of food production

More than 800 million people worldwide—11% of the global population-are affected by hunger. The vast majority are in the developing world, with 520 million in Asia and 240 million in Africa. But hunger also be sets many low-income households in rich nations, including more than 40 million people in the United States. The UN has set a goal of banishing hunger by 2030. To achieve that, the agricultural sector will need to step up innovations in technology and management to improve yields, and food companies will have to create affordable, nutritious foods and reconfigure distribution systems to get those foods onto the tables of people who need them. Africa is home to exciting innovations in all these arenas.

Consider BabbanGona (in Hausa, "great farm"), a Nigerian social enterprise serving networks of small holders. Its members receive development and training, credit, agricultural inputs, marketing support, and other key services. Since its founding, in 2010, BabbanGona has enlisted more than 20,000 Nigerian farmers, who have, on average, more than doubled their yields and increased their net income to triple the national average. Participating small holders who are typically considered a high credit risk, have a 99.9% repayment rate on credit obtained through the program. BabbanGona's founder, Kola Masha, aims to enlist one million farmers in the program by 2025, thus providing livelihoods for 5 million people. Other small holder-focused programs are being launched across the continent, and large commercial farms are also boosting their scale and output. Together these efforts could banish famine in Africa forever.

Our analysis shows that the yield increases facilitated by BabbanGona, if replicated across the continent would be enough to feed Africa's growing population and export to other regions. Africa's "green revolution" is being accelerated by a new breed of tech entrepreneur. One such is Sara Menker, an Ethiopia-born former Wall Street commodities trader. Sherealized that farmers and investors lacked the information needed to choose crops and markets, manage weather and other risks, and identify where and when to invest in infrastructure. So she created GroIntelligence, which she describes as "a Wikipedia for agriculture, but with a very deep analytical engine built on top of it. " With offices in Nairobi and New York, the company has clients ranging from some of the world's largest sovereign-wealth and hedge funds to individual commodity traders in Africa and around the globe. Other digital start-ups are providing farming advice, weather forecasts, and financial tips and helping farmers measure and analyze soil data so that they can apply the right fertilizer and optimally irrigate their farms.

Affordable accessible consumer products

Growing more food is a key step in banishing hunger but it's just as important that ordinary people have access to nutritious, affordable meals. Readers of this magazine maybe familiar with Indomie noodles-one of Nigeria's most successful consumer products. Sold in single-serving packets for the equivalent of less than 20 cents, the noodles can be cooked in under three minutes and combined with an egg to produce a nutritious meal. DullPrima Foods introduced them to Nigeria in 1988. They took off, and the company soon shifted from importing to manufacturing locally. CEO Deepak Singhal told us, "We created a food that was relevant for Nigeria. And in 10 to 15 years we became a household name. "

Dufil has also driven fundamental innovation in getting Indomie noodles to consumers throughout Nigeria. It has a "feet on the street" distribution network of more than 1,000 vehicles, including motorcycles, trucks, and three-wheelers. When distributors can't go any farther by vehicle, they continue on foot. That was a critical innovation because the company's route to consumers was through thousands of small, often informal outlets rather than an organized supermarket network. Dufil's distribution approach has garnered global attention: In 2015 Kellogg invested $450 million to acquire a 50% stake in the west African sales and distribution arm of Indomie's parent company, Tolaram Africa, and in 2018 it ponied up $420 million more for a stake in Tolaram's food-manufacturing business.

Again, innovations in Africa's consumer sector are be example is the ecommerce start-up Jumia Launched in 2012, it now has more than 2 million active customers in 13 African countries, and sales are doubling each year. Although Jumia has yet to deliver fully on its business model-or to make a profit-it has attracted hundreds of millions of dollars in investment from Goldman Sachs and others. Sacha Poignonnec, Jumia's France-born co-CEO, points out that Africa has 60,000 people for each formal retail outlet, whereas the United States has only about 400 people per store. He told us, In the U. S., e-commerce is slowly changing centuries-old shopping habits. Here it is creating habits People are making their first big buys, such as smartphones and their first online purchases simultaneously.

To encourage these habits, Jumia created the JForce sales program, in which agents go door-to-door with Wi-Fi-connected tablets, taking orders from customers who lack internet access. "It allows agents to become entrepreneurs," Poignonnec said, "effectively operating their own online retail business right from home. " In addition, Jumia created a logistics service to fulfill its e-commerce orders; in 2017 it delivered 8 million packages many of them to remote rural areas. And it built an in-house payment platform to help African consumers gain trust in online payments. These innovations could help Africa by pass costly brick-and-mortar retail and go directly to an e-commerce model that brings consumers greater choice and lower prices wherever they live.

Future-Focused Capability Building

With so many young people entering Africa's workforce, innovations in education and skills development are essential. They are also globally relevant: More than75 million young people worldwide are unemployed, while many companies can't find people with the skills needed for entry-level jobs. This happens in part because many education systems don't provide either the technical or the behavioral skills needed to succeed and adapt in the rapidly changing world of work.

One African solution to the youth skills gap is Generation Kenya, a nonprofit with 180 local employer partners, which operates 37 training locations across the country. Each offers immersive "boot camp" programs lasting six to eight weeks aimed at building job readiness in areas such as retail and financial sales, customer service, and apparel manufacturing. The programs not only teach relevant technical skills they also use role-playing and team exercises to impart behavioral and mindset skills such as punctuality and resilience. By 2017 more than 8,000 young Kenyans had gone through a Generation program, with 89% of them finding formal employment within three months of graduation heartening evidence that smart development programs can quickly equip young people, wherever they are, to become high-performing employees in modern businesses (Disclosure: Generation, today a global nonprofit, was founded by McKinsey, and we continue to support it, alongside philanthropic groups such as USAID).

Other African education innovations are decidedly high-tech. GetSmarter is a South African start-up that offers online certification courses to students around the world, supported by remote tutors and coaches. In 2017 it was acquired by the U. S. -based ed-tech company 2U for $103 million. Another example is the African Leadership University, or ALU. Its campuses in Mauritius and Rwanda empower students to manage their own education using technology, peer-to-peer learning, and four-month internships with partner companies, enabling ALU to get by with a small teaching staff. Founder Fred Swaniker is a Stanford-educated Ghanaian who set about creating a business model for higher education from scratch. "Our university produces talent that competes with students from Harvard and Stanford, he told us. " But we do it using one-tenth of the real estate and at one-tenth to one-twentieth of the cost. "

How to Scale and Sustain Innovation

In our consulting work we've watched a diverse cohort of entrepreneurial and corporate innovators in Africa and beyond create remarkable businesses on the continent. Although those innovators differ widely in geographic reach and sector focus, they all see challenges as a spur to innovation and unmet market demand as room for growth other markets could profitably apply to their own growth. They have honed mindsets and practices that companies strategies. That should start with a granular, empathetic understanding of potential customers' needs-recall what M-KOPA did for people who lacked electricity and what Indomie noodles did for consumers seeking cheap, nutritious, and convenient meals. It also means rethinking the business model to truly engage with customers, as Equity Bank did through its agency banking model and its innovations in cell phone banking. These examples point to an additional activity needed for success: harnessing technology in imaginative ways, including to drive down costs and price points.

We've also observed that successful African innovators far from being starry-eyed, are more aware than anyone else of the barriers to success and that they build long-term resilience into their business models. Dufil's Deepak Singhal says that it takes a "lion's heart" to succeed in a market like Africa. We have our own logistics company, our own raw material, our own plants, and our own packaging facilitie's he told us. Controlling our supply chain is very important. In a global survey of executives, we found that such steps were closely correlated with reported growth and profitability in Africa (see Figure 6- 4). Given the world's increased volatility-in politics, markets trade, and even weather-innovative firms everywhere would do well to consider such approaches.

Companies also need to take a firm stand against another tough barrier to business: corruption, which remains widespread in Africa. We advise clients to stick to their values no matter what. We faced a test of that principle ourselves in South Africa, where we briefly explored partnering with a local firm to support Eskom, the national electricity utility only to learn that the firm was owned by a questionable character linked to a national corruption scandal. Although we terminated the discussions we learned hard lessons from the experience, including how critical it is to deeply understand the context of any potential engagement and the actors involved.

High-performing companies actively manage the challenges they face. Shown below are results form a survey of executives whose companies do a significant amount of business in Africa.

Share of respondents who say their organization does the following to overcome barriers to conducting business in Africa:

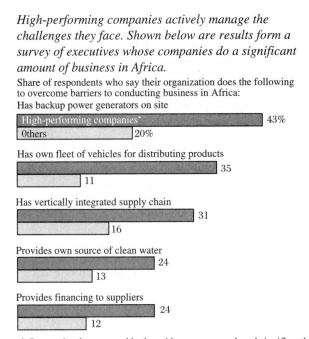

Figure 6-4　Measures to Overcome Barriers to Conducting Business in Africa

Source: McKinsey Insights executive survey on business in Africa, 2017.

What motivates Africa's innovators to get out of bed each morning, navigate this complex terrain, and keep building their businesses? What they have in common, in our experience, is a deeper purpose. When faced with Africa's high levels of poverty and its gaps in infrastructure, education, and health care, they don't see only barriers to business; they see human issues they feel responsible for addressing. Take Strive Masiyiwa, the chairman of the pan-African telecom, media, and technology company Econet Group. There is no doubting his business ambitions: He is the major shareholder in the fast-growing Liquid Telecom, Africa's largest broadband infrastructure and data services company. But Masiyiwa has put equal energy into philanthropic initiatives for example, he has used his wealth to provide scholarships to more than 250,000 young Africans. "To be successful, you need to be more than a businessman; you need to bea responsible citizen," he told us. "If you see a problem, think about how you can solve a piece of it" He added "The exciting part is asking 'What is the root cause of this problem? What can we do to address that root cause?'"

Graca Machel, an international human rights advocate (and the chancellor of ALU), points to business's responsibility to help meet the UN's Sustainable Development Goals. "Those goals are an ambitious universal call to end poverty protect the environment, and ensure that all members of our global family enjoy peace and prosperity," she told us. They require that we leave no one behind? "Machel sees an opportunity for the private sector to partner in poverty eradication efforts and collaborate with the public sector and civil society to drive job creation on a massive scale. That will" require a change in mindset in all of, "she said. " Entire industries and leaders themselves have to meaningfully transform-it can no longer be business as usual. Her late husband Nelson Mandela would have agreed. As he famously wrote, There is no passion to be found playing small-in settling for a life that is less than the one you are capable of living. "

Humankind has never before had such resources, knowledge, and technology at its disposal-yet it is a long way from translating those advances into decent livelihoods and dignified lives for all the world's people We believe that innovation by businesses large and small can play a central role in solving the world's greatest challenges and ushering in an era of shared abundance. Addressing the deprivation that is still widespread in Africa will be an important step toward that goal. But the challenges Africa is known for are present to a surprising degree in every other region of the globe. That makes the innovations born in the African test lab critically important for the rest of the world.

(Source: Africa—A Crucible for Creativity [J]. Harward Business Review, November-December, 2018: 116-125.)

Questions:

Please discuss what opportunities the six types of innovation bring for technology transfer to Africa?

6.5　Expanding Reading

Reading-1

Apple Has Over 1,000 People in Its Four China R&D Centers

Apple Inc on Sunday said that it has already recruited over 1,000 people in its four research and development centers in China, as part of the United States tech giant's broader push to better leverage local talents to grow its business.

This marks the first time for Apple to disclose updates of its R&D centers in China after the company announced its plan of building R&D facilities in Beijing, Shenzhen, Shanghai and Suzhou more than two years ago.

"We are continuing grow the scale of the four R&D centers in China and welcome more talents to join us," Isabel Ge Mahe, managing director of China at Apple, said.

Ge made the remarks on the sidelines of the China International Big Data Industry Expo 2019, which kicked off in Guiyang, Southwest China's Guizhou province, on Sunday.

Apple said earlier it has committed to invest 3. 5 billion yuan ($500 million) in these R&D centers, so as to better tap into China's talents in manufacturing, app development, design and other sectors.

According to Ge, Apple has about 13, 000 employees in China, and the construction of the company's first China data center in Guizhou province is going well, as scheduled.

Apple's plan is to invest $1 billion in the new data center, which is in Guian New Area, Guiyang. It will be operated by Guizhou-Cloud Big Data Industry Co Ltd, a company owned by the Guizhou provincial government. The data center is scheduled to be put into use in 2020.

Apple also is working hard to help more rural students in China access digital technologies. Last year, Apple said it would donate 25 million yuan to the China Development Research Foundation as part of its efforts to help students in the nation's less-developed areas.

The money is used to support the foundation's digitalization program and help more than 300, 000 students from kindergarten to middle school in less-developed areas find a way out of poverty.

(Source: chinadaily, May 27, 2019.)

Reading-2

BMW Teams up with Chinese Companies to Drive R&D of Autonomous Vehicles

BMW is speeding up its efforts to develop autonomous driving vehicles in China, its largest market worldwide, as the German premium carmaker continues to transform itself into a technology company.

On Friday, it announced a deal with Chinese technology firm Tencent Holdings to build a computing center that will help develop self-driving vehicles in the country.

The center, which will start operations by the end of the year, will leverage Tencent's capabilities in cloud computing and big data to develop autonomous driving technology and products adapted to Chinese road and traffic conditions, said BMW in a statement.

The two companies did not disclose the investment in the center and Reuters, citing sources familiar with the deal, said the center will be built in the city of Tianjin.

The deal with Tencent came one week after an agreement with NavInfo, a Beijing-based high-definition mapping service provider, and another with China Unicom for 5G technology in early July.

"We are convinced that China is already at the forefront of defining future mobility. We at BMW will actively leverage our comprehensive research and development competency to support smart mobility and smart city development in China," said JochenGoller, president and CEO of BMW Group Region China.

"Together with our Chinese partners, we are jointly shaping the future of mobility," he said.

BMW received its autonomous driving permit in China in May 2018, the first among international premium carmakers, which has since enabled it to test its fleet on public roads in Shanghai.

The carmaker said China has the most complex traffic in the world and that has made its research facilities in the country essential.

Its teams in Beijing and Shanghai have nearly 100 engineers focusing on the development and validation of automated driving functions based on typical traffic scenarios in China.

BMW is already offering Level 2 autonomous driving functions in some of its models including the all-new 3 Series and 7 Series sedans.

The Level 3, or hands-off and eyes-off functions, will come in 2021 when the carmaker starts to mass-produce the iNEXT concept vehicle.

By then, BMW said it will have collected around 5 million kilometers of real-life driving data from its test fleet vehicles, and 240 million kilometers of simulation-generated data.

It is planning to conduct Level 4 fleet tests starting from 2021 in a number of countries including China. Level 4 can enable drivers to be hands-off, eyes-off and minds-off.

BMW is also introducing China-oriented connectivity features into its models.

Earlier this year, it announced the integration of Alibaba's smart voice assistant Tmall Genie into the on-board system of its vehicles.

Goller said BMW is sticking to its 2 + 4 strategic approach in China, which represents the two brands of BMW and MINI as well as the four fields of autonomous driving, connected vehicles, electrification and sharing services.

China is BMW's largest market worldwide. It delivered 350,070 BMW and MINI-branded vehicles in the country from January to June, up 16.8% year-on-year.

(Source: Li Fusheng, BMW teams up with Chinese Companies to Drive R&D of Autonomous Vehicles, China Daily, July 22, 2019.)

Reading-3

GM Looks to the Future by Investing in Technology

At 10 years old, GM's China Advanced Technical Center is working to fuel the automaker through the next decade by progressing in the research and development of cutting—edge technologies and advanced materials.

Founded in 2009 in Shanghai, where GM China is headquartered, the ATC is a member of GM's global engineering and design network. It includes research and development, design, vehicle engineering and battery laboratories, and develops solutions for GM on a domestic and global basis while supporting the company's vision.

"Being committed to delivering safer, better and more sustainable ways for people to get around, GM is empowered by its vision of the future with zero crashes, zero emissions and zero congestion. We believe technology is the key to turn the vision into reality," said Matt Tsien, GM executive vice-president and president of GM China, on Tuesday in Shanghai.

Improving research and development of new materials, battery testing, concept car design and the localization of global technologies, the GM China ATC will focus more on new energy vehicles, intelligent connected cars and advanced materials in an effort to meet Chinese customers' needs, the company said.

The technical center is equipped with a team of highly-qualified designers, scientists and engineers. They work together to develop mobility solutions and technologies, and are committed to promoting the application of the technologies, Tsien said.

Wang Jianfeng is a chief researcher of advanced materials and manufacturing at the GM China ATC.

He said automobiles are the synthesizer of diverse modern materials. His team is working to develop lightweight, yet strong materials at affordable prices.

The technical center has developed a third-generation steel with enhanced strength, which helps a vehicle reduce its weight by 20%.

Doctorate holder Hu Bin at the technical center has developed a high-performance cast aluminum alloy, which has greatly improved ductility and tensile strength. And the new material is named after Hu Bin, which is called the HuCrAlloy.

The HuCrAlloy has been used in the CT6 V-Sport, a Cadillac model on sale in North America, as well as the 2020 Corvette Stingray.

Compared with conventional cast aluminum alloy used by General Motors, the HuCrAlloy is 40% lighter. Rich in raw materials and with fast-paced technology, China is at the forefront of innovation in metals and metallurgical processes. This helps lay a solid foundation for the technical center's research and development, according to Wang.

A remote laser-welding technology was also developed by the technical center.

It has improved the welding efficiency by three to four times and cut carbon dioxide emissions by 50%, according to the carmaker.

As the automobile industry leans toward electrification and intelligent connectivity, the automaker said there are higher requirements for auto materials.

The aim is to help ensure the operation of electrified and internet-connected devices.

For instance, precise and corrosion-resistant materials are needed by the battery, the cell and the motor to help reduce risks, improve efficiency and gain strength.

William Hotchkiss, director of GM China Engineering, said the ATC is transforming into a hub of intelligent connected vehicles. The automaker will invest a great deal of engineering resources there to shape the future, he added.

According to GM, it is set to join hands with China Intelligent and Connected Vehicles (Beijing) Research Institute.

They aim to help build a vibrant ecosystem of intelligent connected vehicles.

"Based on our own technical strengthen and resources, we hope to develop integrated mobility solutions with the Chinese partners. And the cooperation with CICV is a good example," Tsien noted.

Hotchkiss added that innovation and cooperation are key to building the future of personal mobility. Intelligent connected vehicles have inspired them to focus on technological harmony and develop integrated technical solutions so as to improve road safety and travel efficiency.

Super Cruise is an advanced intelligent driving assistance system developed by GM. It entered the Chinese market in 2018, being used in the Cadillac CT6.

Before that, the automaker collaborated with its local partners in China to localize the technology.

The ATC is a pivotal design center for GM, which is mainly composed of Chinese local designers and aids in its global product design and development.

Designers also take part in market research to capture what's happening in China and the tastes of its customers, according to the carmaker.

Focusing on designing electric cars and concept vehicles for the Chinese and global markets, the technical center is scheduled to recruit more local designers and further improve its design capability.

Growing in its size and capability, the GM China ATC is charting a bold course for the automaker's next decade by continually meeting customers' aspirations, the automaker said.

(Source: Zhang Dandan, GM Looks to the Future by Investing in Technology, China Daily, August 5, 2019.)

Quick Quiz

1. International technology transfer is the transfer of three technological factors, namely skill, techniques and (   ).

2. Technology transfer policies in developed countries mainly contains (   ), restriction policies and prohibition policies.

3. (   ) is mix of direct investment technology transfer.

   A. Equity Joint-Venture   B. Joint Production

   C. Technical Co-Ordination   D. License Transaction

4. The dimensions of the technological environment currently facing international management might contain (   ).

   A. biotechnology

   B. e-business

   C. international trade

   D. telecommunications

   E. technology, outsourcing, and offshoring.

5. Two types of oversea R&D institutes established by TNCs are (   ).

   A. global innovation institute

   B. research institute attached to TNCs' oversea branches

   C. research institutes separated from productive enterprises

   D. institutes for technology dissemination

Answers:

   1. knowledge

2. encouragement policies

3. A

4. ABCDE

5. BC

Endnotes

［1］ Zhang Xiaoyu. Handbook for Transnational Corporation Management ［M］. Beijing：Central Compilation & Translation Press，2017：355-376.

［2］ Fred Luthan，Jonathan P. Doh. International Management—Culture，Strategy and Behavior ［M］. Beijing：Mechanical Industry Press，2018：40-58.

［3］ Wang Ruixu，Zhang Xiaolin. Environmental Analysis and Model Option of Human Resource R&D of Transnational Corporations ［J］. Economic Management. 2003，4.

［4］ Wan Xiaolan and Wang Weiyi. New Analysis on Transnational Corporations ［M］. Beijing：Economic Science Publishing House. 2003.

［5］ Trevino，L.，& Weaver，G. R.. The role of human resources in ethics/compliance management：A fairness perspective ［J］. HRM Review，2001，11 （1），113-134.

［6］ Brown，M.，& Trevino，L.. Ethical leadership：A review and future directions ［J］. The Leadership Quarterly，2006，17 （6），595-616.

［7］ Brown，M.，Trevino，L.，& Harrison，D. Ethical leadership：A social learning perspective for construct development and testing ［J］. Organizational Behavior and Human Decision Processes，2005，97 （2），117-134.

［8］ Fors，Gunnar，Zejan Mario. Overseas R&D by Multinationals in Foreign Centers of excellence ［J］. Econstor. eu，working paper，1996.

［9］ Marc A. Cohen，Dean Peterson. The Implicit Morality of the Market and Joseph Heath's Market Failures Approach to Business Ethics ［J］. Journal of Business Ethics，2019，159 （1）：75-88.

［10］ Pedro Vazquez. Family Business Ethics：At the Crossroads of Business Ethics and Family Business ［J］. Journal of Business Ethics，2018，150 （3）：691-709.

［11］ Juelin Yin，Ali Quazi. Business Ethics in the Greater China Region：Past，Present，and Future Research ［J］. Journal of Business Ethics，2018，150 （3）：815-835.

［12］ Brian Berkey. Business Ethics and Free Speech on the Internet ［J］. 2017，45 （3）：937-945.

Chapter 7 Leadership and Organization Innovation

Learning Objectives

1. Master the definition of leadership
2. Recognize the leadership of transnational corporation
3. Master the leadership behaviors and styles
4. Understand the leadership in different nationalities
5. Understand the definition of organization innovation and styles of research
6. Understand the types of innovation
7. Understand the transformational leadership and organizational innovation

Opening case

Google's Business Leadership and Organizational Culture

Google Inc. has received a lot of attention and acclaim for its unusual organizational culture, which is designed to encourage both loyalty and creativity. Google has created many significant products through this emphasis on innovation, including the Google search engine, Google Maps and the Google Chrome Web browser. The company is now much larger than it was when the organizational culture first developed, forcing some changes to the original model.

Leadership Structure at Google

Google's corporate structure is not particularly unusual other than the existence of a few unique leadership positions such as Chief Culture Officer and Chief Internet Evangelist. The company is overseen by a board of directors, which passes instructions down through an executive management group. This group oversees several departments such as Engineering, Products, Legal, Finance and Sales. Each of these departments is divided into smaller units.

For instance, the Sales department has branches dedicated to the Americas, Asia Pacific, and Europe, the Middle East and Africa. Despite the use of a standard corporate organizational structure, Google has developed a corporate culture based on giving employees substantial leeway to develop new ideas without excessive oversight.

The 70/20/10 Rule

All Google employees follow a rule called the 70/20/10 rule, under which they are expected to devote 70% of every work day to whichever projects are assigned by management, 20% of each day to new projects or ideas related to their core projects, and 10% to any new ideas they want to pursue regardless of what they might be. The company credits this rule with being the driving force behind many of Google's new products and services, because programmers, salespeople and even executives are given enough space to be creative.

When the company became too large to easily manage the flow of new ideas and projects, it instituted a schedule of meetings between employees and the company's founders and chief executives. At these meetings, employees can pitch new ideas and projects directly to the top executives.

Criticisms of Google's Culture

Although the culture of creativity at Google has resulted in many new products, critics such as Gene Munster from the Piper Jaffray Investment Bank charge that most of these products have not produced substantial new revenue. Because advertising on search engine result pages produces much of Google's revenues, many of its products are offered for free to encourage the use of the Google search engine.

Google initially paid employees less than many other Silicon Valley firms, but used other perks to attract employees. For instance, Google employees receive free food cooked by a company chef, are provided with bus rides to work and are allowed to travel through the building on scooters and bicycles. They also have access to company daycare facilities, exercise gyms and other amenities. These perks are intended to help create a fun and creative atmosphere.

In addition, Google now offers stock plans and higher wages that have brought its compensation package into the same range as other companies in the same industry.

Gender Disparity in the Workforce

The company, as with most of Silicon Valley firms, has been criticized for gender disparities in its workforce. The criticisms revolve around two key issues: fairness of the pay scales between men and women in similar jobs, and the harassment of women in the workforce. Google has acknowledged both issues and taken steps to address them. For example, it now conducts an annual salary review of all employees in an attempt to eliminate any gender disparities in pay.

Google's Unofficial Motto

Google's unofficial motto is "Don't Be Evil," and many of its policies and corporate decisions are based on trying to live up to this motto. Although it may seem eccentric to pursue such an approach in a business environment where profit is always the final concern, employees report feeling very differently about working at Google as opposed to other companies.

(Source: Scott Thompson; Reviewed by Michelle Seidel, B. Sc., LL. B., MBA; Updated March 09, 2019.)

7. 1　Leadership of Transnational Corporation

7. 1. 1　Concept Definition

1. Defining Leadership

Leadership has different meanings to different authors. Harry Truman, former American President, said that leadership is the ability to get men (women) to do what they don't like and like it. In this book, leadership is defined as influence, that is, the art or process of influencing people so that they will strive willingly and enthusiastically toward the achievement of group goals. Ideally, people should be encouraged to develop not only willingness to work but also willingness to work with zeal and confidence. Zeal is ardor, earnestness, and intensity in the execution of work; confidence reflects experience and technical ability. Leaders act to help a group attain objectives through the maximum application of its capabilities. They do not stand behind a group to push and prod; they place themselves before the group as they facilitate progress and inspire the group to accomplish organizational goals. A good example is an orchestra leader, whose function is to produce coordinated sound and correct tempo through the integrated effort of the musicians. The performance of the orchestra will depend on the quality of the director's leadership.

Leadership and Supply Chain Implementation in South Korean Firms

As you read the chapter, you will see that leadership is an extremely critical aspect of any organization's Success. By acting appropriately, a leader can retain and motivate employees to do their best. However, leadership does not only affect employees. The implementation of key projects in any company is also affected by company leaders.

In recent study of 142 South Korean firms, the authors examined the characteristics of leadership and effective supply chain implementation. As noted in Chapter 5, a supply chain is simply the list of activities hat company undertakes to manufacture products from the design aspect to after sales support Companies devote significant resources to ensuring that supply chain activities are designed appropriately, as well as to ensuring desirable supply chain outcomes such as low cost, flexible market responsiveness, and trust with customers.

In the study, the authors argue that integrative leadership on the part of the CEO, chief information officer, and supply chain officer is critical for successful supply chain implementation. Integrative leadership refers to the extent to which these key executives have high levels of collaboration and interact in a dynamic manner. The results of the study in South Korea showed that integrative leadership is indeed related to many key supply chain outcomes. Integrative leaders share critical operational and strategic information that allows the company to better implement its supply chain to achieve better value for customers while also enhancing the flow of information within the company.

(Source: Based on Youn, S. Yang, M. G. and Hong, P. 2012. "Integrative leadership for effective supply chain implementation: An empirical study of South Korean firms." International Journal Production Economics, 139, 237-246.)

2. Leadership of Transnational Corporation – Global Leadership

The rise of transnational corporations and the dependence of even the smallest corporations on international trade have created a need for a new type of leader. This global leader must have the skills and abilities to interact with and manage people from the diverse cultural backgrounds that populate his or her transnational corporation.

Let us consider some of the characteristics of this new breed of leader. According to experts on managing cultural differences, the successful global leader is:

(1) Cosmopolitan: Sufficiently flexible to operate comfortably in pluralistic cultural environments.

(2) Skilled at intercultural communication: Conversant in at least one foreign language and understands the complexities of interaction with people from other cultures.

(3) Culturally sensitive: Experienced in different national, regional, and organizational cultures needed to build relationships with culturally different people

while understanding his or her own culture and cultural biases.

(4) Capable of rapid acculturation: Able to rapidly acculturate or adjust to different cultural settings.

(5) A facilitator of subordinates' intercultural performance: Aware of cultural differences in work and living and able to prepare subordinates for successful overseas experiences.

(6) A user of cultural synergy: Takes advantage of cultural differences by finding a synergy that combines the strengths of each cultural group and by using performance standards understandable across cultural groups, resulting in increased levels of organizational performance than those produced by culturally homogeneous companies. Consider the following Case in Point.

(7) A promoter and user of the growing world culture: Understands, uses, and takes advantage of the international advances in media, transportation, and travel that support the globalization of business.

(8) Emotionally intelligent: Able to accurately perceive his or her emotions and to use them to solve problems and to relate to others.

7.1.2   Leadership Behaviors and Styles

Leader behaviors can be translated into three commonly recognized styles: (1) authoritarian, (2) paternalistic, and (3) participative. Authoritarian leadership is the use of work-centered behavior that is designed to ensure task accomplishment. This leader behavior typically involves the use of one-way communication from manager to subordinate. The focus of attention usually is on work progress, work procedures, and roadblocks that are preventing goal attainment. There is a managerial tendency toward lack of involvement with subordinates, where final decisions are in the hands of the higher-level employees. The distance translates into a lack of a relationship where managers focus on assignments over the needs of the employees. At times, the organizational leadership behavior is reflective of the political surroundings, as indicated in one study which focused on Romania. Leaders in this region were slightly more authoritarian (55%), which could have been influenced by the Romanian communistic roots that stressed the importance of completing planned productions. Although this leadership style often is effective in handling crises, some leaders employ it as their primary style regardless of the situation. It also is widely used by Theory X managers, who believe that a continued focus on the task is compatible with the kind of People they are dealing with.

Paternalistic leadership uses work-center behavior coupled with a protective employee-centered concern. This leadership style can be best summarized by the statement, Work hard and the company will take care of you. Paternalistic leaders expect everyone to work hard; in return, the employees are guaranteed employment and given security benefits such as medical and retirement programs. Usually. this leadership behavior satisfies some employee needs, and in turn subordinates tend to exhibit loyalty and compliance.

Studies have shown that this behavior is seen throughout Latin America, including Argentina, Bolivia, Chile, and Mexico, but also in China, Pakistan, India, Turkey, and the United States. Mexico appears to be a country that has high paternalistic values, owing in part to Mexican cultural values of respect for hierarchical relations and strong family and personal relationships and the fact of the absence of welfare or employment benefits. There is also some evidence that paternalistic leadership is still a common leadership approach in greater China, stemming from Confucian ideology, which is founded on social relations, such as "benevolent leader with loyal minister" and "kind father with filial son". In Malaysia, paternalistic leadership acts as a positive reinforcer because paternalistic treatment is contingent on subordinates' task accomplishment. More broadly, paternalistic leadership has been shown to have a positive impact on employees' attitudes in collectivistic cultures because the care, support, and protection provided by paternalistic leaders may address employees'need for frequent contact and close personal relationships.

Participative leadership is the use of both work-centered and people-centered approaches. Participative leaders typically encourage their people to play an active role in assuming control of their work, and authority usually is highly decentralized. The way in which leaders motivate employees could be through consulting with employees, encouraging joint decisions, or delegating responsibilities. Regardless of the method, employees tend to be more creative and innovative when driven by leaders exhibiting this behavior. Participative leadership is very popular in many technologically advanced countries. Such leadership has been widely espoused in the United States, England, and other Anglo countries, and it is currently very popular in Scandinavian countries as well. At General Electric, managers are encouraged to use a participative style that delivers on commitment and shares the values of the firm. Recent research has shown how participative leadership contributes to employees' performance, especially in the presence of psychological empowerment on the part of subordinates who are managers themselves and trust in the supervisors in the case of nonmanagerial subordinates.

One way of characterizing participative leaders is in terms of the managerial grid, which is traditional, well – known method of identifying leadership styles, as shown in Figure 7-1. Perspectives on and preferences toward where leaders perform on the grid can be influenced by culture. The next section explores this idea as a way to better illustrate the managerial grid.

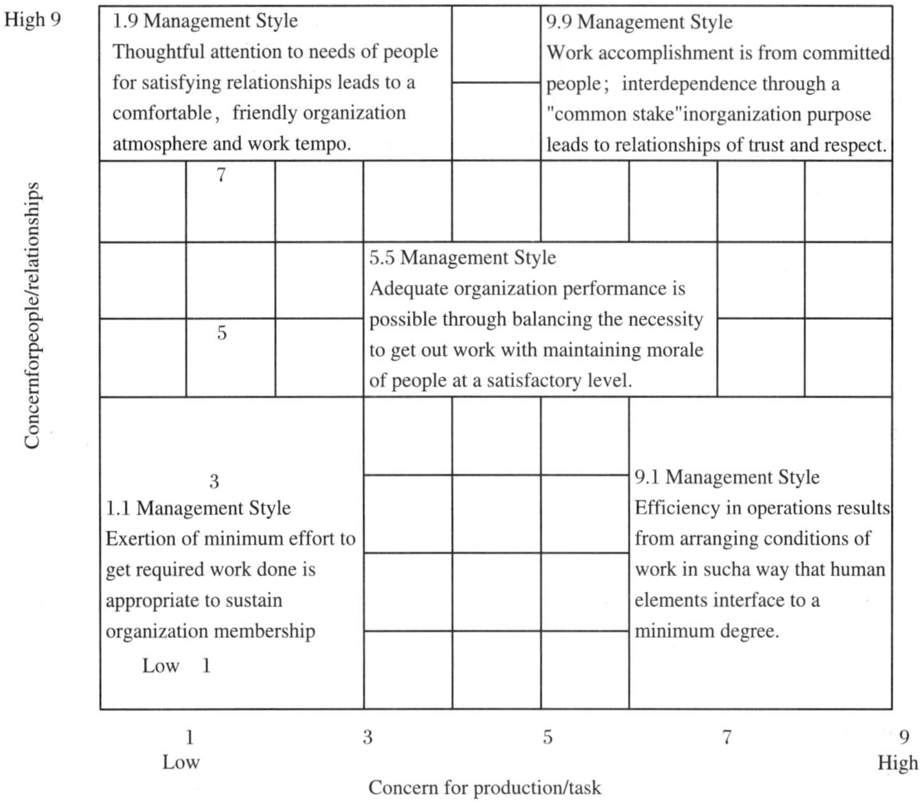

| High 9 | 1.9 Management Style
Thoughtful attention to needs of people for satisfying relationships leads to a comfortable, friendly organization atmosphere and work tempo. | | 9.9 Management Style
Work accomplishment is from committed people; interdependence through a "common stake"inorganization purpose leads to relationships of trust and respect. |

Concern for people/relationships

7

5.5 Management Style
Adequate organization performance is possible through balancing the necessity to get out work with maintaining morale of people at a satisfactory level.

5

3
1.1 Management Style
Exertion of minimum effort to get required work done is appropriate to sustain organization membership

9.1 Management Style
Efficiency in operations results from arranging conditions of work in sucha way that human elements interface to a minimum degree.

Low 1

1   3   5   7   9
Low   High
Concern for production/task

Figure 7-1 Managerial grid

Source: Adapted from Robert S. Blake and Jane S. Mouton. Managerial Facades [J]. Advanced Management Journal, July 1966, P. 31.

7. 1. 3 Leadership in Different Nationalities

1. Attitudes of European Managers toward Leadership Practices

In recent years, much research has been directed at leadership approaches in Europe. Most effort has concentrated on related areas, such as decision making, risk taking, strategic planning, and organization design, which have been covered in previous chapters. Some of this previous discussion is relevant to an understanding of leadership practices in Europe. For example, British managers tend to use a highly participative leadership approach. This is true for two reasons: (1) the political background of the country favors such an approach and (2) because most top British managers are not highly involved in the day-to-day affairs of the business, they prefer to delegate authority and let much of the decision making be handled by middle-and lower-level managers. This preference contrasts sharply with that of the French and the Germans, who prefer a more work-centered, authoritarian approach. In fact, if labor unions had no legally mandated seats on the boards of directors, participative management in Germany likely would be even less pervasive than it is, a problem that currently confronts firms like Volkswagen that are trying to reduce sharply their overhead to meet increasing competition in Europe. Scandinavian countries, however, make wide use of participative leadership approaches, with worker representation on the boards of directors and high management-worker interaction regarding workplace design and changes.

As a general statement, most evidence indicates that European managers tend to use a participative approach. They do not entirely subscribe to Theory Y philosophical assumptions, however, because an element of Theory X thinking persists. This was made clear by the Haire, Ghiselli, and Porter study of 3.641 managers from 14 countries. The leadership-related portion of this study sought to determine whether these managers were basically traditional (Theory X, or system 1/2) or democratic-participative (Theory Y, or system 3/4) in their approach. Specifically, the researchers investigated four areas relevant to leadership:

(1) Capacity for leadership and initiative. Does the leader believe that employees prefer to be directed and have little ambition (Theory X), or does the leader believe that characteristics such as initiative can be acquired by most people regardless of their inborn traits and abilities (Theory Y)?

(2) Sharing information and objectives. Does the leader believe that detailed, complete instructions should be given to subordinates and that subordinates need only this information to do their jobs, or does the leader believe that general directions are sufficient and that subordinates can use their initiative in working out the details?

(3) Participation. Does the leader support participative leadership practices?

(4) Internal control. Does the leader believe that the most effective way to control employees is through rewards and punishment or that employees respond best to internally generated control?

2. Japanese Leadership Approaches

Japan is well known for its paternalistic approach to leadership. Japanese culture promotes a high safety or security need, which is present among home country-based employees as well astransnational corporation expatriates. For example, one study examined the cultural orientations of 522 employees of 28 Japanese-owned firms in the United States and found that the native Japanese employees were more likely than their U. S. counterparts to value paternalistic company behavior. Another study found that Koreans also value such paternalism. However, major differences appear in leadership approaches used by the Japanese and those in other locales.

For example, the comprehensive Haire, Ghiselli, and Porter study found that Japanese managers have much greater belief in the capacity of subordinates for leadership and initiative than do managers in most other countries. In fact, in the study, only managers in Anglo-American countries had stronger feelings in this area. The Japanese also expressed attitudes toward the use of participation to a greater degree than others. In the other two leadership areas, sharing information and objectives and using internal control, the Japanese respondents were above average but not distinctive. Overall, however, this study found that the Japanese respondent scored highest on the four areas of leadership combined. In other words, these findings provide evidence that Japanese leaders have considerable confidence in the overall ability of their subordinates and use a style that allows their people to actively participate in decisions.

In addition, the leadership process used by Japanese managers places a strong emphasis on ambiguous goals. Subordinates are typically unsure of what their manager wants them to do. As a result, they spend a great deal of time over preparing their assignments. Some observers believe that this leadership approach is time-consuming and wasteful. However, it has number of important benefits. First is that the leader is able to maintain stronger control of the followers because the latter do not know with certainty what is expected of them. So they prepare themselves for every eventuality. Second, by placing the subordinates in a position where they must examine a great deal of information, the manager ensures that the personnel are well prepared to deal with the situation and all its ramifications. Third, the approach helps the leader maintain order and provide guidance, even when the leader is not as knowledgeable as the followers.

Two experts on the behavior of Japanese management have noted that salarymen (middle managers) survive in the organization by anticipating contingencies and being prepared to deal with them. So when the manager asks a question and the salaryman shows that he has done the research needed to answer the question, the middle manager also shows himself to be a reliable person. The leader does not have to tell the salaryman to be prepared; the individual knows what is expected of him.

Japanese managers operate this way because they usually have less expertise in a division's day-to-day business than their subordinates do. It is the manager's job to maintain harmony, not to be a technical expert. Consequently, a senior manager doesn't necessarily realize that E, F, G, and are important to know. He gives ambiguous directions to his subordinates so they can use their superior expertise to go beyond A, B, C and D. One salaryman explained it this way: "When my boss asks me to write a report, infer what he wants to know and what he needs to know without being told what he wants. " Another interviewee added that subordinates who receive high performance evaluations are those who know what the boss wants without needing to be told. What frustrates Japanese managers about non-Japanese employees is the feeling that, if they tell such a person they want A through D, they will never extract E through H; instead, they'll get exactly what they asked for. Inferring what the boss would have wanted had he only known to ask is tough game, but it is the one salarymen must play.

3. Leadership in China

In the past few years a growing amount of attention has been focused on leadership in China. In particular, international researchers are interested in learning if the country's economic progress is creating a new cadre of leaders whose styles are different from the styles of leaders of the past. In one of the most comprehensive studies to date, Ralston and his colleagues found that, indeed, new generation of Chinese leaders is emerging and they are somewhat different from past leaders in work values.

The researchers gathered data from a large number of managers and professionals (n =869) who were about to take part in management development programs. These individuals were part of what the researchers called the "New Generation" of Chinese organizational leaders. The researchers wanted to determine if this new generation of managers had the same work values as those of the "Current Generation" and "Older Generation" groups. In their investigation, the researchers focused their attention on the importance that the respondents assigned to three areas: individualism, collectivism, and Confucianism. Individualism was measured by the importance assigned to self-sufficiency and personal accomplishments. Collectivism was measured by the person's willingness to subordinate personal goals to those of the work group with an emphasis on sharing and group harmony. Confucianism was measured by the importance the respondent assigned to social harmony, virtuous interpersonal behavior, and personal and interpersonal harmony.

The researchers found that the new generation group scored significantly higher on individualism than did the current and older generation groups. In addition, the new generation leaders scored significantly lower than the other two groups on collectivism and Confucianism. These values appear to reflect the period of relative openness and freedom, often called the "Social Reform Era," during which these new managers grew up. They have had greater exposure to Western societal influences, and this may well be resulting in leadership styles similar to those of Western managers.

4. Leadership in the Middle East

Research also has been conducted on Middle East countries to determine the similarities and differences in managerial attitudes toward leadership practices. For example, in a follow-up study to that of Haire and associates, midlevel managers from Arab countries were surveyed and found to have higher attitude scores for capacity for leadership and initiative than those from any of the other countries or clusters. The Arab managers'scores for sharing information and objectives, participation and internal control, however, all were significantly lower than the scores of managers in the other countries and clusters. The researcher concluded that the results were accounted for by the culture of the Middle East region.

More recent research provides some evidence that there may be much greater similarity between Middle Eastern leadership styles and those of Western countries. In particular, the observation was made that Western management practices are very evident in the Arabian Gulf region because of the close business ties between the West and this oil-rich area and the increasing educational attainment, often in Western universities, of Middle Eastern managers. A study on decision making styles in the United Arab Emirates showed that organizational culture, level of technology, level of education, and management responsibility were good predictors of decision-making styles in such an environment. These findings were consistent with similar studies in Western environments. Also, results indicated a tendency toward participative leadership styles among young Arab middle management, as well as among highly educated managers of all ages.

5. Leadership Approaches in India

India is developing at a rapid rate as TNCs increase investment. India's workforce is quite knowledgeable in the high-tech industry, and society as a whole is moving toward higher education. However, India is still bound by old traditions. This raises the question, what kind of leadership style does India need to satisfy its traditional roots while heading into a high-tech future. One study showed that Indian workers were more productive when managers took a high people and high task approach (participative). Meanwhile, the less productive workers were managed by individuals who showed high people orientation, but low focus on task-related objectives. These findings may indicate that it is important in India to focus on the individual but in order to be efficient and produce results, managers need to maintain awareness of the tasks that need to be completed.

Because of India's long affiliation with Great Britain, leadership styles in India would seem more likely to be participative than those in the Middle East or in other developing countries. Haire and associates found some degree of similarity between leadership styles in India and Anglo-American countries, but it was not significant. The study found Indians to be similar to the Anglo-Americans in managerial attitudes toward capacity for leadership and initiative, participation and internal control. The difference is in sharing information and objectives. The Indian managers' responses tended to be quite similar to those of managers in other developing countries. These findings from India show that a participative leadership style may be more common and more effective in developing countries than has been reported previously. Over time, developing countries (as also shown in the case of the Persian Gulf nations) may be moving toward a more participative leadership style. Recently, researchers have suggested there may be some unique management and leadership styles that emerge from the polyglot nature of India's population and some of the unique challenges of doing business there. For example, some suggest that Indian leaders can improvise quickly to overcome hurdles, a concept sometimes referred to here as jugaad.

6. Differences between Japanese and U. S. Leadership Styles

In a number of ways, Japanese leadership styles differ from those in the United States. For example, the Haire and associates study found that except for internal control, large U. S. firms tend to be more democratic than small ones, whereas in Japan, the profile is quite different. A second difference is that younger U. S. managers appear to express more democratic attitudes than their older counter parts on all four leadership dimensions, but younger Japanese fall into this category only for sharing information and objectives and in the use of internal control. Simply put, evidence points to some similarities between U. S. and Japanese leadership styles, but major differences also exist.

A number of reasons have been cited for these differences. One of the most com-mon is that Japanese and U. S. managers have basically different philosoph of managing people. Table 7-1 provides a comparison of seven key characteristics that come from Ouchi's Theory Z, which combines Japanese and U. S. assumptions and approaches. Note in the table that the Japanese leadership approach is heavily group-oriented, paternalistic and concerned with the employee's work and personal life. The U. S. leadership approach is almost the opposite.

Table 7-1   **Japanese vs. U. S. Leadership Styles**

Philosophical Dimension	Japanese Approach	U. S. Approach
Employment	Often for life; layoffs are rare	Usually short – term; layoffs are common
Evaluation and promotion	Very slow; big promotions may not come for the first 10 years	Very fast; those not quickly promoted often seek employment elsewhere
Career paths	Very general; people rotate from one area to another and become familiar with all areas of operations	Very specialized; people tend to stay in one area (accounting, sales, etc.) for their entire careers
Decision making	Carried out via group decision making	Carried out by the individual manager
Control mechanism	Very implicit and informal; people rely heavily on trust and goodwill Shared collectively	Very explicit; people know exactly what to control and how to do it
Responsibility	Management's concern extends to the whole life, business and social of the worker	Assigned to individuals
Concern for employees		Management concerned basically with the individual's work life only

Source: Adapted from William Ouchi, Theory Z: How American Business Can Meet the Japanese Challenge MA: Addison-Wesley, 1981.

7.2   Organizational Innovation and Leadership

7.2.1   The Definition of organization innovation and Styles of research

Organizational innovation has been consistently defined as the adoption of an idea or behavior that is new to the organization (Damanpour 1988, 1991, Daft & Becker 1978, Hage 1980, Hage & Aiken 1970, Zaltman, Duncan & Holbek 1973, Oerlemans et al 1998, Wood 1998, Zummato & O' Connor 1992). The innovation can either be a new product, a new service, a new technology, or a new administrative practice. The research usually focuses on rates of innovation and not on single innovations except in the instance of diffusion studies where the speed of adoption is an issue. The importance of studies of innovation rates rather than a case study of a single innovation must be stressed In the meta-analysis of Damanpour (1991), he found that the greater the number of innovations considered in the research study, the more consistent the findings. This is an important conclusion, namely, that the focus on rates of a phenomenon will produce more consistent results than the analysis of a single event. Here lies one of the major methodological reasons why organizational sociologists have not always been able to observe an accumulation of findings.

Although the definition has remained consistent, the particular kinds of innovation examined have shifted across time as well as have the kinds of problems that have interested people. In the 1960s and 1970s the emphasis was on incremental change in public sector organizations (Allen & Cohen 1969, Daft & Becker 1978, Hage & Aiken 1967, Kaluzny et al 1972, Moch 1976), while in the 1980s and 1990s it has been on radical change in private sector organizations (Collins et al 1987, Cohn& Turyn 1980, Ettlie et al 1984, Gerwin 1988, Jaikumar 1986, Teece 1987, Walton 1987). Examples of the latter include flexible manufacturing (Collins et al 1987, Gerwin 1988, Teece 1987), retortable pouches (Ettlie et al 1984), robotics, automated handling of materials, or computer numerically controlled machines (Jaikumar 1986), and even ship automation (Walton 1987) and shoe production (Cohn & Turyn 1980). Furthermore, the measures for "radical" altered from subjective ones (Kaluzny etal 1972) to more objective ones (Cohn & Turyn 1980, Collins et al 1987, Ettlieet al 1984, Walton 1987).

As this shift in focus occurred, the nature of the problem being investigated so changed. Rather than simply count the number of adoptions within a particular time period, the analytical focus became differential implementation of radical innovations, most typically advanced manufacturing technologies (see Zammuto O' Connor 1992)

7.2.2 Types of innovation

The better we understand different types of innovation, the more accurately we can assess their strategic implications. We need to know, in particular, along which dimensions we should assess innovations.

One insightful way to categorize innovations is to measure their degree of newness in terms of technology and markets. Here, technology refers to the methods and materials used to achieve a commercial objective. For example, Apple integrates different types of technologies (hardware, software, micro-processors, the Internet, and so on) to produce and deliver an array of mobile devices and services. We also want to understand the market for an innovation-e. g., whether an innovation is introduced into a new oran existing market-because an idea or invention turns into an innovation only when it is' successfully commercialized. Measuring an innovation along the technology and market dimensions gives us the framework depicted in Figure 7-2. Along the horizontal axis, we ask whether the innovation builds on existing technologies or creates a new one. On the vertical axis, we ask whether the innovation is targeted toward existing or new markets. Four types of innovations emerge: incremental, radical, architectural, and disruptive innovations.

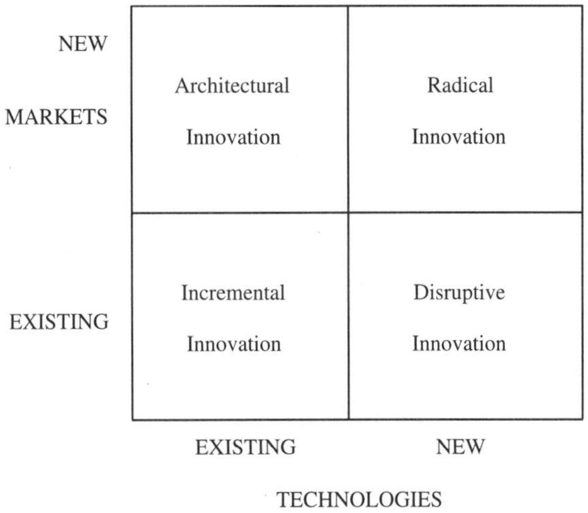

	EXISTING	NEW
NEW MARKETS	Architectural Innovation	Radical Innovation
EXISTING	Incremental Innovation	Disruptive Innovation
	EXISTING	NEW
	TECHNOLOGIES	

Figure 7-2   Innovation Framework

1. Incremental and Radical Innovations

Although radical breakthroughs such as MP3 players and magnetic resonance imaging (MRI) radiology capture most of our attention, the vast majority of innovations are actually incremental ones. An incremental innovation squarely builds on the firm's established knowledge base and steadily improves the product or service it offers. It targets existing markets using existing technology.

The Gillette example shows how radical innovation created a competitive advantage that the company sustained by follow-up incremental innovation. Such an outcome is not foregone conclusion, though. In some instances, the innovator is outcompeted by second movers that quickly introduce a very similar incremental innovation to continuously improve their own offering. For example, although CNN was the pioneer in 24-hour cable news, today it is only the third most popular choice in this category, having been surpassed by Fox News and MSNBC.

On the other hand, radical innovation draws on novel methods or materials, is derived either from an entirely different knowledge base or from recombination of the firm's existing knowledge base with a new stream of knowledge, or targets new markets by using new technologies. Well-known examples of radical innovations include the introduction of the mass-produced automobile (the Ford Model), the X-ray, the airplane, and more recently biotechnology breakthroughs such as genetic engineering and the decoding of the human genome.

Many firms get their start by successfully commercializing radical innovations, some of which, like the airplane, even give birth to new industries. Although the British firm de Havilland first commercialized the jet-powered passenger airplane, Boeing was the company that rode this radical innovation to industry dominance.

More recently, Boeing's leadership has been challenged by Airbus, and today each company has approximately half the market. This stalemate is now being contested by aircraft manufacturers such as Bombardier of Canada and Embraer of Brazil who are moving up-market by building larger luxury jets that are competing with some of the smaller airplane models offered by Boeing and Airbus.

Once firms have achieved market acceptance of a breakthrough innovation, they tend to follow up with incremental rather than radical innovations. Over time, these companies morph into industry incumbents. Future radical innovations are generally introduced by new entrepreneurial ventures.

2. Architectural and Disruptive Innovations

Firms can also innovate by leveraging existing technologies into new markets. Doing so generally requires them to reconfigure the components of a technology, meaning they alter the overall "architecture" of the product. An architectural innovation, therefore, is a new product in which known components, based on existing technologies, are reconfigured in a novel way to create new markets.

For example, in the 1980s Xerox was the most dominant copier company worldwide. It produced high-volume, high-quality copying machines that it leased to its customers through a service agreement. While these machines were ideal for the high end of the market, Xerox ignored small and medium-sized businesses. By applying an architectural innovation, the Japanese entry Canon was able to redesign the copier so that it didn't need professional service-reliability was built directly into the machine, and the user could replace parts such as the cartridge. This allowed Canon to apply the "razor and razor blade" business model, charging relatively low prices for its copiers but higher prices for cartridges. What Xerox had not envisioned was the possibility that the components of the copying machine could be put together in a different way that was more user-friendly.

Finally, a disruptive innovation leverages new technologies to attack existing markets. It invades an existing market from the bottom up. The following examples illustrate disruptive innovations:

(1) Japanese carmakers successfully followed a strategy of disruptive innovation by first introducing small fuel-efficient cars, and then leveraging their low-cost and high-quality advantages into high-end luxury segments, captured by brands such as Lexus, Infiniti, and Acura.

(2) Digital photography improved enough over time to provide higher-definition pictures. As a result, it has been able to replace film photography, even in most professional applications.

(3) Data storage products advanced from the floppy disk to the hard disk to the CD, then to the ZIP drive, and now to flash drives Each new memory device invaded the market from the bottom up and performance improved over time.

(4) Mini computers disrupted mainframe computers; desktop computers disrupted mini computers; laptops disrupted desktop computers now netbooks under $200 are disrupting laptops

(5) Throughout the 1990s, Swatch's low-cost, fun watches disrupted watches that were like expensive jewelry. Today, timekeeping functions of smartphones are replacing wristwatches altogether.

One factor favoring the success of disruptive innovation is that it relies on stealth attack: It invades the market from the bottom up, by first capturing the low end. Many times, incumbent firms fail to defend (and sometimes are even happy to cede) the low end of the market, because it is frequently a low-margin business. The emergence of electric arc furnaces, for example, was a disruptive innovation that allowed so-called mini-mills like Nucor and Chaparral to produce steel in small batches and at lower cost compared with fully integrated steel mills such as U. S. Steel or Bethlehem Steel. Initially, though, the quality of steel produced by mini-mills was poor and could compete only in the lowest tier of the market: steel used to reinforce construction concrete (rebar steel). Once the mini-mills entered segment of the steel market, the integrated mills could no longer be cost-competitive given their high fixed cost; the incumbents happily ceded segment of the market to the entrants because it was low margin-business to begin with. The new entrant is then able to leverage its disruptive technology to continue to invade the existing firm's territory from the bottom up.

Google, for example, is using its new operating system, Chrome, as beachhead to invade Microsoft's stronghold. Chrome OS is optimized to run on netbooks, the fastest-growing segment in computing. To appeal to users who spend most of their time on the web accessing e-mail and other online applications, for instance, it is designed to start up in few seconds. Moreover, Google provides Chrome OS free of charge. In contrast to Microsoft's proprietary Windows operating system, Chrome OS is open-source software, freely accessible to anyone for further development and refinement. In this sense, Google is leveraging crowdsourcing in its new product development, just as threadless uses crowdsourcing to design and market T-shirts and Wikipedia uses the wisdom of the crowds to collectively edit encyclopedia entries.

Another factor favoring the success of disruptive innovation is that incumbent firms often are slow to change. Incumbent firms that listen closely to their current customers will respond by continuing to invest in the existing technology and in incremental changes to the existing products. When newer technology matures and proves to be a better solution, those same customers will switch over. At that time, however, the incumbent firm does not yet have a competitive product ready that is based on the disruptive technology. Although customer-oriented mission statements are more likely to guard against firm obsolescence than product-oriented ones, they are no guarantee that a firm can hold out in the face of disruptive innovation. One of the counterintuitive findings that Clayton Christensen unearthed in his studies is that it can hurt incumbents to listen only to their existing customers.

Although these examples show that disruptive innovations are a serious threat for incumbent firms, some have devised strategic initiatives to counter them. A first option is to invest in staying ahead of the competition. Apple continuously innovates-Steve Jobs has always believed that he knows what customers need even before they realize it. Apple is famous for not soliciting customer feedback or studying markets. A second approach is to guard against disruptive innovation by protecting the low end of the market by introducing low-cost innovations to preempt stealth competitors. Intel introduced the Celeron chip, a stripped-down, budget version of its Pentium chip, in 1998. More recently, Intel followed up with the Atom chip, a new processor that is inexpensive and consumes little battery power, to power low-costnetbooks. A third way to guard against disruptive innovations is to use reverse innovation, rather than wait for others to do it to you. In reverse innovation a firm develops products specifically for emerging markets such as China and India, and then introduces these innovations into developed markets such as the United States or the European Union.

7.2.3   Transformational leadership and organizational innovation

Organizational innovation is the creation of valuable and useful new products/services within an organizational context (Woodman et al., 1993). Since most organizations engage in innovative activity as a competitive weapon, the present study adopts a market-oriented approach and expands this definition to include the returns due to innovation. Accordingly, organizational innovation is the tendency of the organization to develop new or improved products/services and its success in bringing those products/services to the market. This approach is consistent with Damanpour's (1991) definition of product innovations as, "new products/services introduced to meet an external user or market need", and the description provided by the OECD (2004) as, "the successful bringing of the new product or service to the market".

Transformational leaders enhance innovation within the organization; the tendency of organizations to innovate. Leaders use of inspirational motivation and intellectual stimulation is critical for organizational innovation (Elkins and Keller, 2003). Transformational leaders promote creative ideas within their organizations; this behavior reflects the "championing role" of transformational leaders (Howell and Higgins, 1990). These leaders have a vision that motivates their followers increases their willingness to perform beyond expectations, and challenges them to adopt innovative approaches in their work. The resulting heightened level of motivation is likely to enhance organizational innovation (Mumford et al., 2002). A number of empirical studies support such leaders' positive impact on innovation (e.g. Keller 1992; Waldman and Atwater, 1994). These studies examine the relationship between transformational leadership and innovation mostly in R&D units and at the project level. The proposal of an effect of transformational leadership on innovation at the organizational level has become a topic of empirical research only recently. Jung et al. (2003), in a study of 32 companies in Taiwan (China), find that transformational leadership significantly and positively relates to organizational innovation as measured by R&D expenditures and number of patents obtained over the preceding 3 years.

Transformational leaders may also have a positive influence on the market success of the innovations leaders who articulate a strong vision of innovation and display a sense of power and confidence will strive to ensure the market success of the innovation. These leaders mobilize their followers to ensure the innovations' success (Jung et al., 2003). Keller (1992) suggests that leading professional employees might require more than traditional leader behaviors especially in R&D settings where quality rather than quantity is the primary performance criterion.

Furthermore, in addition to the internal roles the transformational leader may be effective in playing external roles such as boundary spanning and entrepreneuring/championing (Howelland Higgins, 1990); these might be important both for understanding the needs of the market and for successful marketing of the innovation.

7.3 Case

Case-1

How to Lead your Fellow Rainmakers

When Daniel was elected managing partner of his consulting firm his colleagues reacted enthusiastically. relatively young and hugely energetic, he had quickly risen to prominence in his firm. He'd garnered widespread support among his peers, especially the younger partners, who felt that some of their older colleagues were "free riding" as they neared retirement. Clients had noticed a decline in the quality of the firms work and were threatening to defect. During his leadership campaign, Daniel had outlined ambitious plans for reinvigorating the firm and restoring it to the number one position in the market. Flattered by his confidence in them and drawn to his vision for the firm, the partners elected Daniel by a substantial majority.

But 18 months later, the partners rejected Daniel's proposals outright and called for his resignation. What had gone wrong?

In conventional corporate settings, leaders are expected to inspire and direct their employees-leading is something they do to followers. But in professional service firms the leadership dynamics are different, because the power relationships are different. Consulting, accounting, and law firms and investment banks tend to be full of highly opinionated rainmakers who don't easily accept the role of follower-and may be just as unwilling to act as leaders. In this context, leadership is a collective, not an individual, endeavor, created through interactions among powerful peers.

Power in organizations belongs to people who control access to key resources.

In professional service firms those resources are specialized expertise, major client relationships, and reputation in the market. Firms may try to codify and capitalize on them, but they cannot exist independently of the people who possess them. In partnerships, which many professional service firms are, this is recognized in the firm's legal structure, because senior professionals own the business.

As a result, power is widely dispersed in professional service firms-autonomy is extensive, and authority is contingent. Senior professionals need considerable autonomy to customize services for their clients. And while they elect or appoint their peers to leadership positions, they cede authority to them only on a conditional basis, reserving the right to challenge, ignore, and even depose them.

That places severe constraints on professional service firm leaders, who are entirely dependent on the continued support of their peers to get anything done. As a partner in a "Big Four" accounting firm told me, among colleagues at his level, "frankly, nobody has to follow anyone. " One senior partner of a law firm described the way he works with his fellow partners like this: "It's not telling them what to do, it's just coming up with the prompts and ideas. So leadership sort happens. "

If you've recently taken on a leadership role at a professional service firm, all this may sound daunting. How can you actually get anything done?

I've been studying and advising the leaders of such firms for the past 25 years. My research includes two major UK government-funded studies of leadership and governance in professional service firms, involving interviews with more than 500 senior professionals from a variety of sectors in 16 countries.

Through this research, and with the help of my colleague Johan Alvehus at Lund University, I've identified three distinct yet interconnected dynamics—establishing legitimacy, maneuvering politically, and negotiating perpetually-that explain how collective leadership actually happens among professionals. At the heart of each lies a tension between the actions of people in leadership positions and how colleagues respond to and interpret their actions. These tensions create an inherently unstable equilibrium. To maintain a balance firm leaders must work constantly with their colleagues to manage these tensions. In the following pages, I'll explain how they can best meet that challenge.

Establishing legitimacy

In conventional organizations rising stars are often advised to demonstrate their potential by seeking out leadership responsibilities. But in a professional service firm, it's wise to be wary. When a boss invites you to take on a "leadership" role, he or she may simply be trying to off-load burden some administrative responsibilities. You risk getting side tracked from income-generating client work and being seen by your peers as a glorified administrator.

Another mistake that professionals often make is to believe they can rise up in their firms just by doing technically brilliant work—by being respected and recognized by colleagues as an expert. That's essential to surviving the progressive culls of staff in the early stages of your career, but the game changes as you approach the rank of partner. It's rare for technical specialists to move into senior leadership roles; the largest law and accounting firms are almost never led by the head of the tax practice, for example.

Among professionals, legitimacy as a leader ultimately depends on your ability to generate revenue—in other words, to be a good rainmaker. My research has found that the people who reach the top of professional service firms are outstanding at winning new business and at managing the most demanding and lucrative clients; they also work harder and longer at earning fees than their peers do (in an environment where extended hours are the norm). Because colleagues see them as role models, they're willing to cede authority to them.

The irony is that many of these role models have very little interest in becoming leaders. They want to focus on the thing they love best—their client work—and are reluctant to put themselves forward as potential leaders of their practiceor their firm.

Christine is a classic example. One of the top rainmakers in her accounting firm, she sold the biggest projects to the best clients. But she was frustrated by the head of her practice area, who had introduced too many controls that got in the way of her client work. In the past Christine had deliberately avoided taking on leadership roles, but her colleagues now asked her to step forward and challenge the practice head-to dismantle his unpopular controls and restore their cherished autonomy.

Christine was reluctant but when she realized the practice head was planning to seek another term, she let it be known she was interested in the position. That was all the encouragement her fellow partners needed. They lobbied the firm's senior partner, saying they had lost confidence in their practice head but were willing to work with Christine. As Christine explained: "People were drawn to me. I had followers before I went into a leadership role because I was the lead partner for a big client. So I created opportunities for people, I was successful, and they enjoyed working with me and my clients. " In other words, she was seen by her peers as a potential leader because she was successful in the market and because she was willing to share her success with them.

Yet, while this gave her the legitimacy to lead, it did not guarantee that Christine would be good at leadership, as she would soon discover. To run their firms effectively, professionals need to understand two other leadership dynamics.

Maneuvering Politically

Although i never asked interviewees specifically about office politics, they were often keen to tell me how much they abhorred political behavior. The chair of one consulting firm in my study declared: "To me, politics smacks of alliance building in the corridors, in offices behind the scenes, of people engineering agendas, which deliver a fait accompli. I would like to think we don't have those behaviors in this firm. "

That chair may have been in denial or simply not telling the truth. In fact, political behaviors were rife in his organization—as they are in most professional service firms I've studied. This isn't necessarily pernicious. In an environment characterized by extensive autonomy and contingent authority, political maneuvering is simply how leadership happens. Leaders need to create and sustain consensus among peers and offer them incentives in private to persuade them to lend their support in public. To carry this off and maintain their authority, leaders need four core political skills: networking ability, interpersonal influence, social astuteness, and apparent sincerity. And many firms enshrine politics within their governance systems, holding elections for senior leadership positions in which candidates issue manifestos, run campaigns, and participate in debates.

Professionals distrust colleagues who seem to want power over them. It's ok to be ambitious for the firm, but you should not seem ambitious for yourself. So as a leader you need to convince colleagues that you're employing your political skills for their benefit rather than your own. If you can do that, then they will not judge you as political but will perceive that you have integrity.

One way to persuade your peers of your integrity is to develop and communicate a compelling vision for the firm. Consider Antonio, who was a partner at a large law firm. Although he led a relatively small practice, he had big ambitions and decided to run for senior partner. He campaigned against eight other candidates and worked hard to win support outside his practice. He met several hundred of his fellow partners, individually and in small groups, listening to their concerns and explaining how his vision would deliver what they most wanted.

At the candidates' debate, he gave a compelling speech, explaining his desire to unleash what he described as the partners' entrepreneurial potential by "giving the partnership back to the partners" and introducing an ambitious investment program to fund new partner-led initiatives. Impressed by what they saw as his passionate commitment to the firm and his belief in their ability his peers elected him by a large majority. The integrity they perceived in Antonio was evident in this description from one colleague. He is not a player. His own motivations in this world are very genuine and clean.

There is a clear link between being a good rainmaker and being a good campaigner. Someone who has the networking ability, interpersonal influence, social astuteness, and apparent sincerity to manage powerful clients can also use those skills to manage powerful partners. But there's much more to leadership in a professional service firm than just that.

Negotiating Perpetually

Striking a balance between exercising autonomy and asserting control is far from straight forward. It involves perpetual negotiating—the third core dynamic of collective leadership in professional service firms. Knowing what actions to take is only part of the challenge. You need to understand when to take them with whom, and how to persuade your colleagues that you're working in their best interests rather than your own.

For example, at the start of the financial year your colleagues may view your attempts to assert control as an unacceptable infringement on their autonomy. But if you wait for financial difficulties to become obvious, they may complain about a "leadership vacuum". If you challenge the inappropriate behavior of a popular and "colorful" partner, your colleagues may protest. But if you fail to reprimand a less likable, more marginalized partner for exactly the same behavior, they may raise questions about your moral leadership. One senior partner in my study explained the problem this way: "Partners say, 'You're too tight, get looser. ' So you get looser, and they say, It's chaotic, get tighter. " One chairman compared the process to " walking a tightrope-helping my partners feel like owners, feel involved, and be engaged, but not dominating them, not getting out infront, and not having a huge ego, which makes them feel like the chairman's kind of on his own trip. At the same time being strong and providing them with a sense of confidence that we're going somewhere. "

Let's return to Daniel, the managing partner who struggled to fulfill his mandate and lost his peers' support. After winning the election, he hired a COO from the corporate sector to undertake a root-and-branch overhaul of his firm's cost base, with a focus on partner spending. Daniel personally led the task force that was redesigning the partner appraisal system, tightening up metrics, clarifying consequences of underperformance, and enhancing rewards for success. In other words he did exactly what his partners had elected him to do: assert control by introducing more performance-oriented financial rigor.

During the election he had talked about making the "free riders" more accountable but had been vague onthe details. once he was in office, his colleagues started to wonder: Which partners did he think were free riders? How many were there? And what exactly did "more accountable" mean? Disaffected partners started whispering that Daniel seemed to be enjoying his new power a little too much and was not showing his peers enough respect. They encouraged colleagues to believe they might be the free riders Daniel was referring to this whispering campaign was effective. When Daniel introduced the new partner appraisal system, his colleagues rebelled, and he was forced to abandon his plans.

Daniel had failed to understand that when his partners had asked him to assert control, they meant control overtheir colleagues but not over them personally. They were prepared to cede some autonomy but not to have it taken away from them. By rejecting his proposals, they were trying to teach Daniel a lesson—that as their elected leader he ultimately worked for them, not the other way around. But having positioned himself as the firm's savior, he had become convinced by his own rhetoric and thought he could do it on his own. He failed to understand that he needed to bring the partners along with him-that leading professional service firms is a collective endeavor, and the mandate to lead your peers must be continually renegotiated and renewed.

An Unstable Equilibrium

In addition to perpetually negotiating, the leader of a professional service firm must keep a constant eye on the other two dynamics which are always in flux. To retain your legitimacy, you need to continue to be successful in the market, despite the fact that you can no longer devote yourself full-time to fee-earning work. You must constantly maneuver politically, as alliances shift among partners and their relative power waxes and wanes. And, remember, it's not just about what you do as an individual leader but how your colleagues interpret and respond to what you are doing (inferring you have leadership ability, perceiving you have integrity, and feeling free to exercise autonomy).

The instability is amplified by the fact that the three leadership dynamics are interconnected. If they discover your political maneuvering, your peers will quickly question your legitimacy. That will undermine your ability to negotiate the balance between control and autonomy as will the failure to convince people you're acting in their interests rather than your own.

Remember Christine? Her colleagues wanted her to take over as leader of their practice because she'd been so successful at winning business. But she was quickly overwhelmed by the complexity of the new role and came to see why the previous practice head had seemed so controlling: There was a lot that needed to be controlled.

She lacked the time and patience to manage the egos of the partners who had supported her and now expected her to support them in their pet projects and peeves. She became distracted from her client work, her core strength. And after she failed to land a couple of major new projects, her colleagues began to see her in a different light. They no longer inferred that she had leadership ability. As her peers withdrew their cooperation, Christine lost her authority and, with it, her ability to get things done. The equilibrium had become destabilized.

And what about Antonio? Fulfilling his election promise, he initiated ambitious spending plans. Profits plummeted, and as the clients became aware of the firm's difficulties, Antonio was unable to win new business. He lost his legitimacy as a leader and so was unable to negotiate effectively. But his political skills, which had helped him win his election against tough opposition, enabled him to save face. When a small group of influential partners called a meeting to demand his resignation, Antonio suggested a deal: He would complete his term as senior partner on the condition that one of them take over as COO to run the firm on his behalf. Rather late in the day, Antonio had come to understand the dynamics of collective leadership.

Collective Leadership in Action

What does collective leadership look like when it works well? Peter and Paul, the senior partner and managing partner of a global law firm, displayed an intuitive understanding of collective leadership when they steered their firm through the greatest crisis in its 70-year history. After the 2008 financial crash, they realized that their firm had to undergo a major restructuring and that a substantial number of its 500 partners would need to be asked to leave. Nothing like that had been done before in the firm, and its rules of governance required that the entire partnership vote on a decision of that magnitude.

Peter and Paul had been among the firm's top rainmakers and were highly respected by their colleagues. Nonetheless, they realized that if they misjudged the mood of their partners and mismanaged the process, they would quickly lose their legitimacy to lead.

The two convened a small group of the firm's most powerful partners and asked them to work together to decide who among their colleagues should be asked to go over the next few months, working in secret, this group analyzed performance data and debated at length the list of candidates for departure. Many partners had worked together for more than 20 years, and some in the group resisted putting the names of longtime friends and colleagues on the list. But gradually, Peter and Paul drew more and more partners into the decision-making process, until eventually 50 of the 500 were involved in the secret deliberations.

Key to the process was the way Peter and Paul intervened selectively, allowing the extended group of partners the autonomy to lead the work but asserting control when they felt its members were not making sufficient progress.

Peter and Paul divided up their roles. as one colleague explained, "Peter worked behind the scenes, speaking to each of us privately and putting pressure on us individually as to whether we had gone far enough. " This approach didn't always work, at which point Paul intervened directly. He said, "I really had to push to ensure there were enough names on the list. But as soon as we had an agreement within a couple of days the list got shorter. I had to go back to them several times and say, 'This is not enough. ' "

Finally, five months after the financial crisis began, Peter and Paul were ready to speak to the partners as a whole. During several hours of one-to-one calls and meetings around the world, they asked 15% of the partners-75 people in total-to leave or accept a reduction in equity. Later that afternoon, Peter and Paul called an emergency meeting of the partnership to announce the departures relieved they hadn't been selected, the remaining partners didn't insist on their right to call a vote about the restructuring.

Peter and Paul were successful because they had worked with an ever-expanding subset of the partner group, ensuring that powerful potential critics were co-opted into the process of making a profoundly difficult decision. Their own track record of market success gave them the legitimacy they needed to persuade colleagues to cooperate. Their political skills enabled them to maneuver their way around the competing views of their peers. And their sense of when to assert control and when to let colleagues exercise autonomy helped them negotiate their way toward consensus.

Although the story of Peter and Paul concerns a one-off crisis, it's important to remember that collective leadership is continuous. Leadership dynamics are constantly in flux as the equilibrium is destabilized and restabilized. Sometimes one individual may step forward and assume leadership, and colleagues will allow him or her to do so. At other times that individual may step back and become a good follower even if he or she is nominally in charge. So collective leadership is not something that is done to followers but is a process done with colleagues.

The leadership team of a professional service firm ineffect includes all the partners; in some firms, collective leadership requires input and support from many hundreds of individuals. When you're a managing or senior partner, your peers may look to you to be their heroic leader, and you may be tempted to take up that mantle. But you need to keep reflecting the leadership challenge back onto them to keep reminding them and yourself that leadership is a collective activity. If it feels lonely at the top that's probably because you're not doing it right.

(Source: Laura Empson. How to Lead your Fellow Rainmakers. Harward Business Review, March-April, 2019: 114-123.)

Questions:

1. According the case above, find ways to maintain a balance firm leaders.

2. As the senior partner and managing partner of a global law firm, what the successful leadership do Peter and Paul embodies?

Case-2

How did IT Match Groups CEO on Innovating In a Fast-Changing Industry

The transformation that has taken place at Match Group since I first began working here, 12 years ago, is incredible to contemplate. Back then dating websites were accessible only from a desktop or a laptop They often required monthly fees and a lot of patience from users, who scrolled through profiles and waited for responses. Online dating also carried a definite stigma, so if a couple had met on Match, they often lied and said they'd met "through friends". Although the sites had rudimentary matching algorithms in their early days most users relied on "open search": They read many profiles that might have little relevance in hopes of finding someone they really wanted to meet.

If you describe that process to a 25-year-old Tinder or Hinge user today, it sounds as antiquated as fax machines. Over the past decade, significant industry wide shifts in technology and business models have occurred-the biggest one being mobile. They have completely changed the way people use our products, which now run almost entirely via apps and smartphones. Those product changes have been accompanied by an attitudinal shift: In the New York Times Weddings section on Sunday, people now routinely mention the dating app on which they met. Research shows that 35% of marriages start online, up from around 3% when I began working here.

The speed of change is one of the things I love about this industry. Each shift has made us completely rethink our approach. I've built my career trying to develop consumer insights and use them to create appealing new products. Match Group is a great place to do that. Perhaps the biggest lesson I've drawn from this experience is that companies need to innovate constantly—with technology, pricing, product features, and business models—to stay ahead of competitors and continue to grow.

Three Big Influences

Not many large companies have female CEOs which has caused me to reflect on why my upbringing compelled me to pursue this kind of career. I count three big influences that led me to my current role. The first is that I grew up in a matriarchal environment. I'm the product of a very strong mother I'm one of three daughters, and I attended an all-girls school while growing up in Dallas. All my early role models were women, and expectations were high for me and my sisters to pursue careers.

The second factor was that I played competitive soccer and was recruited to play for UC Berkeley, which had one of the strongest teams in the country I wasn't the biggest or the fastest player, but I understood team dynamics and could recognize people's strengths and weaknesses and help find ways for us to play better together. Only later did I recognize how useful that skill is when one is leading people—and teams in business.

Finally, I grew up in a very entrepreneurial environment. My father and grandfather owned their own businesses. Looking back, I can't recall any family member who had a traditional 9-to-5 job. That atmosphere taught me the benefits of thinking like an entrepreneur and taking risks.

After college I moved to Israel and worked for a few years at a tech company. I met my first husband while I was there. In 1994 we moved to San Francisco, where I joined Edelman, a large public relations firm. I spent nearly five years working with Silicon Valley tech companies. It was an incredibly exciting time to be in the Bay Area, and I loved working on strategic marketing plans for high-tech companies, but I knew I wanted to run a business and not stay in marketing forever. I realized it was time to move on and enrolled in Wharton's MBA program; my husband and I and our infant daughter moved to Philadelphia.

A week after I signed my student loan, my husband told me he was leaving and wanted a divorce. in an instant my whole world changed. I was alone, without the support system I had expected, in a demanding MBA program, with a one-year-old child. It was a life-changing experience, but I graduated from Wharton stronger than before, and I made lifelong friendships and connections in the process.

As I finished at Wharton, my mom was diagnosed with ovarian cancer. I wanted to move back to Dallas to be with her and my family. While she fought the disease, I became the head of marketing at a B2B tech firm that made supply chain management software. It wasn't the perfect fit, but it was important that I be nearby during what turned out to be the last two years of my mother's life. I also met my current husband at that company.

Two Important Shifts

Soon after my mother died, I got a recruiting call from Match. The company was looking for someone who had a background in marketing to run Chemistry. com, the start-up it had launched to compete with eHarmony, which had launched a few years earlier. To join eHarmony, users had to fill out a lengthy psychological profile, and the site's stated mission wasn't to help people date but to help them marry. Because Match wasn't set up explicitly for finding spouses, eHarmony caused its image to change: match became seen as a site for casual dating, whereas Harmony was for "serious" dating. I ran Chemistry. com from 2006 to 2008. It was my first general management job and I loved building the team. We grew the site quickly.

But even as Chemistry. com expanded, the company's flagship Match. com seemed to be plateauing. So in 2008 management asked me to move over to Match. com and try to reenergize that brand.

Two important shifts were under way that hurt Match. com. First, OkCupid and Plenty of Fish, recent entrants, had pioneered a new business model: Instead of charging users monthly fees, they relied on advertising for revenue. That attracted people who were interested in online dating but reluctant to pay for it, and it marked the beginning of an era in which companies rethought how to price and monetize their platforms.

The second shift involved algorithms. All the early dating websites had search functionality, and all asked users to specify the type of people they hoped to meet. But by 2008 companies were getting more sophisticated about analyzing and understanding users preferences and behavior. We rolled out a feature where by every Match. comuser was sent five daily matches, and we monitored whether people liked them or not. We began hiring more data scientists and changing our algorithms to more closely track users' actual behavior rather than their stated preferences.

For example, if people say they prefer to date tall blondes but they're sending messages to short brunettes, our algorithm should recognize that and send them matches that reflect actual activity patterns. Because our data tells us what types of profiles users like, we also began to encourage them to send messages or likes or winks, rather than just peruse profiles—after all, no dating can actually occur unless someone reaches out first. We began advertising on television, which was very successful because it made online dating seem mainstream.

As these two shifts took place, we initiated a third that became an important driver of our growth. In 2009 Match made its first big acquisition, in the form of a company called People Media. UnlikeMatch, which ran just two websites, People Media had a variety of smaller sites aimed at specific demographics—for example Black Peoplemeet. com and SeniorPeopleMeet. com (now called OurTime. com). Online dating relies on network effects, so in theory a very large site should be more successful. Because it has a deeper pool of people to date. But we'd already seen the advantages of having a variety of targeted brands when the market segmented into "serious" and "casual" dating. Now Facebook and Twitter were bringing more people onto social media, which sparked more interest in online dating, especially from older people. If it was suddenly socially acceptable to meet friends online, why not dates? As the age range of our users began to broaden, providing sites that appealed to various demographics became more important. No one wants to be on the same dating platform as a parent or a grandparent. Over time, Match acquired other brands, including Ok Cupid and Plenty of Fish. Today we have dozens of dating products that operate around the world. When we acquire a new brand, we have a lot of experience to help it grow.

But without a doubt, the biggest technology shift came after 2008. That's when Apple introduced the app Store Smartphones were becoming ubiquitous, and most dating platforms began migrating away from desktops and onto apps. Within a few years that completely changed the face of our industry—a change sparked largely by Tinder.

Tinder's Innovation

In 2012 Tinder came out of an incubator that IAC, Match's parent company, had started; it's now part of our portfolio. It was very different from existing dating products. From the beginning, it was designed for smartphones and existed only as an app. Tinder was location-based, so users could see who was nearby, which brought spontaneity to the industry. Instead of long profiles, which would be hard to read on a mobile device, Tinder relied on photos and a very short bio. Its biggest innovation was swiping-swipe right if you find someone attractive, left if you don't.

When two people swipe right on each other. Tinder notifies both of the mutual attraction. If people know the attraction is mutual, they're more comfortable initiating contact. This was great for women: It was the first time they could filter potential matches and choose whom to talk to, as opposed to getting unsolicited messages.

Tinder introduced its product at an umber of universities. It went viral among college students, and we never imagined how fast it would grow. Before Tinder, relatively few people under 30 used online dating. Today Tinder has tens of millions of users and the majority of them are between 18 and 25. Young people who use it tend to also use two or three other dating apps, which makes our strategy of owning a portfolio of brands even stronger.

Most dating apps, including Tinder, have shifted to a "freemium" or paywall strategy. Joining is free, and users get basic functionality. They can opt to pay premium features such as seeing who likes you and swiping in another city. Last year Tinder's revenue topped $800 million, demonstrating that many people are willing to pay for these features.

When we create a feature that work swell on one of our apps, we roll it out across our other brands. There's a lot of copy catting among our competitors as well. which can make it hard to sustain the competitive advantage created by innovations. When possible, we take steps to protect our intellectual property. In 2017 we patented some of Tinder's key functionality, and since then we've taken steps to defend that IP. ①

The Next Phase of Growth

By 2017 I had led some of Match's biggest brands and the board asked me to become CEO. Today I spend much of my time trying to understand what customers want and need from our products and how we can innovate to help satisfy those needs even better.

Right now we're working on several new strategies that we expect will drive our next phase of growth. I've always thought it ironic that people refer to our industry as "online dating" when no one really ever dates online—at a certain point you meet face-to-face. Too often the spark that was ignited online dies out when people actually meet. The holy grail of our industry is finding ways to use technology to better predict whether that chemistry will persist in real life. If a company could reduce the number of unsuccessful dates, customers would be even more satisfied.

---

① Match Group has filed a lawsuit against Bumble, a dating app created by one of Tinder's original employees, alleging patent infringement. Match Group has also reached settlement agreements with other companies that utilized the swipe.

Video is one of the best tools for that. If you're unaccustomed to talking to people by video, it can feel awkward. But you get used to it. Our company uses video calls extensively—I'd say 90% of my work calls are now done on video.

You can pick up so much more about people when you can see them—how they carry themselves, their sense of humor, their confidence. Using video for online dating isn't a new idea. Years ago we owned a dating platform that let users post videos. People didn't know what to say, so we saw a lot of 10-minute videos of someone reading aloud from a book. That's not very useful. But the market is better able to use video now, Millennials post videos of themselves on Instagram and Snap, so they're naturally comfortable with the format. We've begun allowing users to post video snippets on Tinder, where users tend to be younger; for our brands where users tend to be older and less comfortable posting videos of themselves, were working to find more-natural ways to let their personality come through on video without their feeling embarrassed. Considering how quickly this industry changes, I can only imagine how video may be used on these apps in five years.

We're also expanding in international markets where online dating is less mature. Markets across Asia tend to have lots of young singles with smartphones and evolving dating norms. For Indians of my generation (I'm inmy forties), arranged marriages were common. That's changing. In fact, my second husband is Indian and he was the first person in his family to forgo an arranged marriage. In Japan until recently, a stigma was still attached to online dating. We bought a brand called Pairs, which is the top app for serious dating in Japan, and it's been growing quickly. These markets are very exciting for us as we look to the future.

Match Group has a lot of scale and expertise, and we're trying to use those advantages to be smarter and faster than our competitors. We need to keep innovating, because this is meaningful work. There's an epidemic of loneliness in the world. People are beginning to understand the health implications of that and we need to address it even in a technology-driven society, people crave intimate connections whether that means getting married or just sitting down together for coffee. We help people make those connections. Finding more effective ways to do that has proved very fulfilling.

(Source: Mandy Ginsberg. How did IT Match Groups CEO on Innovating in a Fast-Changing Industry. Harward Business Review, July-August, 2019: 35-39.)

Questions:

1. What is the style of the leadership behavior of Match Groups CEO?

2. According the case above, discuss the relationship between leadership and innovation.

Case-3

HP's CEO Mark Hurd Resigns amid Ethics Scandal

MARK HURD WAS appointed Hewlett-Packard's CEO in the spring of 2005, following Carly Fiorina's tumultuous tenure. He had begun his business career 25 years earlier as an entry-level sales person with NCR, a U. S. technology company best known for its bar code scanners in retail outlets and automatic teller machines (ATMs). By the time he had ascended to the role of CEO at NCR, he had earned a reputation as a low-profile, no-nonsense manager focused on flawless strategy execution. When he was appointed HP CEO, industry analysts praised its board of directors. Moreover, investors hoped that Mr. Hurd would run an efficient and lean operation at HP, to return the company to former greatness and, above all, profitability.

Mr. Hurd did not disappoint. By all indications, he was highly successful at the helm of HP. The company became number one desktop computer sales and increased its lead in inkjet and laser printers to more than 50 percent market share. Through significant cost-cutting and streamlining measures, Mr. Hurd turned HP into a lean operation. For example, he oversaw large-scale layoffs and a pay cut for all remaining employees as he reorganized the company. Wall Street rewarded HP shareholders with 110% stock price appreciation during Mr. Hurd's tenure, outperforming the NASDAQ composite index by a wide margin.

Yet, in the summer of 2010. the HP board found itself caught "between a rock and a hard place", with no easy options in sight. Jodie Fisher, a former adult-movie actress, filed a lawsuit against Mr. Hurd, alleging sexual harassment. As an independent contractor, she worked as a hostess at HP-sponsored events. In this function, she screened attending HP customers and personally ensured that Mr. Hurd would spend time with the most important ones. With an ethics scandal looming, and despite Mr. Hurds stellar financial results for the company, HPs board of directors forced Mr. Hurd to resign.

The HP board of directors found that Mr. Hurd had not expressly violated the company's sexual harassment policy. However, it did find inaccurate expense reports that he allegedly filed to conceal a "close personal relationship" with Ms. Fisher.

The investigation also revealed that HP made payments to Ms. Fisher in instances where there was no legitimate business purpose. Finally, the board alleged that Mr. Hurd leaked private information to Ms. Fisher about the company's intention to acquire EDS, a large information-technology company, months prior to the actual transaction. Following his resignation, Mr. Hurd, who departed with a severance package estimated at $45 million, stated: "I realized there were instances in which I did not live up to the standards and principles of trust, respect and integrity that I have espoused at HP and which have guided me throughout my career."

Reactions were mixed. Some corporate-governance scholars argued that Mr. Hurd should have been fired for cause. Others were not so sure. The most outspoken critic of the board's decision was Larry Ellison, co-founder and CEO of Oracle, who argued, "The HP board just made the worst personnel decision since the idiots on the Apple board fired Steve Jobs many years ago. That decision nearly destroyed Apple and would have if Steve hadn't come back and saved them."

Investors seemed to agree with Mr. Ellison's assessment: HP's market value dropped by roughly $10 billion on the first trading day after Mr. Hurd resigned.

LARRY ELLISON, co-founder and CEO of Oracle, was one of the chief critics of Mark Hurd's ouster as HP CEO. Mr. Ellison and Mr. Hurd are reported to be close personal friends who play tennis together frequently. Just a few weeks after Mark Hurd's resignation from HP, Oracle hired him as co-president and appointed him to the company's board of directors. Oracle's stock market value rose by roughly $10 billion after this announcement. The entire "Hurd saga" led to a stock movement of roughly $20 billion dollars (HP lost $10 billion after Mr. Hurd's ouster and Oracle gained $10 billion after hiring him) plus an undisclosed out-of-court settlement with Ms. Fisher.

In November 2010, HP announced Leo Apothekeras its new CEO. The HP boardroom drama continued, however. Leo Apotheker was let go after only 11 months on the job. Mr. Apotheker, who came to HP from the German enterprise software company SAP, proposed a new corporate strategy for HP. He suggested that HP should focus on enterprise software solutions, and thus spin out its low-margin consumer hardware business. HP's consumer hardware business resulted from the legacy acquisition of Compaq and had now grown to 40% of HP's total revenues of $100 billion. Under Mr. Apotheker, HP also discontinued competing in the mobile device industry, most notably tablet computers—which many viewed as HP capitulating to Apple's dominance with the iPad. Moreover, as part of his new corporate strategy, Mr. Apotheker decided to buy the British software company Autonomy for more than $10 billion, which analysts saw as grossly over valued.

Mr. Apotheker was not able to convince investors of the value of this new corporate strategy; under his 11 months as CEO, HP's stock price dropped by roughly 40%. In September 2011, the HP board appointed Meg Whitman to be HP's new CEO. Ms. Whitman was formerly the CEO at e Bay and had been appointed early in 2011 to HP's board of directors.

1. Given HP's poor performance described in the case, who is to blame? The CEO or the board of directors?

2. What lessons in terms of business ethics, corporate governance, and strategic leadership can be drawn from the case?

7.4　Expand Reading

Reading-1

Profiles of Two Visionaries: Bill Gates and Steve Jobs

Two men who gave their hearts and souls to developing their visions have driven the personal computer (PC) revolution. However, the way in which each of these men went about this quest has been different. Steve Jobs and Bill Gates have changed the way the world does business, but the story of their leadership styles is even more compelling than the success and innovation spawned by Apple and Microsoft.

Bill Gates versus Steve Jobs: The Early Years

Bill Gates started developing his computer skills with childhood friend Paul Allen at Lakeside School in Seattle. At the age of 14, the two had formed their first computer company. After high school, Allen and Gates left Seattle for Boston. Gates went off to Harvard and Allen began working for Honeywell. After only two years at Harvard, Gates and Allen left Boston for Albuquerque to develop a computer language for the new Altair 8080 PC. This computer language would become BASIC and the foundation for Microsoft, which was created as a partnership in 1975.

After five years in New Mexico, Microsoft relocated to Bellevue, Washington, in 1980 with BASIC and two other computer languages (COBOL and FORTRAN) in its arsenal. Later that year, IBM began developing its first PC and was in need of an operating system. Microsoft developed the Microsoft disk operating system (MS-DOS) for IBM while two other companies created competing systems. Gates's determination and persuasion of other software firms to develop programs for MS-DOS made it the default IBM platform.

As Microsoft became more successful Gates realized that he needed help managing the company. His enthusiasm, vision, and hard work were the driving force behind the company's growth, but he recognized the need for professional management. Gates brought in one of his friends from Harvard, Steve Ballmer. Ballmer had worked for Proctor Gamble after graduating from Harvard and was pursuing his MBA at Stanford. Gates persuaded Ballmer to leave school and join Microsoft. Over the years, Ballmer has become an indispensable asset to both Gates and Microsoft. In 1983, Gates continued to show his brilliance by hiring Jon Shriley, who brought order to Microsoft and streamlined the organization structure, while Ballmer served as an advisor and so Microsoft continued to grow and prosper in the 1990s, dominating both the operating system market with its Windows and the office suite software market with Microsoft Office.

Gates recognized that his role was to be the visionary of the company and that he needed professional managers to run Microsoft He combined his unyielding determination and passion with a well-structured management team to make Microsoft the giant it is today.

The other visionary, Steve Jobs, and his friend Steve Wozniak started Apple Computer in Jobs's garage in Los Altos, California, in 1976. In contrast to Bill Gates, Jobs and Wozniak were hardware computer that was affordable and easy to use. When Microsoft offered BASIC to Apple, Jobs immediately dismissed the idea on the basis that he and Wozniak could create their own vision of BASIC in weekend. This was typical Jobs: decisive and almost maniacal at times. Job eventually agreed to license Microsoft's BASIC while pursuing his own vision of developing a more usable and friendly interface for the PC.

Many see Jobs as the anti-Gates. He is a trailblazer and a creator as opposed to Gates, who is more of a consolidator of industry standards. Jobs's goal was to change the world with his computers. He was also very demanding of his employees. Jobs was different from Gates, Allen, and Wozniak. He was not a hard-core computer programmer. He was the person selling the idea of the PC to the public. Jobs made the decision to change the direction of Apple by developing the Macintosh (Mac) using a new graphical user interface that introduced the world to the mouse and on-screen icons, Jobs forced people to choose between the Microsoft-IBM operating system and his Mac operating system. In the beginning, Jobs was the visionary who changed the computer world, and Apple dwarfed Microsoft. With all this success, a major problem was brewing at Apple: Steve Jobs was over confident and did not see Gates and Microsoft as a serious threat to

Apple.

Soon after the release of the Macintosh computer, Jobs asked Microsoft to develop software for the Mac operating system. Gates obliged and proceeded to launch a project copying and improving Apple's user interface. The result of that venture was Microsoft Windows.

This cocky attitude and lack of management skills made Jobs a threat to Apple'ssuccess. He never bothered to develop budgets, and his relationship with his employees was criticized. Wozniak left Apple after the release of the Mac because of differences with Jobs. In 1985, John Scully, CEO of Pepsi Co., replaced Steve Jobs as president and CEO of Apple Computer.

Microsoft and Apple at the Turn of the Century: An Industry Giant and a Revitalized Leader

With the success of Windows, the Office application suite, and Internet Explorer, Microsoft has become a household name and Bill Gates has been hailed as a business genius. The fact that Microsoft's competitors, the press, and the U. S. Justice Department have called Microsoft a monopoly reinforces Gates's determination to succeed. Many people question whether Microsoft could survive the Justice Department's decision. Bill Gates, however, has shown that he is the master of adapting to changing market conditions and technologies.

Apple has gone in the opposite direction in the 1990s. The outdated operating system and falling market share eventually led to a decrease in software development for the Mac Something needed to be done. In 1998, Steve Jobs returned to Apple as the "interim" CEO. His vision, once again, resulted in the innovative iMac. The design is classic Jobs. In the 1980s, he created the simple-to-operate Mac to attract people who were using IBM PCs and their clones. Now he has developed a simple, stylish, and Internet-friendly computer to add some much-needed excitement to the computer market. Jobs had also changed as a manager and a leader. He has matured and looked to his professional staff for advice and ideas. Although he is the interim CEO, Jobs has sold all but one share of his Apple stock. Larry Ellison, Oracle's CEO and Apple board member, attributes Jobs's ability to lead Apple to this fact: He owns only one share of Apple stock, yet he clearly owns the product and the idea behind the company. The Mac is an expression of his creativity, and Apple as a whole is an expression of Steve. That's why, despite the interim in his title, he'll stay at Apple for a long time. Many people believe that this will lead to continued success for Apple and a renewed battle between Gates and Jobs.

(Source: Harold Koontz, Heinz Weihrich. Management [M]. Beijing:

China Renmin University Press, 2014: 310-312.)

Reading-2

China: Copycat or Leader in Innovation?

The world is holding its breath as United States President Donald Trump decides, depending on the results of the trade talks, whether to impose further tariffs on imports from China. There are many intertwined issues between China and the U. S. (and the West in general) but the core issue is how the world (including China itself) should comprehend and cope with the rise of China and its technological giants.

On the U. S. long list of demands, one of the most prominent relates to intellectual property protection and technology transfers. In the heated debate on the subject, Chinese technology giants including Huawei are often depicted as villains, constantly stealing technologies from Western counterparts and competing unfairly, with the backing of the Chinese government's forced technology transfer policy. Of course, there are villains in China, just like anywhere else—but those who argue that China's giants have only risen on the back of foreign technology are like ostriches, burying their heads in the sand and refusing to accept reality.

Learning from the West

China's recent advances in innovation are indeed partly the result of the globalization of innovation. After China's reform and opening-up in the late 1970s, newly arrived Western companies brought with them sophisticated and relevant technologies, presenting domestic Chinese companies with plenty of opportunities for learning by doing, reverse engineering and technological diffusion via talent mobility. Over time the Chinese market became more sophisticated and skills of Chinese labor upgraded, triggering the establishment of R&D centers by Western multinationals, which in turn resulted in more and deeper learning opportunities for China (but also for the Western multinationals as they started to learn new innovation approaches such as "frugal innovation" and business model innovation).

Perseverance in innovation

However, it would be foolish to believe that Chinese technology giants rose purely because of learning from the West. The other part of the story is their R&D which became more apparent in the last decade. At the beginning of the 21st century, only a handful of Chinese companies could afford a large R&D budget. Today, according to the 2018 European Union Industrial R&D Investment Scoreboard, among the 2,500 companies that invest the largest sums in R&D in the world, 438 are Chinese, with Huawei ranking fifth, spending a staggering 11. 3 billion euros ($12. 7 billion) on R&D in 2017/2018. Given this huge investment plus Chinese' entrepreneurial spirit and work ethic, it should not really be a surprise to see China becoming a global leader in e-commerce, high-speed railway, nuclear power generation, telecommunications, quantum cryptography communication, and many other fields.

What has perhaps taken aback many in the West is the sheer speed and scale of the rise of China as a global innovation leader; a non-Western country leading the world is unprecedented in recent human history and the West does not know how to deal with it. Some see China as a strategic threat. I would argue that China is not, as China does not export ideology.

Intellectual Property Protection

To many people in the West, China's rapid rise is a source of unease purely because China is so different and they were often told China encourages a weak intellectual property regime. Sure, China is different, but this does not mean that the West cannot work with it. And yes, China's IP protection system is still young. However, we should recognize the huge strides that China has made in the last few decades. Today it is in China's interest to further improve its IP protection system as they need to attract foreign direct investment and protect their own innovators. And it is certainly encouraging to see the recent move by China's National People's Congress to strengthen legislation that would create an Intellectual Property Court.

Moving up the Value Chain

While Western observers should keep pressing and helping China to further improve IP protection, they must also recognize and appreciate the legitimate concerns of China, and developing countries in general, in upgrading themselves in global value chains. It is morally unacceptable that developing countries should always be constrained to the lower end of global value chains such as simple assembling tasks. Here even the political elite in Washington has a moral deficit (Obama's 2015 statement on the Trans-Pacific Partnership springs to mind—"we can't let countries like China write the rules of the global economy").

Instead of ignoring and dismissing China and other developing countries' concern in upgrading, the West should appreciate their pursuit of higher-end value chain activities such as R&D. In fact, there is a good reason that they should welcome such a move: recent research by my team at the University of Northampton indicated that the latest stages of globalization of innovation actually involved Chinese companies investing in developed countries for R&D and, perhaps counter-intuitively, they have things to teach their partners in the West, therefore also helping the latter to further upgrade their capabilities.

We do not know what future globalization will entail. Whatever it is, the world must address the concerns of both developing and developed countries, and it is only via healthy competition, instead of protection, that we can properly address these two concerns together.

(Source: He Shaowei, China: Copycat or Leader in Innovation, China Daily, March 8, 2019.)

Reading-3

Facebook's Mark Zuckerberg to Face Leadership Vote

A vote calling for Mark Zuckerberg to stand down as Facebook's chairman is expected to take place at the company's annual general meeting on Thursday.

Mr Zuckerberg is both Facebook's chief executive and the chairman of its board of directors.

Those calling for him to step down as chairman say this would help him focus on running the company.

Mr Zuckerberg is very unlikely to lose the vote, because he has 60% of the voting power.

However, the percentage of shareholders who vote against him could indicate how much faith they have in his leadership.

Trillium Asset Management owns about $7m (£ 5.5m) worth of Facebook shares, and works with other businesses that control "hundreds of millions" of dollars worth of the company's shares.

The company is one of those advocating for Mr Zuckerberg to step down.

"He's holding down two full-time jobs in one of the most high-profile companies in the world right now. And if he can focus on being the CEO, and let somebody else focus on being independent board chair, that would be a much better situation," said Jonas Kron, senior vice-president at Trillium.

"He has examples in Larry Page and Alphabet, Bill Gates and Microsoft, of what it can look like for a founder not to be the chairman of the board.

"I realise that it may not be an easy step to take, but it's an important step that would be to his benefit and to his shareholders' benefit. "

'Too much power'

In May, Facebook's former security chief Alex Stamos called for Mr Zuckerberg to step down as chief executive.

"There's a legit argument that he has too much power," Mr Stamos told the Collision Conference in Canada.

Mr Zuckerberg previously defended his leadership of Facebook.

In April, he said: "When you're building something like Facebook, which is unprecedented in the world, there are things that you're going to mess up.

"What I think people should hold us accountable for is if we are learning from our mistakes."

(Source: BBC, 31st May 2019.)

Quick Quiz

1. Leadership is defined as influence, that is, the art or process of influencing people so that they will strive willingly and enthusiastically toward _____ .

2. An _____ innovation squarely builds on the firm's established knowledge base and steadily improves the product or service it offers.

3. _____ is the creation of valuable and useful new products/services within an organizational context.

4. Which type of leadership uses work-center behavior coupled with a protective employee-centered concern?

A. Authoritarian leadership

B. Participative

C. Decentralization

D. Paternalistic

5. The main characteristics of Japanese leadership approaches are _____ .

A. the manager's job is to maintain harmony

B. managers have much greater belief in the capacity of subordinates for leadership

C. subordinates are typically unsure of what their manager wants them to do

D. managers expressed attitudes toward the use of participation to a greater degree than others

E. leaders have considerable confidence in the overall ability of their subordinates

Answers:

1. the achievement of group goals

2. incremental

3. Organizational innovation

4. D

5. ABCDE

Endnotes

［1］ Frank T. Rothaermel. Strategic Management ［M］. Beijing: China Renmin University Press, 2015: 332-350.

［2］ Fred Luthan, Jonathan P. Doh. International Management—Culture, Strategy and Behavior ［M］. Beijing: Mechanical Industry Press, 2018: 455-461.

［3］ John B. Cullen, K. Praveen Parboteeah. Multinaional Management ［M］. Beijing: China Renmin University Press, 2017: 390-412.

［4］ Harlod Koontz, Heinz Weihrich. Essentials of Management—An International and Leadership Perspective ［M］. Beijing: China Renmin University Press, 2014: 294-301.

［5］ Yashu Duan. Research on the Impacts of Humble Leadership on R&D Team Innovation Performance based on the Social Information Processing Perspective ［C］. Proceedings of the 1st International Symposium on Economic Development and Management Innovation（EDMI 2019）, Atlantis Press, 2019.

［6］ Azhar Serikkaliyeva. Chinese leadership and innovations: a capacity for technology transfer to Kazakhstan ［C］. Proceedings of the 3rd International Conference on Social, Economic, and Academic Leadership, Atlantis Press, 2019.

［7］ Fahriözsungur. The impact of ethical leadership on service innovation behavior ［J］. Asia Pacific Journal of Innovation and Entrepreneurship, 2019 （01）: 73-88.

［8］ Mitsuru Kodama. Innovation through dialectical leadership—case studies of Japanese high-tech companies ［J］. Journal of High Technology Management Research, 2005 （02）: 137-156.

［9］ Jean-Philippe Deschamps. Different leadership skills for different innovation strategies ［J］. Strategy & Leadership, 2005 （05）: 31-38.

［10］ Peter R. A. Oeij, Jeff B. R. Gaspersz, Tinka van Vuuren, Steven Dhondt. Leadership in innovation projects: an illustration of the reflective practitioner and the relation to organizational learning ［J］. Journal of Innovation and Entrepreneurship, 2017, 6 （1）: 1-20.

［11］ George W. Joe, Jennifer E. Becan, Danica K. Knight, Patrick

M. Flynn. A structural model of treatment program and individual counselor leadership in innovation transfer [J]. BMC Health Services Research, 2017, 17 (1).

[12] Maria-Gabriella Baldarelli, Mara Del Baldo. Ethics, gift and social innovation through CSR and female leadership in business administrationin Italy [J]. uwf Umwelt Wirtschafts Forum, 2016, 24 (2-3): 141-150.

[13] J T Hage. Organizational Innovationand Organizational Change [J]. Annu. Rev. Sociol 1999, 25: 597-622.

[14] Lale Gumusluoglu, Arzu lIsey. Transformational leadership, creativity, and organizational innovation [J]. Journal of Business Research, 2009, 62: 461-473.

Chapter 8   Strategy Implementation: Human Resource Management

Learning Objectives

1. Recognize the source of human resources
2. Understand the criteria of selecting expatriate managers
3. Master the recruitment methods for international managers
4. Understand the implications for the TNC's training and development
5. Understand the main content of training
6. Master the approaches to manager development
7. Understand the criteria of performance appraisal for international managers
8. Recognize the objectives of international compensation policies
9. Master the common elements of compensation packages
10. Understand the job design in different forms of culture
11. Master the process of developing a personal strategy
12. Recognize the source of stress in workplace
13. Understand the stresses of expatriates

Opening case

U. S. Style Training for Expats and Their Teenagers

One of the major reasons expatriates have trouble with overseas assignments is that their teenage children are unable to adapt to the new culture, and this has an impact on the expat's performance. To deal with this acculturation problem, many U. S. MNCs now are developing special programs for helping teenagers assimilate into new cultures and adjust to new school environments. A good example is provided by General Electric Medical Systems Group (GEMS), a Milwaukee based firm that has expatriates in France, Japan, and Singapore. As soon as GEMS designates an individual for an overseas assignment, this expat and his or her family are matched up with those who have recently returned from this country. If the family going overseas has teenage children, the company will team them up with a family that had teenagers during its stay abroad. Both groups then discuss the challenges and problems that must be faced. In the case of teenagers, they are able to talk about their concerns with others who already have encountered these issues, and the latter can provide important information regarding how to make friends, learn the language, get around town and turn the time abroad into a pleasant experience Coca-Cola uses a similar approach. As soon as someone is designated for an overseas assignment, the company helps initiate cross-cultural discussions with experienced personnel. Coke also provides formal training through use of external cross-cultural consulting firms that are experienced in working with all family members.

A typical concern of teenagers going abroad is that they will have to go away to boarding school In Saudi Arabia, for example, national law forbids expatriate children's attending school past the ninth grade, so most expatriate families will look for European institutions for these children. GEMS addresses these types of problems with a specially developed education program Tutors, schools, curricula, home-country requirements and host-country requirements are examined, and a plan and specific program of study are developed for each school-age child before he or she leaves.

Before the departure of the family, some MNCs will subscribe to local magazines about teen fashions, music, and other sports or social activities in the host country, so that the children know what to expect when they get there. Before the return of the family to the United States, these MNCs provide similar information about what is going on in the United States, so that when the children return for a visit or come back to stay, they are able to quickly fit into their home-country environment once again.

An increasing number of MNCs now give teenagers much of the same cultural training they give their own managers; however, there is one area in which formal assistance often is not as critical for teens as for adults: language training. While most expatriates find it difficult and spend a good deal of time trying to master the local language, many teens find that they can pick it up quite easily. They speak it at school, in their social groups, and out on the street. As a result, they learn not only the formal language but also cliches and slang that help them communicate more easily. In fact, sometimes their accent is so good that they are mistaken for local kids. Simply put: The facility of teens to learn a language often is greatly underrated. A Coca-Cola manager recently drove home this point when he declared: "One girl we sent insisted that, although she would move, she wasn't going to learn the language. Within two months she was practically fluent."

A major educational benefit of this emphasis on teenagers is that it leads to an experienced, bicultural person. So when the young person completes college and begins looking for work, the parent's MNC of tenis interested in this young adult as a future manager. The person has a working knowledge of the MNC speaks a second language, and has had overseas experience in a country where the multinational does business. This type of logic is leading some U. S. MNCs to realize that effective cross-cultural training can be of benefit for their workforces of tomorrow as well as today.

(Source: Fred Luthans, Jonathan P. Doh. International Management [M]. Beijing: China Machine Press, 2018, 11: 520.)

8.1   Recruitment and Selection

8.1.1   Source of Human Resources

TNCs can tap four basic sources for positions: (1) home-country nationals; (2) host country nationals; (3) third-country nationals; and (4) inpatriates. In addition, many MNCs are outsourcing aspects of their global operations and in so doing are engaging temporary or contingent employees. The following sections analyze each of these major sources.

1. Home-Country Nationals

Home-country nationals are managers who are citizens of the country where the MNC is headquartered. In fact, sometimes the term headquarters nationals isused.

These managers commonly are called expatriates, or simply "expats," which refers to those who live and work outside their home country. Historically, TNCs have staffed key positions in their foreign affiliates with home-country nationals or expatriates. Formany companies and for the most senior positions, that trend persists. Major U. S. and European companies such as Cisco Systems have been sending expats to India, and according to a recent estimate, about 1,000 expat senior managers are there now, almost seven times that of two years ago. However, some research has shown that in many instances, host-country nationals may be better suited for the job. Richards, for example, investigated staffing practices for the purpose of determining when companies are more likely to use an expatriate rather than a local manager. She conducted interviews with senior-level headquarters managers at 24 U. S. multinational manufacturing firms and with managers at their U. K. and Thai subsidiaries. This study found that local managers were most effective in subsidiaries located in developing countries or those that relied on a local customer base. In contrast, expatriates were most effective when they were in charge of larger subsidiaries or those with a marketing theme similar to that at headquarters.

There are a variety of reasons for using home-country nationals. One of the most common is to start up operations. Another one is to provide technical expertise. A third is to help the TNC maintain financial control over the operation. Other commonly cited reasons include the desire to provide the company's more promising managers with international experience to equip them better for more responsible positions; the need to maintain and facilitate organizational coordination and control the unavailability of managerial talent in the host country; the company's view of the foreign operation as short lived; the host country's multiracial population, which might mean that selecting a manager of either race would result in political or social problems; the company's conviction that it must maintain a foreign image in the host country; and the belief of some companies that a home country manager is the best person for the job.

In recent years, there has been a trend away from using home-country nationals, given the costs, somewhat uncertain returns, and increasing availability of host-country and third-country nationals and inpatriate.

2. Host-Country Nationals

Host-country nationals are local managers who are hired by the TNC. For a number of reasons, many TNCs use host-country managers at the middle-level and lower-level ranks. One reason in particular is that many countries expect the TNC to hire local talent, and the use of host-country nationals is a good way to meet this expectation. Also, even if an TNC wanted to stall all management positions with home-country personnel, it would be unlikely to have this many available managers, and the cost of transferring and maintaining them in the host country would be prohibitive.

In some cases government regulations dictate selection practices and mandate at least some degree of "nativization. " In Brazil, for example, two-thirds of the employees in any foreign subsidiary traditionally had to be Brazilian nationals. In addition, many countries exert real and subtle pressures to staff the upper-management ranks with nationals. In the past, these pressures by host countries have led companies such as Standard Oil to change their approach to selecting managers. These regulations have substantial costs in that shielding local employees from international competition may create a sense of entitlement and result in low productivity.

Sony is trying the host-country approach in the United States. Employees are encouraged to accept or decline styles that emerge from Japanese headquarters, depending on American tastes. Furthermore, innovative creations are birthed at the U. S. site, all with an American flavor. Sony believes that local citizens are the best qualified for the job, as opposed to Japanese managers, because they already have a working knowledge of the language and culture, and it may be difficult for Sony to understand preferred styles otherwise. The nearby International Management in Action box, "Important Tips on Working for Foreigners," gives examples of how Americans can better adapt to foreign bosses.

3. Third-Country Nationals

Third-country nationals (TCNs) are managers who are citizens of countries other than the country in which the TNC is headquartered or the one in which they are assigned to work by the TNC. Available data on third-country nationals are not as extensive as those on home-or host-country nationals.

A number of advantages have been cited for using TCNs. One is that the salary and benefit package usually is less than that of a home-country national, although in recent years, the salary gap between the two has begun to diminish. A second reason is that the TCN may have a very good working knowledge of the region or speak the same language as the local people. This helps explain why many U. S MNCs hire English or Scottish managers for top positions at subsidiaries in former British colonies such as Jamaica, India, the West Indies, and Kenya. It also explains why successful TNCs such as Gillette. Coca-Cola, and IBM recruit local managers and train them to run overseas subsidiaries. Other cited benefits of using TCNs include:

(1) TCN managers, particularly those who have had assignments in the headquarters country, can often achieve corporate objectives more effectively than expatriates or local nationals. In particular, they frequently have a deep understanding of the corporation's policies from the perspective of a foreigner and can communicate and implement those policies more effectively to others than can expats.

(2) During periods of rapid expansion, TCNs can not only substitute for expatriates in new and growing operations but also offer different perspectives that can complement and expand on the sometimes narrowly focused viewpoints of both

local nationals and headquarters personnel.

（3）In joint ventures, TCNs can demonstrate a global or transnational image and bring unique cross-cultural skills to the relationship.

There are different advantages and disadvantages of the personnel from the different source, as shown in Table 8-1.

Table 8-1   Advantages and Disadvantages for the Personnel from Home Countries, Host Countries and Third Countries

Home Countries	Advantages	a. Organizations can make control and coordination; b. Provide promising managers with exercises to acquire international experiences; c. Home countries' personnel are most suitable because of special skills and experiences; d. Ensure that subsidiaries observe the companies' targets and policies
	Disadvantages	a. Host countries' personnel have limited promotion chances; b. It takes long time to adapt to host countries; c. Host countries' staff may apply some inappropriate methods of headquarters to subsidiaries; d. Different salary levels between host and home countries' personnel
Host Countries	Advantages	a. No language or other obstacles; b. Reducing the recruitment cost and no need for labor license; c. Increasing the continuity of management due to the long working time of local staff; d. Meeting the governments' policy requirement of employing local staff; e. Host countries' personnel would have higher morale when they realize their career potential
	Disadvantages	a. Headquarters' control and coordination may be hindered; b. Host countries' personnel have limited career chance outside the subsidiaries; c. Local employment may restrict the opportunities for home countries' personnel to gain overseas working experiences; d. Local employment may facilitate "federalism" other than global development
Third Countries	Advantages	a. Lower demand for salary and allowance than home countries' personnel; b. More familiar with local environment than home countries personnel
	Disadvantages	a. Possible ethnic hatred should be taken into consideration; b. Governments of host countries may be against the use of other countries' staff; c. Other countries' personnel may be unwilling to return to their own countries

Source: Zhao Shuming et al. Human Resource Management in Transnational Corporations, P62, China Renmin University Press, 2002.

4. Inpatriates

In recent years, a new term has emerged in international management——inpatriates. An inpatriate, or inpat, is an individual from a host country or a third-country national who is assigned to work in the home country. Even Japanese TNCs are now beginning to rely on inpatriates to help them meet their international challenges. Harvey and Buckley report:

The Japanese are reducing their unicultural orientation in their global businesses. Yoichi Morishita, president of Matsushita, has ordered that top management must reflect the cultural diversity of the countries where Matsushita does business. Sony sells 80% of its products overseas and recently recognized the need to become multicultural. It has appointed two foreigners to its board of directors and has plans to hire host-country nationals who are to be integrated into the top management of the parent organization. At the same time. The Chairman of Sony has stated that in five years the board of directors of Sony will reflect the diversity of countries that are important to the future of the company. Similarly, Toshiba plans to have a more representative top management and board of directors to facilitate long-run global strategies.

This growing use of inputs is helping TNCs better develop their global core competencies. As a result, today a new breed of multilingual, multiexperienced, so-called global managers or transnational managers is truly emerging. These new managers are part of a growing group of international executives who can manage across borders and do not fit the traditional third-country nationals mold, With a unified Europe and other such developments in North America and Asia, these global managers are in great demand. Additionally, with labor shortages developing in certain regions, there is a wave of migration from regions with an abundance of personnel to those where the demand is strongest.

8. 1. 2 Selecting Expatriate Managers

Selecting the wrong person for any job can lead to failure and can be a major expense for the company. This problem is even more pronounced for expatriates because a failed expatriate assignment can cost the company from two to five times the assignee's annual salary. In fact, it is estimated that each expatriate failure through early departure can cost a company more than $1 million. Furthermore, it has even been argued that improperly selected employees who cannot perform adequately but who remain on assignment can be more damaging to the company than those who leave prematurely. Companies are therefore becoming more aware of the strategic need to select the right person for the job the first time.

Traditionally, multinational companies have assumed that domestic performance predicts expatriate performance. This assumption leads companies to search for job candidates with the best technical skills and professional competence. When these factors become the major, if not the only, selection criteria for international assignments, companies often overlook other important criteria.

Several experts on international HRM have identified key success factors for expatriate assignments. In addition to professional and technical competence, these factors are relational abilities, family situation, motivation, and language skills.

（1）Technical and managerial skills: Often an expatriate assignment gives managers more tasks and greater responsibilities than similar-level assignments at home. Additionally, the geographical distance from headquarters can result in the manager's having more decision-making autonomy. Only managers with excellent technical, administrative, and leadership skills have a strong likelihood of success in such position.

（2）Personality traits: A foreign assignment inevitably comes with a host of unexpected problems and new situations. To be able to deal with such uncertainties and novelty, the expatriate has to be flexible, be willing and eager to learn new things, be able to deal with ambiguity, have an interest in other people and cultures, and have a good sense of humor. Extroversion also is critical to success. Extroverts are more likely to be sociable and talkative, and thus motivated to communicate and develop relationships with locals. Relationships with locals can not only help expatriates adjust better in the new country, they can also provide access to important information regarding appropriate behavior.

（3）Relational abilities: Relational abilities help employees avoid a major pitfall of international assignments: the failure to adapt to different cultures. People with good relational skills have the ability to adapt to strange or ambiguous situations. They are culturally flexible and sensitive to cultural norms, values, and beliefs. They also have the ability to modify their own behaviors and attitudes to fit in with a new culture. They favor collaborative negotiation styles and avoid direct confrontation.

（4）Family situation: Selection for an international assignment also must weigh the potential expatriate's family situation. An overseas assignment affects the spouse and children as much as the employee, so a family situation favorable to the assignment is crucial for expatriate success. Key factors to consider are the spouse's willingness to live abroad, the impact of the potential posting on the spouse's career and the children's education, and the spouse's relational skills. Because of the increasing number of dual-career couples, multinational companies may need to offer two positions or compensation for the spouse's lost income to ensure a successful assignment.

(5) Stress tolerance: Adapting to a new culture and work environment can be extremely stressful. The ability to tolerate stress is a crucial quality that can help an expatriate succeed on an international assignment. Expatriates who can maintain their composure in the face of extreme stressors are more likely to succeed in their new assignments.

(6) Language ability: The ability to speak, read, and write the host country language enhances many of the other key success factors. Managers with good language skills are well prepared to apply their technical and managerial skills. They have heightened success in dealing with local colleagues, subordinates, and customers. Knowledge of the local language also increases the understanding of local culture and reduces the stress of adapting to a new cultural environment.

(7) Emotional intelligence: Research suggests that emotional intelligence is a crucial success factor. Emotional intelligence is the ability to be aware of oneself, to understand and relate to others, and to be empathetic and manage one's emotions. Expatriates inevitably need to relate to presence. Those with high emotional intelligence are likely to be able to relate others and manage their own to locals and show the appropriate emotions when adjusting locally.

8. 1. 3   Recruitment Methods for International Managers

Recruitment, especially for international managers, is the most important duty for TNCs human resource departments, as well as the key link for the companies development. Facing with current fierce competition for talents, TNCs' international manager recruitment has stepped out the old mode of waiting for applicants and created a lot of new recruitment methods and approaches through practices.

1. Traditional Recruitment Methods

(1) Advertising on the newspapers and magazines. Because classified advertisements on the papers are disorderedly edited without clear requirements, employers cannot get the target effects.

(2) Recruitment meetings in human resource markets. This method requires large labor and time input, by which applicants consult ceaselessly, but cannot deeply communicate with recruitment staff. By this method companies cannot get qualified talents.

(3) Through human resource markets set up by governments. Because the HR

markets are not socialized enough and their service facilities are not completed, the probability of high-level professionals hunting for jobs in HR markets is low.

（4）Head-Hunting companies. Due to the uneven development and lack of standardized operation of head-hunting companies as well as their expensive fees, sometimes employers may fail to get high-quality employees at high expenses.

2. Modern Recruitment Method: Internet Recruitment

The extensive use of the Internet has greatly changed the lifestyle and working methods of our times, and has caused fundamental changes in the field of recruitment. Nowadays, recruitment through Internet has become the main approach for TNCs to recruit talents.

（1）Features of internet recruitment: the information of Internet recruitment has dynamics, for information can be released, collected, updated and searched at any moment; it has no time or space limitations and has interactivity, and recruitment information can be timely revised according to market feedback; job websites have sample CV, which is time-saving; post-informing system can automatically inform the vacancies; recruitment process is digitally managed.

（2）Characteristics of internet users of online recruitment: according to statistics, more than 85% of internet users graduate from junior colleges or above; 88% age between 18 and 35; most of them have professional skills, master foreign languages, and possess the sense of innovation and forward-thinking; most users are in Shanghai, Beijing, Tianjin, Jiangsu Zhejiang, Guangdong and other coastal regions, and have strong international sense. These people are targets of TNCs recruitment.

（3）Job websites are developing very fast. The largest American recruitment website, Monster. com, boasts an annual turnover of $8 billion, and the largest Japanese recruitment website has an $800 million annual profit. Chinese recruitment websites are still in their infancy phase, and nowadays one famous job website has annual profit worth only $100 million. But China recruitment websites enjoy a great market, numerous job-hunters and fast-developing employer companies. Internet recruitment will gradually replace tradition recruitment channels with great prospects. But at this time, the Internet in China is not that popular, and therefore traditional recruitment approaches are still needed. The papers are still an important channel for recruitment. Professional recruitment advertising supplemented by Internet recruitment is the most effective method of the day.

8. 2   Training and Development

8. 2. 1   An Overview

Within a country, training and development needs vary widely, affected by different industries, technologies, strategies, organizational structures, and local labor market conditions. However, broad national differences in training and development do exist.

The cross-national differences in training and development are most closely associated with institutional differences in national educational systems, which create large differences in recruits' qualifications in basic skills and in attitudes toward work. For example, more than 90% of the 25-year-olds to 34-year-olds in Norway, Japan, and South Korea finish secondary school. By contrast, Turkey and Portugal have only 24 percent. For another example, consider Germany, which has a strong technical education program and an apprenticeship system that originated with the guild system of the Middle Ages.

Cross-cultural training and development differences are also associated with the type of emphasis placed by national governments. For instance, the Australian government requires companies above a certain size to spend 1. 5% of their payroll expenses on training. The Chinese government is also heavily involved in training; companies are encouraged to train their workers before they are offered full-time jobs. The Chinese have gone even further by establishing 13 public vocational training institutes for those who do not have access to higher education. Cultural values regarding types of educational credentials and other personnel practices, such as lifetime employment, also affect training and development needs. For example, the Japanese retain the ideal of long-term employment, though it is threatened by economic practicalities and often maligned as inefficient. For companies like Ricoh, which continues to avoid layoffs at all costs, long-term employment allows management training and development to take place slowly, through extensive job rotations. Managers learn by doing, with many different job assignments early in their careers. Table 8- 2 gives an overview of work-related training systems in use through out the world.

Table 8-2   **Training Systems around the World**

Type	Example Countries	Features and Source of Institutional Press
Cooperative	Austria, Germany, Switzerland, and some Latin American countries	Legal and historical precedents for cooperation among companies, unions, and the government
Company-based voluntarism/high labor mobility	United States and U. K	Lack of institutional pressures to provide training. Companies provide training based on own cost benefits
Voluntarism/low labor mobility	Japan	Low labor turnover encourages investment in training without institutional pressure
State-driven incentive provider	South Korea, Singapore, China, Australia	Government identifies needs for skills and uses incentives to encourage companies to train in chosen areas
Supplier	Developing countries in Asia and Africa transition economies	No institutional pressures for companies to train. Government provides formal training organizations.

Source: Adapted from International Labor Organization (LO). 1999. World Employment Report 1998-99. Geneva: International Labor Office.

8. 2. 2 Implications for the TNC's Training and Development

Before setting up operations in a host foreign country, the TNCs' managers must consider the quality of the workers and sometimes of the managers in the host country. They must also examine the feasibility of exporting their company's training techniques to the host country. For example, a transnational company might need workers with basic skills in mathematics and science to staff future plants. Rather than invest in basic education to train a low-cost workforce, the company can locate in countries with the best educational systems. Thus, for example, TNCs with a requirement for technical workers might examine which educational systems produce the best students in mathematics and science.

The adaptation of management-development practices to different national contexts depends significantly on the intended use of host country managers. If host country nationals are limited to lower management levels, then TNCs may follow local management-development practices. This would be alikely approach for TNCs with a polycentric IHRM orientation. Such companies develop local managerial talent for careers in one country. Host country managers often never expect to work at the TNCs' headquarters or in another country.

When TNCs allow and expect host country nationals to rise to higher levels of management, however, the parent company's corporate culture dominates management-development policies, and such TNCs expect managers of all nationalities to be, for example, Motorola or Ford managers-not British or Mexican or Malaysian.

8. 2. 3   Main Content of Training

1. Cross-cultural Training

According to a famous cross-cultural institute's research in 2000, 75% of the expatriate managers in the world have received cross-cultural trainings carefully arranged by their companies before going abroad. Normally cross-cultural training requires the participation of their families, because according to the above-mentioned research, among the three major reasons to the expatriate manager's task failure: a. Spouse inconvenience (96%); b. Family concerns (93%); c. Adaptability weakness (93%), two are related to family factors. TNCs like AT&T, P&G, GE, Microsoft, GM are all providing various cross-cultural and language trainings for expatriate staff before they getting abroad to step over the "cultural shock" and adapt to local life more quickly. Generally speaking, main content of cross-cultural training should include:

(1) Understanding and cognition of the host country's national culture and the parent company's culture;

(2) Culture sensitivity and adaptability training;

(3) Language training;

(4) Training of cross-cultural communication and conflict solving ability;

(5) For Chinese personnel, the host countries'advanced management method and business philosophy are also needed.

2. Management

Adapting to different business principles; solving communication problems in terms of management, technology, finance and marketing: managing the employees who are dissenting or not familiar with the parent companies' business method; being familiar with foreign political, economic, ordinary laws and company law, meeting the requirements of long-distance travel.

3. Accounting and Auditing

Converting and unifying the accounts of overseas subsidiaries: implementing report and control systems; adapting to foreign accounting procedures and requirements; implementing international auditing system.

4. Financing

To be able to raise money for export from banks; to be able to attract foreign capital; to be able to contact foreign banks; to master the foreign currency operations, to be able to properly handle matters relating to the protection of foreign financial assets, to know very well the procedures of transferring capital and profit to home countries.

5. Marketing

Being able to work together with foreign distributors and agents; being able to understand foreign market conditions and sales; being familiar with tariff and non-tariff barriers.

6. Investment

Being able to discuss investment plans with foreign governments and agents; being able to discuss investment and license trade with foreign partners; being able to select courageous foreign joint venture partners to work with; being able to deal with matters such as nationalization.

7. Other Aspects

To be familiar with the destination country's facilities of shop, medicine and education and other conditions such as food, climate, custom, currency, attitude toward foreigners, religion and parties, etc.

Besides, there is specialized training for female employees. When female employees work abroad, they always encounter some unique and gender-related problems. Therefore, it is conducive to reducing their troubles to let them understand host country's culture, custom and women status, under what circumstances gender would hinder their work, how to get along with male colleagues and customers with different cultural background.

Generally speaking, TNCs should determine the training content according to different working tasks, working environments and the specific conditions of the candidates (including individual experiences, foreign language proficiencies, individual characters and attitude toward host countries' culture). For example, since it is the main reason of poor performance of American TNC staff that the expatriate managers and their families cannot adapt to overseas working and living environment, accordingly, these TNCs should enhance the language communication and cultural adaptability training for the candidates and their families. But for Japanese expatriate personnel whose poor performance is mainly because of "Status Shock" and poor independent management, TNCs should enhance the training of management and individual decision-making capacity for the candidates.

8. 2. 4   Approaches to Manager Development

1. Job Rotation

The purpose of job rotation is to broaden the knowledge of managers or potential managers. Trainees learn about the different enterprise functions by rotating into different positions. They may rotate through (1) nonsupervisory work, (2) observation assignments (observing what managers do, rather than actually managing), (3) various managerial training positions, (4) middle-level "assistant" positions, and even (5) various managerial positions in different departments such as production, sales and finance.

2. Creation of "Assistant-to" Positions

"Assistant-to" positions are frequently created to broaden the viewpoints of trainees by allowing them to work closely with experienced managers who can give special attention to the development needs of trainees. Managers can, among other things, give selected assignments to test the judgment of trainees. As in job rotation, this approach can be very effective when superiors are also qualified teachers who can guide and develop trainees until they are ready to assume full responsibilities as managers.

3. Temporary Promotions

Individuals are frequently appointed as "acting" managers when, for example, the permanent manager is on vacation, is ill, or is making an extended business trip, or even when a position is vacant. Thus, temporary promotions are a developmental device as well as a convenience to the enterprise.

When the acting manager is given the authority to make decisions and to assume full responsibility, the experience can be valuable. On the other hand, if such a manager is merely a figure head, makes no decisions, and really does not manage, the developmental benefit may be minimal.

4. Committees and Junior Boards

Committees and junior boards, also known as multiple management, are sometimes used as developmental techniques. These give trainees the opportunity to interact with experienced managers. Furthermore, trainees, usually from the middle but sometimes from the lower level, become acquainted with a variety of issues that concern the whole organization. They learn about the relationships between different departments and the problems created by the interaction of these organizational units. Trainees may be given the opportunity to submit reports and proposals to the committee or the board and to demonstrate their analytical and conceptual abilities. On the other hand, trainees may be treated in a paternalistic way by senior executives and may not be given opportunities to participate, an omission that might frustrate and discourage them. The program would then be detrimental to their development.

5. Coaching

On-the-job training is a never-ending process. A good example of on-the-job training is athletic coaching. To be effective, coaching, which is the responsibility of every line manager, must be done in a climate of confidence and trust between the superior and the trainees. Patience and wisdom are required of superiors, who must be able to delegate authority and give recognition and praise for jobs well done. Effective coaches will develop the strengths and potentials of subordinates and help them overcome their weaknesses. Coaching requires time; but if done well, it will save time and money and will prevent costly mistakes by subordinates. Thus, in the long run, it will benefit all—the superior, the subordinates, and the enterprise.

6. Conference Programs

Conference programs may be used in internal or external training. They expose managers or potential managers to the ideas of speakers who are experts in their field. Within the company, employees may be instructed in the history of the firmand its purposes, policies, and relationships with customers, consumers, and other groups. External conferences may vary greatly, ranging from programs on specific managerial techniques to programs on broad topics, such as the relationship between business and society.

These programs can be valuable if they satisfy a training need and are thoughtfully planned. A careful selection of topics and speakers will increase the effectiveness of this training device. Furthermore, conferences can be made more useful by including discussions, as two-way communication allows participants to ask for clarification of topics that are particularly relevant to them.

7. University Management Programs

Besides offering undergraduate and graduate degrees in business administration, many universities now conduct courses, workshops, conferences, and formal programs for training managers. These offerings may include evening courses, short seminars live-in programs, a full graduate curriculum, or even programs tailored to the needs of individual companies. Some executive development centers even provide career development assistance with programs designed to fit typical training and development needs of first-line supervisors, middle managers, and top executives.

These university programs expose managers to theories, principles, and new developments in management. In addition, there is usually a valuable interchange of experience among managers who, in similar positions, face similar challenges.

8. Business Simulation and Experiential Exercises

Business games and experiential exercises have been used for some time, but the introduction of computers has made these approaches to training and development even more popular. The computer, however, is only one of several tools; many of the exercises do not require any hardware at all.

The great variety of business simulations is best illustrated by the topics discussed at meetings of the Association for Business Simulation and Experiential Learning (ABSEL). The approaches range from behavioral exercises dealing, for example, with attitudes and values to simulations in courses such as marketing, accounting, decision support systems, and business policy and strategic management.

9. E-Learning

E-learning has been successfully used in knowledge-intensive companies, such as IBM's Basic Blue e-learning approach. More recently, e-training is employed for teaching skills. The U. S. Internal Revenue Service uses Web-based training, and so does Neptune Orient Lines, the large transporter of containers. The container company has to train its global workforce in various countries in Europe, Asia, South America, and other regions. Instead of sending trainers around the world, it uses live e-learning as a cost-effective alternative.

The trend of e-learning is just in its early stages. More research will have to be done to make it more effective and to find the proper balance between self-paced learning and instructor-led training.

8.3 Performance Appraisal and Compensation

8.3.1 Performance Appraisal

1. Performance in Accomplishing Goals

In assessing performance, systems of appraising against verifiable pre-selected goal shave extraordinary value. Given consistent, integrated, and understood planning designed to reach specific objectives, probably the best criteria of managerial performance relate to the ability to set goals intelligently, to plan programs that will accomplish those goals, and to succeed in achieving them. Those who have operated under some variation of this system often claim that these criteria are inadequate and that elements of luck or other factors beyond the managers control are not excluded when arriving at any appraisal. In too many cases, managers who achieve results owing to sheer luck are promoted, and those who do not achieve the expected results because of factors beyond their control are blamed for failures. Thus, appraisal against verifiable objectives is, by itself, insufficient.

2. Criteria of Performance Appraisal for International Managers

(1) Traditional Criteria.

①It confuses the appraisal for the subsidiaries themselves and for the managers. For many foreign companies, there are many factors, such as the changes in host countries' policies and regulations for foreign companies, adjustments on the companies' strategies, are all out of the managers control, so the ROI of the subsidiaries does not totally depend on the managers. Therefore, we should distinguish between the appraisal for the subsidiary managers and for the subsidiaries themselves (as an investment).

②Subsidiaries' business conditions can to some extent reflect the performance of decision-makers and senior managers, but it is difficult to appraise the work of middle-level and grass-root managers.

③Even if we take the subsidiaries' business result as the basis to appraise the subsidiary managers, subsidiaries' short-term financial indicators cannot be the only concern, and their acts in protecting the companies' reputation, promoting the relationship between the company and host country's government and personnel cultivation, etc., should also be taken into account. It is wrong to appraise subsidiary managers only based on the subsidiaries' short-term profit, and sometimes this evaluation policy may mislead the subsidiaries' behavioral direction.

④The use of price transfer and other managerial methods usually causes that the subsidiaries' book profits do not truly reflect the subsidiaries' business results. Besides, when appraising the subsidiaries' business results, the choice of currency also affect the review of the subsidiaries business results, the result counted by the home countries' currency is always distorted due to the exchange rate fluctuation.

（2） Strategic Appraisal Criteria. The strategic appraisal of international managers is complicated. All the related factors should be taken into consideration to objectively appraise the subsidiary managers. There are four factors worth special attention:

① The appraisal of subsidiaries and subsidiary managers should be distinguished, and the effect of "uncontrollable variables" （namely the factors that cannot be changed by the managers） should be taken into consideration.

② When appraising the subsidiaries' business condition, except for the numeral conditions such as profit, market share, production cost, etc., the subsidiaries' other strategic acts should be taken into account. Competitive global strategy emphasizes the global achievement, rather than the regional profit in certain countries or regions. Therefore, although a subsidiary is a strategic business unit （SBU） and an independent profit center, the subsidiaries' manager cannot be appraised as the person in full charge of the independent profit center.

③Considering the establishment of a set of accounts that have been adjusted by accountants, less affected by exchange rate fluctuations, cash flows, asset management, price transfer and other managerial methods, thus truly reflecting the subsidiaries business achievements. These accounts can be the financial basis for appraising the subsidiaries.

④ Since the subsidiaries have different strategic positions and business environments, the same subsidiary has different environmental conditions and business objectives in different periods, and since the currency conversion process may be distorted, the comparison of financial indicators between different subsidiaries cannot be the basis for the evaluation of subsidiaries business results. Instead, we should set different business objectives for different subsidiaries according to the company's strategic plans, and appraise the senior managers on the basis of the completion of planned objectives. While for the grass-root managers, their performance should be judged by their supervisors.

3. Performance Appraisals around the World

The Best International Human Resource Management Practices Project provides extensive evidence on cross-national differences in performance appraisal purposes in Australia, Canada, Indonesia, Japan, South Korea, Latin America, Mexico, China and the United States.

Table 8-3 shows the top four countries/regions for each performance appraisal purpose. The project asked respondents to rate the importance of 12 purposes of performance appraisals, and the results revealed significant differences among countries. However, the most striking finding is that Australia, Canada, and the United States are among the top four countries for all performance appraisal purposes; these countries are very high on individualism, meaning that they place heavy emphasis on the development of the individual. As such, performance appraisals are seen as the most effective method to gauge how well an employee is doing and how that person's performance can be improved. However, it is also interesting to see that countries and regions such as Latin America figure prominently on the list. Their presence suggests the possible effects of social institutions such as government and trade agreements. Because these countries are emulating Western-based systems to satisfy trade agreements and other competitiveness requirements, they are perhaps seeing performance appraisal systems as critical.

Table 8-3   Cross-National Differences in Purposes of Performance Appraisals: Top Four Countries and Regions for Each Category

Performance Appraisal Purpose	Countries and Regions			
Determine pay	Canada	United States	China	Japan
Document performance	Australia	United States	Latin America	Canada
Plan development activities	Australia	Latin America	Canada	Mexico
Salary administration	Latin America	United States	Canada	Indonesia
Recognize subordinate	Australia	United States	Canada	China
Discuss improvement	Australia	Latin America	Canada	United States
Discuss subordinate	Australia	Canada	United States	Mexico
Views				
Evaluate goal achievement	Australia	Latin America	Canada	Japan

Continued

Performance Appraisal Purpose	Countries and Regions			
Identify strengths and weaknesses	Latin America	Australia	United States	Canada
Let subordinate express feelings	Australia	Canada	China	United States
Determine promotion potential	South Korea	Latin America	Australia	Japan

Source: Adapted from Geringer, J. Michael, Colette A. Frayne, and John F. Milliman. 2002. "In search of 'best practices' in international human resource management: Research design and methodology. " Human Resource Management, 41 (1), pp 5-30.

8.3.2 Compensation

1. Objectives of International Compensation Policies

(1) The policies should be consistent with the TNCs' overall strategies, and the need of the institutions and companies.

(2) These policies can attract talents to the TNCs' most needed places and keep them there. Therefore, these polices should be competitive and be clear role of factors such as incentive for abroad service, tax equity and reasonable cost reimbursement.

(3) These policies would help the companies to move expatriate staff by the most economical means.

(4) These policies should take the fairness and convenience of administration into account.

2. Common Elements of Compensation Packages

There are five common elements in the typical expatriate compensation package base salary, benefits, allowances, incentives and taxes.

(1) Base Salary. Base salary is the amount of money that an expatriate normally receives in the home country. In the United States this has often been in the range of $200,000- $300,000 for upper-middle managers in recent years, and this rate is similar to that paid to managers in both Japan and Germany. The exchange rates, of course, also affect the real wages. Expatriate salaries typically are set according to the base pay of the home countries. Therefore, a German manager working for a U. S. MNC and assigned to Spain would have a base salary that reflects the salary structure in Germany. U. S. expatriates have salaries tied to U. S. levels. The salaries usually are paid in home currency, local currency or a combination of the two. The base pay also serves as the benchmark against which

bonuses and benefits are calculated.

(2) Benefits. Approximately 1/3 of compensation for regular employees is benefits. These benefits compose a similar, or even larger, portion of expat compensation. A number of thorny issues surround compensation for expatriates, however. These include: Whether TNCs should maintain expatriates in home-country benefit programs, particularly if these programs are not tax-deductible; Whether TNCs have the option of enrolling expatriates in host-country benefit programs or making up any difference in coverage; Whether host-country legislation regarding termination of employment affects employee benefits entitlements; Whether the home or host country is responsible for the expatriates' social security benefits; Whether benefits should be subject to the requirements of the home or host country; Which country should pay for the benefits; Whether other benefits should be used to offset any shortfall in coverage; Whether home-country benefits programs should be available to local nationals.

(3) Allowances. Allowances are an expensive feature of expatriate compensation package. One of the most common parts is a cost-of-living allowance—a payment for differences between the home country and the overseas assignment. This allowance is designed to provide the expat with the same standard of living that he or she enjoyed in the home country, and it may cover a variety of expenses, including relocation, housing, education and hardship.

(4) Incentives. In recent years, some TNCs have also been designing special incentive programs for keeping expats motivated. In the process, a growing number of firms have dropped the ongoing premium for overseas assignments and replaced it with a one-time, lump-sum premium. The lump-sum payment has a number of benefits. One is that expats realize that they will be given this payment just once—when they move to the international locale. So the payment tends to retain its value as an incentive. A second is that the costs to the company are less because there is only one payment and no future financial commitment. A third is that because it is a separate payment, distinguishable from regular pay, it is more readily available for saving or spending.

(5) Taxes. Another major component of expatriate compensation is tax equalization. For example, an expat may have two tax bills, one from the host country and one from the U. S. Internal Revenue Service, for the same pay. IRS Code Section 911 permits a deduction of up to $80,000 on foreign-earned income. Top-level expats often earn far more than this, however; thus, they may pay two tax bills for the amount by which their pay exceeds $80,000. Usually, TNCs pay the extra tax burden. The most common way is by determining the base

salary and other extras that the expat would make if based in the home country. Taxes on this income then are computed and compared with the taxes due on the expat's income Any taxes that exceed what would have been imposed in the home country are paid by the TNC, and any windfall is kept by the expat as a reward for taking the assignment.

Huawei Welcomes Remarkable Graduates with Competitive Salaries

Huawei announced its decision in a statement outlining plans to apply an annual salary management mechanism to certain outstanding graduates in 2019.

The eight fortunate students have mostly majored in cutting-edge fields related to artificial intelligence, and are given an annual salary spanning between 896,000 yuan ($130,000) to a staggering 2.01 million ($290,000).

The notification said that Huawei must win the technology and business war in the future, with its core motives rooted in innovation. Global talents must therefore be brought in to confront the toughest challenges while earning the highest salaries in order to provide the innovative soil.

Among the eight new employees, the highest salary goes to Zhong Zhao, Ph. D from the University of Chinese Academy of Sciences.

Zhong majored in pattern recognition and intelligent systems both in his post-graduate and doctoral studies, according to Liu Chenglin, Zhong's doctoral supervisor and deputy head of Institute of Automation, Chinese Academy of Sciences.

Liu attributed the high salary to Zhong's research direction, which is a new trend some believe to be very practical.

"His research focuses on automated designs of in-depth neural network structures, which means developing how to make the machine learn neural network structures automatically. The AI designs may have better performance than human designs, with a promising future. Few are doing this research in the current stage, which I think pushes Huawei to value it so much," said Liu.

He Rui, another graduate in the lucky list from the same university as Zhong, majored in computational mathematics.

Guo Tiande, deputy head of the School of Mathematical Sciences, University of Chinese Academy of Sciences, said in the interview that "Huawei recruiting Ph. D graduates with fat salaries shows the eagerness for high level talents in China's science and technology industry field, and is a symbol of the advancement of Chinese science and technology standards."

Huawei's CEO Ren Zhengfei highlighted that the company planned to bring in 20 to 30 young talents across the world, and was considering attracting another 200 to 300 in the next year.

Huawei's move will possibly influence college students while choosing their research areas, said Liu, although career success is nevertheless determined by multiple personal as well as professional qualities.

These lucky students should keep their past glories in mind. The school is expecting to see them doing a great job at work and make great contributions for the country's technological development, Guo added.

(Source: Huawei welcomes remarkable graduates with competitive salaries, China Daily, July 25, 2019.)

8.4　Employee Relationship Management

8.4.1　Job Design

1. Concept

Job design consists of a job's content, the methods that are used on the job, and the way in which the job relates to other Jobs in the organization. Job design typically is a function of the work to be done and the way in which management wants it to be carried out. These factors help explain why the same type of work may have a different impact on the motivation of human resources in various parts of the world and result in differing qualities of work life.

2. Job Design in Different Forms of Culture

In Japan, there is strong uncertainty avoidance. The Japanese like to structure tasks so there is no doubt regarding what is to be done and how it is to be done. Individualism is low, so there is strong emphasis on security, and individual risk taking is discouraged. The power-distance index is high, so Japanese workers are accustomed to taking orders from those above them. The masculinity index for the Japanese is high, which shows that they put a great deal of importance on money and other material symbols of success. In designing jobs, the Japanese structure tasks so that the work is performed within these cultural constraints. Japanese managers work their employees extremely hard. Although Japanese workers contribute many ideas through the extensive use of quality circles, Japanese managers give them very little say in what actually goes on in the organization (in contrast to the erroneous picture often portrayed by the media, which presents Japanese firms as highly democratic and managed from the bottom up) and depend heavily on monetary rewards, as reflected by the fact that the Japanese rate money as an important motivator more than the workers in any other industrialized country do.

In Sweden, uncertainty avoidance is low, so job descriptions, policy manuals, and similar work-related materials are more open-ended or general in contrast with the detailed procedural materials developed by the Japanese. In addition, Swedish workers are encouraged to make decisions and to take risks. Swedes exhibit a moderate-to-high degree of individualism, which is reflected in their emphasis on individual decision making (in contrast to the collective or group decision making of the Japanese). They have a weak power-distance index, which means that Swedish managers use participative approaches in leading their people. Swedes score low on masculinity, which means that interpersonal relations and the ability to interact with other workers and discuss job-related matters are important. These cultural dimensions result in job designs that are markedly different from those in Japan.

Cultural dimensions in the United States are closer to those of Sweden than to those of Japan. In addition, except for individualism, the U. S. profile is between that of Sweden and Japan. This means that job design in U. S. assembly plants tends to be more flexible or unstructured than that of the Japanese but more rigid than that of the Swedes.

This same pattern holds for many other jobs in these three countries. All job designs tend to reflect the cultural values of the country. The challenge for TNCs is to adjust job design to meet the needs of the host country's culture. For example, when Japanese firms enter the United States, they often are surprised to learn that people resent close control. In fact, there is evidence that the most profitable Japanese-owned companies in the United States are those that delegate a high degree of authority to their U. S. managers. Similarly, Japanese firms operating in Sweden find that quality of work life is a central concern for the personnel and that a less structured, highly participative management style is needed for success.

8. 4. 2 Career Strategy

The personal strategy should be designed to utilize strengths and overcome weaknesses in order to take advantage of career opportunities. Although there are different approaches to career development, it is considered here as a process of developing a personal strategy that is conceptually similar to an organizational strategy.

1. Preparation of a Personal Profile

One of the most difficult tasks is gaining insight into oneself, yet this is an essential first step in developing a career strategy. Managers should ask themselves: Am I an introvert or an extrovert? What are my attitudes toward time, achievement, work, material things, and change? The answers to these and similar questions and a clarification of values will help in determining the direction of the professional career.

2. Development of Long-Range Personal and Professional Goals

No airplane would take off without a flight plan including a destination. Yet how clear are managers about the direction of their lives? People often resist career planning because it involves making decisions. By choosing one goal, a person gives up opportunities to pursue others; if an individual studies to become a lawyer, he or she cannot become a doctor at the same time. Managers also resist goal setting because uncertainties in the environment cause concern about making commitments. Furthermore, there is the fear of failing to achieve goals because failure is a blow to one's ego.

But by understanding the factors that inhibit goal setting, one can take steps to increase commitment. First, when the setting of performance goals becomes a part of the appraisal process, identifying career goals is easier. Besides, one does not set career goals all at once. Rather, goal setting is a continuing process that allows flexibility; professional goals can be revised in light of changing circumstances.

Another factor that reduces resistance to goal setting is the integration of long-term aims with the more immediate requirement for action. For example, the aim of becoming a doctor makes one accept the study of boring subjects that are necessary for the medical degree.

3. Analysis of the Environment: Threats and Opportunities

In the analysis of the environment, internal and external, many diverse factors need to be taken into account. They include economic, social, political, technological, and demographic factors; they also include the labor market, competition, and other factors relevant to a particular situation. For example, joining an expanding company that usually provides more career opportunities than working for a mature company is not expected to grow. Similarly, working for a mobile manager means a higher probability that the position of the superior will become vacant, or one might "ride on the coattails" of a competent mobile superior by following him or her through a series of promotions up the organizational hierarchy. At any rate, successful career planning requires a systematic scanning of the environment for opportunities and threats.

One has to be concerned not only about the present, but also about the future environment. This requires forecasting. Since there are a great many factors that need to be analyzed, planning one's career necessitates being selective and concentrating on those factors critical to personal success.

4. Analysis of Personal Strengths and Weaknesses

For successful career planning, the environmental opportunities and threats must be matched with the strengths and weaknesses of individuals. Capabilities may be categorized as technical, human, conceptual, or design. The relative importance of these skills differs for the various positions in the organizational hierarchy, with technical skills being very important on the supervisory level, conceptual and design skills being crucial for top managers, and human skills being important at all levels.

5. Development of Strategic Career Alternative

In developing a career strategy, one usually has several alternatives. The most successful strategy would be to build on one's strengths to take advantage of opportunities. For example, if a person has an excellent knowledge of computers and many companies are looking for computer programmers, he or she should find many opportunities for a satisfying career. On the other hand, if there is a demand for programmers and if an individual is interested in programming but lacks the necessary skills, the proper approach would be a development strategy to overcome the weakness and develop the skills in order to take advantage of the opportunities.

It may also be important to recognize the threats in the environment and develop a strategy to cope with them. If a person with excellent managerial and technical skills is working in a declining company or industry, the appropriate strategy might be to find employment in an expanding firm or in a growing industry.

6. Consistency Testing and Strategic Choices

In developing a personal strategy, one must realize that the rational choice based on strengths and opportunities is not always the most fulfilling alternative.

Although one may have certain skills demanded in the job market, a career in that field may not be congruent with personal values or interests. For example, a person may prefer dealing with people to programming computers. Some may find great satisfaction in specialization, while others prefer to broaden their knowledge and skills.

Strategic choices require trade-offs. Some alternatives involve high risks while others involve low risks. Some choices demand action now; other choices can wait Careers that were glamorous in the past may have an uncertain future. Rational and systematic analysis is just one step in the career-planning process, for a choice also involves personal preferences, personal ambitions, and personal values.

7. Development of Short-Range Career Objectives and Action Plans

So far, concern has centered on career direction. But the strategy has to be supported by short-term objectives and action plans, which can be a part of the performance appraisal process. Thus, if the aim is to reach a certain management position that requires a Master of Business degree, the short-term objective may be to complete a number of relevant courses.

Objectives often must be supported by action plans. Continuing with the example, the completion of the management course may require preparing a schedule for attending classes, doing the homework, and obtaining the understanding and support of the spouse for sacrificing family time to attend the course. It is obvious that the long-term strategic career plan needs to be supported by short-term objectives and action plans.

8. Development of Contingency Plans

Career plans are developed in an environment of uncertainty and the future cannot be predicted with great accuracy. Therefore, contingency plans based on alternative assumptions should be prepared. While one may enjoy working for a small, fast-growing venture company, it may be wise to prepare an alternative career plan based on the assumption that the venture may not succeed.

9. Implementation of the Career Plan

Career planning may start during the performance appraisal. At that time, the person's growth and development should be discussed. Career goals and personal ambitions can be considered in selecting and promoting and in designing training and development programs.

10. Monitoring Progress

Monitoring is the process of evaluating progress toward career goals and making necessary corrections in the aims or plans. An opportune time for assessing career programs is during the performance appraisal. This is the time not only to review performance against objectives in the operating areas but also to review the achievement of milestones in the career plan. In addition, progress should be monitored at other times, such as at the completion of an important task or project.

8. 4. 3 Stress Management

1. Source of Stress in Workplace

The workplace is an important source of both demands and pressures causing stress, and structural and social resources to counteract stress.

The workplace factors that have been found to be associated with stress and health risks can be categorised as those to do with the content of work and those to do with the social and organizational context of work (see figure8-1). Those that are intrinsic to the job include long hours work overload time pressure difficult or complex tasks, lack of breaks, lack of variety, and poor physical work conditions (for example, space, temperature, light).

Unclear work or conflicting roles and boundaries can cause stress, as can having responsibility for people. The possibilities for job development are important buffers against current stress, with under promotion, lack of training and job insecurity being stressful. There are two other sources of stress, or buffers against stress: relationships at work, and the organizational culture. Managers who are critical, demanding, unsupportive or bullying create stress whereas a positive social dimension of work and good team working reduces it.

An organizational culture of unpaid overtime or "presenteeism" causes stress. On the other hand, a culture of involving people in decisions, keeping them informed about what is happening in the organization, and providing good amenities and recreation facilities reduce stress organizational change, especially when consultation has been inadequate, is a huge source of stress. Such changes include mergers, relocation, restructuring or "downsizing", individual contracts, and redundancies within the organization. Employees working in TNCs constantly face these stresses.

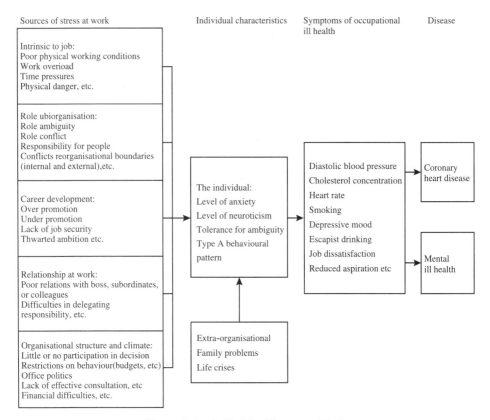

Figure 8-1 A Model of Stress at Work

Source: S Michie. Causes and Management of Stress at Work [J]. Occup Environ Med, 2002, 59: 67-72.

2. Stresses of Expatriates

Despite the economic recession of 2008 ~ 2010, most TNCs continue to make overseas. A survey in 2009 found that 95% of TNCs responding to GMAC Global Relocation Services' 13th annual Global Relocation Trends Survey said they are optimistic about their global business outlook and plan to send more employees on overseas assignments in the future. The survey of 154 multinational companies, with a total worldwide employee population of 4.3 million, found that 68% of the corporations are ramping up their employee assignment efforts. Apparently, this optimism was driven in part by assessments of the growth of emerging markets, especially China as well as the continued integration of the European Union, allowing continued consolidation and integration of European operations. "The survey identified three significant challenges facing corporations: finding suitable candidates for assignments, helping employees-and their families-complete their assignments, and retaining these employees once their assignments end," said Rick

Schwartz, president and chief executive officer of GMAC Global Relocation Services in Woodridge, Illinois.

Not surprisingly, family concerns were cited as the most common reason for assignment refusal, with 89% of those surveyed identifying families as the primarily reason employees turn down an assignment. This was followed by spousal career concerns indicated by 62%. Family-related concerns also were important in the duration of international assignments and were the main driver of early returns from assignments. "Not surprisingly, children's education, family adjustment, partner resistance and difficult locations were identified as the top four critical family challenges in this year's survey," Schwartz said. "That's underscored by the fact that 61% of respondents noted that the impact of family issues on early returns from assignment was very critical or of high importance."

The lack of relevance of assignments to one's career progress was also identified as a major issue. In addition, the general inconveniences caused by assignments were also identified as not fully appreciated by their companies. Moreover, some employees lack opportunities to leverage their international experiences into better positions within their companies. Finally, the annual turnover rate for expatriates on assignment is 25%. In addition, it's 27% for expatriates within one year of completing assignments, compared to 13% average annual turnover for all employees. Other findings from the survey included:

(1) 19% of expatriates were women; the historical average was 15%.

(2) 50% of expatriates were 20 to 39 years old.

(3) 60% of expatriates were married, less than the 66% historical average. The percentage of married men, 51%, was the lowest in the report's history.

(4) 51% of expatriates had children accompanying them, matching the previous all-time low in the 2003 ~ 2004 report; the historical average was 57%.

(5) Spouses and partners accompanied 83% of expatriates, compared to the historical average of 85%.

(6) 54% of spouses were employed before an assignment but not during it; 12% were employed during an assignment but not before; 20% were employed both before and during the assignment.

(7) 56% of expatriates were relocated to or from the headquarters country, below the historical average of 65%.

(8) The United States, China, and United Kingdom were the most frequently cited locations for expatriate assignments.

(9) China, India, and Russia were the primary emerging destinations.

（10）China, India, and Russia also were cited as the most challenging locations for administrators overseeing employee relocations.

3. Stress Management Methods

（1）Individual Stress Management. Most interventions to reduce the risk to health associated with stress in the workplace involve both individual and organizational approaches. Individual approaches include training and one-to-one psychology services—clinical, occupational, health or counselling. They should aim to change individual skills and resources and help the individual change their situation. Training helps prevent stress through：

①becoming aware of the signs of stress.

②using this to interrupt behavior patterns when the stress reaction is just beginning. Stress usually builds up gradually. The more stress builds up, the more difficult it is to deal with.

③analyzing the situation and developing an active plan to minimize the stressors.

④learning skills of active coping and relaxation, developing a lifestyle that creates a buffer against stress.

⑤practising the above in low stress situations first to maximize chances of early success and boost self confidence and motivation to continue.

A wide variety of training courses may help in developing active coping techniques—for example, assertiveness, communications skills, time management, problem solving, and effective management.

（2）Organizational Stress Management. The prevention and management of workplace stress requires organizational level interventions, because it is the organization that creates the stress. An approach that is limited to helping those already experiencing stress is analogous to administering sticking plaster on wounds, rather than dealing with the causes of the damage. An alternative analogy is trying to run up an escalator that's going down! Organizational interventions can be of many types, ranging from structural (for example, staffing levels, work schedules, physical environment) to psychological (for example, social support, control over work, participation).

The emphasis on the organization, rather than the individual, being the problem is well illustrated by the principles used in Scandinavia, where there is an excellent record of creating healthy and safe working environments. Assessing the risk of stress within the workplace must take into account：

①the likelihood and the extent of ill health which could occur as a result of exposure to a particular hazard.

②the extent to which an individual is exposed to the hazard.

③the number of employees exposed to the hazard.

Increasingly, legislation requires employers to assess and address all risks to employee health and safety, including their mental health (for example, the European Commission's framework directive on the introduction of measures to encourage improvements in the safety and health of workers at work). Creating a safe system of work requires targeting equipment, materials, the environment and people (for example, ensuring sufficient skills for the tasks). It also require shaving monitoring and review systems to assess the extent to which prevention and control strategies are effective.

8.5 Case

Case-1

Managers Can't be Great Coaches All by Themselves

In a utopian corporate world, manager slavish a constant stream of feedback on their direct reports. This is necessary, the thinking goes, because organizations and responsibilities are changing rapidly, requiring employees to constantly upgrade their skills. Indeed, the desire for frequent discussions about development is one reason many companies are moving away from annual performance reviews: A yearly conversation isn't enough.

In the real world, though, constant coaching is rare. Managers face too many demands and too much time pressure, and working with subordinates to develop skills tends to slip to the bottom of the to-do list. One survey of HR leaders found that they expect managers to spend 36% of their time developing subordinates, but a survey of managers showed that the actual amount averages just 9% —and even that may sound unrealistically high to many direct reports.

It turns out that 9% shouldn't be alarming, however, because when it comes to coaching, more isn't necessarily better.

To understand how managers can do a better job of providing the coaching and development up-and-coming talent needs, researchers at Gartner surveyed 7,300 employees and managers across a variety of industries; they followed up by interviewing more than 100 HR executives and surveying another 225. Their focus: What are the best managers doing to develop employees in today's busy work environment?

After coding go variables the researchers identified four distinct coaching profiles:

Teacher Managers coach employees on the basis of their own knowledge and experience, providing advice-oriented feedback and personally directing development. Many have expertise in technical fields and spent years as individual contributors before working their way into managerial roles.

Always-on Managers provide continual coaching, stay on top of employees development, and give feedback across a range of skills. Their behaviors closely align with what HR professionals typically idealize. These managers may appear to be the most dedicated of the four types to upgrading their employees' skills-they treat it as a daily part of their job.

Connector Managers give targeted feedback in their areas of expertise; otherwise, they connect employees with others on the team or elsewhere in the organization who are better suited to the task. They spend more time than the other three types assessing the skills, needs and interests of their employees, and they recognize that many skills are best taught by people other than themselves.

Cheerleader managers take a hands-off approach, delivering positive feedback and putting employees in charge of their own development. They are available and supportive, but they aren't as proactive as the other types of managers when it comes to developing employees' skills.

The four types are more or less evenly distributed within organizations, regardless of industry. The most common type, Cheerleaders, accounts for 29% of managers, while the least common, Teachers, accounts for 22%. The revelations in the research relate not to the prevalence of the various styles but to the impact each has on employee performance.

The first surprise: Whether a manager spends 36% of her time on employee development doesn't seem to matter. "There is very little correlation between time spent coaching and employee performance," says Jaime Roca, one of Gartner's practice leaders for human resources. "It's less about the quantity and more about the quality."

The second surprise: Those hypervigilant Always-on Managers are doing more harmthan good. "We thought that category would perform the best, so this really surprised us," Roca says. In fact, employees coached by Always-on Managers performed worse than those coached by the other types and were the only category whose performance diminished as a result of coaching.

The researchers identified three main reasons for Always-on Managers' negative effect on performance. First, although these managers believe that more coaching is better, the continual stream of feedback they offer can be overwhelming and detrimental (The Gartner team compares them to so-called helicopter parents whose close oversight hampers children's ability to develop independence). Second, because they spend less time assessing what skills employees need to upgrade, they tend to coach on topics that are less relevant to employees' real needs. Third, they are so focused on personally coaching their employees that they often fail to recognize the limits of their own expertise, so they may try to teach skills they haven't sufficiently mastered themselves. "That last one is a killer—the manager doesn't actually know he solution to whatever the problem is, and he's essentially winging it and providing misguided information," Roca says.

When the researchers dove deep into the connection between coaching style and employee performance, they found a clear winner: Connectors. The employees of these managers are three times as likely as subordinates of the other types to be high performers.

To understand how Connectors work, consider this analogy from the world of sports: a professional tennis player's coach may be the most important voice guiding the player's development, but she may bring in other experts—for strength training nutrition, and specialized skills such as serves lobs and backhands—instead of trying to teach everything herself. Despite this outsourcing, the coach remains deeply involved, identifying expertise, facilitating introductions, and monitoring progress.

Encouraging managers to adopt Connector behaviors may require a shift in mindset. "Historically, being a manager is about being directive and telling people what to do," Roca says. "Being a connector is more about asking the right questions, providing tailored feedback, and helping employees make a connection to a colleague who can help them." The most difficult part is often self-knowledge and candor: Being a connector requires a manager to recognize that he's not qualified to teach a certain skill and to admit that deficiency to a subordinate. "That isn't something that comes naturally," Roca says.

To get started, the researchers say, managers should focus less on the frequency of their developmental conversations with employees and more on depth and quality. Do you really understand your employees' aspirations and the skills needed to develop in that direction? Next, instead of talking about development only one-on-one, open the conversations up to the team. Encourage colleagues to coach one another, and point out people who have specific skills that others could benefit from learning. Then broaden the scope, encouraging subordinates to connect with colleagues across the organization who might help them gain skills they can't learn from teammates.

For employees, one message from this research is that you're better off working for a Connector than for one of the other types. So how can you recognize whether someone is in that category—ideally before accepting a position? Roca suggests asking your prospective boss about his coachings tyle and discreetly talking with his current direct reports about how he works to upgrade subordinates' skills.

For managers and subordinates the research should redirect attention from the frequency of developmental conversations to the quality of interactions and the route taken to help employees gain skills. Says Roca: "The big takeaway is that when it comes to coaching employees, being a Connector is how you win.

(Source: Gartner. Managers Can't be Great Coaches All by Themselves. Harvard Business Review, May-June 2018.)

Questions:

1. Why are Always-on Managers harmful for performance improvement?

2. What is the right way to be Connectors and raise the effectiveness of training?

Case-2

"We're Giving Ownership of Development to Individuals" Roundtable with Chief Learning Officers

Sankaranarayanan Padmanabhan, Executive chairman, Tata, Business excellence group Samantha Hammock, Chief learning officer, American Express Nick van Dam, Retired global chief, learning officer, McKinsey & Company To understand how the "personal learning cloud" is changing the way companies think about developing executive talent, HBR editor Amy Bernstein and senior editor Daniel McGinn spoke with three heads of learning and development (L&D). Sankaranarayanan "Paddy" Padmanabhan is the executive chairman at Tata business Excellence Group. Samantha Hammock is the chief learning officer at American Express. Nick van Dam was formerly the global chief learning officer at McKinsey Company, where he is currently an external senior adviser; he was recently named chief learning officer at IE University (Disclosure: The three firms are or have been clients of HBR's parent company, Harvard Business Publishing, which sells executive development programs). Edited excerpts follow.

HBR: Paddy, how is leadership development changing at Tata?

PADMANABHAN: Back in the 1960s we created the Tata Management Training Centre, and for many years that was the primary way we developed leaders. But in the past 15 years we've gone beyond that. For very senior leaders the C-level people in our businesses and often the next level down-we look to outside institutions, including Harvard Business School, Stanford the University of Chicago, the Indian Institute of Management, and London Business school. We nominate people for development programs at those schools, and employees are eager to attend. Because Tata is a $110 billion holding company with dozens of operating companies, we also run a leadership culturalization program. It's very important that people be exposed to various companies within Tata, so we send executives to spend two or three days in different parts of the group. They immerse themselves, meet people, and create informal networks. We also do a lot through webinars. Development has gone far beyond the classroom: Today it's more of a conversation, with a lot of emphasis on building a knowledge network.

Samantha, what are the biggest changes at American Express?

HAMMOCK: Traditional learning and development has gone from instructor-led classroom training to virtual, global, scalable options. We've done this because work has changed. Companies aren't only more global; they are more virtual. More people work from home, which makes it impossible to do constant classroom training. The virtual approach also gives people flexibility and appeals to the fact that they want to learn differently. Some employees do the programs at night. Others want to do them during working hours. The biggest thing we get from virtual programs is that people can fit them into their lives.

Nick, what about at McKinsey?

VAN DAM: We're in the intellectual capital business. so we need continual development and learning. That is the central part of our core talent strategy. McKinsey is often referred to as a leadership factory; we have more than 440 alumni serving as CEOs of multibillion-dollar companies. The biggest change in the past five years is the growth of demand for development. Our culture is now very inclusive in this regard: We look at all 28, 000 of our people to determine how they can develop themselves. That requires broadening and deepening our capabilities. Clients expect us to be on the leading edge of thinking and doing and sharing insights so we need to accelerate the development of people's capabilities.

With careers becoming less linear, is it hard to know what skills people need?

PADMANABHAN: When you have flatter organizations and fewer career "ladders", growth can become a challenge. We cope with that by creating a competency framework that addresses the skills and attributes required for every leadership role. If you're going to be the head of our U. S. business, it spells out the capabilities and attributes you must have. If you're going to be the production manager of a motor facility you need different skills and attributes. These frameworks are only 50% or 60% perfect. A person's attitude, behavior, and presence also matter, so we give people opportunities to develop those, too. As ladder promotions become less common, career growth happens through movement across our group companies. This isn't a challenge at the c-suite level; it becomes a challenge a level or two down, when people have 10 to 15 years of experience and are ready to become a unit head or take P&L ownership. That's where bottlenecks can occur.

Is anything lost as talent development programs shift online?

HAMMOCK: You can never replace face-to-face interaction. The feedback from our big in-person sessions shows the value of bringing people together. But it's no longer possible or effective to have that be 80% of your model. Technology is creating better ways to conduct learning virtually. People can join from anywhere and feel like they're in class together.

In your programs, has the mix of soft and hard skills changed?

VAN DAM: It's difficult to cite a percentage, because a lot of development isn't about what happens in the classroom or on a digital learning platform. Leadership development is an ecosystem. There's learning on the job; there's client experience; there's staffing, apprenticeship, mentoring. Each is a building block. So is our performance culture. We have very clear expectations of people at different points in their careers, and we give extensive feedback that provides ongoing development goals. That lets people personalize their development; we call it Making Your Own McKinsey. The goal is to ensure that people are leading their own careers, exploring what they want to do, and making their own choices. We're giving ownership of development to individuals.

HAMMOCK: In terms of hard versus soft skills, they might shift in the future, but I don't think they have changed drastically to date. What has changed is how quickly hard skills can become obsolete, especially in technical roles. People struggle to stay ahead on the technical side, and they tend to be reactive-waiting to see how technology evolves so that they know what they need to learn next.

How challenging is it to personalize talent development?

VAN DAM: There are challenges. One relates to how you define people's career paths. Development experiences will vary according to career paths, and different roles require different competencies. Even in a classroom environment, different people will require different levels of proficiency. When it comes to digital learning, we curate content that we believe is the best fit for people's capability development. Our people like to know what's expected of them, and they don't want to spend a lot of time trying to figure out which of the 50 digital learning objects might be right for them. They want us to direct them to the best most relevant content. Some people like to learn by watching a video rather than reading a PDF. That's another level of personalization. Finally, personalization is also about how much time people can allocate to learning programs.

When employees are learning virtually, how important is it to form relationships with other participants?

HAMMOCK: Cohorts are critical. Even with virtual work, a top success factor is a well-rounded diverse cohort that helps people feel engaged. We put a lot of care into assembling these groups so that our employees have a positive experience.

With the shift to digital learning, do you worry about whether people are taking the time to participate?

PADMANABHAN: For mid level employees and below, most knowledge is delivered via digital media. Every company has its own method. Take a store manager in a retail chain. That person will receive content on his or her smartphone that's focused on building the capabilities necessary to manage the store. That kind of content is largely about convenience, so there might be 15-minute modules. The convenience increases utilization. For people who are 25 or 30, who grew up on YouTube and online this form of learning is prevalent, so utilization isn't a problem. For people over 45 and at senior levels, digital learning isn't as common. For them, leadership development continues to be in the classroom and on the job, partly because that provides better networking opportunities.

How do you measure L&D's success?

PADMANABHAN: For the CEOs who lead Tata Group's 100 or so businesses, we assess it on the basis of their performance. Within a couple of years of moving into the job, can the CEO manage multiple stakeholders? Is the CEO comfortable in the role? Many things contribute to how each CEO develops but we look at whether learning and development programs and job rotations have contributed to creating an effective CEO, CXO, or group head. It's very difficult to measure the effectiveness of these programs for leaders. At lower levels there are more-measurable skills-a link to productivity, or better customer satisfaction. But at high levels it's hard to attribute leadership to the effectiveness of training in any systematic manner.

VAN DAM: For us, it's about how we can make sure we have more impact for our clients and how we can expand the scope. Can we do it better? We can grow only if we have more partners in the firm, so one measure is how well we are developing people to become partner. We also see the value of investments in L&D when we are attracting people. Today more people decide to join an organization because they believe it's a place where they can take their skills to the next level, so L&D is linked to recruiting. Nobody at McKinsey would ever ask me to do a purely financial return-on-investment calculation about every dollar we spend on learning and development; you can't do that. But we know there is an ROI and a huge client impact. We also know that formal leadership development is only one piece of the pie. Globally and across industries the typical person spends something like 40 hours a year in formal learning programs, out of 1,800 hours on the job. So there's a tremendous opportunity in many organizations to advance on-the-job development by turning the workplace into a learning place.

Is the cost of developing talent hard to justify when people are likely to leave the firm for their next job?

HAMMOCK: We've spent a lot of time debating that, particularly in the past year, when we made a large investment in our flagship leadership program. Ultimately we decided that we want to grow great leaders, and we want American Express to be known for that. For instance, we encourage employees to list the certifications they earn on their LinkedIn page, even though that increases their visibility externally. Ideally we want them to find their next opportunity internally, but we know some of them will move on and that's OK.

(Source: We're giving Ownership of Development to Individuals. Harvard Business Review, Marh-April, 2019.)

Questions:

1. According to the content of this roundtable, by what means will individuals can achieve their development?

2. How can we measure L&D's success in TNCs?

Case-3

How to Hire

I really dislike the term "A player. " It implies a grading system that can determine who will be best for a position. HR people always ask how Netflix, where I served as chief talent officer from 1998 to 2012, managed to hire only A players. I say, "There's an island populated exclusively by A players, but only some of us know where it is."

In truth, one company's A player may be a B player for another firm. There is no formula for what makes people successful. Many of the people we let go from Netflix because they were not excelling at what we were doing went on to excel in other jobs.

Finding the right people is also not a matter of "culture fit". What most people really mean when they say someone is a good fit culturally is that he or she is someone they'd like to have a beer with but people with all sorts of personalities can be great at the job you need done. This misguided hiring strategy can also contribute to a company's lack of diversity, since very often the people we enjoy hanging out with have backgrounds much like our own.

Making great hires is about recognizing great matches and often they're not what you'd expect. Take Anthony Park. On paper he wasn't a slam dunk for a Silicon Valley company. He was working at an Arizona bank, where he was a "programmer", not a "software developer", and he was a pretty buttoned up guy. We called Anthony because in his spare time he'd created a Netflix-enhancing app, which he had posted on his website. He came in for a day of interviews, and everyone loved him when he got to me late in the day, I told him he would be getting an offer. He seemed overwhelmed, so I asked if he was all right. He said, "You're going to pay me a lot of money to do what I love!" I did wonder how he'd fit in with the high-powered team he was joining; I hoped it wouldn't burn him out.

A few months later I sat in on a meeting of his team. Everyone was arguing until Anthony suddenly said, "Can I speak now?" The room went silent, because Anthony didn't say much, but when he did speak, it was something really smart- something that would make us all wonder, Damn it, why didn't I think of that? Now Anthony is a vice president. He's proof that organizations can adapt to many people's styles.

In this article I'll describe what I've learned about making great hires during my 14 years at Netflix and in subsequent consulting on culture and leadership. The process requires probing beneath the surface of people and their resumes; engaging managers in every aspect of hiring; treating your in-house recruiters as true business partners; adopting a mindset in which you're always recruiting; and coming up with compensation that suits the performance you need and the future you aspire to my observations may be especially relevant to fast-growing tech-based firms, whose rapid innovation means a continual need for new talent. But organizations of all types can benefit from taking fresh look at their hiring and compensation practices.

Probe Beneath The Surface

At Netflix we had to be creative about where we searched for talent, because we often needed people with rarefied technical skills. When we began looking for big data experts, for example, no one even really knew what "big" meant. We couldn't just search resumes and do keyword matching. We had to think about all the different kinds of companies-many were insurance or credit card companies-that handled masses of data. What's more, our recruiting team lacked the in-depth knowledge to assess people's technical skills.

Our best recruiter of technical people was Bethany Brodsky. She knew virtually nothing about technology before coming to Netflix, but she was great at understanding our business and the root problems we had to solve. She also understood that a candidate's approach to problem solving was more important than previous experience.

One of Bethany's best interviews was with someone working at Lawrence Livermore—a government research center focused on nuclear science. This was when Netflix was beginning to stream on Xbox, Roku and TiVo. When interviewing candidates, Bethany would tell them we had signed up a million subscribers in just 30 days on one of those devices and ask which one they thought it was. TiVo was taking off then, so most people said, "TiVo, for sure." But this candidate asked whether any conditions were attached to getting a Netflix subscription on any of the devices. She told him that Xbox subscribers needed a gold membership. He reasoned that it must be Xbox, because its users were already willing to pay a premium. He was right, and she knew he was our guy.

I had a similar "aha" moment when I interviewed Christian Kaiser, who was managing a group of 25 programmers at AOL. I had tried to hire quite a few people from his group, because they were doing the kind of technical work we needed. But they all wanted to stay at AOL. Netflix was a much sexier place to work, so I was perplexed. When I asked them about it, they would say, "I have the most amazing boss! He's the best communicator I've ever known. I can't bear the thought of leaving him." I told my recruiters, "Go get that guy."

Christian wasn't what I'd expected. He had a thick German accent, and he stuttered. This was the great communicator? On top of that, he was clearly nervous. Our conversation was painful for him and for me. But when I asked him to explain, in simple terms, the technical work he was doing, he was transformed. He still stuttered, but he gave me a riveting explanation, and I realized, That's it!

He's great at making really complicated things understandable. We hired him, and he's been an amazing team builder.

We always tried to be creative about probing people and their resumes. Bethany once decided to analyze the resumes of our best data-science people for common features. She found that those people shared an avid interest in music. From then on she and her team looked for that quality. She recalls, "We'd get really excited and call out, Hey, I found a guy who plays piano!" She concluded that such people can easily toggle between their left and right brains—a great skill for data analysis.

Engage Managers Fully

Many companies rely on outside recruiters. Netflix was growing so quickly that we opted for a different strategy: We formed an internal team of experienced recruiters. The sad truth is that most companies treat recruitment as a separate, nonbusiness, even non-HR function, and many young companies outsource it. Building a talented team of internal recruiters was a substantial investment but I could make an irrefutable business case for doing so: I could clearly show what the return would be from eliminating head hunter fees. We saved bundles of money over time.

The technical nature of our business meant that managers needed to be highly engaged in the hiring process. But that should be required at all companies. Every hiring manager should understand the company's approach to hiring and how to execute on it, down to the smallest detail.

Our recruiters' job involved coaching our hiring managers. The recruiters created a slide deck to use with each manager, one-on-one. They would ask, "What does your interview process look like? What does your interview team look like? What is your process for having candidates come in?" People don't have to approach interviewing or recruiting in the same way, but we insisted that they have a plan and not just improvise.

In the end, the manager would make the hiring decision. Team members provided input, and my team and I also weighed in. But the ultimate responsibility was the managers, as was the performance of the team he or she was building.

All this should be modeled from the top. Bethany once worked with our CEO, Reed Hastings, to fill a director-level position. They met on a Thursday morning to discuss what type of candidate they needed. Friday afternoon Reed e-mailed her to say he had sent messages to 20 prospects he'd found on LinkedIn and had gotten three responses. He'd interviewed one via Skype, really liked him, and wanted him to come in on Monday.

When hiring managers are as engaged as reed was, recruiters up their game even more. After getting Reeds e-mail, Bethany was determined to find someone even better (We ended up hiring Reed's guy, and Reed gloated about it for years).

Treat Recruiters as Business Partners

For the approach I'm describing to work, recruiters must be considered vital contributors to building the business. They need to deeply understand the needs of the business, and hiring managers need to treat them as business partners.

Getting the two groups to work together optimally may require holding hiring managers' feet to the fire. One day I heard one of my best recruiters complain about a new executive: "He doesn't return my calls or e-mails I send him resumes but he doesn't respond I'm frustrated because we really need to build him a great team. " I walked up to her and said, "I think you need to work with someone else. I'll take care of this. Then I sent him an e-mail saying I had reassigned his recruiter: "I've put her on another project, because you appear to have a methodology for hiring and don't seem to need her help Let us know when we can step in and assist Love Patty. "

Within minutes he was at my desk, fuming. "What the hell?" he demanded. I asked him. "Is it true that she set up two meetings with you and you canceled?" He snapped, "I'm a busy guy. I'm doing the work of 10 people. " I asked, "Is it true that she sent you a number of qualified candidates and you didn't respond? It's your job to build the team, not hers. By the way, there are three people who are delighted that she's not spending time on you. She's a great partner; she could really make this work for you. But if you don't need her, that's cool. " Realizing that he did need the recruiter to help grow his team, he changed his tune and began treating her with respect.

It infuriates me when hiring managers dismiss the value of good HR people. Usually when I asked managers why they weren't engaging more with recruiters, they'd say, "Well, they're not that smart, and they don't really understand what's going on in my business or how the technology works. " My response would be "Then start expecting—and demanding—that they do!" If you hire smart people; insist that they be businesspeople; and include them in running the business, they'll act like businesspeople.

On occasion, I even advise companies to hire a businessperson, not an HR specialist, to run HR. Just like any other department or division head, your HR chief should understand the details of your business, how you earn your revenue, who your customers are, and your strategy for the future.

Always be Recruiting

At Netflix we had a saying: "Always be recruiting! Candidates came from everywhere-from professional conferences from the sidelines of a kids soccer game, from conversations on airplanes. But certain fundamentals were strictly enforced. The interview and hiring process gives a powerful first impression about how your company operates, for good or bad. So I had an ironclad rule that if people saw a stranger sitting alone at headquarters waiting for an interview, they should stop and say, "Hi, I'm...Are you here for an interview? Let's look at your schedule, and I'll help you find the next person?" If I was late coming to meet with a candidate and said, "Sorry-I hope someone talked to you," he or she would say, "Six people talked to me."

Recruiting was so important that interviews trumped any meeting a hiring manager was scheduled for, and they were the only reason people could miss our executive staff meetings. Candidates are evaluating you, just as you're evaluating them. People forget that. Our goal was to have every person who came for an interview walk away wanting the job. Even if we hated candidates, we wanted them to think wow that was an incredible experience. It was efficient, it was effective, it was on time, the questions were relevant everyone was smart, and I was treated with dignity. I would tell people, "Even if this person isn't the right fit, we might love his next-door neighbor?"

We acted as quickly as possible once the decision was made: no running the hire by two levels of management, the compensation department, and HR. My team worked directly with hiring managers to determine compensation, title and other details. Recruiters laid the groundwork; managers made the offers speed and efficiency often meant we could land candidates who were interviewing with other great companies.

Set Compensation That Makes Sense for You

Competitive salaries are obviously needed to lure top talent. Every business would like to mark its salaries to the market, but that can be challenging. There are amazingly sophisticated resources to tap for salary information; industry surveys cover every domain and give elaborate breakdowns by level. But jobs are not widgets, and neither are people. Roles are specialized in ways that survey descriptions cannot account for, and a candidate may have skills, such as good judgment and collaborative prowess that can't be measured by surveys.

Say you need a software engineer. Do you want a senior programmer fluent in the best new techniques in search engine development? And this person will be managing a staff of five? Oh, and this person also needs to understand online advertising systems well enough to work with marketing on an online advertising strategy a survey is not going to tell you how much such a person is paid currently-

or should be paid by you.

Compensation departments spend gobs of time comparing descriptions and adjusting for other factors. However, that process gives you only a baseline understanding of the market landscape. How many people with those qualifications are available? To get the person you want, you often need to throw your calculations away and respond to actual market demand.

But market demand may not in itself be an adequate guide, because it reflects the present moment, and hiring should be about the future. The prevailing compensation system is often behind the times; it's based on the historical value of what employees have produced rather than on their potential to add value in the future.

Imagine that your recruiter manages to find a software engineer with all the credentials you need and your team loves her, but she has an offer from your main competitor that's $35,000 more than what you were prepared to pay. In determining what to offer, consider the difference it might make to the future of your business if you bring her in rather than settle for your second choice-who may be a distant second, and whom it will take three months to hire because you'll keep looking for someone with the skills and talent of your first choice. How much added revenue might that great first choice produce? Might she ensure that you beat your competitor on the launch of a fabulous new search system-especially if she gets started now rather than three months down the road? How much ad revenue might she bring in by improving your targeting? What about the value of her management experience-might a key member of her team who gets an offer from another firm decide to stay because she's a great leader? And what about the value to you of her not working you're your competitor, particularly if your domain is undergoing rapid innovation?

Current market demand and salary surveys can't help you calculate these future gains. I'm not saying there's no value to benchmarking, but I advise forgoing elaborate calculations based on what other companies are paying right now; that's comparing apples and oranges. It's better to focus on what you can afford to pay for the performance you want and the future you're heading toward.

Once you've made an offer and hired someone you need to keep assessing compensation. I learned this during a period when Netflix was losing people because of exorbitant offers from our competitors. One day I heard that google had offered one of our folks almost twice his current pay, and I hit the roof. He was a really important guy, so his manager wanted to counter. I got into a heated e-mail exchange with his manager and a couple of VPs. I wrote, "Google shouldn't decide the salaries for everybody just because they have more money than god!" We bickered for days. They kept telling me, "You don't understand how good he is!" I was having none of it.

But I woke up one morning and thought, Oh, of course! No wonder Google wants him. They're right! He had been working on some incredibly valuable personalization technology, and very few people in the world had his expertise. I realized that his work with us had given him a whole new market value. I fired off another e-mail: "I was wrong, and by the way, I went through the P&L, and we can double the salaries of everybody on this team. " That experience changed how we thought about compensation. We realized that for some jobs we were creating expertise and scarcity, and rigidly adhering to internal salary ranges could harm our best contributors, who could make more elsewhere. We decided we didn't want a system in which people had to leave to be paid what they were worth. We also encouraged our employees to interview elsewhere regularly. That was the most reliable and efficient way to learn how competitive our pay was.

People often tell me, "We can't pay top dollar. That was great for Netflix, because the company was booming. But we're not growing that way, and we don't have the margin. " Fair enough. Maybe it's not possible to pay top of market for every position. In that case I suggest identifying the positions with the greatest potential to boost your performance and paying top dollar to fill them with the very best people you can get. Think about it this way: What if by paying top of market you could bring in one supremely talented person who could do the job of two people or add even more value than that? Consider the 80/20 rule about sales teams: that 20% of your salespeople will generate 80% of your revenue. It may apply to other employees. I've seen a similar effect on team after team.

Another objection I often hear to hiring star performers at top pay is that their salaries will be much higher than those of their teammates. Managers at Netflix used to complain about that. Say we wanted to bring in someone whose salary would be twice that of everybody else on the team. Department heads would sometimes ask, "Does that mean I'm paying people half of what they're worth?" I'd say, "Well, is this new person going to be able to move us faster, maybe even twice as fast? And when we hire him, who on your team could take his place at his former company?" The answers were usually "Yeah, we'll be able to move much faster" and "None of them could replace him because they don't have his experience. "

This focus on the value-add of an individual star is especially important when a company is scaling up. I recently got a call from a CEO whose company employs 150 people. He said it would be growing to 300 and asked my advice on getting there I said, "That's a precise number of people. What's it based on?"

He said his company would need to do twice as much work. I asked would the new people be doing the same kinds of work as the current staff or would there be new things? Would the company be launching a product line? And if teams were getting bigger, might he need more-experienced managers? Did twice as much work mean reaching twice as many customers? If so, he would have to ramp up customer service. But that might not mean hiring twice as many reps; maybe outsourcing would be better. Then I asked the question I've found to be the most thought-provoking in these consultations: "Instead of 150 new people, are you sure you don't want 75 people whom you pay twice as much because they have twice as much experience and can be higher performers?"

I've found that if you focus intently on hiring the best people you can find and pay them top dollar, chances are your business growth will more than make up for what you spend on compensation.

(Source: Patty McCord. How to Hire. Harvard Business Review, January-February, 2018.)

Questions:

1. According to the case, what are the key factors to be an effective recruiter?

2. Combined with the case, how do TNCs set competitive salaries to attract overseas talents?

8.6　Expanding Reading

Reading-1

Multinational Recruiters Face Host of Challenges

Domestic companies increasingly competitive in terms of salary and career advancement opportunities.

Whether multinational companies are still as attractive to candidates as they were some 20 years ago is an open question nowadays.

US headhunting company manpower has been monitoring multinational companies' hiring demand in China since 2005. However, the hiring willingness has been declining since 2010.

Multinational companies' conservative attitude towards the Chinese market is one possible reason holding up their recruitment plans. According to the survey released by German Chamber of Commerce in China in late November 2017, more than half of the 423 surveyed German companies said they did not have any plans to invest in new locations in China in 2018, hitting a record high since statistics are available.

Besides, a number of well-known multinational companies have withdrawn from the Chinese market in various ways. German toymaker Autec announced in January last year that it will move all its production lines back to Germany. In the same month, US data-storage company Seagate announced that it will shut down its plant in Suzhou. At the end of October, Japanese digital camera maker Nikon closed its plant in Wuxi.

At the same time, multinational companies are faced with fierce competition for talents from Chinese domestic companies, according to global recruitment agency Hays. As Simon Lance, managing director of Hays in China explained, domestic companies are seeking all possible ways to look for and retain the right talents by offering better payment, stock options and the promise of opportunities for further development, he said.

Lu Yue used to be the human resources vice-president of a US technology company in China. However, the company adjusted its strategy in the country four years ago, cutting much of its headcount and forcing Lu to look for another job opportunity.

She soon landed a job at a local internet finance company in Shanghai. One year later, she relocated to Beijing to work as the human resources vice-president at a domestic internet entertainment and technology firm.

"It will be impossible for me to go back to the system at multinational companies right now," she said, adding that the payment and empowerment she currently receives from executives "are something that can be hardly found in multinational companies".

Liu Naiying, human resources vice-president of Coca-Cola Greater China and South Korea Region, admitted that the company's recruitment has been somewhat affected by the rise of the domestic companies, especially e-commerce companies.

"Shortly after the reform and opening-up policy took effect in China (in the late 1970s), it was quite easy for multinational companies to hire the right talents here thanks to our more competitive compensation packages. But now, the younger generation show greater interest in working at emerging industries," she said.

However, Coca-Cola will still adopt a recruitment plan in China that Liu considers a bit more aggressive than the company employed last year, hiring more hands in marketing as well as research and development.

"We can still attract the talents we want. But the problem for us now is, the turnover rate is so low at the company that we lack a little bit of vitality," she said.

Pete Chia, managing director of recruitment service provider BRecruit in China, said that multinational companies are not seen as the ideal choice for candidates right now, given that domestic companies have caught up and even overtaken them in terms of technology, pay, overseas job opportunities and social recognition. The advantages of domestic firms are especially apparent in the internet and technology sectors.

Meanwhile, multinational companies usually have a longer brand history than domestic ones and thus their personnel structure is more stable. Younger staff anxious for promotions may have to wait a longer time than they would at domestic companies before achieving their career goals. The comparatively longer waiting time will force some people to give up the opportunity at multinational companies and opt for domestic ones, Chia said.

But he also pointed out that multinational companies have been changing over the past decades in terms of their requirement for talents. In the early days of reform and opening up, the positions opened to the Chinese market were preliminary ones such as factory workers. But now, they increasingly need more candidates with professional knowledge and skills, he said.

"It is true that domestic companies have learned a lot from multinational companies over the past few decades. But the story should be the other way round now. Multinational companies should learn from the domestic ones to know more about the Chinese market, get more localized, and pass on the message to the global headquarters more efficiently," he said.

(Source: Shi Jing, Multinational Recruiters Face Host of Challenges, China Daily, Feburary 28, 2018.)

Reading-2

Expatriate Success in China

Most research on HRM orientation has focused mostly on multinationals based in developed countries expanding into either developed or developing economies.

However, the current environment is seeing the emergence of multinationals from emerging markets. Consider the case of India, with companies such as Infosys and Tata. Both companies are becoming formidable competitors in their own right.

As such, it is important to see how these smaller emerging market multinational, which are often at early stages of internationalization, are adopting

IHRM strategy.

A recent study suggests that emerging markets multinationals face two forms of liabilities that developed multinationals do not necessarily face. First, in entering a new country, emerging market multinationals face the liability of foreignness whereby they have to work harder in a host country to succeed because they are seen as being foreign. Second, emerging markets multinationals also suffer from the liability of country of origin. Specifically, emerging market multinationals also suffer from the poor image perception of their country of origin.

In the face of such barriers, emerging market multinationals have to approach adoption of IHRM strategy differently. For instance, if they operate in developed markets, they can seldom use the "forward diffusion" strategy typical of developed market multinationals. While developed market multinationals often have superior home country practices that they can transfer to other countries, emerging market multinationals are often more likely to want to learn from practices in developed markets and to transfer those practices to other countries. As such, they are more likely to adopt more polycentric or regiocentric approaches where they hire host country managers with local knowledge. Lessons learned from the various locations are then transferred back to home subsidiaries as an improvement mechanism.

However, if an emerging market multinational is entering other emerging markets, it may not have access to the necessary individuals with the needed technical and management skills at the local level. In such cases, emerging market multinationals are more likely to adopt an ethnocentric approach, whereby they transfer home HRM practices in other subsidiaries worldwide.

(Sources: Based on Thite, M., A. Wilkinson, and D. Shah. "internationalization and HRM strategies across subsidiaries in multinational corporations from emerging economies: A conceptual frame-work." Journal of World Business, 2012 (47), 251-258.)

Quick Quiz

1. ____ are managers who are citizens of the country where the MNC is headquartered.

2. Nowadays, recruitment through ____ has become the main approach for TNCs to recruit talents.

3. The purpose of job rotation is to ____ .

4. ____ is the process of evaluating progress toward career goals and making necessary corrections in the aims or plans.

5. What are the key success factors for expatriate assignments that international

HR considered?

    A. technical competence

    B. relational abilities

    C. family situation

    D. motivation

    E. intelligence quotient

6. The main content of cross-cultural training should include ＿＿ .

    A. understanding and cognition of the host country's national culture and the parent company's culture

    B. language training

    C. training of cross-cultural communication and conflict solving ability

    D. enterprise system

    E. culture sensitivity and adaptability training

7. There are four factors of strategic appraisal worth special attention ＿＿ .

    A. the effect of "uncontrollable variables" should be taken into consideration

    B. grass-root managers' performance should be judged by themselves

    C. considering the establishment of a set of accounts that have been adjusted by accountants

    D. we should set different business objectives for different subsidiaries according to the company's strategic plans

    E. the subsidiaries' other strategic acts should be taken into account

Answers：

    1. Home-country nationals

    2. internet

    3. broaden the knowledge of managers or potential managers

    4. Monitoring

    5. ABCD

    6. ABCE

    7. ACDE

Endnotes

[1] Harlod Koontz, Heinz Weihrich. Essentials of Management—An International and Leadership Perspective [M]. Beijing: China Renmin University Press, 2014: 252-257.

[2] John B. Cullen, K. Praveen Parboteeah. Multinaional Management [M]. Beijing: China Renmin University Press, 2017: 282-325.

[3] Fred Luthan, Jonathan P. Doh. International Management—Culture, Strategy and Behavior [M]. Beijing: Mechanical Industry Press, 2018: 490-504.

[4] Zhang Xiaoyu. Handbook for Transnational Corporation Management [M]. Beijing: Central Compilation & Translation Press, 2017: 257-290.

[5] Som Sekhar Bhattacharyya. Comparative Cross Cultural Study of Indian Managers' Perspectives on Doing International Business in Bedouin and Guanxi Culture [J]. International Journal of Asian Business and Information Management, 2019 (03): 1-21.

[6] Goudarz Azar, Rian Drogendijk. Ex-post Performance Implications of Divergence of Managers' Perceptions of " Distance " From " Reality " in International Business [J]. Management International Review, 2019, 59 (1): 67-92.

[7] Dimitri Golovko, Jan H. Schumann. Influence of company Facebook activities on recruitment success [J]. Journal of Business Research, 2019 (06): 161-169.

[8] Channah Herschberg, Yvonne Benschop; Marieke van den Brink. Precarious postdocs: A comparative study on recruitment and selection of early-career researchers [J]. Scandinavian Journal of Management, 2018 (10): 301-310.

[9] Fabricia Silva Rosa, Rogério João Lunkes, Kelly Saviatto. Effect of using public resources and training for the sustainable development of Brazilian municipalities [J]. Environmental Monitoring and Assessment, 2019, 191 (10): 1-11.

[10] Dussault Gilles. Reflections on Health Workforce Development Comment on "Health Professional Training and Capacity Strengthening Through International Academic Partnerships: The First Five Years of the Human Resources for Health Program in Rwanda" [J]. International Journal of Health Policy and Management, 2019 (04): 245-246.

[11] Ruichao Zhang, Hongshan Liu; Jiajing Zhang. A Brief Study on the Problems and Development Countermeasures of China's International Trade Talents Training [J]. Modern Economy, 2017 (12): 1575-1579.

[12] Mei-yung Leung, Qi Liang, Isabelle Y. S. Chan. Development of a Stressors-Stress-Performance-Outcome Model for Expatriate Construction Professionals [J]. Journal of Construction Engineering and Management, 2016 (10).

[13] Stefan Schmid, Frederic Altfeld. International work experience and compensation: Is more always better for CFOs? [J]. European Management Journal, 2017 (10).

[14] Andreas Kuhn. International Evidence on the Perception and Normative

Valuation of Executive Compensation ［J］. British Journal of Industrial Relations，2017（01）：112-136.

［15］Haiying Kang，Jie Shen. Transfer or localize? International reward and compensation practices of South Korean multinational enterprises in China ［J］. Asia Pacific Business Review，2015（02）：211-227.

［16］ John B. Cullen，K. Praveen Parboteeah. Multinaional Management ［M］. Beijing：China Renmin University Press，2017：390-412.

Chapter 9 Business Ethics

Learning Objectives

1. Understand the connotation of international business ethics
2. Master the factors that raise ethical standards in business
3. Recognize the way to become an effective and ethical strategic leader in business
4. Understand the connotation of social responsibility
5. Master the ethics and social responsibility in cross-cultural management
6. Understand the differing ethical standards across cultures

Opening Case

Advertising or Free Speech? The Case of Nike and Human Rights

Nike Inc, the global leader in the production and marketing of sports and athletic merchandise including shoes, clothing, and equipment, has enjoyed unparalleled worldwide growth for many years. Consumers around the world recognize Nike's brand name and logo. As a supplier to and sponsor of professional sports figures and organizations, and as a large advertiser to the general public, Nike is widely known. Nike was a pioneer in offshore manufacturing, establishing company-owned assembly plants and engaging third-party contractors in developing countries.

In 1996, Life magazine published a landmark article about the labor conditions of Nike's overseas subcontractors, entitled, "On the Playgrounds of America, Every Kid's Goal Is to Score: In Pakistan, Where Children Stitch Soccer Balls for Six Cents an Hour, Their Goal Is to Survive. " Accompanying the article was a photo of a 12-year old Pakistani boy stitching a Nike embossed soccer ball. The photo caption noted that the job took a whole day, and the child was paid US $60 for his effort. Up until this time, the general public was neither aware of the wide use of foreign labor nor familiar with the working arrangements and treatment of laborers in developing countries. Since then, Nike has become a poster child for the questionable unethical use of offshore workers in poorer regions of the world. This label has continued to plague the corporation as many global human interest and labor rights organizations have monitored and often condemned Nike for its labor practices around the world.

Nike executives have been frequent targets at public events, especially at universities where students have pressed administrators and athletic directors to ban products that have been made under "sweatshop" conditions. Indeed, at the University of Oregon, a major gift from Phil Knight, Nike's CEO, was held up in part because of student criticism and activism against Nike on campus.

In 2003 the company employed 86 compliance officers (up from just three in 1996) to monitor its plant operations and working conditions and ensure compliance with its published corporate code of conduct. Even so, the stigma of past practices—whether perceived or real-remains emblazoned on its image and brand name. Nike found itself constantly defending its activities, striving to shake this reputation and perception.

In 2002 Marc Kasky sued Nike, alleging that the company knowingly made false and misleading statements in its denial of direct participation in abusive labor conditions abroad. Through corporate news releases, full-page ads in major newspapers, and letters to editors, Nike defended its conduct and sought to show that allegations of misconduct were unwarranted. The action by the plaintiff, a local citizen, was predicated on a California state law prohibiting unlawful business practices. He alleged that Nike's public statements were motivated by marketing and public relations and were simply false. According to the allegation Nike's statements misled the public and thus violated the California statute. Nike countered by claiming its statements fell under and within the protection of the First Amendment, which protects free speech. The state court concluded that a firm's public statements about its operations have the effect of persuading consumers to buy its products and therefore are, in effect, advertising. Therefore, the suit could be adjudicated on the basis of whether Nike's pronouncements were false and misleading. The court stated that promoting a company's reputation was equivalent to sales solicitation, a practice clearly within the purview of state law. The majority of justices summarized their decision by declaring, "because messages in question were directed by a commercial speaker to a commercial audience, and because they made representations of fact about the speaker's own business operations for the purpose of promoting sales of its products, we conclude that these messages are commercial speech for purposes of applying state laws barring false and misleading commercial messages" (Kasky v. Nike Inc., 2002). The conclusion reached by the court was that statements by a business enterprise to promote its reputation must, like advertising be factual representations and that companies have a clear duty to speak truthfully about such issues.

In January 2003, the U. S. Supreme Court agreed to hear Nike's appeal of the decision in Kasky v. Nike Inc. from the California Supreme Court. In particular, the U. S. Supreme Court agreed to rule on whether Nike's previous statements about the working conditions at its subcontracted, overseas plants were in fact "commercial speech" and, separately, whether a private individual (such as Kasky) has the rig to sue on those grounds. Numerous amici briefs were filedon both sides. Supporters of Kasky included California, as well as 17 other states, Ralph Nader's Public Citizen Organization, California's AFL/CIO, and California's attorney general. Nike's friends of the court included the American Civil Liberties Union, the Business Roundtable, the U. S Chamber of Commerce, other MNCs including Exxon/Mobil and Microsoft, and the Bush administration (particularly grounds that it does not support private individuals acting as public censors).

Despite the novelty of this First Amendment debate and the potentially wide-reaching effects for big business (particularly MNCS), the U. S. Supreme Court dismissed the case (6 to 3) in June 2003 as improvidently granted due to procedural issues surrounding the case. In their dissenting opinion, Justices Stephen G. Breyer and Sandra Day Connor suggested that Nike would likely win the appeal at the U. S. Supreme Court level. In both the concurring and dissenting opinions, Nike's statements were described as a mix of "commercial" and "noncommercial" speech. This suggested to Nike, as well as other MNCs, that if the Court were to have ruled on the substantive issue, Nike would have prevailed.

Although this case has set no nationwide precedent for corporate advertising about business practices or corporate social responsibility (CSR) in general, given the sensitivity of the issue, Nike has allowed its actions to speak louder than words in recent years. As part of its international CSR profile, Nike has assisted relief efforts and advocated fair wages and employment practices in its outsourced operations. Nike claims that it has not abandoned production in certain countries in favor of lower-wage labor in others and that its factory wages abroad are actually in accordance with local regulations, once one accounts for purchasing power and cost-of-living differences. The Nike Foundation, a nonprofit organization supported by Nike, is also an active supporter of the Millennium Development Goals, particularly those directed at improving the lives of adolescent girls in developing countries (specifically Bangladesh, Brazil, Ethiopia, and Zambia) through better health, education, and economic opportunities.

As part of its domestic CSR profile, Nike is primarily concerned with keeping youth active, presumably for health, safety, educational, and psychological/esteem reasons. Nike has worked with Head Start (2005) and Special Olympics Oregon (2007), as well as created its own community program, NikeGO, to advocate physical activity among youth. Furthermore, Nike is committed to domestic efforts such as Hurricane Katrina relief and education, the latter through grants made by the Nike School Innovation Fund in support of the Primary Years Literacy Initiate.

Despite Nike's impressive CSR profile, if the California State Supreme Court decision is sustained and sets a global precedent, Nike's promotion or "advertisement" of its global CSR initiatives could still be subjected to legal challenge.

This could create a minefield for multinational firms. It could effectively elevate statements on human rights treatment by companies to the level of corporate marketing and advertising. Under these conditions, it might be difficult for MNCs to defend themselves against allegations human rights abuses. In fact, action such as the issuance and dissemination of a written company code of conduct could fall into the category of advertising declarations. Although Kaskyv. Nike was never fully resolved in court, the issues that it raised remain to be addressed by global companies.

Also to be seen is what effect a court decision would have on Nike's financial success. Despite the publicity of the case at both the state and Supreme Court levels, and the lingering criticism about its labor practices overseas, Nike has maintained strong and growing sales and profits. The company has expanded its operations into different types of clothing and sports equipment and has continued to choose successful athletes to advertise its gear. Nike has shown no signs of slowing down, suggesting that its name and logo have not been substantially tarnished in the global market.

(Source: Lawrence Beer, W. P. Carey School of Business, Arizona State University as the Basis for Class Discussion.)

9.1 Ethics and Business

9.1.1 Concepts and Theory

1. International Business Ethics

Before you can understand the ethical dilemmas faced by multinational managers, you need a working definition of business ethics. Most experts consider business ethics as an application of the broader concern for all ethical behavior and reasoning, which pertains to behaviors or actions that affect people and their welfare. A decision by managers to knowingly sell a useful but dangerous product is an ethical decision. Ethics deal with the "should" of life-that is, the rules and values that determine the goals and actions people should follow when dealing with other human beings.

Although economic logic (i. e., making money) dominates business decision making, most business decisions have consequences for people (workers, suppliers, customers and society). Thus, ethical decision making permeates organizational life. For example, decisions such as those regarding product safety, layoffs, closing or relocating a plant, or the truthfulness of an advertisement have consequences for people. When managers make such decisions, they make decisions with ethical consequences—whether consciously or not.

However, ethical questions seldom have clear or unambiguous answers that all people accept. For example, producing automobiles that are safer than those currently on the market is possible. However, if such vehicles were required by law, they would be extremely expensive (only the rich could drive), they would probably result in smaller automobile production plants (putting people out of work), they would likely require larger engines (increasing oil consumption and pollution), and they would likely reduce profits (violating the ethical responsibilities of the managers to stockholders). So automobile manufacturers always deal with the ethical dilemma of whether a vehicle is sufficiently safe versus sufficiently affordable.

International business ethics pertain to the unique ethical problems faced by managers conducting business operations across national boundaries. International business ethics differ from domestic business ethics on two accounts. First, and perhaps most important, international business is more complex because business is conducted cross-nationally. Different cultural values and institutional systems necessarily mean that people may not always agree on how one should behave in a given situation. Expatriate managers may face situations where local business practices violate their culturally based sensibilities or home country laws. Second, very large multinational companies often have powers and assets that equal those of some foreign governments. Managers in these large and powerful multinationals may encounter challenging ethical dilemmas regarding how to use this power.

General Electric and Code of Conduct

General Electric (GE) is ranked sixth among the Fortune 500 companies and eleventh among the Fortune Global 500 companies. It is involved in varied industries. such as transportation equipment manufacturing, electrical products manufacturing media, and healthcare products manufacturing. It produces such things as turbines, trains, TVs and ultrasound machines, and also provides financial services. It also operates in a large number of countries that have widely different norms and standards. However, despite this variety of industries and countries, it is seen as a company with high ethics and integrity. How can it maintain such consistency? GE follows a number of important principles:

Committed leadership and leading by example: One of the key reasons why GE can maintain consistency worldwide is that top executives are committed to performance with integrity. All executives are committed to ethics and show such commitment in all activities. Furthermore, top executives are also held to the same strict standards as everyone in the company. In two cases, GE did not hesitate to terminate top executives who violated GE ethics, although these executives had valuable in-depth country knowledge. Such actions send an important message that no one can violate the ethics standards under any circumstances.

Going beyond financial, legal and country rules: In order to maintain the same standards worldwide, GE will often adopt the most rigorous standards that are applied consistently worldwide. The company consults with stakeholders to determine those critical areas that need to be addressed. GE has instituted a corporate risk committee made up of top officers. The committee meets regularly to discuss which areas need standards and to determine the most rigorous to be applied.

Staying ahead of regulators: GE also makes sure that it is constantly being pro active to stay ahead of regulators. It has a team of employees that constantly reviews trends worldwide to determine what new regulations might be passed. It then reviews its own regulations to ensure that it stays ahead of new rules.

Assigning responsibility to all employees: GE ensures that everyone is responsible for leadership in their own areas. Instead of the typical procedure of assigning ethics responsibility to employees in the legal or finance department, GE acknowledges that employees are more aware of ethical dilemmas in their work than others. As such, employees are given the authority and responsibility of maintaining and improving ethical standards in their respective areas. For example, plant managers are formally responsible for environmental, health, and safety issues in their plants.

Letting employees have a say in ethics: GE discovered that educating and training employees, especially in newly acquired companies or emerging markets, is extremely critical. However, such training cannot function effectively unless employees can also voice their concern about current standards or new ethical issues. GE therefore gives employees several channels to voice their concerns. For example, GE has an ombuds system that lets employees voice their views without fear of retaliation.

Holding leaders accountable with ethics metrics: GE ensures that employees receive the necessary feedback regarding integrity and ethics. Each and every business leader is evaluated in terms of how they have fulfilled their ethics responsibilities. Have the proper systems been implemented? Have the leaders set appropriate goals? Have they integrated high ethics in all areas? Based on such evaluations, GE then rewards employees as appropriate.

(Sources: Based on Ethisphere Institute. 2012. "Ethisphere Institute unveils the 2012 World's Most Ethical Companies". http://ethisphere.com/ethisphere-institute-unveils-2012-worlds-most-ethical-companies/; Heineman, B., Jr. "Avoiding integrity land mines. " Harvard Business Review, April, 2007, 100-108.)

2. Ethics Theories and Philosophy

There are a range of ethical theories and approaches around the world, many emanating from religious and cultural traditions. Here we review three tenets from Western philosophy, and briefly describe Eastern philosophy, which can be used to evaluate and inform international management decisions. The nearby International Management in Action feature explores how these perspectives might be used to inform the ethics of a specific international business decision.

Kantian philosophical traditions argue that individuals (and organizations) have responsibilities based on a core set of moral principles that go beyond those of narrow self-interest. In fact, a Kantian moral analysis rejects consequences (either conceivable or likely) as morally irrelevant when evaluating the choice of an agent: "The moral worth of an action does not lie in the effect expected from it, nor in any principle of action which requires to borrow its motive from this expected effect. " Rather, a Kantian approach asks us to consider our choices as implying a general rule, or maxim, that must be evaluated for its consistency as a universal law. For Kant, what is distinctive about rational behavior is not that it is self-interested or even purpose driven, though all actions do include some purpose as part of their explanation. Instead, rational beings, in addition to having purposes and being able to reason practically in their pursuit, are also capable of evaluating their choices through the lens of a universal law, what Kant calls the moral law, or the "categorical imperative" (Kant 1949). From this perspective, we ought always to act under a maxim that we can will consistently as a universal law for all rational beings similarly situated.

Aristotelian virtue ethics focus on core, individual behaviors and actions and how they express and form individual character. They also consider social and arrangements and practices in terms of their contribution to the formation of good character in individuals. A good, or virtuous, individual does what is right for the right reasons and derives satisfaction from such actions because his or her character is rightly formed. For Aristotle, moral success and failure largely come down to a matter of right desire, or appetite: "In matters of action, the principles of initiating motives are the ends at which our actions are aimed. But as soon as people become corrupted by pleasure or pain, the goal no longer appears as a motivating principle: he no longer sees that he should choose and act in every case for the sake of and because of this end. For vice tends to destroy the principle or initiating motive of action." It is important to have an understanding of what is truly good and practical wisdom to enable one to form an effective plan of action toward realizing what is good; however, absent a fixed and habitual desire for the good, there is little incentive for good actions. There is also an important social component to virtue theory in so far as one's formation is a social process. The exemplars and practices one finds in one's cultural context guide one's moral development. Virtue theory relies heavily on existing practices to provide an account of what is good and what character traits contribute to pursuing and realizing the good in concrete ways.

Utilitarianism—a form of consequentialism—favors the greatest good for the greatest number of people under a given set of constraints. A given act is morally correct if it maximizes utility, that is, if the ratio of benefit to harm (calculated by taking everyone affected by the act into consideration) is greater than the ratio resulting from an alternative act. This theory was given its most famous modern expression in the works of Jeremy Bentham (1988) and John Stuart Mill (1957), two English utilitarians writing in the 18th and 19th centuries, both of whom emphasized the greatest happiness principle as their moral standard. Utilitarianism is an attractive perspective for business decision making, especially in Western countries, because its logic is similar to an economic calculation of utility or cost-benefit, something many Western managers are accustomed to doing.

Eastern philosophy, which broadly can include various philosophies of Asia, including Indian philosophy, Chinese philosophy, Iranian philosophy, Japanese philosophy and Korean philosophy tend to view the individual as part of, rather than separate from, nature. Many Western philosophers generally assume as a given that the individual is something distinct from the entire universe, and many Western philosophers attempt to describe and categorize the universe from a detached, objective viewpoint. Eastern perspectives, on the other hand, typically hold that people are an intrinsic and inseparable part of the universe, and that attempts to discuss the universe from an objective viewpoint, as though the individual speaking were something separate and detached from the whole, are inherently absurd.

In international management, executives may rely upon one or more of these perspectives when confronted with decisions that involve ethics or morality. While they may not invoke the specific philosophical tradition by name, they likely are drawing from these fundamental moral and ethical beliefs when advancing a specific agenda or decision. The nearby International Management in Action box regarding an offshoring decision shows how a given action could be informed by each of these perspectives.

9. 1. 2   Factors that Raise Ethical Standards in Business

The two factors that raise ethical standards the most, according to the respondents in one study, are (1) public disclosure and publicity and (2) the increased concern of a well-informed public. These factors are followed by government regulations and by education to raise the professionalism of business managers.

For ethical codes to be effective, provisions must be made for their enforcement unethical managers should be held responsible for their actions. This means that privileges and benefits should be withdrawn and sanctions should be applied. Although the enforcement of ethical codes may not be easy, the mere existence of such codes can increase ethical behavior by clarifying expectations. On the other hand, one should not expect ethical codes to solve all problems. In fact, they can create a false sense of security. Effective code enforcement requires demonstration of consistent ethical behavior and support from top management. Another factor that could raise ethical standards is the teaching of ethics and values in higher education institutions.

The way of encouraging ethical corporate behavior is through whistle-blowing, which means making known to outside agencies unethical company practices. Black's Law Dictionary defines a whistle-blower as "an employee who refuses to engage in and/or reports illegal or wrongful activities of his employer or fellow employees. " There is even a whistle-blower website that discusses whistle-blowing issues, including legal matters and protection. This whistle-blowing center is a nonprofit organization that helps enforce environmental laws and works for the accountability of business and government organizations. Its primary objective is to protect and defend persons who disclose actions harmful to the environment and public health.

9. 1. 3 The Way to Become an Effective and Ethical Strategic Leader in Business

Every board of directors and the shareholders they represent want effective strategic leadership for their company. According to the upper-echelons theory, it's the top management team (at the upper echelons of an organization) that primarily determines the success or failure of an organization through the strategies they pursue. This leads us to consider the source of strategic leadership: How do you become an ethical and effective strategic leader? Is it innate? Can it be learned? The upper-echelons theory favors the idea that strong leadership is the result of both innate abilities and learning. It states that executives interpret situations through a lens of their unique perspectives, shaped by personal circumstances, values, and experiences. Their leadership actions reflect characteristics of age, education and career experiences, filtered through their personalized interpretations of the situations they face.

Given the prestige, power, and compensation of top-level executives, many aspire to be effective strategic leaders. In his bestseller *Good to Great*, strategy researcher and consultant Jim Collins identified *great companies* as those that transitioned from an average performer to achieving a sustained competitive advantage. He measured that transition as "cumulative stock returns of 6. 9 times the general market in the fifteen years following their transition points. " Collins found patterns of leadership among the companies he studied, as pictured in the Level-5 leadership pyramid in figure 9-1. The pyramid is a conceptual framework that shows leadership progression through five distinct, sequential levels. Interestingly, Collins found that all companies he identified as great were led by Level-5 executives.

According to the Level-5 leadership pyramid, effective executives go through a natural progression of five different levels. Each level builds upon the prior one, meaning the executive can move on to the next level of leadership only when the current level has been mastered. Characteristics of the five levels are:

(1) The Level-1 manager is a highly capable individual who makes productive contributions through motivation, talent, knowledge and skills.

(2) The Level-2 manager masters the skills required at Level I, but is also a contributing team member who works effectively with others in order to achieve synergies and team objectives.

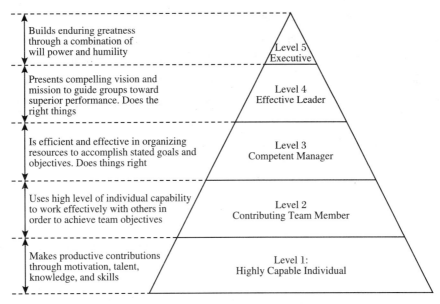

Figure 9-1   The Level-5 Pyramid

Source: Adapted from J. Collins (2001), Good to Great: Why Some Companies Make the Leap...And Others Don't (New York: HarperCollins), P. 20.

(3) The Level-3 manager is a well-rounded and competent manager, a highly capable individual who is an effective team player and organizes resources effectively to achieve predetermined goals. He or she "does things right".

(4) At Level 4, the effective manager from Level 3 turns into a leader who determines what the right decisions are. The Level-4 leader presents and effectively communicates a compelling vision and mission to guide the firm toward superior performance. He or she "does the right things".

(5) Finally, at Level 5, the manager reaches a leadership pinnacle, turning into a strategic leader. An effective strategic leader is an executive who builds enduring greatness into the organizations he or she leads.

A strategic leader who has mastered Level 5 simultaneously combines and reconcile stremendous will power and personal modesty. Such leaders, says Collins, "channel their ego needs away from themselves and into the larger goal of building a great company. It's not that Level 5 leaders have no ego or self-interest. Indeed, they are incredibly ambitious—but their ambition is first and foremost for the institution, not themselves. " Indeed, Jim Collins goes so far as to argue that the greatness of a strategic leader can truly be judged only if their organizations are able to sustain a competitive advantage in the years after the successful executive has departed from the organization.

Taken together, you become an effective and ethical leader by sequentially mastering each of the five steps in the strategic leadership pyramid. Your training in college allows you to become a highly capable individual who can make productive contributions. If you take a first job immediately after your undergraduate degree, you will likely begin your corporate career in a functional area that was your focus or major in college (e. g. , accounting, operations management, marketing, finance). As you move down the learning curve through group work in college and on-the-job training, you develop the ability to work effectively with others to achieve team objectives. With these skills, you move to Level-2 leadership. As responsibilities come to you, you will be able to develop and demonstrate the ability to organize resources efficiently and effectively to achieve strategic objectives. At Level 3, you have become an effective manager—someone who produces results.

Levels 4 and 5 require a stronger element of strategic leadership than the prior levels. When given the chance to work as a general manager (someone who has profit-and-loss responsibility for a unit or group), you will need Level-4 strategic leadership qualities.

9.1.4 Social Responsibility

Closely related to business ethics is the concept of corporate social responsibility, which is the idea that businesses have a responsibility to society beyond making profits. Corporate social responsibility means that a company must take into account the welfare of other constituents (e. g., customers, suppliers) in addition to stockholders. While business ethics usually concern the ethical dilemmas faced by managers as individuals, corporate social responsibility is usually associated with the ethical consequences of a company's policies and procedures. Monitoring the working conditions of your suppliers, paying for the education of the children of workers, and donating money to the local community are examples of corporate social responsibility in action.

In practice, ethics and social responsibility are not easily distinguished. Usually, procedures and policies in a company regarding social responsibility reflect the ethical values and decisions of the top management team. Furthermore, the ethical and social responsibility issues faced by multinational companies are complex and varied. Table 9-1 identifies some of the stakeholders in a multinational company and shows typical problems that multinational companies face and that affect their stakeholders. As the table shows, multinational companies have both primary and secondary stakeholders. Primary stakeholders are directly linked to a company's survival and include customers, suppliers, employees, and shareholders. In contrast, secondary stakeholders are less directly linked to the company's survival and include the media, trade associations, and special interest groups. Although secondary stakeholders may seem to have less potential impact on multinational companies, recent examples show that they are as important as primary shareholders in terms of their effect. Consider, for example, that Shell Oil has been forced to acknowledge its relationship with a corrupt government in Nigeria. Similarly, the agricultural giant Monsanto has been forced to deal with secondary stakeholders such as Greenpeace and Friends of the Earth as it tries to develop agricultural biotechnology products. Such examples show that addressing the needs of both groups of shareholders is critical.

Table 9-1   **Areas of Ethical and Social Responsibility Concerns for TNCs**

Stakeholder Affected	Ethical/Social Responsibility Issue	Example Problems for the TNCs
Customers	Product safety	Should an TNC delete safety features to make a product more affordable for people in a poorer nation?
	Fair price	Should a sole supplier in a country take advantage of its monopoly?
	Proper disclosures and information	Should an TNC assume the cost of translating all its product information into other languages?
Stockholders	Fair return on investment	If a product is banned becauseit is unsafe in one country, should it be sold in countries where it is not banned to maintain profit margins?
		What should a company do if it is found that the corporate executives have been involved in accounting scandals? What protection measures should be taken to protect shareholders' interests?
		How much should CEOs be paid?
		Should shareholders ignore extremely generous severance packages?
	Fair wages	Should a company pay more than market ages when such wages result in other people living in poverty?
	Safety of working conditions	Should a company be responsible for the working conditions of its suppliers'employees?

Continued

Stakeholder Affected	Ethical/Social Responsibility Issue	Example Problems for the TNCs
Employees	Child labor	Should an TNC use child labor if it is legal in the host country?
	Discrimination by sex, race, color or creed	Should a company assign a woman to a country where women are expected to remain separate from men in public?
	Impact on local economics	Should an TNC use transfer pricing and other internal accounting measures to reduce its actual tax base in a foreign country?
Host country	Following local laws	Should an TNC follow local laws that violate home country laws against discrimination?
	Impact on local social institutions	Should an TNC require its workers to work on religious holidays?
	Environmental protection	Is an TNC obligated to control its hazardous waste to a degree higher than local laws require?
Society in general	Raw material depletion	Should TNCs deplete natural resources in countries that are willing to let do no?

Johnson & Johnson's Challenges with Ethical Business Practices

we believe our first responsibility is to the doctors, nurses and patents to mothers and fathers and all others who use our products and services. In meeting their needs everything we do must be of high quality. We must constantly strive to reduce our costs in order to maintain reasonable prices. Customers' orders must be serviced promptly and accurately. Our suppliers and a distributors must have an opportunity to make a fair profit.

We are responsible to our employees, the men and women who work with us throughout the world. Everyone must be considered as an individual. We must respect their dignity and recognize their merit. They must have a sense of security in their jobs. Compensation must be fair and adequate, and working conditions clean, orderly and safe. We must be mindful of ways to help our employees fulfill their family responsibilities. Employees must feel free to make suggestions and complaints. There must be equal opportunity for employment, development and advancement for those qualified. We must provide competent management, and their actions must be just and ethical.

We are responsible to the communities in which we will live and work and to the world community as well. We must be good citizens—support good works and charities and bear our fair share of taxes. We must encourage civic improvements and better health and education. We must maintain, in good order, the property we are privileged to use, protecting the environment and natural resources.

Johnson Johnson (J&J) has experienced its fair share of ethical dilemmas over the past 25 years. The first occurred in 1982 in Chicago, Illinois, when bottles of extra-strength Tylenol capsules were found to belaced with cyanide. J&J looked to its credo of "the customer always comes first," and quickly responded to the tragedy only three days after the second tainted bottle was discovered. A recall of an estimated 31 million bottles swept the nation and lightened J&J's wallet as it experienced losses of about $100 million and an almost 30% drop, bringing it to single digits, in market share for pain relievers. By 1986 an almost full recovery showed J&J with a 33% market share for pain relievers when another unfortunate poisoning occurred. At this point, J&J recalled all Tylenol capsules and still maintained 96% of sales despite the setback. J&J is often cited for its impressive response to this crisis. More recently, J&J disclosed that "improper payments in connection with the sale of medical devices" were made in some units. Adding insult to injury, Janssen, a J&J subsidiary, inappropriately marketed a psychiatric product targeted for use in children, resulting in a combined $117 million in costs to the Texas Medicaid program. More recently, J&J has faced several scandals. In January 2010, the U. S. Justice Department charged J&J with paying millions of dollars in kickbacks to Omnicare, the nation's largest pharmacy that specializes in dispensing drugs to nursing home patients so its Risperdal antipsychotic would be widely prescribed. In April 2010, J& J's Ortho-McNeil Pharmaceutical and Ortho-McNeil-Janssen Pharmaceuticals subsidiaries agreed to pay $81 million in order to resolve criminal and civil lawsuits charging the units with illegally promoting the Topamax epilepsy drug for so-called off-label use. The government alleged that the company promoted Topamax for off-label psychiatric uses through a program called "Doctor-for-a-Day" in which the J&J unit hired outside physicians to join sales reps in visiting other doctors and to speak at meetings and dinners about prescribing Topamax for unapproved uses and doses. Also in April 2010, the FDA found quality problems at a J&J facility, prompting a broad-based recall affecting about 70% of the market for over-the-counter paediatric liquid medications, including Tylenol, Motrin, Benadryl and Zyrtec, among dozens of others. Why is Johnson & Johnson facing continued problems of this sort? Is the credo helping J&J to resolve these issues?

(Source: Johnson & Johnson website, http://www pharmalot. com.)

9. 1. 5 Arguments For and Against Business Involvement in Social Actions

Although there are arguments for business involvement in social activities, there are also arguments against it, as shown in Table 9-2.

Table 9-2   Arguments For and Against Social Involvement of Business

Arguments for social involvement of business
1. Public needs have changed, leading to changed expectations. Business, it is suggested, received its charter from society and consequently has to respond to the needs of society.
2. The creation of a better social environment benefits both society and business. Society gains through better neighborhoods and employment opportunities; business benefits from a better community, since the community is the source of its workforce and the consumer of its products and services.
3. Social involvement discourages government regulation and intervention. The result is greater freedom and more flexibility in decision-making for business.
4. Business has a great deal of power that, it is reasoned, should be accompanied by an equal amount of responsibility.
5. Modern society is an interdependent system, and the internal activities of the enterprise have an impact on the external environment.
6. Social involvement may be in the interests of stockholders.
7. Problems can become profits. Items that may once have been considered waste (e. g. , empty soft-drink cans) can be profitably used again.
8. Social involvement creates a favorable public image. As a result, the firm may attract customers, employees, and investors.
9. Business should try to solve the problems that other institutions have not been able to solve. After all, business has a history of coming up with novel ideas.
10. Business has the resources. Specifically, business should use the talents of its managers and specialists, as well as its capital resources, to solve some of society's problems.
11. It is better to prevent social problems through business involvement than to cure them. It may be easier to help the hard-core unemployed than to cope with social unrest.
Arguments against social involvement of business
1. The primary task of business is to maximize profit by focusing strictly on economic activities. Social involvement could reduce economic efficiency.
2. In the final analysis, society must pay for the social involvement of business through higher prices. Social involvement would create excessive costs for business, which cannot commit its resources to social action.
3. Social involvement can create a weakened international balance-of-payment situation. The cost of social programs, the reasoning goes, would have to be added to the price of the product. Thus, socially involved companies selling in international markets would be at a disadvantage when competing with companies from other countries that do not have these social costs to bear.
4. Business has enough power, and additional social involvement would further increase its power and influence.
5. Business people lack the social skills to deal with the problems of society. Their training and experience are with economic matters, and their skills may not be pertinent to social problems.
6. There is a lack of accountability of business to society. Unless accountability can be established, business should not get involved.
7. There is not full support for involvement in social actions. Consequently, disagreements among groups with different viewpoints will cause friction.

Source: Based on a variety of sources, including william C. Frederick, Keith Davis, and James Post, Business and Society, 6th ed, New York: McGraw-Hill, 1985.

Today, many businesses are involved in social actions. A good example is the Ben& Jerry ice cream company, which contributes to the conservation of the rainforest. The company also purchases nuts from tribes in the rainforest so that they do not rely on cutting trees for survival. A decision as to whether companies should extend their social involvement requires careful examination of the arguments for and against such actions. Certainly, society's expectations are changing, and the trend seems to be toward greater social responsiveness.

9.2   TNCs' Business Ethics and Social Responsibility Under the Cross-Cultural Background

9.2.1   Ethics and Social Responsibility in Cross-Cultural Management

Unbiased ethical decision-making processes are imperative to modern cross-cultural business practices. It is difficult to determine a universal ethical standard when the views and norms in one country can vary substantially from others. Ethics, the study of morality and standards of conduct, is often the victim of subjectivity as it yields to the will of cultural relativism, or the belief that the ethical standard of a country is based on the culture that created it and that moral concepts lack universal application.

The adage "When in Rome, do as the Romans do" is derived from the idea of cultural relativism and suggests that businesses and the managers should be have in accordance with the ethical standards of the country they are active in, regardless of TNC headquarter location. It is necessary, to some extent, to rely on local teams to execute under local rule; however, this can be taken to extremes. While a business whose only objective is to make a profit may opt to take advantage of these differences in norms and standards in order to legally gain leverage over the competition it may find that negative consumer opinion about unethical business practices, not to mention potential legal action, could affect the bottom line. Dilemmas that arise from conflicts between ethical standards of a country and business ethics, or the moral code guiding business behavior, are most evident in employment and business practices recognition of human rights, including women in the workplace, and corruption. The newer area of corporate social responsibility (CSR) is closely related to ethics. Ethics is the study of or the learning process involved in understanding morality, while CSR involves taking action.

Furthermore, the area of ethics has a lawful component and implies right and wrong in a legal sense, while CSR is based more on voluntary actions. Business ethics and CSR maybe therefore viewed as two complementary dimensions of a company's overall social profile and position.

9.2.2 Differing Ethical Standards across Cultures

Ethical as well as legal standards differ, particularly between nations and cultures. For example, certain nations permit privately owned companies to make monetary contributions to political parties, campaigns, and candidates (which is prohibited in the United States). In some countries, payments to government officials and other persons with political influence to ensure favorable handling of a business or other transactions are regarded not as bribes but as payments for services rendered. In some cases, payments made in order to win a contract are even looked upon as a normal and acceptable way of doing business. Consider the Quaker Oats Company, which faced a situation in which foreign officials threatened to close its operation if the demand for "payouts" was not met; or a company may find itself in a predicament where its plant manager's safety will be in jeopardy if payoffs are not made. The question facing responsible foreign business managers is: What ethical standards should they follow? For example, guanxi, which pertains to informal relationships and exchange of favors, influences business activities in China and East Asia. There is no question of what to do in similar situations in the United States: executives have to refuse the suggestion of putting money in a "paper bag". But in a country where such practices are expected and are common, American executives are faced with a difficult problem. With the passage of laws by the U. S. Congress and the adoption of regulations by the Securities and Exchange Commission, not only must American firms report anything that could be called a payoff but also anything else that can be construed as a bribe is unlawful. The Foreign Corrupt Practices Act (FCPA) Antibribery Provisions state: "U. S. firms seeking to do business in foreign markets must be familiar with the FCPA. In general, the FCPA prohibits corrupt payments to foreign officials for the purpose of obtaining or keeping business. " Thus, the United States has attempted to export its standards for doing business to other countries which can improve ethical standards abroad.

Truth in Advertising Regulations Differ in Various Countries

Advertising in China is getting tougher. Proctor Gamble (P&G) claimed that its

Pantene product makes the hair ten times stronger. Government authorities demanded proof which was difficult to show through objective studies. Consequently, P&G withdrew the advertising. In the past, advertisers in China were relatively free in making claims for their products. Yet, a 1995 Chinese law stated that statistical claims should be accurate and true.

Advertising regulations differ among countries. In the U. S., for example, the Federal Trade Commission provides an oversight. Moreover, competitors also watch for and expose questionable claims of their adversaries. In most European countries. industry is guided by self-regulation as well as strong governmental regulation.

9. 2. 3   TNCs' Social and Organizational Responsibility for Sustainability

TNCs are increasingly engaged in a range of responses to growing pressures to contribute positively to the social and environmental progress of the communities in which they do business. One response is the agreements and codes of conduct in which TNCs commit to maintain certain standards in their domestic and global operations. These agreements, which include the U. N. Global Compact, the Global Reporting Initiative, the social accountability "SA8000" standards, and the ISO 14000 environmental quality standards, provide some assurances that when TNCs do business around the world, they will maintain a minimum level of social and environmental standards in the workplaces and communities in which they operate. These codes help offset the real or perceived concern that companies move Jobs to avoid higher labor or environmental standards in their home markets. They may also contribute to the raising of standards in the developing world by "exporting" higher standards to local firms in those countries. Another interesting trend among businesses and NGOs is the movement toward increasing the availability of "fairly traded" products. Beginning with coffee and moving to chocolate, fruits, and other agricultural products, fair trade is an organized social movement and market-based approach that aims to help producers in developing countries obtain better trading conditions and promote sustainability.

In the boardroom, the term sustainability may first be associated with financial investments or the hope of steadily increasing profits, but for a growing number of companies, this term means the same to them as it does to an environmental conservationist. Partially this is due to corporations recognizing that dwindling resources will eventually halt productivity, but the World Economic Forum in Davos, Switzerland, has also played a part in bringing awareness to this timely subject. While the January 24, 2007, gathering obviously put profit at the top of the agenda, it was closely followed by the concern for global warming and environmentally damaging practices, marking a new era with sustainability as a high priority concern. While the United States has the Environmental Protection Agency to provide information about and enforce environmental laws, the United Nations also has a division dedicated to the education, promotion, facilitation, and advocacy of sustainable practices and environmentally sound concerns called the United Nations Environment Programme (UNEP), The degree to which global awareness and concern are rising extends beyond laws and regulations, as corporations are now taking strides to be leaders in this "green" movement.

Walmart, one of the most well-known and pervasive global retailers, has begun to recognize the numerous benefits of the adage. "Think globally, act locally". Working with environmentalists, it discovered that changes in production and supply chain practices could reduce waste and pollution and therefore reduce costs. By cutting back on packaging, Walmart saves an estimated $2.4 million a year, 3,800 trees, and 1 million barrels of oil. Over 80,000 compete to put their products on Walmart shelves, which means that this company has a strong influence on how manufacturers do business. And Walmart's efforts are truly global. The company is buying solar and wind power in Mexico, sourcing local food in China and India, and analyzing the life cycle impact of consumer products in Brazil. Alleviating hunger has become a goal of Walmart's charitable efforts, and so with CARE it is backing education, job-training, and entrepreneurial programs for women in Peru, Bangladesh, and India. Walmart is attempting to change global standards as it offers higher prices to coffee growers in Brazil and increases pressures on the factory owners in China to reduce energy and fuel costs. As noted in this chapter's opening discussion, GE has pursued an aggressive initiative to integrate environmental sustainability with its business goals through the "ecomagination" program. Management styles again are changing as agendas are refocused on not only seeing the present but also looking to the future of human needs and the environment.

9.2.4 The Implications of CSR for Chinese TNCs' Competitiveness

1. CSR Development in China

The CSR movement was introduced into China in the mid-1990s. when brand names started to impose various supplier codes of conduct to the textiles and garment factories under the pressure from anti sweat shop activities abroad. China's CSR development illustrates two opposite forces, drastically increasing profile of CSR on one hand and continuous strong resistance on the other.

Reluctant to follow suit in addressing social issues related to business operation the same way the westerners do, the Chinese leadership emphasizes sustainability policies in other terms at macro-level, such as promise to the world that by 2020 it will quadruple its economic growth while only doubling its energy use; and domestically, the government advocates the idea of encouraging businesses contribute to sustainable social and economic development. In 2004, the Chinese government announced a new green measurement of GDP taking into account the wider social and environmental costs of China's economic growth, demonstrating China's willingness to catch up with sustainable development policies.

Among businesses, most Chinese companies are actually just getting started with a learning process on CSR initiatives, but CSR takes ground in China expeditiously, in particular among managers of export-oriented factories. Many large-sized enterprises recognize an increasingly active CSR engagement will offer them a chance to become globally competitive, for example, participation in the global Compact. However, it's important to note that Chinese companies are expecting short term business interest in participating in CSR initiatives, and largely motivated by the benefits of securing contracts from international buyers.

CSR engagement presents a geographical disparity in China due to level of economic development and sectoral focus. The most advanced region in terms of CSR awareness and engagement is evidently the South China Guangdong province, which accounted for 1/3 of nation's total exports and where most foreign invested enterprises are based. China's CSR engagement has not yielded any systematic approach so far, and the notion of sustainable development is still a new concept to many business managers. Most companies taking philanthropy as substitute of CSR, and others hold a "wait and see" attitude for government regulatory pressures.

2. What does CSR Imply to TNCs from China

Supported by the government policies of "going global" and of creating 30 ~ 50 internationally competitive "global champions" firms, an increasing number of Chinese firms are now among the largest TNCs from developing countries, in terms of foreign assets: in 1994, only 7 Chinese enterprises were among the top 50 largest TNCs from developing countries; by 2001, 12 TNCs were in the top 50, and 6 of them had foreign assets of above $2 billion.

Chinese TNCs are picking up a fast-track learning process of CSR. Till 2004, Haier was the only Chinese brand recognized in the Global Name Brand List edited by World Brand Laboratory, one of five world brand evaluation agencies. Its brand building in the 1980s focused on technical qualities and in the 1990s on innovation. During its globalization process in which Haier expanded its manufacturing bases overseas, it clearly experienced the pressure from environmental regulation and safety standards. Green marketing and consumption now dominates the senior managements agenda, for example, in the R&D of central air conditioner products, Haier prioritizes "energy saving and health" as two major themes. Its senior management has developed new concept of running business that emphasizes contribution that Haier should make to the society, their focus has changed from the 1980s' "Flawed products are nothing but a waste" to today's "Haier will become an integral part of the society".

The Economic Weekly of the People's Daily conducted a comparative analysis between China's 500 strong enterprises with those of the world. It pointed out the threat to China's long-term competitiveness that China's high-speed economic growth has been done at a big price of resources and environment. "In 2003, the per unit GDP consumption of energy resources was 10 times that of Japan, 5 times of the USA and 3 times of Canada, and the metal consumption was 2 ~ 4 times that of the world average".

UNCTAD survey found the main driving force for Chinese TNCs' internationalization is "the need to bypass trade barriers" and "the need to utilize domestic production capacity" because the home market for their products is too small, are key drivers of internationalization. The future "Chinese giants", will unavoidably encounter the CSR challenges when they move to a market with higher social standards, and what left to Chinese TNCs, and other developing-country TNCs, is to find out how to apply CSR to enhance their visibility and marketability through intangible assets building and technology and management innovation.

9.3　Case

Case-1

How to Design an Ethical Organization

From Volkswagen's emissions fiasco to Wells Fargo's deceptive sales practices to Uber's privacy intrusions, corporate wrongdoing is a continuing reality in global business. Unethical behavior takes a significant toll on organizations by damaging reputations, harming employee morale, and increasing regulatory costs—not to mention the wider damage to society's overall trust in business. Few executives set out to achieve advantage by breaking the rules, and most companies have programs in place to prevent malfeasance at all levels. Yet recurring scandals show that we could do better.

Interventions to encourage ethical behavior are often based on misperceptions of how transgressions occur and thus are not as effective as they could be. Compliance programs increasingly take a legalistic approach to ethics that focuses on individual accountability. They're designed to educate employees and then punish wrongdoing among the "bad apples" who misbehave. Yet a large body of behavioral science research suggests that even well-meaning and well-informed people are more ethically malleable than one might guess. When watching a potential emergency unfold, for example, people are much more likely to intervene if they are alone than if other bystanders are around—because they think others will deal with the situation believe that others are more qualified to help, or fail to recognize an emergency because others don't look alarmed. Small changes to the context can have a significant effect on a person's behavior. Yet people in the midst of these situations tend not to recognize the influence of context. In Stanley Milgram's famous obedience experiments, participants who were told by an authority figure to deliver increasingly powerful electric shocks to another person progressed to a much higher voltage than other people predicted they themselves would deliver. Context is not just powerful, researchers have learned; it is surprisingly powerful.

Pillars of an Ethical Culture

CREATING AN ETHICAL culture thus requires thinking about ethics not simply as a belief problem but also as a design problem. We have identified four critical features that need to be addressed when designing an ethical culture: explicit values, thoughts during judgment, incentives, and cultural norms.

EXPLICIT VALUES. strategies and practices should be anchored to clearly stated principles that can be widely shared within the organization a well-crafted mission statement can help achieve this, as long as it is used correctly. Leaders can refer to it to guide the creation of any new strategy or initiative and note its connection to the company's principles when addressing employees, thus reinforcing the broader ethical system. Employees should easily be able to see how ethical principles influence a company's practices. They're likely to be have differently if they think the organization is being guided by the ethos of Mr. Rogers, the relentlessly kind PBS show host, versus that of Gordon Gekko, the relentlessly greedy banker in the film Wall Street. Indeed, in one experiment, 70% of participants playing an economic game with a partner cooperated for mutual gain when it was called the Community Game, but only 30% cooperated when it was called the Wall Street Game. This dramatic effect occurred even though the financial incentives were identical.

A mission statement should be simple, short, actionable, and emotionally resonant. Most corporate mission statements today are too long to remember, too obvious to need stating, too clearly tailored for regulators, or too distant from day-to-day practices to meaningfully guide employees. A statement can't be just words on paper; it must undergird not only strategy but policies around hiring firing, promoting, and operations so that core ethical principles are deeply embedded throughout the organization. Patagonia's mission statement, for instance, is "Build the best product, cause no unnecessary harm, use business to inspire and implement solutions to the environmental crisis. " Its Worn Wear initiative implements its mission by enabling employees to help consumers repair or recycle their products. Patagonia also developed a standardized metric, posted on its website, to evaluate the environmental impact of its entire supply chain. Zappos says its number one core value is to "Deliver WOW through service" to customers, according them respect and dignity. It implements this value by not measuring the average length of customer service calls (the industry standard), so employees can spend as much time with customers as necessary. Mission statements like these help keep an organization's values crystal clear in employees' minds.

THOUGHTS DURING JUDGMENT. Most people have less difficulty knowing what's right or wrong than they do keeping ethical considerations top of mind when making decisions. Ethical lapses can therefore be reduced in a culture where ethics are at the center of attention You might know that it's wrong to hurt someone else's chances of being hired but fail to think of the harm you cause to unknown applicants when trying to help a friend, a family member, or a business school classmate land a job. Behavior tends to be guided by what comes to mind immediately before engaging in an action, and those thoughts can be meaning fully affected by context. Should someone remind you that helping a friend necessarily hurts the chances of people you don't happen to know, you might think twice about whether your advocacy efforts are appropriate.

Several experiments make this point. In one, people were more likely to tell the truth when an honor code came at the beginning of a form-thereby putting ethics top of mind as they completed the form-than when it was posted at the end. In a large field experiment of approximately 18,000 U. S. government contractors, simply adding a box for filers to check certifying their honesty while reporting yielded $28. 6 million more in sales tax revenue than did a condition that omitted the box. And in a simulation that asked MBA students to play the role of financial adviser, having them complete an ethics checklist before recommending potential investment funds significantly decreased the percentage who recommended what turned out to be the Madoff feeder fund. When ethics were top of mind, the students were more alert to the possibility that the fund was too good to be true.

As a counter example, Enron was notorious for its constant focus on stock price, even posting it in the elevators. Reflecting on his own misdeeds, its former CFO Andy Fastow said, "I knew it was wrong...But I didn't think it was illegal... The question I should have asked is not what is the rule, but what is the principle. " People working in an ethical culture are routinely triggered to think, Is it right? rather than Is it legal?

INCENTIVES. It is a boring truism that people do what they're incentivized to do, meaning that aligning rewards with ethical outcomes is an obvious solution to many ethical problems. That may sound simple just pay people for acting ethically, but money goes only so far, and incentive programs must provide a variety of rewards to be effective.

Along with earning an income, employees care about doing meaningful work, making a positive impact, and being respected or appreciated for their efforts. In one experiment hospital staff members were more likely to follow correct hand washing procedures when a sign above the sink reminded them of consequences to others ("hand hygiene prevents patients from catching diseases") than when it reminded them of personal consequences. Nevertheless, managers may easily overlook the importance of nonfinancial incentives. When asked how important such incentives were to employees, customer service managers at one Fortune 500 firm tended to dramatically underestimate what they meant to their reports.

In addition to aligning financial incentives with desired outcomes, ethical cultures provide explicit opportunities to benefit others and reward people who do so with recognition, praise, and validation. If, for instance, your employees are making people's lives meaningfully better in some way, pointing that out will encourage future ethical behavior. It may even improve performance, because the reward is aligned with ethical motivation. In one experiment, salespeople for a large pharmaceutical company performed dramatically better after participating in a prosocial bonus system, which encouraged them to spend a small award on their teammates, compared with a typical "proself" bonus system, in which they spent the award on themselves.

This approach to incentives may have ancillary HR benefits. People tend to underestimate both how positive they will feel about connecting with others in a prosocial way and the positive impact their behavior will have on other. In a field experiment with Virgin Atlantic pilots, a bonus system for increasing fuel economy was structured so that the bonus went to a charity of their choosing. The resulting increase in their job satisfaction was similar in magnitude to the effect of moving from poor health to good health. Companies that use prosocial incentives are likely to produce happier, more satisfied, and more loyal employees. An ethical culture not only does good; it also feels good.

CULTURAL NORMS. Most leaders intuitively recognize the importance of "tone at the top" for setting ethical standards in an organization. Easily overlooked is "tone in the middle", which may actually be a more significant driver of employees' behavior. Good leaders produce good followers; but if employees in the middle of the organization are surrounded by coworkers who are lying, cheating, or stealing, they will most likely do the same, regardless of what their bosses say. So-called descriptive norms—how peers actually behave—tend to exert the most social influence. In one field experiment conducted by a UK government agency, 13 versions of a letter were sent to delinquent taxpayers, including versions that referenced moral principles, the ease of paying taxes or financial penalties. The most effective letter compared the recipient's behavior with that of fellow citizens: "Nine out of ten people in the uk pay their taxes on time. You are currently in the very small minority of people who have not paid us yet. "

People often fail to appreciate the power of social norms. When researchers were interested in determining how best to encourage energy efficiency among a group of Californians, for instance, they first asked a group of nearly 1,000 residents to predict the effectiveness of various approaches, including appeals to environmental protection, personal financial benefits, societal benefits, and social norms (what percentage of neighbors conserved energy by using fans). These residents expected that the environmental appeal would be most persuasive and the social norm appeal least persuasive. But when the researchers sent about 1,000 other residents one of the four appeals, the social norm had by far the biggest effect on reducing energy use.

Leaders can encourage an ethical culture by highlighting the good things employees are doing. Although the natural tendency is to focus on cautionary tales or "ethical black holes", doing so can make undesirable actions seem more common than they really are, potentially increasing unethical behavior. To create more ethical norms, focus instead on "ethical beacons?" in your organization:

people who are putting the mission statement into practice or behaving in an exemplary fashion.

Putting Ethical Design into Practice

A LEADER DESIGNING. An ethical culture should try to create contexts that keep ethical principles top of mind, reward ethics through formal and informal incentives and opportunities, and weave ethics into day-to-day behavior. Precisely how this is achieved will vary among organizations, but here are a few examples.

HIRING. First impressions are inordinately powerful. For many employees, an organization's values were revealed during the hiring process. Although interviews are typically treated as opportunities for identifying the best candidate, they also begin the acculturation process. At one Fortune100 firm, for instance, interview questions are designed around a core value, such as putting customer needs first. In one interview script, candidates are told of this value and then asked, "Tell me about a time when you uncovered an unmet need of a customer that you were able to address. " We don't know if this question identified people who are good at treating customers respectfully, but that's not necessarily the point. Highlighting values in the interview reveals their importance to the organization. It is one piece of a broader system that draws attention to ethics.

EVALUATION. Ethics can also be woven into the design of performance evaluations to highlight their importance to an organization as well as to reward and encourage good behavior. At Johnson&Johnson, for instance. each executive's 360-degree evaluation is built on the four components of the company's famous credo, which expresses commitment to customers, employees, communities, and stakeholders. In one version of the evaluation we saw each executive was rated on items such as "nurtures commitment to our credo", "confronts actions that are or border on the unethical" and "establishes an environment in which uncompromising integrity is the norm".

COMPENSATION. Aligning financial incentives with ethical outcomes may sound easy in principle, but it is tricky in practice. This is where a mission statement can help. Southwest Airlines has used an executive scorecard to tie compensation to its four core values: every employee matters, every flight matters, every customer matters, and every share holder matters. Each value is demonstrated by an objective measurement—"every employee matters " by voluntary turnover; "every flight matters" by ontime performance. This scorecard highlights how well core ethical values align with business success, helps keep employees' attention on them, and suggests the behaviors needed to realize them.

Leaders can reward ethical actions by showing employees the positive impact of their work on others and recognizing their actions in presentations and publications. They can also create opportunities within the organization to behave ethically toward colleagues. In one recent field experiment, managers were randomly assigned to perform five acts of kindness for certain fellow employees over a four-week period. Not only did this increase the number of kind acts observed within the organization, but recipients were more likely than controls to subsequently do kind things for other employees, demonstrating that ethical behavior can be contagious. These acts of kindness improved well-being for those performing them as well as for recipients. Perhaps most important, depressive symptoms dropped dramatically among both groups compared with the control condition, a result that continued for at least three months beyond the initial one-month intervention.

Ethics, by Design

NO COMPANY WILL ever be perfect because no human being is perfect Indeed, some companies we've used as examples have had serious ethical lapses. Real people are not purely good or purely evil but are capable of doing both good and evil. Organizations should aim to design a system that makes being good as easy as possible. That means attending carefully to the contexts people are actually in, making ethical principles foundational in strategies and policies, keeping ethics top of mind, rewarding ethical behavior through a variety of incentives, and encouraging ethical norms in day-to-day practices. Doing so will never turn an organization full of humans into a host of angels, but it can help them be as ethical as they are capable of being.

(Source: Nicholas Epley, Amit Kumar. How to Design an Ethical Organization? Harvard Business Review, May-June, 2019.)

Questions:

1. What is the impact of unethical behavior for an organization?

2. What is the significance of pillars of an ethical culture for TNCs?

3. In addition to the ways offered in the material, what other ways do you know to practice ethical design?

Case-2

Calculating the Value of Impact Investing

An evidence-based way to estimate social and environmental returns

As concerns about scarcity and inequality become increasingly urgent, many investors are eager to generate both business and social returns—to "do well by doing good" . One avenue is impact investing: directing capital to ventures that are expected to yield social and environmental benefits as well as profits. But there's a problem: Although the business world has several universally accepted tools, such as the internal rate of return, for estimating a potential investments financial yields, no analogue exists for evaluating hoped-for social and environmental rewards in dollar terms. Forecasting gains is too often a matter of guesswork.

Investors hoping to use a company's track record on social and environmental impact to assess future opportunities will similarly find little useful data to evaluate The reporting of environmental, social and governance issues is now standard practice at nearly three-quarters of the world's large and mid-cap companies, but it is usually confined to information about commitments and process and rarely scores actual impact.

Over the past two years the organizations we work for the rise Fund, a $2 billion impact-investing fund managed by TPG Growth, and the Bridgespan Group, a global social impact advisory firm-have attempted to bring the rigor of financial performance measurement to the assessment of social and environmental impact. Through trial and error, and in collaboration with experts who have been working for years in the field, the partnership between Rise and Bridgespan has produced a methodology to estimate—before any money is committed—the financial value of the social and environmental good that is likely to result from each dollar invested. Thus social-impact investors, whether corporations or institutions, can evaluate the projected return on an opportunity. We call our new metric the impact multiple of money (IMM).

Calculating an IMM is not a trivial undertaking, so any business that wishes to use it must first determine which products, services, or projects warrant the effort. As an equity investor, Rise does a qualitative assessment of potential investments to filter out deals that are unlikely to pass the IMM hurdle, just as it filters out deals that are not financially promising companies with a social purpose and a potentially measurable impact get a green light for IMM evaluation. Rise will invest in a company only if the IMM calculation suggests a minimum social return on investment of $2. 50 for every $1 invested. Businesses that adopt this metric can set their own minimum thresholds.

To be clear, numerous assumptions and choices are involved in this process, precluding any claim that our method can provide a definitive number. But we believe that this approach provides valuable guidance regarding which investments will or will not have a significant social impact.

In the following pages we explain how to calculate an IMM during an investment-selection process. The method consists of six steps.

1. Assess the relevance and scale

Investors should begin by considering the relevance and scale of a product, a service, or a project for evaluation a manufacturer of home appliances may want to consider investing in energy-saving features in its product lines. A health clinic provider may want to assess the potential social benefits of expanding into low-income neighborhoods.

With regard to scale, ask, how many people will the product or service reach, and how deep will its impact be? Rise's experience with calculating the product reach of the educational-technology company EverFi, one of its first impact investments, provides a good example (The financial and participation data in this article is representative; the actual numbers are confidential). Rise identified three EverFi programs that already had significant reach: Alcoholedu-an online course designed to deter alcohol abuse among college students, which was given at more than 400 universities; Haven, which educates college students about dating violence and sexual harassment and is used at some 650 universities; and a financial literacy program that introduces students to credit cards, interest rates, taxes, insurance and is offered at more than 6,100 high schools. On the basis of projected annual student enrollments in these programs, Rise estimated that an investment in EverFi could affect 6.1 million students over a five-year period beginning in 2017.

Of course, a program's impact is not just about the number of people touched; it's about the improvement achieved. Fewer people touched deeply may be worth more than many people hardly affected. Consider another rise investment, Dodla Dairy, which procures and processes fresh milk every day from more than 220,000 smallholder farmers across rural southern India. The number of farmers affected was known so what Rise needed to assess was how much milk dodla was likely to buy from them and at whatprice. With projected sales of 2.6 billion liters of milk over five years, Rise estimated that investments in Dodla would increase farm families' annual incomes by 73%, from $425 to $735. Smallholder farmers with a reliable buyer for their milk spend less time and money marketing and have the predictability and support needed to make long-term investments, increasing milk yields and, therefore, income.

2. Identify target social or environmental outcomes

The second step in calculating an IMM is identifying the desired social or environmental outcomes and determining whether existing research verifies that they are achievable and measurable. Fortunately, investors can draw on a huge array of social science reports to estimate a company's impact potential. Over the past decade foundations, nonprofits, and some policy makers (including the U. S. Department of Education's Investing in Innovation Fund) have relied heavily on research results to guide funding for social programs. This "what works" movement has spurred the development of an industry around social-outcome measurement led by organizations such as MDRC, a nonprofit social-policy research organization; the Abdul Latif Jameel Poverty Action Lab (J-PAL), at MIT; and Mathematica Policy research, basedin Princeton, New Jersey.

For AlcoholEdu we drew on a 2010 randomized controlled trial demonstrating that students who had been exposed to the program experienced an 11% reduction in "alcohol-related incidents" such as engaging in risky behaviors, doing or saying embarrassing things, or feeling bad about themselves because of their drinking. That would amount to some 239, 350 fewer incidents. According to the National Institutes of Health, alcohol-related deaths account for about 15% of all deaths among college students in the United States. Rise estimated that AlcoholEdu would save 36 lives among the approximately 2. 2 million students who were projected to engage with the program over a five-year period. (Lives saved, arguably the most important impact of less drinking are relatively straight forward to monetize. But reducing alcohol abuse clearly has additional benefits for individuals and society.)

For Haven we focused on the prevention of sexual assault. Some 10. 3% of undergraduate women and 2. 5% of undergraduate men experience sexual assault every year. According to a 2007 study that evaluated the effects of an in-person course on preventing sexual assault that was taught at a college in the northeastern United States, assault declined by about 19% for women and 36% for men among those who took the course.

Applying this data to 2. 6 million students expected to experience the Haven program over five years, and assuming that an equal number of college women and men participated, Rise estimated that the program would avert 25, 869 incidents of sexual assault among women, and 12, 029 incidents among men.

3. Estimate the economic value of those outcomes to society

Once they have identified the target outcomes, social impact investors need to find an "anchor study" hat robustly translates those outcomes into economic terms. Cellulanta regional African provider of a mobile payments platform used by banks, major retailers, telecommunications companies, and governments, is a good example. Cellulant worked with the Nigerian Ministry of Agriculture to redesign a corruption-plagued program that provided seed and fertilizer subsidies. The company developed a cell phone App that allows farmers to pick up their subsidized goods directly from local merchants, reducing the opportunity for graft. The program had been losing 89% of funds to mismanagement and corruption. Cellulant's app now enables delivery of 90% of the intended aid.

Our task was to understand the economic impact on farmers when they received the subsidized seed and fertilizer. We used a reliable study that compared one seasons outcomes for farmers enrolled in the subsidy program with those for similar farmers who were not enrolled. The study found that participating farmers earned an additional $99 that season by improving maize yields.

To choose an anchor study we look at several key features. First, its rigor: Does the study systematically evaluate previous research results to derive conclusions about that body of research? Alternatively, does it present findings from a randomized controlled trial-which compares groups with and without a designated intervention? Both types of research are preferable to observational or case studies. Just as important is relevance: Does the study include people living in similar contexts (urban, say, or rural) and in the same income bracket? The closer the match the better. Recent studies are better than older ones. And studies frequently cited in the research literature deserve extra consideration.

When uncertainty or a lack of reliable research stalls your work, seek guidance from an expert in the field. For example we sought advice from the Center for Financial Services Innovation, in Chicago, when we could not locate appropriate studies demonstrating the impact of helping people establish a regular savings habit—one of three impact pathways we were examining for Acorns, a fintech company for low-and middle-income individuals. That callled us to research showing that even modest savings among the target group can reduce the use of high-cost payday loans.

To translate the outcomes of AlcoholEdu into dollar terms, we turned to the U. S. Department of Transportation's guidance on valuing the reduction of fatalities or injuries which uses a measure called the value of a statistical life. According to this anchor study a fatality is worth $5.4 million. Thus AlcoholEdu could expect to generate social value of at least $194 million by saving 36 lives.

In the case of haven we found that researchers at the National Institutes of Health have done quite a bit of work on the economic impact of sexual assault. In fact, the NIH has pegged the legal, health, and economic costs of a single assault at $16,657, adjusted for inflation. Rise multiplied the NIH figure by the estimated number of sexual assaults. Haven would avert (37,898) to get close to 632 million. Because sexual assault is under reported, Rise believes that Haven's impact may be even greater.

For EverFi's financial literacy program we relied on a 2016 study that looked at a similar program for high school students. It found that program participants had an average of $538 less in consumer debt at the age of 22 than a similar group of students who hadn't been exposed to the program. On average, interest paid on that additional debt came to about $81 over five years. Assuming that 1.3 million students completed the EverFi program over five years and they all saved $81, the economic value of the program would total $105 million.

We estimated that the social impact of the three EverFi programs combined had a five-year economic value of about $931 million: $194 million for AlcoholEdu, $632 million for Haven, and $105 million for financial literacy.

4. Adjust for Risks

Although we have proved to our satisfaction that social science research can be used to monetize social and environmental benefits, we recognize the risk in applying findings from research that is not directly linked to a given investment opportunity. Therefore we adjust the social values derived from applying the anchor study to reflect the quality and relevance of the research. We do this by calculating an "impact realization" index. We assign values to six risk categories and total them to arrive at an impact-probability score on a 100-point scale.

Two of the index components relate to the quality of the anchor study and how directly it is linked to the product or service. Together these accounts for 60 of the possible 100 points. Anchor studies based on a meta-analysis or a randomized controlled trial merit top scores, whereas observational studies rate lower. AlcoholEdu's study was in the former category; Haven's and the financial literacy program's studies were in the latter.

Establishing the linkage between an anchor study and the desired outcome of a product or service sometimes requires making assumptions and with more assumptions comes greater risk. For example, the anchor study for EverFi's financial literacy program clearly linked the training to lower student debt, resulting in a maximum rating. But AlcoholEdu and Haven relied on studies with less clear linkages AlcoholEdu assumes that its training leads to fewer negative alcohol incidents, resulting in lower rates of alcohol-related death. The anchor study for Haven assumes that sexual-assault-prevention training leads to fewer assaults, and thus to fewer of the consequences of those assaults.

The four remaining index components, each of which gets a maximum score of 10, are context (Does the study's social environment correspond to the project's? For instance are they both urban, or is one rural?) country income group (Are the populations of the study and the project in the same country income bracket as determined by the World Bank?) product or service similarity (how closely do the activities in the study correspond to what the project provides? For example, is the product or service delivered to the same age group in both?) and projected usage (Is there a risk that once a product or service is purchased, it will not be used as intended? Consider that gym memberships have a high drop-off rate.).

In applying the index to EverFi's programs, Rise calculated impact-probability scores for AlcoholEdu, Haven and the financial literacy program at 85%, 55%, and 75% respectively. Then it adjusted their estimated monetary impact accordingly, arriving at $164 million for AlcoholEdu, $348 million for Haven, and $77 million for the financial literacy program. The risk-adjusted impact for all three programs totaled $589 million, down from $931 million.

Constructing the index proved challenging. We refined the risk categories and the values assigned to each many times on the basis of feedback from experts in evaluation and measurement. For example one version emphasized the importance of comparing study results according to geography-say, country or continent. But experts advised that a more accurate comparison would juxtapose studies of similar income groups, regardless of country or living circumstances (urban versus rural).

The impact-realization index attempts to capture the most important elements of risk, but we recognize that it does not capture every threat to impact or all the nuances of risk between anchor studies and a company's product or service. We expect to make refinements as others bring new ideas to the table.

5. Estimate Terminal Value

In finance, terminal value estimates a business's worth in dollars beyond an explicit forecast period and typically accounts for a large percentage of the total projected value of a business. It is, however, a new concept in social investment, where attention usually focuses on quantifying present or historical impact. To be sure for many projects (dispensing chlorination tablets, for example) the social impact (safer water) does notlong outlive the program. But others (such as installing solar panels) can have a longer-term impact (the panels save energy long after they're installed). In some cases, therefore, it makes sense to estimate a terminal value.

Here's how Rise addresses this question: Starting with the estimated value of impact in the final year of investment, Rise assesses the probability that both output (people reached) and social value will continue undiminished for five more years. Companies with high probabilities on both counts get a discount rate of 5%, meaning that yearly residual value falls by 5%. Those that score low get a discount rate of 25%.

To estimate the terminal value of EverFi's programs for a post-ownership period from 2022 to 2026, Rise assumed that their estimated $159 million in total impact for 2021—the last year of its investment—would also be generated in each of the following five years. That figure was then discounted by 20% per annum compounded, reflecting assumptions about the number of users graduating from the programs and the likely duration of the trainings impact. This resulted in a terminal value of $477 million—the five-year residual value. Rise could claim—for the three programs. Rise added that amount to the risk-adjusted $589 million in impact realized during the investment holding period to get a total impact of about $1.1 billion.

6. Calculate social returnon Every Dollar Spent

The final step in calculating an IMM differs for businesses and investors. Businesses can simply take the estimated value of a social or environmental benefit and divide it by the total investment.

Suppose a company invests $25 million to launch a line of low-cost eyewear for rural residents of developing countries and its research leads to an estimate of $200 million in social benefits, based on increased customer productivity and income. The company would simply divide $200 million by $25 million. Thus the eyewear generates $8 in social value for every $1 invested. The IMM expresses this as 8X.

Investors, however, must take an extra step to account for their partial ownership of companies they are invested in. Suppose Rise invests $25 million to buy a 30% ownerships take in a company projected to generate $500 million in social value. It can take credit only for the proportion of hat value reflected by its stake: $150 million. Rise divides $150 million by its $25 million investment and arrives at $6 in social value for every $1 it invested—an IMM of 6X.

Rise invested $100 million for 50% of EverFi. It adjusted its share of EverFi's projected risk-adjusted $1.1 billion in social value to $534 million and divided that amount by its investment to arrive at an IMM of approximately 5X. The great advantage of deriving an IMM is that it enables direct comparisons between investment opportunities. It's important, however, to realize that the number is not a precise multiple, like a traded stock's price-earnings multiple. For all the rigor that may lie behind a given IMM calculation, it is possible that some other analyst will rely on a different, equally valid anchor study that leads to a quite different number. Treat the IMM as a directional measure instead. And make all the steps in your calculation transparent when others understand your assumptions, they can help you refine them to generate more robust numbers. We also recommend using sensitivity analysis to show what happens to an IMM if you change the underlying assumptions. This process will help you identify the key drivers of social value.

Speaking at the 2017 Global Steering Group for Impact Investment Summit, Sir Ronald Cohen, a leading impact investing innovator and advocate, contended that the field's rapid growth will reach a tipping point and "spark a chain reaction in impact creation," touching investors, big business, foundations, and social organizations. That could hasten the adoption of impact assessment in day-to-day business processes and operations. But first businesses and investors must develop better ways to assess social and environmental impact. This is apriority concern not just for impact investors but for all those who want to see more private capital flow toward solving pressing social needs. We've embarked on this experiment to demonstrate the value of putting impact underwriting on the same footing as financial underwriting. It's a model that rise and Bridgespan seek to share with other investors and businesses, a commitment that led rise to launch a new entity to foster research and aggregate studies needed to inform impact-investment decisions. In a world where more and more CEOs talk about profit and purpose, the IMM offers a rigorous methodology to advance the art of allocating capital to achieve social benefit.

(Source: Chris Addy, Maya Chorengel, Mariah Collins, Michae Etzel. Calculating the Value of Impact Investing [J]. Harvard Business Review, January-February, 2019.)

Questions:

According to the article, how should we understand the value of impact investing in TNCs?

Case-3

Colgate's Distasteful Toothpaste

Colgate is a well-known consumer products company based in New York. Its present products are in the areas of household and personal care, which include laundry detergents such as Ajax and Fab, health care products manufactured for home health care, and specialty products such as Hill pet food. The household products segment represents approximately 75% of company revenues, while the specialty segment accounts for less than 7%. Colgate's value has been set in excess of $5.6 billion. Through both recessionary and recovery periods in the United States, Colgate has always been advocated by investment analysts as a good long-term stock.

Colgate's domestic market share has been lagging for several years. In the 1970s, when diversification seemed to be the tool to hedge against risk and sustain profits, Colgate bought companies in various industries, including kosher hot dogs, tennis and golf equipment, and jewelry. However, such extreme diversification diverted the company's attention away from its key money-making products: soap, laundry detergents, toothpaste, and other household products. The product diversification strategy ended in 1984 when Reuben Mark became CEO. At the young age of 45, he ordered the sale of parts of the organization that deviated too far from Colgate's core competency of personal and household products. He followed consultant Tom Peters's prescription for excellence: "Stick to the knitting. "

Colgate's International Presence

Colgate traditionally has had a strong presence overseas. The company has operations in Australia, Latin America, Canada, France and Germany. International sales presently represent one-half of Colgate's total revenue. In the past, Colgate always made a detailed analysis of each international market for demand. For instance, its entry into South America required an analysis of the type of product that would be most successful based on the dental hygiene needs of South American consumers. Because of this commitment to local cultural differences. The company has the number-one brand of toothpaste worldwide, Total.

To gain a strong share of the Asian market without having to build its own production plant, Colgate bought a 50% partnership in the Hawley and Hazel group in August 1985 for $50 million. One stipulation of this agreement was that Colgate had no management prerogatives: Hawley and Hazel maintained the right to make the major decisions in the organization. This partnership turned out to be very lucrative for Colgate, with double-digit millions in annual sales.

Enter the Distasteful Toothpaste

Hawley and Hazel is a chemical products company based in Hong Kong (China). The company was formed in the early part of the twentieth century, and its only product of note, believe it or not, was called "Darkie" toothpaste. Over the years, this had been one of the popular brands in Asia and had a dominant presence in markets such as China's Taiwan, China's Hong Kong, Singapore, Malaysia, and Thailand.

"Darkie" toothpaste goes back to the 1920s. The founder of this product, on a visit to the United States, loved Al Jolson, then a very popular black-faced entertainer (i. e., a white person with black makeup on his face). The founder decided to re-create the spirit of this character in the form of a trademark logo for his toothpaste because of the character's big smile and white teeth. When the founder returned to Asia, he trademarked the name "Darkie" to go along with the logo. Since the 1920s, there has been strong brand loyalty among Asians for this product. One housewife from China's Taiwan whose family used the product for years remarked, "The toothpaste featuring a Black man with a toothy smile is an excellent advertisement. "

The Backlash against Colgate

"Darkie" toothpaste had been sold in Asia for about 65 years. After Colgate became partners with Hawley and Hazel and its distasteful product, however, there was a wave of dissatisfaction with the logo and name from U. S. minorities and civil rights groups. There really has been no definite source on how this issue was passed to U. S. action groups and the media; however, a book entitled Soap Opera: The Inside Story of Procter and Gamble places responsibility in the hands of Procter& Gamble in an effort to tarnish Colgate's image and lower its market share.

The Americans' irate response to "Darkie" was a surprise to the Hawley and Hazel group. The product had always been successful in their Asian markets, and there had been no complaints. In fact, the success of "Darkie" had led the firm to market a new product in Japan called "Mouth Jazz," which had a similar logo. A spokesperson for Hawley and Hazel remarked, "There had been no problem before; you can tell by the market share that it is quite well received in Asia. "

ICCR, the Interfaith Center on Corporate Responsibility, started the fight against Colgate about 10 years ago when it received a package of "Darkie" toothpaste from a consumer in Thailand. ICCR is composed of institutional investors that influence corporations through stock ownership. At the time the movement against Colgate's racially offensive product started. Three members of ICCR already owned a small amount of stock in the company, and they filed a shareholder petition against Colgate requesting a change in the logo and name.

In a letter to Colgate, the ICCR executive director summarized the position against the distasteful toothpaste as follows:

"Darkie" toothpaste is a 60-year-old product sold widely in the Far East. Its packaging includes a top-hatted and gleaming-toothed smiling likeness of Al Jolson under the words "Darkie" toothpaste. As you know, the term "Darkie" is deeply offensive, We would hope that in this new association with the Hawley and Hazel Chemical Company, that immediate action will be taken to stop this product's name so that a U. S. company will not be associated with promoting racial stereotypes in the Third World.

In response to this letter, R. G. S. Anderson, Colgate's director of corporate development, replied, "No plans exist or are being contemplated that would extend marketing and sales efforts for the product in Colgate subsidiaries else where or beyond this Far East area. " Anderson then went on to explain that Darkie's founder was imitating Al Jolson and that in the Someone view, imitation was the "highest form of flattery. " The ICCR then informed Colgate that if the logo was not changed, the organization would create a media frenzy and help various civil rights action groups in a possible boycott.

Because Colgate still refused to remove the logo, ICCR did form a coalition with civil rights groups such as the NAACP and the National Urban League to start protest campaigns. The protest took many forms, including lobbying at the state and local levels. At one point, after heavy lobbying by the ICCR, the House of Representatives in Pennsylvania passed a resolution urging Colgateto change the name and logo. Similar resolutions had been proposed in the U. S. Congress.

The pressures at home placed Colgate in a difficult position, especially as it had no management rights in its agreement with Hawley and Hazel. In the Asian market, neither Colgate nor Hawley and Hazel had any knowledge of consumer dissatisfaction because of racial offensiveness, despite the fact that the local Chinese name for "Darkie" (pronounced heiren yagao) can be translated as "Black Man Toothpaste. " The logo seemed to enhance brand loyalty. One Asian customer stated, "I buy it because of the Black man's white teeth. "

The demographics of the Asian market may help to explain the product's apparent acceptance. There are a relatively small number of Africans, Indians, Pakistanis and Bangladeshis in the region; therefore, the number of people who might be offended by the logo is low. Also, some people of color did not seem disturbed by the name. For example, when asked about the implications of "Darkie" toothpaste, the secretary of the Indian Chamber of Commerce noted, "It doesn't offend me, and I'm sort of dark-skinned. "

Initially, Colgate had no intentions of forcing Hawley and Hazel to change the product. R. G. S. Anderson issued another formal statement to the ICCR as follows: "Our position...would be different if the product were sold in the United States or in any Western English-speaking country, which, as I have stated several times, will not happen. " Hawley and Hazel concurred with the stance. The alliance was very fearful of a loss of market share and did not believe that the complaints were issues relevant to Pacific Rim countries. A spokesperson for the alliance referred to the protest campaign as "a U. S. issue. " The trade-off for revamping a successful product was deemed to be too risky and costly.

Colgate's Change of Heart

The issue did not go away. As U. S. leaders in Congress began to learn about this very offensive logo and name, the pressure on Colgate mounted. Interestingly, however, the value of Colgate's stock increased throughout this period of controversy. Wall Street seemed oblivious to the charges against Colgate, and this was another reason why Colgate took no action. Colgate management believed that an issue about overseas products should not have a negative effect on the company's domesticimage. However, pressures continued from groups such as the Congressional Black Caucus, a strong political force. Colgate finally began to waver, but because of its agreement with Hawley and Hazel, it felt helpless. As one Colgate executive remarked, "One hates to let exogenous things drive your business, but you sometimes have to be aware of them. "

Colgate CEO Reuben Mark eventually became very distressed over the situation. He was adamantly against racism of any kind and had taken actions to exhibit his beliefs. For instance, he and his wife had received recognition for their involvement in a special program for disadvantaged teenagers. He commented publicly about the situation as follows: "It's just offensive. The morally right thing dictates that we must change. What we have to do is find a way to change that is least damaging to the economic interests of our partners?" He also publicly stated that Colgate had been trying to change the package since 1985, when it bought into the partnership.

Colgate's Plan of Action to Repair the Damage

The protest campaign initiated by ICCR and carried further by others definitely caused Colgate's image to be tarnished badly in the eyes not only of African Americans but of all Americans. To get action, some members of the Congressional Black Caucus (including Rep. John Conyers, D-Mich.) even by passed Colgate and tried to negotiate directly with Hawley and Hazel. To try to repair the damage, two years after ICCR's initial inquiry, Colgate, in cooperation with Hawley and Hazel, finally developed a plan to change the product. In a letter to ICCR, CEO Mark stated, "I and Colgate share your concern that the caricature of a minstrel in black-face on the package and the name 'Darkie' itself could be considered racially offensive. "Colgate and Hawley and Hazel then proposed some specific changes for the name and logo. Names considered included Darlie, Darbie, Hawley and Dakkie. The logo options included a dark, nondescript silhouette and a well-dressed black man. The alliances decided to test-market the options among their Asian consumers; however, they refused to change the Chinese name ("Black Man

Toothpaste"）, which is more used by their custermers.

They decided that changes would be implemented over the course of a year to maintain brand loyalty and avoid advertising confusion with their customers. There was the risk that loyal customers would not know if the modified name/logo was still the same toothpaste that had proven itself through the years. Altogether, the process would take approximately three years, test marketing included. Colgate also decided to pay for the entire change process abandoning its initial suggestion that the change be paid for by Hawley and Hazel.

Colgate and Hawley and Hazel then made a worldwide apology to all insulted groups. Although Hawley and Hazel was slow to agree with the plan, a spokesperson emphasized that racial stereotyping was against its policy. It also helped that Hawley and Hazel would pay no money to make the needed changes. It felt that the product was too strong to change quickly; thus, three years was not too long to implement the new logo and name fully into all Asian markets. Further, it insisted that as part of the marketing campaign, the product advertising use the following statement in Chinese, "Only the English name is being changed. Black Man Toothpaste is still Black Man Toothpaste. "

Response Worldwide

Colgate and Hawley and Hazel still suffer from the effects of their racially offensive product. In 1992, while dealing with its own civil rights issues, the Chinese government placed a ban on Darlie toothpaste because of the products violation of China's trademark laws. Although the English name change was implemented across all markets, the retained Chinese name and logo still were deemed derogatory by the Chinese, and the government banned the product. Also, Eric Molobi, an African National Congress representative, was outraged at the toothpaste's logo on a recent visit to the Pacific Rim. When asked if Darlie toothpaste would be marketed in his country, the South African representative replied, "If this company found itself in South Africa it would not be used. There would be a permanent boycott. "

Today, the name of Colgate cannot be found anywhere on the packaging of what is now called Darlie toothpaste. In a strategic move, Colgate has distanced itself completely away from the controversial product.

In the Thailand and Indonesia health-products markets, Colgate even competes against Darlie toothpaste with its own brand.

（Source: Reprinted with permission of Alisa L Mosley. Cogate's Distasteful Toothpaste, Free Case Study Solutions, www. freecasestudysolutions. com/case-study-Cogates-Distasteful-Toothpaste. aspx. ）

Questions：

1. Identify the major strategic and ethical issues faced by Colgate in its partnership with Hawley and Hazel.

2. Is it possible for Colgate and Hawley and Hazel to change the toothpaste's advertising without sacrificing consumer brand loyalty? Is that a possible reason for Colgate's not responding quickly to domestic complaints?

9.4 Expanding Reading

Reading-1

China Hosts Conference to Promote AI Ethical Standards

BEIJING-China is keen on ensuring that ethical standards take hold in the booming artificial intelligence industry, says Chen Xiaoping, director of the Robotics Lab at the University of Science and Technology of China.

As AI is increasingly seen as a significant source of productivity and opportunities, the discomfort or even pessimism regarding the technology cannot be ignored, according to the leading AI scientist.

Last year, Chen was asked to set up the Professional Committee for AI Ethics under the Chinese Association for Artificial Intelligence, China's state-level AI association, and to draw up AI ethics guidelines.

According to Chen, the industry's capacity to put in place ethical guidelines lags far behind its rapid technological development.

So, how do you balance the improved production efficiency brought about by automation with the social costs of the unemployed who lose their jobs?

The stronger AI's abilities, the greater the responsibility those using the technology shoulder. So, what should they ask themselves?

And how do you apply AI technology to help solve major social issues such as upgrading industry, an aging population, uneven distribution of resources and unbalanced economic development?

To deal with these issues, Chen has proposed a new task: to develop an entire system of AI ethics, with ethical guidelines and a set of operating mechanisms to realize them.

At the Global AI Technology Conference in Nanjing of East China's Jiangsu province in May, Li Deyi, CAAI director and academician from the Chinese Academy of Engineering, said he had great expectations of the AI ethics committee and was expecting contribution from overseas experts as well.

Osamu Sakura of Japan's University of Tokyo and Center for Advanced Intelligence Project said attitudes to autonomous technologies, including AI and humanoid robots, differ between the East and the West. And comparative research should be conducted in East Asia.

Wendell Wallach, a leading AI ethics expert from the United States, said self-driving cars provide a good metaphor. Technology is moving into the driver's seat as a primary determinant of human destiny, and people need to think more about the trade-offs entailed in AI technologies.

Wallach, from Yale University's Interdisciplinary Center for Bioethics where he chairs technology and ethics studies, said the International Congress for the Governance of AI is to be held in April 2020 and he looks forward to the participation and engagement of Chinese researchers.

Chen shared his opinion on drafting ethics rules, suggesting that the guidelines should play a role on three levels.

The upper level is the basic mission of AI, which will remain unchanged for a long time.

The middle level is ethical rules, guided by the mission. When ethical rules are applied to specific AI applications, these are the basic level, the compulsory codes of practice, including technical norms, product standards, and industry regulation.

Chen said the mission of AI ethics should be about maximizing benefits, rather than just putting restraints on what can be deployed. It's about directing the technology to improve the condition of humanity and reducing risks and undesirable consequences, and especially solving major social issues.

The CAAI's plan to draft ethics guidelines drew attention from foreign and domestic counterparts. And, Chen said that AI research leaders in tech companies or associations including the China Robot Industry Alliance and Berggruen Research Center of Peking University have expressed support for his plan.

Jeroen Van den Hoven, a professor of ethics at Delft University of Technology in the Netherlands, said he and Wallach agreed that the US and Europe should have more communication and cooperation with China in AI ethics research. And given the important role of AI in the lives of people, international collaboration is going to be essential, he said.

(Source: China Hosts Conference to Promote AI Ethical Standards, Xinhua News Agency, June 19, 2019.)

Reading-2

Google Acknowledges Responsibility in Self-driving Car Accident

Google acknowledged on Monday "some responsibility" in a minor fender-bender crash involving one of its autonomous vehicles earlier this month.

However, in explaining the situation on a street of Mountain View, Northern California, where the technology company is headquartered, Google reasoned that "if our car hadn't moved there wouldn't have been a collision."

The self-driving car, a modified Lexus RX450h, struck the side of a public bus on Feb. 14 while operating on the autonomous mode, resulting in no injuries in the car or on the bus but causing damage to the car's left front fender, front wheel and a driver side sensor.

As Google claimed in November that none of its cars had been the cause of the 17 minor accidents in the six-year-old project, during which about 3. 2 million kilometers were logged in autonomous and manual driving, the latest incident seemed to be the first caused by its fleet of self-driving vehicles.

"Our vehicle was driving autonomously … It then detected sandbags near a storm drain blocking its path, so it needed to come to a stop," the Silicon Valley company said in a written statement. "After waiting for some other vehicles to pass, our vehicle, still in autonomous mode, began angling back toward the center of the lane."

The car was moving at about 3. 2 km per hour, and "made contact" with the side of a passing bus traveling at about 24 km per hour.

The Department of Motor Vehicles of California posted an accident report filed on Feb. 23 by Chris Urmson, director of Google's self-driving car project.

Referring to the accident report, the company said "our car had detected the approaching bus, but predicted that it would yield to us because we were ahead of it."

During the accident, the test driver, whose presence is required by state law, watched the bus in the mirror and expected it to slow or stop, therefore did not take over the wheel.

"This type of misunderstanding happens between human drivers on the road every day," Google said.

Google has been pushing authorities for more extensive road tests of self-driving cars and has joined other companies working on similar projects to make case that most of traffic accidents were the results of human errors.

Since the latest crash, the company said it has "reviewed this incident (and thousands of variations on it) in our simulator in detail and made refinements to our software. From now on, our cars will more deeply understand that buses (and other large vehicles) are less likely to yield to us than other types of vehicles. "

"We hope to handle situations like this more gracefully in the future," it said.

(Source: Google acknowledges 'responsibility' in self-driving car accident, Xinhua Published, Maxch 1, 2016.)

Reading-3

Enterprises in Zhejiang Province Release the 2013 Corporate Social Responsibility Reports, Geely Earn two Honors

The Conference on Corporate Social Responsibility Reports by Enterprises in Zhejiang Province was held on November 25, 2013. During the conference, Geely Holding Group, as an annual representative of the enterprises which release their corporate social responsibility reports, released its own report on the site. Geely also earned two honors during the conference: "Zhejiang Province's Excellent Enterprise in the release of corporate social responsibility reports" and "Best Case Enterprise in Promoting Enterprise Information Disclosure through Boosting Corporate Social Responsibilities in Zhejiang and Shanxi Province".

Yang Xueliang, Chief Public Relations Officer of Geely Holding Group, said in the conference that Geely has established a complete management and governance system in the field of corporate social responsibility management, and integrated the system into corporate development strategies. The current system is able to effectively respond to the appeals from relevant interested parties. "Environmental Protection" and "Talents Education" are two major topics of greatest concern for Geely at the present stage in the field of corporate social responsibilities.

Yang Xueliang expressed that in the environmental protection field Geely upholds the corporate mission of "making the safest, most environmental-friendly and most efficient cars", takes a firm stand in technological innovation of automobile safety and environmental protection and accelerates the development and utilization of technologies in energy conservation and emission reduction and air purification. Take the air quality inside cars for example, Geely has gone from the single control of air quality to the user-friendly integrated management and control of interior environment quality in a quest for improvement of interior air quality. The improved interior air quality control technology has been applied in all Geely car models. In 2012, during a "Healthy Cars" test organized by a third party, Geely's Emgr and EC8 was one of the healthy cars recommended by the "Healthy Cars" test.

Yang Xueliang said that Geely has long been caring about the development of its employees and education of the country's future talents. For this, Geely has not only established Beijing Geely University, Sanya University and Zhejiang Automotive Engineering Institute but also, for many years, continued to pour efforts and donations into the cultivation of talents for the auto industry and the education of future talents for the society. As of 2012, Beijing Geely University and Sanya University have produced a total of 65, 207 graduates for the society. With the help of "Li Shufu Education Assistance Fund", education plans have been funded and special fund established to help poverty-stricken college students continue their studies and bring early education to the left-behind children. Geely has also founded several auto training schools such as Zhejiang Geely Automobile Industry School and Hunan Geely Auto College and trained a large number of applied talents for the auto industry thanks to its "Combination of Production, Learning and Research" mode. Geely believes that employees are the source of innovation of a company and the decisive force for its development. Geely upholds the ideal that "Talent resources are the primary resources" and takes talents as the most valuable asset of the company. Geely also has created four career development paths for its employees and actively helped them plan proper career paths in line with their individual needs in order to build confidence in their career development and realize everyone's personal development goal.

Deputy Director General of Department of Policies, Laws and Regulations of MIIT, Fan Bin believed that corporate social responsibility has been raised to the national strategic level. Related officials from Department of Laws and Regulations of Zhejiang Province Economic and Information Commission noted that the inner driving forces are constantly increasing for enterprises in Zhejiang to build social responsibilities and that corporate social responsibilities have gradually become the strategic awareness of enterprise directors. Some enterprises have even set out to bring social responsibilities into their strategic management system and integrate into enterprise strategic planning and everyday operation and management. They have established social responsibility indicators to achieve institutionalization and standardization in the practice of social responsibilities.

Statistics indicated an increasing initiative of enterprises in Zhejiang Province to release social responsibility reports during recent years. According to incomplete statistics, the number of enterprises in Zhejiang which release social responsibility reports has jumped from 2 in 2007 to 152 in 2013, accounting for 16. 7% of the whole nation. Among the enterprises which release social responsibility reports, private ones take up 62. 7% , 73. 3% come from Hangzhou, Ningbo, Wenzhou and Shaoxing, 86.7% earn more than 1 billion yuan in annual turnover and 85% specialize in manufacturing.

(Source: Enterprises in Zhejiang Province release the 2013 corporate social responsibility reports, Geely earn two honors, Globaltimes. cn Published, December 25, 2013.)

Quick Quiz

1. The two factors that raise ethical standards the most, according to the respondents in one study, are (1) public disclosure and publicity and (2) ____.

2. Corporate social responsibility means that a company must take into account the ____ of other constituents in addition to stockholders.

3. ____ is the study of or the learning process involved in understanding morality, while CSR involves taking action.

4. According to the Level-5 leadership pyramid, which is the character of Level-4 manager?

A. a contributing team member

B. a highly capable individual who makes productive contributions through motivation

C. presents and effectively communicates a compelling vision and mission

D. turns into a strategic leader

5. The arguments for business involvement in social activities are ____

A. Public needs have changed, leading to changed expectations.

B. Social involvement may be in the interests of stockholders.

C. Problems can become profits.

D. The cost of social programs, the reasoning goes, would have to be added to the price of the product.

E. Business has the resources.

Answers:

1. the increased concern of a well-informed public.

2. welfare

3. Ethics

4. C

5. ABCE

Endnotes

[1] Fred Luthan, Jonathan P. Doh. International Management—Culture,

Strategy and Behavior [M]. Beijing: Mechanical Industry Press, 2018: 55-67.

[2] Frank T. Rothaermel. Strategic Management [M]. Beijing: China Renmin University Press, 2015: 357-360.

[3] Harlod Koontz, Heinz Weihrich. Essentials of Management—An International and Leadership Perspective [M]. Beijing: China Renmin University Press, 2014: 42-49.

[4] John B. Cullen, K. Praveen Parboteeah. Multinaional Management [M]. Beijing: China Renmin University Press, 2017: 100-120.

[5] Georges Enderle. Thomas Donaldson, The Ethics of International Business [J]. Business and Human Rights Journal, 2015 (01): 173-178.

[6] Ans Kolk. The social responsibility of international business: From ethics and the environment to CSR and sustainable development [J]. Journal of World Business, 2016 (01): 23-34

[7] Litani Kemala Widhi, Erika Setyanti Kusumaputri. Ethical Leadership and Leader Follower Value Congruence: The Moderating Role of Collectivism [C]. Proceedings of the 1st Annual International Conference on Social Sciences and Humanities (Alcosh 2019), Atlantis Press, 2019.

[8] Stacey Sanders, Barbara Wisse, Nico W. Yperen, Diana Rus. On ethically solvent leaders: the roles of pride and moral identity in predicting leader ethical behavior [J]. Journal of Business Ethics, 2018, 150 (3): 631-645.

[9] Weichun Zhu, Linda K. Treviño, Xiaoming Zheng. Ethical Leaders and Their Followers: The Transmission of Moral Identity and Moral Attentiveness [J]. Business Ethics Quarterly, 2016 (01): 95-115.

[10] Paresh Mishra, Gordon B. Schmidt. How can leaders of multinational organizations be ethical by contributing to corporate social responsibility initiatives? Guidelines and pitfalls for leaders trying to do good [J]. Business Horizons, 2018 (10).

[11] Repaul Kanji, Rajat Agrawal. Building a society conducive to the use of corporate social responsibility as a tool to develop disaster resilience with sustainable development as the goal: an interpretive structural modelling approach in the Indian context [J]. Asian Journal of Sustainability and Social Responsibility, 2019, 4 (1): 1-25.

[12] John R. Nofsinger, Johan Sulaeman, Abhishek Varma. Institutional investors and corporate social responsibility [J]. Journal of Corporate Finance, 2019 (07): 700-725.

[13] Abugre, Anlesinya. Corporate social responsibility and business value of multinational companies: lessons from a Sub-Saharan African environment [J]. Journal of African Business, 2019 (04): 435-454.

Chapter 10　Cross-Border Electronic Commerce

Learning Objectives

1. Recognize the general situation of cross-border E-commerce
2. Understand E-Commerce indeveloping countries
3. Understand Cross-border E-Commerce in China
4. Master the international policies for E-Commerce
5. Understand the standardization on the internet
6. Recognize the situation of fast growing coexist with barriers

Opening Case

Chinese E-commerce giants ought to expand overseas

With significant development experience and the promotion of the Belt and Road Initiative (BRI), China's developed E-commerce giants are facing a great opportunity to set up and extend overseas operations, and they could help drive economic growth in less-developed countries and create jobs for the locals, Chinese experts noted.

"E-commerce development is an inevitable trend for all economies, and China has built up a leading position in the field," Wang Tengfei, an economic affairs officer of the United Nations Economic and Social Commission for Asia and the Pacific (UNESCAP), told the Global Times on Wednesday.

Indeed, it is an opportune time for China's E-commerce giants to seek development overseas and create economic-growth momentum in developing countries. This would be a win-win situation for many people involved, Wang said.

"The E-commerce revolution in Asia-Pacific presents vast economic potential," Wang said on Wednesday at a forum themed on "Trading for Shared Prosperity" which was organized by the Central Asia Regional Economic Cooperation Institute (CAREC), an intergovernmental organization based in

Urumqi, Northwest China's Xinjiang Uyghur Autonomous Region.

Wang cited the example of Kazakhstan, a member of CAREC, whose E-commerce market is growing 55% annually and has a market value of $3.6 billion. Another example of cross-border E-commerce cooperation can be seen in Thailand, where a subsidiary of China's E-commerce giant Alibaba Group signed a purchase deal for at least 800,000 durians from farmers' cooperatives in three eastern provinces.

Wang told the Global Times that as China has one of the biggest markets in the world, there is a great advantage for Chinese E-commerce firms. He added that without Alibaba's cross-border E-commerce contract, the durians could be sold at a much lower price.

In addition, the China-proposed BRI brings a great opportunity for E-commerce industries' development as well, he noted.

Though this is a win-win approach, there are still big challenges for Chinese E-commerce firms going abroad, Wang said.

For example, government's support is a critical foundation, and a convenient customs clearance procedure could speed up the cross-border E-commerce development to a great extent.

Regional organizations including CAREC could also offer support to E-commerce cooperation between different economies, such as market analysis, he said.

China's annual E-commerce turnover totaled 31.63 trillion yuan ($4.42 trillion) in 2018, up 8.5% year-on-year, with cross-border E-commerce imports and exports topping 134.7 billion yuan, up 50% year-on-year, according to the Beijing News in May, citing data from the Ministry of Commerce.

(Source: Song Lin in Xi'an, Global Times Published, August 28, 2019.)

10.1　General Situation and the Development of Cross-border E-Commerce

10.1.1　General Situation

1. E-Commerce

E-commerce is a set of transactions made by computer networks. These transactions most frequently concern the purchase or sale of goods and services ordered electronically, but the payment for and delivery of the goods or services may be performed in any form (also outside the network). The most popular method of carrying out these transactions is through the Internet, hence the name electronic commerce.

Initially, i. e. in the 1980s, E-commerce took place with the help of Electronic Data Interchange (EDI). It was, however, a solution for the largest enterprises. Later, thanks to dynamic development of the Internet, ecommerce became available for almost everyone.

Although trade conducted via the Internet has had short history and, initially, its importance was marginal, it currently constitutes one of the most dynamic and significant areas of the economy of many countries. For the already existing enterprises it has created new possibilities to compete and expand on a larger scale, and for the newly-emerging ones—prospects for fast development. This is possible thanks to low barriers to entry, which encourage more and more companies to sell their products via the Internet.

According to the European Commission, ecommerce is the main factor of economic growth and increasing employment levels in the whole European Union. E-commerce gives jobs, directly and indirectly, to 2 Million people. It is estimated that, altogether, there are approximately 550 thousand E-enterprises in Europe, which send 3. 6 Billion shipments a year. The turnover of ecommerce in Europe was € 423. 8 Billion in 2014, which was a rise of 14% in relation to the previous year.

The level of advancement and popularity of E-commerce varies greatly in individual member states of the European Union (EU). The British market is the largest one in Europe—the total turnover in 2013 amounted to € 96. 2 Billion. Next come Germany (€ 63. 4 Billion) and France (€ 51 Billion).

2. Cross-Border E-Commerce

E-commerce, just like the Internet, is characterized by a lack of borders, thanks to which customers can do shopping via the Internet from the furthest corners of the world. Although most customers who do shopping online still choose national Internet shops, purchases from shops located outside the country enjoy more and more popularity. This is the so-called cross-border E-commerce. Cross-border E-commerce has a huge potential because 37. 5% of the EU population lives in border areas. It accounts for 10% to 15% of the E-commerce market. In 2014 in the European Union (EU) 15% of inhabitants did shopping from sellers from a different country. This translates into a rise in the share of this kind of trade by 25%

in relation to the previous year.

According to the Ecommerce Europe organization (2015), the fact that last year almost all member states of the European Union noted an increase in the share of crossborder E-commerce proves that it will be one of the main factors driving the E-commerce market in Europe and the whole world. The Boston Consulting Group estimates that by 2025 the annual value of the global income from crossborder E-commerce may amount to 250 billion to 350 billion dollars (this income is now valued at 80 billion). According the data of the Nielsen company, in turn, the cross-border commerce is to be worth as many as 308 billion dollars in 2018. It is estimated that Asia (40%) will have the greatest share in cross-border E-commerce, Europe (25%) and North America (20%) will come next.

3. Problems Connected with Cross-border E-Commerce

The main difference between cross-border E-commerce and national trade is that in the case of the former, shopping is done from sellers located in a foreign country. As a result, apart from standard problems which E-shops struggle with in cross-border E-commerce, the following should also be taken into account:

- delivery cost,
- time and quality of delivery,
- communication in a foreign language,
- payment currency,
- payment terms,
- legal and tax conditionings,
- dealing with returns.

One of the greatest barriers in cross-border E-commerce is the delivery cost. This may seriously discourage customers from a decision to purchase in shops located abroad. A low shipment cost is critical from consumers' point of view. Research suggests that 90% of consumers are more willing to re-purchase from the same seller if they find the delivery cost satisfying.

Right after the delivery cost, one of the most important factors affecting customer satisfaction is the order fulfilment time. In the case of cross-border E-commerce, satisfying the customer is more difficult due to the distance between the seller and the customer. Mostly (mainly outside border areas), it is much greater than in the case of national shipments. In international trade, shipments often have to be subjected to additional operations, such as clearing through customs, which prolongs the delivery fulfilment time. What matters to customers besides time is the certainty of having the product delivered. When placing orders in foreign shops, customers are concerned about when, but also if at all and in what condition they will receive the parcel. According to the studies conducted by The European Consumer Centres' Network (2011), 49% of consumers do not decide to buy in foreign E-shops for fear of possible delivery problems.

The website, enquiries about the offer, or dealing with the return of goods are only a few aspects that require communication in a language understood by both sides. Studies suggest that only 61% of E-shops located within the European Union offer information in more than one language. An offer in a language that the customer cannot speak discredits the seller at first contact.

Another issue is the currency in which the products offered by the sellers are priced. Customers are more willing to do shopping at shops that offer their national payment currency. Research proves that, on average, 1/3 of consumers leave the website of an E-shop which presents prices in a foreign currency only, and almost 40% of consumers declare no desire to return to websites of such shops (E4X Cambridge Mercantile Group of Companies 2013).

The form of payment is another issue. The lack of well-known to the customer methods of payment may also lead to the abandoning of a purchase. Even though the substantial improvements in international banking services have been made in recent years (payment procedures simplification, fees reduction, credit and debit cards payments popularization), still not all of the E-shops offer the generally accepted forms of payments. The surveys show that in the European Union (EU) credit card is accepted method of payment in 95% of E-shops, payment via debit card is possible in 65% E-shops, 51% of them supports online payments, 43% accept transfers via banks and payment by the cash on delivery is possible in 20%.

As in the case of international trade, in cross-border E-commerce the law and taxes play an important role. These two elements still are not clear and unambiguous in crossborder E-commerce. The uncertainty of the end price (including all taxes, duties and banking fees) discourages the customers to purchase from the foreign E-shops effectively. The survey of FTI Consulting (2011) conducted on the request of the European Commission shows that the 57% of Europeans do not shop online cross-borders because of the concerns about returning goods and resolving issues with faulty products and uncertainty about consumer.

In case of products ordered from abroad, the return services are particularly important. The return of goods purchased online crossborder is strictly related to the all above mentioned issues: language—returning goods requires a contact with the seller to specify terms of the return and reimbursement (or to find, read and understand the policy of returning goods if the seller has published it on his web page); currency and form of payment—the customer may not be sure how the refund will be processed (changes in currency exchange rates may cause that the customer will not receive exactly the same amount of money that he paid for the product); delivery costs-the customer has to return the products on his own expense, which in case of more expensive international shipment has a significant impact on the attractiveness of the online shopping cross-border; time and delivery quality—the customer receives the reimbursement only after the seller receives the returned product, in case of international shipment this may affect the timing of the refund. The studies show that in online purchases cross-border in 57% of cases customers do not receive the compensation they are entitled to. According to the EU regulation the consumer is entitled to receive the amount of money which is equal to the product price and the delivery costs however still not all of the sellers comply with it.

To keep the dynamic growth of crossborder E-commerce sector, the elimination of the above mentioned issues is required. Public institutions and non-governmental organizations undertake a number of activities to increase the competitiveness of online shopping cross-border. In Europe cross-border E-commerce has been developed for many years by the European Union. The European Commission (EC) is the author of numerous policies and regulations aimed at developing public trust in the E-commerce sector. According to the EC one of key elements which have the greatest impact on the growth of the E-commerce sector is the right delivery service. One of the EC's top priorities is elimination of these constraints to implement the Digital Single Market in the EU. The Digital Single Market Strategy is built on three pillars: (1) better access for consumers and businesses to digital goods and services cross Europe; (2) creating the right conditions and a level playing field for digital networks and innovative services to flourish; (3) maximizing the growth potential of the digital economy. This strategy is aimed at the development of small and medium enterprises (SME) in particular. The EC's activities are intended to regulate consumer rights, increase shipment efficiency and lower delivery costs. Other world regions undertake similar actions. Asia is particularly active in this matter. International trade has been developed in Asia through Free Trade Agreements like ASEAN Free Trade Agreement (AFTA). AFTA is a collaboration between countries of southeast Asia and enables the members to trade internationally on concessional term. AFTA, like the UE, supports cross-border E-commerce development through actions aimed at the reduction of regulations.

10. 1. 2   E-Commerce and Developing Countries

1. The Gains from Internet to Developing Countries

While virtually all countries stand to gain from the opportunities offered by Internet, according to one view, developing countries stand to gain more from it than developed countries. The argument is that these countries are far behind developed countries in terms of information-technology infrastructure. Given the cost savings offered by Internet technology and the relative ease with which it can be provided, they can now skip several stages of technological development through which developed countries had to go. Stated differently, developing countries are much farther inside the current technological frontier and, therefore, have larger potential benefits from moving to it.

In the long run, this is a defensible statement. But it must be acknowledged that the benefits of E-commerce are distributed unevenly not only across countries-both between and among developing and developed countries-but also over time. Given that three fourths of the current E-commerce is concentrated within the United States, perhaps this single country has benefited most from it. In contrast, for many poor countries in Africa, the telecommunications infrastructure is so poorly developed that it will take a long time before they are able to benefit significantly from E-commerce.

The benefits from E-commerce to a particular developing country, both domestically and internationally, depend on the volume of demand for, and supply of, goods and services that can be potentially traded on Internet. Despite all the excitement surrounding Internet, it is likely that for many developing countries the demand and supply factors do not promise large gains, at least in the foreseeable future. Due to a lack of electronic means of payment such as credit cards, payments will still have to be made by conventional means. This factor alone is likely to limit considerably the scope of domestic electronic transactions. Moreover, the domestic demand for services that are electronically delivered is likely to be limited. Due to low costs of internal movement of natural persons, even businesses, which have heavy needs for customized software, are likely to rely on the physical presence of personnel. In these countries, even if Internet were widely available, E-commerce, as distinct from email and other communications, will not be a big success immediately.

In assessing the potential benefits from international E-commerce to a country, analysts often focus only on the goods and services that it can export. This is an incorrect approach, however, since benefits can arise from a reduction in the cost of imports as much as from an increase in the price received for exports. Even if a country does not export any services, it can benefit from imports of services, paying for them in terms of goods. Cheaper availability of medical, engineering and architectural services, long-distance learning and reduced costs of transactions can confer benefits even if the country does not immediately export the services traded through Internet.

To the extent that Internet effectively opens markets that were previously closed, it is tempting to think of it as another form of trade liberalization. But, in fact, it is much more: it amounts to a technical improvement that lowers costs of transactions and, as such, generates far larger benefits than the triangular efficiency gains from trade liberalization. Indeed, the decline in costs increases potential benefits from trade liberalization in many services sectors.

Among developing countries, the countries best situated to benefit from E-commerce through export expansion are those with a substantial pool of skilled labour, capable of working on or near the frontier of computer technology. The case of India, which is already benefiting from E-exports in a big way, best illustrates this point.

Because the international movement of natural persons is subject to severe restraints, the value of marginal product of skilled labour in developed countries is far higher than in developing countries. Though numerical estimates are not available, the potential gains from the increased mobility of natural persons are astronomical. Developing countries in general, and India in particular, have long sought a relaxation of restrictions in developed countries on the movement of natural persons. But they have not achieved a notable success in this effort.

By making the sales of skilled labour abroad, possible without actually moving natural persons physically, Internet has at last brought developed country demand for skilled labour to developing countries. This has resulted in a large capital gain on the investment India has made in higher education during the last four decades. Thus, what had seemed to be a poor allocation of resources for decades, ex post, promises to turn into an excellent investment.

2. Policies for the Expansion of Ecommerce

Development of E-commerce should not be treated as a goal in itself. Some countries are better positioned than others to achieve a rapid expansion of E-commerce for the same amount of resource invested. Since resources have alternative uses, one must compare the rate of return in ecommerce to those in other activities before committing resources to this sector. This consideration remains valid even if investment decisions are made by private agents, but the policies chosen by the government have significant effects on those decisions. For instance, policies facilitating the development of E-exports are likely to yield higher returns in a country like India, which has a significant pool of skills to export, than in a country lacking such skills.

For developing countries that find the expansion of E-commerce a desirable instrument for achieving its social and development goals, action must be taken at three levels. First, the hardware and software necessary to develop electronically sellable services should be available at reasonable prices. Second, the basic infrastructure necessary for the smooth functioning of Internet must be in place. Here "infrastructure" is defined broadly and includes facilities to conduct financial transactions on the Internet. Finally and most importantly, developing countries must negotiate access to developed country markets in sectors to which they can export services by electronic medium.

Countries can ensure the access to hardware and software by liberalizing the imports of the relevant products. This, in turn, can be accomplished by either signing the Information Technology Agreement or liberalizing the imports of the relevant products selectively, outside of that agreement. Note that this recommendation is made taking as given, the desirability of the expansion of E-commerce in the first place. We must bear in mind that when there are high trade barriers on other products, as is likely in many developing countries, this liberalization itself may misallocate resources and consumer expenditure. In such circumstances, the benefits from the expansion of E-commerce must outweigh the costs of the misallocation.

It is presumably in the area of infrastructure development that developing countries need to do most to assist in the development of E-commerce. Without adequate telecommunications systems and the availability of inexpensive telephone services, Internet and E-commerce cannot flourish. At present, the telecommunications network in many developing countries is rather poorly developed. A large majority of individuals do not have access to telephones, and those who do must pay very high rates for telephone calls. Unlike in the United States, local telephone calls are metered and charged at fairly high rates so that even if the Internet access is cheap, the expense of local telephone calls, necessary to connect to the internet access provider, can raise the overall cost of Internet use.

There is also the issue of power supply. In India, for instance, publicly supplied power has been so unreliable that many software firms in Banaglore had to resort to their own generators to ensure a continuous flow of power. Frequent and long interruptions in power flows can have a devastating effect on the transmission of data.

At present, in the large majority of developing countries, Internet access is also expensive and unreliable. Often telecommunications services are supplied by a public monopoly, which also becomes the monopoly provider of Internet access. Unable to expand service sufficiently, under public pressure, it makes many more connections than the capacity of the system. The result is a failure of many customers to access the service for which they have paid.

The solution to this problem is to simply allow private Internet service providers into the market. As long as these access providers can be obliged to give inter-connections to one another through proper regulation, there are no benefits to having a monopoly supplier of the access service. This is clearly an area in which the private market can function efficiently.

The prevalence of a legal framework, centred on paper-based contracts and handwritten signatures can also impede the growth of E-commerce. The United Nations Commission on International Trade Law (UNCITRAL) had drawn attention to this issue as early as 1985 and called upon governments to consider the possibility of permitting, where appropriate, the use of electronic means of authentication. Subsequently, UNCITRAL developed a Model law on Electronic Commerce, which was approved by the United Nations General Assembly in December 1996. The Model law lays out what constitutes the equivalent of a written document, signature and original in the electronic environment. It also sets forth rules governing the admissibility and evidential weight of electronic messages, the retention of data messages, the formation and validity of contracts, and attribution. Many countries have either adopted the Model law or introduced legislation related to electronic facilitation issues. The countries that have not yet introduced legislation along these lines are likely to need to do so.

Finally, assuming the provision of reliable Internet service at reasonable rates domestically can be ensured, additional policy measures are required to facilitate E-commerce. In many developing countries, electronic means of payment, including credit cards, are virtually non-existent. This means that even when products can be ordered or services delivered by Internet, payment must be made by conventional means. This slows down the completion of transactions considerably, reducing potential benefits.

In the case of foreign purchases, this problem becomes even more acute. Many developing countries do not have current-account convertibility so that ordering goods on Internet from abroad is not a practical option except perhaps in the case of large firms, which may have ready access to foreign exchange. Even in countries such as India, which have current-account convertibility but not capital-account convertibility, individuals do not have ready access to foreign exchange. Thus, as far as imports of goods and services are concerned, the Internet option is likely to remain limited to larger firms. The solution is not entirely clear since the issue of giving access to foreign exchange to individuals has serious implications for the ability to control capital outflows, especially in times of crisis. Even if access is provided for current-account transactions only, it becomes easy to disguise capital-account transactions as current-account transactions. This may be even easier when the purchase is that of services rather than goods.

The final step in ensuring access to international E-commerce is to have access to communication networks and markets for electronically tradable goods in foreign countries. At present, there is sufficient excess capacity in the networks in developed countries. Therefore, access is unlikely to be a problem. It is possible however, that as the use of Internet grows worldwide, the expansion of capacity may fail to keep up with demand. Normally, one would expect the price mechanism to manage the demand for access, but there may be phases when networks begin to congest heavily. Under such circumstances, developing countries will need to ensure that their access rights are not violated. While, personally, I do not expect this to become a serious problem, some caution in this regard may prove valuable.

The more important access issue relates to liberalization commitments by developed countries in the services that developing countries can export electronically. Developing countries are largely importers of these services. Commitments in electronically traded services, which developing countries can potentially export have been limited. For some developing countries, the potential for exports of services through electronic means is very substantial. Starting with simple data entry services in the 1980s, the supply of back office services from developing countries has grown to include electronic publishing, website design and management, customer call centres, medical records management, hotel reservations, credit card authorizations, remote secretarial services, mailing list management, technical on-line support, indexing and abstracting services, research and technical writing, and technical transcription.

Internet also offers developing countries the opportunity to become exporters of products purchased by foreign governments. In the past, it would have been difficult for potential developing country suppliers to find information on these purchases. However, many developed country governments are now beginning to post tenders for procurement of goods and services on Internet. This gives suppliers from developing countries better access to yet another sector in developed countries. Though the establishment of credibility may take some time for the small and medium firms, large firms in developing countries can certainly bid and compete successfully for these contracts.

10. 1. 3 Cross-border E-Commerce in China

1. Development of Cross-border E-Commerce in China

Cross-border E-commerce generally refers to transactions between different countries or regions who communication via the Internet, email or other forms. It is a new international trade patterns which is smaller, more often and faster than before. Currently, China's E-commerce is in a period of great development. cross-border E-commerce in China whose main body is center enterprise is developing well, and with its strong vitality growing. Cross-border E-commerce is a new pattern of cross-border trade which takes electronic as means. It is very young and has incomparable advantages. But it is the same with other new things, there are some problems and bottlenecks. How to solve these problems is a better electronic the basic requirements for business. The financial crisis is becoming a catalyst for the development of E-commerce. The development of cross-border E-commerce in China plays a role as a forerunner. A lot of experience and models are cross-border E-commerce can directly reference.

In recent years, development of cross-border E-commerce has attracted the close attention of the community. The government is also took highly concerned about the future development of China's cross-border E-commerce, and actively guides enterprises to participate in cross-border E-commerce. The rapid development of cross-border trade is inseparable from promoting E-commerce platform. Currently, there are some platform which could provide service of cross-border E-commerce in China, including ebay, Alibaba's AliExpress. There are many hands to build the core national policy promoting reform, such as the Belt and Road, Free Trade Area (FTA), the internationalization of RMB, Chinese manufacturing 2025, Internet + and the coordinated development of regional economy. Cross-border E-commerce could make distance shorten between product and market in time and space. It will be the main mean of promoting trade a facilitation, upgrade trade development and promote the effective implementation of national policy.

Expansion of national policy will gradually solve the problems of cross-border E-commerce which are clearance, settlement, billing, logistics, financing, taxation and open up new markets and avoid trade barriers and a series of bottlenecks. The implement and carry out of cross-border E-commerce will help drive policy. On the external hand, cross-border E-commerce strategy is from trade to investment to gradual currency. On the internal hand, cross-border E-commerce strategy is simplifying administration and decentralization, optimize investment environment, upgrading of industrial structure fully and optimize production capacity. Linkage between inside and outside is for cross-border trade facilitation and deepening economic ties. We could output the excess products and access to obtain resource and market. Through these two processes to promote the RMB as an international settlement currency, and ultimately enhance the international influence of Chinese economy.

Currently, the global trade is undergoing profound changes. Cross-border E-commerce has become the main way trade growth. Trade accounts for 14% of China's total import and export trade, and 23% of exports, 3.9% of imports. Cross-border E-commerce growth rate is 16 times the general trade, export 7.3 times, 98 times that of imports. Business to Business (B2B) accounts 88% of cross-border E-commerce. Cross-border B2B refers to the small customize and wholesale business through E-commerce between different borders businesses. The rapid growth of cross-border B2B business described in the global information flow, logistics, capital flow increasingly demand convenience and differentiation, the background of rising costs, fragmentation of trade, trend apparent terminal. The enterprises who follow the trend would have the opportunity to integrate the value chain and market terminal, and form a new competitive advantage. Conversely, the enterprises who could not restructuring timely would be replaced.

Cross-border E-commerce retail exports account for 37% of global market share in China. There are obvious manufacturing capacity advantages on "made in China", but the development space is still big to the industry. Cross-border E-commerce is export-oriented whose outlet is 6.8 times to the amount of imports. It is dual results of market supply and demand relationship and the policy-oriented. From the actual market situation, the current cross-border E-commerce is limited categories of imports, which is focusing on maternal, Beauty and light extravagance and luxury. Because China is a manufacturing power country, most of the production and living necessities domestic supply to meet the market demand. From a regulatory perspective, China's regulatory authorities, the same as the other importing countries, have to meet the impact of natural sources of revenue (import duty, excise duty and VAT[①]) and import industry from cross-border E-commerce. At the same time, it is responsible for product safety regulatory responsibilities. Regulatory authorities, while promoting imports to meet consumption, must also be keeping guard at the door, so take a relatively cautious reforms are necessary.

In 2014, there is a rapid growth on cross-border E-commerce business scale of the cross-border E-commerce. There is total 3. 75 trillion, and increasing 39%, of which exports is 3. 27 trillion, and increasing 37%, of which imports is 0. 48 trillion, and increasing 59%. Cross-border retail is 0. 45 trillion, an increase of 44 percent, in of which exports 0. 32 trillion, an increase of 30% and imports 0. 13 trillion, an increase of 60%. China's major trading partners are the United States, Britain, Australia and Brazil.

Finnair to Go Online in China'e Commerce Giant JD. com

BEIJING, Oct. 26 (Xinhua) —Finnair jointly announced the establishment of a strategic partnership with China's E-commerce giant JD. com in Beijing on Thursday, becoming the first foreign airline on the online platform.

The cooperation shows Finnair's commitment to the Chinese market, as well as its dedication to offering more choices and better services to Chinese consumers, Finnair said.

"Finnair highly values China as a prominent aviation market with increasing numbers of passengers. We will jointly explore opportunities by combining air travel with E-commerce," said Juha Jarvinen, Finnair's CCO.

Finnair will become the first overseas airline to set up a flagship online store on JD Travel at the beginning of 2018, according to the Memorandum of Understanding between the airline and JD. com.

Customers will be able to book and pay for air tickets on the store. A membership and loyalty program will be launched between JD. com and Finnair Plus members, allowing points to be exchanged between two parties.

"JD. com has 260 million high-quality active users and a modern logistics system. We will join hands with Finnair to step forward into the global tourism market," said Frank Sun, general manager of JD. com's Life and Travel department.

Finnair became the first Western European airline to open a direct flight route to China when it began the Helsinki-Beijing direct flight in 1988.

To date, it has six routes to China. In June 2017, it extended Wi-Fi services to

---

① value added tax

all routes to the country.

(Source: Mengjie. Finnair to Go Online in China'e Commerce Giant JD. com, Xinhua net, October 26, 2017.)

2. Development Bottleneck

The problems facing both exports and imports is a single window, and it is still hard to realize information exchange, mutual recognition of regulatory, law enforcement mutual aid. Talent of cross-border E-commerce is shortage, and the tax contribution is small. Problems faced by cross-border E-commerce exports are mainly about price competition and shrinking profit. Otherwise, it is hard to parcel tax rebates, overseas ware house construction costs are high and stocking financial pressure. Financing is very difficult to cross-border E-commerce enterprises. Marketing cost is high for independent website overseas. The markets are disturbed by speculative mentality, fake, sub-standard, not the integrity of transactions. Problems faced by cross-border E-commerce imports are mainly about the impact of existing sources of tax revenue and circulation systems, it is more controversial. Regulatory pressure is big for sea Amoy direct mail. The contradiction among bonded stocking, aging and security. Electronic fence needs highly information technology for businesses and regulatory departments. These are no doubt problems which stop the development of cross-border E-commerce.

3. The Development Trend of Cross-Border E-Commerce in China

To start cross-border E-commerce business well, we must first carry out a rational market position, the goal is to occupy the terminal markets, then to the global market and integration of the value chain. We also should build the value chain, carding and supplement. Furthermore, synthesized service platform of cross-border E-commerce should be built to train young backbone of the business, and they should master the skills of cross-border E-commerce. Cross-border E-commerce is facing opportunities and challenges. And there is a huge space for development and potential. In the future, there will be mainly five trends of cross-border E-commerce to develop as following.

(1) Role in promoting of national strategies for cross-border E-commerce. With the commencement of national policy, China will strive to the right of leading of international rules and speak of cross-border E-commerce. China will also support the promotion of the Belt and Road (B&R) and some related regions to do the infrastructure construction of cross-border E-commerce. This will gradually solve the problems of which cross-border E-commerce is facing, including clearance,

settlement, billing, logistics, financing, taxation, explore new markets and avoid trade barriers and a series of bottlenecks.

(2) Cross-border E-commerce localization is forced by the strengthen supervision. With the influx of a large number of countries through cross-border E-commerce commodities manner, the problems of source of revenue, product quality and consumer protection are shown. Some governments have attracted the attention. In 2014, Russia increase imported goods tax policy of cross-border E-commerce greatly, which makes China meet very large impact. Countries strengthen the supervision of cross-border E-commerce. And the-border E-commerce business will be forced to develop localization, and the "sea Amoy" to combine online and offline "local" E-commerce businesses.

(3) Value chain of cross-border E-commerce business is extension by market demand-driven. With the growing of global consumer cross-border shopping, the demand of timeliness, type and offline services is increasing, too. Currently, packet-based direct mail business model could only sale the products of both volume and weight small, and without the need of a large number of offline services. If we want to meet the demand of consumers, the cross-border E-commerce companies need to move logistics chain to domestic, then increase big-ticket goods, improve distribution efficiency and reverse logistics processing capabilities. Offline experience and service centers should be established to improve service and customer experience by the way of O2O.

(4) Trade enterprises will become the new force of cross-border E-commerce business. Foreign trade enterprises in their respective areas have the advantage ability to control supply chain. They are familiar with foreign regulatory approach, and have a certain financial strength, have the advantage in terms of cross-border B2C business. Meanwhile, cross-border B2B will become a major marketing channel of traditional foreign trade enterprises. Advantage in marketing of internet will be used by foreign companies to cross the intermediate links to end distributors, retailers or service providers directly. This could improve income and reinforce the ability to respond to changes in market demand.

(5) Comprehensive services of cross-border E-commerce will rise up. Foreign trade enterprises will be converged with integrated services cross-border E-commerce platform, forming a comprehensive cross-border E-commerce services. It is a realistic way of sustained, healthy and rapid development for cross-border E-commerce. Integrated services of cross-border E-commerce is developing to payment, logistics, credit, product quality insurance and finance other direction based on the existing information and transaction services through the integration of industrial chain, trade chain, chain of custody and data link. It provides a full range of integrated services for whole process of cross-border online trade, and it could push comprehensive services to promote integration and development of traditional processing trade and cross-border E-commerce.

In logistics, cloud computing, networking and other new generation of information technology is used in cross-border E-commerce, which will enhance the information level of logistics and efficiency, reduce logistics costs.

In terms of credit, relying on resources and modern information technology, large-scale E-commerce platform opens up new avenues for the credit system.

In terms of Internet financial, relying on the big data resources, for example transaction, logistics and payment, E-commerce platform understands credit conditions and operating conditions of foreign trade enterprises deeply. It could provide supply chain finance, reduce the cost of financing for small and micro enterprises, and promote foreign trade enterprises to enhance overall competitiveness.

Alibaba Launches Undergraduate E-commerce Program for African Students

China's E-commerce giant Alibaba on Wednesday launched its first undergraduate cross-border E-commerce program for African students.

The 22 students from Rwanda arrived in the eastern Chinese city of Hangzhou, where Alibaba is headquartered, Tuesday, the 20th anniversary of the tech giant.

"You came at the right time and to the right place," said Zeng Ming, president of Alibaba Business School with the Hangzhou Normal University, at the opening ceremony.

The school is not a traditional business school, but one that focuses on the internet economy, said Zeng.

"Foreign students can take courses related to the internet, global trade and cross-border E-commerce and also gain firsthand experience of the development of China's digital economy," he said.

"This opportunity will change our lives," said 18-year-old Mike Manzi. He said that after graduation, he hopes to set up an E-commerce platform back in his country that helps simplify tax declarations and customs clearance for cross-border trade.

The program is part of a cooperation agreement between the Rwandan government and Alibaba under the latter's Electronic World Trade Platform (eWTP) initiative.

Rwanda and Alibaba launched the eWTP in October 2018, making Rwanda the first African country to launch the platform.

Since the launch of the eWTP, Rwanda's coffee and tourism products have been sold on Alibaba's E-commerce platforms, including coffee from Rwandan company "Land of a Thousand Hills."

The eWTP demonstrates the friendly development concept of China's Belt and Road Initiative and help connect the world through the internet, said Virgile Rwanyagatare, the Charge d'Affaires at the Rwandan Embassy in China, at the ceremony.

China sells goods to the world through E-commerce, and African countries will soon be able to connect to these online platforms, said Rwanyagatare.

"The eWTP is an opportunity for Rwandans, and I believe it will help Rwanda's development in terms of economy and E-commerce," said Manzi.

Rwanda wants to become a middle-income nation by embracing digitalization and smart business transactions through the eWTP, said Sanny Ntayombya, head of communications and marketing at Rwanda Development Board, in a written interview with Xinhua.

The prospects of the eWTP are high in Rwanda, said Ntayombya, and the country hopes the partnership results in more trade with China and the world.

"With four-year systematic learning, we hope Rwandan students can integrate into China's digital economy and become a backbone for Rwanda after graduation," said Huang Mingwei, vice president of Alibaba.

Over the past year, Alibaba has provided E-commerce training programs for officials, business owners, entrepreneurs, and college teachers from Rwanda. The company has jointly developed E-commerce courses with Rwanda's African Leadership University.

Rwanyagatare said he expects the students to become strong leaders and develop successful businesses in the future and to teach people back home what they have learned in China.

(Source: Alibaba Launches Undergraduate E-commerce Program for African Students, Xinhua Published, September 12, 2019.)

10. 2　Focus on the Practice of Cross-border E-Commerce

10. 2. 1　International Policies for E-Commerce

1. Which Multilateral Discipline: GATT, GATS or Both?

The degree to which countries can regulate international trade via the Internet, what taxes they can impose on it, and in what way they can discriminate in favor of the domestic suppliers of similar items will depend on the WTO discipline the member countries decide to apply to it. The WTO report mentioned in footnote two raises the possibility that, in principle, the "digits" traded on Internet could be viewed as goods, services or even something else. Which of these characterizations is chosen determines whether this trade is subject to the rules laid down in the General Agreement on Tariffs and Trade (GATT), General Agreement on Trade in Services (GATS), a combination of these two or an entirely new agreement.

It may be noted at the outset that there is no ambiguity at present regarding the status of the goods ordered and paid for on Internet but delivered physically in the conventional manner. Except for the order and payment themselves, these transactions are treated as goods trade and the GATT discipline applies to them. The ambiguity arises only when the goods are delivered on Internet. On the face of it, any deliveries made by Internet would seem to resemble services. Nevertheless, as already noted in the introduction, there are products delivered by Internet that have counterparts in physical, merchandise trade. The obvious examples are books, videos, music CDs and computer software. When imported in physical form, these products are treated as goods with the GATT discipline applied to them. But can they be treated as services when delivered by Internet? Or, in conformity with their physical counterparts, should they be treated as goods?

One extreme possibility is to characterize all transmissions on Internet as goods with GATT discipline applied to them. Such a characterization accompanied by a ban on custom duties on the transmissions, currently in place, would amount to the WTO members committing themselves to complete free trade in all transactions routed by Internet. This is because national treatment and MFN status are general obligations under GATT. By accepting the GATT discipline, under national treatment, the member countries would give up their right to discriminate against Internet imports as far as domestic taxes are concerned. In addition, the ban on customs duty would bind their tariffs on Internet imports at zero. However, at present, no one is considering such a proposal. The member countries made their commitments in the UR and post-UR negotiations on services based on the assumption that most of those transactions were services rather than goods.

At the opposite extreme, we could abandon both GATT and GATS and develop an entirely new discipline for Internet trade. Once again, virtually no one is advocating this position. For a search for a new discipline for E-commerce makes little sense. Internet services, which include Internet service providers and phone lines on which transmissions flow, are already subject to GATS and the Agreement on Basic Telecommunications. All electronic transmissions that flow on Internet, on the other hand, have counterparts in either goods trade or services trade. As such, the rules necessary to regulate that trade can be found in GATT or GATS.

Thus, the real choice is between applying GATS to all Internet trade, or GATT to that trade for which physical counterparts also exist, and GATS to all other E-trade. In my judgement, on balance, it makes more sense to define all electronic transmissions as services. At one level, it may be argued that at the time Internet transmissions cross the border between two countries, they do not have a physically traded counterpart. The eventual transformation of the transmission into a good such as a book or CD does not negate the fact that at the border the transmission did not have a physically traded counterpart. Indeed, in many cases, the transmission may not be turned into the physically traded counterpart at all. For example, the recipient may continue to store it in the digital form with books read on the screen and music played directly on the computer.

But this is not the primary reason why leaning in favour of treating all Internet trade as service trade. The key advantage of adopting the across-the-board definition is that it is clean and minimizes possible disputes that may arise from countries wishing to have certain transmissions classified as intangible goods and others as services. Under a mixed definition, in any trade dispute involving Internet trade, panels will have to first decide whether the object of dispute is a good or a service to determine whether the rules of GATT or GATS are to be applied in evaluating the dispute. The adoption of the across-the-board definition automatically resolves this issue.

The across-the-board definition, nevertheless, raises some efficiency issues that must be addressed. Thus, consider first the issue of tariffs, which are applicable to products imported in physical form but not when transmitted electronically. As long as the cost of electronic transmission is lower than that of physical delivery, the presence of tariffs on the latter poses no problem. Effectively, the electronic transmission offers the product to the country at a price lower than that available through physical delivery. This change is equivalent to an improvement in the country's terms of trade and, leaving aside some general-equilibrium considerations, improves welfare unambiguously.

But for many countries, especially backward ones, this is an unlikely scenario. In these countries, most consumers do not have computers or Internet access. A likely scenario, therefore, is one in which a handful of independent entrepreneurs will receive the product by Internet, convert it into physical form such as CDs and sell the latter to consumers.

2. Access to E-Commerce

Access to E-commerce, which in the WTO parlance often means access to E-exports, has two components that must be distinguished sharply: access to Internet services and access to services that can be traded electronically. The former deals with access to Internet infrastructure while the latter relates to specific commitments in electronically tradable services. In goods trade, we can liken these components, respectively, to access to transportation networks (including ports, ships, roads, railways and air transport) and access to specific goods markets through a lowering of trade barriers such as tariffs and quotas. For lower trade barriers to result in more imports, access to transportation networks is necessary.

The access to Internet infrastructure depends on two factors: (i) availability of communications networks, hardware and software and (ii) access to the existing communications networks. Let us consider briefly each of these factors.

(1) Availability of infrastructure, hardware and software. At the basic level, access to Internet by the residents of a country depends on the level of development of the telecommunications sector and the availability of hardware and software. In the remote villages of many developing countries, even the basic telecommunications services may not exist. To bring Internet and, hence, ecommerce to these villages, one will need first to bring telecommunications services there. But even when telecommunications services exist, additional hardware that links up the individual user to Internet must be put in place. Finally, one needs to ensure access to equipment such as computers, modems and software. Generally speaking, an open trade regime with respect to information technology equipment is likely to facilitate access to this equipment. This is perhaps the reason why some countries chose to sign the Information Technology Agreement (ITA), which requires the signatories to open up trade in a large number of information-technology products.

(2) Access to communications networks. There are three principal WTO provisions that govern access to communications networks: GATS Article VIII on monopolies and exclusive service suppliers, GATS Annex on Telecommunications, and the Reference Paper on regulatory principles in the Agreement on Basic Telecommunications. In addition, specific commitments on national treatment and market access made by countries in the basic telecommunications sector have implications for access to Internet. GATS Article VIII and the Annex apply to all WTO members uniformly. The Reference Paper applies to approximately 60 countries that incorporated it into their specific commitments in the agreement on basic telecommunications services. A total of 69 countries made specific commitments in

the basic telecommunications sector. Of these, ten countries made specific commitments with respect to Internet access providers.

Article VIII, which applies to all services, is designed to deal with monopoly suppliers who can potentially frustrate a Member's MFN and specific market access commitments. For instance, suppose telephone lines in a Member country are owned by a single entity and the Member has made market access commitments to other countries in the provision of Internet services. Article VIII requires this entity not to limit access to phone lines to service suppliers from other Members or discriminate among them. It also requires this entity to ensure that the commitments made by the Member in other service sectors are not frustrated.

Article VIII is limited in its application to cases in which a monopolist supplies the service in question. GATS negotiators recognized, however, that basic telecommunications services are central to the smooth flow of trade in a large number of other services. Therefore they introduced further provisions in the Annex on Telecommunications to widen access rights in the use of public telecommunications transport networks and services (PTTNS).

The Annex requires each Member government to ensure that suppliers of other Members are given reasonable and nondiscriminatory access to and use of PTTNS for the supply of a service included in the Member's schedule. The term "nondiscriminatory" is defined here to include both national treatment and MFN. The Annex, thus goes beyond Article VIII in two respects. First, for a service listed in the Member's schedule, it gives foreign suppliers nondiscriminatory access to PTTNS even though the Member has not committed to national treatment in that service. Second, the access provision applies to PTTNS irrespective of whether these services and networks are supplied by a monopolist or competitive firms.

The concern that telecommunications markets would be dominated by large operators, capable of frustrating market access commitments, remained central during basic telecommunications negotiations. This led the participants to lay down a set of regulatory principles in a Reference paper, aimed at reigning in the behavior of the major suppliers of telecommunications services. Some 60 participants incorporated this Reference Paper into their commitment schedules.

The regulatory principles in the Reference Paper oblige major suppliers to provide interconnection on nondiscriminatory terms. They are to provide also services in sufficiently unbundled form that those seeking interconnections do not have to pay for unnecessary components and facilities. The Reference Paper also lists rules governing anti-competitive cross-subsidization, the misuse of information, licensing criteria and transparency.

Finally, Internet access also depends on the degree of liberalization in basic telecommunications undertaken by Members. 69 countries signed the Agreement on Basic Telecommunications in February 1997. Counting the European Communities as one, this produced 55 schedules. Many of the negotiated undertakings represent a pre-commitment to liberalize in the future.

In addition to the Internet access services just discussed, Internet offers the opportunity for trade in two additional areas. First, many services outside of the telecommunications sector, such as those in the banking, insurance and computer programming sectors can be delivered electronically. Second, Internet can be the vehicle for the provision of distribution services with goods and services purchased through Internet but delivered by other means. For transactions in the first category, GATS discipline applies fully. In contrast, transactions in the second category are similar to those by telephone or mail order. When delivered physically, goods are subject to the usual GATT discipline including customs duties.

While national treatment and market access commitments in national schedules do matter in that they restrain the importing country's ability to discriminate in its tax policies in favour of domestic suppliers or among various foreign suppliers, in the case of Internet trade, they play a less crucial role. To the extent that governments do not have effective control over what is traded on Internet, especially when transactions are from business to consumers, the value of these commitments is limited.

Instead, the bulk of the expansion of E-commerce will depend on countries granting recognition to the education or experience obtained, requirements met, or licenses or certificates granted in another country. Article VII of GATS allows for such recognition even on a discriminatory basis, in the sense that it allows Members to extend such recognition on a selective basis. For instance, the United States may give recognition to accountancy degrees from Europe but not India. This could signal potential buyers that it is hazardous to buy accountancy services in India even though the latter may be capable of supplying them competitively. In this regard, Article VII gives some flexibility to excluded countries, which developing countries should exploit as much as they can. In particular, if a Member gives recognition to the standards prevailing in another Member in a specific area, and a developing country's standards in the same area happen to be at par, under Article VII provisions, it should be granted similar recognition.

10. 2. 2　Standardization on the Internet

Given the very large and rapidly growing number of Internet users in many countries there is an enormous growth potential for online commerce in both the B2B and B2C markets. Attractions exist for managers in terms of cost savings in the online domain and efficiency effects of market transactions.

For Singh and Boughton (2002) a standardized web site entails "the same web content, in the same language, for both domestic and international users. Standardized websites do not prominently display any information about their international operations. " It is suggested that online standardization leads to cost savings. Website adaptation is potentially a costly undertaking. Incorporating culturally responsive features in a website necessitates the employment of culturally experienced staff and expert linguists not only to undertake the initial design and launch of country specific websites but also to provide continuous analysis and interpretation of cues and generate insights from online dialogue and interaction with customers residing in culturally diverse environments. If, as Tsikriktsis (2002) concludes, culture plays a "...significantly less important role in Web site quality expectations compared with traditional service quality expectations..." , then the payoff to cultural adaptation in web design and operation may not be that large. Forrester Research reinforce this view by observing that repeat visitation of websites is predominantly determined by interactivity, trust, the right composition of quality content, ease of use, speed and frequency of updating, while cultural dimensions and appeals are of negligible importance. An additional argument for website standardization can be provided in terms of developing scale and scope economies by pursuing global product and branding strategies. Yip and Dempster (2005) point out that higher levels of Internet-use is related to higher levels of firm performance, thus supporting scale-and scope efficiencies.

The proponents of online standardization also claim that it will strengthen the brand image of the company amongst its potential online customers. Furthermore, it is the preferred strategy to " push" visitors through the conversion process from "surfers" to "purchasers" . This is essentially due to cost consideration as cultural online adaptation is relatively costly and as long as the target conversion rate is not very high it can be achieved by transmitting a standardized online presence. On the other hand, proponents of the adaptation strategy contend that standardization does not generate distinctiveness in web-communication, and hence cannot maximize market potentials in respective markets and thus risks losing competitive advantage.

Adapted websites exhibit specific time, date, zip code and number formats. These sites have country specific templates reflected in the country-specific unique resource locators (URL's) such as, . de (Germany), . com (U. S), and. co. uk (United Kingdom). Furthermore, these country-specific sites feature visibly on the level of the parent company websites and pay detail attention to culture specificities, most notably language issues. Proponents of website adaptation believe that information technology competences and capabilities of companies such as operating websites or conducting business online can easily be replicated by competitors. Competitive advantages on the Internet are therefore not likely to remain sustainable and companies must seek differentiation advantages. Kotha (1998) suggests that uniform communication patterns may not be sufficient to maintain healthy profit margins and competitive advantage. Yip and Dempster (2005) concur with Porter and suggest the establishment of a " unique set of activities"; they claim that companies in global industries must "…carefully monitor how rivals are making use of the Internet, and lead or match rivals' activities. "

As Kotha et al. (2004) show, buyer's online experience is critical to website competitiveness. This induces the firm to create various "relationship services" . As conceived by Kotha et al. (2004) relationship services are a mechanism to create a bond with online customers and engender buyer trust. Other scholars have similarly maintained that buyer trust is a critical underpinning of a positive online experience. Although previous studies are mostly concerned with trust in an E-commerce context, without necessarily focusing on cross-border transactions, it is reasonable to assume that trust is at least as crucial in this context as it is in domestic E-commerce.

In the cross-border context, the creation of relationship service implies adaptation or differentiation. Relationship services are provided as a part of making the website more culturally sensitive and specific to the target market. Cultural adaptation does have the potential to improve the effectiveness of websites. Yamin and Sinkovics (2006) reason that website interactivity entails a degree of cultural adaptation and that such cultural adaptation is beneficial in terms of sustaining the buyer/seller "dialogue" . Others have suggested that whilst ICT-enabled standardization may improve coordination and control for TNCs, a level of subsidiary autonomy and initiative taking is still beneficial for TNCs, as might be induced by adaptation of local websites. Looking at the profiles of Internet buyers in 20 countries, it has been suggested that "…even with increased electronic interactions, people still need to feel engaged (culturally or contextually) with vendors, even online. Consequently, companies that have an understanding of and an ability to 'mirror' the culture of their target country will have a competitive global advantage. " (Lynch and Beck, 2001). Samiee's (1998) suggestion that culture can have a main impact on the success of E-marketing efforts appears to be valid in the online contexts, too.

In a more empirical vein, a number of studies show that culture does influence the design of websites. Empirical evidence is further provided by Luna et al. (2002), who show that exposure to culturally appropriate websites, reduces the cognitive efforts required from the customer. The enhanced quality and frequency of online contact is likely to result in conversion efficiency. Chakraborty et al. (2005) provide empirical evidence from a B2B context, which suggests that "one shoe fits all" approaches in website design should be avoided and websites should be custom-built to geographical regions.

In all, the debate over online adaptation or standardization has not yet provided a consolidated view on the issue, which suggests there is scope for fruitful empirical examination of online adaptation or standardization following a cultural perspective.

10. 2. 3　Fast Growing Coexist with Barriers

The Boston Consulting Group cataloged the barriers to E-commerce in Breaking

Through the barriers to Online growth (BCG article, June 2013). The article's conclusion bears restating here: when theE-commerce channel is fully developed, retailing will be a multichannel activity, withonline the leading channel for domestic and cross-border sales in most product categories (see Figure10-1).

Nowhere is the rapid expansion of E-commerce more apparent than in Asia. China is leading the way, shedding its identity as solely a production center and emerging as a burgeoning consumer market, with an increasingly affluent and populous middle class eager to embrace online technologies and adopt the developed world's consumption styles. Asia's E-commerce growth rates are in the double digits in most product categories. and it's no coincidence that china is the only major market where the largest retailer, Alibaba, is a pure-play internet service.

The main growth, so far, is mostly domestic, as barriers to cross-border transactions are constraining the growth of cross-border E-commerce in Asia as well as in Western markets. These barriers include the following:

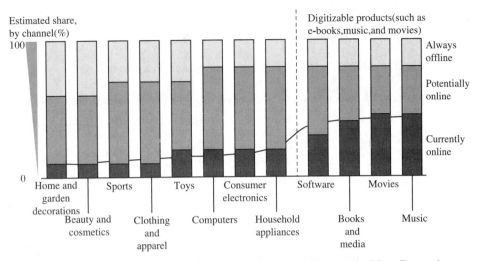

Figure 10-1   E-Commerce Will Become the Dominant Channel in Most Categories

Source：BCG analysis.

Note：The estimate is for Westem European markets；online growth in other markets will vary depending on their individual dynamics.

1. Unreliable and Lengthy Transit Times

Consumers want shorter, more precise, and more reliable delivery windows for both domestic and cross-border purchases.

2. Complex and Ambiguous Return Processes

Fully tracked, easy-to-arrange returns should be a standard option on all E-commerce sites.

3. Customs Bottlenecks

At present, dissonant customs practices create significant scheduling uncertainty for shippers. Customs regimes need to be harmonized and their timing made more predictable.

4. Limited Transparency on Delivery

Some parcels aren't tracked at all, and the tracking information that does exist lags the actual delivery by about six hours. Tracking is linked to specific delivery windows, decreasing the value of the information for short transit times.

5. Price Opacity

International shipping options are often complicated by VAT and customs charges, and shoppers can't determine the final landed cost of an item, even after they click "buy. " This uncertainty discourages purchasing.

6. Limited Ability to Alter Delivery Times and Locations

At present, if consumers' plans change, they cannot change delivery times or locations for internationally shipped goods if the parcel is already in transit, as they can with most domestic deliveries.

With so much at stake and with so many competitors jostling for a piece of the E-commerce action, it's only a matter of time before a number of players in the cross-border E-commerce ecosystem find ways to surmount these barriers at an acceptable cost, with encouragement from public-sector bodies such as the EU. An integrator might be able to manage down the costs of its end-to-end service, or postal operators might collaborate to act as quasi integrator to take advantage of their low-cost residential delivery. Commercial airlines may have a role to play connecting domestic residential networks to international senders. Intermediaries are already stepping into link electronic retailers and domestic carriers for cross-border service, while integrated online retailers and order retrieval companies are preparing to offer cross-bor derdelivery services to third parties.

Cross-border E-commerce currently accounts for 10% to 15% of total E-commerce volume, depending on region. That share is sure to expand as the barriers are dismantled. By 2025, annual global cross-border E-commerce revenues could swell to between $250 billion and $350 billion—up from about $80 billion today. Asia will account for some 40% of those cross-border revenues, making it far and away the center of the E-commerce world Europe will account for about 25% of revenues, followed by North America at 20%.

The current figure might look small compared with domestic E-commerce flows but it turns out that domestic E-commerce isn't so domestic after all. Already, roughly 70% of the revenues of domestically anchored carriers in midsize European countries have some kind of cross-border component. In some cases, that component is a direct infeed from a foreign player; in others, a foreign player uses local fulfillment to complete a delivery; in still others, a domestic company assembles and ships goods with international content (see Figure10-2).

When the barriers to cross-border E-commerce fall away, it will no longer matter to consumers if they buy domestic or cross-border. At that point, retailers will have a golden opportunity to organize their sales not by region but by customer needs, selling products and services matched to particular markets regardless of location. Carriers have a critical role to play in bringing this new world into being, acting both independently and collectively to surmount cross-border barriers, standardize service offerings and improve service quality. Individually, they face the task of determining what kind of cross-border players they want to be, depending on their competitive positions and ambitions. Most will likely opt to position themselves some where within the cross-border ecosystem and thus avoid the risk of becoming no more than a domestic subcontractor. Once they determine their place within the greater network, carriers can make the needed investments in it, sales and marketing and other functions essential to their service.

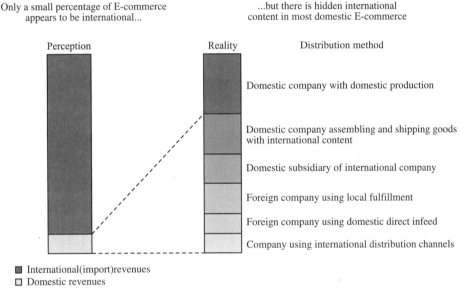

Only a small percentage of E-commerce appears to be international...

...but there is hidden international content in most domestic E-commerce

Perception   Reality   Distribution method

Domestic company with domestic production

Domestic company assembling and shipping goods with international content

Domestic subsidiary of international company

Foreign company using local fulfillment

Foreign company using domestic direct infeed

Company using international distribution channels

■ International(import)revenues
□ Domestic revenues

Figure 10-2   Most Domestic E-Commerce Has an International Component

Source: BCG analysis.

Note: Based on BCG experience in midsize European countries.

10. 3   Case

Case

The New Sales Imperative

Most B2B sellers think their customers are in the driver's seat—empowered, armed to the teeth with information, and so clear about their needs that they don't bother to engage with suppliers until late in the process, when their purchase decision is all but complete.

Customers don't see it that way. They may be better informed than ever, but CEB research shows that they're deeply uncertain and stressed. Buying complex solutions, such as enterprise software or manufacturing equipment, has never been easy. But with a wealth of data on any solution, a raft of stakeholders involved in each purchase, and an ever-expanding array of options, more and more deals bog down or even halt altogether. Customers are increasingly overwhelmed and often more paralyzed than empowered.

In our work with companies around the world, we've seen decision makers pushed into unproductive, open-ended learning loops by the deluge of information. With each iteration they work harder to ensure that they fully understand the requirements and the alternatives. More information begets more questions, with the result that customers take longer and longer to make a purchase decision—if they ever do.

At the same time, the number of people involved in B2B solutions purchases has climbed from an average of 5.4 two years ago to 6.8 today, and these stakeholders come from a lengthening roster of roles, functions, and geographies. The resulting divergence in personal and organizational priorities makes it difficult for buying groups to agree to anything more than "move cautiously", "avoid risk", and "save money". One CMO has memorably referred to this as "lowest common denominator purchasing".

Finally, the expanding range of options that B2B customers face requires increasing amounts of time for evaluation as stakeholders deliberate over the trade-offs. Research shows that for individual consumers, greater choice isn't necessarily a good thing; the same principle applies to big B2B purchases. No matter the choice, some stakeholders will always find aspects of an alternative more appealing. In addition to slowing the purchase process, an excess of options leads to post-purchase anxiety: "Did we do the right thing? Would another choice have been better?" Our research shows that such second-guessing occurs in more than 40% of completed B2B purchases.

That customers struggle to buy comes as a surprise to many suppliers. At CEB we've asked thousands of senior executives at companies around the world to describe the complex-solutions purchase process in one word. Among their responses are "hard", "awful", "painful", "frustrating", and "minefield". We find that a typical solutions purchase takes twice as long as customers expect it will. What's more, 65% of customers tell us that they spent as much time as they'd expected to need for the *entire* purchase just getting ready to speak with a sales rep. Clearly, much of what makes the process so hard has nothing at all to do with suppliers and everything to do with customers themselves.

The solution? Make buying easier.

Suppliers have of course been working on simplifying sales since the dawn of selling—and the majority in our surveys assume they're succeeding. Unfortunately, the very tactics they think will increase ease of purchase often do the opposite. Our research finds that the vast majority of sales professionals believe that giving customers more information helps them make better decisions; that they must flexibly respond to a customer's direction (even when they disagree with it); and that it's "extremely important" to help customers consider all possible alternatives. Sellers are striving to be more responsive than ever—taking the customer's lead and providing whatever support is requested. They ensure that customers have all the data, cases, and testimonials they might need to guide their decision making, and they lay out a suite of options, continually adjusting the offering as customer demand evolves. This approach seems like the right one, and it's in keeping with suppliers' desire to be more customer-centric. Yet it drives an 18% *decrease* in purchase ease, according to our survey of more than 600 B2B buyers. Piling on more information and options just makes things harder.

A Powerful Prescription

We evaluated the impact of dozens of selling tactics on the purchase process and saw a clear pattern: Whereas the responsive approach typically depressed purchase ease, a proactive, prescriptive approach increased purchase ease by 86%. Prescriptive suppliers give a clear recommendation for action backed by a specific rationale; they present a concise offering and a stable view of their capabilities; and they explain complex aspects of the purchase process clearly. A simple prescription might sound like this: "One of the things we've learned from working with customers like you is that purchasing folks are going to get involved, and probably late in the process. And when they come in late, things tend to blow up. So you'll want to bring them in earlier. When you do that, they will have two main questions: X and Y. Here's how to answer them. "

Not surprisingly, customers perceive prescriptive salespeople as being one step ahead, anticipating and eliminating obstacles. That translates directly into business results: Suppliers that make buying easy are 62% likelier than other suppliers to win a high-quality sale (one in which the customer buys a premium offering). In fact, purchase ease is by far the biggest driver of deal quality we've found across three large studies. What's more, customers who complete a prescriptive, easy sales process are dramatically less likely to regret their purchase or to speak negatively of the supplier, and are more likely to repurchase, than customers in conventional sales interactions.

At CEB we've worked with hundreds of sales organizations globally and have run frequent workshops on how to be a prescriptive sales organization. Although every deal is different, all deals are typically more similar than not—especially within a particular industry, across a specific customer segment, or for a given offering. The most effective prescriptive sellers learn from the purchase processes and challenges of a handful of customers to effectively prescribe to a wide range of similar customers, scaling their capability. Selling prescriptively is less an individual rep skill than an organizational aptitude that can be deployed across channels, from sales conversations to marketing content to customer diagnostic exercises.

Prescription may take many forms, but the companies that have mastered it employ the same practices: They work to deeply understand the customer's purchase journey; identify the most significant customer challenge at each buying stage; arm their salespeople with tools to help overcome each challenge; and trace the customer's progress so that they can intervene at any moment to keep the process on track.

Let's look at each step in detail.

1. Map the Journey

Most B2B marketing executives will tell you that they already map customers' buying journeys. But the mapping they commonly do is insufficient to support a prescriptive sales strategy. Conventional journey maps typically include four main steps—awareness, consideration, preference, and purchase—often depicted as a funnel narrowing to the sale of the supplier's solution. At CEB we call this the customer *purchase-from-us* journey, because of its focus on the supplier's process and offering. In this model, if we were to ask, "Awareness of whom?" the answer would be "Of us, the supplier." "Consideration of whom?" "Of us, the supplier." and so on.

But recall that the obstacles customers face often have nothing to do with the supplier, because they lie early in the purchase journey, long before the supplier has entered the picture. Thus a supplier-oriented perspective fails to expose many of those obstacles and is of relatively little help in determining what steps sellers should take. That's why we advise companies to construct supplier-agnostic journey maps for their customers.

At the outset, think of the typical purchase journey as spanning three phases: early, middle, and late. In the first phase, customers are simply identifying whether they have a problem that merits attention—for example, whether their CRM system needs upgrading or replacing. This first phase might involve identifying, sizing, and prioritizing competing business challenges. In the middle phase, customers assess various approaches to addressing their highest-priority problems. They might explore build-versus-buy options, technology-versus-people solutions, and the implications of integrating various solutions with existing systems. In the late phase, having agreed on a suitable solution, the customer considers suppliers and engages, often for the first time, with a sales rep.

Your goal is to uncover struggles that customers would have with any supplier.

Across these three phases—each broken into discrete steps—customers study a wide range of information, explore numerous options, and work to align diverse internal stakeholders. Each step may contain land mines. A detailed understanding of customers' activities during these steps, regardless of who ultimately lands the contract, is therefore essential. ①

The task of creating journey maps has typically fallen to marketing. But that function tends to approach the job from the supplier's perspective. Many of the supplier-agnostic maps we've helped design are developed by sales operations or sales enablement. That said, the most effective commercial teams work collaboratively across functions and with customers to create a comprehensive map couched in language that is readily understood throughout the organization. High-performing sales reps are instrumental in refining the maps, because they often have superior insight into their customers' processes. Additionally, a supplier's established customers are often willing to collaborate in the exercise, since they stand to benefit from the supplier's improved understanding of their processes. Gathering customer information needn't be complicated: Suppliers can conduct interviews, focus groups, or surveys to ask straightforward questions about a past purchase, such as "What sources of information did you consult?" "What information was most or least helpful?" "Who was involved in the purchase, and when did they become involved?"

Beyond following the framework outlined here—work across functions, tap star reps' expertise, involve customers—there's no rigid blueprint. We have seen many variations on the theme as companies tailor the process to their circumstances.

One provider of workforce management solutions we worked with was relying

---

① A word of caution: Although precision is important in fleshing out a journey map, we find that 5 to about 10 steps is ideal; beyond 10, the map may be too cumber some to use effectively, especially by individual reps.

heavily on its top reps to identify the key steps in customers' journeys. Its leaders assumed that because deals are so different, a common buying map would be too general to be helpful. But after weeks of debate, the team converged on a nine-stage map that worked for a broad range of customers. The more they used the map, the more clearly they saw its applicability to virtually any purchase of their complex solution.

Another CEB client, a global logistics company, used this same map as a starting point and found that it described much of the company's own customers' buying process, despite the very different industry. The sales enablement team held a daylong workshop to customize the map to the needs of sales leaders, creating a pilot version in a matter of hours. To achieve this, the team members identified similarities in buying behavior across diverse deals—an approach that allowed them to build a map with wide application.

The marketing department at an e-learning and training provider took a different approach to map development. That team focused less on the details of specific buying stages and more on understanding the concerns of individual customer stakeholders. Starting with a rudimentary map of three buying stages— early, middle, and late—the team interviewed the stakeholders, teasing out what information they sought, where they looked, and what challenges arose at each step in the process.

2. Identify Barriers

We've treated mapping as distinct from identifying obstacles to purchase. But as the example of the e-learning firm suggests, the two often overlap. Particularly when customer interviews are part of the journey mapping, questions about pain points in the process can be integrated.

Customer surveys or in-person interviews should explore questions such as: "What specific challenges did you encounter in the process and at what stages?" "What information would have helped you make faster progress or a better decision?" "Was there anyone who was not involved, or involved late, who should have participated or have been brought in sooner?" "If you were starting over, what would you do differently?" and "What advice would you give others embarking on a similar purchase?" Remember that the goal is not to learn about the problems customers encounter in dealing with you (such as your complex contracting process or hard-to-navigate website) but, rather, to uncover the struggles they would have with any supplier.

As suppliers gather data, they may be tempted to act on input from a single customer. But it's smart to consider answers from many and to look for patterns that reveal the few higher-order obstacles that give rise to a disproportionate amount of buying difficulty. For example, stakeholders at one company might have trouble making an effective business case for change; those at another might struggle with getting internal buy-in for a course of action; and those at a third might have difficulty dislodging a particular function, such as finance, from an alternative point of view. In aggregate these challenges might speak to a broader problem buyers have in assembling clear, quantifiable evidence. Or they might indicate a very specific category of purchase requirements that the supplier failed to consider— something, perhaps, that seemed only tangentially related to its solution but proved to be essential to the purchase. In addition to helping the supplier focus its prescription efforts on high-ROI targets, attacking a small number of big problems reduces the burden for reps who are already inundated with new tools, systems, and rules.

We have identified common themes among the challenges customers most often encounter. In the early stages, as they engage in learning and research, they are likely to struggle with information-based challenges—for example, drawing clear conclusions from often conflicting data or recommendations. In the middle stages, as more stakeholders find their way to the table, communication breakdown tends to be a major obstacle. This may include failing to uncover all stakeholder concerns—perhaps by overlooking a compliance team's focus on data vulnerability or IT's interest in system integration when selling a new app to the head of sales. Other challenges include aligning decision makers' competing priorities—such as operations' focus on efficiency with safety's concerns about injury—and reconciling conflicting interpretations of business needs or leadership directives. Finally, in the late purchase stages, customers often bog down when considering options and selecting a course of action. Challenges here might include an inability to agree on a specific plan for implementation (such as a pilot versus a large-scale rollout) or a disagreement about the ROI of various product options or configurations, such as on-premises versus cloud-based CRM.

Consider how one mobile-technology solutions provider mapped customers' single greatest challenge at each of six buying stages. The provider, which sells radio-frequency identification, wireless networking, and other products and services for real-time collaboration across dispersed systems and staffs, encountered a host of obstacles. For example, it found that customers sometimes get derailed in the first stage of the journey as they simply seek to understand and prioritize the value of connecting a widely dispersed workforce. Until they have a clear grasp of the technology's benefits, they won't move to the next buying stage. The provider also discovered that in the second stage, various customer stakeholders across IT, operations, and finance often had differing ideas about the solution's uses and its value to their function and to the company. Without a common understanding, no deal with any supplier is likely to proceed. That's not because the provider fails to meet customer expectations but because the customer stalls on the journey before a specific solution is even on the table.

By clearly identifying the principal obstacles to purchase, this provider was able to devise an effective prescription sales strategy, as we'll discuss in the next section.

3. Design Prescriptions

Prescriptive approaches vary widely and are delivered through a range of channels: content produced and distributed by marketing; live customer conversations; workshops led by reps, specialists, or executives; customer diagnostics; and self-assessment exercises. For example, customers might complete a benchmarking survey that shows their performance is falling short relative to that of similar companies with comparable goals.

However they're delivered, prescriptive efforts must meet three requirements. First, they must be unbiased and credible. If they're principally promotional, they'll not only fail to help customers buy but will be regarded with suspicion. A customer's natural reaction to effective prescription is never "I see what you're trying to do there..." but, rather, "Wow, you just made my life so much easier!" Second, they must reduce indecision and compel action. Therefore, an effort should systematically focus customers on a manageable set of considerations and make concrete, evidence-based recommendations. And third, without explicitly promoting the supplier's solutions, prescriptions should facilitate progress along a purchase path leading to a solution that the supplier is uniquely able to provide.

Let's return to the mobile-technology solutions provider. After identifying half a dozen key customer roadblocks, sales and marketing collaborated to develop targeted interventions for each. These included a diagnostic tool to help customers evaluate shortcomings in their current collaboration systems, workshops to help align internal stakeholders on the need for change, and a "rollout readiness assessment" to help customers identify the step-by-step path they would need to follow.

National Instruments, a producer of testing and measurement systems used in production and research facilities, faced a similar challenge. The company found that potential deals often stalled early on because a typically diverse array of customer stakeholders, from CTOs to R&D leaders to design and production managers—all with differing or even conflicting priorities—disagreed on the urgency of upgrading outdated equipment.

Rather than directly pitch the company's solution, National Instruments' sales enablement team built an assessment tool to help customers establish a data-driven view of their own "business and technical maturity," diagnosing areas of underperformance, revealing risks, and identifying the potential business impact of various improvements. The tool serves to simplify purchasing, regardless of which supplier the customer ultimately selects, while also laying out a decision-making framework designed to maximize National Instruments' ability to help. It objectively gauges competency across 15 parameters in three areas—people, process, and technology—and produces a maturity score that can be compared with the scores of National Instruments' global client base. The assessment's impartial nature cuts through customers' opinions and personal biases, reducing sources of contention and allowing stakeholders to zero in on the company's true challenges and opportunities.

Prescriptive efforts must reduce indecision and compel action. Meanwhile, data-backed "what if" scenarios help customers quickly reach consensus by modeling the financial impact they might expect from taking specific actions (or no action) across a range of scenarios—from completely upgrading their measurement and evaluation systems with the latest technology to making various piecemeal improvements to making no changes at all.

4. Track Customer Progress

To eliminate obstacles to purchase, you must know exactly where your customers are on their purchase journey. With this information, suppliers can spot problems before customers encounter them and determine which interventions will maintain momentum and maximize purchase ease.

To this end, suppliers rely on "customer verifiers" —clear indicators that a customer has advanced from one purchase stage to the next. Good verifiers share three attributes: (1) They require active participation—customers must take clear steps confirming that they've committed to advancing the purchase process. (2) They are binary and objective, minimizing the potential for misinterpretation—the customer either did or didn't engage in a diagnostic, commit resources, or approve next steps in writing. (3) They signal at each step a customer's deepening commitment to moving away from the status quo. Verifiers range from the fairly general, such as acknowledging the need for change, to the explicit, such as signing a contract.

Below are two approaches to designing customer verifiers. The first uses a diagnostic tool as both a prescriptive device and a verifier. The second relies on a written commitment to progress through defined steps toward purchase.

National Instruments' assessment tool, in addition to aligning stakeholders and suggesting paths forward, pinpoints two early positions on the customer's journey map: acknowledgment of the need for change and degree of stakeholder alignment. For this verifier to be both binary and objective, customers must engage with the diagnostic on a specified date and provide formal executive-level signoff up front. That serves as a clear go/no-go signal. Simply expressing interest in taking the diagnostic is not a strong verifier.

A more structured approach, often used by IT suppliers in the mid to late stages of a purchase, involves creating a staged plan of required supplier and customer actions. This document is developed in close collaboration with customer stakeholders and identifies each step necessary to advance the buying process, with dates and owners indicated for each item and opportunities for the customer to exit the agreement at predetermined points. Steps might include "agree on preliminary success criteria", "present cost estimate", "begin legal review", "review draft proposal", and so on. The document is a highly detailed and customer-specific expansion of the journey map.

Once the plan is set, the customer commits to it in writing, establishing a precise position midway in the buying journey. The completion of each subsequent step serves as a robust verifier of progress.

Conclusion

Today's best suppliers help customers consider not just what to buy but how. Here we've described the key tactics they use: mapping the journey, identifying barriers, designing prescriptions, and tracking progress. But they also share two overarching organizational characteristics: First, they avoid focusing on getting customers to buy from *them* and instead concentrate on how customers make purchase decisions. This may seem like a minor distinction, but in fact it's a profound one, and fundamental to the best practitioners' success. Second, they tightly align their sales and marketing teams to support the customer journey from start to finish—breaking down the historical barriers between those functions in the process. As a result, these companies create consistent and relevant tools, messaging, and guidance to shape and simplify the purchase journey, drive sales, and ultimately increase customer loyalty.

(Source: Nicholas Toman, Brent Adamson, Cristina Gomez. The Sales

Imperative [J], Harvard Business Review, March-April 2017.)

Questions:

1. According to the case, what are the different opinions between suppliers and customers on B2B purchasing?

2. As global sales organizations, how to make it easy for their customers to buy?

10.4   Expanding Reading

Reading-1

E-commerce Empowers Expatriates to Spend more

Overseas students check out shoes on the Taobao platform at a restaurant in Dalian, Liaoning province.

When I relocated from Mumbai to Beijing in September 2015, little did I realize not only is vegetarian food, including Indian cuisine, easy to find but e-stores in China sell Indian groceries and even rare Indian vegetables like drumsticks!

By then, I was already a registered user of a million online marketplaces and service providers in India. But nothing had prepared me for the wondrous world of Chinese e-shopping. I still feel I've explored only a strait in a vast ocean.

Every time I open the Taobao or JD app, I see there's some new feature or another. Its videos, colorful graphics, live streamed promotions remind me of the joke that in the beginning, God created the heaven and the Earth, and after that, everything else was made in China. Fool-proof packaging and super-efficient logistics reinforce that feeling.

My love affair with Chinese E-commerce continues. I'm not sure if my never-married status-single and, yay, happy—is to blame. Is a girlfriend really more expensive than shopping on Taobao, Tmall, JD and Pinduoduo combined?

Talking of expenses, I don't keep track anymore. Artificial intelligence, which has become integral to e-shopping, does. The platforms are so intuitive and easy to use that once you figure out the simple one-two-three-four stepwise process, you could emerge an e-shopping champion, even without knowing Chinese. It's tech that got me hooked in spite of the language barrier.

So, when Alibaba founder Jack Ma told Tesla's Elon Musk the other day that he is not unduly enamored of tech, I almost chuckled. The Alibaba Group and its affiliates rely on tech, including big data and AI, so much it can annoy consumers sometimes.

Moments after you buy a product, would you want to be bombarded indefinitely with hundreds of recommendations for similar or same products? I find this aspect of AI, and in-app search results, primitive, amusing, dumb and inexplicable.

As an expat, I'll concede, however, that it's relatively easier to register on and use tech-driven Chinese apps, websites and services. Last month, I was aghast to note India's new-age mobile and internet services provider does not accept a valid passport as proof of identity to issue a new SIM card. It insists on an ID that India's Supreme Court had already ruled is inessential or optional. Suffice to say the Chinese ecosystem is definitely better geared to innovate technology for making life easier for common people.

In China, I buy almost everything I need, and then some, on E-commerce platforms-groceries, snacks, accessories, cutlery, crockery, outerwear, innerwear, footwear, household stuff, electronics, data storage devices, mobile phones, gifts, medicine, wellness and health products, fruits, novelties, what have you.

Deep-discount coupons on WeChat groups tempt me into buying goods that I later realize I don't really need. But then, they also sensitize me to some other useful products that I did not even know were manufactured. The Singles Day shopping festival on Nov 11 (11-11) no longer enthralls me.

Inferior, substandard or fake products are not uncommon, while refunds and replacements aren't difficult either; but, low-value items could mean you'd prefer not to bother returning the broken stuff but lump the losses. It's best not to buy fruit, fresh dairy, cheap wine, and certain electronics online.

Initially, dirt-cheap Taobao deals seemed irresistible. Now, however, in line with the ongoing consumption upgrade, and encouraged by the ease of using Chinese tech, I am beginning to explore more e-shopping options.

A direct communication channel with the e-shopping platform itself (not just sellers) and a multilingual option can add value to e-shopping in China. Single-language apps are a shame, and a colossal disservice to the consumption upgrade drive.

(Source: Siva Sankar, E-commerce Empowers Expatriates to Spend more, China Daily, September 6, 2019.)

Reading-2

B2B Cross-border E-commerce in China Drives the
Industry Forward "The Millennials are Coming!"

It was a great honor and pleasure to speak about cross-border e-commerce (CBE) trends and opportunities during APEC SME Summit by DHgate and during WECC 2016 World Ecommerce Conference organized by the CECIA. The later event was held on March 14 in Shenzhen, and the latter one on April 11-13 in Yiwu.

In my presentation I shared research data from DHgate in collaboration with University South California (USC) and ABAC, but also from Cross-border E-commerce Community (CBEC) partners, Payvision and Acapture, and last but not least, my own views on the subjects.

Cross-border E-business in China is estimated to reach 6.5 trillion yuan (US $1.02 trillion) in 2016, with an increase of 30% growth rate and 20% in the ratio of China's total import and export trade, according to Chinese Ministry of Commerce. Nearly 40% of apparel products sold in the US are imported from China. In the US apparel counts for only 3% of the total B2B E-commerce.

Starting 2012, as co-founder and chairman of the CBEC knowledge platform, I started collecting in-depth research data to help merchants to lower their barriers for cross-border E-commerce. Not for profit and with the main objective to educate the industry and boost the cross-border eco-system globally.

As economies want to grow their CBE share, working together in a disruptive collaborative model and "educate" the market is one of the best approaches. The CBEC offers a platform where partners from all over the world can share research and best practices to assist manufacturers (B2B) and merchants (B2C) in boosting import and export trade.

WHY do you want to do CBE as a manufacturer?

CBE and omnichannel are the main trends of the global market. Let's take a look at the reasons why the values of CBE are widely recognized among APEC economies and why CBE is empowering SMEs to enter the global value chain. Asia-Pacific region has become the dominant region in the global economy, growing faster than any other, at a rate of 35.2% year on.

The values of CBE to global SMEs are recognized among APAC economies because of two major reasons. First is the disruptive force in economies that are undergoing *massive political*, *social and economic changes* to support CBE. Even traditionally "closed" economies are putting CBE at the highest priority on their digital 2020 agenda. Second, SMEs are fast-growing due to disruptive innovation. By applying new sets of rules, values and models which ultimately disrupt and/or overtake existing markets by displacing earlier technologies and alliances, these innovative SMEs create new markets.

International research conducted by University of South California revealed that 74% of businesses surveyed considered CBE as the key disruptive force on their economy over the next three years, 82% indicated that CBE would have great impact on SMEs over the next three years, and 48% said that CBE would have greater priority for their company strategy and development.

Domestic markets have become mature and saturated. CBE is the most logical way for future growth. Governments around the world have recognized e-commerce as an engine of future economic growth, especially in supporting SMEs to expand cross-border. Supportive policies boost the development of CBE.

International research conducted by Payvision showed that 70% of companies surveyed indicated that selling products and services overseas has proven to be profitable. While 40% indicated that emerging markets were their primary focus, and 45% indicate that China will be their main focus in the future.

CBE is empowering SMEs to enter global value chain, to survive in a mature and saturated competitive domestic market, increase their speed of development and broaden their business opportunities.

SMEs with high internet and technology usage grow 2.1 *times faster than SMEs that do not leverage technology, regardless of the industry.* 60%~80% of e-commerce exporters survive their first year in business compared with a 30%~50% survival rate for traditional businesses. E-commerce firms on average export to 30-40 different economies compared with 3-4 economies for traditional exporters. That's 10 times more opportunities for business growth.

Using CBE the business risks are reduced to a level with lower intensity of competition in overseas markets, and wider reach of global markets. CBE offers more flexibility and lower barriers, no geographical restrictions, thus it increases the profit margins for sellers and saves money for global buyers.

Under CBE industry, B2B is the leading force in driving the industry forward.

Let's take a look at the number of global B2B. According to Frost and Sullivan report (LINK), it is estimated that in 2020, the total global transactional volume in B2B business will be twice the size of B2C business, with 6.7 trillion USD revenue.

According to 2015 e-commerce marketplace data, in China, in terms of cross-border sales, B2C revenue dwarfed with $221m in B2B. Chinese e-commerce market reached USD 2.3 trillion in 2015 and almost 70% came from B2B (China Internet Watch).

In absolute terms, the European B2B e-commerce market is growing at a faster rate than the B2C sector. Yet, the B2B sector still has major growth opportunity. More than 50% of companies make purchases through e-commerce, but less than 22% of companies are actually selling through e-commerce.

So, why is B2B the winner?

With the integrated online B2B platforms, a complete service chain is moved online, shortening the purchasing cycle and cutting the cost through less middlemen. Buying in bulk also means an enhanced logistics efficiency. And with larger order size, businesses are more inclined to enter this business with more profit margins.

Did you know that Prada makes about 20% of their collection in China? Miuccia Prada told the Wall Street Journal, "*Sooner or later, it will happen to everyone because Chinese manufacturing is so good. Their skill set is better, their finishing is better, and they can handle that type of fashion.*" This example illustrates the demand from overseas markets for Chinese high quality products. I believe with the increasing productivity and improved product quality, made-in-China products will be tested and recognized with good reputation in the global markets! Over 40% of apparel sold in the US is made in China. For B2B demand by the rest of the world for machinery parts that are made in China will be double that of the US by 2022. Quality reputation is being restored.

Around the world, Computers and other Machinery, Automotive, Pharmaceutical, Petroleum & Minerals, are leading the B2B rankings for many years, as the early adopters. But let's be clear about these numbers; lately many new categories are on the rise. Look at apparel, only ranking around 5% is already bringing solid business to China. Good quality products will grow every industry/sector in CBE.

Future perspectives

Although consumers will have the largest number of devices, the greatest value will be driven through B2B spending until 2020 when this is predicted to level out. Business-to-business IoT devices and applications will capture more value initially—over 60% in 2016—than consumers, although consumer applications, such as fitness monitors and self-driving cars will grow at a fast pace, and by 2020 will generate more value than B2B. As adoption grows, consumers will become more confident with payment security and will spend on higher value items. On top of that, we reached the turning point where millennials in the age of 18 ~ 34 are the digital natives, able to analyze and understand information incredibly fast. This business model will be highly acceptable for them. They bring in buying power with 'no border' mentality and higher demand for convenience and user experience.

The main barriers to adopting an integrated Internet of Things strategy is privacy security, and the main barriers to B2B cross-border e-commerce are lack of awareness, business intelligence and technical skills.

The B2B e-commerce industry needs support with education and expertise for growth. As economies grow, working together in a disruptive collaborative model is best, to "educate" the market wherever we can. Partners from all over the world can share research and best practices to assist manufacturers (B2B) and merchants (B2C) in boosting import and export trade. This is where the CBEC can play a significant role.

Nowadays, manufacturers and merchants focus on being present on many channels and platforms; online, offline, mobile, social and everything in between. This makes the landscape very fragmented and it pushes merchants to multi-vendor operations. The East is way ahead of the West when it comes to integrated platforms and aiming for a better user experience. I've been in China many times and I am a frequent user of the integrated in-app solutions such as WeChat. It's used by the entire population because it's convenient, efficient and all-in-one solution for daily purposes such as chatting, sharing experiences and photo's with friends, video conferencing, ordering taxis, finding information on theater, train and flight tickets, paying with one click for the tickets, buying on marketplaces, you name it and its possible, all-in-one.

My advice to SMEs is finding ways to connect to, or stick to one vendor that can accommodate your specific omnichannel needs that fits to your business. *From a payment provider perspective, omnichannel is still in its early stages because all elements of the experience are fragmented.* In this increasingly omnichannel retail landscape, SMEs' main challenge is often the jointed processing systems they use, the independent fulfilment and CRM systems for each channel, the different settlements dates, reports, contacts and so on. With such disparate operations, uniting the user experience can be impossible. Merchants should unite their channels so customers can be approached as a single, identifiable customer. By *moving from multi-vendor strategies*, integrating and connecting the processing systems and collecting visitors' data, merchants can better understand their customer's desires and needs and add new services to their offering. Payment providers are very well positioned to gather this data and make it available for their retailers to integrate it in the shopping experience.

(Source: B2B Cross-border E-commerce in China Drives the Industry Forward, CBEC, April 28, 2016.)

Quick Quiz

1. E-commerce is a set of transactions made by ____ .

2. Because the ____ is subject to severe restraints, the value of marginal product of skilled labour in developed countries is far higher than in developing countries.

3. Apart from standard problems which E-shops struggle with in cross-border E-commerce, what factors should also be taken into account ____

A. delivery cost

B. payment terms

C. communication in a foreign language

D. legal and tax conditionings

E. time and quality of delivery

4. Currently, China's E-commerce is in a period of great development, which mainly manifests in ____

A. government is also took highly concerned about the future development of China's cross-border E-commerce

B. there are some platform which could provide service of cross-border E-commerce

C. cross-border E-commerce strategy is from trade to investment to gradual currency

D. there are many hands to build the core national policy promoting reform

E. Cross-border E-commerce retail exports account for 37% of global market

5. Which is not the trend of cross-border E-commerce to develop in China ____ ?

A. Role in promoting of national strategies for cross-border E-commerce

B. Value chain of is extension by consumer demand-driven

C. Trade enterprises will become the new force

D. Localization is forced by the strengthen supervision

E. Comprehensive services of cross-border E-commerce will rise up

Answers:

1. computer networks

2. international movement of natural persons

3. ABCDE

4. ABCDE

5. B

Endnotes

[1] Wenlong Zhu, Jian Mou, Morad Benyoucef. Exploring purchase intention in cross-border E-commerce: A three stage model [J]. Journal of Retailing and Consumer Services, 2019 (10): 320-330.

[2] Xinyu Zhang. Coordinated Development of China's Cross-border E-commerce and Manufacturing Cluster Against the Background of "Internet Plus" and "the Belt and Road" [C]. Proceedings of the 3rd International Conference on Culture, Education and Economic Development of Modern Society (ICCESE 2019), Atlantis Press, 2019.

[3] Xuan-Xuan Zhang, Guo-Hua CAO. Electronic Word of Mouth, Cross-Border Logistics Way and Imports Retail E-commerce [C]. DEStech Transactions on Economics, Business and Management, 2019.

[4] Kakali Chatterjee, Asok De. A novel multi-server authentication scheme for E-commerce applications using smart card [J]. Wireless Personal Communications, 2016, 91 (1).

[5] Xvming Lou, Dan Bai, Bao Meng, Yanan Zhao. Research on Influencing Factors of Consumers' Willingness to Use Cross-border E-commerce Websites Continuously [C]. Proceedings of the 2018 International Seminar on Education Research and Social Science, Atlantis Press, 2018.

[6] Sylwia Talar. Cross-border E-commerce—problems in identification and measurement [J]. Contemporary Economy, 2017 (03): 13-27.

[7] Lunan Zhao, Shui Jin. China's Dilemma of Cross-border E-commerce Company—Take Amazon China as an example [C]. Proceedings of the 2016 International Seminar on Education Innovation and Economic Management, Atlantis Press, 2016.

[8] Guy H. Gessner, Coral R. Snodgrass. Designing E-commerce cross-border distribution networks for small and medium-size enterprises incorporating Canadian and U. S. trade incentive programs [J]. Research in Transportation Business & Management, 2015 (10): 84-94.

[9] Estrella Gomez-Herrera, Bertin Martens, Geomina Turlea. The drivers and impediments for cross-border E-commerce in the EU [J]. Information Economics and Policy, 2014 (10): 83-96.

[10] Kawa A, Zdrenka W, Conception of integrator in cross-border E-commerce [J]. LogForum 2015: 12 (1), 63-73.

［11］ Wanxin Xue, Dandan Li, Yilei Pei. The Development and Current of Cross-border E-Commerce ［C］. Wuhan International Conference on e-Business, Summer, 2016.

［12］ Rudolf R. Sinkovics, MoYamin, Matthias Hossinger. Cultural adapation in cross border E-commerce ［J］. Journal of Electronic Commerce Research, 2007, 8 (04).